THE FLOWERING
OF MYSTICISM

A five-volume series

**THE PRESENCE OF GOD:
A HISTORY OF WESTERN CHRISTIAN MYSTICISM**

THE FLOWERING
OF MYSTICISM

MEN AND WOMEN IN THE NEW MYSTICISM (1200–1350)

Vol. III of
The Presence of God:
A History of Western Christian Mysticism

by
Bernard McGinn

A Crossroad Herder Book
The Crossroad Publishing Company
New York

The Crossroad Publishing Company
370 Lexington Avenue, New York, NY 10017

Printed in the United States of America

Library of Congress Cataloging-in-Publication Data

McGinn, Bernard, 1937–
    The flowering of mysticism : men and women in the new mysticism,
1200–1350 / by Bernard McGinn.
        p.   cm.–(The presence of God ; vol. 3)
    Includes bibliographical references and indexes.
    ISBN 0-8245-1742-3 (hardcover : alk. paper). – ISBN 0-8245-1743-1
(pbk. : alk. paper)
    1. Mysticism–History–Middle Ages, 600–1500. 2. Mysticism–
Catholic Church–History. 3. Catholic Church–Doctrines–History.
I. Title. II. Series: McGinn, Bernard, 1937– Presence of God ;
vol. 3.
BV5075.M37 1994 vol. 3
[BV5075]
248.2'2'09022–dc21   97-52986
                                                               CIP

*This volume is dedicated
to my colleagues at the Divinity School
of the University of Chicago
past and present:
"An ancient and honorable company of scholars."*

A Note on the Cover Illustration

The stigmata received by Francis of Assisi, traditionally on September 14, 1224, is the most famous experience of identification with the passion of Christ in the history of Christian mysticism. Thomas of Celano, the saint's first biographer, fittingly described it as a "new and amazing miracle," one that helped define the new mysticism described in this volume. Hundreds of later depictions of the reception of the stigmata survive. Particularly influential were those painted by Giotto di Bondone (ca. 1266–1337), which helped spread Bonaventure's interpretation of the miracle in which the seraph takes on the appearance of the crucified Christ. This panel painted by Giotto and his workshop about 1300 (and signed by him: OPVS JOCTI FLORENTINI) was originally made for the church of S. Francesco in Pisa and is now in the Louvre. (Photo courtesy of Art Resource.)

Contents

Contents

Preface

Whenhen I first conceived the possibility of writing this history of Christian mysticism, I was already convinced from my previous reading and teaching that the year 1200 marked a major turning point in the mysticism of Western Christianity. New styles of religious life, especially the mendicants and the beguines, new forms of mystical expression, as well as the sudden emergence of a more powerful role for women, all pointed to an important shift. My original plan was to devote a volume to the development of mysticism before 1200, a story largely revolving around the contribution of monastics to the foundation and growth of mysticism as a distinct element in Christianity. The second volume was to treat the period between 1200 and roughly 1600, the rich centuries of the flowering of what I have come to call the "new mysticism" of the late medieval and early modern periods. The third volume was to deal with the crisis of mysticism in the seventeenth century, its marginal position in the eighteenth and nineteenth centuries, and its revival in our own time.

Habent sua fata libelli—"Books have their destinies"; so does the writing of books. The richness of the search for deeper and even immediate experience of the presence of God by Christians between the third century and the end of the twelfth century made it impossible for me to do any real justice to the early history of mysticism in a single volume as I had planned. The writing eventually led to two substantial books: *The Foundations of Mysticism* (1991) and *The Growth of Mysticism* (1994). Given that modification, I was not surprised when it became clear to me that what was originally conceived of as the second volume of *The Presence of God* also needed to be split into at least two parts.

Initially, I conceived of these two parts in an essentially chronological way. The first would deal with the period 1200–1350, arguably the richest era for the production of mystical literature in the whole history of Christianity. The second part would deal with subsequent developments from about 1350 to 1600, since I consider sixteenth-century mysticism, even that of the great Spanish mystics, to be in basic continuity with the major lines of the new mysticism created in the thirteenth century.[1] Volume 3 of the reconceived series was to have treated primarily three broad traditions or movements during the period 1200–1350: Franciscan mysticism; female mystics; and the speculative mysticism associated with Meister Eckhart and his followers. During the course of my research and writing for the first part of the volume that I called *The Flowering of Mysticism,* however, the variety and creativity of the mystical texts of the period, especially those created by women, necessitated a further change in my plans. In order to do justice to the movements beginning about 1200, particularly the "mystical conversation" between men and women that was central to the evolution of the new mysticism, I discovered that it would not be possible to treat all three traditions in a single volume, even one of considerable size. Since the third tradition, that of speculative mysticism, was chronologically later than the other two, not originating until the latter part of the thirteenth century, I have found it necessary to postpone its treatment until the following volume of this history. Although the mystical teaching initiated by the German Dominicans certainly had links to aspects of the mystical life and literature of early-fourteenth-century women, the two central strands or traditions treated here can, on the whole, be understood independently of the study of Eckhart, his predecessors, and followers.

Hence, in this volume entitled *The Flowering of Mysticism: Men and Women in the New Mysticism (1200–1350),* the reader will not find Meister Eckhart or his predecessors (among whom Albert the Great and Thomas Aquinas must be numbered, at least in some respects). Nor will one find chapters devoted to his followers, such as Henry Suso and John Tauler among the Dominicans, and even the great John Ruusbroec, who, despite his independence of mind, was touched by Eckhart's thought. The important male mystics who lived and wrote between 1300 and 1350 will appear in the next volume, entitled *Continuity and Change in Western Mysticism.* This fourth volume will overlap chronologically with the present book in its first part, but extend well beyond it through the late medieval and early modern periods.[2] Volume 4 of *The Presence of God* will also consider the ongoing contribution of women mystics in the late Middle Ages, not only well-known names like Catherine of Siena and Julian of Norwich but also many who are lesser known. Nor did the history of Franciscan mysticism end with 1350; the tradition carried forward, among both male and female Franciscans. These too will be treated in the next volume.

The patient reader who has perused volumes 1 and 2 of *The Presence of God* will recall the deliberately broad understanding of mysticism that has been my touchstone in writing this history.[3] Naturally, the comments and critiques of reviewers, conversations with students, friends, and colleagues about mysticism and different aspects of its story, as well as my own continuing reading, have led me to further, and I hope deeper, insights about the promise and some of the problems of this approach. Mechthild of Magdeburg, one of the beguine mystics treated in this volume, provided a warning that all (especially scholars) should heed when she said: *Dú trumpheit behaget ir selbe alleine, dú wisheit kan niemer volleleren,* "Foolishness is satisfied with itself alone; wisdom can never learn enough."[4] Nevertheless, even in an era like the late Middle Ages when discussion of the nature and meaning of union with God was widespread, I think that there are still distinct advantages to maintaining the notion of consciousness of God's presence in a deeper and more immediate way as the fundamental category for coming to terms with the full range of Christian mysticism, including the many ways of understanding *unio mystica*.

The subtitle of this volume expresses what I have come to see as central to the creation of the new mysticism of the period after 1200. In responding to reactions to the first two volumes in this history (at least those that accept the modern construct of "mysticism" as a tool for making sense of this aspect of the Christian past), I have at times been taken to task for neglecting the role of women. The historical theologian, however, is limited not to what should have been and what even may have been but does not survive, but only to what the evidence actually conveys to us. While recent scholarship has done much to recover the history of women before 1200, the evidence for a *major* contribution by women to mysticism prior to the thirteenth century is lacking.[5] It is in the decades immediately after 1200 that we witness the beginnings of a flood of writing about and by women mystics that was to reach epic proportions by the end of the century.

The treatment of the women mystics of the later Middle Ages, both in this volume and that to follow, reflects a different perspective from that of many of their recent investigators and supporters. Without the contributions of contemporary feminist scholarship, the history of medieval thought would probably not have come to a deeper appreciation of most of these women, especially those whose stories have been all too easily dismissed as impossible and extreme. Even the women mystics who were themselves authors have left us writings that are often difficult to decipher by historians of theology more habituated to linear, scholastic modes of thinking. Despite the many ways in which I have profited from feminist scholarship on medieval women mystics, however, *The Flowering of Mysticism* is written not from a feminist perspective but from that of a historical theologian attempting to do justice to the full range of late medieval mysticism. From this perspective it does not seem fruitful, or even possible, to identify a single "women's mysticism" in the later Middle Ages. There are, to be sure, mystical themes and practices that were pioneered by women, and there are significant differences in how women used language to express their sense of the mystery of God. But rarely, if ever, do we find an aspect of the new mysticism that belongs to women alone. Even more significant is the amazing variety that characterized the women, again notwithstanding the many themes they shared in conveying their message about how to attain loving union with God. It seems far more important to celebrate the diversity of the contribution of women than to search for an elusive unity.

Along with this emphasis on difference, three other aspects of the role of women in the flowering of mysticism have emerged more clearly to me as this volume was being written. The first is the way in which the impossible task of expressing how God encounters humans in some direct way encouraged mystics to question the gender roles and ways of understanding and expressing them that characterized medieval society. Beginning with Caroline Walker Bynum's research of two decades ago,[6] down through much recent literature which will be cited below, scholars have come to recognize the gender malleability by which mysticism challenged medieval society and continues to challenge us as well. Once again, however, we should note that this quest to modify, to transmute, and even to transcend gender was by no means restricted to women.

A second aspect concerns the variety of genres and perspectives in the evidence at our disposal. While hagiography played a role in the development of Christian mysticism before 1200 (think of Athanasius's *Life of Antony*, or Gregory the Great's presentation of Benedict in the second book of the *Dialogues*), this complex genre becomes much more important in the era of the new mysticism.[7] A good deal of the evidence for the contribution of women is to be found in the lives written about them by their male clerical confessors and guides, though as the period wore on women also began to compose *vitae* about other holy women. The fourteenth century saw the development of what some scholars have termed "autohagiographies," that is, narratives in which an author presents aspects of her or his own life as a model of suffering in imitation of Christ's passion and the reception of "divine consolations."[8] All hagiography is didactic, intended not so much to give a historical account of a life as to teach a lesson about how to live. The male-authored lives of holy women tell us how men wanted to present the message contained in the lives of these *mulieres sanctae*, something that was often not quite the same as what the women thought about themselves, or how they formulated their own teaching, whether in hagiographical form or not.[9] It is not that there is no relation between the two perspectives, but rather that we always need to be sensitive to both the variety of viewpoints and the interchanges between men and women present in the evidence at our disposal.

It is precisely because of this interchange that I have appealed to the model of conversation as a helpful way of understanding the complexity of the roles of men and women in the new mysticism. Conversation as encounter, as dialogue, as interchange of horizons which opens up the conversation partners to change and adaptation seems to me not only evident in the mystical texts of the time but also significant in the creation of the new forms of religious life that formed the historical matrix of the new mysticism. It is my hope that *The Flowering of Mysticism* will help us to overhear these conversations–perhaps even to take a part in them–as we continue to learn from this amazing era.

The limits that hamper attempts to overhear these conversations are many and serious. All our efforts will be unsatisfactory in many ways. What we can recover is always partial–but some participation is better than none. The mystical quest for deeper contact with God of its very nature involves failure, both in attainment and in expression. Augustine of Hippo, who was read and admired by almost all the mystics studied in this volume, knew this well. In his *Enarrations on the Psalms* he put it this way:

> Conticescant humanae voces, requiescant humanae cogitationes; ad incomprehensibilia non se extendant quasi comprehensuri, sed tamquam participaturi; participes enim erimus.

> Let human voices keep silent, let human thoughts take their rest; they reach out to incomprehensible things not as if they could take them in their grasp, but only to share in them; and share in them we shall.[10]

Many colleagues, students, and friends have contributed to this volume in the course of its writing. In addition, parts of the book have been given as lectures in a number of venues, and versions of some sections have appeared in article form. Rather than listing here at the start all the names of those to whom I owe a profound debt of gratitude for their contributions to *The Flowering of Mysticism*, I will try to thank those who have read and commented on different sections in the appropriate places in the notes. There are, however, some whose help went beyond any single section or part and whose generosity needs to be singled out here. I want to thank my wife, Patricia, especially for her assistance as a keen-eyed stylistic editor. My three most recent research assistants, Edward Howells, Kevin Hughes, and Scott Johnson, gave invaluable help in the research, as well as in the editing stages. And finally, sincere thanks to Michael Leach of Crossroad for his constant support.

Bernard McGinn
University of Chicago
November 1997

Abbreviations

AA.SS.   Acta Sanctorum. Antwerp and Brussels: Various publishers, 1643–1940. Reprint Brussels: Lebon, 1965. 68 vols. This will be cited by month and day and then page number.

CCCM   *Corpus Christianorum. Continuatio Mediaevalis.* Turnhout: Brepols, 1971–.

DIP   *Dizionario degli Istituti di Perfezione.* Rome: Edizioni Paoline, 1974–. 9 vols. to Ve.

DS   *Dictionnaire de spiritualité ascétique et mystique doctrine et histoire.* Edited by Marcel Viller et al. Paris: Beauchesne, 1937–94. 16 vols.

MGH   *Monumenta Germaniae Historica inde ab a.C. 500 usque ad a. 1500.* Hanover and Berlin, 1826–. Various publishers and sections. What will mostly be cited here is the section SS (*Scriptores*) by volume and page.

PL   *Patrologiae cursus completus. Series latina.* Paris: J. P. Migne, 1844–64. 221 vols.

SC   *Sources chrétiennes.* Paris: Cerf, 1940–. 350 vols. to date.

Vg   Vulgate version of the Bible. See *Biblia sacra iuxta Vulgatam Versionem.* Stuttgart: Deutsche Bibelgemeinschaft, 1983.

Introduction:
Apostolic Renewal
and the New Mysticism

ew things about the study of history are more misleading than periodization. When did the Roman Empire fall? What are the chronological parameters of the Middle Ages? Where should we place the beginnings of modernity? Discussions about such questions can weary all but the most obsessive of historians. Much depends on the perspective brought by the examiner, as well as the issue addressed and type of evidence educed. The art historian Ernst Kitzinger once declared, "Classical art became 'medieval' before it became Christian,"[1] that is, the aesthetic shift that marked the transition to the transcendental style typical of early medieval art took place in Roman art before Constantine's conversion.

Medievalists have long pointed to the twelfth century, often broadly defined as stretching from Pope Gregory VII (1075–1084) through Pope Innocent III (1198–1216), as the beginning of a new period in the history of the Middle Ages, what has been called the High Middle Ages.[2] This may well be the case, but from the perspective of the history of Christian mysticism, the date 1200 is more significant than 1100 for marking the new stage in the history of Western Christian mysticism that is the subject of this volume, the era of the "Flowering of Mysticism." To be sure, the mystics who will be studied here (those active between ca. 1200 and ca. 1350) were deeply indebted to the tradition of monastic mysticism initiated by the church fathers and developed by the monks of the medieval West. This monastic phase or layer of mysticism reached its fulfillment in the twelfth century, especially among the Cistercians and the canons of the Abbey of St. Victor outside Paris. There were significant new elements added by both these groups of mystical authors, such as the stress on the role of experience and the importance of erotic love-language among the Cistercians, and the attempt to introduce scholastic modes of ordering the doctrine of *contemplatio* among the Victorines. Twelfth-century visionaries also hinted at things to come in their emphasis on the authentification of their teaching through visionary experience. Nevertheless, for mysticism at least, a more decisive shift is evident around the year 1200. This transition introduced so many new elements and new emphases into the Western mystical tradition that it marks a real turning point.

The major characteristics of this "new mysticism" can be illustrated by the lives of some extraordinary individuals born in the last decades of the twelfth century and active in the first quarter of the thirteenth century. Their understanding of the path to perfection shaped Christianity throughout the later medieval period and in some cases long after. Before we turn to an investigation of these men and women in chapter 1, however, it will be helpful to investigate some aspects of the historical and ecclesiastical context that formed the foundation for the new stage in the history of mysticism, as well as to introduce some of the themes that were particularly important to its development.

The Context[3]

Europe in 1200 was quite a different society from what it had been in 1000, or even in 1100. Politically, it was less fragmented and more efficiently organized and administered. Powerful kingdoms, such as the realms of France, England, and Norman Sicily had emerged in the course of the previous century and had introduced new forms of bureaucratic rationalization, especially into judicial and financial administration. Political historians have looked back on these developments for the origins of the modern state.[4] The German Empire, with its claims to universal rule inherited from ancient Rome, had been revived by the new Hohenstaufen dynasty after a period of decline attendant upon the struggle between the empire and the reformed papacy in the late eleventh and early twelfth centuries. Frederick II (1194–1250), the dominant political figure of the first half of the thirteenth century, was arguably the last effective medieval emperor.

Europe was also different economically. In 1200 most of the West was in the midst of a period of expansion (one might almost say a "boom time" were it not for the periodic threats of bad harvest, plague, and war). This had begun in the eleventh century and was to continue until the early part of the fourteenth century. The most significant aspect of this demographic and economic expansion for the religious life of the time was the urbanization encouraged by the growth of trade and commerce and the gradual transition to a profit economy based on money and banking rather than the gift economy that had characterized the early Middle Ages.[5]

Christianity had originally spread through the urban centers of the ancient Roman Empire, but had had to adapt to the de-urbanized world of the early Middle Ages in ways that had a powerful effect on its piety and practice.[6] The Benedictine monasticism that had dominated religious life in the West since the eighth century was admirably suited to the dispersed rural life and the feudal structure of early medieval society, but it was ill suited to the commercial world of the towns and growing cities of the later Middle Ages. At the start of the thirteenth century Western Christianity was confronted with the necessity of "re-urbanizing," that is, of creating appropriate religious responses, both institutional and spiritual, to answer the needs of a rapidly changing, urbanizing society.[7] Some of these adaptations had to do with the moral dilemmas raised by the profit economy itself.[8]

A third difference in the Europe of 1200 in comparison with even a century before was a change in methods of advanced education coupled with growing literacy, especially in the vernacular. The late eleventh and the twelfth century saw the emergence of scholasticism, the new scientifically organized and academically professional mode of seeking the understanding of faith (*intellectus fidei*).[9] The contrasts–not oppositions–between the older form of theology practiced in the monasteries and the new theology of the urban schools were real, but there was also significant interaction between the two. While the world of monastic theology reached its height in the twelfth century, especially in the writings of the Cistercians, it faded after 1200 with the triumph of scholasticism. The traditional date for the founding of the University of Paris, 1215, the year in which Pope Innocent III's legate confirmed the statutes granting the body of the masters (*universitas magistrorum et scolarium*) the right to act as a corporate body under papal control, is a benchmark of this victory.[10] Soon even the monks established houses in Paris so they could train their men in the regnant mode of theology.

In discussing education, however, we should not forget a wider and more diffuse but equally important educational process at work–the growing literacy among the laity.[11] Italy and Flanders led the way, especially through the development of town schools. (These were the same two areas that saw the rise of the new forms of religious life to be discussed below.) We have no way of knowing what percentage of the population was literate, or even what kind of literacy was enjoyed.[12] Certainly the aristocracy and the upper bourgeoisie had the largest numbers (particularly the professional class among the latter, such as lawyers, clerks, notaries, and merchants). The percentage of women, either religious or lay, who could read is even more difficult to ascertain, but the evidence of the thirteenth-century mystics indicates that there were probably more literate women than previously suspected.[13] Despite these uncertainties, we can agree with M. B. Parkes that "[w]hatever date one wishes to assign to the emergence of the general reader, the process began in the 13th century, when the pragmatic reader began to look beyond his immediate professional horizons."[14] The new literacy was a necessary foundation for the emerging vernacular theology of the mystics to be discussed below.

These developments in politics, economics, and education, which served as the context for the shift in the nature of mysticism about 1200, had their counterparts in the religious life of the era. Here too important changes are evident—even the evaluation given to change was changing! The early medieval opposition to change, the myth that what is old is good and what is new must be bad, had come under increasing question during the twelfth century, especially in relation to the formation of new religious orders. By the thirteenth century, as Beryl Smalley put it: "The champions of novelty have moved from defence to offense. They glory in novelty and have no idea of sneaking it in under cover of a mere return to the past."[15] Such a change of mentality, of course, did not put an end to argument. The theological debates of the early thirteenth century, those that helped shape the new mysticism, were concerned with the differences between good and bad innovation.

At the beginning of the thirteenth century the Latin church enjoyed immense success at the same time that it confronted unparalleled challenges. The papal reform movement begun in the mid-eleventh century had made the bishop of Rome the ultimate doctrinal and judicial authority in a more effective way than ever before. No occupant of the See of Peter was better prepared to exercise this power, both for good and for ill, than the able young Italian canonist and theologian Lothario Segni, elected Pope Innocent III in 1198.[16] Innocent's legitimate triumphs were equal to his tragic defeats. His judicial expertise made him supreme among the medieval lawyer-popes and his concern for furthering pastoral reform shows that he was more than a narrow legalist. Although his maneuverings to enhance the status of the papacy in the power politics of the day make him often seem like a "world ruler" in clerical garb, one also has to take into account the world-denying piety evident in his writings, such as the *Misery of the Human Condition*, as well as the support he gave to new religious movements which rejected human systems of domination.[17] Innocent's role in the creation of effective means for the suppression of heresy (the institution we call the Inquisition), terrible as it seems to us today, needs to be measured against his efforts to bring dissidents back to the *Ecclesia Romana et Catholica* by correcting abuses and trying to negotiate differences of opinion that did not involve doctrine. The breadth of the pope's vision for the church was admirably reflected in the great reform council he summoned to meet in Rome toward the end of his pontificate, the Fourth Lateran Council (November 1215). The pronouncements of this council touch on most of the religious issues of the early thirteenth century. They can be summarized under two general headings: apostolic life (*vita apostolica*) and pastoral renewal (*cura animarum*).

No ideal was more central to the spirituality of the later Middle Ages than that of the *vita apostolica,* that is, to live as Christ and the apostles had lived.[18] The imperative of apostolicity, as we may call it, though certainly given impetus by the Gregorian reform of the papacy in the late eleventh century, came from below as much as from above. Although the *vita vere apostolica* was praised by popes and bishops in official documents, it began as the rallying cry of less highly placed reformers and their followers, originally monks and priests, but increasingly in the twelfth century lay persons as well.[19] The attitude of the official church toward these movements was mostly one not of initiation but rather of investigation leading to either approbation or disapproval. Lateran IV witnesses to this. The only one of the seventy-one constitutions of the council that directly concerns the issue of new institutional attempts to realize the *vita apostolica* was a negative one, Constitution 13, which forbade new religious orders.[20] Whether or not this represented the mind of Pope Innocent, and despite the fact that the constitution was understood as excepting the new mendicant orders, it was a clear sign of the growing tension in the thirteenth century between hierarchical attempts to limit and control the variety of ways to live the religious life, on the one hand, and the power of the appeal found in the *vita apostolica* on the other.

The claim to follow Christ and the apostles, of course, was not a new one. In the early Middle Ages monks had traditionally identified their way of life with the *vita apostolica.* Basing their arguments on the picture of the first Christians in Jerusalem in the fourth chapter of the Acts of the Apostles, they asserted that the model of a stable community of prayer and common ownership of goods was the example given to all later ages by the apostolic church. In the twelfth century this view began to be challenged, first in the debates between monastics and clerics over whether monks had the right to preach, and then by defenders of canonical reform, who insisted that preaching and evangelization of the world were not merely permissible but were central to a *truly* apostolic way of life. This shift from centering on inward-looking community to outward-looking encounter with the world was of major moment for later medieval spirituality and mysticism.[21]

One of the most remarkable things about this new understanding of the *vita apostolica* in the twelfth and thirteenth centuries is how rapidly the evangelical ideal, which found its scriptural warrant in the picture of Christ sending out the disciples to preach without "purse, or wallet, or sandals" in Luke 10:1–12 and parallel passages, spread to all levels of society. Lay desire for the *vita apostolica* goes back at least to the end of the eleventh century, as we can see from the chronicler Bernold of Constance's reference to a bull of Pope Urban II which praised the "innumerable multitude" of men and women who took up the "common life" (*communis vita*) according to "the form of the primitive church."[22] As the twelfth century progressed, more and more laity were attracted to the evangelical rather than to the communal model of the apostolic life. The wandering preachers like Stephen of Muret, Bernard of Tiron, Robert of Arbrissel, and Norbert of Xanten, whose peregrinations cut across much of northern Europe in the early part of the twelfth century, attracted large numbers of lay followers. Many of these preachers became revered founders of religious houses and orders. Others, like Henry of Lausanne and Tanchelm of Antwerp, appear to have begun their careers as reformers and preachers of penance, but to have developed (or perhaps been forced into) positions criticizing clerical corruption and current church practice, positions that were eventually condemned as heretical. The new stage in the understanding of the *vita apostolica* is inseparably linked to the growth of popular heresy in the twelfth and thirteenth centuries.[23]

The essential components of the evangelical understanding of the *vita apostolica* were penance, poverty and preaching. Penance for sin, both one's own sins and those of the world, was too deeply ingrained in the medieval Christian outlook ever to be directly questioned or condemned. (The fact that heretics were often denounced as *false* ascetics alone gives evidence of this.) Poverty and preaching, however, while always seen as important religious practices, were more open to dispute as to their appropriate form and importance. The career of Peter Valdez of Lyon can be used to illustrate these ambiguities.

Valdez was a wealthy merchant who experienced a conversion in the early 1170s after hearing the story of St. Alexis, the legendary beggar saint. When he asked a master of theology about the way to perfection, the priest repeated the same text that nine centuries before had been effective in the case of the wealthy young Egyptian farmer, Antony—"If you will be perfect, go, sell what you have and give to the poor" (Matt. 19:21). Both Antony and Valdez took the evangelical counsel in literal fashion, but their further efforts to achieve perfection diverged radically. Antony began to practice a withdrawn ascetical life that eventually led him to set forth alone into the deep desert; Valdez began to preach publicly in towns and cities by both word and example and to beg for his sustenance. He soon gathered followers, as the *Chronicle of Laon* notes:

> [Valdez], . . . having taken a vow to the God of heaven henceforth and throughout his life never to possess either gold or silver or to take thought for the morrow, began to gather associates in his way of life. They followed his example in giving their all to the poor and became devotees of voluntary poverty. Little by little, both publicly and privately, they began to declaim against their own sins and those of others.[24]

Valdez and his followers went to Rome in 1179 and received the approbation of Pope Alexander III for their voluntary poverty, though the pope forbade "preaching either by Valdez himself or his followers unless welcomed by the local priests."[25] Valdez's preaching and manner of life did, however, raise the suspicions of his local bishop. (Southern France at that time was troubled with the rising power of the dualist heresy of the *Cathari,* or pure ones, whose leaders also lived lives of poverty and asceticism as they wandered from place to place preaching their message.) We still have the profession of faith Valdez signed in 1181, testifying to his opposition to Catharism. Soon after, however, in the face of a prohibition by the bishop against his preaching, Valdez, citing the evangelical precept, "Preach the Gospel to every creature" (Mark 16:15), elected to continue proclaiming his message and moved from reform to heresy. As the later Dominican Inquisitor Stephen of Bourbon put it: "Valdez and his followers fell first into disobedience by their presumption and their usurpation of the apostolic office, then into contumacy, and finally under the sentence of excommunication."[26]

The usurpation of the apostolic office of preaching mentioned by Stephen reveals the core of the problem. In the medieval church, preaching was the prerogative of the ordained successors of the apostles, that is, the bishops, and through license by the bishop, also to priests. No layman had the functional qualification for preaching the word of God, at least if preaching be understood in the formal sense of proclamation of doctrine (*articuli fidei*). There was, however, another and broader understanding of public witness to the gospel available at the time that might have avoided the confrontation between Valdez and his bishop. About 1155, the *Dialogue between Two Monks* of Idung of Prüfening distinguished between the *officium docentis*, or office of teaching, by which every human is obligated to correct the intellectual and moral errors of his brethren, and the *officium praedicandi*, or public teaching, which is reserved to bishops and priests in their churches and abbots in their monasteries.[27] Innocent III himself was to use this form of distinction between doctrinal preaching and moral exhortation (*verbum exhortationis*) in the first decade of the thirteenth century in order bring some of the followers of Valdez back into communion with Rome.[28] Many of the higher clergy of the later Middle Ages, however, seemed to think it safer to restrict all forms of preaching to the ordained.

The issue of the proper understanding of the *paupertas vitae* practiced by Valdez and others was as complicated as their preaching.[29] Benedictine monks took a vow of poverty, which entailed giving up all their personal possessions when they entered the monastery, but the monastery itself needed land and resources to survive. The wealth accumulated by Benedictine monasteries through much of the Middle Ages led to a style of living that was sometimes far more opulent than that enjoyed by all but the greatest of the aristocracy. Much of the monastic reform of the eleventh and twelfth centuries was a protest against such affluence in the name of more rigid views of monastic poverty.

Similarly, many of the lower clergy who served the faithful in town and country were doubtless as poor as their flock, but the bishops and higher clergy often possessed considerable wealth. Though the Gregorian Reform was primarily directed against clerical marriage (nicolaitism) and the buying of ecclesiastical office (simony), it also was bound to raise questions about the appropriateness of clerical wealth. Finally, the growing role of liquid capital in late-twelfth-century society, often gained by what the church defined as usury, helped precipitate a religious crisis over the issue of poverty evident in the lives of Valdez and in his younger contemporary, Francis of Assisi. Poverty had been traditionally understood in a relatively limited way, as a form of moral control or one necessary ascetic practice among others, but toward the end of the twelfth century this confluence of issues began to give it a more potent force. For many poverty became nothing less than "the proper institutional condition of the kingdom of God in this world," as M.-D. Chenu put it.[30]

If the *vita apostolica* and the debates it engendered reflect the "ascending" aspects of the religious ferment that reached a culmination about 1200, the issue of the *cura animarum*, or pastoral reform, moved in the other direction; that is, it represented the "descending" effort of the official clerical hierarchy to encourage a more fervent Christianity among their flock. There is evidence for a rather important shift in concerns for implementing effective pastoral care in the years between the Third and the Fourth Lateran Councils (1179–1215), seen, for example, in the beginnings of the flood of *pastoralia,* or pastoral guides for the clergy.[31] Here, too, the decrees of Lateran IV represent a watershed. In contrast to its suspicion of new orders representing divergent understandings of the *vita apostolica,* the council set forth a full and positive program of what we would call today pastoral renewal. The best-known aspect of this was Constitution 21, which prescribed the yearly reception of the sacrament of penance and the Holy Eucharist from one's parish priest; but a host of other constitutions dealt with pastoral issues such as the obligation to preach (Constit. 10), the importance of care for the sick (Constit. 22), regulations about matrimony (Constit. 50-52), and precautions about the cult of relics (Constit. 62). A large number of the constitutions dealt with reform of the clergy, always a necessary condition for a more effective *cura animarum.*

Pope Innocent had been a student at Paris in the last decades of the twelfth century during the time of the flourishing of what has been called the "biblical-moral" school of Paris masters.[32] Great teachers (if not exactly original thinkers), like Peter Comestor, Peter Cantor, and Stephen Langton, building on the theological program first laid out by the Victorines, emphasized that the new scientific theology was ultimately worthless unless it served to improve the general education and preaching ability of the clergy. Peter Cantor's moral compendium, *The Abbreviated Word,* captures the pastoral concern of these theologians. For example, chapter 62 protests against "the evil silence, especially of prelates," that is, their failure to preach the gospel, while chapter 65 deals with the proper qualifications for a good confessor.[33] The latter includes an appropriate story about Pope Alexander III's response when someone praised him for being a good pope—"Alexander answered in his native tongue and said to him: 'If I knew that I fasted well, preached well, and did penance, then I would know I was a good pope.' Thus he set forth the entire office of a prelate in these three things."[34]

The major concerns of the pastoral renewal so important to popes like Alexander III and Innocent III included both negative and positive aspects. The most significant negative aspect was the necessity of combating heresy, the major growing internal threat to the Christian world order (the external threat of Islam and the crusade ideology used against it need not concern us here). The positive aspects were legion, but for this general account we can summarize them under three headings: preaching, sacraments, and devotionalism.

Preaching was central to the religious life of the later Middle Ages.[35] The

concern for more effective preaching that took place in the late twelfth and
especially in the thirteenth century is evident in many ways.[36] For example,
Maurice of Sully, the bishop of Paris, published his Sunday homilies on the
gospels in French in the 1170s as a guide to other preachers.[37] Soon handbooks of preaching also began to appear. Alan of Lille, a Paris master who
died a Cistercian in 1202, preached against the Cathar heretics in the 1180s
and then composed one of the earliest of such works, *The Art of Preaching*. In
it he places preaching at the summit of a seven-stage ladder of perfection,[38]
defining it as "open and public instruction in faith and morals for the purpose of human formation, deriving from the road of reason and the well-
spring of authority."[39] The impetus for improved preaching was given the
highest approbation at Lateran IV, which proclaimed:

> Among the things which pertain to the salvation of the Christian people the
> food of the word of God is known to be especially necessary, because the soul
> is nourished by spiritual food just as the body is by material food, so that "not
> by bread alone does man live, but by every word that comes forth from the
> mouth of God" (Mt. 4:4). . . . Therefore, we command that fitting men be
> ordained in cathedrals and other conventual churches whom the bishops may
> have as assistants and cooperators not only in the office of preaching, but also
> in hearing confessions, assigning penances, and the other things that pertain to
> the salvation of souls.[40]

The new mendicant religious orders, both Dominicans and Franciscans,
were soon to offer themselves as the most "fitting men" for this pastoral
imperative.[41]

The message preached centered on the sacramental life of the church,
particularly on penance and the Eucharist. The new theology of the sacraments worked out in the scholastic debates of the twelfth century bore fruit
in the sacramental renewal of the thirteenth century. Part of this emphasis
was defensive. The Catholic sacramental system was under severe attack,
both from reformist heretics, who, like the Donatists of old, denied the
validity of the sacraments performed by unworthy priests, and in an even
more serious way by the Cathar dualists, whose rejection of the material
world led to a condemnation of the Eucharist and the other sacraments.
The same Fourth Lateran Council that fostered the renewal of preaching
and commanded the yearly reception of penance and communion also
defined the reality of the presence of Christ's Body and Blood in the
Eucharist through adopting the new term "transubstantiation."[42]

The preaching of penance for sins was nothing new, but the growth and
development of the penitential system in the later Middle Ages was
remarkable.[43] Though the view is still controverted, there is good evidence

to suggest that the practice of confession was not really universal before the pastoral renewal centering on Lateran IV. The power to forgive sins and assign penances, to excommunicate and to remit penance through indulgences, was part of a vast and intricate system of social control, but it was also, for most believers at least, a moral and spiritual discipline that gave them hope for salvation.[44] The positive, pastoral side is especially evident in the numerous manuals for confessors that began to be produced around 1200. Alan of Lille was one of the first into the lists with a large *Book of Penance* written in the 1190s.[45] Once again, the new orders of mendicants soon took up the task of administering the sacrament with enthusiasm and expertise.[46]

The obligation of yearly confession was tied to the annual reception of the sacrament of Christ's Body and Blood. According to Miri Rubin, "The eucharist . . . was refigured in the eleventh and twelfth centuries to create a new structure of relations, thus modifying the symbolic order, and the social relations and political claims which could be attached to it." The result was that, "[t]he eucharist emerged as a unifying symbol for a complex world. . . . it possessed universal meaning."[47] This new "eucharistic symbolic order" was centered on what has been described as "a piety of presence,"[48] because for the most part actual reception of the Body and Blood of Christ was less important than demonstrating faith in the real presence of Christ by seeing and worshiping the Host. (The saintly King Louis IX of France, for example, took Communion only four times a year.) An exception to this rule is found among the women mystics to be studied in this volume, many of whom insisted on frequent reception of the sacrament and who often developed striking forms of eucharistic mysticism.[49] Indeed, the new liturgical feast of Corpus Christi, which celebrated Christ's real presence in the sacrament and became the lynchpin of the piety of presence, grew out of the efforts of one such mystic, Juliana of Mt. Cornillon.[50] Along with the new feast, the late Middle Ages produced a host of paraliturgical devotional practices witnessing to the significance of the Eucharist.

The pastoral renewal of the early thirteenth century seems to have been instrumental in encouraging the growth of many such devotions. According to Richard Kieckhefer, "Perhaps the most significant development in late medieval Christianity was the rise of devotionalism," seen as the complex of attitudes, prayers, and practices that constitute a middle way between officially recognized public liturgical actions and purely private and internal piety.[51] The devotional explosion of the late medieval period, far too varied and complex to be summarized here, was in many ways a reaction of the whole body of the faithful to the official program of a renewed *cura ani-*

marum set forth in Lateran IV and encouraged by thirteenth-century church leaders. Many of these devotions eventually received some form of official recognition; others did not, and some even came to be seen as superficial, superstitious, and dangerous to true faith. A number of them, particularly devotion to the passion of Christ and devotion to Mary, are very important for late medieval mysticism.[52] Their history witnesses to the interaction between clergy and laity, between men and women, that is also to be seen in the flowering of new forms of mysticism around the year 1200.

The New Mysticism[53]

Within the context of these changes, both in society and in the Western church, new ways of understanding and presenting the direct consciousness of the presence of God become evident in the early thirteenth century. Before considering them in detail, it will be helpful to give a brief heuristic sketch of major aspects of these developments and some of the methodological issues they raise for the study of mysticism. These developments can be summarized under three headings: (1) new attitudes toward the relation between world and cloister; (2) a new relationship between men and women in the mystical path; and, finally, (3) new forms of language and modes of representation of mystical consciousness.

The first great tradition or layer in the history of Western Christian mysticism, the monastic mysticism studied in *The Foundations of Mysticism* and *The Growth of Mysticism*, was created for the most part by a religious elite who fled from the world in order to find in the cloister a model here on earth of the Heavenly Jerusalem. The greatest figures in early Latin mysticism, particularly Ambrose and Augustine, and later Gregory the Great, were monastics, but they were also bishops engaged in the guidance of the Christian community, and therefore they encouraged all Christians to aspire to some form of more direct, or mystical, contact with God.[54] Nevertheless, up to the end of the twelfth century, their writings were preserved and read largely within monasteries and hence served primarily to guide those who had fled the "shipwreck of the world," as Gregory called it. Bernard of Clairvaux himself, the premier mystic of this century, theoretically expressed the view that every soul may find in itself "a source . . . whence it may dare to aspire to the nuptials of the Word,"[55] but, practically speaking, Bernard's message of loving union with Christ was directed to his fellow monks. Early medieval mysticism was dominated by the motif of withdrawal from the world in order to join a spiritual elite.

This emphasis begins to change in the early thirteenth century as we witness the first stirrings of a process of democratization and secularization that was to grow over the next five centuries. By democratization, I mean a conviction that it was practically and not just theoretically possible for all Christians, not just the *religiosi,* to enjoy immediate consciousness of God's presence. By secularization, I mean that flight from the world was not considered a necessary precondition for attaining such divine grace—God could be found in the secular realm and in the midst of everyday experience.[56] A phrase found in the *Life of Ida of Leeuw,* one of the early beguines, puts it in a nutshell: "She remained at home, living in the world, but did not live in a worldly way" (*domi manens, vivens in saeculo non saeculariter se deduxit*).[57]

This shift was neither immediate nor universal. Indeed, we can detect an ongoing tension between some late-medieval mystics who showed democratizing and secularizing tendencies and others who continued to insist on the necessity for physical withdrawal into an elite community for real mystical experience. (The latter position is argued, for example, in the Middle English *Cloud of Unknowing.*) This tension fostered debates that continued down to the early-twentieth-century neoscholastic discussions about whether or not mysticism was open to all believers.[58] But the evangelical movement out into the world represented by the new ways of understanding the *vita apostolica* made possible a growing conviction that God could be found anywhere and by anyone, if the proper dispositions were present and grace was given. Let us note here just a few witnesses from the thirteenth and fourteenth centuries.

One of the earliest texts about Francis of Assisi, the *Sacred Exchange* (*Sacrum Commercium*), perhaps written in 1227, tells the story of the meeting of the saint and his brethren and Lady Poverty. Toward the end of the work, after Lady Poverty has had a sparse banquet with the friars, she goes to sleep. The text continues: "She slept a very peaceful and sober sleep. She quickly arose and asked to be shown the cloister. They took her to a certain hill and showed her the whole world to be seen from there, saying, 'This, Lady, is our cloister.'"[59] Here we can see an important inversion of the traditional picture of the relation between world, cloister, and heaven. In monastic mysticism, one fled the world to enter the cloister, where, through spiritual exercise, it might become possible to enjoy the foretaste of paradise. In the *Sacred Exchange,* the Franciscan practice of absolute poverty allows the whole world to be seen as a cloister, and even a paradise! Lady Poverty tells the brethren that "[i]t seemed to me today as though I were with you in God's paradise," because "[o]n earth I am joined with those who represent for me the image of him to whom I am espoused in heaven."[60]

At the end of the thirteenth century and in the early decades of the four-

teenth century, the German Dominican Meister Eckhart repeatedly insisted
that God could be found, directly and decisively, anywhere and by anyone.
One of the most striking texts comes from a vernacular sermon preached
on 1 John 4:9:

> Truly, when people think that they are acquiring more of God in inwardness,
> in devotion, in sweetness and in various approaches than they do by the fire-
> side or in the stable, you are acting just as if you took God and muffled his
> head up in a cloak and pushed him under a bench. Whoever is seeking God
> by ways is finding ways and losing God, who in ways is hidden.[61]

In another vernacular sermon, Eckhart speaks of the ineffable joy that God
takes in any person who leaves or abandons himself and all things in perfect detachment or "separatedness" (*abegescheidenheit*), concluding:

> But I say yet more (do not be afraid for this joy is close to you and is in you):
> there is not one of you who is so cross-grained, so feeble in understanding or
> so remote but he may find this joy within himself, in truth, as it is, with joy
> and understanding, before you leave this church today, indeed before I have
> finished preaching; he can find this as truly within him, live it and possess it,
> as that God is God and I am a man.[62]

Eckhart's view of mysticism, as Reiner Schürmann and others have argued,
is decidely an inner-worldly one.[63] It is also directed to all Christians.

Catherine of Siena's mysticism with its highly visionary and ecstatic
emphasis is quite different from Eckhart's, but the Dominican tertiary also
witnesses to the movement out into the world with a universal message.
Karen Scott has shown how Catherine viewed herself as an *apostola* who
combined contemplative union with Christ and a divinely-given active apostolate of preaching and peace-making.[64] Even the *Major Life* of Catherine
written by the Dominican friar Raymond of Capua between 1384 and 1395,
which concentrates on the saint's mystical gifts, stresses the fact that these
were given to her not only in private but also in the public forum of worldly
activity—"From that time on the Lord began openly and familiarly to show
himself to his spouse not only in secret, as he had formerly done, but also in
public, while she was both on the road and when she was staying some-
where."[65] Obviously, this form of *unio mystica* is in continuity with the ancient
tradition, insisted on by many monastic mystics, that the highest form of spiritual attainment was to be seen in some combination of action and contemplation.[66] Still, action and contemplation had traditionally been viewed as
successive aspects of a total life dedicated to God, aspects often in tension with
one another; they had not been conceived of as being capable of complete
fusion within the sphere of public activity, as in Catherine's case.

The second major shift in late medieval mysticism involves gender: it is only after 1200 that women begin to take a prominent place in the mystical tradition. I emphasize the word "tradition" here (that is, what is handed on in a public way to become accessible to later generations), because we obviously cannot exclude a role for women in the monastic layer of Western mysticism. The problem is that we have very little written evidence. Outside of a few pieces of hagiography, the writings of one or two remarkable women, like Hildegard of Bingen, and some texts directed primarily to women, like the twelfth-century German *Teaching of the Loving Knowledge of God,* there is little in the recorded tradition.[67] Nothing is more stiking about the new mysticism beginning about 1200 than the important role that women assume, both in terms of hagiographical accounts and texts produced by women themselves. Without denying that there have been important women, and even women writers, in Christianity from its earliest years, it is fair to say that the great age of women's theology begins in 1200.[68]

This new role for women raises a number of issues that will recur in the course of this book and in later volumes in this history. Perhaps the most prominent, as well as the most difficult to answer, is whether it is possible to discern a distinctive women's mysticism. Obviously, any remotely satisfactory answer to this question must come as the result of the kind of detailed investigation that this and the following volumes will attempt to conduct. Here it is important to set out some methodological guidelines for such an investigation, particularly those that deal with the dangers to be avoided.[69]

The first, perhaps obvious, maxim is to avoid undue generalization and essentialization. The fact that some, or even many women may tend to use language in a certain way, or to adopt distinctive kinds of symbols, or to construct their gender identity and its relation to God according to particular patterns, does not necessarily mean that all women or no men will do so. From this perspective, it is difficult to imagine that there could be *one single* form of mysticism characteristic of all women, and only of women, either in the late Middle Ages, or in any other period in the history of the tradition. It may be possible, of course, to discern patterns of presentation of mystical consciousness—both of the immediate experience of God and of the path to it and the effects it produces—that are first associated with women, or whose earliest appearance is in the writings of women mystics, and that remain more consistently realized in the case of women than in that of men. A number of studies of aspects of late medieval women's mysticism have been successful in pointing to such patterns, such as those relating to food and eating studied in Caroline Walker Bynum's *Holy Feast and Holy Fast.* Nevertheless, it is misleading to move on to general conclusions about the differences between how men and women use language and symbol on the basis of any single pattern, form of language, symbol, or the like.[70]

A second helpful maxim is to avoid privileging the present. The rediscovery of medieval women mystics, at least in part, has been fueled by contemporary feminism and feminist theology, which have discovered in these often forgotten female voices valued predecessors and conversation partners. There is nothing wrong with this—all historical investigation involves a spiraling dialogue between the questions and concerns of the historian and the evidence she or he seeks to understand and present. But there are also dangers. Our issues are often widely different from those of the medieval mystics. Forgetting this can all too easily lead either to neglect of beliefs and practices that were central to the medieval figures but marginal or troubling to us (e.g., the role of virginity, or the practice of certain forms of asceticism), or else to reading back contemporary issues into the medieval world through a skewed selectivity of evidence or a confusion between ambiguous similarities and possible real convergences. All historical reconstruction is selective, but some selections are more representative and illuminating than others. The historian of medieval women's spirituality needs to strive for as wide and sensitive a presentation as possible, as Caroline Walker Bynum has noted:

> The task for future historians of women's piety is not only to devote more detailed study to texts by women but also to pay attention to the full range of phenomena in these texts, no matter how masochistic or altruistic, unattractive or heroic, peculiar, amusing, or charming such phenomena may seem, either by modern standards or by those of medieval men.[71]

Bynum's point here serves to introduce a third methodological caution needed for investigating the role of women in medieval mysticism—the need to be attentive to the gender perspective of the evidence under investigation.

Much of what we know about medieval women mystics comes from the pens of their male admirers. These texts tell us what men wanted to think about holy women. This is true of most of the thirteenth-century lives, though by the fourteenth century women had also begun to produce substantial amounts of hagiography, as in the case of the Dominican *Sister Books* to be treated in the final chapter.[72] The same male perspective is also at least partly evident in the case of the important texts in which a confessor or spiritual advisor took down a mystical account given him by a woman.[73] Other texts, of course, are rightly thought of as the direct product of a woman's literary activity, though even here medieval concepts of authorship were different from ours in important ways.

Medieval conceptions of gender must also be understood in context. On the one hand, we are constantly and rightly warned against thinking that medieval women merely internalized the mostly misogynist view of their sex that was the cultural given of their time,[74] while on the other hand, we should remember that it is a modern prejudice to think that often they may not have agreed with these cultural biases. It is also quite likely that some male authors came to modify or stretch their inherited views of women's nature–and human nature–by what they learned from the *mulieres sanctae* they so much admired. It is only by a subtle and searching attentiveness to the particularities of presentation in our texts that we will gain more insight into the true role of women in late medieval mysticism.

It is my conviction that the best model for approaching the issue of the relation between men and women in late medieval mysticism is that of an overheard conversation, rather than that of argument or confrontation (though these cannot be excluded from the record either). Just as remarkable as the sudden emergence of women at this time is the evidence that this emergence was characterized by new forms of cooperation between women and men, in terms of both a shared dedication to the pursuit of the *vita apostolica* and a joint concern for attaining the "loving knowledge of God."

Within the context of the medieval church it was virtually impossible for women to create new ways of living the gospel without the cooperation and approval of men.[75] So too, the voices of medieval women mystics only rarely reach us in the form of a direct address written "from her own point of view," so to speak. Rather, in so many cases (Mary of Oignies, Beatrice of Nazareth, Angela of Foligno, Mechthild of Magdeburg, to mention only some prominent thirteenth-century examples) what we hear comes to us in the form of a dialogue in which the contributions of male and female voices are both present in varied ways, often in a mutually enriching fashion.[76] Such records of a lost dialogue are frequently frustrating and difficult to decipher. As the historical novelist Marguerite Yourcenar observed, "Too few people are aware of the extent to which human speech is relayed to us from the past in stages–staggering along, infected with miscomprehensions, eaten away by omissions, and encrusted with additions. . . ."[77] Even when it is possible to catch hints of these conversations, we cannot deny that dialogue, then as now, was often either a prelude to, or a mask for, the monologic triumph of the authoritative male voice of ecclesiastical authority. We shall see examples of this in the chapters that follow. But it is not the whole story–and not, I suggest, its most lasting part.

The succeeding chapters will contain many illustrations of these conversations, most often only implicitly presented and therefore difficult to retrieve. Let me cite here just one explicit example of the process. The Austrian beguine Agnes Blannbekin lived in Vienna from about 1260 until her death in 1315. Although she was sufficiently literate to read the Divine Office, her mystical visions and auditions were written down after her death by her confessor, a Franciscan friar, under the title of *Life and Revelations*.[78] In chapter 118 of the work the friar recounts a meeting between him and Agnes beginning as follows:

> One day I was reading her some passages of St. Bernard's *Sermons on the Song of Songs* about how the soul of the bride, renouncing all other desires, rests wholly and only on love. As she thought about this, she wondered at how she ought not strive after honor, because among St. Bernard's sayings one also finds that God, insofar as he is the Bridegroom, asks only to be loved. As she turned this over in her mind, she heard a voice within saying to her, "The devout soul who is in the bridal chamber of contemplation as the bride strives only for love."[79]

The chapter goes on to recount, however, that such a soul is not only a bride but also a mother and provider in the household (*materfamilias in domo et procuratrix*), and therefore she needs to combine active and contemplative love. The fascinating aspect of this vignette is how Agnes and her confessor deal with mystical issues through their joint attempt to understand the message contained in Bernard by way of a new revelation from the ultimate source in God.

Some contemporary feminists may find the investigation of the medieval sources, with the complex interchange they demonstrate between male and female mystics, largely fruitless if it does not lead us closer to the identification of a "true" women's mysticism. Others, like Danielle Régnier-Bohler, suggest a wider vision when they affirm that "[t]his cooperation between men and women marked an important step in the development of a capacity for self-analysis and self-expression" among women.[80] From the perspective of the history of mysticism, I would argue that the mutual enrichment that came precisely from this unprecedented dialogue was one of the most remarkable characteristics of the new mysticism of the later Middle Ages.[81]

The issue of the role of women and the complexities of gender are inseparable from the third major area that deserves comment—that of forms of language and modes of representation found in mystical texts. Throughout this history of mysticism I have insisted that the immediate object of study is not mystical experience as such but the mystical text, both written and (increasingly in the late Middle Ages) visual.[82] This conviction about the textual and linguistic foundation of mysticism is even more central to the present volume, because after 1200 the forms of mystical language become far more diverse with the move into the vernacular languages, a transition that allowed the modes of representation of mystical experience to take on remarkable new configurations.[83] The rich, though never static, equilibrium found in the major twelfth-century mystical traditions, especially those of the Cistercians and Victorines, was based in part on the common learned language of a largely male cultural and religious elite. The picture was to grow more diverse, more striking and flamboyant, at times more extreme, and certainly far more controversial in the world of vernacular mystical theology that we find beginning in the thirteenth century.[84]

The course of medieval theology can be understood according to the model of three interactive modes of appropriating the meaning of faith–the monastic, the scholastic, and the vernacular.[85] For the better part of a century, modern investigation of medieval thought recognized only one kind of theology: the professional, scientific, and academic theology of the Schoolmen, the theology that arose in the eleventh and twelfth centuries. The pioneering work of Jean Leclercq and others around the middle of the present century helped medievalists to discern the lineaments of a monastic theology that flourished from the time of Gregory the Great down through the twelfth century, a theology whose contributions to the history of mysticism were studied in *The Growth of Mysticism*. The research of the past several decades, however, has begun to make clear the existence of a third form of medieval theology, equally important, if more diffuse and difficult to describe: vernacular theology. Some might prefer to say vernacular "theologies"; different linguistic matrices shaped different actualizations of an understanding of faith that was not bound to the professional schools or the cloister. Still, taking a clue from the writings of Erich Auerbach, one could argue that there was some unity to vernacular theology, despite the many national tongues in which it came to expression, because of the singleness of spirit that fueled these attempts to appropriate the Christian story set forth in the Bible.[86] This narrative, as Auerbach showed, from the beginning contained the germs of a new style, that of the *sermo humilis,* "an entirely new kind of sublimity, in which the everyday and the low were included, not excluded, so that, in style as in content, it directly connected the lowest with the highest."[87]

All forms of medieval theology tried to be true to two goals–deepening the understanding of faith (*intellectus fidei*) and enkindling charity (*experientia caritatis*), so that the believer could arrive at the higher understanding of love (*intelligentia amoris*). They did so, however, by employing different genres and patterns of presentation, produced by theologians who were authenticated in different ways and who often addressed rather different audiences. The technical genres of Latin scholastic theology, such as the *lectio, quaestio, disputatio,* and *summa,* are well known; so too are the monastic genres of biblical commentary, letter-treatise, and written rhetorical sermons, such as those that make up Bernard's great commentary on the Song of Songs.[88]

It is more difficult to describe the genres of the new vernacular theology, once again because they are less technically precise and identifiable than those used by scholastic and monastic thinkers. Of course, much vernacular theology was communicated through hagiography, one of the broadest, most investigated, yet still misunderstood forms of medieval literature.[89] Saints' *vitae* may perhaps be seen as something like modern film—a protean medium of communication and entertainment containing many forms, but one in which certain modes of representation remain characteristic of the whole. If films intend primarily to entertain, *vitae* may at times entertain but always in the service of instruction. Some pieces of hagiography, like *cinema verité,* do their best to imitate the appearance of reality, though the modern reader should not confuse this form of representation with real life, any more than we would do in the case of films that pretend to imitate everyday occurrences. Most saints' lives, however, involve a heightening of the presentation of events according to certain conventions that were as well understood by their medieval audience as the adaptations of reality that contemporary viewers accept in film. Most of these implicit rules for reading hagiography pertained throughout the Middle Ages, though there were also innovations in the period after 1200, such as the "autohagiographies" created in the fourteenth century.[90]

Another important genre, though it too is fluid in expression, is the vision, sometimes standing alone, at other times inserted into saints' lives, or linked with other visions and commentary to form a quasi-genre, the visionary collection or compendium, as illustrated by mystics like Hadewijch in the thirteenth century and Julian of Norwich in the fourteenth. At times these visionary collections take the form of spiritual "diaries," as we find in Margarite Ebner and Agnes Blannbekin in the fourteenth century. Though there is no way of being sure, this may have been true of the lost vernacular account of her visions by Beatrice of Nazareth in the early decades of the thirteenth century. A number of mystics also adapted prose or poetic versions of courtly personification dialogues, as we find in the cases of Mechthild, Hadewijch, and Marguerite Porete among the women, and Henry Suso among the men.[91] The use of poetry to express mystical consciousness, though not unknown in the earlier tradition, grew in significance in vernacular theology, as the figures of Hadewijch, Mechthild, and

Jacopone da Todi show. Many brief treatises, letters, and, of course, vernacular sermons (often quite different from the logically organized Latin sermons of the scholastic mode) also form part of the picture. This list is not meant to be exhaustive—it merely suggests that in the world of vernacular theology genre was important but not easy to characterize.

Even less easy to describe in any general way is the rich variety of linguistic strategies that the vernacular theologians utilized in the presentation of their message. Though the learned language of Latin possessed distinct advantages in terms of its weight of sacrality,[92] its scholastic precision, its homogeneity, cultural universality, and ability to maintain a link between past and present, Latin suffered from important disadvantages as well.[93] Latin was at best half-alive in the Middle Ages—never the language of first acquisition, always bound to a male-dominated cultural elite, and regulated by inherited models of linguistic propriety that made innovation difficult, though never impossible. The vernacular languages that were beginning to become literate in the full sense around 1200 offered, on the contrary, remarkable potential for creative innovation. The mystics were in at the creation. In terms of some literary vernacular traditions—Dutch, for example—mystical texts are among our earliest witnesses, and in almost every early vernacular literature of Western Europe we can point to major monuments that are examples of the new vernacular theology, most often of a mystical character.[94]

The mode of attaining an authoritative voice—becoming an *auctoritas* in one medieval sense—was also different in vernacular theology from what it was in scholasticism or among the monks. The most obvious difference, of course, is that so many of the vernacular theologians were women. There was no institutionally approved way by which a woman could gain the authority to teach in an official way,[95] but, given Christian belief that the Holy Spirit is the true source of all divine truth, women could not be totally excluded from all forms of teaching. About 1290 the Paris master Henry of Ghent, disputing the question "Whether a woman can be a doctor of theology?" distinguished between teaching *ex officio* and teaching *ex beneficio* (i.e., from the gift of grace). Women were excluded from the former, but "[s]peaking about teaching from divine favor and the fervor of charity, it is well allowed for a woman to teach just like anyone else, if she possesses sound doctrine."[96] Henry wished to limit such teaching to the private sector and to other women; not all women were to abide by these rules, both among the suspect, like Marguerite Porete, and among the accepted, like Catherine of Siena. By the early fifteenth century there were even voices raised claiming that teaching *ex beneficio* and in the vernacular was really all that was needed. The Franciscan Giovanni Bonvisi of Lucca gave the sisters of Monteluce this authorization: "Speak in charity and you will speak theologically (*per teologia*). One may understand the Scriptures without *grammatica*, namely by a certain light from God. *Grammatica* is nothing but language."[97]

The ways in which women gained such authority within the realm of vernacular theology were as many and varied as the women themselves and need to be investigated case by case before any generalizations can be made. We also must remember that men who did not qualify as teachers according to the normal ecclesiastical and academic channels also had to create similar new models of authority. While many vernacular theologians, like the German Dominicans, could appeal to their clerical and academic status, other figures, like the unordained fourteenth-century English hermit, Richard Rolle, enjoyed no such position. Rolle, therefore, had to work out a complex and carefully prepared claim to authority in his writings, as Nicholas Watson has shown.[98] Other lay male mystics, like the German merchant Rulman Merswin, were less subtle and also less successful in their attempts to claim authorization.

Vernacular theology, then, employed different genres from the scholastic and monastic theologies and was put forth according to new modes of claiming authority *ex beneficio* (that is, from grace). It also was directed to a different audience—one both wider and narrower than that of the technical scholastic Latin. The vernacular audience was wider, of course, because it addressed any person, male or female, high or low, who was literate in the particular vernacular employed. But the audience was also narrower because it did not use the learned language which guaranteed texts a broad dissemination across linguistic barriers. This contrast, however, needs to be qualified by two important considerations that also help illumine the vitality and variety of the new mysticism.

First of all, a number of mystical texts were produced in a form of Latin that can be said to reflect the new vernacular theology in terms of authorship, style, and content, even though they were written down in the language of the learned. The writings of Francis of Assisi, for example, are certainly not the product of a scholastic mind, or even of one trained in monastic thought, though they bespeak a deep theological vision set forth in a dramatic new "vernacular" way of using language.[99] The same is true for the mystical text of Angela of Foligno, the *Memorial* taken down in Latin by a Franciscan friar—a fascinating example of a work created by a typical conversation between a male and a female author.[100] Another example can be found in Henry Suso, who produced first a German and then a rather different Latin version of his longest mystical treatise, *The Clock of Wisdom* (*Little Book of Eternal Wisdom,* in Middle High German).

The second qualification against making too simple a contrast between Latin and the vernacular is that vernacular theological texts that were found particularly impressive were often translated into Latin in order to give them a more universal and permanent status as a part of high culture. The first of these was Beatrice's *Seven Manners of Loving,* available in the Latin *vita* of this Cistercian nun written about 1275; the second was Mechthild of Magdeburg's *Flowing Light of the Godhead,* written between 1250 and 1280 and translated into Latin by admiring Dominicans in the 1290s. Translations were made both of works considered dangerous, like Marguerite Porete's *Mirror of Simple Souls,* and of mainstream ones, like John Tauler's sermons and John Ruusbroec's treatises. In the case of Meister Eckhart's German sequence "The Mustard Seed" (*Granum sinapis*), we have the unusual example of a learned Latin commentary being made on the vernacular poem, probably by one of his Dominican confreres. Careful study of the vernacular and Latin versions of the same mystical texts (they are rarely simple translations), as in the case of the texts of Beatrice and Mechthild, reveals interesting differences between male and female perspectives and casts new light on the relationships between the various forms of medieval theology.

What this all suggests is that while Latin was no longer totally adequate, it was still necessary. In the same way that much of the new mystical vernacular theology was the product of a conversation between men and women which we overhear only in snatches in the records that survive to us, so too the new mysticism developed to a large degree through an analogous dialogue between Latin, mostly of the scholastically precise form rather than the proto-humanist rhetorical variety,[101] and the burgeoning vernaculars. Dante, the figure in whom the vernacular first directly challenged Latin for cultural dominance, provides a good illustration of the complexity of the relationship. In his vernacular treatise of ca. 1304–1308, *The Banquet (Il Convivio),* the great poet began with an argument for the superiority of Latin in a text written in Italian (*Conv.* I.5), though the case was subtly undercut in the succeeding chapters of book 1 by his argument for the inappropriateness of writing a Latin commentary on vernacular poems and by his defense of his natural love of his native tongue.[102] In his treatise *On Vernacular Eloquence (De vulgari eloquentia),* on the other hand, Dante directly defended the illustrious character of the vernacular, but he did so in Latin, the universal language of culture.[103] Although Dante was the most forceful proponent of the creativity of the vernacular, the fact that he chose to present his message in Latin is a sign that the bond between the two forms of expression was still a symbiotic one.[104]

Finally, the conversation between men and women, as well as between Latin and the vernacular, undercuts not only simplistic attempts to uncover the feminine voice in all its purity but also the claims of some students of medieval mysticism that overstate the difference between mysticism in the vernacular languages and the Latin mysticism of the inherited tradition. I do not believe that mysticism really *first* comes into its own in its vernacular expression in the late Middle Ages, primarily because this view implies that biographical or autobiographical descriptions of personal visionary experience constitute the real core of mysticism.[105] There are differences, to be sure, between texts that reflect more on the theological conditions for the possibility of the direct encounter with God in this life and those that attempt to present these conditions through descriptions of personal experience. There are also, as I have tried to suggest above, significant changes and developments that become evident when mysticism moves into the vernacular languages. But to define "real" mysticism primarily as the "experiential" and visionary mysticism found in late medieval vernacular texts is to impoverish the richness of the Western mystical tradition and to hinder rather than to assist the task of attempting to understand the new mysticism itself. Its very novelty is constituted in terms of its dialogue with the older tradition.[106]

If movement out into the world—a democratization and secularization as I have termed it—represents the external and social dimension of the new mysticism, and if gender issues, especially the new role of women in vernacular theology, are crucial to its internal constitution, what is to be said, if only in introductory fashion, about the message conveyed in this new stage in the history of Western mysticism? What are the contours of its teaching about how God may or may not become present in this life? How are these related to previous forms of mystical teaching? What do these texts have to tell us about these mystics and their view of God? Answers to these questions will be possible only on the basis of the investigation that follows in this and subsequent volumes of *The Presence of God*, but one issue that raises important questions about the very nature of mysticism needs to be taken up here, if only in preliminary fashion—the significance of the late medieval predilection for biographical and autobiographical accounts of a visionary nature for the history of the mysticism.

One of the most striking aspects of the new mysticism is the explosion of accounts of what German scholars have called "experiential mysticism" (*Erlebnismystik*). Aspects of this stress on the presentation of direct "experience," especially of a visionary kind, had already appeared in the twelfth century. The Bernardine appeal to the *liber experientiae,* as pointed out in *The Growth of Mysticism,* introduced a significant new dimension in Western mysticism, though the Cistercian's emphasis on the mutuality of the biblical book and the experiential one made his appeal to experience different from that found in most of the women mystics of the thirteenth century. This difference went beyond the fact that women could never be professional scriptural exegetes as Bernard himself and Richard of St. Victor were.[107] Similarly, autobiographical accounts of properly mystical visionary experiences began to appear in the twelfth century, both among men, like Rupert of Deutz and Joachim of Fiore,[108] and among women. Some of Hildegard of Bingen's descriptions of her unusual states of consciousness fit this category,[109] as do those of a figure like the English anchoress, Christina of Markyate (died after 1154).[110]

These developing trends scarcely prepare us for the flood of visionary narratives, especially by and about women, that begin to appear shortly after 1200. Many of these texts contain descriptions of direct encounters with Jesus that signal a new form of mystical consciousness, or mystical knowing—more direct, more excessive, more bodily in nature than older forms.[111] It is only within the past decade or so that the extravagant corporeal manifestations of the medieval mystics, largely female, have been hailed as indications of a breakthrough beyond the more restrained, "intellectualized" conceptions found in the earlier mystical tradition, rather than as indications of some form of personal imbalance, even hysteria.[112] Such visions and visionaries were to remain controversial among those mystics who downplayed the importance of paranormal occurrences as well as among the clerics who emphasized the necessity for "testing the spirits" (*discretio spirituum*). There can be no question, however, of their impact on the religious life of the time. Of the many issues that this proliferation of visionary accounts raises, two stand out for discussion here. To what extent can these narratives be considered descriptions of real experiences? And, are all medieval visions (whether "real" or not) to be considered mystical? Let me take them up in reverse order.

As I have already argued in *The Growth of Mysticism,* it seems incorrect to me to treat all late medieval accounts of visions as mystical, if the term mysticism is to retain enough specificity to allow it to characterize a continuing tradition in the beliefs and practices of the Christian religion. The visionary and the mystical elements in Christianity are distinct, though obviously interconnected, trajectories. If all experiential accounts of visions and auditions from the celestial realm, no matter *whom* they involve (God, Christ,

Mary, angels, saints), and *what* they teach (messages about reform of the church, or about future events, doctrinal disputes, etc.), are to be considered mystical, then the mystical element in Christianity is in danger of losing connection with what most mystics themselves have claimed to be essential, that is, a special consciousness of the presence of God that by definition exceeds description and results in a transformation of the subject who receives it. Mysticism should not be reduced to the history of more or less autobiographical claims to have received some kind of visual manifestation of the other world, varied as these have been.[113] To accept such a definition would compel us to view most of what the earlier Christian tradition taught about *contemplatio* and *theologia mystica* as peripheral to true mysticism: at best a theological preparation, a *Mystologie* or *Mystagogie* as some German authors call it, to the *real* mysticism. My conviction throughout this history has been that real mysticism has been present in Christianity from an early era, though expressed in varying ways and with greater degrees of explicitness over the course of the centuries. The visionary mystics of the thirteenth and fourteenth centuries themselves witness to this continuity in their deep dependence on the rich inheritance of received teaching about *contemplatio,* despite the new elements they introduced.

The fundamental error behind the equation of mysticism with visionary narrative lies in the assumption that there is some kind of inner division between the "experiential" and the "theological" aspects of the Christian mystical tradition. Fortunately, the notion that mystical texts are screens or distorting coverings that must be penetrated or peeled away to uncover the "religious" experience behind the veil of the text has come under increasing fire in recent study. Without entering into the theoretical deficiencies of this approach to mysticism, it is enough to note here that the medieval mystics themselves never admitted such a separation. As Alois M. Haas put it: "It is not carelessness when Christian mystics do not want to make a distinction between mystical experience and the meaning or the teaching about this experience; it is intentional."[114]

The mystical element within Christianity, as I have argued throughout this history, centers on a form of immediate encounter with God whose essential purpose is to convey a loving knowledge (even a negative one) that transforms the mystic's mind and whole way of life. This view, I believe, can provide categories sufficiently specific and yet flexible enough to include in one broad tradition both the usually nonvisionary and non-autobiographical monastic mysticism dominant prior to 1200 and the mystical aspects of the visionary explosion of the later Middle Ages. Thus, mysticism is characterized primarily by a sense of an immediate relation to God and the transformation this effects in the consciousness of the recipient–not by visions or auditions, which constitute, at best, as Antoine Vergote puts it, "the remnants of perceptual experiences or surpassed imaginative productions and premonitions of the union they anticipate and desire."[115] Hence, it is not so much the *fact* that someone makes claims to visionary experience as it is the *kind of vision* presented, the *purpose* for which it is given, and the *effect* it has on the recipient that will determine whether or not any particular vision may be described as mystical. This was a message well known to medieval mystics, even those like Angela of Foligno and Julian of Norwich who experienced many such showings.[116]

The second question prompted by the visionary explosion beginning around 1200 concerns the extent to which these accounts can be accepted as direct reporting of the experiences of the purported authors themselves or of close associates of the saints whose lives are being presented. In short, how "real" are they? Throughout its whole history medieval culture was intensely visionary. "Visions were," as Christopher Holdsworth put it, "one aspect of the continuing revelation of God."[117] The reality of visionary experience was scarcely questioned in the Middle Ages, but we must remember that the kinds of visions that people actually experienced and especially the ways in which they communicated the meaning of visions to others were shaped by theological and cultural forms that we can at best only partially recover.

Medieval authors knew the difference between visions that were presented as literary fictions, whether dream-visions or not, and visions whose mode of presentation purported to be rooted in personal experience.[118] In the case of the latter, Dinzelbacher has demonstrated that the most popular type of vision changed in the later Middle Ages. The form of vision that was widespread prior to ca. 1150–1200 was the tour of heaven and hell, the genre that was transformed to a new and higher level in Dante's *Divine Comedy*. A significant alternate form of vision began in the twelfth century, however, and grew in importance throughout the later Middle Ages. This involved ecstatic transport to the supernatural realm, where a revelation in pictorial form was given to the seer, most often by a heavenly being. These experiences tended to be repeatable apparitions consciously prepared for and expected.[119] Such visions, whether mystical or not, had many uses. From the recipient's viewpoint, they were important for the supernatural authority they provided for her message. From a broader cultural perspective they also seem to point to changes in the perception of the relationship

between this world and the next, a conviction that in the case of some specially graced individuals the usual barriers between the earthly and the
heavenly were more permeable than had been previously supposed.

The theology underpinning visionary claims to teaching *ex beneficio* was
well known in the thirteenth century. The clerical hagiographers were
aware that many earlier medieval saints had received visions. They were
also acquainted with the theology of visions laid down by Augustine and
refined by twelfth-century theologians like Richard of St. Victor.[120] This
background helps us understand why visionary recitals were so frequently
employed as proofs of the authority and sanctity of particular figures, but it
does not give us much assistance in discovering why the mode and content
of visionary recitals shifted away from a predominance of descriptions of
lengthy visits to heaven and hell in the direction of repeatable encounters
with a variety of heavenly figures. As noted above, these new visions were
often (though not always) mystical, involving personal, deeply emotional,
and even erotic encounters with Jesus, the Divine Lover.[121] But did they
really happen? Or, more accurately, can these accounts of "experienced
visions" be automatically taken as some kind of direct reporting?

The misplaced issue of the "reality" of medieval visions was the subject
of some debate in the 1980s, especially between the historian Peter Dinzelbacher and scholars of Middle High German mystical texts, such as Siegfried Ringler and Ursula Peters.[122] On the basis of his study of the *Sister
Books,* that is, the *vitae* of the German Dominican nuns produced in the first
half of the fourteenth century, Ringler argued that the use of literary conventions and compositional structures in this genre of what seems at first
glance like direct reporting of visions makes it difficult to recover the
"authenticity of the experience" (*Erlebnisechtheit*) portrayed.[123] Dinzelbacher
attacked this viewpoint by insisting that such accounts must be grounded in
historical reality,[124] but Ringler defended his position by invoking the wider
methodological implications of the necessity of recognizing the role of
reception and literary structure in late medieval visionary accounts.[125] As he
pointed out, the "reality" of any literary text is much more complex than
the question of whether it portrays things "as they actually happened"—
"'The real' is not only the historical substratum that underlies the literary
presentation; in a much more powerful measure the real is often the literary
presentation itself, even in its fictive part insofar as it is a product of historically effective forces and above all insofar as it becomes historically effective itself."[126] While it is certainly true, as Dinzelbacher noted, that
"[w]ithout their underlying [mystical] experience these textual expressions
would not exist,"[127] this observation needs to be qualified to be really help-

ful in the investigation of visionary mystical accounts. Without *some* kind of claim to an underlying experience these textual expressions would probably not have come into existence and certainly would not have won acceptance; but to say that every expression of such a claim was intended as a more or less literal account of a divinely given vision is neither provable nor required in order to demonstrate how the new modes of *presenting* visions argue for a new stage of Western mysticism.

Reflection on the kind of contact with God that is suggested in a text and how this contact is presented cannot be adequately investigated through simple contrasts between experience and theory or by invoking simplistic divisions between underlying mystical content and overlying literary form. We must continue to insist that we have no *direct* access to the experience of thirteenth-century mystics—or any other mystics for that matter. We should always remember that medieval mystics placed far less value on the significance of "experience" than many modern theories of mysticism do. Furthermore, medieval mystics lived within a total religious world. Even in the case of "illiterate" women, the mediation of a living tradition, beginning with the Bible and including liturgy, other forms of prayer and iconography, as well as the consultation with clerical advisors, must always be taken into account as significant factors in determining the kinds of "experiences" these mystics may have enjoyed.[128] To be sure, the mediation of the prior mystical tradition never set absolute boundaries for what states of consciousness were possible in the search for God, especially in a religion where God remains ever more than can be conceived or expressed even by what is given in revelation. (As Lateran IV put it: "Between Creator and creature one can never affirm as much likeness as there is unlikeness.")[129] Nevertheless, the reception of tradition was crucial in shaping the forms of mystical communication that were judged effective and accepted.

The student of mysticism has to avoid two false extremes. The first naively misses the point that much late medieval literature, including mystical literature, involves what Franz Bäuml has described as "the creation of the fiction that a fiction is not a fiction."[130] But even "fiction" can have a real didactic purpose, especially in the kind of overarching worldview within which late medieval mystics lived. The second extreme suggests that all linguistic stylization, such as the use of *topoi* or of implicit quotations of earlier authoritative texts, indicates that we are dealing with purely literary creations independent of the contemplative and ecstatic modes of consciousness enjoyed by real individuals. Every description is rooted in assumptions about what is possible and what has been experienced, as well as about how the two can be described. Greater attention to the role of genre, the anticipated audience, the styles of representation, and especially the possibilities and limits of the nascent vernacular languages in comparison with Latin, will help us appreciate more fully the hermeneutical situation within which medieval mystical consciousness is textually mediated to us.[131]

Specifically with regard to visions, I suggest that it is helpful to think of them primarily as "visualizations," in the sense of powerful imaginative creations based on intense meditation on the imagery of the Bible and the liturgy, as well as artistic representations of Christ, the angels and saints, heaven and hell, and so on. Michael Camille has noted how the world of Gothic art involved a "new way of seeing" that shaped every aspect of the visual culture of the thirteenth and fourteenth centuries.[132] Medieval nuns were among the virtuosi practitioners of this new mode of seeing—"Nuns were probably among those members of society with the most sophisticated visual skills of comparison and juxtaposition, precisely because every aspect of their lives, from attending mass, private devotions, and prayer, was lived in the constant presence of images."[133] Hence, it is not surprising that the religious women of the late Middle Ages, such as the beguines Hadewijch and Mechthild, the Cistercian nuns of Helfta, and the German Dominican nuns of the first half of the fourteenth century, produced such powerful and original new visions, or visualizations, of the inner meaning of salvation history and of the mystical relation between God and humans. It is understandable that they would have conceived of their imaginative constructions and the dialogues that accompanied them as divinely given insofar as these produced new theological and spiritual insights useful for themselves and their readers. But theological evaluations of these visions, both in the Middle Ages and in the present century, have never insisted that such presentations need be taken at face value or in a purely literal way.[134]

These observations are not meant to deny the innovative character of the visionary, ecstatic, excessive aspects of the new mysticism that began about the year 1200, any more than we should question the fact that the new movement was pioneered by women and came to expression in the nascent vernacular theology. Recent excitement over these innovations, however, has not always kept them in perspective, especially because of lack of attention to the forms of dialogue that were essential to their development—the dialogue between men and women, between Latin and the emerging vernaculars, between spirituality and theology, and finally that between the inherited wisdom of the ancient contemplative tradition and the creative energies of a new era. As Hans-Georg Gadamer once put it: "To stand within a tradition does not limit the freedom of knowledge but makes it possible."[135]

CHAPTER 1

Men and Women and the Origins of the New Mysticism

The introduction has surveyed the new mysticism in terms of its historical context and some of the methodological issues it has evoked in recent scholaship. It is now time to investigate the origins of this new stage in the history of Western mysticism through the lives and writings of those responsible for it.

There is much that is surprising about the story of these beginnings. They were sudden and brief—effected in a period of roughly two decades. They involved the cooperation of both men and women, in varying ways, right from the start. Finally, although they occurred mainly in two widely separated parts of Europe, there were important connections, geographical and personal, especially in terms of common goals, among the leaders.[1] The bonds that related new religious movements in Lotharingia and Umbria were not genetic in the sense that one movement caused the other; but they do demonstrate how much the new mysticism had common roots in the renewal associated with the *vita apostolica.*

The more one considers the evidence from a synoptic point of view, the more one senses a surprising inner unity in the first moments of the new layer in the history of Christian mysticism. The connections are evident not only in terms of common spiritual values but also with regard to gender dynamics. An investigation of two pairs of spiritual leaders—Francis and Clare in Umbria, and Mary of Oignies and James of Vitry in Lotharingia—will demonstrate this claim. Although the polarity of the gender relation is different in the two cases—Francis was the model and exemplar for Clare, while Mary was responsible for

James's conversion to a higher life and functioned as his saintly protector and teacher—the story of the creation of the Franciscans and the beguines shows that the success of these religious reforms and the mystical spiritualities they fostered was the work of leaders of both sexes.[2] I will begin with Mary and James since they are chronologically prior.

The Beguines of Lotharingia:
Mary of Oignies and Her Clerical Supporters

The beguine style of the *vita apostolica* ranks among the most creative innovations of late medieval religion.[3] Though there are obvious connections between the beguines and the female pursuit of the apostolic life that had produced the Cistercian nuns and Praemonstratensian canonesses in the twelfth century,[4] key aspects of beguine life, especially their existence outside the cloister and their independence of established religious rules of life, gave them a special character.

The beguine movement began in Lotharingia (the ancient middle division of the Carolingian Empire), starting in present-day Belgium and soon spreading to the Rhineland.[5] Demographic features were certainly at work, such as the movement of rural women into the growing towns to find employment, but this provides a factor, not an explanation.[6] Since the early twentieth century, it has been customary to distinguish four chronological phases in the institutional development of the beguines: (a) individual women living alone or with their parents; (b) small communities in a parish setting; (c) larger groups of enclosed beguines in the service of hospitals and other good works; and (d) independent beguine parishes (called *curtes*) with large communities of women and associated personnel, such as found in the Belgian *begijnhof* that have survived down to the present day.[7] Recent research indicates that for the southern Low Countries, at least, the third and fourth stages were not late developments in reaction to the condemnation of the movement in the early fourteenth century, as has often been claimed. Rather, they originated in the second quarter of the thirteenth century as ecclesiastical authorities sought to regularize this new movement of female piety.[8] An early witness to the roots of the beguine movement can be found among the lay followers of a parish priest of Liège, Lambert le Bègüe (the Stammerer).[9]

The diocese of Liège was remarkable in the Middle Ages for the spiritual energy displayed by its inhabitants—it produced far more than its share of reform movements and new devotions over several centuries.[10] Lambert was ordained priest about 1160 and began to repair his half-ruined church and to attract groups of pious laity, especially women, through his preaching and translation of parts of the Bible and saints' lives into the vernacular. He appears to have been an ardent reformer in the tradition of Gregory VII, denouncing the evil lives of the clergy and calling for moral and sacramental renewal, though very much on a grassroots level. Lambert's activities, however, upset his unreformed bishop, who about 1175 imprisoned him on charges of heresy. Lambert wrote to the Antipope Callixtus III (then reigning in Rome), defending himself against these accusations. The pope supported Lambert, who was released and died in 1177. It would be saying too much to call Lambert the founder of the beguines–the movement's special character was to have no founder, no established rule, as well as (originally at least) no cloister or enclosure to separate women and protect them within a sacred space. But the thirteenth-century Cistercian chronicle of Alberic of Trois-Fontaines was not totally wrong in describing Lambert as "the most fervent preacher of the new religious life (*religio*) which flourished in Liège and its neighborhood,"[11] not least for the priest's concern for spreading the call for a more devout life through the vernacular and especially to women.[12]

The urban and vernacular form of the *vita apostolica* evident in the career of Lambert doubtless was also found in other towns and cities of the area toward the end of the twelfth century, but it is only in the early thirteenth century that we can begin to speak of the beguines as a distinctive form of life, one that also included a strong mystical element within its understanding of how to live the gospel. The archetype of the early stages of beguine life, and especially of beguine spirituality, is to be found in Mary of Oignies (1176–1213).[13]

Mary was born of well-to-do parents in Nivelles in the diocese of Liège. She was educated, at least enough to read. Married at the age of fourteen, she convinced her husband sometime in the early 1190s to join her in making a vow of chastity (not unusual among the very devout), and (more typical of the new piety) in undertaking a life of apostolic activity rather than retreating into male and female religious houses. It is particularly interesting to note that like the young Francis of Assisi about a decade later, the couple gave themselves to service of the outcasts of society, the lepers– "Totally abandoning themselves for the Lord's sake, for a time they served some lepers for the Lord near Nivelles in a place called Williambrouck."[14] Mary remained there for a number of years, apparently until about 1207, as her growing reputation for sanctity began to attract like-minded women to come live with her (we do not hear more about her husband in the *vita*). Her holiness is described in terms both traditional (for example, with reference to ecstatic states induced by seeing the crucifix and in the reception of the gift of tears), and in more unusual terms, such as her "shouting like a woman giving birth from an intense disturbance of heart" when she went to confession.[15] Eventually, since "she who desired only to be free for the Lord was no longer able to bear the press of people who came to her out of devotion,"[16] Mary took up a more secluded form of life by fleeing to the house of Augustinian canons at the church of St. Nicholas at Oignies. The *Supplement* to her life describes this as "the humble place of Oignies amidst those faithful flocks of beguines (*oves Beghinarum*) whom worldlings (*Aegyptii*) despise."[17] Here Mary became a kind of lay nun, or *conversa*, though she did not live an enclosed life. We are told that she freely traveled about to engage in apostolic work, especially visiting the sick and dying.[18] Such dedication to a life that combined evangelical action and ecstatic contemplation was to be typical of many later women mystics.

Both at Williambrouck and at Oignies, Mary was the center of a group including both other holy women and educated clerics that found in her and her miraculous gifts a living example of the *vita apostolica*. This pattern, to be repeated by Mechthild of Magdeburg, Angela of Foligno, Bridget of Sweden, Catherine of Siena, Catherine of Genoa, and others, is a distinctive mark of many of the women of the new mysticism. A number of these clerics are well known as staunch proponents of new forms of religious life for women.[19] The one who stands out, since it is his account on which we mainly rely for what we know of Mary, is James of Vitry.[20]

James was born sometime between 1160 and 1170 possibly at Reims. He studied in Paris, where he was influenced by the new concern for the *cura animarum*, especially the vernacular preaching of Fulk of Neuilly. James was not satisfied with the easy path to ecclesiastical preferment followed by many Paris clerics. Like his later friends Fulk, the Archbishop of Toulouse, and Cardinal Hugolino, who became Pope Gregory IX (both key ecclesiastical supporters for the new forms of religious life), James had inner tensions and self-doubts that seem to have found some relief and consolation when he put himself under the care of the ecstatic and miraculous *mulier sancta* Mary of Oignies.

About 1208, attracted by her fame, James came from Paris to meet Mary at Oignies.[21] The meeting shaped the rest of his life. It seems to have been with her encouragement that he finally offered himself for ordination about 1210.[22] He then returned to Oignies and joined its community in 1211. Since James seems to have owed much of his later fame and ecclesiastical preferment to his ability as a preacher, it is significant to note that in his *Life of Mary* he gave her all the credit for his homiletical skill. James tells us that when he began preaching he was ineffective and lived in constant fear of failure until Mary noticed his depression and encouraged him with an apt parable.[23] As a woman, Mary could preach only by example and the "word of exhortation"; in James she found her official mouthpiece, as she reportedly claimed on her death-bed.[24]

Sometime in 1211, Archbishop Fulk of Toulouse arrived in Liège. Fulk was another important figure in the web of contacts and relationships that helped shape the new mysticism.[25] Born ca. 1150 in Marseilles, he had been a rich merchant and famous troubador before his conversion to religious life and entry into the Cistercian order in 1196. The Cistercians had become the major weapon in the papal campaign against the widespread Cathar heresy in Provence, so it comes as no surprise that Fulk, who was something of a thirteenth-century media expert, was made bishop of the "dead diocese" of Toulouse in 1205. There he promptly formed a lay confraternity to attack heresy and usury. Fulk worked closely with the Cistercians sent to preach against the heretics; more importantly, he encouraged the new group of poor preachers centered around Bishop Diego of Osma and his canon Dominic in their efforts to combat false doctrine.[26] In 1207 Fulk and Dominic even preached together in a public debate with the heretics held at Pamiers.

The era of irenic preaching, however, ended in early 1208, when Peter de Castelnau, one of the papal legates in Provence, was murdered by the Cathars. Pope Innocent III then declared a crusade against the heretics.[27] Fulk, who continued to be the major episcopal supporter of Dominic and his preachers, went on the road as a crusade preacher after his exile from his diocese at the hands of Count Raymond. He traveled north to raise money and attract knights to the cause of the suppression of heresy. It was in this capacity that he first came to the "Promised Land of Liège" (*terra promissionis in partibus Leodii*) and met James of Vitry, as well as Mary and a number of the other *mulieres sanctae* of the region. In the prologue he addressed to Fulk at the beginning of his *Life of Mary,* James, with perhaps some exaggeration, says of the bishop:

> [He] came as far as the diocese of Liège, drawn, as it were, by the odor and fame of certain people fighting for God in true humility. He did not cease to admire their faith and devotion, especially the holy women who with the greatest desire and reverence venerated Christ's church and the church's sacraments which in his own territory were either totally rejected or under-appreciated by almost everybody.[28]

Fulk's interest in the witness of the holy women was no pious invention. The bishop had been the sponsor of the convent that Dominic founded at

Prouille in 1206 to provide a refuge for converts from Catharism and a place to educate girls who might be in danger of falling into heresy.[29] The bishop's commitment to this work of support for female piety is evident in the two subsequent trips he made to Lotharingia in 1213 and 1217.[30]

Mary of Oignies died in June of 1213. James of Vitry immediately embarked on writing her life, a task that may have taken some time, since he himself was called on to preach against the heretics in the same year. The text was finished by the time he was named archbishop of Acre in the Holy Land in 1216. James's *Life of Mary of Oignies* was a manifesto for the new form of beguine life and its mystical piety. Though scarcely a triumph of organization, it was popular and highly influential on subsequent accounts of the *mulieres sanctae*. The work falls into three parts: the prologue addressed to Fulk, which announces the antiheretical theme and trumpets the praise of the holy women of the Lotharingia;[31] book 1, providing a somewhat disorganized account of Mary's life and piety up to her final illness; and book 2, which recounts her death after showing the conformity of her new form of piety to tradition. James does this by illustrating how Mary manifested the working of the seven gifts of the Holy Spirit, the charisms identified with the pursuit of perfection since the time of Gregory the Great.[32]

The antiheretical impetus behind the praise for the new mysticism is evident throughout the *Life,* especially in the prologue.[33] Neither James of Vitry nor Fulk of Toulouse was a mystic; they were pious and discerning ecclesiastics who saw in the graces manifested in the holy women evident signs of divine favor and an ideal weapon to use against the dualist heresy in which women had taken an important role.[34] Part of the fascination of the mysticism of the beguines is how its novelty allowed it to be suspected of heresy at the same time as it was used in the fight against heresy.

James's *Life of Mary* portrays a new kind of mystic, who is as apostolic as she is ecstatic. Though many women favored with divine gifts had appeared in the diocese of Liège, "I find," says James, "the fullness of almost all graces in one precious and surpassing pearl."[35] Much of both the first and the second book of the *Life* applies familiar hagiographical themes to the description of this "pearl"—for example, compunction and tears (1.5), fasting (1.8), prayer (1.9), humility (2.2.47), chastity (2.5.75), and especially penance and satisfaction for sin springing from deep devotion to Christ's passion (1.7, 1.9.28, 1.10, 1.13.40, 2.3.61, 2.5.74–75). Mary performs miracles, both nature miracles (e.g., 1.9.28, cf. VMOS 2.8–9) and miracles of healing (e.g., 2.3.55, cf. VMOS 1.6–7); she also makes miraculous prophecies (2.6.80, 2.10.95) and casts out demons (e.g., 1.2.31). The description that James gives of these traditional practices, however, often displays an "excessive" character that will also be found among many other late medieval women mystics. Consider, for example, his account of her cutting off a piece of her own flesh to do penance for the delight she had once taken in bodily nourishment:

> As if she were drunk in fervor of spirit, she scorned her own flesh for the sake of the sweetness of the Paschal Lamb. With impunity she cut off a large piece with a knife and hid it in the ground for modesty. Because while afire with such a great fervor of love she had conquered the pain of the flesh, she beheld in her ecstasy of mind one of the seraphim standing next to her.[36]

Such combination of extravagant ascetical practice and ecstatic rapture is another mark of the new mysticism.[37]

Other elements in the picture canon James paints of the woman he called his *magistra* (2.2.48) point to forms of piety that had begun to emerge in the late twelfth century, such as her frequent visions of angels and saints (e.g., 1.8.24, 1.10.35, 2.3.51–53, 2.8.89–91, 2.9.94, 2.10.97, 2.12.103), of the devil (e.g., 1.8.23, 1.9.30–32, 2.3.50–52 and 56–61, 2.4.70, 2.7.83 and 85, 2.12.108), and of the souls of the deceased (e.g., 1.9.27, 2.3.51, 2.12.104).[38] Mary is described as having a love for the sacrament of penance (1.6) and an even greater devotion to the reception of Christ in the Eucharist. James tells us that "[i]t was like dying to her if she had to be separated from this sacrament for long through abstaining."[39] Like other beguines, she sees Christ as a child at the elevation of the Host (2.4.72 [655CD], cf. 2.8.91). James records a lengthy ecstatic rapture triggered by reception of Communion:

> Once she rested sweetly with the Lord for thirty-five days in a sweet and blessed silence, taking no corporeal food and totally unable to speak a word for days save for "I want the Body of Our Lord Jesus Christ." When she received it, she remained in her silence with the Lord for whole days. In those days she used to feel as if her spirit were separated from her body. . . . Thus, she was drawn away from sensible objects and rapt above herself in an ecstasy (*excessus*). Finally, after five weeks she returned to herself, opened her mouth, and to the wonder of those about her spoke and received corporeal food.[40]

What is most remarkable about this passage in the light of the history of mysticism is not so much Mary's ability to survive on the miraculous sufficiency of eucharistic nourishment,[41] but how James describes the trance-like state that accompanied this prolonged lack of ordinary food with the traditional vocabulary associated with the heights of monastic *contemplatio* (e.g., *separatus a corpore, a sensibilibus abstracta, in excessu rapta*). The monastic understanding of such contemplative encounter with God, as taught by Gregory the Great, Bernard of Clairvaux, and others, had always emphasized the necessary brevity of such immediate experiences of God.[42] I know of no earlier text in which we find an account of such a prolonged ecstatic rapture.

There are about a dozen other passages in the *Life of Mary* that recount similar ecstatic states.[43] In considering Mary's possession of the "spirit of knowledge," James makes use of the traditional topos of union of spirits based on 1 Corinthians 6:17, beginning with the words, "Another time when she sweetly and pleasantly had been made one spirit with the Lord, adhering to the same Lord with the glue of fear," and going on to cite the language of Song of Songs 2:7 about sleeping with the Divine Lover. Here too, however, a new note creeps in. While the beguine follows tradition in her willingness to abandon the sleep of contemplation in order to serve those in need, James's account of this departure involves a note of violence with distinctive somatic effects:

> When she heard strangers approach, in order not to scandalize anyone she tore her spirit away from the sweet delight of contemplation, the embrace of her Spouse, with such great pain that she did violence to herself. Sometimes, as if her insides split open, she vomited or spit up a large mass of pure blood, preferring to undergo this martyrdom rather than disturb the peace of the brethren and especially of pilgrims.[44]

Under the "spirit of understanding," James describes states of "suspension" (*suspendium*) for whole days when Mary "beheld the Sun of Justice like an eagle" and "received into her soul simple and divine forms as if in a pure mirror without any phantasm or image."[45] While this passage seems to reflect the language of Augustinian intellectual visions, it goes on to emphasize Mary's loving pursuit of God through a rich invocation of pictorial images of paradise and the use of erotic themes. James seems less interested in showing how Mary fits into the traditional hierarchy of visions than in presenting a new model of contact with God, one that concentrates on visual representation and intense somatic effects that witness to the saint's immediate experience of God.

This approach becomes especially clear toward the end of the *Life,* when James recounts the ecstasies that represent the beguine's reception of the highest gift of the Holy Spirit, the "spirit of wisdom," as well as in his account of her preparation for death. Mary's possession of the spirit of wisdom is described in terms of tasting, eating, drinking, mystical inebriation, and insatiable hunger (citing one of the proof-texts for mystical *epektasis,* or constant desire for God, namely, Ecclesiasticus 24:29). The intense visualization of her contact with Christ accords with the liturgical feasts being celebrated—as baby that she hides within her breasts, as young boy at the time of the presentation in the Temple, or as the dying Lord on the cross (2.8.87–88 [659D–660A]). James's presentation of Mary's *spiritus sapientiae* is a kind of *omnium-gatherum* of all her other visionary experiences of Christ, saints, and angels recounted throughout the text (2.8.90 [660CE]). James never questions the nature of any of Mary's visionary experiences, while Thomas of Cantimpré, perhaps in response to a growing debate on the visions recounted by other beguines, later defended Mary as the only visionary "in the area of Lotharingia" who was never deceived by the devil in any way because of her possession of the grace of "discretion of spirits" (*discretio spirituum*).[46]

James pictures the beguine's experiences as increasing in intensity as death approaches. In the last year of her life she feels that "her whole body seemed to burst from the fullness of her heart," so that she can look at the physical sun without injury to her eye, because she "is ravished more powerfully than usual" in her desire to die and to be with the Lord.[47] The mystical drama reaches its conclusion in the presentation of her fifty-three-day death agony, especially the heavenly song or *iubilus* that she sings for three whole days.

The connection between mystical states of consciousness and singing–whether liturgical song or personal outbursts of melody–has yet to receive adequate attention, either in Christianity or in other mystical traditions.[48] But prior references to the role of a song of jubilation (*iubilum* and later *iubilus*) in the history of Christian mystical literature do not prepare us for James of Vitry's extended description of Mary's singing as the promised time of her death drew near–"She began to sing in a high and clear voice and did not cease for three days and nights to praise the Lord with thanksgiving."[49] The song that "our tambourine player" (*tympanistria nostra*), as James calls her, sings is spontaneous praise of God, the angels, the saints, her friends–something she does not have to prepare or think about, but that flows out of her as if she were one of the seraphim. After getting hoarse from one day's constant performance, she is cured by an angel and sings higher and clearer the next day, beginning with the mystery of the Trinity, and gradually descending to the humanity of Christ, the Blessed Virgin, the angels and saints, ending with revelations about her friends–all sung rhythmically in her native vernacular (*lingua Romana*). Mary's song here is not a wordless *iubilus,* however, of the kind that is witnessed to in the lives of a number of other holy women.[50] Rather, "she expounded in a new and wonderful way certain things about the divine scriptures, subtly explaining many things about the Gospel, the Psalms, and the Old and New Testaments that she never heard."[51] In other words, it is sung mystical doctrine. On both the

Thursday and the Saturday before her death on Sunday, June 23, she returned to singing. The last song was apparently one of wordless rejoicing— "She began to sing the Alleluia in a sweet voice and for almost that whole night she was in joy and exultation as if she had been invited to a banquet."[52]

If Mary of Oignies is portrayed by James of Vitry, and later by Thomas of Cantimpré, as a new kind of ecstatic mystic, she is no less an apostolic woman, a contemporary *apostola*. The beguine is presented as a model of penance for sin, even to the extreme of cutting off pieces of her own flesh to do penance for her sins and those of others, as we have seen. But, as a "little poor woman" (*paupercula*) she is also described as devoted to poverty in terms that echo those used by Francis and the early mendicants.[53] Indeed, James says that the canons of St. Nicholas restrained her from taking up a wandering life of begging only with great difficulty (2.2.45). Mary does not scorn to work with her hands (1.12.38), and both James's *Life* and the *Supplement* written by Thomas emphasize how her entire life was lived in the service of others.[54]

The beguine is presented both as a teacher (*magistra*) and as a preacher, though James never actually uses the word of her. The fundamental way in which Mary preaches, of course, is through her miraculous activity as witnessed to by the *Life*, which is merely the extension of what James and his contemporaries saw in her daily activities. Her very appearance is a book that reveals the action of the Holy Spirit:

> With her head bowed down and her glance toward the ground, she would walk humbly with a slow and mature gait. The grace of the Holy Spirit shone forth in her face from her heart's fullness to such a degree that many were spiritually nourished by her appearance and moved to devotion and to tears. Reading the unction of the Holy Spirit in her face, as if in a book, they recognized that power came forth from her.[55]

If Mary can be described as a living *liber experientiae*,[56] a flesh-and-blood sermon, that does not prevent her from also preaching in a more formal sense, though indirectly, through her devotion to preachers. This was especially the case, as we have seen, with James of Vitry, who was proud to have her declare him her "one and only preacher" (2.4.69 [655A]).[57] This emphasis on Mary as a true preacher also may help explain why James stresses her love for scripture, something that was considered a necessary part of any good preacher's life.[58]

James of Vitry's portrait of Mary of Oignies marks a new departure in Western hagiography and mysticism. Although he recognizes her excesses and warns that she is more to be admired than imitated in certain things,[59] he expresses no doubts about the divine authority displayed in her life and actions. This is even the case when she seems to become a law unto herself, for example, when she changes the rules of fasting.[60] But not all of the *mulieres sanctae* who attained the "spirit of liberty" (*spiritus libertatis*) which allowed them "to judge all things but to be judged by no one" (1 Cor. 2:15; cf. 2 Cor. 3:17) were to be treated with equal forbearance.

Francis and Clare of Assisi[61]

In 1216 James of Vitry left Lotharingia and crossed the Alps, called to accept the see of Acre in the Holy Land. On his journey to the papal court, he had the opportunity to witness firsthand a number of the new expressions of the *vita apostolica* that were spreading through Italy. In October, while at the papal court in Perugia, he petitioned the new pope, Honorius III (Innocent had just died and James got to see his corpse laid out for burial), to approve the form of life of the *mulieres sanctae* that he had fostered in the North. Though the approval was only verbal, we have no reason to doubt James's account that it was given and that he had been central in gaining official approbation for the new movement.[62] At the same time, James made contact with the highest circles in church administration, specifically with Cardinal Hugolino, later Pope Gregory IX (1227–1241). Thomas of Cantimpré tells the story he heard from James himself about how he later cured his friend Hugolino of his temptations to the "spirit of blasphemy" by giving him the most precious and powerful relic in his possession—the finger of Mary of Oignies.[63]

James described the various apostolic groups he had encountered in his *Western History* (*Historia Occidentalis*), a handbook of the forms of religious life of his time. His outlook was positive—"Day-by-day the state of the Western church is being reformed for the better, and those who long sat in darkness and the shadow of death are being illumined through the word of the Lord."[64] Not the least of the spiritual men (*viri spirituales*) and apostolic groups that James eagerly sought out was the one he described as "the religion of the poor men of the Crucified One and the order of preachers we call lesser brothers" (*fratres minores*).[65] He also recounts how in 1219, while he was in the East at Damietta during the Fifth Crusade, "We saw the first founder and master of this order, whom all the others obey as their supreme prior, a simple and unlettered man, beloved of God and men, called Brother Francis, who was rapt to such great ecstasy of drunkenness and fervor of spirit."[66] The complex interactions between powerful church officials, like James of Vitry, Fulk of Toulouse, and Cardinal Hugolino, on the one hand, and the founders of the new forms of religious life, like Mary, Dominic, and Francis, on the other, may not fully explain the dramatic changes in religious life that took place during the first two decades of the thirteenth century, but they do help us understand how these new movements were so rapidly accepted by the official church.

The most famous of the new spiritual leaders was Francis of Assisi.[67] Born Francesco Bernardone, a few years after Mary of Oignies, probably in 1181, he too was from wealthy stock, his father a successful cloth merchant of Assisi. Other contemporary leaders of the new forms of the *vita apostolica* have faded from popular memory, kept alive by diligent historians, local cults, or the religious orders they founded. Francis of Assisi remains larger than life. Like the elusive historical Jesus, the historical Francis has been the subject of intense debate for over a century since Paul Sabatier first challenged the traditional hagiographical picture in his *Vie de S. François* of 1893.[68] The layers of documentation that give us access to the saint are multiple—beginning with his own writings (largely ignored until the present century), moving through the witness of his early companions insofar as these are recoverable, as well as the stages of the creation of the standard hagiographical picture in the thirteenth century, and ending with the delightful stories about the "Little Poor Man" (*Il Poverello*) enshrined in the ever-popular *Little Flowers* (*Fioretti*) (still the most read work about the saint).[69] Recent scholarship has rightly insisted that we must evaluate the "historical" Francis primarily on the basis of his authentic writings, recognizing that the hagiographical materials are expressions of the developing image of Francis and are closely tied to disputes within and without the order over the meaning of the saint for his followers.[70] Always bearing this in mind, it is necessary to admit that one cannot tell the story of Francis's life without appealing to these lives and story collections, though they must be used with caution, especially when it comes to interpreting the saint's spiritual teaching. The directness and seeming simplicity of Francis's own writings, as well as the combination of charming naivete and theological reconstruction found in the lives, compound the difficulties involved in trying to understand a figure whose elusiveness equals his perennial appeal.

The brief account that follows does not pretend to solve all the problems connected with the life of Francis. It is impossible, however, to tell the story of the new mysticism without paying careful attention to *Il Poverello*, if only because he came to be represented as the mystic *par excellence*, the one rapt into unique union with the suffering Christ. We need to try to see what made this hagiographical picture so powerful. We must also investigate, on the basis of his writings, to what extent it may be legitimate to speak of

Francis himself as a mystic. Both questions are as complicated as most of the other issues that surround his life.

The basic facts and dates concerning Francis's conversion to the *vita apostolica* are well established. As a young man he pursued a thoughtless, if scarcely vicious, life until about 1204. Setting out on a military expedition bound for Apulia in southern Italy, he is said to have experienced a dream vision that sent him back home to ponder his future. The most valuable witness to his conversion, however, comes from Francis himself at the beginning of the *Testament* that he dictated shortly before his death in 1226. The year he speaks of must have been 1205.

> The Lord gave it to me, Brother Francis, this way to begin doing penance. Because, when I was in sins, it seemed very bitter to me to see lepers. And the Lord himself brought me among them and I made mercy with them. And when I withdrew from them, what had seemed bitter to me was changed to sweetness of body and soul to me. And after this, I stayed a little while and left the world.[71]

As Raoul Manselli among others has shown,[72] this text is central to understanding Francis's witness over the next twenty-one years as he grew from a troubled young man whom his family thought foolish or mad to become the "madman" whose sanctity was so universally recognized that his formal canonization remains among the fastest on record.[73] The *Testament* reveals that for Francis two things remained essential: the conviction that God himself "gave" him what to do; and that he was called to share the life of society's outcasts. The "life of the gospel of Jesus Christ," as he later called it,[74] was not *just* penance, poverty, and preaching, though these remained hallmarks of Francis's witness: it was a total acceptance of the core of the gospel message as identity with the abject Christ on the cross. To be sure, this was not a new value in Christianity—preachers since Paul had made the motif of being crucified with Christ central to their lives (see, e.g., Gal. 2:19; 5:24; 6:14). Francis's originality rests in the totally uncompromising way in which he tried to fulfill what it meant to follow the crucified Christ by witnessing to the gospel in the world.[75]

Before taking up the major issues concerning mysticism that must concern us here, an introduction to the two decades of Francis's public life will be helpful to set the context within which these questions need to be examined. The basic facts of his career are well known, though their meaning is still subject to dispute in many cases.

In 1205 the young Francis began to give away his possessions and to withdraw from society to live the life of a penitent performing charitable services for lepers and beggars in the vicinity of Assisi. The process was

apparently a gradual one. Later hagiographical accounts (not Francis himself) speak of several experiences that encouraged him in his free-form life
of penance, especially hearing the voice of Christ as he knelt before a crucifix in the half-ruined church of San Damiano. According to the *Legend of the
Three Companions:*

> When he entered the church he began to pray fervently before an image of
> the Crucified and heard a voice addressing him devoutly and tenderly: "Fran-
> cis, don't you see that my house is destroyed? Go, then, and repair it for me."
> In awe and wonder he said: "I'll do it gladly, Lord." He understood what was
> said to him in reference to that church which was threatening to fall down
> because of its extreme age.[76]

Francis's new lifestyle clashed with his family's expectations, and so
apparently in late 1205 or early 1206 his father locked him up at home
hoping to bring him to his senses. All the biographies recount the dramatic
story of how his father hauled him before the city magistrates of Assisi, who
handed the case on to the bishop since it involved a person who had
already indicated his intention to enter God's service. In the presence of
Bishop Guido, his father, and a large crowd, Francis sealed his conversion
by handing over all his remaining money to his father, stripping off his
clothes, and acknowledging God alone as his Father. Francis's striking symbolic action—the literal exemplification of the ancient adage *nudus nudum
Christum sequi*—was matched by that of Bishop Guido, who covered him
with his mantle expressing the church's sponsorship and protection.[77]

Francis's gradual conversion initially emphasized withdrawal from the
world, loving concern for the rejected and marginalized, penance, and now
total poverty. In fact, the young man had taken on a form of life well recognized in the Middle Ages, that of a hermit (*eremita*).[78] Francis's desire to find
solitary places outside the control of the Assisi commune where he could
pray more fervently to God is an important theme of his early converted
life,[79] and one that remained strong throughout his career, as is evident
from *The Rule for Hermitages* that he composed late in life.[80] But Francis was
not a typical hermit. The pull of newer conceptions of the *vita apostolica* was
also strong as he struggled to find the best way to follow the naked Christ.[81]

During the period 1206–1208 other key elements in Francis's new mode
of gospel life become evident, especially preaching, service to the church
and clergy, and devotion to the Eucharist. While still living in a quasi-
eremitical way, Francis began to work at restoring San Damiano, publicly
begging for the supplies needed to accomplish the task. According to the
hagiographers, one day (probably early in 1208), while listening to the

gospel at mass, he was struck by the apostolic imperative in Christ's words to his disciples to take neither silver nor gold, nor traveling bag, nor spare tunic, shoes or staff on the way as they went to preach (see Matt. 10:9–10). "Filled with indescribable joy, he said: 'This is what I want to fulfill with all my strength.'"[82] Casting off the traditional hermit's garb, he followed the injunction literally, content with one miserable tunic and a cord. The *Legend of the Three Companions* notes the significance of this conversion to the apostolic life—"By divine inspiration, he began to live as one who proclaims evangelical perfection and to preach penance in a simple way in public."[83]

Francis's conversion to apostolic poverty and preaching thus far bore a similarity to that of Peter Valdez discussed above (pp. 6–8). Like Valdez, too, his witness soon attracted followers. In the Spring of 1208 he was joined by a rich layman, Bernard of Quintavalle, and a priest, Peter Catanii. At this critical juncture, the beginning of the *fraternitas* that was to carry the Franciscan understanding of the gospel message all over the world,[84] Francis and his companions, unsure of how to proceed, made use of the *sortes apostolicae,* a Christian version of an ancient divinatory rite. Going to the church of St. Nicholas in Assisi early one morning, they prayed, and then Francis opened the Bible at random three times to consult the will of God as to how they should live. All three texts he hit upon were classic proclamations of the "evangelical" understanding of the *vita apostolica:* "If you wish to be perfect, go, sell what you have and give to the poor" (Matt. 19:21); "Take nothing for your journey" (Luke 9:3); and "He who wishes to come after me, must deny himself" (Matt. 16:24).[85] The event appears to be reflected in the *Testament,* where Francis says: "And afterward the Lord gave me brethren. No one showed me what I ought to do, but the Most High himself revealed to me that I ought to live according to the form of the Holy Gospel."[86]

The manner of life of the early *fraternitas,* while bearing similarity to other apostolic movements of the era, contained elements of striking originality, as we can see from the primitive regulations available to us in the *Early Rule.* Like the Waldensians, the brothers were to sell their possessions and give the proceeds to the poor before submitting to the obedience of the *fraternitas* (RnBu 2). They were to avoid all contact with money, save in the case of alms necessary for the care of sick brothers and lepers (RnBu 8). But the brethren were also encouraged to work in ways that would contribute to what David Flood has called their new "economics of service" (RnBu 7).[87] In their solidarity with the poor and the outcasts, they were not to be ashamed to beg for alms, because "alms are a legacy and a just right due to the poor" (RnBu 9.8). The brethren were also encouraged to wander through the world, giving an example of peacefulness, poverty, and humil-

ity (RnBu 14), even to the extent of going out "among Saracens and other
non-believers" (RnBu 16.3) in a missionary impulse.[88]

It is clear from the *Testament,* as well as from the hagiographical witnesses, that Francis was on guard from the beginning against any conflict
with the clergy as he and his growing group of companions began to preach
penance publicly and to work and beg for their sustenance in and around
Assisi and neighboring towns in Umbria. Whether or not he was aware of
the history of Valdez and other followers of the apostolic life who had
clashed with the hierarchy, Francis's reverence for the clergy and his insistence on obeying them in all things was a mark of the *fraternitas* from the
beginning. This reverence, however, appears to have been rooted not so
much in a love of hierarchy for hierarchy's sake as in the saint's devotion to
the Eucharist. In discussing why he "does not wish to consider sin in them
[i.e., the clergy]" (always a starting place for Donatist-style movements),
Francis said in the *Testament,* "And I do it for this reason, because I see nothing corporeally of the Highest Son of God himself in this world, except his
most Holy Body and most Holy Blood, which they receive and they alone
minister to others."[89] Francis's devotion to the reality of Christ's presence in
the Eucharist, evident both in his own writings and in the *vitae,* brings him
close to the *mulieres sanctae* of his time.[90]

It was probably in 1209 that Francis took his *fratres de paenitentia* with
him to Rome, where (improbable as it may seem today) they did get to
meet with Innocent III. They received the pope's verbal approval for the
brief rule of life that Francis had caused to be written down, as well as the
"license to preach everywhere" (*licentia ubique praedicandi*).[91] This first Rule,
since lost,[92] was most likely a collection of the Gospel texts on which Francis had based his way of life. Its approval prior to Lateran IV's decree ban-
ning new religious orders was an important protection for the growing
movement. As Francis later insisted, and as astute observers like James of
Vitry remarked, this was *not* a new rule in the manner of other founders of
religious orders. Rather, Francis and his brothers had gone back to the
essential rule of all Christian living, the gospel—"If we diligently observe the
state and order of the primitive church, [the Lord] did not so much add a
new rule as renew the old one."[93]

The evangelical way of life pioneered by Francis proved increasingly
attractive to the men who flocked to his group. How could it not also have its
effect on women, especially in this era of the flowering of what has been
called the "Women's Movement" (*Frauenbewegung*)? In 1211 the young daughter of a noble family of Assisi, Chiara (Clare) di Offreduccio, approached
Francis through her cousin, Ruffino, who had already joined the *fraternitas,*

concerning her desire to adopt Francis's form of the evangelical life.[94] It is difficult to know how far Francis may have anticipated such a possibility.[95] Given the hand-to-mouth mendicancy and asperity of his life, as well as medieval views of the necessity for the separation of the sexes and protection of women, it was impossible for him to conceive of women becoming full members of the wandering brothers. But what is significant is that Francis did not reject Clare's overture; he rather began to meet with her in secret, instructing her and working out an alternative model which would allow Clare and others who might follow her a share, if necessarily in a somewhat different way, in his understanding of the evangelical life. Given Francis's later opposition to direct legal association between the women who subsequently imitated Clare and the developing *fraternitas* of male Franciscans, it seems logical to think that he conceived (then or later?) of distinct male and female models of his understanding of following the gospel.[96]

According to the *Legend of St. Clare* composed shortly after her death in 1253:

> The Father Francis encouraged her to despise the world, showing her by his living speech how dry the hope of the world was and how deceptive its beauty. He whispered in her ears of a sweet espousal with Christ, persuading her to preserve the pearl of her virginal purity for that blessed Spouse whom Love made man.[97]

All this was fairly standard virtuous advice that would fit any medieval nun. What was new was Francis's encouragement of Clare's desire to live in absolute poverty, as well as his willingness to have her swear obedience to him alone as the master of this form of life. On the night of Palm Sunday in 1212, Clare stole away from her house and went down the hill from Assisi to the little church of St. Mary of the Portiuncula, which the bishop of Assisi had given to Francis and his followers. Here Francis, contrary to church law (he was neither priest nor bishop), cut off her hair, the symbol of her rejection of the world, and Clare was clothed in the rough garb and cord of the poor brothers.[98] He then sent her to live with nearby Benedictine nuns, until she was joined by several members of her family and other women and could be settled permanently in a dwelling prepared for them at San Damiano.

At first, their mode of life appears to have been not very different from that observed by Mary of Oignies and the early beguines. James of Vitry witnesses to their engagement in active good works and their manual labor.[99] Soon, however, they came under pressure to follow the standard enclosed model of religious life for women. Clare seems to have acquiesced (perhaps not altogether contentedly) in this move toward claustration. What she refused to compromise on was her commitment to a life of total poverty. Sometime about 1215, she induced Francis to give the "poor ladies" (*dominae pauperae*) of San Damiano a "form of life" (*forma vitae*) expressing this central spiritual value. The document was approved by Innocent III in a special "Privilege of Poverty," which, for the first time in ecclesiastical history, allowed a female community the unheard-of license to live without property—"the privilege to live without privilege," as Marco Bartoli put it.[100] We can catch some of the words of this original form of life in the *Rule* that Clare later composed and struggled, with eventual success, to have approved by the papacy:

> When the Blessed Father saw that we feared no poverty, labor, tribulation, debasement, or the world's contempt, but rather held them as great delights, moved by piety he composed a *Form of Life* for us in this manner: "Because by divine inspiration you have made yourselves daughters and handmaids of the Most High King, the Heavenly Father, and you have espoused yourselves to the Holy Spirit by choosing to live according to the perfection of the Holy Gospel, I resolve and I promise through myself and my brothers that I will always have as much loving care and special solicitude for you as for them."[101]

In the years between 1205 and 1212, then, Francis had established a new form of the evangelical life that began to spread rapidly throughout Italy, one that proved attractive to men and women and to clergy and laity. Like the Cistercians, his movement had an appeal to uneducated laity; unlike the Cistercians, who relegated the illiterate to the ranks of the *conversi*, or working brothers, Francis accepted all on the same footing.[102] Francis even invited those who, without electing to divest themselves of everything, heeded his call to penance and wished to live a more devout and austere life. His two *Letters to the Faithful* were directed to such "penitents" and demonstrate his concern for the wider effect of his witness to the gospel, a concern that eventually helped produce the "Third Order" of Franciscans.[103] Indeed, it is striking to note that what the Franciscan scholar Thaddée Matura has identified as one of the two best summaries of Francis's theological vision occurs in the *Second Letter to the Faithful.*[104]

Francis may have been present in Rome for the Fourth Lateran Council in November 1215. A more decisive moment for the future of his followers came in May of 1217 at the general chapter of the brethren when it was decided to send missions outside Italy, north over the Alps and across the Mediterranean to the Holy Land and Tunisia to try to convert the Muslims. Francis himself, who appears to have always nourished a desire to wander for Christ, intended to go abroad. After retiring to pray about the decision, he addressed the assembly (according to the *Legend of Perugia*), saying: "I choose the province of France where the people are catholic, and, more than all the other catholics of Holy Church, they display the greatest respect for the Body of Christ, which pleases me greatly. This is why I would gladly go among them."[105] (It is not impossible that Francis's enthusiasm for *Francia* may have had something to do with reports concerning the eucharistic piety of the beguines.) He was not to get his wish, however. Cardinal Hugolino, the close friend of James of Vitry, who had been appointed protector and advisor of the order by Honorius III, met Francis at Florence and convinced him that he was needed in Italy.

Francis was able to go off to the Holy Land in 1218 or 1219, where he boldly preached before the sultan. After his return and in failing health (he had long suffered from malaria),[106] he resigned his position as leader of the *fraternitas* in 1220, though he continued his itinerent preaching with a devoted group of the brethren, the companions (*socii*), and sought to keep his ideal alive through his writings. As the nascent movement continued to grow in numbers and geographical extent, a painful tension developed between Francis's original vision of apostolic spontaneity and the necessity for organization, rationalization, and full ecclesiastical approbation. Cardinal Hugolino has often been seen as the villain responsible for the loss of Francis's original vision in this movement toward structure and accommodation. A key struggle involved the attempt to create a written rule for the order. The *Rule* drawn up by Francis and his consultants about 1221 proved to be too rigorous and so did not receive papal approval (hence it is known as the *Regula non Bullata,* i.e, not given a papal bull of approval). Later, a modified version, the *Regula Bullata,* did gain this recognition on November 29, 1223.[107]

It is unfair to blame Cardinal Hugolino, or any single person, for the difficulties that the Franciscans encountered as they spread so rapidly throughout Europe. It is also impossible to deny the tragic aspects of the last years of Francis's life as he struggled to reconcile his own vision of mendicancy, absolute poverty, and abjection of life with the institutionalization process already well under way. That process would make the Franciscans into one religious order among many, however much they strove for a century to prove that, through the practice of apostolic poverty, the order was different from and superior to other religious groups.

One of the most difficult problems in approaching the "historical Francis" is how to balance his willingness for accommodation (*condescensio*) on some issues with his apostolic intransigence regarding what he insisted had been directly given him by God.[108] For about two years (ca. 1222–1224) Francis wrestled with these problems in a period of inner and outer trial and temptation.[109] During the late summer of 1224, he spent a forty-day period in retreat and fasting on the Monte Alverna in Tuscany, which had been given to the brethren by a local nobleman. Here, traditionally on September 14, he received the stigmata, the physical wounds of the crucified Lord. Discussion about whether or not this is the first recorded account of *some* kind of stigmata in Christian religious history (it is not) has clouded the essential issue: Francis's stigmata became *the* universal model and archetype of this sign of divine favor. In the later Middle Ages and for centuries afterward, his reception of Christ's wounds was seen as the most cogent proof of Francis's special status as an exemplar of Christ.

Francis's health took an even worse turn in the spring of 1225, as he became almost blind from a form of eye disease he had contracted in Egypt. The last year-and-a-half of his life was spent in great pain and suffering, from doctors as much as from illness. He spent some time at San Damiano with Clare and her community in mid-1225, where he composed his most noted vernacular work, the "Canticle of Brother Sun." Finally, knowing death was near, he had himself carried to the Portiuncula church outside Assisi. Here he dictated his *Testament,* the most direct and revealing of all his works, in which he summarized his life's work and strictly forbade his followers to add glosses, explanations, or excuses to the *Rule* or his last wishes: "Just as the Lord gave me to speak and to write the Rule and these words simply and purely, so you should understand them simply and without a gloss and observe them in holy working unto the end."[110] In preparation for death and perhaps to complete the prophetic action of stripping before the bishop at the beginning of his career, he had himself laid naked upon the naked earth, before organizing a "last supper" for his brethren.[111] Francis died on the morning of October 4, 1226. According to Thomas of Celano, as his body was laid out for burial, his followers saw the marks of the stigmata made glorious as in an anticipated resurrection body:

> In truth there appeared in him the form of the cross and of the passion of the Lamb without blemish, who washes away the sins of the world, for he seemed as though he had been recently taken down from the cross. . . . They saw his flesh, which before had been dark, now gleaming with a dazzling whiteness and giving promise of the rewards of the blessed resurrection by reason of its beauty.[112]

Was Francis a mystic? The traditional picture of the stigmatic rapt in contemplation of God makes *Il Poverello* one of the most noted Christian mystics, but a perusal of Francis's own writings gives sparse evidence of emphasis on the mystical element in Christianity, either of the monastic *contemplatio* model, or of the ecstatic excess of beguines like Mary of Oignies.

In order to try to understand the role of Francis in the history of Western mysticism, we must look at the interaction of the various layers of evidence that make his inner mystery accessible, beginning with his own writings (some of which, at least, are probably products of consultation with his closest brethren),[113] and moving on through the layers of hagiography, popular and learned, whose complexities remain elusive despite so much study.[114]

Francis may well be thought of as one of the first major vernacular theologians, as recent scholarship has begun to indicate,[115] but it is difficult to claim that his writings can, in general, be called mystical literature, despite the efforts of some to make them so.[116] Yet if Christian mysticism is grounded in the entire faith of the believer, then any expression of the latter (especially one as rich as the comprehensive vision of the Christian life found in Francis's authentic works), can be said to have an implied mystical element, especially if it serves as the foundation for a more explicit mystical theory and practice in others.[117]

Despite the considerable body of research that has been produced on Francis's writings in recent years, it is still difficult to present any synoptic view of his theology. Deceptively simple at first glance, the apparent verbal poverty of his writings, especially his prayers, hides unusual theological riches. What is most striking is the distance between Francis the writer and Francis the saint as portrayed by the hagiographers. To be sure, many themes are common to both presentations, such as the insistence on poverty and its concomitant virtues of humility and obedience. But in Francis's works even such shared themes take on their own complexion because they appear within a theological perspective that is rather different from that found in the writings of his followers, no matter how much they tried to be faithful to his witness. Some aspects of the hagiographical picture of the saint, such as his role as perfect *imitatio Christi,* and his emphasis on the concrete visual presentation of the mysteries of Christ's life (e.g., the Christmas crib at Greccio)—while not without historical evidence in his life—are not found in any explicit way in his own writings.[118]

Francis's theological vision is deeply trinitarian and christological, so rooted in traditional scriptural and liturgical materials that Thaddée Matura has aptly characterized it as "archaic."[119] He does not speculate on the mystery of the Trinity, but rather concentrates on the presence of the Trinity in the three great acts of the history of salvation: creation, redemption, and final consummation.[120] The terms "Creator," "Redeemer," and "Savior," a leitmotif of his thought, apply to the whole Trinity: "Therefore, let us desire nothing else, let wish for nothing else, let nothing else please us and delight us save our Creator and Redeemer and Savior, alone true God, who is the full good, the whole good, the total good, the true and highest good. . . ."[121] Over and over again in his works, Francis turns to praise of the three divine persons of the Trinity, and especially the Father as the source of all within and without the Trinity, when he wishes to summarize the goal of the Christian life.[122]

Francis does not depart from the biblical perspective that it is Christ alone, God made man, who gives us access to the Father during the course of salvation history. Christ is both Lord and Servant, exalted and abject, in his life on earth. In his role as the Word and Beloved Son of the Father, he is our Master, our Wisdom, and our Light.[123] Nevertheless, Francis, deeply influenced by the Johannine and Pauline teaching that it is only in and through the Paraclete, the "Spirit of Christ," that we can truly recognize and follow the Redeemer, also insists throughout his works on the role of the Holy Spirit. Those who see Jesus only according to his humanity are condemned, because it is only "the Spirit of the Lord, who lives in his faithful," who allows us to see that he is true Son of God and is present body and blood, humanity and divinity, in the Eucharist (Adms 1.6–12). The same Spirit as "Spirit of scripture" (*spiritus divinae litterae*) enables true religious to discern the real meaning of the Bible, that is, "not to appropriate any text which they know or seek to know to the body, but by word and example to render them back to the most high Lord God to whom every good belongs."[124] Francis's theology, then, may be described as containing a strong emphasis on a form of biblical Spirit-Christology.

All Christians are called upon to follow after Christ (*sequi Christum*),[125] an imperative that Francis describes as an ever-deeper rooting in a threefold relation to the God-Man based on Matthew 12:50 and that he typically places within a trinitarian perspective:

> And they will be sons of the Heavenly Father whose works they perform [cf. Matt. 5:45]. And they are spouses, brothers and mothers of our Lord Jesus Christ [cf. Mark 2:18–19; Matt. 12:50]. We are spouses when the faithful soul is joined to Jesus Christ by the Holy Spirit. We are brothers when we do the will of his Father who is in heaven. We are mothers when we bear him in our heart and body [see 1 Cor. 6:20] through love and pure and sincere conscience, [and when] we give him birth through holy action which ought to shine as an example to others [see Matt. 5:16].[126]

It is worth noting that this appeal, containing, if not elaborating upon, the traditional mystical themes of being espoused to Christ, of divine filiation, and the birth of Christ in the soul, appears not in a document directed to the *fraternitas,* but in one addressed to the whole body of the faithful.[127] The implied mystical element in Francis's theology is certainly a democratic one.

Our conformity to Christ is realized through the practice of the fundamental virtues of penance, obedience, and humility, following the model of the self-emptying (*kenōsis*) of the Word made flesh. Francis, who had begun his ministry by sharing the abjection of lepers and outcasts, remained true to this central insight throughout his life. True poverty (which he mentions less often than obedience) was never more than a means to this end.[128] The account of Francis's description of true joy, which appears to be an authentic dictation, is a perfect expression of the core of his teaching about the proper dispositions required for living the evangelical life.[129]

The apostolic dimension of Francis's vocation is quite evident in his authentic writings, especially in his exhortation that all the brothers should preach by deeds (*Omnes tamen fratres operibus praedicent* [RnBu 17.3]). The saint's stress on preaching according to "the form and institution of holy church," his repeated emphasis on respect for the clergy, as well as his insistence on the necessity for orthodox belief,[130] demonstrate the care with which he sought to preserve his followers from the excesses of some of the other groups who were pursuing the new understanding of the *vita apostolica*. All of this is ample evidence for the richness of the theology of *Il Poverello*, but not, I submit, for explicit and developed mystical teaching.

Those who have sought to find a mysticism in Francis have adopted three different approaches. First, many writers over the past century have presented a picture of Francis as mystic based on vague understandings of mysticism and a willingness to consider all sources, however late, as equal evidence for Francis's mysticism.[131] More recently, Ewert Cousins has made the case for a variety of new forms of mysticism appearing in Francis on the basis of a discriminating evaluation of both the saint's own writings and aspects of later theological interpretation, especially by Bonaventure.[132] Finally, the Franciscan scholar Octavian Schmucki proposed a more restricted range of evidence, arguing that the best case for Francis's mysticism must rest upon his own writings independent of the hagiographical accounts. On this basis, Schmucki identified ten themes that he considered characteristic of the mystical message of *Il Poverello*.[133]

No one would deny that many of the themes singled out by Schmucki are among the doctrinal foundations of Western mysticism, such as the understanding of human nature as *imago Dei*, the insistence on passivity to divine action, the role of God conceived of as Love and as the *summum bonum*, devotion to the Eucharist, and the divine indwelling presented in terms of the trinitarian formula of relating to God as "spouse-brother-mother."[134] Nevertheless, there is a difference between expressing fundamental theological truths that underlie mysticism and a teaching that sets out a program of mystical transformation, whether expressed in exegetical, theoretical, or biographical terms. From this perspective, it does not seem that the majority of Francis's writings are explicitly mystical.

There may, however, be a few exceptions to this, especially among the saint's prayers. The most striking is the "Canticle of Brother Sun" (also called the "Praise of the Creatures"), the poem Francis composed in his native Umbrian dialect toward the end of his life.[135] This noted verse, the earliest surviving religious poem in Italian, is a paradigm of the rest of the saint's writings in its ability to mask subtle and profound theology under a deceptively simple presentation. A number of recent authors have made it central to their interpretation of his mysticism.[136] The canticle reflects the saint's attitude toward the natural world as displayed in the numerous animal stories found in the hagiographical accounts (though animals are not mentioned in the poem). While it is true that Francis was an innovator in Christian attitudes toward the environment, his vision of the "enfraternization" of the whole created world, that is, the mutual interconnection of all creation, must be seen in the context of his fundamental theological belief in God as Creator, Redeemer, and Savior revealed in Jesus Christ as Lord and as crucified Servant.[137]

The canticle falls into four parts. In the first, or properly theological, section dealing with God, one strophe is devoted to direct praise of God in terms typical of the saint's Latin writings, while the second sets up the paradox of all attempts to praise God: "No man is worthy to name you" (Italian *mentovare* = Latin *nominare*). This introduction is followed by a cosmological section of seven strophes devoted to praise of the Creator as revealed "with" (*cun*) and "through" (*per*) his creatures, with the sun (the central manifestation of divine light and goodness) being given the primary role:

> Laudato sie, mi signore, *cun* tucte le tue creature,
> spetialmente messor lo frate sole,
> lo qual'è iorno, et allumini noi per loi.
> Et ellu è bellu e radiante cun grande splendore,
> de te, altissimo, porta significatione.
> Laudato si, mi signore, *per* sora luna e le stelle,
> in celu l'ài formate clarite et pretiose et belle.

> Praised be you, My Lord, with all your creatures,
> especially Sir Brother Sun,
> who is the day and through whom you enlighten us.
> And he is beautiful and shining with great splendor,
> of you, Most High, he bears the likeness.

> Praised be you, My Lord, through Sister Moon and the stars,
> in heaven you formed them shining and precious and beautiful.[138]

The first three stanzas deal with the heavenly realm of the sun, moon, and stars, each of which is characterized by three attributes, while the next four stanzas describe the four elements of terrestrial medieval cosmology (air, water, fire, earth), assigning four attributes to each. The continuous repetition of the preposition *per* reveals much about the canticle's complexity. Who is the one giving praise and how, especially in light of Francis's use of the passive imperative (*laudato*) rather than the active? In other writings (e.g., 2 EFi 61) Francis invites all creatures to praise God, and some have seen a similar sense of agency in the *per* in the canticle, but the passive construction suggests that causal and instrumental connotations of *per* are more powerful here—that is, humans are called upon to praise God *because* he has created such wonderful creatures and especially *by means of* the creatures who manifest his glory. In light of the apophatic insistence at the outset of the canticle, however, we can agree with Giovanni Pozzi, who emphasizes that in the deepest sense the *per* signifies that God alone is able to give himself true praise in and through the entire enfraternized universe he has created.[139]

In the third, or anthropological, part (traditionally said to have been added by Francis to celebrate a truce between the bishop and the mayor of Assisi), two strophes praise those who pardon others for love's sake and those who bear infirmity in peace, what we might describe as the fundamental active and passive dimensions of Francis's understanding of following Christ. Finally, in the last, or eschatological part, composed shortly before his death, Francis praises God in three strophes through "Our Sister Bodily Death," expressing his hope to die in God's most holy will. Bodily (*not* spiritual) death carries no fear for the person who has understood the true meaning of praise.

Though Francis obviously knew and depended on the creation psalms and canticles of the Old Testament, his song strikes a new note both because of the solidarity it expresses between the human and cosmic order and because of the way in which it conveys an experience of the world as a single harmonious theophany of God.[140] We can, along with Ewert Cousins, speak of the canticle as expressing a form of theophanic nature mysticism, which is to say that Francis's consciousness of the world is more than just a sense of integration with the cosmos conceived of as in some way divine, as found in some forms of ancient classical mysticism (e.g., the *Asclepius*), or in modern nature mystics, like Richard Jeffries.[141] Francis presents a specifically Christian nature mysticism in which God's presence is experienced as luminously real and immediate in the cosmos as a whole and in each of its elements insofar as they reflect some aspect of the divine fullness. In discussing how the corporeal eye of the resurrected body will see God in heaven, Augustine's *City of God* had spoken of the possibility of seeing "the material bodies of the new heaven and new earth in such a manner that we shall see God as present everywhere and governing all bodies."[142] We need not think that Francis knew this discussion, or John Scottus Eriugena's treatment of the world as theophany, in order to find in these themes a resource for grasping how the Christian mystical tradition prepared the way for his new presentation of a distinctive form of theophanic nature mysticism.[143] Giovanni Pozzi puts it well: "We moderns who encounter this text of Francis must not do so on the level of sentimentality, but rather on the level of relentless probing into the essence of things, in order to touch there the presence of God."[144]

In order to appreciate the full impact of Francis on the new mysticism, however, we cannot restrict ourselves to his own writings, but we must also utilize the picture of the saint found in the hagiography, because it was primarily this image that influenced subsequent Western mystical traditions. Two aspects of this picture are of central importance: Francis as ecstatic contemplative; and Francis as literal image of Jesus, especially through his reception of the stigmata.

Francis's writings provide no accounts of his own visions, though the saint insisted on his direct access to God regarding the form of life he conveyed to his brothers. If Francis had visionary and ecstatic experiences, it is salutary to know that he did not think them worth writing about. (This marks him as belonging to the older Christian tradition in which depth of spiritual teaching was more important than personal charisms or accounts of one's own experience of God.[145]) The hagiographical materials about Francis, however, portray him as a remarkable visionary, one who shows interesting analogies to the experiences ascribed to Mary of Oignies and other contemporaries. For example, a developed picture of Francis as visionary is found in the *Legend of the Three Companions,* a text that some have seen as containing early materials emanating from reminiscences of the townfolk of Assisi and Francis's most intimate companions. Whatever the validity of this claim, the *Legend* is a good witness for the hagiographical picture of Francis the visionary mystic.

In the *Legend,* Francis is depicted as undergoing a form of ecstatic initiation culminating in the *ne plus ultra* experience of identification with the suffering Christ through the reception of the stigmata. Earlier accounts of the saint's life, such as the *First Life* of Thomas of Celano, had already identified the stigmata as the acme of Francis's itinerary to God, but the *Legend* is the first compilation to orchestrate the experience on Monte Alverna as the final chapter in a series of divine manifestations. According to the *Legend,* Francis began his visionary career by receiving two dream manifestations prior to his conversion—one promising him that he would become "a great leader," the other advising him to return to Assisi and not to seek his fortune in military adventures.[146] The young Francis then was favored with a waking experience of the sweetness of the Lord, which the author of the *Legend* interprets as the beginning of his marriage to his true spouse, the *vera religio* of Franciscan poverty of life.[147] In Francis's fourth experience, a voice from heaven prepares him for his encounter with a leper and the choice of the life of an outcast that is later witnessed to in his own *Testament.*[148]

The fifth mystical moment, which comes at the center of this itinerary (with four prior and four subsequent experiences), has Christ address Francis from the cross as he prays in the church of San Damiano. This marks a transition to a new stage, one that the hagiographer (as noted above) explicitly relates to the final experience of identity with Christ in the reception of the stigmata.[149] Francis, having made his commitment to renounce the world while still continuing to live in it, now begins to have his true task revealed to him. The author of the *Legend,* not unlike James of Vitry in his *Life of Mary,* is anxious to portray Francis as someone "drunk with divine love" (7.21) and "filled with prophetic spirit" (7.24, 10.36) as he goes about his task of founding the *fraternitas.* It is noteworthy, however, that the three visionary experiences that the author of the *Legend of the Three Companions* places in the "public life" of Francis are all dream visions, which have a relatively restricted importance in the other hagiographical sources.[150] The final vision, that of the stigmata, is crucial to all accounts and will be taken up below.

The other major sources for the life of Francis, both official documents like the *First Life* and *Second Life* of Thomas of Celano and the two *Legends* written by Bonaventure, as well as the compilations of stories, like the *Compilation of Assisi* and the *Mirror of Perfection,* all describe Francis as enjoying special experiences of God. These include dream visions,[151] along with waking ecstasies.[152] The use of the traditional language of monastic *contemplatio* to describe Francis's experiences reaches its culmination in later theological interpretations, especially those of Bonaventure, but it is spread throughout the hagiographical materials.

Thomas of Celano's *First Life* speaks of a transformative ecstasy of ca. 1208 in which Francis was given conviction that his sins were forgiven and then was "raptured above himself and absorbed in a certain light so that his interior mind was enlarged and he could clearly see what was to come."[153] In subsequent texts Celano speaks of Francis as "raised up in contemplation" (1Cel 83), or wishing "to pass over completely" to the heavenly state (1Cel 92), or being "in frequent ecstasy" (1Cel 103), or contemplating Christ "in rapture of mind" (1Cel 115). Through the saint's mediation, other friars were also given visionary and ecstatic experiences, thus demonstrating the sanctity of their leader (e.g., 1Cel 47–48 and 110). As we might expect, such descriptions only increase in the long *Second Life* that Celano was commissioned to write by the minister general Crescentius of Jesi about 1246–47.[154]

Hagiographical accounts of Francis's ecstatic experiences, however, are only part of the story. Two other aspects of the picture of Francis given in this literature provide help for understanding his major contribution to the new mysticism. The first is Francis's devotion to literal imitation of the events in the historical life of Jesus, what Ewert Cousins has called "the mysticism of the historical event."[155] The second is the way in which his followers used the most literal aspect of his following of Christ, the stigmata, to forge a picture of *Il Poverello* not just as another follower of Christ but, according to Thomas of Celano, as the "true image of the cross and passion of the Lamb without blemish" who has become "the pattern of salvation" for all Christians.[156] Modern biblical criticism has investigated how in the case of Jesus "the proclaimer became the proclaimed," that is, Jesus the eschatological preacher became the preached message of the first Christians. This shift bears an analogy to how Francis the *follower* of the evangelical way of life became Francis the "true imitator and disciple of the Savior" (*verus imitator et discipulus Salvatoris*), that is, the person all should follow in order to come closer to Christ.[157]

In his own writings Francis had insisted both on the necessity for all believers to follow Christ and on fidelity to the form of apostolic life for his own followers. But in these works he never used the phrase *ad literam,* so that much modern study of Francis's "literalism" seems exaggerated or misplaced.[158] Likewise, there is nothing in his writings explicitly dwelling on the imaginative recreation of the events of Christ's life, which Cousins describes as the essence of the mysticism of the historical event.[159] Nevertheless, there is a foundation for later Franciscan emphasis on contemplative reliving of the events of the gospel in two aspects of the hagiographical picture of the saint's final years–the Christmas crib scene he created at Greccio in 1223,[160] and the reception of the stigmata on Monte Alverna nine months later.

Two things should be noted about this aspect of the message of *Il Poverello*. The first is that emphasis on concrete recollection of the events of

Christ's life and appropriation of their religious meaning by the believer often through literal imitation was part of a long trajectory in medieval spirituality. Some earlier manifestations, appearing in figures like Peter Damian and the Cistercians, have been considered in *The Growth of Mysticism*.[161] How much of a development Francis himself made in this tradition is difficult to say,[162] though there can be no question that the Franciscans, especially through the writings of Bonaventure and through the pseudo-Bonaventurean *Meditations on the Life of Christ*, were major proponents of this theme in later medieval spirituality. What is significant about the Greccio incident is not that it constitutes the earliest appearance of a visual recreation of the birth of Christ (such presentations were already known in Italy), but that Francis orchestrated the *tableau vivant* in relation to the celebration of the Eucharist, thus emphasizing that imaginative recreation of the historical event finds its true meaning in the sacrament in which Jesus, God and man, becomes present to those who recognize him in the Spirit of the Lord.

The second issue is how far we may wish to speak of such meditative and contemplative practices as mystical. Given the flexible notion of mysticism used in this history, I have no difficulty in seeing a "mysticism of the historical event" as one form of Christian mysticism, and Francis (both the real Francis and the hagiographical model) as playing an important role in its evolution. I would suggest, however, that such intense pictorial realizations of the events of Christ's life should be seen as belonging more to the preparation for a direct and often non-pictorial consciousness of identification with Christ, both human and divine, at the summit of the mystical path, than as constituting its core. However we evaluate the significance of the "mysticism of the historical event," one thing is clear: the Franciscan contribution to mystical identification with Christ, especially his passion, depended primarily on Francis's unprecedented identification with the Savior through his reception of the stigmata, the physical marks of the five wounds of the crucified Jesus. All the accounts of Francis's life stress this as the culminating seal of his holiness.[163]

Emphasis on bearing the wounds of Christ, really or metaphorically, was nothing new. Paul himself set the stage with his statement "I bear the marks of Jesus in my body" (*ego enim stigmata in corpore meo porto* [Gal. 6:17]).[164] *Stigmata*, however, was used in a fairly generic way until the twelfth century, when the growing devotion to the sacred humanity of Christ and especially to his passion seems to have initiated a shift in the understanding of the term toward identification with the specific five wounds exhibited by Christ on the cross. There is evidence from the early thirteenth century of several figures who inflicted the marks of the crucifixion on themselves, either by self-crucifixion or else as a form of ascetic practice. The ambigious nature of such activity is indicated by the fact that a man who had crucified himself in England around 1222 was condemned to be immured as a heretic,[165] while several other pre-1224 self-stigmatics were hailed as holy men.[166] All this is quite different from what Thomas of Celano hailed as "the new and amazing miracle" (*novo et stupendo miraculo* [3Cel 2.2]) manifested in Francis.

The stigmata received by Francis are still unique in the history of Christianity, not so much because these marks were not self-induced (at least several score later stigmatics fall into this category), but primarily because the event was used by Francis's followers to put the seal on his model of following Jesus in a way that no other subsequent report of stigmata, authentic or inauthentic, ever approached.[167] Francis remains *the* stigmatic. As Dante put it in his "Paradiso," this sign was "the final seal received from Christ and borne by his limbs for two years when it pleased God, who had given him such good, to draw him up to the reward he deserved by making himself humble."[168]

Modern discussions of Francis's stigmata have revolved around attempts to determine the authenticity of the details of the various secondary reports of the event, as if we could ever know what really happened and what Francis chose not to talk about directly (even in his most personal document, the *Testament*). From the perspective of the history of mysticism, it is important to begin with some theological observations that will help frame the issue of the significance of the stigmata. Two basic principles have guided subsequent theological evaluation of claims to stigmata. The first is that the stigmata are not, in themselves, necessarily miraculous, because it is not possible to rule out a psychological origin (indeed, there have been modern cases in which the stigmata have appeared outside a specifically Christian context).[169] Second, and following from this, reception of the stigmata does not, of itself, constitute direct proof for special sanctity of life or of some immediate contact with God.[170] In cases like that of Francis, where the stigmata constitute an integral part of a deeply devout Christian life, we can invoke a third principle expressed in John of the Cross's observations about the nature of such divine communications.

John's treatment of the "wound of love" in the second stanza of *The Living Flame of Love* distinguishes between a purely internal cauterization of the soul effected solely by the Holy Spirit and "another and most sublime way" of burning in which the soul is wounded interiorly in such a manner that the flame of divine love fills it entirely so that "it seems to the soul that the whole universe is a sea of love in which it is swallowed." In this latter case,

God may allow the effect of this interior love to pass outward into the senses, "as was the case when the seraph wounded St. Francis; when the soul is wounded by love with five wounds, the effect extends to the body and the wounds are marked on the body, and it is wounded just as the soul is."[171] When this happens, John insists that the character of the exterior manifestation will be directly proportional to the strength of the interior manifestation. Thus, for John of the Cross, priority is always given to the invisible interior wound,[172] though he suggests that the intensity and exemplary character of Francis's bodily manifestation of Christ's wounds gives him a special place as a religious "founder."[173]

Such theological analysis of the meaning of Francis's stigmata as a sign of his interior transformation extends beyond the canons of historical investigation, though it should not lead us to neglect what historical study can say about the events under discussion. The sources seem to present us with at least three layers of evidence.[174] The first concerns the basic facts granted by all. There is agreement that Francis received the stigmata in September of 1224 during a forty-day period of fasting on Monte Alverna, where he was staying in the company of a few chosen companions. There is also consensus that he bore the signs of the passion during the rest of his life and that these marks were seen by many at the time of his death.

A second layer of evidence concerns the seraph vision, which traditionally came to be seen (and pictured) as precipitating the appearance of the marks on the saint's body. Chiara Frugoni suggests that a careful study of the early accounts indicates that the seraph vision was originally separate from the appearance of the stigmata.[175] This seems likely, though we have no way of determining what interval may have separated the two, and all the evidence suggests that they both are associated with the retreat on Monte Alverna. (In this connection, it is worth noting that the account of the stigmata found in the encyclical letter said to have been published by the minister general Elias shortly after Francis's death in 1226 does not mention the seraph vision.) Octavian Schmucki suggested the formation of what he calls a "canonical description" underlying the other reports which fused the two events from an early period,[176] but J. A. Wayne Hellmann has recently argued in more convincing fashion that it was Thomas of Celano in the extended description he gave of the Alverna events in his *First Life of St. Francis* who first connected the seraph vision with the stigmata.[177] The seraph is also mentioned in the note that Brother Leo, who was present on Alverna, wrote on the parchment blessing he had been given by the saint, but this is a later witness. Finally, a third layer of evidence for both the stigmata and its relation to the seraph vision consists in subsequent theological descriptions of the events and analysis of the character and meaning of the wounds, often written in response to attacks on the veneration of the stigmata and therefore of less historical weight, however much they have to tell us about the developing hagiography regarding the event.[178]

Immediately after Francis's death, Brother Elias issued an encyclical letter announcing the fact and beginning the canonization process of *Il Poverello*. In this text, of which only a very late witness survives, Elias put the stigmata at the center of his message:

> I announce a great joy to you [Luke 2:10] and a new miracle. Such a sign has been unheard of from the beginning [John 9:2], save only in the Son of God, who is Christ the Lord. Not long before his death, our brother and father appeared crucified, bearing the five wounds which are truly the stigmata of Christ in his body [Gal. 6:17]. For his hands and feet had as it were, the puncture wounds of the nails, pierced on both sides, retaining the scars and showing the blackness of the nails. His side appeared to have been lanced and it frequently seeped blood.[179]

Beginning with Thomas of Celano's *First Life,* subsequent reports elaborated on how the scars on Francis's hands and feet appeared to have had fleshly or cartilagenous extrusions, which seem to be what Elias had in mind through his mention of "the blackness of the nails." Though this description underwent considerable hagiographical development, it does parallel similar extrusions of flesh that have been reported on later stigmatics (or are these rooted in the popularity of the Francis legend?).[180]

From the perspective of their mystical significance, the character of the wounds is less important than the meaning of the inner experience that produced them. As John of the Cross suggested, for believers the external appearance of such wounds was a sign of the more important interior identification with Christ crucified that some of the hagiographical sources contend began with the San Damiano experience. This "crucifixion complex," as Herbert Thurston called it, was also reflected in the saint's own composition, the "Office of the Passion of the Lord," as well as in some other of his writings.[181] The passion certainly played an important part in Francis's dedication to following Christ, but his spirituality always centered on the total process of salvation more than on any single event or mystery.

Another dimension of this experience is manifested in the mysterious vision of the figure of the seraph. Celano's *First Life* recounts how Francis "in a vision of God" (Ezek. 8:3) saw a six-winged seraph above him with hands and feet extended and fixed to a cross (the various accounts combine aspects of two fundamental angelic manifestations of the Old Testament,

Isaiah 6 and Ezekiel 1). "When the blessed servant of the Most High saw these things, he was filled with the greatest wonder, but he could not understand what this vision should mean to him." Francis's experience is described, as many other mystical visions have been, as combining great joy because of the beauty and kindness of the seraph along with sharp pain at the suffering of crucifixion. It was while he was considering the "novelty of this vision" (*visionis huius novitas*), according to Celano, that "the marks of the nails began to appear in his hands and feet, just as he had seen them shortly before on the crucified man above him."[182] Celano's account of the seraph vision does not identify the seraph with Christ and does not give the seraph the role of actually causing the wounds that later iconography and tradition did.[183] We are left to wonder about the relationship between the angelic manifestation and the appearance of the stigmata.[184]

In ancient Christian tradition, Christ himself had sometimes been seen as an angel, specifically "the Angel of Great Counsel" (*angelus magni consilii* [Isa. 9:5 in LXX and liturgical texts]), and even as one of the seraphim of the vision of Isaiah 6.[185] Some early medieval portrayals of Christ on the cross contain attending seraphim. More importantly, the seraph, as the highest form of angel, had come to be identified with the overwhelming power of fiery love by the twelfth century.[186] Hence, we may suggest that Francis's seraph vision, later interpreted as precipitating the appearance of the stigmata, originally signified a revelation of the mystery of the heavenly Father's love sending the Son into the world to redeem fallen humanity.[187] This would locate the meaning of the "original" vision solidly in Francis's archaic theology. It also seems to be confirmed by the evidence of the highly biblical hymn to God which the saint is said to have composed in response to his visionary experience, the "Praises of God Most High," which preface the "Blessing given to Leo."[188] Thomas of Celano in the *First Life* developed a full theological picture of the seraph, using it as a device to invite his readers to participate, along with Francis, in the practice of virtue and contemplative vision of God revealed in the passion (see 1Cel 114–15).[189]

Once again, however, we sense a real gap between what we can discover, in partial fashion at best, about Francis's own understanding of his experience of God and what was made of it by his followers, even those closest to him. Whatever the relation of these two mysterious events, Francis's reception of the stigmata of the Suffering Savior and its connection with the seraph vision became *the* sign to his followers that he had achieved the status of the highest angels through transforming love—Francis, as Bonaventure later described him, was truly the *vir angelicus* (1Bon 13.5).

This "new and amazing miracle," which can also be described as a new form of mystical union, assured *Il Poverello* an important role in subsequent Christian mysticism.

The theme of finding Christ in and through Francis was central to all later Franciscan piety and mysticism. No more perfect example of this is to be found than in Clare of Assisi (1193–1253), Francis's first female convert to the evangelical way of life and the founder of the "Poor Ladies of San Damiano," the source of all the later groups of women who identify them-selves as Franciscan.[190] As she put it in the *Testament* that she wrote late in life in imitation of that left by Francis: "The Son of God became our way, which our most holy father Francis, his true lover and imitator, showed and taught us by word and example."[191]

Francis's special love for Clare, whom he used to call "the Christian,"[192] is evident in his own writings and in all the hagiographical accounts.[193] A number of recent treatments, influenced by contemporary gender studies, have explored the dynamics of their interaction, seeking to show how Francis found in Clare a feminine complement to his own single-minded devotion to following the gospel and suggesting that they are best viewed as joint partners in the creation of the new apostolic form of life.[194] It is a strik-ing example of the important interactions between men and women in the beginnings of the new mysticism.[195]

The emerging image of Clare as a spiritual leader offers an analogue to attempts to discover the "real" Francis in the midst of the differences between *Il Poverello*'s own writings and the images developed in the Francis hagiography. Clare's authentic writings, though not extensive (only a third as long as those ascribed to Francis), are not only varied in genre but also display a rather diverse picture of her from that revealed in the subsequent hagiographical accounts.[196] Though brief, these writings provide us with real access to her own voice (as contrasted with what we know of Mary of Oignies, for example). Most medieval and modern conceptions of Clare have been more shaped by the famous *Legend* of her life written not long after her death and (in recent historiography) by the valuable "Process," that is, the official document recording the testimonies presented in evi-dence for her canonization,[197] but the investigation of the "real" Clare, like that of the historical Francis, needs to begin with her own writings.

The appeal to Francis found in Clare's authentic writings is a helpful starting place for grasping her mystical theology. All of Clare's writings date to after Francis's death; it is obvious that the role that he plays in them is in part polemical—Clare was using the image of her canonized friend to defend her own (perhaps better, *their* own) understanding of absolute poverty against those who wished to modify it.[198] This is why Francis is omnipresent in the *Testament* that Clare wrote to guarantee the continuity of their mutual vision, while only moderately strong in her *Rule,* and almost absent from the *Letters to Agnes* that summarize her own spiritual teaching.[199] The depth of Clare's personal attachment to Francis is brought out in a vision reported in the *Process* for her canonization. According to the testimony of Sister Filippa, Clare recounted to some sisters a vision she had in which she saw herself carrying a jug of hot water and a towel to Francis (probably a reminiscence of her nursing him during his illness of 1223 when he stayed at San Damiano). The vision, whether a dream-vision or not (we are not told), suddenly switches scenes, and, instead of Clare serving Francis, she sees herself as climbing a ladder to reach Francis who is standing at the top. Then Francis, in the manner of the maternal figure of an abbot made popular by Bernard of Clairvaux and others,[200] nourishes Clare from his own breast in a striking portrayal:

> And when she reached Saint Francis, the saint uncovered his breast and said to the virgin Clare, "Come, take, and suck." And when she had sucked, the saint admonished her to suck again. While she sucked, what she was sucking was so sweet and delightful that she had no way to describe it. When she had sucked, the nipple or mouth of the breast from which the milk came remained in blessed Clare's lips. And when she took what remained in her mouth in her hands, it seemed to her that it was gold so bright and clear that she saw everything there as if in a mirror.[201]

The powerful symbols of this account express a remarkable reversal of genders as Clare is nourished by the heavenly milk of "Mother Francis."[202] Her sense of identity with Francis as a babe at his breast helps explain Clare's practice of referring to herself in diminutives in the course of her writings–*plantula beatissimi patris Francisci* (ReCl 1.3; cf. TeCl 37 and 49, and BeCl 6), as well as *ancilla* (eleven times), *famula* (three times), and *serva* (once).[203] The golden nipple that becomes a mirror (mirrors are a central symbol in Clare, as we shall see below) appears to represent their common *forma vitae,* that is, the dedication to poverty which reflects, or gives meaning to, "everything" (*tucta*) in their lives.

Clare of Assisi was the first woman to write her own rule for religious life, and (what is more remarkable) to have it receive ecclesiastical approbation.[204] That she could not have done this without Francis–Francis alive and Francis dead–in no way detracts from her own genius and energy. Francis alive provided the *forma vitae* that was the core of her vision of a new kind of religious life for women; Francis dead and in heaven was the celestial patron she used with remarkable astuteness to overcome papal opposition

to the regularized form of a life of absolute poverty for women that she
managed to see approved on her deathbed.

The fundamental characteristics of Clare's ground-breaking rule, especially its emphasis on absolute poverty, manual labor, and the common life,
have been studied by Marco Bartoli among others.[205] Clare's *Form of Life*
(she did not call it a *Rule* herself) is no more a mystical document than any
other rule for the religious life, monastic or mendicant, however much it
was designed to provide a context designed to foster intense encounter with
God. Her own interior life, like that of Francis, is largely hidden in the *Rule,*
as it also is in her *Testament,* which is more a public exhortation than an
interior revelation. Fortunately, a series of four letters that Clare wrote ca.
1230–1253 to Agnes of Hungary, daughter of the king of Bohemia, who
had rejected marriage to Emperor Frederick II in order to join the houses
following the poverty of life of the community of San Damiano, provide
more direct insight into her own life with God.

The *Letters to Agnes* are written in an ornate style different from that found
in the *Rule* and *Testament,* one reminiscent of the marriage of supple Latinity
and spiritual expressivity in Cistercian and Victorine authors of the twelfth
century. Reputable authorities have noted that these relatively brief letters
do not concentrate on the theme of contemplation, but then few letters
from monastic contemplatives did. As a woman, and therefore an *illiterata*
(i.e., someone untrained in either the monastic or scholastic modes of theology),[206] she could scarcely be expected to leave extensive mystical commentaries on scripture. Nevertheless, the mystical elements enshrined in
these letters guarantee Clare a significant role in the contribution of thirteenth-century women to mysticism, though perhaps not completely to the
"new" mysticism. Clare's teaching looks back to the twelfth century at least
as much as it shares in the new developments found in contemporary
female authors.

Clare was not primarily a visionary in the manner of so many other
thirteenth-century women. Not only does she not describe such experiences
in her own works, but the only major vision ascribed to her in the canonization process was the vision of Francis noted above.[207] The *Process* is even
quite chary of speaking of her ecstatic experiences, mentioning only a rapture that kept her insensible for more than a whole day one Good Friday.[208]
While Clare certainly shows a respect for the Eucharist, she was not fundamentally eucharistic in her prayer life, as were so many other female mystics of the time.[209] Finally, while she makes considerable use of the nuptial
language of the soul as spouse of Christ (which appears rarely in Francis),
she does so more in accordance with twelfth-century erotic mysticism

(though with some variations), rather than in the manner of the "excessive" eroticism that characterizes many thirteenth-century women.

The nuptial aspect of Clare's mystical piety is rooted in her adoption of the formula found in Francis concerning the individual Christian as "mother, sister and spouse of Christ."[210] This mode of describing our relation to Christ is in turn founded on the theology of the indwelling of Christ in the soul, as is evident from a passage from the third *Letter to Agnes:*

> So, it is clear that by God's grace the soul of a faithful person, the most worthy creature, is greater than heaven, since heaven and other creatures are not able to grasp the Creator and only the faithful soul is his dwelling and throne, and this is possible only through the charity that the wicked lack.[211]

For Clare this indwelling theme is presented within a Marian setting—the Blessed Virgin is the first and exemplary "cloister" (*claustrum*) that contains Christ the Creator (3ECl 17–19 and 24–26).[212] The sister who is a mother of Christ due to the charity that lives within her and which she expresses by mutual love for all,[213] by that very reason also shows herself to be Christ's spouse.

Clare develops the theme of the mystical marriage both in traditional accents of the Song of Songs and with a new tonality expressive of the Franciscan emphasis on the love of the poor and crucified Jesus. Six key passages in the *Letters to Agnes* describe spiritual experience in the language of nuptial union.[214] Although Francis's *forma vitae* had identified the poor ladies as spouses of the Holy Spirit (see ReCl 6.2), Clare herself always speaks of Christ as the Bridegroom. A number of the nuptial texts in the *Letters* are rhetorical evocations of the power of mutual love in a manner not unlike those found in the Cistercian mystics.[215] Other passages, however, display new notes. In the second of the *Letters,* for example, Agnes is invited as a "poor virgin to embrace the poor Christ." She is to gaze upon and follow the one who was made contemptible for her. Clare continues:

> Most noble queen, look upon, consider, contemplate and desire to imitate your Spouse, "beautiful beyond the sons of men" (Ps. 44:3), who, for your salvation, was made the vilest of men, despised, beaten and scourged in many ways over his whole body, dying in the midst of the agonies of the cross.[216]

This emphasis on the love of the crucified Christ, of course, was also important to Francis, but he never developed it in the context of the spousal motif. Also noteworthy in this text is the fourfold program beginning in two forms of visual meditation (*intuere–considera*) and moving on to contemplation (*contemplare*) for the purpose of imitation (*desiderans imitari*).

Two extended passages on Agnes as bride in the third and fourth of the letters present aspects of the marital relation between Christ and the virginal soul that demonstrate why Clare, despite the brevity of her writings, can be numbered among the significant female mystics of the thirteenth century. In the third *Letter to Agnes* an extended passage (3ECl 5–28) summarizes her spiritual teaching and introduces a key mystical theme not found in Francis— the notion of the *speculum,* or mirror.[217] Clare praises Agnes both at the beginning and at the end of this lyrical passage (3ECl 5–11 and 24–28) for the virginity and devotion to poverty that have enabled her to outwit the devil. Within this envelope of praise she includes an invitation to a deeper understanding of what it means to be a Bride of Christ:

> Place your mind in the mirror of eternity; place your soul in the splendor of glory; place your heart in the figure of divine substance and transform your-self totally through contemplation into the image of his divinity so that you may feel (*sentias*) what friends feel in tasting the hidden sweetness which God himself has reserved from the beginning for those who love him.[218]

So, the contemplation of God in Christ (as the references to Heb. 1:3, and 2 Cor. 3:18 indicate) is the means whereby the bride is transformed into Christ and comes to taste the divine sweetness. The highly visual emphasis found in most of Clare's teaching on the experience of Christ here also involves a synaesthetic richness typical of the evocation of the spiritual senses present in such classic monastic mystics as Gregory the Great and Bernard of Clairvaux.[219] The second part of the inclusion (3ECl 15–23) pro-vides another view of this transformation by its teaching (cited above) on the divine indwelling by which the virgin bride becomes a mother of God after the archetype of Mary.

The mirror image occurs again in the final letter, which the dying Clare sent to her beloved Agnes. Here the mirror describes Christ as both the Divine Lover and the model and inspiration for the Franciscan way of life. Once again, Clare begins from the text of Hebrews 1:3, here combined with Wisdom 7:26, a reference to Christ as Eternal Wisdom:

> She [i.e., Christ as Wisdom] is the "splendor of eternal glory" (Heb. 1:3), "the brightness of eternal life, and the mirror without stain" (Wis. 7:26). Gaze daily into this mirror, O Queen, Spouse of Jesus Christ, and always behold your face there so that you may adorn yourself, within and without, "with a many-colored garment" (Ps. 44:10). . . .[220]

In an extended allegory, Clare invites Agnes to behold the three essential virtues of the Franciscan life in the Christ-mirror. The poverty and humility Divine Wisdom manifested in being born in a manger appear at the "begin-ning" (*principium*) or edge of the mirror. The surface (*medium*) of the mirror continues to display these virtues in the later events of his life, while the depth (*finis*) of the mirror allows Agnes to "contemplate the ineffable charity by which he willed to suffer on the wood of the cross and there to die the most shameful of deaths."[221] Such contemplation of the events of Christ's life in the mirror that is he himself aims toward heightening desire for erotic contact with the Divine Lover, something that Clare sets out in the language of the Song of Songs (4ECl 30–32). Though she does not say so here, a passage from the *Testament* shows that Clare insisted upon the reciprocal nature of gazing into the mirror. By attentive contemplation of the Christ-mirror the sisters of San Damiano come to be established as "a form in example and mirror for others, but also for our own sisters whom the Lord will call to our vocation [e.g., Agnes and her community], so that they may serve as a mirror and example for those living in the world."[222]

This important text leads us to the final issue concerning Clare's relation to the new mysticism. Many, though not all, of the themes of Clare's mysticism come from the treasury of the earlier medieval teaching on *contemplatio;* it may also seem that Clare's retreat from the world into the enclosure of San Damiano was also typical of monastic separation and is therefore at odds with the democratizing and secularizing tendency of the new mysticism noted earlier. This is not the case, however, especially because Clare conceived of her commitment to Francis's *forma vitae* as involving a new public responsibility for the entire church.

The fifth and eleventh chapters of Clare's *Rule* give feminine enclosure both a more flexible interpretation and a less central place than the rules that Gregory IX and Innocent IV had attempted to impose on San Damiano.[223] As Jean-François Godet puts it, Clare's model was "a life of withdrawal, not a life of confinement."[224] A measure of withdrawal was necessary so that the practice of humility, poverty, and mutual charity enshrined in the apostolic *forma vitae* of the Poor Ladies could shine more brightly as a mirror for women and men still living in the world, as both the *Testament* and a passage in the third *Letter to Agnes* make clear (see 3ECl 7–8). The paradoxical way in which Clare and her followers withdrew from the world in order to become a more manifest example of light and love to it was not lost upon her hagiographer (see the *Legend,* especially 1.10–11), but it was never expressed with more lyric intensity than in the Bull of Canonization. These lines can serve to summarize key values of the new apostolic forms of mysticism that began to flourish shortly after 1200.

> She was kept inside, and remained outside. Clare was hidden, yet her way of life was open. Clare kept silent, but her fame cried out. She was concealed in a cell, but she was taught in the cities. It is no wonder that so bright and gleaming a light could not be hidden, but must shine forth and give clear light in the Lord's house.[225]

Early Franciscan Mysticism and Bonaventure's Synthesis

HE TRANSITION FROM THE PRIMITIVE *fraternitas* of Francis and his first companions to the established Franciscan order was well under way in the saint's own lifetime.[1] The approval given by Pope Honorius III to the modified *Rule* (*Regula bullata*) on November 29, 1223, was a key step in this process. A hundred years later, on November 12, 1323, Pope John XXII issued another bull (*Cum inter nonnullos*), which condemned the teaching that Christ and the apostles had owned nothing either in private or in common, the so-called doctrine of absolute poverty upon which many Franciscans had based the distinctiveness of their order.[2] John's condemnation not only precipitated a crisis within the order, but also brought to an end a century of Franciscan life as notable for its contentiousness as it was for its spiritual creativity.

Much has been written about the first century of Franciscan history and especially about the debates over poverty.[3] There is also an extensive literature dealing with the contribution of the Franciscans to medieval piety and theology during this century.[4] I cannot attempt to survey this material here, but in order to comprehend some of the key issues in early Franciscan mysticism, it will be helpful to begin with a brief look at the poverty debate insofar as it forms a necessary background to the first century of Franciscan mysticism.[5]

The long history of specialized forms of religious life within Christianity shows nothing to equal the drama and conflict of the first century of the Franciscan order—the *ordo sine ordine* (order without order) as it has been ironically termed. The debate over what it meant to follow the example of Francis as the "true imitator" (*verus imitator*) of Jesus, especially in his practice of poverty, was unique, not only because of the cultural and religious significance of the Franciscans, but also because of the way in which this quarrel allowed Francis to take on a more powerful role than that enjoyed by any other religious founder. The paradox by which Francis, whose central desire was to share in Christ's total abnegation, became the Francis whose patronage was necessary to prove that those who no longer fully followed his example could still share in his unique relation to Christ, remains one of the most intriguing chapters in the history of Christian attempts to live the apostolic life. The easy solution to this paradox is to convict those who claimed they were following Francis but who really wound up modifying his ideal of being guilty either of bad faith or radical misunderstanding. While neither of these options can be ruled out, it is difficult to think that personal failings give the full explanation for why so many sincerely religious people became convinced that important changes in the original model of the *fraternitas* were necessary. Similar tensions between ideals and reality have marked all institutional attempts to realize the Gospel. The unique aspect of the Franciscan debate was the way it centered on the significance of "Lady Poverty" (*Domina Paupertas*).[6]

The debate over the meaning of Francis and his witness was played out in a variety of contexts. The major arena, of course, was within the new *ordo* itself, both the "first order" of men, and the "second order" of Clare and her followers. The immense success of the Franciscans, however, made the debates over the meaning of following Francis important for both church and society. The thirteenth-century papacy needed the Franciscans and the other mendicant orders, especially the Dominicans, in order to vindicate its desire to encourage more effective forms of the *cura animarum*. The religious energy unleashed by Francis and his companions, however, introduced elements of evangelical "freedom of the spirit" (*libertas spiritus*, 2 Cor. 3:17) that the increasingly bureaucratic Roman curia found problematic, given its emphasis on structure and obedience. The position of the thirteenth-century papacy as arbiter of all reform and guardian of orthodoxy meant that the meaning of following Francis could not be settled by the Franciscans alone.

In the *Rule* (*Regula bullata*) that was finally accepted by Rome, Francis had admonished the ministers of the order to be accessible as the servants of all at the same time that he encouraged the brethren to "pursue what they should desire above all things–to have the Spirit of the Lord and his holy manner of working."[7] There could be little disagreement about such general obligations; but on other issues, especially concerning the practice of poverty and the role of papal dispensation in the evolving life of the order, disputes soon emerged. A focus for such disagreements was the status of Francis's *Testament,* dictated on his deathbed. In this document the saint had enjoined absolute obedience to the *Rule* and his final wishes:

> The Minister General and all the other ministers and guardians are held through obedience not to add to or take away from these words. . . . Through obedience I firmly command all my brothers, clerical and lay, not to place glosses upon the *Rule* nor upon these words saying: "They are to be understood in this way." Just as the Lord gave me to speak and to write the *Rule* and these words in simplicity and purity, so too you should understand them in simplicity and without a gloss and you should observe them with a holy manner of working to the end.[8]

But could any merely human document, even one by Francis, enjoy such authority? Could Francis's words constrain the freedom of future Franciscan leaders and especially of the papacy to legislate for the good of the order? Francis's former friend and protector, Cardinal Hugolino, now Pope Gregory IX, declared otherwise in his bull *Quo elongati* of 1230.

This bull was a turning point in the history of the order, not only because of its rejection of the authority of the *Testament* (a point never accepted by some Franciscans) but also because of its introduction of the distinction between ownership (*dominium*) and use (*usus*). The pope's interpretation of the *Rule* was that the Franciscan life demanded the renunciation of all right of ownership but not of the necessary use of houses, books, furniture, and food, goods that a later papal bull, *Ordinem vestrem* of Innocent IV (1245), determined were actually owned by the papacy itself. "From this moment," according to John Moorman, "the Order set out on the path of a modest security,"[9] one that not only facilitated the growth of the movement but also encouraged the entry of the friars into the intellectual life of the new universities.[10]

The rapid changes in the order did not proceed without opposition. By the late 1230s resistance to the relaxation of poverty and longing for the simpler life of the early *fraternitas* is evident in some groups, especially in Italy, where members of Francis's own circle, like Brothers Leo, Rufino, and Angelo, as well as Giles of Assisi, provided a link with the past. Soon thereafter younger men, such as Conrad of Offida, James of Massa, and John of Parma, also represented the tendency that later came to be known as the "Spiritual" wing of the order as contrasted to the "Community," or majority party. The use of the term *spirituales* for the former group reflects another significant development in the order that seems to have begun about 1240–the adoption of ideas initiated by Joachim of Fiore as a part of Franciscan ideology.

Joachim, who died in 1202, left a rich legacy of biblical commentaries and treatises centering on predictions of the imminence of Antichrist and the coming end of the second *status* of history, the time ascribed to the second person of the Trinity. The Calabrian abbot broke with earlier Christian theologies of history, however, in looking forward to a coming third *status,* the time when the Holy Spirit would be poured out more fully upon a perfect contemplative church. Joachim's monasticized vision of history also included prophecies concerning coming orders of *viri spirituales,* or "spiritual men," who would preach against Antichrist and lead the church into the promised utopia of the third *status.* Joachim's predictions were ready-made for those Franciscans who saw their order as the culminating form of religious life which was destined play a decisive role in the imminent crisis of the age. Works pseudonymously ascribed to the abbot identified the *viri spirituales* with the friars and trumpeted apostolic poverty as their characteristic mark. An apocalyptic role was also found for Francis, who was identified with the angel of the sixth seal of Apocalypse 7:2, "ascending from the rising of the sun and having the seal of the living God," that is, the marks of the stigmata upon him.[11]

The power of this ideal is evident in the career of John of Parma, who served as minister general from 1247 to 1257. Though John supported the clericalizing and intellectualizing tendencies among the Franciscans, he suspended the implementation of some of the papal privileges and made the practice of actual "poverty of life" (*paupertas vitae/usus pauper*) the center of his efforts. Unfortunately, John became controversial when one of his protégés studying theology at Paris, the young friar Gerardo di Borgo San Donnino, produced an edition and commentary of Joachim's writings called the *Introduction to the Eternal Gospel.* Gerardo not only advanced the date of 1260 for the advent of the third *status,* but he also explicitly declared that the Franciscan way of life was the harbinger of a more perfect form of church that would triumph in the era to come. A group of secular priests serving as masters of theology at Paris (no friends of the friars, who had become increasingly important in the university) attacked Gerardo and all the mendicant orders as heretics and agents of Antichrist. The papacy rallied to the support of the new orders, but Gerardo was condemned and imprisoned for life and his patron John was compelled to step down.[12]

At this critical moment the order called upon its most gifted member, the Paris master John of Fidanza, or Brother Bonaventure (1217–1274), to take up the position of minister general. Like Augustine, Gregory the Great, and Bernard of Clairvaux, Bonaventure gives the lie to the common view of mystics as reclusive or anti-institutional figures. His careful mediation between the opposing groups in the order, his theological justification for the Franciscan claim to follow the absolute poverty of Christ and the apostles,[13] and his creation of a moderate form of Joachite theology of history to counter the excesses of Gerardo without losing the advantages Joachitism gave to the Franciscans led him to be termed "the second founder of the order." Bonaventure's rescue operation seemed complete when the Franciscan order received a strong vote of confidence against its detractors in the papal bull *Exiit qui seminat* of Nicholas III in 1279. The same bull approved Bonaventure's teaching about the absolute poverty of Christ and the apostles and his understanding of the distinction between *dominium* and *usus*.[14]

The inner tensions in the order, however, soon led to renewed disagreement. The Spiritual party, strong in Provence and central Italy, insisted on the authority of Francis's *Testament* and the practice of the strictest form of *usus pauper,* or "poor use," of goods. The Community party, on the other hand, was content with a style of life that differed little from that of other religious orders as long as they could maintain the claim that the Franciscans alone practiced the lack of dominion introduced by Christ and the apostles. The popes and Franciscan leaders usually sided with this position. Peter John Olivi (1248–1298), the theological leader of the Spirituals, who preached and wrote extensively in support of the "poor use" and the apocalyptic significance of the Franciscan order, was condemned both in his lifetime and after his death.

The period 1290–1310 witnessed increasingly acrimonious conflict between the Spirituals and the Community. In 1294 Pope Celestine V allowed some Spirituals to separate from the order to found their own group, the Poor Hermits of Celestine, but this permission was rescinded by Boniface VIII, who began a persecution of those Spirituals who sided with his ecclesiastical opponents. Ubertino of Casale, a Tuscan Spiritual leader, attacked Boniface and his successor, Benedict XI, as dual manifestations of the "Mystical Antichrist" foretold by Olivi. Apocalyptic speculation had now resulted in strong opposition to the institutional church itself. Clement V attempted to reach a compromise between the two parties by summoning the order to reform in his bull *Exivi de Paradiso* (1312), but his message went unheeded.

The aged canonist who followed him on the throne of Peter, John XXII (1316–1334), determined to settle the Franciscan problem once and for all. Pope John began by issuing a bull entitled *Quorumdam exigit* in 1317, which decided in favor of the Community position in disputed issues of poverty involving clothing and granaries. It closed with the ominous warning: "Great is poverty; greater is chastity; but the greatest good is obedience if it is kept unbroken."[15] True to his warning, in 1318 Pope John ordered four Spirituals who refused to accept the authority of the bull burned as heretics at Marseilles. The minister general Michael of Cesena initiated a suppression of the Spirituals throughout the order, while the Inquisition pursued their lay supporters (called "beguins" in southern France). The remnants of the Spiritual party, now known as the heretical *fraticelli*, continued to rail against the papal Antichrist for decades.

Pope John's zeal went even further. He decided to open a theological investigation of the heart of Franciscan claims to the superiority of their order, the assertion that they alone followed Christ and St. Francis in eschewing all forms of right to possession. Though accepted by Nicholas III in *Exiit qui seminat*, the lack of scriptural basis for the doctrine, as well as the obvious gap between Franciscan claims and the actual life of the friars, had led many to question this teaching. In a startling series of decrees, John first of all asserted his power to alter the decisions of his predecessors (bull *Quia nonnumquam* of March 1322), then denied that the papacy really owned the things used by the Franciscan order (*Ad conditorem canonum* of December 1322), and finally declared a heresy the teaching that Christ and the apostles did not possess both the right of possession and actual ownership of some material goods (*Cum inter nonnullos* of November 1323). The pope's sometime ally Michael of Cesena and many of the Conventual party joined their former enemies among the Spirituals in denouncing the pope as Antichrist and fleeing to join the ranks of his political opponents. It was against the background of these controversies and dramatic events that the golden age of Franciscan mysticism developed.

Ecstatic Contemplation among the Early Franciscans

As mentioned in the previous chapter, the hagiographical picture of Francis found in the early lives and stories places emphasis on his ecstatic visionary experiences, though the saint's own writings do not refer to them. It is not surprising that a number of early Franciscans, especially among his most intimate followers, were also credited with ecstatic experiences.[16] Among these figures, one stands out—Giles of Assisi, the third member of the *fraternitas*.

Giles (ca. 1190–1262), pilgrim and missionary, preacher and contemplative, lived through the early part of the tumultuous history traced above.[17]

He is unique among Francis's first followers in having his own hagiographical and sayings tradition, with three rather different lives and four surviving
collections of *Sayings (Dicta)* ascribed to him.[18] Giles was considered to be a
critic of developments in the order, as indicated by the stories about his
opposition to the erection of the great basilica to house Francis's remains at
Assisi and his statement that Paris had destroyed the order of St. Francis.
Evidence in the *Sayings* also hints at a discomfort with overemphasis on the
cult of Francis to the detriment of recognizing the divine mystery present in
all things.[19] Giles is a significant figure in the development of Franciscan
mysticism, not only because the *Life of Blessed Giles* portrays him as an independent ecstatic in a way that allowed for the development of alternative
models within the Franciscan tradition but also because his *Sayings* establish
a link with the Thomas Gallus, the last great Victorine and a pivotal figure in
the theoretical construction of the new mysticism of the period after 1200.

While other accounts concentrate on how Giles served as a model for
Franciscans in his active life, Leo's *Life* emphasizes Giles the ecstatic.
According to this text, Giles began to receive visions during his first period
in a hermitage some six years after his conversion,[20] but it was only after
the death of Francis, while he was at the hermitage of Cetona near Chiusi
in the winter of 1226–27, that he moved into a life of full ecstatic contact
with God. In Leo's account, Francis appeared to Giles in sleep, counseling
him to "Look to himself" (*stude tibi*). After intense preparation, the Lord
then appeared to Giles three days before Christmas. "At his appearance,"
we are told, "Brother Giles let out great cries because of the surpassing
odor; and because he was not able to bear it, it seemed to him that his very
being was failing."[21] This was the beginning of a series of experiences of
divine presence that lasted until Epiphany.[22] The language employed here,
as well as the length of the experience, recalls hagiographical accounts
more common to women mystics. Leo's version of Giles's reaction to these
raptures rings true because it conforms to a message also found in the *Sayings* about the necessity for silence, reticence, and indirection in speaking
about such mystical gifts.[23] These divine visitations during the winter after
the death of Francis gave Brother Giles, "the simple and unlearned peasant" (*homo idiota et sine literis, rusticus et simplex*), an overpowering and sometimes frightening sense of being under the direction of God rather than
self.[24] They also granted him a profundity of insight evident in the many
dicta found both in the lives and sayings collections. To those who praised
the greatness of God's manifestations to St. Peter, St. Francis, and to himself, Giles responded with a homespun apophaticism: "It is true that these

are great things; but God's works are one thing, and he is something else."[25] Toward the end of his life, when someone reminded him that Francis had said that every servant of God should always want to die a martyr's death, he reflected that he had once shared this view when he went off to preach to the Muslims in Tunisia, but now, "I don't wish to die a better death than that of contemplation"–an interesting reprisal of the ancient theme of the "mystical death" (*mors mystica*).[26]

Brother Giles's reputation as a mystic grew over the next three decades. Bonaventure, who interviewed him for stories about Francis not long before his death, spoke of him as a simple unlearned person who was "lifted up to the summit of the highest contemplation" in frequent raptures.[27] A story about the meeting of Bonaventure and Giles near Perugia recorded in the *Chronicle of the Twenty-Four Generals,* a fourteenth-century source based on earlier materials, emphasizes the new democratized mode of mystical consciousness implied in the reputation for ecstasy of such an *idiota et simplex.* Giles is reported to have asked Bonaventure, "Can a simple person love God as much as a learned one?" To which the general responded, "An old woman can do so even more than a master in theology." The text goes on: "Then Brother Giles arose in fervor of spirit and went into the garden near the part which looked toward the city and cried out: 'Poor little old woman, simple and unlearned, love the Lord God and you will be greater than Brother Bonaventure!'"[28] Giles's reputation as an ecstatic also involves a humorous side, as we are told that the boys of Perugia loved to send him into ecstasy by yelling "Paradiso! Paradiso!" whenever they saw him.[29]

Given the emphasis on Giles's lack of education, we might be tempted to see him as the representative of some kind of mysticism from below, a challenge to the learned tradition of speculation on contemplation. The most famous of his *Sayings,* however, refutes such a contention and reveals a significant point of intersection between new theoretical developments in Western mysticism and early Franciscan ecstatics. In chapter 13 of the *Sayings* Giles is recorded as responding to an inquiry concerning contemplation by distinguishing seven stages:

> "Fire," I say, is a kind of light which precedes in order to enlighten the soul. Then there is the "unction of ointments" from which arises a marvelous odor which follows that light and of which it says in the Song of Songs, "In the odor of your ointments . . ." [Song 1:3]. After this is "ecstasy": when the odor is perceived the soul is raptured and drawn away from bodily sensation. There follows "contemplation," for after the soul is drawn away from the bodily senses it contemplates God in a wonderful way. Then follows "taste," for in contem-

plation the soul feels a wonderful sweetness, as the Psalm says, "Taste and see
..." [Ps. 33:9]. After this is "rest," because the soul rests in that sweetness
when its spiritual palate has been soothed. Finally, "glory" follows, because
the soul glories in such great rest and is refreshed with immense joy, as the
Psalm says, "I will be satisfied when your glory appears" [Ps. 16:15].[30]

This pattern of seven stages emphasizing the progressive action of the
spiritual senses, with taste and a total experience of touch involving rest and
repletion at the height, was later adopted by Bonaventure, who twice used
it in discussions of the nature of contemplation.[31] It also is found in a brief
treatise often ascribed to Bonaventure entitled *The Seven Stages of Contemplation.* The treatise, however, is not by the Franciscan doctor, but is the product of the pen of Thomas Gallus, a Victorine canon resident in northern
Italy during the early years of the spread of the Franciscan movement.[32]
The use of Gallus's seven-stage motif by Giles and Bonaventure may seem
a minor moment in the exciting story of the new styles of mystical life of
the early thirteenth century, but it is actually of considerable significance,
because Gallus is an essential figure for understanding late medieval mysticism, especially that of the Franciscans.

Thomas Gallus and the New Dionysianism[33]

Whether or not Thomas Gallus knew Giles of Assisi personally, there is
no doubt that he was a friend of Antony of Padua (1191–1231), the Por-
tuguese canon who became a friar in 1220 and to whom Francis had given
the charge to provide theological instruction to Franciscan clerics.[34] Gallus's
ties to the early Franciscans are important for grasping why the last major
Victorine mystical author was a crucial figure connecting the twelfth-
century contemplative tradition and what I have called the new mysticism.
     Before his twentieth-century rediscovery by the Dominican scholar
Gabriel Théry, Thomas Gallus (i.e., "the Frenchman"), also known as
Thomas of St. Victor and Thomas of Vercelli, was a figure lost to history.
Part of this may have been because Gallus is not easy to read. A prolix
writer with a vocabulary and style that emulate the idiosyncratic originality
of his master, Pseudo-Dionysius, he can tax even devoted students. But
Gallus was well known and widely read in the later Middle Ages, primarily
as a commentator on the Dionysian writings but also as an exegete of the
Song of Songs. On the basis of the Dionysian commentary tradition begun
by his Victorine predecessors, Hugh and Richard, he combined Dionysian
apophaticism with an affective reading of the Song to form a potent new

mystical theory that was influential not only on many Franciscans but also on a wide variety of other late medieval mystics.

At the risk of oversimplification, we can say that two broad streams of the interpretation of Dionysius can be found in the later Middle Ages: the speculative Dionysianism initiated by the Dominican master Albert the Great, and what is often referred to as the "affective Dionysianism" first given systematic formulation in the writings of Thomas Gallus.[35] The Frenchman's role in initiating this latter tradition suggests why he deserves treatment here. Born in France sometime in the late twelfth century, Thomas became a canon at St. Victor and moved to Italy in 1219, eventually to become abbot of the Victorine house at Vercelli in Piedmont in 1226.[36] His involvement in the quarrels between the popes and the emperor Frederick II eventually forced him into exile in Ivrea in 1243. He died in 1246. Obviously well educated in the Parisian theology of the early thirteenth century and in the learned tradition of the canons of St. Victor, Gallus wrote extensively between about 1218 and the time of his death.[37]

Gallus's mystical theory is quite systematic: a clear debt to the scholastic impetus of the Victorine tradition.[38] His desire for organization resulted in a position on the relation between love and knowledge in mystical consciousness that was to be both influential and debated in the later Middle Ages. Gallus was one of the first authors, if not the first, to hold that affectivity tends to exclude rather than subsume human knowledge in the highest stages of the mystical itinerary.[39] The Victorine came to this view through his attempt to show that the Dionysian writings and the Song of Songs were not only mutually compatible but were really two sides of the same coin: the positive and negative versions of the higher knowledge of God that alone can lead to uniting with God (*unitio*) in this life. As he put it in the beginning of his *Commentary II on the Song of Songs:*

> There are two forms of knowledge of God. The one is intellectual and works through consideration of creatures, as in the book of Ecclesiasticus according to the worthy doctor Master Hugh's exposition, who was a canon of our church of St. Victor at Paris. . . . The other knowledge of God, incomparably better, is described by Dionysius in the *Divine Names* 7. . . . This superior wisdom is by way of the human heart. . . .

These two forms of knowledge, which he identified with the terms *scire* and *nosse* found in a passage in Jeremiah 9:24, are both necessary for humanity, but only the experiential super-intellectual *nosse* can lead to union. This higher knowledge has two aspects, and (in good scholastic fashion) two textbooks:

On the basis of the teaching of Paul, the great Dionysius the Areopagite wrote the theoretical part (*theorica*) of this superintellectual wisdom—insofar as it can be written—in his book *Mystical Theology.* .... But in this book [the Song of Songs] Solomon treated of the practical part (*practica*) of the same mystical theology, as is evident from its whole content.[40]

Gallus's entire program is outlined in this brief comment. Though both the textbooks he points to had been important among Christian mystics for centuries, no one had ever combined them in quite the same way.

The revival of the mystical interpretation of the Song of Songs, among the most significant achievements of twelfth-century mysticism, was certainly known to Gallus. Though he does not reproduce the details of Cistercian readings of the Song, his emphasis on the Bride's speaking from experience (*experientialiter loquitur* is a favorite phrase) marks a connection with the exegesis pioneered by Bernard of Clairvaux and William of St. Thierry.[41] Just as Bernard had invented the phrase "the book of experience," in commenting on Song of Songs 5:2, Thomas speaks of the "ears of experience":

"The voice of my Beloved beating." While I am thus engaged in spiritual practices, the voice, that is, the influx of the Beloved beating (I cannot express it in any other way) sounds in a superintellectual manner in the ears of my experience. It does not say that he is speaking, or persuading, because by the fire of his ray he beats upon the highest door, not of the intelligence, but of the affection.[42]

Like the Cistercians, especially Bernard, Thomas Gallus sees the Song as a key to unlock the central message of the whole Bible, citing hundreds of correlative texts from the Old and the New Testaments to underline the message he discovers. What is unique about his reading, however, is the way in which he uses Dionysius as the foundation of the entire program: the Areopagite is the key that unlocks the key. Thus, Thomas's commentaries assume the form of an extended dialogue between the Song text and the Dionysian corpus.

Gallus's Dionysianism rests on two significant innovations: a reinterpretation of the ascent to the unknown God which places the experience of affective love above all cognition, and a process whereby the angelic hierarchies are treated primarily as the inner powers of the soul to be energized and set in order to achieve loving union. Both these shifts are rooted in the thought of the former masters of St. Victor, but in Gallus they reach a new level of sophistication and systematization.

At the end of the first chapter of the *Mystical Theology,* Dionysius speaks of how Moses, the archetypal mystic, breaks free of all that can be perceived by body or mind in order "to plunge into the truly mystical cloud of unknowing." He continues: "Here, being neither oneself nor someone else, one is supremely united to the Unknown by an inactivity of all knowledge, and knows beyond the mind by knowing nothing."[43] This is how Gallus paraphrases the text in his *Extract:* "Separated from all things and from oneself, as it were, one is united to the intellectually unknown God *through a uniting of love which effects true knowledge* by means of a knowledge much better than intellectual knowledge, and, because intellectual knowledge is left behind, one knows God above intellect and mind."[44] The underlined phrase concerning the uniting of love represents, as Paul Rorem has shown, a new, specifically Latin Christian interpretation of the intellectual ascent found in Dionysius.[45] In line with Augustine, Gregory the Great, and the major twelfth-century Western mystics, Gallus insisted that because God is unknowable but reveals himself as Love (1 John 4:16), love has special access to him. As he put it in his *Commentary on Isaiah 6:* "The power of loving (*affectus*) is inestimably more profoundly and more sublimely drawn by God into God than is the power of understanding (*intellectus*), because angels and humans love more than they can investigate or understand."[46] Of course, most previous mystics had assigned love priority over intellect in attaining God, but the way in which the Victorine understood the priority of love had new accents not found in previous mystical teachers.

Gallus's affective Dionysianism is based upon a misreading, though one not without foundation in the *corpus dionysiacum*. There is little language about love in Dionysius's account of the ascent to God; but a noted text about the transcendental and cosmic nature of love (*erōs*) in the fourth chapter of the *Divine Names,* one that I have argued is central to the metaphysical foundations of Christian mysticism,[47] provided him with at least some basis for his interpretation. In this passage Dionysius vindicates the name of *erōs/agapē* for God as the primary cataphatic denomination, constituting the inner meaning of the divine name of "Goodness." Because God is Eros, the universe that is his manifestation must also be erotic, with the Divine Eros serving as both the object of its love, and, in participated form, the power by which it moves toward the goal. "He is Eros on the move, simple, self-moved, self-acting, preexistent in the Good, flowing out from the Good onto all things and returning once again to the Good."[48] It was not by accident that Gallus cited this passage *in extenso* in the third and most detailed of his commentaries on the Song of Songs in order to justify his inserting the affective erotic language of the Song into the vision of cosmic eros described by Dionysius.[49] He followed through on this reinterpretation by infusing the whole Dionysian ascent process with the language of yearning desire, as well as by adding a new upper floor, or level, to the powers of the soul, the "high point of the power of attraction," or the "spark of the synderesis" (*apex affectionis/scintilla synderesis*), that is, the affective summit "which alone is capable of being united with the Divine Spirit."[50] This notion of the "spark of the soul," which Gallus defined as "the principle and pure participation of divine goodness," was to have a considerable future in medieval mysticism.[51]

As typical with the Victorines, Thomas Gallus was much concerned with the role of the powers of the soul in the ascent to God. Like the masters of the twelfth century, he was convinced that both love and knowedge were necessary to attain God, but his thought on the relation of love and knowledge marks an important departure from earlier conceptions. Previous mystics had taught that love goes further than knowledge in attaining God, but they had also insisted that the love by which we reach God implies a form of knowing above ordinary reason. Gregory the Great coined the slogan for this when he said, "Love itself is a kind of knowing" (*amor ipse notitia est*). The exact nature of this knowing had been richly explored in the twelfth century, especially by Bernard of Clairvaux, William of St. Thierry, and Richard of St. Victor.[52] These thinkers generally held that the "understanding of love" (*intellectus amoris*) was built upon all the mystic's prior efforts to know and love God, and that, consequently, lower forms of knowing God were subsumed and transformed in the higher state. As William put it in his *Exposition on the Song of Songs:* "In the contemplation of God where love is chiefly operative, reason passes into love and is transformed into a certain spiritual and divine understanding which transcends and absorbs all reason."[53] Gallus's understanding of the relation of knowledge to the higher uniting of love differs from this by emphasizing a separation, or cutting off, of all knowing before the flight into the amorous *unitio deificans*.[54] In other words, love no longer *subsumes* preparatory forms of knowing, however necessary, but *discards* or *rejects* them. (Some of his followers were to question whether any preparatory knowing was either needed or helpful.) Therefore, although Gallus says that the downward influx (*influitio*) from the experience of uniting conveys both love and knowledge to the lower powers of the soul,[55] it is not easy to say in what sense the union itself may be characterized as cognitive, despite the fact that he does refer to it as a superintellectual "knowing" (*cognitio*) in some places.[56] Whatever we make of this downward movement of knowing, it is clear that Gallus has broken the link between knowing and loving on the *upward* path to God.

One way to understand what this *cognitio superintellectualis* may involve is to look at what Gallus has to say about the names of God, especially in relation to the revelation given to Moses, an archetypal mystic. Exodus 3:14, a foundational text for Christian metaphysics, declares: "The Lord said to Moses, 'I am who am,' and he said, 'Thus shall you say to the children of Israel, "Who is" sends me to you.'" Gallus, at least in his more mature works,[57] makes an original distinction between the two names given here—*ego sum qui sum* and *qui est*. The latter belongs to the realm of intellectual knowledge of God (*scire*), that is, knowledge of God as the cause of all things; but the former, "existence as reflective on itself," is a "unitive name known only to the united."[58] It is an incommunicable name that "is most correctly imprinted on the highest point of the primary power of loving and does not descend below it."[59] Hence, whatever "knowledge" it is that may exist on the superintellectual level, it is so purely personal that it can never be conveyed to anyone else.

Gallus's analysis of the relation between knowing and loving in the path to God involved subtle, but significant, shifts from the previous tradition of Western mysticism, changes that were important both in themselves and because they announced coming strife between the proponents of love and the defenders of knowledge in later mysticism.[60] A more complete understanding of this shift, both in the interpretation of Dionysius and in his influence on later mystics, especially among the Franciscans, emerges when we look at what the Victorine has to say about the role of the angelic hierarchies in the soul's ascent to God. Dionysius, let us remember, was the master not only of negative theology but also of angelic theology. In the *Celestial Hierarchy,* his most widely read work in the Middle Ages, he defined hierarchy as: "A sacred order, a state of understanding and an activity approximating as closely as possible to the divine," that is, "an image of the beauty of God which sacredly works out the mysteries of its own enlightenment."[61] As a trinitarian manifestation, every hierarchy in the created universe must be both one and three, exercising the purifying, enlightening, and perfecting activites that lead back to God—initiating action, mediating action, and being acted upon. In Dionysius's thought, angelic mediation plays a key role in human ascent, not so much because we are made into angels, but rather because by our effort to understand the angels as manifestations of God we participate in their anagogic mediation.[62] The Victorines, however, beginning with Hugh's *Commentary on the Celestial Hierarchy* and continuing with Richard's *Mystical Ark,* initiated a process of "angelization," whereby the soul itself *becomes* angelic by a process of "transforming into itself the figure of heavenly and winged animals and transfiguring their image in itself," as Richard put it.[63]

This process was accompanied by a shift in the meaning given to the seraphim, the highest of the nine orders, whereby they came to represent the dominance of *affectus* in the soul's return to God, as we have already noted in the previous chapter in speaking of the seraph vision of Francis (p. 63). This change is evident as early as Hugh's *Commentary* of ca. 1135. In analyzing biblical teaching concerning the seraphim in chapter 7 of his *Celestial Hierarchy* (CH 7.1), Dionysius had employed the language of fire and heat to describe their activity—they are the "heat-makers" (*calefacientes* in Eriugena's translation). There is no direct mention of love in the Dionysian analysis, but Hugh of St. Victor, anxious to draw Dionysius closer to Western mystical thinkers, provided a comment on the text which interpreted the relation between the two highest orders of seraphim and cherubim in terms of the priority of love over knowledge, concluding: "Love surpasses knowledge and is greater than understanding, for one loves more than one understands and love enters in and draws near where knowledge remains outside."[64] The fire or heat of the seraphim was henceforth to be understood as the fire of burning love.

On the basis of this new reading of the highest angelic hierarchies and the "angelization" process found in Richard's *Mystical Ark,* Thomas Gallus set out an account of how the internalization of the angelic hierarchies is integral to the soul's path to God. In *The Seven Degrees of Contemplation* he even employs the term, stating: "Fortunate indeed is he who attains the height of this degree [the fourth]; he is fully 'angelified' in the present and has already begun the future life."[65] This program is already present in his earliest work, the *Commentary on Isaiah 6.*[66] Since "the intention of hierarchy is assimilation and uniting to God, that is, to assimilate all habits and operations to God and to be united to him,"[67] the nine hierarchies, or orders, of angels can be found in every spirit, both angelic and human. In a key text in book 10 of the *Celestial Hierarchy* Dionysius had said as much, but he had not developed the point. Gallus seized upon this as the authorization for his program showing how everything said of the angels can also be applied to humans.[68] Insofar as the hierarchies are identified with the powers of the soul and their operations, the language that the soul speaks in its pursuit of God is a "hierarchized" one. Thus Gallus says that the bride of the Song of Songs "speaks now in one hierarchy of her mind, now in another; now in one order, now in another."[69] We can grasp how this interaction among the nine orders functions in the ascent process through the following chart.[70]

CHART 1

NATURE
{
Angels: *nuntio* (apprehension of good and evil)
Archangels: *dictatio* (natural choice of apparent good)
Principalities: *ductio* (opening of intellect and will to
divine truth and goodness)
}

INDUSTRY (nature-grace)
{
Powers: *ordinatio* (choice of divine good and orientation
of powers to God)
Virtues: *roboratio* (strengthening of intellect and will)
Dominations: *imperatio* (perfect activity of intellect
and will toward God: *extensio*)
}

GRACE
{
Thrones: *susceptio* (reception of infused graces)

Cherubim: *revelatio* (infused illumination: perfection
of will and intellect)
Seraphim: *unitio* (intellect cut off: realm of *apex affectus-
scintilla synderesis*)
}

There is no need to follow the details of Gallus's presentation of the soul's *cursus amoris* to God in order to grasp how its systematic structure, its treatment of the relation between nature and grace in the mystical path, and its stress on the superiority of ecstatic love made it useful for later mystical authors like Bonaventure. The Frenchman's revision of the Dionysian hierarchies infused dynamic energy into the mystical analysis of the role of the powers of the soul.[71]

Gallus also made major contributions to the understanding of the goal of the mystical itinerary, loving union with God. His treatment of *unitio deificans* has both conservative and innovative aspects. The stress on union with God puts the canon clearly in line with his predecessors, especially Richard of St. Victor, as does his use of the traditional terminology of *excessus mentis, ecstasis, and raptus.*[72] As is clear from the chart above, Gallus recognized two forms of *excessus,* one that pertains to the orders of thrones and cherubim involving *both* love and understanding, and one of love *alone* on the level of the seraphim.[73] Like the twelfth-century mystics, he insisted that the experience of ecstasy in this life must always be of brief duration, or *separabilis,* as he put it.[74] Though he does not present any extended analysis of the onto-logical mode of uniting with God, his discussions indicate that he understood it in much the same way as Bernard of Clairvaux and Richard of St. Victor, that is, as an *unitas spiritus* involving loving union of wills, which brings us into the life of the Trinity, but not some form of indistinct identity with God.[75]

If all this looks fairly standard in relation to the major twelfth-century theories of mysticism, other aspects of the Victorine's writings demonstrate new directions. First of all, we must remember that Dionysianism and its peculiar vocabulary, despite its place in the thought of John Scottus Eriugena, had exercised a relatively restricted role in medieval theology and mysticism thus far.[76] This changed in the thirteenth century, and Thomas Gallus was a major figure in what has been called the "Dionysius renaissance" of that time.[77] His writings display a rich vein of the peculiar vocabulary that marks this tradition in the history of mysticism, such as the compounds produced with the prefixes *super, supra,* and *sursum*–clear indicators of the anagogic impetus of Dionysian thought. But Gallus's contribution was more than one of mere terminology. His exploration of the apophatic dimensions of the mystical encounter with God, from the perspective of both the divine and the human, is original and worth examination.

In commenting on the text from the Song of Songs, "I am black but beautiful" (Song 1:4a), Gallus departed from twelfth-century commentators like Bernard and William by reading the passage as signifying the necessity for the soul to empty herself of all lower powers of knowing in order to plunge into the Dionysian cloud of unknowing to attain God. Here both the soul and God become *incontemplabilis,* that is, unable to be contemplated or comprehended: "She herself speaks to these inferior powers in her inability to grasp heself, 'I am black,' that is, enveloped in the superlucent cloud of divine incomprehensibility."[78] This mutual transcendence of knowledge may be the root of another important apophatic motif found in Gallus, one that was to have an extensive future in medieval mysticism. Several texts in the *Commentary II on the Song of Songs* read the reference to the desert in Song 3:6 as indicating the necessity for the soul to become an inner desert in order to be ready for the encounter with God–a frequent theme of twelfth-century monastic authors.[79] In the third commentary, however, Gallus adds a new dimension by speaking of the desert as "the trackless and unique solitude of the eternal supersubstanial Trinity."[80] Although references to God as desert had been found in John Scottus Eriugena and Isaac of Stella before him, Gallus's adaptation of the motif of the divine-human desert doubtless had its influence on the development of this theme in later thirteenth- and fourteenth-century mysticism.[81]

There is a third aspect to Gallus's stress on the mutuality of the *unitio* that joins God and human, one that again testifies to the importance of Diony-sius's cosmic eros for his thought. In book 4 of the *Divine Names,* the logic of Denys's position that God is characterized by the longing associated with eros led him to make the remarkable statement that the divine must be, in some sense, ecstatic to the world, that is, "carried outside himself in the lov-ing care he has for everything." Of course, Dionysius insisted that such divine ecstasy must be viewed in a dialectical way—the cataphatic mode by which we can metaphorically speak of God's ecstasy is rooted in his apophatic "supernatural and ecstatic capacity to remain . . . within him-self."[82] Thomas Gallus was typical of the monastic mystics of the twelfth cen-tury in his concern for investigating the loving *ecstasis* of the soul; but he differed from them by accepting the notion that God too must become ecstatic—and precisely in his love for humans, not merely in a universal cos-mic way. "Love is of such power," as he put it, "that not only does it place one outside oneself in relation to God, but (if we can say it) it draws God outside himself to the human person, as it were, so that the Infinite may unite things that are distant."[83] These three aspects of the Victorine's teach-ing on union constitute an important opening to the rich exploration of fully mutual love between God and humans, both men and women, found in the new mysticism of the thirteenth century.

In the preface to his *Extract* of the writings of Dionysius, Thomas Gallus spoke of the difficulty of "expressing in a common style the meaning which in these books I have conceived throughout twenty years—with what sleep-lessness, what labor!"[84] No less effort seems to have gone into his obsession with showing how the Song of Song, rightly understood, gave exactly the same sense. The indefatigable commentator's efforts were not to go totally unrewarded, as will be evident from many of the mystics to be considered in this volume.

Bonaventure's Mystical Synthesis

Bernard of Clairvaux and Bonaventure—the *doctor mellifluus* and the *doctor seraphicus*—may be justly described as the two premier mystical teachers of the medieval West.[85] Both were important ecclesiastical officials who were forced to be men of action, as well as of contemplation. Both wrote on a variety of theological and church-political topics, as well as on how the soul attains God in this life. Bonaventure's theology is more extensive and more systematic than Bernard's (not surprising given his scholastic career),[86] and this confronts any study of his mysticism with a major difficulty of presenta-tion. As Etienne Gilson put it, in the case of a teaching such as that of St.

Bonaventure, "the totality of the system means so much that the mere notion of fragments has no meaning at all. You can either see the general economy of his doctrine in its totality, or see none of it."[87] It is obviously impossible to try to give any remotely adequate account of the Franciscan's system in a brief compass, but still, given the close integration of his mystical theory with his general theology,[88] it is necessary to touch on some of the foundational themes of the Bonaventurean synthesis if one wishes to grasp the genius of the writer whom Pope Leo XIII called "the prince of mystical theology."[89]

Theological Foundations

Early in his *Collations on the Hexaemeron,* the "last will and testament" that Bonaventure preached to his brethren at the Franciscan convent in Paris in the spring of 1273 before setting out for the Council of Lyons, there is a text that provides a summary of the essential themes of his thought:

> The Word expresses the Father and the things made through him, and he is foremost in leading us to the unity of the Father who brings all things together. For this reason he is the Tree of Life, because through this center (*medium*) we return and are given life in the fountain of life.... This is the metaphysical center that leads back and this is the sum total of our metaphysics: concerning emanation, exemplarity and consummation, that is, being illuminated by spiritual rays and being drawn back to the Highest Source. And thus you will be a true metaphysician.[90]

It may seem odd that Bonaventure talks about the Word here as being the key to metaphysics, but for the Seraphic Doctor there is both a philosophical and a theological metaphysics, with the former finding its culmination in the latter, so that the Trinity and Christology are *the* essential metaphysical truths intended by philosophy and realized in theology.[91] The three dynamic principles at the heart of this dual metaphysics—*emanatio, exemplaritas, consummatio*—give us the key to Bonaventure's system.

Emanation describes the activity of God as the *summum,* or First Principle, characterized by what Bonaventure calls "fountain-fullness" (*fontalis plenitudo*). In analyzing the "highest primacy" of the Trinity, in his *Disputed Questions on the Mystery of the Trinity* Bonaventure cites an axiom from the Proclean *Book of Causes* and insists that because "the more prior a being is the more powerful and actual it is, therefore the First Principle is necessarily most actual and most powerful." He goes on to distinguish between two ways in which God is said to possess the most actual and powerful fontality. All three persons of the Trinity have fontality with respect to creation.

"But," he continues, "insofar as it [fontality] declares an absence of personal origin, it belongs only to the Person who is not capable of being generated, that is, the Father, in whom is the fountain-fullnesss for the production of the Son and the Holy Spirit. This fontality is the origin of the other."[92] The Franciscan's insistence on the fecundity of the Father as the source of all production—first, the emanation of the Word and the Spirit in the Trinity, and then the creation of the universe—is the foundation of his theological metaphysics.

Innascibilitas (unbegottenness), the proper attribute of the Father, though grammatically negative, in reality signifies the positive aspect of "primacy, and hence it also means fountain-fullness with respect to personal production."[93] Supreme primacy demands the highest actuality in terms of production, the highest fontality in terms of emanation, and the highest fecundity in terms of generation. This triple dynamism of overflowing goodness found in the Father realizes itself perfectly and fully in two intrinsic modes of production that must be coequal, coeternal, and consubstantial: "The mode of nature and the mode of will, that is, of the Word and of Love."[94] Bonaventure's trinitarian theology, then, is developed on the basis of a powerful reprisal of the Dionysian motif of the goodness that necessarily diffuses itself (*bonum est diffusivum sui*).[95] This is the reason why the Franciscan, unlike his contemporary Thomas Aquinas, distinguishes the three persons in terms of their origin (i.e., by the processions within the Godhead), rather than through their opposed relations (i.e., paternity and filiation).

The Father is the foundation, but not the "expression," or content, of Bonaventure's thought, because the Father as Father cannot be expressed. The only means we have of speaking about this ultimate mystery is through the Father's "Expressive Word" (*verbum expressivum*), the second person of the Trinity.[96] To go back to the passage from the first of the *Collations on the Hexaemeron* cited above, *emanation,* or the production of all things from the First Principle, demands *exemplarity,* that is, expression or manifestation of the hidden source which is, by that very reason, the exemplary cause of all else.[97] This is why it is legitimate to speak, with Ewert Cousins, of Bonaventure's mysticism as involving a "mysticism of language," as long as we recognize that we are dealing with more than human expression.[98]

A passage in Bonaventure's *Commentary on the Sentences of Peter Lombard* defines *verbum* thus: "A word is nothing other than an expressed and expressive likeness conceived by the power of an intelligent spirit by which it knows itself or another."[99] In another place the Franciscan notes that likeness (*similitudo*) can be understood in two ways: as the agreement of two beings in a third reality, or as the resemblance of one being to another. In the latter mode (which alone can be predicated of God), one thing can resemble another by an "imitative likeness" (the way that creatures imitate God), or by an "exemplative likeness" (the way in which "the exemplary idea in the Creator is a likeness of the creature").[100] While the goal of philosophical metaphysics is to know God as the exemplary cause of all things, the realm of theological metaphysics allows us to grasp the primordial exemplarity of the *Verbum* in the Trinity.

In his *Commentary on John's Gospel,* Bonaventure explains that the denomination *verbum* is the most fitting one for the second person of the Trinity. The reason is because while the term *filius* expresses a relationship only to the Father, "*Verbum* declares [1] a relationship to the speaker, [2] a relationship to what is said through the word, [3] a relationship to the voice which it uses, and [4] a relationship to the teaching which it causes in another by the word's mediation."[101] The term *filius* expresses the hypostatic equality of the second person with the Father in full possession of divinity (*similitudo hypostatica*); *imago* points to how he reveals the Father's hidden reality as the one unique and absolutely pure expression of the person of the Father (*similitudo expressa*). *Verbum,* however, as the *similitudo expressiva,* names all four aspects of the second person: his relationship to the Father as speaker; to the world understood as what the Word forms in his role as exemplary cause; to the human nature he puts on in the incarnation to declare his message to fallen humanity; and finally to his teaching enshrined in the words of scripture.[102] The Word, therefore, is God knowing himself as the "expressive likeness of all things" (*similitudo expressiva omnium*), a role he is able to take on precisely insofar as he is the Father's perfect expression.[103] "In the very same Word in which the Father speaks himself, he speaks whatever he speaks," as Bonaventure summarizes in the *Disputed Questions on the Trinity.*[104]

As the middle person in the Trinity, the Word is also the "metaphysical center" (*medium metaphysicum*) between God and creation. Bonaventure succinctly declares: "The Word, which is the imitative likeness of the Father and the exemplative and operative likeness of things, thus holds, as it were, the central position and the Father is said to work through the Word."[105] The mediating function of the Word as the supreme center, which was more and more stressed by Bonaventure in his later works, can be illuminated through the Franciscan's distinction of the three "states" of the *Verbum*. The third collation of the *Collations on the Hexaemeron* declares: "The key of contemplation is a threefold understanding—that of the uncreated Word through which all things are made, that of the incarnate Word through which all things are restored, and that of the inspired Word through which all things are revealed."[106] It was through the mediating activity of the uncreated Word that the universe was made. In Adam's unfallen state humanity was able to recognize this supreme exemplarity by reading the book of nature, but, given the Fall, it is necessary for the uncreated Word to take on flesh as the incarnate Word and to present his message throughout history through the inspired Word of the Bible.[107] The only way back to the source, the *plenitudo fontalis,* is through the center or *medium* who has become the *mediator,* namely, Jesus Christ.[108] "It is not the same thing to say 'mediator' and 'medium'; nevertheless, there is no mediator without someone in the center."[109]

The mediating activity that expresses the return implies the third essential metaphysical principle, *consummatio,* that is, "being led back to the Highest Source" (*reduci ad summum*). Like emanation and exemplarity, consummation, or *reductio* (which we might describe as being "being drawn back into the Principle"), is essential to all true metaphysics. Reduction is both an ontological principle and a method of philosophical analysis.[110] Bonaventure provides formal discussions of reductive analysis, specifying five different modes of such philosophical exercise in the second book of his *Sentence Commentary.*[111] As Jacques Bougerol puts it: "To reduce . . . the truth of any judgment amounts to bringing back this judgment, from condition to condition, to the eternal reasons upon which it is established."[112] Reduction, and its correlative principle of universal analogy,[113] forms the heart of the Franciscan's mode of argumentation, which, in its ceaseless piling up of ternary formulations often may seem arbitrary to those who have not grasped the basic structure of the Bonaventurean synthesis. Reduction is not the same as Aristotelian demonstration, as Alexander Gerken reminds us: "The method of *reductio* goes back to the basic principle; it proves nothing but it shows something. It shows, namely, what is present in cognition; it shows that the foundation . . . demands an immortal being, an eternal origin."[114]

Reduction as a mode of argumentation, however, is secondary to reduction as a metaphysical principle. If emanation and exemplarity comprise Bonaventure's understanding of the traditional theological category of *egressus* or *exitus,* that is, how all things come forth from God, then *consummatio/reductio* is his way of exploring the return—the *regressus* or *reditus* which restores all things to the *plenitudo fontalis.* The whole of the Franciscan's mystical theology can be seen as an attempt to present the proper understanding of our *reductio* to God. Reduction, like production, must be christological in nature. As a text from the treatise *The Reduction of the Arts to Theology* puts it:

> It is necessary to establish a center in the going forth and the return of all things. But the center in going forth should be more on the side of the one producing, while the center in the return is more on the side of the one returning. Therefore, just as things went forth from God through the Word of God, so it is necessary for a complete return that the Mediator of God and humans be not only God but also man to lead humans back to God.[115]

A passage from the first book of the *Commentary on the Sentences* applies the action of *reductio* both to the Son and to the Holy Spirit.[116] It is not surprising that the Spirit, as the bond of love (*nexus*) between Father and Son, is sent into the world to carry on the work of Christ in his church;[117] but Bonaventure understands this in terms of the role that the Spirit plays in the universal process by which we realize the identity given to each human person in the exemplary activity of the Word. We become who we were meant to be through the Spirit's action helping us to actualize the *reductio* offered us by the incarnate Word.[118] (In this connection, it is worth noting that Bonaventure sometimes follows Francis in identifying the Holy Spirit as the Bridegroom of the soul, though, of course, he also uses the more traditional identification with Christ, the incarnate Word.)[119] Thus, all three persons of the Trinity are always at work in our lives, as Bonaventure aptly summarizes at the beginning of his treatise called the *Soliloquy*, where he offers a prayer to the Trinity calling to mind, once again, the three general themes of his theology—emanation, exemplarity, and consummation:

> At the beginning of every good work not without reason should we invoke him from whom every good comes forth as from its origin, through whom every good is produced as from its exemplar, and to whom every good is brought back as its end. This is the ineffable Trinity, Father, Son and Holy Spirit.[120]

There are many other themes of the Franciscan's theology that might be taken up to shed further light on how this *reductio*, or "the mind's journey/pilgrimage into God" (*itinerarium mentis in Deum*), functions as the organizing principle of his synthesis. Some of these are directly connected with his mystical teaching, such as his understanding of the spiritual interpretation of scripture;[121] others have a more distant, but still significant, relation to the journey and its goal. However, if we keep in mind the understanding of Trinity and Christology rooted in the three essential principles of emanation, exemplarity, and consummation, we will have a sufficient basis for grasping the inner harmony between the Seraphic Doctor's general theology and his explicitly mystical teaching.

Francis as the Exemplar of the Crucified Christ

Much of Bonaventure's mystical theology is traditional: the Franciscan's powerful mind acted as a kind of reservoir into which all the major streams of earlier Western mysticism—Augustinian, Dionysian, Gregorian, Cistercian, Victorine—emptied in order to provide a resource for the generations to come.[122] But Bonaventure's mysticism did more than just summarize and synthesize earlier Western mystical traditions. It transformed them. This transformation was due in large part to Bonaventure's meditation on the meaning of Francis's relation to the *Verbum incarnatum*. Taking a clue once again from the theme of expressive exemplarity so central to his thought, we can lay out the logic of his position in the following way:

> Since the universe is the expression of the Trinity produced
>   through the *Verbum increatum,*
> and since the *Verbum incarnatum* expresses himself best in
>   dying for humanity on the cross,
> then Francis, as the ideal expression of the crucified Jesus,
>   is the exemplar of our journey, or reduction, back into God.

Many investigators have noted the experiential character of Bonaventure's theology, especially after 1257, when he left the university of Paris to take up the position of minister general of the Franciscan order. Bonaventure begins with Christian experience: his own experience, the experience of his audience, and the experience of one special Christian, Francis of Assisi. His many sermons on Francis, his *Large Life of St. Francis* (1261), the appeal to Francis in the *Collations on the Hexaemeron,* and lastly the role that Francis played as the inspiration for and in a sense the content of Bonaventure's greatest mystical work, *The Mind's Journey into God,* all present the same message that *Il Poverello* is more than just another saint—he is "the mirror of sanctity and the exemplar of all evangelical perfection."[123]

At the beginning of the *Itinerarium* (1259), Bonaventure tells how, "following the example of the most blessed Father Francis," he withdrew to Monte Alverna in the thirty-third year after the saint's death to seek peace and to reflect on the various forms of mental ascent to God. His meditation upon the miracle of the appearance of the six-winged seraph in the form of the crucified Jesus provided a flash of insight for synthesizing all these forms of *mentales ascensiones in Deum*—"I saw at once that this vision fully revealed the father's suspension in the act of contemplation and the way to reach it."[124] This path is nothing other than "the most burning love of the Crucified" which transformed Paul and blazed forth in Francis in the marks of the stigmata he carried for the last two years of his life, thus demonstrating that "no one rightly enters onto the path except through the Crucified" (prol. 3).

The lengthy exposition of the six stages of ascent symbolized by the six wings of the Christ-Seraph, however, makes no explicit reference to Francis until near the end when, in discussing the culmination of ecstatic passage (*transitus*) into God achieved through contemplation of Christ on the cross, Bonaventure says:

> This was also shown to blessed Francis when he was enraptured in contemplation on the high mountain. . . . There he passed over into God through contemplative rapture and was established as an example of perfect contemplation, just as he had been previously of action. And so, like another Jacob and Israel, through him God might invite all other truly spiritual men to this kind of passing over and ecstasy of mind, more by example than by word.[125]

Bonaventure's treatment of the stages of contemplative ascent (to be considered in more detail below) is nothing more than a laying out of what had taken place in the soul of Francis as a model for all ecstatics.

The appeal to the "spiritual men" (*viri spirituales*) in this text is also a telling one. Though the term had a long history as a description for contemplatives, in the context of the contemporary debates in the Franciscan order over Joachite theology of history and in light of the presentation of Francis in the *Life* and the *Collations on the Hexaemeron*, it demonstrates that Bonaventure identified Francis as the model for both action and contemplation in the light of his position in salvation history. Francis's exemplarity, then, has both a vertical and a horizontal pole. The vertical pole, centering on the conception of Francis as the *vir hierarchicus* or *vir angelicus* ascending to full experience of God,[126] is of obvious Dionysian provenance, depending specifically on the new Dionysianism of Thomas Gallus.[127] The horizontal or historical pole, in which Francis is identified as the Angel of the Sixth Seal of Apocalypse 7:2, who marks the faithful in preparation for the end, is an expression of Bonaventure's Joachite theology of history.[128] The stigmata that was "impressed" on the saint is the "expressive" sign of both dimensions—*illa apparitio Seraph . . . quae fuit expressiva et impressa* (*Hexaem.* 22.23). An investigation of the *Life* and *Collations* will spell out these two dimensions in greater detail.

The Major Life of Francis, once dismissed by some because of its "unhistorical" character, has been reevaluated in recent years as a hagiographical and theological masterpiece.[129] In it Bonaventure weaves together what I have called the vertical and the horizontal poles of his view of Francis as not only the model to be imitated, but as the very "book" that reveals the meaning of the *Verbum incarnatum* as we approach the end of the age.[130] As in the earlier *Mind's Journey into God,* in the *Major Life* the Seraphic Doctor again invokes his own experience at the outset, appealing to Francis's intercession in curing him from a childhood disease as a factor which enabled him "to experience his power in myself" (*Leg. maj.* prol. 3). A passage from the prologue highlights the dual aspects of Francis:

> He was totally ignited by a seraphic flame and like a hierarchic man he was borne upward by a fiery chariot, as the course of his life richly shows. This is reasonable proof that he came "in the spirit and power of Elijah" (Lk. 1:17). Therefore, like that other "friend of the Bridegroom" (Jn. 3:29), John the Apostle and Evangelist, he is well designated according to a true prophecy under the likeness of the Angel who ascends from the rising of the sun bearing the sign of the living God (Apoc. 7:2).[131]

If the brief references to Francis in *The Mind's Journey into God* emphasize the ascensional role of the saint, what is remarkable about the *Life* is how it never loses sight of both the vertical and the horizontal aspects. The very structure of the text itself demonstrates this.[132] Bonaventure's comment that he intends to follow a primarily thematic approach (*Leg. maj.* prol. 4) should not be taken to mean that chronology is neglected. Rather, in chapters 1–4 and 13–15 a chronological review of the initial and the final stages of Francis's journey into God encloses an account of his virtues (chaps. 5–12). This moral section seems to represent the three traditional stages of the spiritual life: purgation, illumination, and perfection or union. In other words, the traditional ascensional patterns of Dionysian spirituality are incorporated within a concrete life, that of Francis, a story that is of profound significance for the course of salvation history insofar as it "expresses" the imminent crisis of this age and the coming of a new contemplative age before the end.[133] In this connection, a passage from the later *Defense of the Poor Mendicants* (1269) underlines why Francis's role in salvation history gives him a status that no other saint enjoyed:

> And so it was fitting that Christ, by means of the Seraph's appearance, impressed the stigmata as his seal of approval on this poor little holy man. He did it that he might show an open sign of perfection for us in the face of the dangerous cloud of the last times—one that might lead us back (*reducimur*) to Christ, the exemplar and goal of perfect virtue. . . .[134]

Bonaventure, as Ewert Cousins puts it, "is ultimately concerned with the way in which Francis developed spiritually through assimilation into the mystery of Christ."[135] This development centers on the saint's progressive identification with Christ crucified until, by the reception of the stigmata, "he is totally transformed into the likeness of Christ crucified, not through the martyrdom of the flesh but through conflagration of mind" (*Leg. maj.* 13.3). The Seraphic Doctor introduces seven manifestations of the cross into the *Life,* some given to Francis himself and some accorded to others about him (see *Leg. maj.* 1.3, 1.5, 2.1, 3.5–6, 4.9, 4.10, and the stigmata account in 13). These mark stages in an itinerary of deepening understanding of the meaning of the cross which leads on to the decisive event of the stigmata, whose account (briefly announced in chapter 4.11 and fully described in chapter 13) frames the treatment of the saint's virtues in chapters 5–12. These seven visions of the cross correspond to the seven stages of ascent of *The Mind's Journey into God:* "like six steps leading to the seventh in which you finally reach your resting place, . . . the summit of evangelical perfection" (*Leg. maj.* 13.10). In true Franciscan fashion, however, Bonaventure links the full imitation of the Crucified to the practice of total poverty. As he put it in another context: "Poverty is the virtue necessary for the integrity of perfection to such a degree that no one is able to be perfect without it, as the Lord says."[136]

During the course of the *Life,* Bonaventure often dwells on Francis's ecstatic experiences (e.g., 1.5, 2.1, 3.6, 8.10, 9.2, 10.1–4, 11.13, 12.1). It is clear that he sees the stigmata as the highest of these. But the reception of the wounds of Christ through the appearance of the "Seraph . . . with the figure of a man crucified" (13.3-4) has an eschatological-apocalyptic meaning as well as an ecstatic-contemplative one.[137] Bonaventure had already compared Francis with Enoch and Elijah. Both were noted contemplatives due to their ascents into heaven, and they were also eschatological figures identified with the two witnesses of Apocalypse 11 who would preach against Antichrist in the last days (see, e.g., Prol. 1, 4.4, 15.8). The stigmata, however, establishes Francis as an even more potent apocalyptic figure, the angel of Apocalypse 7:2, who seals God's chosen ones with the *TAU* mark of the cross.[138] For a full understanding of the meaning of this identification, we must turn to the theology of history found in the *Collations on the Hexaemeron,* which contains a revised form of the corporate apocalyptic mysticism created by Joachim of Fiore in the late twelfth century.[139]

The exuberant richness of the spiritual exegesis of the *Collations* makes them difficult reading for students of medieval theology more used to logical distinctions and syllogistic demonstrations. But if the scholastic mentality was primarily directed toward theological synthesis based on systematic organizing principles, Bonaventure's *Collations* should be considered one of its high points–a masterpiece of symbolic and mystical theology. The *Collations* have a special place in the literature of Western mysticism because they incorporate a theology of mystical encounter into a view of history that looks forward to an imminent contemplative age as the goal of all human hopes.[140]

Mystical theologians of the patristic era, especially Augustine, had also been concerned with setting forth the structure and meaning of history. Gregory the Great had seen God's plan for human history as the story of the various states of contemplation,[141] while the visionary Joachim of Fiore, though he contributed little to the theory of mystical states, has a place in the history of mysticism by reason of his conviction that the coming *status* of the Holy Spirit would witness a universal age of perfect contemplation. Bonaventure's *Collations* represent perhaps the most significant–though by no means the final–exploration of this "social-mystical" trajectory.[142]

The *Collations* combine traditional Augustinian theology of history with a rich vein of Joachite speculation to create something new. The Franciscan portrays history–the *expressio* of the Word–as comprising six ages, the standard "World Week" pattern based on a parallel between the six days of creation and universal history (*Hexaem*. 15.12–18). But in *Collation* 16 he adopts a schema initiated by Joachim of Fiore using three interrelated successions of sevens: the seven days of creation; the seven ages of the Old Testament; and the seven ages of the New Testament. The Franciscan's development of this view of history utilizes two principles ultimately derived from the thought of Joachim.[143] The first is Joachim's system of *concordiae*, that is, exact historical parallels between events in the eras of the Old and of the New Testaments. This allowed Bonaventure to interpret the biblical text, especially the Apocalypse, as both *demonstrating* what had already taken place in history and as *demonstrative* or prophetic of things to come (see *Hexaem*. 15.22, 16.1 and 11–31). The second major aspect of Joachim's thought that Bonaventure transformed for his own purposes was the abbot's hope for a coming time when the "spiritual understanding" (*intelligentia spiritualis*) of the letter of both the Old and the New Testaments would flower in a monasticized church given over to contemplation. Joachim had tied this hope to his teaching concerning the imminent third *status*, or age, of history–the time ascribed to the Holy Spirit. Recognizing the dangers implied in the crude version of this teaching put forth by Franciscan Joachites like Gerardo di Borgo San Donnino, Bonaventure's Christocentric revision insisted that "[a]fter the New Testament there will not be another, nor can any sacrament of the New Law be abrogated, because it is the Eternal Testament."[144] While Bonaventure thus rejected any talk of a coming age of the Holy Spirit or a new church, he did not jettison the optimism of Joachim's program, nor the special role that such apocalypticism gave to Saint Francis.

Apocalyptic thought always manifests an interaction between optimism and pessimism—a sense of crisis brought on by the impending threat of the forces of evil and a confidence rooted in the conviction that God has already planted the signs of his coming vindication in concrete persons and events. Bonaventure's theology of history convinced him that his own time was late in the sixth era of the church, a time of both crisis and promise (*Hexaem.* 16.16, 19, and 29–30). The crisis was especially evident in the growing threat of the false uses of the philosophy of Aristotle, which Bonaventure painted in dark, apocalyptic colors for the young frairs studying at Paris (see, e.g., *Hexaem.* 6.1–6, 18.25–28, 19.12–18). The great positive sign of the coming triumph of contemplation was the appearance of Francis, the Angel of the Sixth Seal.

On the basis of the concordance between the sixth day of creation (the day of humanity's formation), the sixth time of the Old Testament (i.e., the era of the prophets), and the sixth age of the church, "the time of clear doctrine in which there would be a prophetic style of life," Bonaventure concludes:

> It was necessary that in this time one order, that is, a prophetic disposition similar to the order of Jesus Christ, would come. Its head would be the "Angel ascending from the sunrise having the sign of the living God" (Apoc. 7:2) and conformed to Christ. And he [i.e., Bonaventure] said that he [i.e., the Angel] had already come![145]

As the completion of the prophecy found in the Apocalypse, Francis has a unique historical role. His perfect conformity to Christ, manifested in the stigmata as the sign of his angelic contemplative status, makes him also the "seal-bearer" who not only announces but also creates the new *ordo* of contemplatives. This order is present initially only in himself, but is now being realized in all those who follow his example. Bonaventure believed that this new order was soon to be more fully revealed, as later sermons in the *Collations* indicate.

In *Collation* 22 the Seraphic Doctor, again making use of the thought of Thomas Gallus,[146] compares the nine angelic hierarchies with the various orders in the history of the church. Of the triple comparisons he employs, the most important for the historical development of mysticism is the third, the comparison according to practice (*exercitia*).[147] Three orders of active laity correspond to the lowest hierarchy of angels-archangels-principalities and are ascribed to the Father (*Hexaem.* 22.16–18), while three orders of clergy, leading a life of mixed action and contemplation, correspond to the middle hierarchy of powers-virtues-dominations and are ascribed to the Son (22.19). Finally, three orders of contemplatives ascribed to the Holy Spirit correspond to the highest hierarchy. The monastic orders, dedicated to supplication, match the thrones; the Dominicans and Franciscans, who practice both speculative examination of scripture and active piety, are linked to the cherubim (22.20–21). He concludes:

> The third order is of those contemplating God according to the mode of elevation, that is, the ecstatic or excessive mode. . . . This is the seraphic order. It seems that Francis belonged to this. . . . In these people the church will be consummated. But what this future order is to be, or if it already exists, is not easy to know.[148]

Bonaventure's caution in the face of the crisis of his age and with regard to a future known only to God, however, cannot hide the enthusiasm with which he looks forward to the full manifestation of the *ordo contemplativus*.

Francis, then, is not only the ideal contemplative but also the initiator of a new order in which perfect contemplation will flourish and a deeper understanding of scripture will be given to "a multitude."[149] Following the model of Christ and his perfect imitator, Francis, this order will only reach its fulfillment "through tribulation" (*per tribulationem*). It too is marked with the sign of the cross. The order should be thought of in an inclusive, not an exclusive way: it embraces not only those Franciscans who truly follow Francis into ecstatic contemplation but also all who are marked with the *TAU* of contemplative conformity to the crucified Christ.[150] Though these members may be hidden in the present moment, we must not mute the historical character of Bonaventure's social and corporate apocalyptic mysticism. Like Joachim of Fiore, he believed that a new contemplative age was dawning through the continuing agency of St. Francis whose work he summed up in the *Life* with the following encomium:

> O most Christian of men, who strove by perfect imitation to be like the living Christ when alive, like the dying Christ in dying, and like the dead Christ after death—and therefore merited to be adorned with his expressed likeness![151]

Bonaventure's devotion to Francis, however, was never an end in itself. Francis was always the channel to the *Verbum incarnatum*. As Zachary Hayes has shown, a speculative Christology is at the heart of Bonaventure's spiritual vision and therefore also of his mysticism.[152] A treatment of the ontological and psychological aspects of the hypostatic union realized in Christ is not required here, but we do need to examine briefly the function of the mysteries of Christ's life in the process of our *reductio* to the divine source, since they are crucial to Bonaventure's mysticism.

The prologue to the first book of the *Sentence Commentary* expresses the role of the Incarnation in the following way: "The Incarnation of the Son of God is said to be a river, because just as a circle joins the end to the beginning, so too in the Incarnation the highest is joined to the lowest."[153] Bonaventure was in agreement with the patristic authorities who emphasized redemption as a total process embracing all the events of Christ's life on earth, as well as his ongoing activity in the church until the end of time.[154] Nevertheless, within this single great act the mysteries of the Word's birth and death take on special importance insofar as they "express" the essential meaning of the whole. As he put it in a sermon preached on the Nativity: "In order to make a perfect peace the most faithful Mediator first gave himself totally to humanity in the Nativity and afterwards offered and gave himself totally to God on humanity's behalf in the Passion."[155] There is a sense, then, in which Bonaventure, like Francis, stresses the historical events of Christ's life, especially the defining moments of its beginning and end, as the necessary foundation for all mystical contact with God.

Within this overarching sense of the economy of salvation Bonaventure gave special emphasis to the passion. In this he is both representative of a significant shift in late medieval devotion, and, given the impact of his thought, one of the founders of the passion piety that meets us almost everywhere in late medieval literature and art.[156] Although he insists that both the resurrection and the passion are necessary for our justification,[157] the passion is the complete expression of the mystery of kenotic love by which God empties himself into human poverty—even unto ignominious death on the cross—in order to open access to the *fontalis plenitudo* of God's own life.[158] As the Franciscan put it in his treatise *The Mystical Vine:*

> Conquered by the bonds of love, he was drawn down from heaven to earth to take up the bonds of the cross. Conversely, we who desire to be drawn from earth to heaven first must be gathered to our Head by the bonds of the passion so that through this we may reach the bonds of love and be made one with him.[159]

This principle explains why Francis's Christomimesis culminated in his being marked with the wounds of Jesus and why *The Mind's Journey into God* insisted that no one can enter on the path that Francis trod "except through the Crucified" (prol. 3). The whole of the Christian life, of course, should be conceived of as an *imitatio Christi,* but this is a-fortiori the case with regard to the necessity of imitating the passion.[160] Some of the Seraphic Doctor's most moving language is to be found in his devotional treatises, especially *The Tree of Life* and *The Mystical Vine,* where he encourages his readers to appropriate the mystery of the cross in their own lives through meditation and contemplation.[161] At the beginning of the former work he invites us to become conformed to the crucified Savior employing, as Bernard of Clairvaux before him had, the language of Song of Songs 1:12: "My Beloved is a bundle of myrrh to me; he will dwell between my breasts."[162] Here the crucifixion is described as Christ's wedding day (*in hunc diem nuptiarum tuarum* [*Vit. myst.* 5.4]), and the often-repeated encouragement to enter into the very wounds of Christ has a powerful, though not overt, erotic undertone.[163] Bonaventure employs every rhetorical means at his disposal to fix his reader's attention on the cross, because it is the sole means of access to the eternal beatitude of heaven: "We draw near to you sitting on the throne of majesty, O good Jesus, as far as we can in our minds, praying that we may merit to be brought to you and by you there where the thief, who confessed you on the throne of the cross, has already entered."[164] The address that he puts into Christ's mouth at the end of *The Mystical Vine* summarizes this passion-centered piety:

> I, who in my divinity was unseen and invisible and in a manner not loved, was made a visible human being so that I might be seen and loved by you. Give yourself as the prize for my incarnation and passion—you for whom I was both made flesh and made to suffer. I have given myself to you. Give yourself to me.[165]

The Road to Passing Over (transitus)

The message of the cross is sufficient in and of itself. This is evident in the way Bonaventure praises the early years of the *fraternitas* when Francis and his first followers needed only to read "the book of Christ's cross" to attain God (*librum crucis Christi* in *Leg. maj.* 4.3). But Bonaventure recognizes that this heroic simplicity is not for all; most will need further instruction. His spiritual and mystical treatises may be conceived of as theological meditations on the inner meaning of the cross directed to a universal audience,[166] but especially to his Franciscan brethren whose task was to help others along this most important *itinerarium,* the path that leads to what he called transformation, "passing over" (*transitus*) into God.[167]

In his discussion of the inner relation between scripture and the other sciences in *The Reduction of the Arts to Theology,* Bonaventure argues that all these forms of illumination contain three basic truths: the eternal generation and incarnation of the Word; the correct way of living; and the soul's union with God.[168] As the goal of the Christian life, mystical union, "the study of contemplatives" (*studium contemplativorum*), was of paramount importance for Bonaventure.[169] While there are many discussions of the nature of ecstasy, rapture, and union in Bonaventure's *Commentary on the Sentences*, his fullest teaching about spiritual progress and its goal is found in the two treatises written in 1259, *The Mind's Journey into God* and *The Three-fold Way*.[170] Both works are relatively brief but extremely rich, synthesizing the mystical theology of the past at the same time that they summarize aspects of the new mysticism of the later Middle Ages.

The Threefold Way is less well known to modern readers, but appears to have been the more popular work in the Middle Ages.[171] The notion of dividing any process into three parts seems rooted deep in human thought; the specific threefold distinction of the spiritual journey into the stages of purgation, illumination, and perfection/union was introduced into Christianity by Origen and was given its classic formulation in the writings of Dionysius.[172] Bonaventure's chief concern in the treatise is to create a map of how the three essential spiritual practices of meditation, prayer, and contemplation are to be employed in an integrated way throughout the three hierarchical ways or stages in order to lead the devout soul to the point where she is so enflamed through "the love of his supreme desirable presence" that she is lifted above "everything sensible, imaginable, and intelligible" to the incomprehensible mystery of the Trinity (*Tripl. via* 1.15–17).[173] The structure of the work, gradually unfolding like a series of Chinese boxes in which the whole is always mirrored in each part, is announced in the prologue and reemphasized at the beginning of the third chapter:

> After speaking of how we ought to work toward wisdom through meditation and prayer, now let us briefly touch on how we come to true wisdom through contemplation. For through contemplation our mind journeys into the heavenly Jerusalem upon which the church has been formed. . . . For it is necessary that the church militant be conformed to the church triumphant. . . . In glory there is a triple gift in which the perfection of reward is to be found: eternal possession of supreme peace; open vision of supreme truth; and full enjoyment of supreme goodness or charity.[174]

The appeal to the conformity between the earthly and the heavenly churches demonstrates once again Bonaventure's concern for the ecclesial and historical dimension of the journey to God. There is no such thing as a private experience of God in the sense of one that takes place independent of the corporate and historical life of the church.[175] Since the goal is the simultaneous possession of peace, truth, and charity, the three stages or steps (*gradus*) that lead to it are not successive but simultaneous and mutually interactive. The purgative way consisting in the expulsion of sin, the illuminative way consisting in the imitation of Christ, and the unitive way consisting in the receiving of the Spouse are all equally necessary and continuous (3.1). As he put it in his slightly earlier *Commentary on the Gospel of Luke:* "The whole of mystical theology, as Dionysius says, . . . consists in ecstatic love according to a threefold hierarchic power: purgative, illuminative, and perfective."[176]

The reading of scripture (*lectio*) and the *meditatio* that accompanied it in the monastic tradition are the first practice that purifies, illumines, and perfects the soul. It utilizes the "goad of conscience" to purge the soul, the "ray of understanding" to illumine it, and finally the "little fire of wisdom" to gather the soul together, to enflame it, and to lift it up to the Divine Lover. "All our meditation," he concludes, "should be fixed here, because this is the goal of all knowing and doing; it is true wisdom in which there is knowledge through true experience."[177] Wisdom, as "experiential knowledge of God," is the highest of the seven gifts of the Holy Spirit and one of the central categories of Bonaventure's mystical theory. In his discussion of the seven gifts in book 3 of the *Sentence Commentary,* the Franciscan insists that wisdom involves both an act of the affection for uniting and an act of knowledge for apprehending, though "it begins in knowledge and is consummated in affection insofar as the taste or savoring is an experiential knowledge of what is good and sweet." Since it is directed to the experience of infinite divine sweetness, one can never have too much of it, as is evident in the lives of the contemplatives, "who from the power of too much sweetness are sometimes elevated to ecstasy and sometimes even lifted up as far as rapture, though this happens to very few."[178]

The second fundamental practice to be exercised in all three stages is prayer (*oratio*). Here, too, Bonaventure's treatise summarizes a rich tradition and connects with numerous other discussions throughout his writings.[179] Prayer is purgative in deploring our misery, illuminative in imploring mercy, and perfective in leading the soul into ecstasy (*excessus* [2.3]) by offering God fitting adoration.[180] Finally, in the third chapter, Bonaventure turns to *contemplatio,* the richest and most protean term in the traditional mystical vocabulary. In his many treatments of contemplation, Bonaventure shows little interest in defining the word, and, like many other mystical teachers, he uses a variety of models or maps of the forms of contemplation.[181] Two things should be noted about his discussion here. First, *contemplatio* is a broad term that can be used of exercises found in the purgative and illuminative aspects of the Christian life, as well as in the perfective-unitive aspect; second, *contemplatio,* especially in its highest stages, expresses the relationship between the soul and the angelic orders by which the believer internalizes the hierarchies in approaching God–the process of "angelization" that we have seen in Thomas Gallus.

Bonaventure offers two different models for the progress of contemplation (which we might best translate as "attentive regard"). The first is based on three series of sevens: seven purgative contemplations that lead to the repose of peace (3.2); seven illuminative ones directed to Christ on the cross that give access to the splendor of truth by revealing seven hidden mysteries (3.3–5); and finally seven contemplations received from the Holy Spirit as the Spouse of the soul v hich lead to the sweetness of love (3.6–7). This last enumeration, which features a rich invocation of mystical texts from the Psalms and the Song of Songs, begins with *consideratio,* or mental investigation, but proceeds by means of the power of affection or attraction (*affectio*).[182] "Vigilance investigates how fitting, how rewarding, how delightful it is to love God, and from this is born a trust which gives rise to desire, which in turn bears the ecstasy which reaches even unto the bond, the kiss, the embrace."[183]

The second map of modes of contemplation is described as being distinguished "according to difference of three times three corresponding to the threefold hierarchy" (3.9), that is, of the angelic orders. Bonaventure does not develop the angelic connection in this discussion, saving his explicit invocation of the comparison between the soul and the nine choirs of angels until the end of the treatise. This invocation of hierarchy, however, highlights one of the constant themes of his mysticism, that of the *anima hierarchizata,* the soul that has appropriated the ascending activities of the angelic hierarchies even as far as "embracing the Truth through a kiss and love that belongs to the seraphim" (3.14).[184] Although the Franciscan always insisted that love has the highest role in our path to God, *The Threefold Way* also emphasizes the important role that knowledge plays by closing with a brief treatise on the manner in which the "gaze of Truth" (*aspectus veritatis*) illuminates the mind by a double contemplation of the mystery of the Trinity.[185] The positive way, taught by Augustine, distinguishes the common, proper, and appropriated names of God (3.11–12). Concerning the "more eminent" negative way of Dionysius, Bonaventure says:

> This is the most noble mode of elevation. But in order to be perfect, it demands that the other precede it, just as perfection needs illumination and negation needs affirmation. The more intimate the ascending force, the more powerful the mode of ascent; the closer affection is to it, the more fruitful it becomes.[186]

The Threefold Way is a carefully crafted summary of mystical teaching, but

Bonaventure was capable of more. *The Mind's Journey into God* manages to take up all the themes found in *The Threefold Way* (though not, to be sure, in the same way), as well as to add to them not only an emphasis on St. Francis as the exemplar of the mystical life but also a profound treatment of the cosmic and anthropological dimensions of the process of *reductio* to the divine source. Perhaps no other treatise of comparable size in the history of Western mysticism packs so much into one seamless whole.[187] Bonaventure draws deeply on both Augustine and Dionysius for his fundamental theological perspective, but his model of the path to God is a unique fusion of itineraries taken from both major mystical traditions of the twelfth century—the Cistercian and the Victorine.

While *The Threefold Way* made sporadic use of images where helpful, one reason for the heightened synthetic power of the *Itinerarium* can be ascribed to the way in which Bonaventure uses archetypal symbols, especially of the journey within and above, to orchestrate such a variety of materials into a symphonic whole. The journey motif is expressed in two master symbols: that of the six-winged seraph signifying the ascent to God; and that of the tabernacle described in Exodus (e.g., Exodus 26–27 and 38–39) symbolizing the process of interiorization to the God who is present in the depths of the soul.[188] Ascension and introversion, however, are in reality one, as Bonaventure, following Augustine and other mystics, insisted:

> In the human soul the inmost part and the highest part are the same. This is evident because it is according to both its highest and its inmost part that it especially draws near to God, so the more that it returns to its interior, the more it ascends and is united to things eternal.[189]

There is probably no better illustration in medieval thought of how the genius of the symbolic imagination also involves deep speculative insight.[190]

Meditation on the seraph that appeared to Francis on Monte Alverna provided the flash of insight that enabled Bonaventure to present both the goal of "suspension in contemplation" and "the road that leads to it" in one synoptic picture (*Itin.* prol. 2). The seraph's six wings represent six levels of illumination leading from creatures to God, a path that can be completed only by saints like Paul and Francis who are totally consumed by burning love for the Crucified (prol. 3). The multivalent aspects of the seraph symbol become evident in chapter 1 where Bonaventure's concise development of the theme almost defies summary. The nature of creation as an expression of God or theophany, that is, a world of signs meant to lead us back to the *fontalis plenitudo* is the basis for his development:

The universe is a ladder for ascending into God. Some created things are vestiges; some images . . . . In order to come to an investigation of the First Principle, . . . we must pass through (*transire*) the vestige which is corporal, temporal and outside us. . . . We must enter into (*intrare*) our mind which is the image of God, everlasting, spiritual and within us. . . . And we must go beyond (*transcendere*) to the eternal and most spiritual above us by gazing upon the First Principle.[191]

The mind's three essential modes of perception reflect these three basic movements. Sense knowledge (*sensualitas*) is directed toward material objects; as spirit (*spiritus*) we go within to know ourselves; and finally as *mens* in the proper sense we direct ourselves above to knowing God (1.4). Each form of perception, however, can be realized in two different ways, depending on whether we see God *in* a mirror or *through* a mirror, "so the small world [i.e., the human as microcosm] is led to the rest of contemplation in a most orderly way by six successive stages of illumination."[192] The dynamic interrelationship of these six activities of mind—specified by their objects (see 1.4), useful for their mode of manifesting God (1.5), and grounding the distinction of the three forms of theology (symbolic, proper and mystical [see 1.7])—displays the influence of Richard of St. Victor's distinction of the forms of contemplation found in *The Mystical Ark*.[193] But the names that the Franciscan gives them—*sensus, imaginatio, ratio, intellectus, intelligentia*, and what he calls *apex mentis* or *synderesis scintilla* (see 1.6)—show dependence on the Cistercian Isaac of Stella's fivefold ascent to God as mediated through the pseudo-Augustinian treatise *On the Spirit and the Soul*.[194] The affective power at the top of the ladder (*apex mentis-apex affectus-synderesis scintilla*)[195] is a contribution of Thomas Gallus. The many aspects of this complex ascensional map can be sketched out in the diagram given on the next page.

The genius of Bonaventure's treatise, however, lies not so much in the ingenious architecture of his plan as in the rich texture of its development. The work represents a theological meditation on the theophanic nature mysticism pioneered by Francis (see especially 2.12), a christological reworking of the traditional models of ascent to God, an original treatment of the respective roles of knowing and loving in the journey into union, a treatise on the centrality of the passion as the essential mystery of mystical transformation, and (as noted above) a presentation of the meaning of Francis to the world. Like *The Triple Way*, it contains a major restatement of Bonaventure's trinitarian theology, but it goes further than that tract in its discussion of the nature of loving ecstasy or "excess" (*excessus*) by which the soul dies into God.

CHART 2

Chap.	Gradus	Manifest God	Aspect of Mens	Object	Action	Theology
7	apex mentis	ecstasis	mens (proprie)	(supra nos) Deus (ens spiritualissimum)	trans-cendere	mystica
5–6	intelligentia	per/in lumen				
4	intellectus	in imagine	spiritus	spiritualia (intra nos)	intrare	propria
3	ratio	per imaginem				
2	imaginatio	in vestigio	sensualitas	(extra nos) corporalia	transire	symbolica
1	sensus	per vestigium				

The discussion of the three lowest modes of cognition occupies chapters 1-3. Chapter 1 treats of how the exterior senses provide us with knowledge of God through reason, faith, and intellectual (i.e., natural) contemplation (1.10–15). The level of imagination in chapter 2 demonstrates how God is contemplated in his creaturely vestiges, that is, as he is in them by essence, power, and presence (2.1). The movement within the mind begins in chapter 3, where reason proper is analyzed as the *imago Trinitatis* through its three powers of memory, intellect, and will.[196] Contemplation of the First Principle in ourselves by means of discernment (*intellectus*) brings us to the level of grace in chapter 4. What has gone before was, in a sense, an ideal picture—what contemplation would have been like had it not been for the Fall of Adam and Eve, which traps humans in sins, cares, and the senses, so that the mind cannot refer things to God and "re-enter into itself as the image of God" (4.1). Christ alone restores the possibility of contemplative ascent: "Our soul was not able to rise perfectly from the things of sense to the coequal grasp (*contuitus*) of itself and of the Eternal Truth in itself, unless Truth, assuming human form in Christ, made a ladder of itself to repair the former ladder broken in Adam."[197] Through the action of the threefold Word (*Verbum increatum-Verbum incarnatum-Verbum inspiratum*) the three theological virtues restore the spiritual senses that allow us, like the Bride, "to sing the Song of Songs which was composed for the practice of contemplation on this fourth stage" (4.3).[198] Such a soul has traversed the threefold path of purgation, illumination, and perfection and has been made hierarchical by being conformed to the anagogic operations found in the nine choirs of angels (4.4).[199]

Though these stages should be thought of as simultaneous and interactive in actual life, the logic of Bonaventure's map views what Bernard of Clairvaux and others had seen as the height of the mystical path, that is, attaining the status of the Bride, as the entry into the level of mystical theology proper, where the mind transcends itself. This takes place first in the cognitive activity of suprarational *intelligentia* contemplating God *through* the divine light (chap. 5) and then *in* the divine light (chap. 6), and finally by passing over into God *per excessum mentalem et mysticum* (chap. 7).

In these chapters the imagery of the entry into the Holy of Holies of the tabernacle where the two cherubim face each other over the *propitiatorium,* or Mercy Seat, becomes dominant (see Exod. 25:10–22). The cherubim represent the highest form of knowing–"two modes or steps of contemplating the invisible and eternal things of God, one concerned with the essential attributes of God, the other with those proper to the Persons" (5.1). In these modes of contemplation the mind has passed beyond the world of rational logic to a form of Neoplatonic dialectical thought that invokes the coincidence of opposites realized in all attempts to speak of the nature of God.[200] Bonaventure's contemplation of the primary essential attribute of divinity (i.e., *esse;* see Exod. 3:14) is reminiscent of the "necessary reason" argument for God's existence found in Anselm's *Proslogion,* an analysis of why "being itself is so supremely certain in itself that it cannot be thought not to be" (5.3). But the Franciscan is not really interested in proving God's existence; rather, he wishes to arouse admiration in the mind by teasing out all the implications of the most pure and absolute Being which is "the universal efficient, exemplary, and final cause of everything" (5.7). The consideration of the second cherub in chapter 6 shows that "the Good itself is the most principal foundation of the contemplation of the emanations" in God (6.1). Following the Dionysian principle that "the Highest Good must be most self-diffusive,"[201] Bonaventure advances a demonstration for the Trinity influenced by the third book of Richard of St. Victor's treatise on the mystery and also dependent on the arguments used in his own *Disputed Questions on the Trinity* of 1254. Again, however, the object of his discussion is not intended to let the contemplator think that he has comprehended the incomprehensible, but rather is meant to induce "amazed admiration" (*stupor admirationis*) at the coincidence of opposites implied in the six properties of divine self-diffusion (6.3).

Bonaventure has now set the stage for the remarkable conclusion of the *Itinerarium,* arguably the most powerful text in his mystical writings. Contemplating the fact that the two cherubim face each other with their countenances turned toward the Mercy Seat (Exod. 25:20), he identifies the latter with the "totally wondrous union of God and man in the unity of the person of Christ" (6.4). He then asks his reader *to become* each cherub in turn in order to contemplate the paradoxical coincidences involved not just in the dialectical fusing of opposite predicates in the divine nature, but also by their union with all the attributes proper to humanity in Christ, the *Verbum incarnatum* (6.5–6). In other words, we must contemplate Christ precisely as both God and human in order to reach *excessus mentis.*[202] This shift from objective theological analysis in the third person to invitation in the second person underlines the fact that the *Itinerarium* is not to be read as an academic presentation of theological truths; rather, it must be personally appropriated through contemplative practice. "In this investigation," he concludes, "is the perfection of the mind's illumination . . . on the sixth step, as if it had reached the sixth day [of creation]. Nothing remains save the day of rest in which through *excessus mentis* the human mind's discernment rests from all the work which it has done."[203]

In order to know any truth in secure fashion, Bonaventure insists, the human mind needs to have a direct, if not necessarily clear, contact with Truth itself, the *Divina Ars.* In other words, we need to have an implicit "contuition" of the Uncreated Word in any act of affirming the truth.[204] This innate presence of the Word can be made explicit and conscious through the practice of the "contemplative contuition" sketched out in the *Itinerarium:*

> After our mind has contuited God outside itself through vestiges and in vestiges, and within itself through the image and in the image, and above itself through the likeness of the divine light shining above us and in the light itself, . . . when finally in the sixth step it reaches the point where it beholds in the First and Supreme Principle and in Jesus Christ, the Mediator of God and humanity, those things whose likenesses cannot be found among creatures, . . . it remains for it to surmount and pass beyond not only the sense world but itself in beholding these things. . . .[205]

This transcendent "passing beyond" (*transitus*) can be attained only in and through Christ's *transitus,* or *pascha,* that is, his death on the cross (7.2).[206] This was the mystery revealed to and in Francis in the seraph vision and his reception of the stigmata. As in Thomas Gallus, it is an essentially affective experience:

In this passing beyond, if it is perfect, it is necessary that all intellectual operations be left behind and that the *apex affectionis* be totally transferred and transformed into God. This is mystical and most secret—"No one knows it who has
not been given it" (Apoc. 2:7).[207]

As he attempts to describe this ineffable conclusion of the journey to
God, Bonaventure emphasizes its character as a divine donation given in
darkness, one that brings death (7.5–6). It is a *donation*—nature, effort,
inquiry, words, and writing can do little or nothing; the Spirit gives it to
whom he wills. It is an experience of "the superessential ray of the divine
darkness"—the Franciscan can find no better way to express this than by
including a lengthy quotation from the first chapter of Dionysius's *Mystical
Theology* at this point. So, although the Seraphic Doctor generally emphasizes the role of illumination and the expressivity of the *Verbum* in his mystical itinerary, at the end light passes into cloud and darkness and all
speaking into sleep and silence.[208] As in Dionysius, negation reigns at the
end. What is not Dionysian in Bonaventure's presentation is the centrality
of the *death* motif, or more exactly, what we might call *dying into love*. The
"ecstatic anointings and totally enflamed affections" (*excessivis unctionibus et
ardentissimis affectionibus*) that carry us over into God are enkindled by
Christ "in the heat of his totally enflamed passion." Our love for his death
leads to our sharing in the archetypal *mors mystica:* "Let us die and enter
into the darkness . . . ; with Christ crucified let us pass out of this world to
the Father" (cf. John 13:1).[209] As Denys Turner puts it: "Bonaventure locates
that *transitus* in the broken, crucified Christ, in a 'similarity' so 'dissimilar'
as to dramatise with paradoxical intensity the brokenness and failure of all
our language and knowledge of God."[210]

Although Bonaventure does not say so explicitly in the *Itinerarium*, it is
clear here and elsewhere that, like Thomas Gallus, he held that there were
really two related forms of mystical contemplation, a primarily intellectual
(though suprarational) one represented by the cherubim, and a higher,
affective stage symbolized in the crucified seraph who is Christ.[211] It is the
latter that he usually describes as *excessus mentis*, and more rarely as *ecstasis*.[212] What is the relationship between the two? No aspect of the Seraphic
Doctor's mystical theory has produced so much disagreement, especially
concerning the role of love and knowledge at the culminating point.[213]

Despite the influence of Thomas Gallus, it seems to me that Bonaventure
is close to the great mystics of the twelfth century in stressing the necessity
for the ongoing collaboration of both loving and knowing in the mind's
journey into God. Knowing is never cut off; it is necessary, but insufficient.
However, it is clear that the Franciscan was deeply influenced by the new

form of Dionysianism of Gallus, which interpreted mystical darkness in terms of burning love, specifically the love of Christ crucified. The apophatic exigence present in Dionysian mysticism, then, becomes transmuted in Bonaventure primarily into the language of love, expressed better through metaphors of tasting and touching than of seeing.[214] Since the *apex affectus* itself is not an intellectual power, it is clear that we need to take Bonaventure seriously when he says that the culminating point is reached in love "*with all intellectual operations left behind*" (*Itin.* 7.4). Nevertheless, the Franciscan sometimes uses the term *cognitio* in a transferred sense to describe the ecstatic contact with God that takes place at this high point, as when he says, "Ecstasy is the ultimate and most noble mode of knowing."[215] What becomes present in the *apex* cannot be known and expressed—it is "the new name which no one knows to whom it has not been given" (Apoc. 2:13). But the *apex* still bears some kind of relation to knowledge and to what can be expressed in language, both because it draws up into itself all the preparatory cognitive operations that are part of the journey into God just at the moment it leaps beyond them,[216] and also because although *what* is received is incommunicable, the person who receives it is transformed by this contact in a way that enables him or her to be a better channel of divine illumination.[217] This is why Bonaventure always insists that in the beatific vision, the highest state of immediate contact with God, we will *both* love and know him.[218]

In ecstasy, then, contemplatives are fixed upon no creaturely image, so that "they truly feel more than they know."[219] It seems that this loving absorption does not take place through a created effect the way the intellectual contemplation symbolized in the cherubim does; it is realized in a direct contact where "what is known takes the knower captive."[220] This stress on ecstasy as the imageless consciousness of divine love helps explain Bonaventure's rather negative attitude toward visions, which he said "were more to be feared than desired."[221]

What is known in ecstasy is the God who is Trinity.[222] Of course, the experience of "feeling" the trinitarian life that the mystic gains cannot be communicated—it is "wisdom without a form" (*sapientia nulliformis* [*Hexaem.* 2.28–30]). Such presence is different from the beatific vision. It is dark and obscure, while the light of glory is complete illumination. The beatitude of heaven is permanent; on earth "we cannot stay long in any one state" (*Hexaem.* 22.40).

Ecstasy, however, does not exhaust all the possibilities for immediate consciousness of God in this life. Although Bonaventure always differentiated between the contact with God possible here below and that to come in heaven, and though he understood contemplation as comprising a broad continuum of increasing contact with God culminating in the loving ecstasy described in the *Itinerarium* and elsewhere, a number of texts in his writings distinguish between *excessus/exstasis* and *raptus*.[223] For example, in the *Collations on the Hexaemeron,* while the fourth of the sixth illuminations leading to the heavenly seventh day is "suspension in contemplation," the series culminates in "the vision of the understanding absorbed in God through rapture." Here Bonaventure notes: "This uplifting makes the soul as like to God as it can be in this life. Ecstasy and rapture are not the same. Hence, as they say, [those who possess the latter] do not have the habit of glory but only an actuation of it."[224] Paul, Job, and Dionysius are mentioned here as those who have enjoyed rapture; Moses was also traditionally included in the ranks of "the very few" (*paucissimorum* [*Hexaem.* 3.24]) who experienced it.[225] Rapture, then, is a foretaste of the glory of heaven in this life, a brief reception of the light of glory in the soul, but not the permanent habit found among the blessed. It is so rare and special that this may explain why Bonaventure did not mention it in the *Itinerarium,* which is best viewed as a general invitation to all Christians to follow the way of Francis leading to *excessus mentis*.[226]

Discussion of the various forms of mystical union and the proper way to understand its nature had become widespread by the thirteenth century. Bonaventure uses the language of union in various place in his *Sentence Commentary,* speaking, for example, of the "expressed uniting" (*expressa unitio*) with God that we acquire through charity,[227] and analyzing the modes of union primarily to demonstrate the singular nature of the union of God and humanity in the person of the Word.[228] It is obvious, however, that the Franciscan did not think that an analysis of forms of union was an important task for the mystical theologian.

As befits the eminently practical character of even his deepest speculations about the journey into God, Bonaventure's primary intention was to encourage himself and his readers to follow Francis upward into the mystery of the cross. In the prayer that closes *The Disputed Questions on the Knowledge of Christ,* he summarizes the modes of knowing concentrated in the unique mind of Jesus, the God-man, especially the knowledge *per excessum* of someone rooted in the charity which Dionysius praises in his *Mystical Theology* and which Bonaventure refers to by his signature text from Apocalypse 2:13. "This true and experiential wisdom" is not to be found in exterior speech, but in internal silence. He concludes:

> And therefore this is the place to stop speaking and to begin praying to the Lord that he may grant us to experience what we speak about.[229]

CHAPTER 3

Men and Women in the Franciscan Mystical Tradition

T HE PROFUNDITY OF BONAVENTURE'S mystical theory, rooted in one of the greatest theological syntheses of the thirteenth century, guaranteed him immense influence in the later Middle Ages. This is evident as much from the numerous pseudonymous works that circulated under his name as from the impact of his authentic treatises.[1] The importance of the Seraphic Doctor is evident in the case of the mystics connected with the tradition of the Spiritual Franciscans, as well as in those who represented the Community perspective during the struggle over poverty. Nevertheless, because of the variety in the mystical writings produced by Franciscans in the first century of the existence of the order, some texts show no trace of the influence of Bonaventure and are not even very "Franciscan," if we identify Franciscan mysticism with emphasis on the importance of Francis, the centrality of poverty, and the role of the passion as the mystery that gives us access to God.

The German friar David of Augsburg (d. 1272) is a good example. David was a contemporary of Bonaventure and thus could scarcely be expected to show much influence from the Seraphic Doctor, but it is still noteworthy how far his ascetical and mystical teaching is from what we think of as characteristically Franciscan. David was the master of novices in the Franciscan houses at Regensburg and Augsburg.[2] A noted preacher, he was also the traveling companion of Berthold of Regensburg, perhaps the most important vernacular homilist of the era. David's major work, written in the 1240s, bears the cumbersome title *The Composition of the Interior and Exterior Man according to the Triple State of Beginners, Proficient, and Perfect*. It is composed of three different treatises whose dates and relationships are difficult to determine.[3]

This primarily ascetic and often pedestrian composition was vastly popular, with close to four hundred manuscripts of the whole or parts surviving along with numerous translations. It, too, was sometimes ascribed to Bonaventure, though it has quite a different tone and content.

The popularity of David's work rests on the fact that it was an ideal handbook for religious of any congregation or order. This work is dependent on the classics of the earlier monastic tradition, especially Gregory the Great, Bernard, and William of St. Thierry, and there is little emphasis on the usual Franciscan themes.[4] The novice master's wisdom is sober, moderate, and practical. The outer man needs to be disciplined by cloister life before he can turn to the inner life in which he may become a "friend of God" who can become "one spirit with God" (1 Cor. 6:17).[5] It is not until the end of the third book describing seven stages in the progress of the interior man that we find teaching that can be described as properly mystical in nature.[6]

David divides prayer into three basic types–set vocal prayer, spontaneous vocal prayer, and interior prayer (3.53–57). "The fruit and final goal of all prayer is to be joined to the Lord and to become one spirit with him through the melting action of the most pure love and through the gaze of the clearest knowledge and through being hidden from the tumult of the world in God's countenance in the calm ecstasy of enjoyment."[7] The states of prayer discussed in 3.63 begin with three that involve the purification of the basic powers of the soul, that is, (1) control of the imagination or memory, (2) illumination of the understanding, and (3) centering love on the *Summum Bonum* in order to attain true wisdom. David describes this as a progressive union with God, using traditional language of the embrace of the Divine Spouse and of inebriation. The complete possession of God as "the form of the soul" (*forma enim animae Deus est*) will only be given in heaven–"On earth perfection clearly lies in a perfect beginning of all this."[8] David then turns his attention to four "higher states of contemplation" spoken of in scripture and spiritual writers–ecstatic shout (*iubilus*), inebriation of spirit (*ebrietas spiritus*), spiritual delight (*spiritualis iucunditas*) and liquefaction or melting (*liquefactio*)–briefly defining each and discussing their nature with appropriate biblical citations (3.64.1–5).[9] The Franciscan's teaching here is a summary of classic monastic teaching on the higher stages of mystical contemplation.

Perhaps the most interesting part of the conclusion of David's treatise is his discussion of visions, revelations, and ecstatic experiences (3.66-68). "The less we meddle in such matters," he begins, "the less opportunity there will be for deception,"[10] though he does not deny that many saints were given visions for the purposes of special consolation and devotion. It is clear that David was particularly worried about contemporaries whose visions involved embracing, kissing, and "being caressed in other less decent ways" by Christ or Mary in a manner that affected both the interior and the exterior person.[11] He also attacked the "sickening endless spate of prophecies foretelling the coming of Antichrist" associated with Joachim and his followers.[12] These broadsides, as well as his psychologically astute treatment of sensible consolations (3.68.1–2) and the physical weakness that can come from vehemence of devotion (3.69.1), witness to an early stage in the debate over the nature of mystical states of consciousness that seems to have been sparked by the excessive forms of mysticism found in some men but especially among women.

David of Augsburg's real originality, however, rests in another aspect of his oeuvre, his mystical treatises in the vernacular. Although there has been some question as to how many of the Middle High German works ascribed to him are authentic, Kurt Ruh has made a good case for the genuine character of at least some of these, and they have not hitherto received adequate attention in the history of mysticism.[13] David provides us with an early opportunity to study the conversation between learned Latin mystical texts and the developing vernacular mystical theology. It is not just the fact that he composed mystical treatises in Middle High German (and, in the case of *The Seven Stages of Prayer,* both Latin and German versions of the same text), but also the way in which he experimented with creating new terminology for trinitarian speculation that marks him out as a pioneer, "Meister Eckhart's most important predecessor," according to Ruh.[14]

The Seven Stages of Prayer, like the mystical section of *The Composition of the Interior and Exterior Man,* is primarily an expression of monastic mysticism, dependent on Bernard of Clairvaux and William of St. Thierry's *Golden Letter* (cited under the name of Bernard).[15] Its originality rests in the skillful way in which it creates a new vernacular form for the impassioned language of the soul's ascent to various forms of mystical contact with God. Two stages of vocal prayer prepare the way for the passage through four ascents of interior prayer (*suspiria interna-mens suspensa-alienatio mentis-excessus mentis*). The highest form of prayer, face-to-face vision, will be reached only in heaven, though some great saints, like Paul, received a taste of it in this life. A comparison of the two versions, for example, regarding the sixth stage, shows that the German version drops the learned quotations of sources (though often paraphrasing the message) and frequently expands on the basic content given in the Latin, especially by explanations that emphasize the state of the soul in mystical union. In describing the *unitas spiritus* that is the highest state of contact with the divine presence, both the Latin and the German cite a central passage from William's *Golden Letter* (underlined below), but the German makes an interesting and typical expansion:

> *There the soul is so united with God,* that she is what God is, although she is not God–yet one heart, one will, one love, one spirit with God–*not only with the union by which she thereupon wills only what God wills, but that she cannot will otherwise than God does.*[16]

David of Augsburg's linguistic creativity is especially evident in the treatise *Concerning the Manifestation and Salvation of the Human Race,* which contains the beginnings of speculative trinitarian mysticism in German.[17] With the precision of a trained theologian, the Franciscan sets out the traditional "Abelardian" triad of attributed trinitarian names, that is, power-wisdom-goodness (*maht-wîsheit-güete*)–something also found in the twelfth-century German text *A Teaching of the Loving Knowledge of God.*[18] But David goes beyond previous vernacular treatments in his discussion of the trinitarian processions, especially in the way in which he adopts an analogy, first found in Anselm, to a dynamic Dionysian expression of the inner trinitarian life. His treatment has analogies with what we have seen in Bonaventure, and it also announces themes to be developed by Meister Eckhart, among others. David expresses it thus:

> The Father is the fountain (*brunne*) and the principle (*ursprunc*) of the divine flowing; the Son is the river and the brook which flows out from the fountain; the Holy Spirit is the sea which flows out from the fountain and the river. The Father is the beginning, the Son the middle, the Holy Spirit the end of the divine flowing. Because the highest good cannot remain standing in place, it bestows itself and shows itself to be the best in goodness and power.[19]

This dynamic picture of the divine flowing (*fluzze*) within the Trinity was to have a long history in German mysticism.

In the Wake of Bonaventure

David of Augsburg wrote in a pre-Bonaventurean era. Soon a flood of Bonaventure's works and others ascribed to him, both in Latin and in many vernaculars, were to be found in Germany and throughout Europe.[20] Most of the late-thirteenth- and early-fourteenth-century Franciscan mystics were deeply influenced by this Bonaventurean wave, though they naturally reflect it in varying ways. Four popular spiritual handbooks often ascribed to Bonaventure, two from Germany and two from Italy, provide examples of the mystical themes common to the second half-century of Franciscan mysticism.[21]

Little is known of the life of the German friar Rudolph of Biberach (ca. 1270–ca. 1330), a contemporary of Meister Eckhart. His *Seven Roads of Eternity,* probably written around 1300, is an example of a form of mystical text pioneered in Bonaventure's *Soliloquy,* that is, a handbook of traditional wisdom on the nature of the path to contemplative contact with God. Two interesting features of Rudolph's popular work (over one hundred Latin manuscripts are known, and there was also a German translation made about 1350) are the range of his sources (over forty authorities are used) and the scholastic complexity of his arrangement.[22] Augustine, Gregory the Great, Bernard, and the Victorines (and even Origen) are cited, often in detail, but the single most quoted authority is Thomas Gallus—a sign of how much the new Dionysianism had influenced the Franciscans. Rudolph's learned treatise often seems tedious in comparison with the vibrancy of contemporary vernacular works, but it was the kind of text whose popularity was to grow in the later Middle Ages. Spiritual directors needed the proper theological materials to guide their charges on the path to union with God, what Rudolph called "the eternal and intrinsic secret" (*aeternum et intrinsecum secretum*).[23]

Bonaventure's treatise on the life of Christ, *The Tree of Life,* had pioneered the use of the tree symbol in Franciscan circles, though the notion of organizing sermons and treatises according to a "treelike" structure of branches and sub-branches was widely popular in the later Middle Ages: *praedicare est arborisare* ("To preach is to make a tree"), as one authority put it. About 1300 an anonymous German author, most probably a Franciscan, composed a sermonlike treatise in Latin called *The Tree of Love,* which was soon also translated into Middle High German and Middle Dutch.[24] As in Rudolph of Biberach's treatise, we see here a trained scholastic mind at work synthesizing Old Testament allegories of the mystical life (Jacob, Moses, Esther, Job, the Bride of the Song of Songs, etc.) with a rich vein of traditional mystical teaching drawn from Augustine, Gregory the Great, Bernard, and Hugh of St. Victor. The theological image that distinguishes the branches of love is the seven characteristics of the love of seraphim as analyzed in Hugh of St. Victor's commentary on Dionysius's *Celestial Hierarchy,* chapter 7.[25] Love is "mobile" in always seeking the beloved, "unceasing" in its prayer, "warm . . . in order to enliven, incite and enflame sensation."[26] It is also "acute" in penetrating to the fullness of knowledge, "fervent" when it begins "to boil over . . . into melting and sickness," then "superfervent" when borne outside itself in "failing away and rapture" (*defectus et raptus*), and finally "inaccessible." Although *The Tree of Love* does not cite Thomas Gallus directly, the description of the triumph of love and total failure of knowledge in this final stage echoes his thought and also hints at the objections some had to his teaching: "I fear many objections if I were to call the rejoicing of love (*iubilum amoris*) inaccessible, and its two branches ecstasy or alienation of mind and the blinding of all reason, such that one is led by the affection like a blind man by a puppy."[27]

Italian Franciscans also contributed to the flood of Pseudo-Bonaventurean spiritual literature that inundated the later Middle Ages. Some of these treatises not only were widely popular but also made significant contributions to the history of mysticism. As in the German examples cited above, these books were often first written in Latin and then given vernacular form. The treatise known as *The Goad of Love,* written by James of Milan, exists in several Latin versions and was translated into Italian, French, Spanish, German, English (a very free rendering by Walter Hilton late in the fourteenth century), and even Gaelic.[28] *The Goad* was more popular in form than Rudolph of Biberach's *Seven Roads of Eternity,* with no scholastic structure nor apparatus of learned authorities. This mélange of ascetical and mystical teaching was deeply influenced by Bonaventure, especially in its devotion to the passion,[29] but it goes beyond the Seraphic Doctor in the more graphic way in which it encourages the reader to enter into visual meditation on the events of Christ's life.[30] A constant theme is veneration of the wounds of Christ (*vulnera Christi*) introduced in the prayer at the beginning of the work:

> Transfix the vitals of my soul, most sweet Lord Jesus Christ, with the most sweet and saving wound of your love. Wound the inmost organs of my soul by true, fraternal, and apostolic charity so that it may burn and languish; let my soul always dissolve only with love and desire for you.[31]

Throughout *The Goad* the tone is one of similar heightened, at times perhaps cloying, rhetoric, especially in some of the purple passages inviting the reader to become one with Christ on the cross. Nevertheless, Friar James has much sane and moderate advice for contemplatives (such as in chap. 11 entitled "A Contemplative Should Not Judge Others"), and he puts forth several original ideas in discussing mystical states, such as his distinction between two forms of inebriation in chapter 9.[32] The democratic universality of James of Milan's view of the mystical contact with Christ made possible by fleeing to Christ's wounds is evident in the final chapter, which rather daringly discusses how one can become perfect in a brief time (*Quod homo in brevi tempore potest esse perfectus*)![33]

Another pseudo-Bonaventurean treatise illustrates even more forcefully the trajectory of graphic imaginative meditation on the events of Christ's life found in Bonaventure's treatises, especially *The Tree of Life*. The *Meditations on the Life of Christ* was widely disseminated and sometimes accompanied by a rich series of illustrations.[34] The text appears to have been written by an anonymous Tuscan friar to a Poor Clare about 1300.[35] The original language was Latin, but a Latin much influenced by the vernacular. The work was translated into Italian, English, and French, as well as later into German, Dutch, Spanish, Catalan, and Swedish.[36]

There has been some question about whether or not the *Meditations* should be considered a mystical text.[37] If we allow for a "mysticism of the historical event" in the Franciscan tradition, as argued for by Ewert Cousins and others, it seems difficult to exclude the *Meditations* from the story of Franciscan mysticism. The work can be described as a classic of imaginative recreation of the events of Christ's life with the intention of achieving communion with the God-man and penetrating to the inner meaning of the mysteries of salvation.[38] Both text and pictures are designed to invite the reader to become an eyewitness to the events of Christ's life, that is, to learn to practice what the author calls "contemplation of the humanity of Christ."[39] For the author of the *Meditations* (much like Bernard of Clairvaux, who is far and away the most frequently cited source), such contemplation, a form of *amor carnalis Christi*, is not the end of the mystical quest. Rather, it is meant to prepare the soul for the higher stages of "contemplation of the celestial court" and "contemplation of the divine majesty."[40] All three forms, the author insists, citing Bernard's Sermon 49 on the Song of Songs, involve "the two raptures of mind (*excessus mentis*), that is, the intellectual and the affective."[41] At the conclusion of the work, the author once again appeals to Bernard's teaching on the necessity of beginning with the *amor carnalis Christi*. Here, however, a difference emerges. Despite another invocation of Bernard, the *Meditations* give greater weight to the continuing necessity for carnal meditation-contemplation of Christ's humanity than did the abbot of Clairvaux:

> You see how this meditation is carnal with respect to spiritual meditation. You take it up not to decrease devotion, but that fervor might grow to greater things to which you ought to come, nevertheless, by passing through these modes. . . . Let meditating be your whole and only intent, your rest, your food, your study. . . . Even those who ascend to greater contemplation ought not to renounce it, at the right place and time. . . . Remember what you have read above, in the treatise on this kind of contemplation, that is, on the humanity of Christ, that the Blessed Bernard, the highest contemplator, never renounced it.[42]

The Franciscan character of the text is evident in the prologue, which lifts up both Francis and Clare, "your mother and leader" (*virgine Clara matre ac ducissa tua*), as examples of patience under suffering. Francis is singled out as a model contemplative:

> Therefore, he was so ardently drawn to it [i.e., meditation on Christ's life] that he was like a picture of it. In all the virtues he imitated it as perfectly as he could, and at last, completing and perfecting [himself] in Jesus through the impression of the sacred stigmata, he was totally transformed into him.[43]

Although the length of the *Meditations* allows for a full treatment of all the events of Christ's life, the concentration on the nativity and especially on the passion seems to be a mark of Bonaventure's influence.[44] Finally, the stress given to true poverty "rooted and established in the heart," and especially the insistence that Christ and the apostles themselves did not *use* money, indicates that the text is probably the product of a friar sympathetic to the Spiritual cause.[45]

Mystics among the Spirituals[46]

Although a few of the Spiritual leaders, like Angelo of Clareno in his *History of the Seven Tribulations of the Order of Minors,* criticized Bonaventure for his role in the downfall of the Spiritual hero John of Parma,[47] most of the Spiritual party were deeply indebted to the Seraphic Doctor.[48] Peter John Olivi (1248–1298), the intellectual leader of the Spirituals, had heard Bonaventure in Paris and always considered himself a faithful follower. Olivi is a figure of considerable complexity, and recent research has vindicated the importance of his theology and apocalyptic thought.[49] The history of the Spiritual movement indicates that he was a religious leader of an intensity that might even allow employing that overused word "charismatic."

Olivi's scholastic works contain treatments of the nature of contemplation, where he insists both on the reciprocal activity of intellect and will and on the superiority of the latter. Here, as well as in his discussion of the superior status of the mixed life of contemplation and action, he largely conveys traditional teaching.[50] Olivi also composed some tracts on ascetical and moral issues, such as his *Letter to the Sons of Charles II,*[51] but he did not write special treatises on mystical topics, with the possible exception of a small work concerning the rules for discerning true and false visions and spiritual experiences, *The Remedies against Spiritual Temptations.*[52] Where the Provençal friar's knowledge of mystical literature is most evident, not unexpectedly, is in his exegesis, especially his *Exposition on the Song of Songs.*[53] This neglected work makes heavy use of such traditional authorities as

Bernard and Hugh of St. Victor, but it essentially follows the lead of Thomas Gallus in combining Dionysian apophaticism with the Song's language of love.[54] For example, in commenting on Song 1:5, the Bride's statement *nigra sum,* Olivi, like Gallus, ties the text to the darkness of separation from all lower intellectual activity:

> The best mode of seeking God is to be rightly drawn upward in a superintellectual way, until the mind's apex, separated from all being, understands the Supersubstantial Existent above all things and knows through full ignorance the things that are beyond ignorance. Perfect unknowing is the knowing of him who is beyond all that is known. This is entering the darkness, or cloud, along with Moses.[55]

What is new about this by now traditional teaching is how Olivi, from time to time, gives a historical and apocalyptic dimension to the story of the loving soul recounted in the Song of Songs.[56]

Olivi's fame as the leader of the Spirituals gave him a reputation as a visionary, especially with regard to a revelation of the meaning of the Bible supposedly granted during his student days at Paris (perhaps not unlike Joachim of Fiore's showing about the inner coherence of the biblical concordances).[57] Olivi was certainly interested in visions, and he used revelations given to holy friars and laywomen to authenticate controversial aspects of his teaching, such as his belief in the coming resurrection of St. Francis from the dead.[58]

The most interesting aspect of Olivi's thought for the history of mysticism, however, is his notion of an imminent age of perfect contemplation, another form of the corporate, or social, apocalyptic mysticism found in Joachim of Fiore and in Bonaventure. Olivi's scriptural commentaries, especially his *Interpretation of the Apocalypse* (*Lectura super Apocalypsim*), completed shortly before his death, advance a theology of history dependent on Joachim and Bonaventure but with distinctive elements.[59] Like both his predecessors, Olivi saw exact historical parallels between seven ages of the Old Testament and seven of the New Testament, but unlike Bonaventure he adopted Joachim's view of a coming third *status* of the Holy Spirit, though in a guarded way. Olivi also accorded Francis an apocalyptic role as the Angel of the Sixth Seal of Apocalypse 7:2, the figure in whom the imminent era of full contemplation has actually begun. Unlike Bonaventure, he gave the controversial Joachim of Fiore a somewhat similar role because of "the great light given to him in the dawn, as it were, of the third age." In his scholastic treatments of contemplation, Olivi had stressed an ongoing historical transition from the stage of faith, through the growing contemplative grasp of divine truth, which he characterized especially as a "tasting" (*gustus*), down to the final vision to come in heaven. He believed this "gusta-tory and tactile experience" of the mystical meaning of the Bible and a heightened interior consciousness of God in which "the whole world will enter into Christ" would soon be realized. As a text from his unedited *Inter-pretation of John* puts it: "Christ wishes to say that all his external doctrine, according to which he has taught them about divine things as a man up to now, is more or less parabolic and enigmatic or metaphorical and obscure when compared with what he will do shortly afterward through his Spirit."[60]

Ubertino of Casale (ca. 1259–ca. 1330) was at the Franciscan *studium* at Florence ca. 1285–89 with Olivi before being sent on to Paris (ca. 1289–98), where he was a contemporary of Meister Eckhart.[61] But Ubertino rejected the scholasticism of Paris. He was much more influenced by his encounters with the aged John of Parma and a number of the women mystics con-nected with the Franciscan movement. A powerful preacher in Tuscany, Umbria, and the Marche, Ubertino's devotion to the Spiritual cause led to his suspension from preaching in 1304. He retired to Monte Alverna for a year, where he completed his masterpiece, the lengthy *Tree of the Crucified Life of Jesus*. The first four books of the work contain a series of considera-tions of the mysteries of the life of Jesus, very much in the vein begun by Bonaventure's *Tree of Life* and continued in the *Meditations on the Life of Christ*. The fifth book is a commentary on the Apocalypse, summarizing the Franciscanized interpretation of Olivi, but going beyond the latter in the acerbity of its attacks on the representatives of the carnal church who opposed the Spirituals' interpretation of the Franciscan way of life.[62] Olivi was the creator of the dual view of the imminent Antichrist–the Mystical Antichrist, a false pope (or popes) who would attack the Franciscan *Rule*, and the Great Antichrist comprising political persecutors. Ubertino went further in actually naming the Mystical Antichrist–none other than the con-temporary popes Boniface VIII and Benedict XI, whose respective cruelty and deceit summarized the evils of this final enemy of Christ.[63] Ubertino was deeply involved in the dramatic events of the condemnation and sup-pression of the Spirituals. His daring eventually led to an order for his arrest as a heretic in 1325, at which time he fled Avignon and became lost to history.

The *Tree of the Crucified Life of Jesus* is many things, not least a treatise summarizing key elements of Franciscan mysticism.[64] Most of these we have seen before: the importance of the role of Francis as exemplar through his reception of the stigmata;[65] the significance of poverty and humility, both interior and exterior, as the essential virtues of the Christian life;[66] the centrality of imaginative participation in the events of Christ's life, above all the passion; a strong Marian piety; belief in an imminent general age of contemplation;[67] the artful combination of material drawn from the monastic contemplative tradition, especially Bernard of Clairvaux, with Bonaventure's mystical teaching; and, finally, the conception of the highest form of life as involving the fusion of action and contemplation, for which both Francis and Giles of Assisi are taken as models.[68] Ubertino synthesizes these themes masterfully, often intensifying them through the ardor of his devotion to the Spiritual cause. Though the sheer size of the work prevented the *Arbor* from having as wide a dissemination as some of the other Franciscan mystical works studied above, there are a number of manuscripts, versions, partial translations, and one early printing at Venice in 1485. Dante knew the *Arbor,* and it was influential on Bernardino of Siena and later Franciscan mystics, like Francis of Osuna.[69]

In his first prologue (*Arbor* 3a–7b), Ubertino provides a spiritual autobiography in which he pays homage to those who helped his progress in the inner appropriation of the saving life of Jesus, even unto the "third cross" discussed in book 4. Among these were John of Parma, Peter of Siena, and the holy woman Cecilia of Florence, "who," Ubertino says, "frequently taught me the whole path of higher contemplation concerning the life of Jesus and the hidden things of my heart and much else about the infant Jesus." Once again, the image of the "learned" friar being instructed by the divinely guided female adept is important. From Olivi, as a good disciple of Bonaventure, he learned "to behold the Beloved" not only in every form of knowledge, but also "in every aspect of any creature whatever in almost every place," and "always to think along with Jesus crucified in mind and body."[70] Even more striking is the testimony he gives to the effect of his meeting with Angela of Foligno, whose counsel completely renewed his life after his stay in Paris had reduced his spiritual fervor, "so that from that time on I was not the person I had been" (*ut iam ex tunc non fueram ille qui fui* [5a]).[71] In these comments about the major influences on his spiritual development we again catch hints of the forms of conversation and mutual instruction between men and women that were so important for late medieval mysticism.

The second prologue (7b–9b) outlines the mystical intent of the *Tree of the Crucified Life,* nothing less than the *amor exstaticus* which Dionysius ascribed to Paul in the fourth book of the *Divine Names.* Ubertino quotes Dionysius's *Divine Names* 4.13 (in the version of Robert Grosseteste) and adds: "Ecstasy means 'making outside the self'; hence spiritual men are called ecstatics, i.e., 'made outside themselves,' by thinking of God, not themselves, in everything." Such ecstatic love can be directed only to the three Persons of the Trinity, who, Ubertino claims, are all contained in the name Jesus (*unctus*)–"In which the Father is understood as the one anointing, the Holy Spirit as the anointing itself, and the anointed one as Christ the man."[72] The true ecstatic, like Paul (see Gal. 2:20), belongs to God not to self.

Ecstatic love of God, then, is the goal of Ubertino's meditative-contemplative considerations of the mysteries of the *Verbum increatum* (book 1) and the *Verbum incarnatum* (books 2–4). As might be expected, the central mystery that provides the clue to salvation history is found in Christ on the cross–"Christ does not invite you to perform miracles, but to follow his footsteps and to ponder and embrace the scandal of his cross."[73] Therefore, the lengthy chapter entitled *Christus cruce ditatus,* "Christ made rich by the cross," is the center of the work.[74] Here the Franciscan introduces an original concept of five different forms of the cross: the cross of Jesus, the cross of Mary, the cross of the perfect, the cross of the proficient, and the cross of beginners.[75] "Note that the cross, insofar as it is taken up by Christ and distributed to his sons, declares sorrow and joy in a proportionate measure proceeding from the love of the Holy Spirit equally dispensing both of these."[76] Because Christ the God-man has the highest measure of the "inflowing" (*influxus*) of the love of the Holy Spirit, his cross possesses the supreme measure of this paradoxical union of sorrow and joy, abnegation and triumph. Mary's unique devotion to her Son makes her cross the next in power.

Ubertino's treatment of the cross of the perfect summarizes his understanding of mystical union. The Franciscan echoes earlier mystics, such as William of St. Thierry, in rooting union with God in the love that is the Holy Spirit, the embrace and kiss within the trinitarian processions; but he is original, as Kurt Ruh has pointed out, in finding the model for this union in the hypostatic uniting of God and man in Jesus. Just as there is no human person or "supposit" in the philosophical sense in Jesus, but a total emptying of the human personality, "so too ought it to be in you, soul, who wishes to attain the perfection of his cross." Whoever wishes to be united to God by love and will "through perfect abnegation," must surrender all love of self and others, even all will, so that "the Holy Spirit itself seems as if it is your love and your will and you will nothing for yourself, but only for Jesus: you will nothing but him and because of him."[77] Ubertino's notion of annihilation may have been influenced by Angela of Foligno, though his expressions are not as radical.

Ubertino, like Olivi, characterizes union as a form of tasting God (*gustus*),[78] but his favorite mode of describing this highest state is *quies,* which he conceives of as a "true and full tranquillity" (*vera et plena tranquillitas*) in which we surrender ourselves to everything that we encounter because it all issues from divine providence. Like David of Augsburg and Olivi, Ubertino (who attacked the proponents of the "sect of the spirit of liberty" in his preaching in Tuscany) was anxious to distinguish his understanding of such tranquillity from false views. Since *quies* arises from the love of the Holy Spirit manifested in the cross and thus distributes both *gaudium* and *dolor*, it is a mystical experience that does not involve "lack of compassion towards the neighbor in tribulations," nor failure to see sin as sin. "This soul will do very well to flee the pest of that poisonous error—the spirit of liberty, or rather of malignity!"[79] Rather, suffering and sin (either in the case of the self or another) are the source of more intense anxiety precisely insofar as they are viewed from the perspective of quiet abandonment. For one who has achieved such consciousness, Ubertino claims:

> Nevertheless, he takes into himself most strongly with sorrow and the compassion of God all the evils which he sees or feels—the neighbor's injuries and tribulations. The more fully he feels them, the more he is at rest. He conceives this rest of his as the act of bearing all these things, so that the rest grows from the tribulation and the tribulation from the will's resting. This is participation in the sleep of the beloved disciple [John, as the image of the contemplative].[80]

The ardor of the *Tree of the Crucified Life of Jesus* and its at times almost poetic form reveal a dimension of the Franciscan experience, especially in its most uncompromising members, that found powerful expression in two great mystics of the vernacular tradition: Jacopone of Todi, one of the greatest mystical poets of the Middle Ages; and Angela of Foligno, one of its premier women mystics.

Jacopone (ca. 1236–1306) was an educated layman who underwent a conversion after the death of his wife about 1268.[81] For a number of years he traveled the roads of Italy as a "holy fool" (*bizoccone*), leading a life of poverty and penance. In 1278 he became a Franciscan friar, championing the view of poverty held by the Spirituals. In 1297 Jacopone signed the Longhezza Manifesto, which rejected the conclave that had elected Boniface VIII and called for a council to elect a new pope. Boniface excommunicated the signers and eventually captured them after besieging Palestrina for over a year. Jacopone was sentenced to life imprisonment in an underground cell in the monastery of San Fortunato at Todi, where he wrote some of his most impassioned and also most desolate poems—among the treasures of prison literature.[82] He was released from prison by the new pope Benedict XI in 1303 and died three years later.

Although Jacopone knew Latin, his contribution was essentially a vernacular one in poetic form.[83] In the manner of many of the vernacular theologians of the later Middle Ages, he was far more learned in the mystical tradition than he lets on. His *Lauds* are astonishing in their range and their complexity of tone and message. As Elémarie Zolla puts it: "There is no transition between contradictory levels of consciousness. Mystical rapture and animal directness, sublime spiritual enlightenment and devotional trivia appear simply juxtaposed, black and white."[84] Like many of the Spirituals, Jacopone was a fervent apocalyptic thinker (see *Laud* 50), and his devotion to penance often took the form of savage attacks on the body and the senses (e.g., *Lauds* 3, 5–7, 15, 22–24, 27), on the wiles of women (*Laud* 8), as well as including somber meditations on death (*Lauds* 21 and 25). Jacopone never hesitated to express his own inner conflicts, "the two blades of the scissors" that felt like they were cutting him in two (*Laud* 38.61; cf. 39, 47–48, and especially 55). Despite (or perhaps rather because of) these unresolved conflicts, Jacopone's ability to suggest the annihilating power of the experience of divine love has few rivals in the history of Christian mysticism.

Jacopone's fundamental themes of love and annihilation are based on a bedrock of Franciscan theological and mystical motifs.[85] At the heart of his vision is the overwhelming love manifested in God taking on flesh and suffering for us on the cross. This is clearly expressed in *Lauds* 40–42 where a dialogue between Christ, the angels, and the soul discusses the mystery of redemption. Christ says:

I teach love	and this is my art . . .
I am the book of life,	sealed with seven seals,
When I am opened	you will find five signs
Painted red with blood	in which you can study.[86]

Contemplating Christ on the cross leads to embracing abjection and suffering, drinking the "new wine" of love that no cask can contain (*Laud* 75). Francis, with his seven visions of the cross culminating in the stigmata (a theme drawn from Bonaventure's *Major Life*), is the model for the transformation that is the goal of such redemptive love:

The highest divine love	brought you to embrace Christ,
His totally burning affection	swallowed you up
To put a stamp on your heart	like a seal in wax.
The impression was his	in whom you are transformed.
There has never been found	a saint who bore such a sign,
A mystery so deep	that if God had not revealed it,
It would be better to pass over it,	not knowing how to speak.
Those can treat of it	who have tasted it![87]

Christ's emptying of himself through the madness of love is the archetype of the voluntary poverty that is the center of the Franciscan way of life, as the two *Lauds* devoted to poverty demonstrate.[88]

Jacopone also witnesses to the Franciscan adoption of the angelic interiorization pioneered by Thomas Gallus, which in two other *Lauds* combines with the Bonaventurean-inspired use of the tree image.[89] This is the closest that he comes to creating an itinerary of the soul's ascent to God. Ingenious as these poems are (and often filled with flashes of piercing insight), Jacopone was not comfortable with structures and explanations. His metier was rather exuberant presentations of the power of divine love that may have closer analogies with Sufi poets than with most Christian mystical poets.[90]

Jacopone's idiosyncratic poetry has provoked widely differing evaluations among students of Italian literature. Also, because he expressed himself in a difficult Umbrian form of early Italian, few students of the history of mysticism have given him the consideration he deserves.[91] Many difficulties face the interpreter. Given the contradictions he flaunts in his poetry (which his numerous "confessions" only make more complicated), it is easy to pit one side of the Franciscan's thought against another (e.g., the world-negating *Lauds* against *Laud* 82, which praises how the senses find God in the whole creation). The message of the power of love repeats itself with such frequency in the later *Lauds* that it is tempting to engage in a detailed treatment of many of the poems (e.g., *Lauds* 65, 71, 83–85, and 87), each of which contains striking variations on this theme. But Jacopone's presentation of the relation between love and annihilation never achieved greater heights than in *Lauds* 90–92, so a look at these lengthy poems (almost 650 lines) provides a sense of why he is one of the central figures of late medieval vernacular mysticism.[92]

These three *Lauds* comprise a series of fuguelike explorations of divine love as excessive, ecstatic, and annihilating. The longest, *Laud* 90 in eight-verse stanzas (an early form of *ottava rima*), concentrates on the violence of the love that has conquered both God and man. *Laud* 91 describes the union with God attained through such love, emphasizing the annihilation that leads to a state of sinlessness. Finally, *Laud* 92 (in a different poetic form) sets out three stages in the path to self-annihilation. Jacopone's daring formulations regarding overwhelming love, divine nothingness, and a state of sinlessness beyond all willing suggest interesting comparisons with Angela of Foligno (whose work he may well have known), as well as with the French beguine, Marguerite Porete, with whom he could not have been familiar. These shared themes point to a set of issues about the possibility of

attaining a form of indistinct union with God characteristic of much late-
thirteenth- and early-fourteenth-century mysticism.

Amor de caritate, perché m'hai sì ferito?–"Love of charity, why have you
wounded me in this way?" *Laud* 90 begins with an invocation of the torture
that Divine Love brings to the soul (lines 1–18), a condition that results
from the soul's willingness to give up everything for love (lines 19–82).
Such love is Christocentric, leading to a transformation in Christ beyond
the realm of sin. According to Jacopone the soul:

Is transformed in Christ,	as if she were Christ,
Joined to God,	she is totally divine. . . .
There is no more dross	where sin can be found,
What is old has been taken away,	purged of every stench.[93]

As he explores the intensity of this loving union with Christ (lines 115–46),
Jacopone employs mystical paradoxes to help describe the abyss of love:

Once I spoke,	now I am mute;
Once I could see,	now I am blind.
Oh, the depths of the abyss	in which
Though silent, I speak;	fleeing, I am bound;
Descending, I rise;	holding, I am held;
Outside, I am within;	I pursue and am pursued.
Love without limits,	why do you drive me mad?
And destroy me	in this burning furnace?[94]

The second half of the poem (lines 147–290) concerns the tension
between *caritas ordinata,* the ideal of monastic contemplation, and *amor
vehemens,* the excessive power of divine love. Twelfth-century mystics, like
Bernard of Clairvaux and Richard of St. Victor, had struggled to keep these
clashing aspects together;[95] for Jacopone, vehement love sweeps all before
it. Christ upbraids the tortured lover, demanding that her love be put in
order (lines 147–62). The lover responds that this is impossible, and
besides, since the soul is now totally transformed into Christ, he has only
himself to blame for the extravagance and disorder (lines 175–78). Ultimately, it really is all love's fault, because it was love in the first place who
conquered Christ, bringing him down from heaven to earth where, like a
madman drunk with love, "He leaped up on to the cross to embrace us"
(line 215). The soul, then, has no trouble admitting that she too has been
conquered by love to such an extent that she longs for death (lines 227–42).
This desire for annihilation in the love that is Christ is given incantatory
form in the closing lines (243–90), where *amor* is repeated over seventy
times, often in the form of *amor, amor Iesù.* Here Jacopone provides a strik-

ing example of the *iubilus,* the unrestrained outpouring of love found
among so many thirteenth-century mystics, especially women (see also
Lauds 76 and 80):

> Love, Love-Jesus, most desirable,
> Love, I wish to die in your embrace,
> Love, Love-Jesus, my sweet Spouse,
> Love, Love, I demand death from you.
> Love, Love-Jesus, so very delightful,
> You give yourself to me in transforming me into you;
> I sense that I am growing less and less,
> Love, I do not know where I am.
> Jesus, my hope, submerge me in the abyss of love.[96]

Abissame en amore is the heart of the friar's mysticism.

Laud 91 explores the nature of the perfect union achieved in this abyss
(lines 1–104) with particular attention to the sinlessness inherent in such a
state (lines 105–52) and the relation between union and annihilation (lines
153–242). If the language of mystical death was emphasized in the previous
poem, here the concentration is on the "Nothingness" (*alta nichilitate*) in
which the soul becomes identical with God. The daring of Jacopone's
expressions of this identity and his insistence that in this state there can be
no sin (see, e.g., lines 15–16, 114, 124, 139–40, 151) have led some to accuse
him of sharing in the ideas of the so-called "Free Spirit" heretics.[97] The
problems concerning this mystical "heresy" will be taken up in more detail
in chapter 5 below, especially in treating the condemned beguine, Marguerite Porete (pp. 244–46). Here it is enough to say that poetic expressions, even of a daring "autotheistic" flavor, are always difficult to interpret.
One must try to avoid the opposed dangers of either explaining away their
boldness by interpreting them as mere poetic exaggeration to be put right
by prose qualifications, or of failing to recognize that mystics, especially
those like Jacopone, often do challenge conventional orthodox expressions.
It is worth noting that other poems of Jacopone make use of more traditional bridal language about union in language that does not conflict with
what was traditionally orthodox,[98] while (on the other side) Jacopone's
whole life was one that more timid souls could only characterize as
extreme.[99]

In language that reflects the "dazzling darkness" of the Dionysian tradition, the Franciscan speaks of God as "the unimaginable Light ... who
wishes to live in the midst of obscure darkness" (lines 9–10). To attain this
hidden God, human powers have to cease to function and all values need
to be reversed as we are raptured into the annihilation of love. Of those

who are "abyssed in the midst of this sea" (line 27) startling things can be said: "Take possession of everything; you have attained such a transformation through union that you can say, 'Everything is mine.'" Or, "The form that has been given you by God has absorbed you in such a way that you live although you are dead, both conquerer and conquered." Toward the end of the poem, Jacopone even claims:

You possess in being possessed	in such a union
That there is no division	that separates you from him.
You drink and are drunk	in a transformation
Of such perfection	that none can distract you from it . . .
In God you are made infinite	there is none can oppose you.[100]

Two other motifs in this challenging poem are also reminiscent of the language of Marguerite Porete in her condemned book *The Mirror of Simple Annihilated Souls.* Jacopone insists that in order to arrive at this highest state the soul needs to get beyond all willing: "Both willing and not willing are annihilated in you."[101] This implies that our created will must become nothing in order to be merged into the divine *nihil* in some form of indistinction. In such a state the soul wills without a will, desiring nothing and possessing no power in itself. Jacopone concludes:

This supreme height	is founded in nothingness,
Nothingness, formed,	placed in the Savior.
Supreme Nothingness,	your action is so powerful,
It opens all the doors	and enters infinity.

Later in the poem he returns to the same theme of the coincidence of opposites in which supreme height and depth are fused:

Your profound depth	is lifted up so high,
That it is placed upon the throne to reign with God always.	
It is so drowned in the abyss	in that supreme height
That it cannot be found	and does not appear in itself.[102]

This darkness of mutual annihilation, the dual abyss of God and the soul (really the same abyss), brings Jacopone close to one of the major speculative themes of the new mysticism, one found primarily among women mystics, like Hadewijch, Angela of Foligno, and Marguerite Porete, as we will see below.[103]

The third and shortest poem in this trilogy on "deep union" has textual problems, but its general teaching is clear. Jacopone begins by describing how the three theological virtues of faith, hope, and charity effect the annihilation of the soul beyond the "yes" and "no" of the created will (lines

1–14). The *Laud* distinguishes three stages in the path to annihilation (*nel primo e nel secondo e nel megliore* [line 36]). The first is the utter renunciation of the will, already familiar from the previous poem (lines 15–32). The second involves the intellect divesting itself of all its wisdom since it cannot swim in the sea of love (lines 33–74). Though textual corruptions make this section difficult to interpret, it echoes a constant theme of Franciscan mysticism often repeated by Jacopone, that is, the necessity for intellect to yield to love for the final advance into God.[104] The final state, briefly described in highly metaphorical terms (lines 75–86), combines expressions of both pain and tranquil rest in God (*quies*). Commentary on such enigmatic verses could be extensive, but probably superfluous:

> Autumn comes every fourth quarter–
> (This is established and cannot be changed).
> The heavens stand firm,
> Their silence makes me cry out.
> O bottomless sea,   the depth of your abyss
> Has circled me in tight bonds   wishing to annihilate me.[105]

Great poets and great mystics share a desire to express the inexpressible, though they often conceive of what is inexpressible in different ways. Jacopone has eluded interpreters in part because he is among the first Christian mystics (Hadewijch and Mechthild of Magdeburg preceded him) who chose to express his sense of God's paradoxical presence in poetic form– and a vernacular one at that. He remains as challenging to us as he was to himself and his contemporaries.

Jacopone's *Laud* 63, consisting of a brief and unique Latin letter and an equally short poem, is addressed to his friend John of Alverna, who also belonged to the Spiritual camp (legend has it that John miraculously brought Jacopone the last sacraments on his deathbed). John's life reminds us of another aspect of early Franciscan mysticism, that is, the continuing importance of ecstatic experience. Franciscans on both sides of the poverty debate were interested in visions and ecstatic experience, especially the necessity for discriminating between true and false visions.[106]

Though visions and ecstasies were ascribed to other Spirituals, such as the Umbrian leader Conrad of Offida (d. 1306),[107] no member of the Spiritual party acquired a greater reputation for his raptures than John of Alverna (1259–1322), who spent much of his life as a hermit on the Franciscan holy mountain where Francis had received the stigmata.[108] The first book of the Latin *Acts of Saint Francis and His Companions* (what in its Italian form came to be known as the *Little Flowers*) closes with an account of his raptures, many also found in the *Life* written by one of his close associates.

John's experiences comprise a kind of encyclopedia of the various forms of ecstasies found in the major sources of Christian mysticism. Chapter 49 of the *Acts,* for example, tells how Christ appeared to him after a period of trial and darkness and allowed him to kiss first his feet, then his hands, and his holy breast, whereby he "was rapt in ecstasy and utterly consoled and marvellously enlightened."[109] The reference to the triple kiss taught by Bernard of Clairvaux is noted by the author; equally evident is the Bernardine transition from love of Christ's humanity to being "buried in the depths of the Divinity."[110] John sees visions of souls being freed from purgatory (*Acts* 51), of saints on their deathbed, of angels and saints in glory (*Acts* 52). Excessive experiences of fervor and sweetness, sometimes lasting lengthy periods of time, cause him to cry out and shout in a form of *iubilus.* Like St. Benedict, he has a vision of the entire universe from God's perspective,[111] as well as a powerful experience of being assumed into the divine abyss using the traditional metaphor of the drop of wine being absorbed into the sea (*Acts* 56.11–17). Finally, chapter 57 describes a eucharistic vision where Christ appears in the host, not unlike many visions ascribed to the beguines.

John of Alverna's only rival among these later Franciscan male ecstatics allied with the Spiritual camp was Roger of Provence (d. 1287).[112] Roger's *Meditations,* and especially the *Life* written by his confessor Raymond Peter, make frequent ecstatic experience the center of his life (in one place Raymond reports that Roger claimed to have been raptured at least a hundred times during a single Matins!).[113] Monastic mystics like Bernard of Clairvaux had taught that contemplative awareness of the direct presence of God was rare and brief–*rara hora et parva mora.*[114] Beginning in the thirteenth century, first with beguines like Mary of Oignies, a new stress on frequent and lengthy ecstasy appears. This is usually associated with women, but the examples of John of Alverna and Roger show that it was not gender-specific.

Raymond Peter's *Life of Roger* ranks among the more extreme examples of ecstatic biography. Roger's obsessive practice of confessing (twenty times a day or more) and his various forms of guarding the senses are examples of the taste for the excessive that marked many late medieval visionaries. As was the case with John of Alverna, many of Roger's ecstasies took place while he was celebrating Mass. (Raymond says some friars were afraid to serve his Mass for this reason.)[115] The biographer gives us several detailed descriptions of the kind of raptures that led some to think that he was insane (*insanus vel amens factus*). During Holy Week, for example, Roger once wandered about in the garden of the friary for three days crying out, "When will I die, O Lord, when will I die?" When Raymond went out into the garden, "[h]e met me like a man who was drunk, with his entire face so red and enflamed that it was like fire going from it and his eyes did not see me. His face was so terrible that I did not dare to speak to him or to look at him."[116] Perhaps the most unusual form of rapture described in the life is one that is actually quite fitting for a learned friar—ecstatic reading and preaching. According to Raymond, Roger used to read the Bible and mystical authors (e.g., Dionysius, Augustine, and Hugh of St. Victor) aloud in a state of ecstasy while making constant marks in the margins of their texts. Those who heard him were deeply moved. Even more powerful was his ecstatic preaching. After giving a sermon one Sunday evening, he found it impossible to stop preaching, so he took Raymond and two others apart, and "looking up to heaven he began to set forth, as if reading from a book, such deep and profound mysteries unheard of by the world" that no one could really remember them or understand them. The words were so forceful that after two hours one of those present (not Raymond we presume who was game for anything) felt as if his chest was going to split. In fear of dying, he got Roger to break off by shouting to him three times that Matins was about to begin.[117]

Roger's *Meditations,* really a sayings collection like those taken down from Giles of Assisi, match this picture in both style and content. They contain often obscure and frequently ungrammatical "considerations" that at times seem to be experiments in trying to express ecstatic speech, matching their insistence on the ineffability and inexpressibility of God.[118] Though these *dicta* demonstrate Roger's theological background, containing references to Augustine, Dionysius, Bernard, and Bonaventure, the purpose of the *Meditations* is not learned information for confessors and spiritual directors, as we have seen in Rudolph of Biberach for instance, but rather inspiration for friars and laity to enter within to find God. As Roger says in one place:

> See, O man, that the words you have heard are near to silence and so near that they cannot be heard outside silence, because they can only be heard where they are and because they are within silence. Therefore, enter into your inmost self, within your own silence, so that you may go from your silence to God's and his silence beyond thought may speak this to you.[119]

The ecstatic states recounted in the *Life of Roger* and reflected in the obscure texts of the *Meditations* were considered bizarre even by many of his contemporaries, but they represent a dimension of Franciscan mysticism that cannot be ignored.

Any attempt to treat the many-faceted history of Franciscan mysticism in its first century cannot avoid the figure of Ramon Llull (1232–1316). Like

Joachim of Fiore, Llull has been an important and controversial figure in the history of Western thought. For all those who became convinced that his *ars generalis* (General Art) was the key to wisdom, providing the means to integrate the many disciplines of knowledge and convert unbelievers to Christianity, there were always others who judged him long-winded and confused. His role in the history of mysticism is also open to debate.[120] Llull has been called the first great Spanish mystic (Christian Spanish mystic, of course), but the adjective may be exaggerated. Llull's visions were an important factor in his life, and there are a number of works in his vast *oeuvre* of over two hundred and fifty writings that can be considered to contain mystical teaching; but it is doubtful that he played a major role in the development of late medieval mysticism.

Llull was born into an aristocratic family in Palma on the island of Majorca. A married man, courtier, and troubador, he was converted about 1263 by a series of five visions of Christ crucified. Inspired by a sermon on St. Francis, he provided some money for his wife and family, gave away the rest, and devoted himself to the task of "writing a book, the best in the world, against the errors of the unbelievers."[121] This undertaking, which involved his acquiring a rich if idiosyncratic education, consumed the rest of his life. After nine years of study, including learning Arabic, Llull began his writing career, composing the first and longest version of the "best book in the world," what he called *The Book of Contemplation* (ca. 1273–74). Despite its title, this vast work of about a million words is more of a summary of Llull's developing thought than a properly mystical treatise, containing little discussion of contemplation in the mystical sense.[122] In 1274 he received an illumination that gave him the "form and method for writing the aforementioned book against the errors of the unbelievers." This was the *ars generalis,* an approach to learning that can be best described as a new logic of letter and figure combinations designed to clarify the trinitarian structure of reality and to demonstrate the truths of the Christian religion.[123] As a universal technique for discovering and demonstrating the analogies that lead to God, the *ars* formed the theme for almost all of Llull's later works, implicitly or explicitly.

The Catalan polymath spent much of his later life wandering the Mediterranean, though he also visited Paris, where he was allowed to lecture on his "Art." He was instrumental in founding a college for Franciscans on Majorca to train the friars for missions to Muslims, though the project did not flourish. Three times he went to northern Africa, endeavoring to use the Art to convert Muslims, often in peril of his life. In 1283, while at Montpellier, he wrote his famous novelistic romance in Catalan, called *Blaquerna,* which contains his best known mystical work, *The Book of the Lover and Beloved* (*Lo libre d'amich e amat*). At the same time he also composed the short treatise called *The Art of Contemplation*.[124] In 1293, Llull experienced a spiritual crisis in Genoa, during which he asked to be clothed with the Franciscan habit, though this was not granted at the time. Llull's life was essentially that of a wandering penitent (a *bizoccone* like Jacopone). While there is no clear proof that he was ever really a "Franciscan" in any canonical sense, Franciscan tradition is not totally incorrect in claiming this strange witness to poverty and missionary preaching as its own. There is also evidence that Llull had contact with circles of Spiritual Franciscans, as might have been expected from his interests and location.[125] The story that he died a martyr's death on his last trip to Africa has now been discounted as a legend.

Llull was one of the few Latin Christians of the thirteenth century reasonably well acquainted with Islam. The influence on his writings of the great Muslim thinker and mystic Al-Ghazzali (d. 1111), as well as other Sufis, is indisputable. A number of his later works, both in Latin and in Catalan, deal with mystical topics.[126] The writings in which he employs his Art to demonstrate how the soul attains contemplation of God by love and intellect, such as the *Flowers of Love and Flowers of Intelligence,* are scarcely readable today, a kind of "mysticism by the letters."[127] Even the more discursive Latin treatises that deal with contemplation, such as the *Book of the Ascent and Descent of the Intellect* and the treatises in *The Contemplation of Raymond,* are dry structural analyses of how contemplation fits into the vast map of congruences that makes up the Lullian logic.[128] In these works, at least, Llull parts company with the standard Franciscan emphasis on the superiority of *affectus* as the power giving final access to God. Instead, he stresses an intellectualist and universalized understanding of *contemplatio* befitting his missionary program of proving the truth of Christianity by necessary reasons.[129] The intellect desires knowledge, and when knowledge is attained it produces devotion in the will; there is no *apex affectus* that surpasses intellect.[130] Also, despite the vision of Christ on the cross that sparked his initial conversion, Llull had little interest in salvation history. Meditation on the events of Christ's life, while present, is not a prominent theme.[131]

It is only in the brief aphoristic work *The Book of the Lover and Beloved* that we find a text that is both accessible to the modern reader and closer to the affective language found in many Franciscans. Here Llull explicitly admits to following the example of the Sufis, who "offer words of love and brief *exempla* that inspire a person to great devotion."[132] The singular grace and mysterious charm of many of these aphorisms do rival the love language of the Sufis and constitute a new genre in Christian mystical literature. Here are three examples of Llull's insights into love of God:

> 26. Birds were singing the dawn; the Lover who is the dawn awoke. The birds finished their song; the Lover died in the dawn for the Beloved.

> 235. Love is a sea with violent winds and waves, but without any shore or harbor. The Lover runs great risks at sea, but in this danger his torment dies and his final reward is born.

> 350. The Lover looked at himself as a mirror for seeing his Beloved. He looked at his Beloved as a mirror for knowing himself. So the question arises: which of the two mirrors was closest to his Intellect?[133]

Like Jacopone, Llull emphasizes the pain and suffering that the Beloved visits upon the Lover (e.g., nn. 9, 35, 52, 72, 115, 132, 178, 179, 232, 303, 340). Traditional themes, such as love's disinterest and mutuality are explored (e.g., nn. 62, 118, 160, 190), and there are several aphorisms dealing with the nature of the union attained with the Beloved (nn. 50, 211). Even in this small gem of meditations on love of God, however, it is doubtful that Llull intends to give the will an intrinsically superior position to memory or intellect. Rather, the Augustinian triad always seems to function in an interactive, if sometimes vague, way: "The love between the Lover and the Beloved bound itself up with Memory, Intellect, and Will, so that the Lover and the Beloved would not separate. The cord that bound their love was made of anguish, longing sighs, and weeping."[134]

Franciscan Women Mystics

As pointed out in chapter 1, the example of Clare, the first female follower of Francis, demonstrates the powerful appeal of his witness for women as well as men. During the century after his death, thousands of women joined the communities inspired by Francis and Clare. Doubtless even more shared in the Franciscan way of life by becoming associated with the widespread penitential movement that developed into what came to be called the third order.[135] Most of these women remain anonymous, but a few became famous for their sanctity and hence were the subjects of veneration and candidates for hagiographical *vitae*. Such lives often repeat standard phrases about the prayer life and contemplative prowess of their subjects, but this scarcely allows us to speak of all the early holy women of the Franciscan family as mystics. In several cases, however, the *topoi* pass beyond customary expressions and give us considerable evidence for mystical states of consciousness. In one example, that of Angela of Foligno, we also possess a remarkable mystical text that ranks among the most important of the thirteenth century.[136]

Several of the early women associated with the *pauperes dominae* of Clare left reputations as contemplatives and visionaries.[137] Important noble patrons of the Franciscans, such as Elizabeth of Hungary (1207–1231), and later Isabelle of France (1225–1270), who founded her own order of Franciscan women in 1255, also achieved the status of saints and were described as contemplatives. But it was primarily in the second half of the thirteenth century that a number of Franciscan women, mostly in Italy, gained fame as visionaries and ecstatics. None of these women belonged to the ecclesiastically approved order of the Poor Clares (*pauperes dominae*) or their equivalents. The greater ecclesiastical control these women lived under may have militated against the originality, creativity, and even the excess exhibited by the *sante* who were in closer contact with the world. These "secular" holy women were Franciscans, but in a variety of ways.

Among the earliest of the Franciscan female mystics after Clare is Douceline of Digne in southern France (1214–1274), the younger sister of Hugh of Digne (1205–1255). Hugh, "the great Joachite" (*magnus Joachita*), as his friend the Franciscan chronicler Salimbene called him, was an early leader of those Provençal friars who pushed for a more rigid observance of poverty of life.[138] Douceline was the subject of an important hagiographical piece, *The Life of the Blessed Saint Douceline Mother of the Ladies of Roubaut* (*Li Vida de la benaurada sancta Doucelina mayre de las donnas de Robaut*), written in Provençal by Felipa de Porcelet, a member of her community. The vernacular form of the work and the fact that it was written by a woman are no less remarkable than the content.[139] Born into a pious merchant family, Douceline lost her mother at an early age and then took on the task of helping her father succor the poor. Once, while she was engaged in this work, Jesus appeared to her in the form of a sick man who asked her to touch his breast. She recoiled from this in modesty, but Christ told her: "Daughter, do not be ashamed of me who was not ashamed to show you to the Father."[140] This first appearance of the Divine Bridegroom in the guise of a poor sick person was matched by another encounter toward the end of the *Life*.[141]

Douceline was deeply influenced by her brother in her search for the best form of *estamen*, or religious state of life. She spent time in a community of Franciscan women in Genoa, but was not satisfied with this. While visiting a hospital in Hyères, she had a vision of three women clothed in black habits and white veils who told her that they belonged to "the order that pleases God" and that she should "take this veil and follow us" (cf. Matt. 16:24). Inspired by this, and doubtless with the advice and help of

Hugh, who was probably familiar with beguines from his trips to northern France, Douceline decided to found a convent of beguines. As the *Life* puts it: "The holy mother wished to be called a beguine from love of the Mother of God, who was her model. She said that she [i.e., Mary] had been the first beguine."[142]

Douceline's way of life as a Franciscan beguine was quite similar to that of the northern beguines, especially those living in community. She practiced severe asceticism, but also engaged in care of the sick since the house was not cloistered (see *Life* 6). The community did not have a chapel, so the women attended the neighboring Franciscan church. Douceline was famous for her gift of tears and for her devotion to the passion of Christ and to the Eucharist. Nevertheless, several new notes appear in the *Life* in comparison with the northern beguines. As might be expected, Douceline showed a particular reverence for St. Francis and the life of poverty (see *Life* 5). It has even been suggested that her words of praise for Francis recorded in the *Life* were inspired by the Joachite Franciscan view of Francis's place in the coming crisis of the sixth age of history.[143] Douceline was also active in secular politics, as were many of the Joachite Franciscans. She had close ties to the person and family of Charles of Anjou, the brother of Louis IX and papally appointed king of Sicily.[144]

Like Mary of Oignies, Douceline was a powerful ecstatic whose states of rapture were quite different from those familiar to the monastic tradition. Two lengthy chapters in the *Life* (9–10, ed. 70–150) revel in recounting the stories of the ecstasies that brought her fame and even notoriety as "the example and mirror of contemplation" (*Life* 10.26, ed., 142). As the *Life* puts it:

> Although she was a simple woman without letters, our Savior raised her to the most sublime heights of contemplation. During long periods of time she was continually fixed on the things of heaven; she was so often lifted up to God in high raptures, as though she were present before him, that she seemed to live the life of an angel rather than a woman.[145]

Similar witness can be found in Salimbene's *Chronicle*, which says: "She obtained the special grace from God to be raptured into ecstasy as the friars saw a thousand times in their church; and if they lifted up her arm, she held it so from morning to Vespers because she was totally absorbed in God."[146] Charles of Anjou, with characteristic cruelty, once had this catatonic state tested by having molten lead poured on her feet when she was in ecstasy. We are told that she felt nothing then, but afterward was crippled for a long time by the effects of the test (*Life* 9.16). These "raptures" (*raubiment*) and "ecstasies" (*tirament*) included states of physical levitation,[147] as well as experiences of loud *iubilus* where she sang in often indecipherable words, one time leading her sisters in a procession as she hymned the beauty of the Heavenly Jerusalem.[148] Contemplation of the blood of Christ, source of our redemption, led her to states of mystical inebriation; hearing words about God or St. Francis–even hearing a bird sing or seeing a beautiful flower (*Life* 9.19 and 13.4)–could send her into a completely alienated state, sometimes for as long as three days (see *Life* 13.12). Douceline is a good example of the growing importance of these new forms of ecstasy in the thirteenth century.

Although female followers of Francis spread rapidly throughout Europe, Umbria remained the spiritual center of the Franciscan movement both for men and for women. The example of two notable female saints of the late thirteenth century shows the essential role the area maintained in the history of Franciscan mysticism. Margaret of Cortona (1247–1297) and Angela of Foligno (ca. 1248–1309) each illustrate, in diverse ways, the power of women ecstatics in late medieval Italy.[149]

Douceline of Digne was portrayed as a saint from birth; Margaret of Cortona is a Magdalene-type (*ut nova Magdalena,* as her *vita* says)–a converted sinner whose intense penance and loving devotion to Christ made up for her early sinful life and provide, if not exactly a model to be imitated, at least a source of hope and patronage for sinners.[150] In the *Life* written by her confessor, the friar Giunta of Bevegnati, she is presented as the model for members of the third order. In its conclusion, Christ is depicted as addressing her with the words: "You are the third light granted to the order of my beloved Francis. He was the first light in the order of friars minor; St. Clare was the second in the order of nuns; and you are third in the order of penitents."[151]

As a young girl of sixteen, Margaret fled an unhappy family life to live for nine years as the mistress of a nobleman of Montepulciano. Upon his death, she fled to Cortona with her young son and put herself under the protection of the Franciscans. Abandoning her son to charity (a move not unknown among female converts to the ascetic life),[152] she was allowed to join the "Order of Penance of St. Francis" in 1275. This implied a public role. When she asked Christ to be allowed to remain in her cell in order to enjoy the fuits of contemplation more fully, he responded:

> Margaret, why are you asking to taste my delights constantly? And why don't you desire the trials that prepare one for tasting them first? Why do you ask me to enclose you in a cell? . . . Go to the place of your father Saint Francis so that there you can hear Mass, reverently adore me and see me in the priest's hands. Go! You may not enclose yourself until I wish to hide you.[153]

This is another illustration of the "secularizing" tendency in late medieval mysticism—the insistence on the mystic's presence in the public world, even if she or he wished to remain in the cell of contemplation. For thirteen years Margaret led a life that combined extraordinary ascetical and mystical practices with public service, such as the founding of a hospital for the poor.[154] She also acquired political importance, particularly in her efforts (very Franciscan) to bring peace to turbulant local factions. About 1289 Margaret withdrew from her more active life to live as a recluse in her final years, possibly as a reaction to changes in the relation between the Franciscan *penitentes* and the friars when the bull of Pope Nicholas IV (*Supra montem*) began the regularization process that resulted in definitive status being given to the third order.[155]

As befits her role as a converted sinner, Margaret's *Life* stresses the ongoing paradox of severe asceticism based on her sense of herself as the worst of sinners and the extraordinary mystical graces Christ gave her as the sign that the last shall be first. The perfect imitation of the passion manifested in Francis and richly developed in the Franciscan tradition was the center of her piety and mysticism, which is expressed in detailed accounts of her conversations with Christ and descriptions of her states of rapture. The lengthy chapter 6 of Fra Giunta's account, "On Christ's Passion, Meditation, and Patience," forms the high point of the text. Here Margaret is described as practicing the form of total present identification with the passion presented in texts like the *Meditations on the Life of Christ,* but with an added dimension fitting her public role as chief penitent and patron of the city of Cortona. Fra Giunta (who always managed to be involved in the major moments of Margaret's mystical career) tells how Christ promised Margaret one night that he would allow her to share in a special way the next day in the pain that Mary felt at the crucifixion. After begging Giunta's prayers, she went into ecstasy the next morning at Terce (about 9:00 A.M.) and relived each aspect of the passion up through Christ's death at 3:00 P.M. This was not a private event, however, but a form of public theater. Doubtless alerted by the Franciscans, the citizens of Cortona gathered to witness the living presentation of the events of salvation enacted in Margaret's body:

> Such a new and moving a spectacle so moved the citizens of Cortona, men and women, that they left everything they were doing—their jobs and even the children and sick they were caring for—to fill our church . . . time and time again that day with their tears and weeping. There they saw Margaret, not alongside the cross, but as if she were on the cross, tortured by severe sufferings. . . . In the terrible excess of suffering she ground her teeth, writhed like a

worm or a twisted wreath, grew as pale as ash, lost her pulse and speech, grew totally cold. Her throat grew so hoarse she could hardly be understood when she came to her senses.[156]

Mystical ecstasy became public in a new way in the thirteenth century.

Though the language of Bride and Bridegroom appears in the *Life,* Kurt Ruh is correct in claiming that there is no traditional erotic mysticism involved.[157] Margaret rather rejoices in being called daughter (*filia*) when cleansed of her sins through general confession (*Life* 2.23). Her immediacy to God centers in her ability to be one with Christ in his passion as "his martyr," with only marginal use of the language of contemplation and union. A summation of this passion-dominated mysticism occurs in the sixth chapter, when Margaret, in the manner of many thirteenth-century mystics, is first praised for her role as Christ's plant, "his daughter, sister, and accomplice" (*filia mea, soror et socia*), who waters the dry plants of other Christians, and then is accorded a vision of Christ on the cross that brings her to heaven:

> Then Christ showed himself to her as though crucified, saying, "Put your palms upon the places of the nails of my hands." When Margaret out of reverence said, "O no, my Lord!", immediately the wound in the side of the loving Jesus opened and in that opening she beheld her Savior's heart. In this ecstasy she embraced the Crucified Lord and was raised up by him into heaven. She heard him telling her, "Daughter, from these wounds you absorb what preachers seek to express."[158]

Margaret is presented here as the *magistra* of a vernacular theology directed to the lay *penitentes* distinct from the scholastic and monastic models.

In the cases of Douceline and Margaret we are dealing with hagiographical accounts, one written by a woman, the other by a man. In both texts learned theology (remember that Felipa's *Life of Douceline* was based on Bonaventure's *Life of Francis*) is used but transformed in the service of new forms of vernacular mystical presentation. This interaction is more evident and more complex in the case of Angela of Foligno, whose *Book* rightly stands as the premier text of all Franciscan women mystics, a judgment confirmed not only by recent scholarship, but also by the role that the work played in later mystical tradition. Douceline was forgotten; Margaret became the object of a local cult; but the controversial Angela was widely read, especially in sixteenth-century Spain, seventeenth-century France, as well as in the modern era.[159]

I like to describe Angela as one of the four "female evangelists" of thirteenth-century mysticism.[160] I use the term "evangelist" in a perhaps provocative way, not only to underline the stature of these four women

(Angela, Hadewijch, Mechthild, and Marguerite Porete) as the most important female mystics of the thirteenth century,[161] but also to emphasize the
bold, quasi-scriptural claims they made for their writings. In order to authenticate their teaching about the path to God each of these women had to
"invent" a form of divine authorization of literally evangelical weight, that is,
they had to claim that their message came directly from God in a manner
analogous to that of the Bible itself. Though they did so in distinctive ways,
there are interesting analogies and some overlaps in the situations they faced
as women teachers, as well as in the strategies they employed in working out
their claims. Such invention of authority was not totally unprecedented.
Hildegard of Bingen had used similar tactics in the twelfth century,[162] but
both the content of her theology and the import of her claims were somewhat different from the four female evangelists of the thirteenth century.
Other thirteenth- and fourteenth-century women also had to wrestle with the
issue of authority, as we shall see in the chapters that follow. Likewise, male
mystics who were not clerics, like Richard Rolle, had to "invent" authority
for themselves, as Nicholas Watson has shown.[163] But the nonclerical men
seem to have been content to aspire to the authority enjoyed by the great
male mystics of the past, such as Bernard of Clairvaux. The women had to
dare more in order to get a hearing. Among these four female evangelists,
Angela stands out in a number of ways, not only because of her specifically
Franciscan identity but also because she was the only one of the four who
was largely untouched by the language of courtly love.

One day in 1291 a commotion erupted at the entrance of the great basilica at Assisi dedicated to St. Francis. A middle-aged Italian woman who
had come there on pilgrimage began screaming and shouting. A friar who
was both her confessor and a relative, ashamed at the spectacle, told her
and those with her they should never dare to come to Assisi again. A short
time later, however, when he returned to his friary in their native town of
Foligno not far from Assisi, he asked the woman to explain the reason for
her actions. As she began to tell him the story of her interior spiritual journey, he felt impelled to write it down, transcribing from her native Umbrian
dictation into Latin and later polishing it up after extended consulation with
her.[164] This is the account of its origin given us in the text of *The Book of
Blessed Angela,* one of the treasures of medieval mysticism and also one of the
best, if most perplexing, examples of the collaboration between an ecstatic
woman and a learned cleric in the production of a mystical text.

The paucity of external references to Angela (though she is mentioned by
Ubertino, as noted above), as well as the complexities of the text itself, have
led to different evaluations of the historicity of Angela and her mystical itin-

erary. Most accounts of medieval mysticism have taken the presentation of *The Book* too much at face value and have not given sufficient attention to the problems inherent in the text for recovering the "historical" Angela. On the opposite side, one recent interpretation goes so far as to claim that it is doubtful that a historical "Angela" ever existed and that we should conceive of *The Book* as a "mystic tale" in which Franciscan Spirituals presented their view of the ideal lover of God.[165] Between these extremes, there is room for a middle ground which attempts to discover Angela's history and to sort out, as far as possible, the contribution of this female visionary and the often apologetic, but still learned, clerical scribe in the production of Angela's *Book*. The best avenue of approach to the text is to recognize the fact that the main "author," Angela, and Brother A. (whoever he may have been), the "co-protagonist" of her communications from God, were both struggling, though in different ways, with the impossible but necessary task of finding words to express the "Unknown Nothing" (*nihil incognitum*) she had encountered. Therefore, we should not wonder that trying to sort out the exact contribution of each to the text has proven to be a fascinating but perhaps inconclusive task.[166]

Angela was born about 1248 in relatively affluent circumstances. She was married with children—a sinner in her eyes, but certainly not a scandal—when she experienced a conversion about 1285, partly aided by a dream in which St. Francis appeared to her (*Memorial* 1; ed., 132). She began to lead a life devoted to deeper perfection, not easy given her circumstances. About 1288 this became easier when her entire family died.[167] With one holy serving woman, Masazuola, as her companion, she began to divest herself of her possessions and to live as a penitent, eventually being accepted into the Franciscan third order probably in 1291. Brother A. appears to have begun writing the *Memorial*, the narrative of her inner journey, in 1292 when she had completed twenty stages (*passus*, or *mutationes*) of her itinerary to God. The first nineteen stages are succinctly described in the first chapter. Brother A. remained with her until 1296 while she completed the higher and more difficult final ten stages, but since it proved impossible for him to understand these fully, he condensed them into seven "supplementary stages" whose description takes up the larger portion of the *Memorial*.[168] In 1298 the text was submitted to Cardinal James of Colonna and eight Franciscans, who gave it their approval.[169] It seems that Brother A. revised it shortly thereafter (1299–1300). The final version of the *Book* appends a series of thirty-six *Instructions* to the *Memorial*. These reflect Angela's teaching between 1296 and her death in early 1309, a period in which she served as the teacher (*magistra*) for a group of laity and Franciscans who gathered around her. Many of these teachings are more conventional in tone and have differences in vocabulary and emphasis from the *Memorial*. This may be the result of redactions by several hands. Nevertheless, the *Instructions* appear to reflect the mystic's teaching, though perhaps at some remove.

A mystical itinerary of thirty stages is unusual (it is possible that the number was suggested to her by John Climacus's *Ladder of Perfection,* which had recently been translated into Latin and then into Italian by Franciscan Spirituals). Even Brother A. was confused, as we have seen. The *Instructions* speak of a threefold transformation that God works in the soul and this structure may be helpful for getting a handle on the more complicated thirty stages of the *Memorial:*

> The first transformation is when the soul attempts to imitate the works of the suffering God-man because in them God's will is and was manifested. The second transformation is when the soul is united to God and has great feelings and great delights from God which still can be conceived or expressed in words. The third transformation is when the soul is transformed within God and God within the soul by a most perfect union. It feels and tastes the highest matters of God to such an extent that they cannot be conceived or expressed in words.[170]

This suggests a pattern somewhat different from the three stages of purification, illumination, and perfection, but one still roughly amenable to that traditional distinction.

In good Franciscan fashion, Angela's path to perfection begins with emphasis on the imitation of Christ on the cross. The first sixteen stages of the itinerary laid out in chapter 1 of the *Memorial* are primarily purgative, though with growing experiences of illuminative contact with Christ. A dominant note in these early stages is that of poverty, the traditional Franciscan imperative to "go naked to the cross."[171] Steps 17 through 19 of the first series, as well as the first six of the supplementary stages, are experiences of union, though forms of uniting with God that Angela feels are still capable of being expressed, however inadequately. The seventh supplementary stage is a union beyond expression, where the Franciscan tertiary joins company with a number of the other daring mystics of her time, both men and women. While it may be artificial to try to contain the originality and concreteness of Angela's narrative in any single set of categories, the fact that the *Instructions* attempted to simplify her complex itinerary shows that this process began in her own lifetime.

It will not be possible here to survey each of these stages in detail. Indeed, in the case of the first nineteen completed by the time Brother A. met Angela in 1291 we can be relatively brief, because the purgative "mutations" are given little attention in comparison with what comes later.[172] Beginning with stage 17, descriptions of more intense forms of contact with God proliferate, such as a revelation about the depth of meaning of a passage in Paul (#17, ed., 150), a screaming *iubilus* (#18; ed., 152), and the illumination in which she experienced both the humanity and the divinity of Christ (#19; ed., 152-54). According to Brother A., Angela was at step 20 when she had the disconcerting Assisi rapture that first brought her to his attention.

The description of the supplementary stages constitutes one of the richest accounts of mystical union presented in autohagiographical form in Christian history. We sense throughout that both Angela and Brother A. were working in constant collaboration to present an original teaching about the divine–human encounter based on the Franciscan penitent's inner life.[173] It will not be possible to describe all these experiences in equal detail, but it will be helpful to give a brief analysis, especially of the higher stages, along with some reflections on the themes they present.

There is much within all the "mutations," even the culminating ones, that is typical of the other Franciscan mystics. For example, Francis continues to play a major role, from Angela's initial conversion down to the end of the itinerary, where he appears as a patron for the final stages begun in 1291.[174] (Later on, in Instruction 21, we find the Poverello addressing Angela with the remarkable statement: "You are the only one born of me.")[175] Concentration on the passion as the central mystery providing access to God is also dominant in Angela's thought. Although the fact that the passion is only explicitly mentioned with regard to the first transformation of the *Instructions* might suggest a journey in which the Crucified Jesus is left behind, further consideration shows that this is definitely not the case. Each of the three transformations, including the final indescribable union, expresses a deepening relation to the passion, as we will see. Angela is also typical of most Franciscans, as well as other thirteenth-century mystical women, in the importance that the Eucharist has in her path to God, as well as in her devotion to the Blessed Virgin.[176] At least three important themes, however, serve to set Angela off from the other Franciscan ecstatics investigated above: her understanding of the role of the Trinity; her appeal to negative theology; and her description of the soul and God as mutual abysses.

The 1291 experience at Assisi marked Angela's entry into the first of the supplementary stages (#20). This involved a manifestation of the Holy Spirit that took place on the road to Assisi in which the Spirit (in the manner of Francis) addressed her as bride: "My daughter and sweet bride . . . I love you more than any other woman in the valley of Spoleto."[177] In somewhat confusing fashion (subsequently explained by a discussion of how the whole Trinity must come into the soul if one Person is there), Angela then heard Christ within her relating the story of his passion. This continuing divine presence made her intensely conscious of her own sinfulness while it also gave her immense joy. The experience reached its culmination when she saw St. Francis portrayed as being embraced by Christ in a stained-glass window in the basilica at Assisi and heard the words: "Thus I will hold you close—much more than can be seen with human eyes. Now the hour has come, sweet daughter, my temple, my beloved, to fulfill what I said to you."[178] It was at the moment when the vision (which Angela can only describe as "an immense majesty . . . which was the All Good" [*omne bonum*]) withdrew that she began to cry out: "Love still unknown, why do you leave me? . . . Love still unknown, Why? Why? Why?"[179]

Upon her return to Foligno she experienced eight days of such indescribable delight in the Lord that she longed for death. During this time she was betrothed to God (it is difficult to say whether this is to Christ or to the Holy Spirit), and her companion saw light radiating from her as she rested on her bed in an ecstatic state. This stage contains two further notices typical of Angela's mystical itinerary, though it is not clear that these events all happened at this time. The first is a vision of Christ on the cross in which he shows her his throat, which is described as of such beauty that she knows it must be divine (a rare reference to the Song of Songs, in this case 5:16). The mention of the beauty of Christ's body led Brother A. to question her about her visions of Christ in the Host and so step 20 closes with an account of a variety of such visions, typical of so many thirteenth-century women mystics.

The second supplementary stage (#21; ed., 200–228) includes further signs of God's loving presence within her soul and closes with more Eucharistic experiences. The third step (#22; ed., 230–54), basically a meditation on the status of "legitimate sons" (i.e., those willing to share in Christ's sufferings), contains one of her disconcerting but typical expressions of identification with the abject Christ.[180] Angela and her servant go to the hospital on Maundy Thursday to wait on the poor, especially the lepers, where, as a gesture of extreme asceticism, they both drink from the water in which they had washed the decomposing limbs of a leper. "We tasted such sweetness," she says, "that the whole way home we went in a sweetness as great as if we had received Communion."[181]

The fourth supplementary step, which lasted from August 1292 through the summer of 1293, is described in chapter 6 (#23; ed., 256–86) and contains three unusual visions. The first takes place during Mass when God reveals his power to her in such a way that she cries out, "The world is pregnant with God!" (ed., 262.65). The second is a total immersion in Christ, "more than I had ever had or experienced that I could recall," which significantly takes place when she receives the Eucharist (ed., 272). In the third vision, which happened as she was gazing at a crucifix, she felt Christ within her embracing her with the arm with which he was crucified. This gave her a certainty about the truth of her manifestations and an abiding joy in Christ's passion–"All my joy is now in this suffering God-man."[182] The passion motif continues in the fifth supplementary step (#24 in chap. 7; ed., 288–334). Here Angela is given ever deeper realizations of the sufferings of Christ, in his soul as well as in his body, to the point that on Holy Saturday of 1294 she found herself in ecstasy (*in excessu mentis*) with Christ in the tomb. She kissed his mouth and placed her cheek on his. The text continues: "Christ placed his hand upon her other cheek and drew her to him, and Christ's faithful one heard him say these words to her: 'Before I lay in the tomb, I held you this tightly.' ... And she was in an undescribable state of the greatest joy."[183] After a number of other visions of Divine Love (including one that lasted for three whole days), this step closes with an analysis of seven modes of increasing intensity by which God enters into the soul, the highest of which is the reception of Christ as pilgrim (ed., 312–24). These modes may be considered a form of summary of the whole thirty stages.

The sixth and seventh supplementary stages are the most complex. First of all, Angela insists that they take place at least in part simultaneously, a fact not easy to understand because these stages represent such differing forms of consciousness. A second difficulty is that the seventh stage marks the transformation to a realm that cannot be conceived of or expressed in words and therefore can only be suggested by a variety of strategies of an original form of apophatic mysticism that transgresses the ordinary bounds of language.[184] The sixth step (#25 in chap. 8; ed., 336–52) is Angela's version of what was later called by John of the Cross the "Dark Night of the Soul." Afflicted by horrible torments and demonic temptations in body and in soul, Angela feels like "a person blindfolded with his hands bound behind him and hung by the neck from a rope, yet remaining alive on the gallows, without aid or any kind of support or rescue."[185] In this state, in which she felt all her old vices revive, Angela raged against herself, beating and punishing her body, and calling out to Christ, "My Son, my Son, do not abandon me" (ed., 340.54; cf. Matt. 27:46). This form of sharing in the abandonment of Christ on the cross (as suggested by the scriptural citation) was to have a considerable future in the history of Christian mysticism.

The sixth stage lasted for more than two years (ca. 1294–96) and was accompanied by the beginnings of the seventh stage, which was to perdure beyond it (#26 in chap. 9; ed., 354–400). This level was one of an indescribable encounter with God, the All Good, "in and with darkness" (*in et cum tenebra*), Angela's innovative expression of apophatic mysticism.[186] Brother A. says that Angela had been elevated to this highest state only three times, a position where she goes beyond love (*et effecta sum non amor* [354.10]) and where "she sees nothing and sees everything altogether" (*et nihil videt, et videt omnia omnino* [356.35]). She is portrayed as being more powerfully drawn into this state than any of her former ecstasies. Here she seems to be standing in the midst of the Trinity, which is what she sees "in the darkness."[187] She remembers no form, not even that of the God-man, but she hears the words, "You are I and I am you" (*Tu es ego et ego sum tu* [362.92–93]).[188] Angela distinguished this infrequent state of darkness from the almost constant state of feeling security in the God-man, which latter experience she also claimed involved no "medium between me and him" (*nihil erat medium inter me et ipsum* [362.101–2]).

The dense and often obscure descriptions of stages 6 and 7 with their formless elevations into the Trinity have similarities to what we find in Angela's contemporary, Marguerite Porete, and also to passages in Meister Eckhart. Like the German Dominican, Angela says that to make even such limited statements seems like speaking blasphemy (e.g., 360.84–85, 380.301–2, 384.345, 388.403–4). Nevertheless, because "the elevations with which she was lifted up sometimes were joined together" (366.132–33), during this period Angela continues to use language of identification with the suffering Christ, such as being with him on the bed of the cross.

Finally, in a carefully elaborated series of further mystical experiences (ed., 378–92), the *Memorial* returns to descriptions of the most profound immersions in the Trinity, and, for the first time begins to invoke the language of the abyss to describe the relation between God and the soul. "I understand that no angel and no creature has the capacity to comprehend these divine works and that deepest abyss."[189] Like other thirteenth-century female mystics, such as Hadewijch and Marguerite Porete (see chapter 5 below), Angela can also describe the soul as an abyss. At this point she even claims that she "is drawn out (*extracta*) of everything she had previously experienced," so that she "finds nothing in the cross in which she used to delight so much" (ed., 380.303–14). From one aspect, then, the seventh stage surpasses everything created, including the humanity of Christ and the cross, though this "surpassing" is not a permanent state. In this deepest state God "produces in the soul many divine operations with much greater grace and with so profound and ineffable an abyss that the presence of God alone, without any other gifts, is the good that the saints enjoy in heaven."[190] Because of the deep identity of indistinction between God and the soul, the latter, like God, is described as being incomprehensible: "And my soul was then unable to comprehend itself, and so if the soul, although it be created and finite and circumscribed, cannot understand itself, how much less can it comprehend the immense and infinite Creator God?"[191] In attempting to find ways to characterize this unimaginable depth within the soul, it is interesting to see Angela employing language similar to Meister Eckhart's "little castle" or "little spark" to characterize the divine ground within the soul. In Angela's words, there is a "chamber" (*camera*) within the soul where the All Good alone resides—"though I blaspheme by speaking about it."[192]

The various forms of deep, mediationless union with God described in the seventh stage—both the relatively rare union "in and with darkness," as well as the more common (almost constant; *millies mille vicibus;* ed., 392.439) union in which she sees "the One who is and how he is the being of all creatures" (ed., 390.410–11)—are passive states into which God alone draws the soul. Although this long chapter in Angela's *Book* contains some of the strongest expressions of *unio mystica* in the history of Christian mysticism,[193] Angela and her co-author are anxious to show the conformity between her states and traditional aspects of Christian life and devotion. For example, she encounters St. Francis in her ecstasies (ed., 374–76). Also, while the seventh stage at times involves the experience of being "extracted" even from Christ's humanity and passion, the more constant form of union has her soul "transformed into the passion of Christ" (ed., 370.189–91). The transports and the messages she receives in these states are still often connected with the Eucharist (e.g., ed., 372–78 and 396–98). Furthermore, the Bible remains the guide to truth for her. Like other women mystics, Angela cannot act as a biblical interpreter, but in her states of union she is given to understand how the scriptures were written and how there are no real contradictions in them (ed., 386).

Angela's essential orthodoxy, despite the almost unprecedented daring of so many aspects of her mystical itinerary, is also highlighted in the *Instructions*. Furthermore, the relation between the two parts of *The Book of Blessed Angela*, that is, the *Memorial* and the *Instructions*, reveals the secret of her claim to authority. The *Memorial*, as already pointed out, is one of the first and certainly the longest and most complex of the autohagiographies of the later Middle Ages. If the original four Gospels presented the story of Jesus and his teaching in order to convey the "good news" of salvation, then the mystical journey of Angela as recounted in the *Memorial* was intended to portray how a woman might become another Christ through identity with the suffering Savior and eventual absorption into the Trinity. The *Instructions* show how the truth of this transformation was accepted by a circle of devout followers, lay and clerical, for whom Angela served as *mater et magistra,* both "mother and teacher."

Angela had become a spiritual teacher whose message was identical with that of Christ. To belong to her circle was to be one with Jesus. In Instruction 23, for example, the Lord tells her: "All those who are lovers and followers of my poverty, suffering, and contempt are my legitimate sons; and these are likewise your sons, and no others." And in Instruction 26 God blesses Brother A. and says to Angela, "You will have sons, and all of them will receive this blessing, for all my sons are yours, and yours, mine."[194] The picture presented in the *Instructions* is the remarkable one of something like a new Jerusalem community, centered not on the apostles, as in the New Testament book of Acts, but on a female teacher who conveys God's saving word.

The more didactic texts found in the *Instructions* contain much that reflects the teaching found in the *Memorial,* especially in relation to identification with the suffering Christ (see, e.g., Instructions 3, 5, 15, 18, 23, 24, 28, 30, 34). An important new note, however, is Angela's opposition to "those who say they are of the spirit of freedom," a point where she joins with Ubertino of Casale and others in denouncing the claim that a mystic can reach a state where nothing is sinful and no ongoing penance is needed.[195] The language of transformation, rarely used in the *Memorial,* appears frequently in the *Instructions,* becoming the major theme in some texts (e.g., 2, 7, 27, 28, 34). Another new note is the growing emphasis on God as "Uncreated Love" (*amor increatus;* see, e.g., Instructions 2, 14, 18, 22, 30), as well as discussions, similar to those found in more traditional mystics, of the relation between love and knowledge in the path to divinization (see, e.g., Instruction 34).

The *Instructions* do not employ the language of darkness that appeared in the seventh supplemental step, but this does not mean that Angela's teaching became any less apophatic. Speaking of God as an abyss becomes more frequent and more powerful. Like Ubertino and Jacopone, Angela uses "abyss" in verbal forms, as in the vision where she sees her followers swallowed up "as if God had totally transubstantiated and 'abyssated' (*inabyssare*) them into himself."[196] Instruction 32 contains a Dionysian analysis of experiencing God more from what cannot be comprehended than from what can be grasped by the human mind (ed., 664). Finally, the account of

Angela's last days, as she lies on her deathbed "absorbed more than usual in the abyss of divine infinity" (Instruction 36; ed., 726.32) has her cry out shortly before the end again and again–"O Unknown Nothingness! O Unknown Nothingness!" (*o nihil incognitum;* ed., 734.124–32).

Angela of Foligno's sense of the overwhelming mystery of God accompanied her to the end. Such emphasis on divine darkness and the way of negation, however, must be balanced with the equally overwhelming message of God's love. As God told her in *Instruction* 23: "My love for you has not been a hoax" (*Ego te non amavi per truffam;* ed., 612.13).

Conclusion

At the conclusion of these two chapters devoted to Franciscans of the first century after Francis it may be worthwhile to raise the question of the character of Franciscan mysticism in general. We should be careful to distinguish between some abstract description of Franciscan mysticism and the mysticism practiced and written about by actual Franciscans. As we have noted, some followers of Francis, like David of Augsburg, really do not manifest the complex of themes typically associated with most Franciscan mystics, such as devotion to Francis the stigmatic, a special role for poverty, and concentration on concrete imitation of the passion. Perhaps any attempt to describe a uniform system of spirituality and mysticism characteristic of most Franciscans is illusory, but if we follow the history of the men and women who have been considered in these chapters, we can, I believe, discern a set of variations on some common themes. While these themes were by no means restricted to the Franciscan order in the later Middle Ages–Francis himself soon became a figure of veneration for all Christians–it is this rich play of variations that constitutes the real contribution of the Franciscan family to the new mysticism of the later Middle Ages.

I would suggest that the survey given here discloses two tendencies that developed and interacted among Franciscans in the first century of the movement. The first of these may be described as a new theology of mysticism which attempted to reinterpret traditional Western mystagogical teaching in the light of Francis as the ultimate manifestation of the crucified Jesus and the most secure mode of access to God. This new model, which involved a strong emphasis on meditation on the mysteries of Christ's life and the *imitatio Christi,* one in which *affectus* or fiery love also took on a special role, was created by Bonaventure. It was made possible, at least in part, by the writings of Thomas Gallus. The immense reputation of the Seraphic Doctor gave this view of the mystical journey considerable importance for centuries, both inside and outside the Franciscan movement. The second trajectory among the Franciscan mystics of the century following the saint's death was that of the excessive states of rapture that were also common to many non-Franciscan mystics, especially women. Francis himself had said nothing about ecstasy in his own writings, but "the new and unheard of miracle" of his stigmata, as well as the reports of his companions and hagiographers about his visions, made Francis into the ecstatic *par excellence.* Later Franciscans, men like Giles of Assisi, John of Alverna, and Roger of Provence, and women such as Douceline, Margaret, and especially Angela of Foligno, achieved fame for manifesting the new forms of ecstasy that distinguish later medieval mysticism from the monastic conceptions of the brevity and rarity of *excessus mentis.*

Mulieres Religiosae: Experiments in Female Mysticism

Dicit ei Jesus: Mulier, quid ploras, quem quaeris? (John 20:15)

Jesus said to her: "Woman, why are you weeping; whom do you seek?"[1]

THESE WORDS ADDRESSED BY JESUS to Mary Magdalene are a fitting introduction to the lives of the women mystics of the thirteenth and fourteenth centuries.[2] For centuries Christian women had imitated Mary Magdalene in devoting themselves to the austerities and penitential tears of the religious life. Like the Magdalene, who had much forgiven her because she loved much (Luke 7:47), such women were not content merely to weep. They also sought for Jesus with an intensity of love that often must have achieved intimate contact with the Divine Bridegroom. Unfortunately, little direct testimony, especially from the women themselves, gives us access to this chapter in the history of Christian mysticism. From 1200 on, however, there is a growing body of literature concerning women who imitated the Magdalene not only in penitential weeping, but also in seeking out and attaining loving union with Christ.[3]

The reasons for the dramatic change in the place of women in the new mysticism that began in the thirteenth century continue to puzzle historians. Certainly, greater access to education and literacy for women, especially women of the upper and middle classes, was a necessary factor behind the upsurge of writing by and about women. Even more significant was the role that women took in the new forms of the *vita apostolica,* as suggested in chapter 1. The result was that the religious opportunities open to women greatly increased during the course of the first half of the thirteenth century. This is true not only in the case of the new female orders that followed ecclesiastically approved rules, such as the Premonstratensians, Cistercians, Carthusians, Franciscans, and Dominicans, but also for the many varieties of *mulieres religiosae,* the blanket term used by contemporaries to cover the less structured forms of devout life for women. Another factor in the growth of this religious "women's movement" was the way in which ecclesiastical officials employed miracle-working women ecstatics as useful counters to the role of women in contemporary heretical movements, especially among the Cathars.[4] Nevertheless, the suddenness and the intensity with which so many women all over Europe began to follow the Magdalene's path of mystical devotion to Jesus remain surprising and mystifying.

The following three chapters will investigate the major female mystics of the thirteenth and the first half of the fourteenth centuries, both those we know about primarily through hagiographical accounts and those who recounted their loving pursuit of God in their own words.[5] Naturally, it will not be possible to treat of every woman mystic here,[6] though I have tried to discuss all those who composed their own mystical texts. As noted in the introduction, I shall avoid any attempt to discover a general form of mysticism common to all women, especially as contrasted to that found in contemporary male mystics. This is not to overlook the fact that there are significant differences between male and female mystics that need to be addressed, but the further one investigates the full range of evidence, the more difficult it becomes to make generalizations.

It is important to remember at the outset that women mystics had to face problems and issues that most male mystics did not. Foremost among these was the issue of what authority the mystic claimed for her writings, as mentioned above in considering Angela of Foligno (pp. 149–50 above). The teachings and life stories of the mystics who are available to the historical record, both men and women, all imply some claim to authority, usually involving the possession of special graces and the call to present a message about attaining God. Within the institutional structure of medieval Christianity it was relatively easy for most male mystics, because of their theological education and clerical status, to make such claims or to have such made about them. Although male authors who did not enjoy the advantages conveyed by sacramental orders and theological degrees also had to struggle to attain recognition, the difficulties were far greater for women.

The misogynistic biases of medieval society and the medieval church are too well known to need discussion here. These prejudices did not prevent some women, at least, from enjoying positions of relative power in medieval Christianity, as we can see in cases like those of the abbesses of monasteries and the noble patronesses of religious houses. But such roles were carefully circumscribed. While they included the possibility of women being put forward as models of sanctity, such presentations traditionally had to adhere to prescribed models. These models did not usually include a case for women functioning as teachers of contemplative wisdom or mystical theology, although both the Blessed Virgin Mary and Mary Magdalene (the *apostola apostolorum,* or "Apostle of the Apostles," as she was sometimes called) were exceptions. In the thirteenth century, however, not only do hagiographical accounts begin to portray women as mystical models in ways not found in the previous tradition (as we have already seen with Mary of Oignies), but women also start taking on the role of mystical teacher, as we have observed in the examples of Clare of Assisi and Angela of Foligno. In order to vindicate their claims to teaching authority, late medieval female mystics had to create new models and to construct new theological categories. An examination of how they did this will be an important part of this and the following chapters.

Among the most common of the strategies employed by the hagiographers (mostly male) and the female mystical writers was the appeal to visionary revelation, as already discussed in the introduction (pp. 24–30). Augustine of Hippo laid the foundations for the theological evaluation of visions by dividing the showings produced by special divine action into three ascending forms based on their relation to materiality: corporeal visions; spiritual visions (i.e., images given interiorly to the soul); and intellectual visions, which constitute an immediate grasp of infallible divine truths.[7] Many of the visions found in late medieval mystical texts, especially by women, tend to collapse the Augustinian hierarchy, not only by merging the spiritual and intellectual visions so that inner images become the immediate source of new insights into divine truths, but also in ways that meld all three modes of vision into direct forms of "total" conscious experience of God realized as much in and through the body as in a purely spiritual way.[8]

Teaching about the spiritual senses, that is, as Origen put it, "a sensuality that has nothing sensual about it," enjoyed an important role in the history of Christian mysticism prior to the thirteenth century.[9] This doctrine, primarily created to deal with the exegetical problem of how to understand the sensuous and anthropomorphic language of the Bible, most especially the Song of Songs, was founded on a distinction between the inner "real" or spiritual person and the outer material body that is an analogue to the distinction between the letter of the biblical text and its internal, or "mystical," meaning. The distinction was often expressed almost in terms of opposition, though recognition of the interrelationships between the two aspects of the human personality (and the meaning of the Bible) was always theoretically present. With mystics like Bernard of Clairvaux, however, who stressed the necessity for full human experience, both carnal and spiritual, in the path to union with God, the sensual language of the Song begins to be used more as the referent for what eventually appears as a single "set" of senses, a sensorium, or general activity of sensation, which was to be progressively spiritualized in the mystical life.[10]

This process was further developed in the descriptions of mystical consciousness, both visual and nonvisual, found in many medieval women mystics (and some men too) after 1200. In these mystics the original biblical referent of the sensual language tends to vanish, and the distinction between the inner and the outer senses often disappears. These authors describe their encounter with God in a concrete and intensely "sensual" way without any appeal to the traditional caveat that the soul "must transform passion into passionlessness," as Gregory of Nyssa once put it in analyzing the role of the spiritual senses.[11] This is most evident, of course, in the startlingly direct use of sexual images and language in many descriptions of nuptial union between Christ, the Divine Lover, and the human soul, female both in linguistic gender and very often in concrete sexuality. The modes of representation of erotic union with God are no longer concerned with signaling the allegorical transformation of sexual terminology, as was the case in monastic mysticism, but rather seek to show that passion *is* passion and passionate union with Christ is its highest form.[12] Whether this represents a shift in the actual consciousness of immediate contact with God, or whether it is to be seen as a new mode of the literary presentation of such encounters, is difficult to determine. Still, the fact that such embodied accounts of attaining God become widespread in the thirteenth-century West, especially among women, is of real significance.[13]

Embodied experience of God, both visionary and nonvisionary, is connected to another aspect of late medieval mysticism characteristic of many women—the "excessive" character of their ascetical practice and loving devotion. In recounting Mary of Oignies' youthful penances, as we have noted (pp. 40–41 above), even James of Vitry admitted, "I am not telling this to commend her excess, but to show her fervor."[14] Similar language appears in many of the accounts of the *mulieres religiosae*.[15] Excess in asceticism was, of course, not unknown among the early desert monastics, and the notion of "the insanity of love" (*insania amoris*) had been explored by Richard of St. Victor in his treatise *The Four Degrees of Violent Charity*.[16] It was the combination of extraordinary penitential practices and what the mystics themselves often spoke of as love's excess, insanity, madness, and folly that was distinctive to the new mystical trends of the era, especially as found among women. Without ever explicitly saying so, many late medieval mystics seem to have abandoned the notion of the *ordo caritatis,* the restoration of the proper harmony between love of God and all other loves,[17] in favor of what might be described as a new form of *epektasis,* that is, an infinite and "insane" pursuit of God, one based on an overpowering love that is subject to no law but itself and able to find no term but its own annihilation.

Madness, infinite longing, annihilation–these are among the motifs that meet us constantly in the women mystics of the thirteenth and fourteenth centuries. If mystical consciousness can be said to take on a totalizing and somatic character in many of the mystical texts of this period, we can also say that the mystical subject or self begins to be portrayed as less limited, less bound to its created nature than hitherto. The madness of love functions, in part, to break down the ordinary boundaries of consciousness and selfhood. Infinite longing reveals that the soul or self is in some mysterious way itself infinite, so that the annihilation of the created will leaves nothing present but God, or rather, the "No-thing" or "No-self" that is the most adequate way to point toward the true God who lies beyond the God of limited human thoughts and aspirations.

New forms of apophatic language that express the mutual infinity of God and the self were pioneered by women mystics. These expressions move beyond the usual accounts of the necessity for eradicating the fallen and sinful will to emphasize that what keeps us from full union with God is the very *created will* itself. Hence, many of the thirteenth-century women seem to find the traditional understanding of *unio mystica,* that of a loving union of spirits, finite and infinite, inadequate to describe the kind of union they wish to attain–an indistinct identity with God in the No-self. As Barbara Newman has recently pointed out, this dissolution of the limits of the created self also led some women to challenge anew what theologians like Origen and Eriugena had also queried–the possibility that the God who is infinite love could condemn someone to hell eternally.[18]

In the case of each of these five aspects of the new mysticism–the problem of authority, the role of visions, totalizing embodied consciousness, excess, and annihilating indistinction–we find evidence for the creative, even initiatory, role of women. We do not, however, discern themes that can be restricted *only* to women.

Attempting to classify the women mystics of the period ca. 1200–1350 is difficult and will always be a bit artificial. A strictly chronological approach would tell us little about the common interests that often existed among the

women. Here I will present the thirteenth- and early-fourteenth-century
female mystics primarily according to the form of religious life they
adopted, beginning with the beguines and other *mulieres religiosae,* who lived
an independent and less-structured mode of religious life (chaps. 4–5), and
moving on to consider the women who lived according to the rule of a recognized order (chap. 6). Nevertheless, an investigation of the scores of mystical women of this century and a half shows that their form of religious
identification was often malleable. Many began as beguines, but subsequently entered established religious houses. Women who lived a cloistered
life in a religious order (*religio*) were often in contact with "religious
women" (*mulieres religiosae*) living in the world and shared their forms of
mystical devotion. In such a rich and protean world, the analysis of individual figures and their interconnections is more significant than attempts to
create artificial divisions, even those based on the forms of religious life that
shaped the spirituality of many of these women.

Because of these interconnections, this chapter will begin with a consideration of a group of women who belonged both to the ranks of the *mulieres
religiosae* and to an established order, the Cistercians. Between ca. 1200 and
ca. 1250 a remarkable flowering of female mystics occurred in Lotharingia,
primarily in the area of present-day Belgium. Because of their personal connections and the limited geographical area of their influence, it seems best
to treat them as a group. The second part of the chapter studies some later
beguine mystics from Germany, as well as one "beguin," that is, a radical
adherent of the Spiritual Franciscans, from southern France. The concluding part of the chapter will treat the mystical literature and mystical saints
found among thirteenth-century ancoresses or *reclusae.* The next chapter
will deal with the three main beguine authors of the thirteenth century–
Hadewijch, Mechthild of Magdeburg, and Marguerite Porete. Finally, chapter 6 will concentrate on the late-thirteenth- and early-fourteenth-century
women mystics who lived as members of ecclesiastically approved orders
following the Benedictine, Cistercian, Carthusian, Premonstratensian, and
Dominican forms of life.

The *Mulieres Religiosae* of Lotharingia

In chapter 1 we have already touched on the role taken by the "middle-
kingdom" of Lotharingia in the production of new forms of religious life for
women, especially the beguines (pp. 31–33). The beguine movement began
in the diocese of Liège, but soon spread throughout the other dioceses of
present-day Belgium and northern France, as well as northward into what

we call Holland and eastward into present-day Germany along the Rhine. The noted comment about Cologne by Matthew Paris in his *Chronicle* summarized their life in the following way:

> At that time, especially in Germany, some people of both sexes, but particularly women, took up a religious way of life, but a light one. They called themselves "religious," professing continence and simplicity of life by a private vow. Nevertheless, they are not bound by a saint's rule, nor are they at this time confined to a cloister.[19]

Matthew Paris recognized the beguines as religious, and although he had trouble locating their form of "religion" in comparison to more standard models, he captured its main characteristics accurately and succinctly. The English monk was apparently unfamiliar with the *curtes* beguinages, that is, the large houses of women that did lead a semicloistered life and, at least sometimes, adopted a local rule of life (*regula*), such as the Great Beguinage at Paris founded under the aegis of Louis IX.[20] During the thirteenth century, however, it was the beguines of the "light religion" who contributed the most to the history of mysticism.

In the Lotharingian heartland, however, another remarkable aspect of the "women's movement" of the age was of almost equal importance for the flowering of mysticism. This was the explosion of female Cistercian houses.[21] Like many of the new orders of the twelfth and thirteenth centuries, the Cistercians displayed a rather ambivalent attitude toward the incorporation of women.[22] During the earliest period (1125–1147), Cistercian leaders like Stephen Harding and Bernard of Clairvaux encouraged private associations between women's houses and the new order of white monks, while from 1147 to 1187 various forms of affiliated status developed. In 1187 the Spanish nunnery of Las Huelgas and its daughter houses were legally incorporated into the Cistercian order by decision of the General Chapter. In 1213 the General Chapter issued a series of regulations designed to guide the incorporation of female houses into the order, but this led to such an explosion of incorporations that in 1228 the Chapter forbade further acceptance of women's houses, though many individual exceptions continued to be made.[23] In the twelfth century, the Premonstratension reform had been the most popular in Belgium (twenty-three male houses and sixteen female), but activity shifted decisively toward the Cistercians, and especially to Cistercian women, after 1200. The number of male houses in Belgium remained relatively small (ten by 1237), but by 1252 there were fifty convents of Cistercian nuns, all but three founded or incorporated after 1200.[24] The first Cistercian nuns remain largely anonymous. Once again, 1200 marks an important shift as the early thirteenth century saw the production of a number of lives of Cistercian women saints, especially in Belgium, as well as the writings of Beatrice of Nazareth, the first Cistercian woman to compose mystical texts.

The power of the medieval women's movement in Lotharingia should not be restricted to beguines and Cistercian nuns, although almost all the women who could be termed mystics either belonged to these two groups or were closely associated with them.[25] The Cistercian women and the beguines in these areas were often related. Many of the Cistercian convents began life as houses of *mulieres religiosae;* individual beguines joined Cistercian houses, early and late in their lives. More tellingly, there is no clear distinction between the forms of mystical piety characteristic of women who lived an enclosed life as demanded by the Cistercian regulations and those who enjoyed the greater freedom of the beguine style of life, as can be seen by a perusal of the sixteen *vitae* of thirteenth-century holy women from the Low Countries that have come down to us.[26] Given the common themes found in these lives (e.g., severe asceticism, devotion to the Eucharist,[27] ecstatic excess, numerous visions both heavenly and infernal, miraculous powers, etc.), it is neither desirable nor necessary to treat all of them. We can get a good sense of what the male clerics found significant about these women through a consideration of three of the lives written by Thomas of Cantimpré.

Thomas himself also illustrates the fluidity of religious life of the time.[28] Born into a noble family about 1200 near Brussels, he entered the Augustinian abbey of Cantimpré in 1217. Thomas was ambitious and erudite, and his encounter with the holy woman Lutgard of Aywières in 1230 changed his life. Thomas joined the Dominicans in 1232 and dedicated the rest of his life (d. after 1262) to spreading the fame of contemporary saints through the writing of five *vitae* and also by including illustrative stories (*exempla*) about them in his massive handbook of Christian behavior, *The Book of Bees,* or *Universal Good Concerning Bees.*[29] Thomas, a keen student of Augustine and the Cistercian mystics, had studied at Paris with Albert the Great. Like James of Vitry, he illustrates the intimate connection between the new styles of feminine mystical holiness and theologically trained clerics and authors. Thomas's *Life of Christina the Astonishing (Mirabilis),* the most bizarre of the four *vitae* he devoted to women ecstatics, is a good test case of the theological limits of ecstatic holiness.

Thomas's *Life of Christina* has not received a good press in twentieth-century views of the Christian mystical heritage. Prior to the recent revival of interest in late-medieval women mystics, one of the few authors who treated Christina in modern times, the learned Jesuit scholar of the physical phenomena of mysticism Herbert Thurston, thought that the inclusion of Thomas's *vita* in the *Acta Sanctorum* was a "conspicuous instance" of a lapse of judgment and that the details set down by the Dominican were "utterly untrustworthy."[30] Recent attempts to understand the intention behind a *vita* like that of Christina, such as viewing the beguine as a living exemplar of purgatorial cleansing and a "fool for Christ's sake" (see 1 Cor. 3:18–19),[31] help illuminate aspects of its meaning, but they do not lessen the difficulty modern readers have with such extreme expressions of impossible ascetic feats and often bizarre mystical phenomena. Perhaps we can view these *vitae* as something close to modern science fiction–presentations of an alternative reality which some readers found valuable or at least entertaining because it illumined aspects of their own hopes and fears for the future–at least in the next life.

Christina was born at St. Trond in 1150 and died there in 1224. Thomas's *vita*, written in 1232, is a carefully constructed and lengthy *exemplum*,[32] as he makes clear at the conclusion:

> What else did Christina proclaim throughout her life, save to do penance and be prepared [for death] at every hour? With many words and tears and laments, with infinite cries, she taught this by the example of her life, she proclaimed it, more than anyone before or since that we have read or heard about.[33]

In a genre of vision widespread in the early Middle Ages, a seer is depicted as dying and going on an extended journey to the other world, before miraculously returning to life and helping effect conversions by telling what he or she had seen of eternal punishment or reward. Thomas adapts and alters this visionary genre. In order to demonstrate that Christina teaches penance more powerfully than anyone else, he has her special religious vocation begin with a death and otherworldly journey (VCM 1.5-7), but then he inserts Christina back into the world in order to become a *living* example of the necessity of purgatorial punishment for sin. But this is only half the message. Thomas also portrays the beguine as a model of the status of the resurrected body already enjoying, at least in part, the vision of God. The ascetic-purgatorial side of the *Life of Christina* has been what has attracted the most interest to date. Along with usual penances, like begging and extreme food deprivation (e.g., VCM 2.22 and 25; 5.50), Christina performs incredible feats, like creeping into fiery ovens, jumping into cauldrons of boiling water, staying in the Meuse river for days in winter, and even rolling herself into a round ball to pray (1.11–13; 2.16; 3.37). None of this abuse, however, harms her body in any way, because Thomas insists that it is *not* a normal body: "People could scarcely tell whether [she was] a spirit or a material body" (4.46 [658B]).³⁴ This accounts for some of the constant themes of the life–Christina's aversion to the smell of human beings (e.g., VCM 1.5 and 9) and her flying abilities. Douceline of Digne and other thirteenth-century saints are portrayed as levitating; Christina flies like a bird to treetops, church roofs and other high places (1.5 and 9; 2.15–16, 2.20; 3.26; 4.46). Her breasts also exude miraculous nourishing oil that both feeds and cures (1.9; 2.19); she is able to sing a heavenly song of "wonderful harmony" (*harmonia mirabilis* [3.34]) from a mysterious somatic source between her breast and her throat. Christina's body, then, is a resurrected body.

Thomas pictures Christina as spiritually adept in the usual practices and graces associated with other contemporary holy women. Like her fellow beguines, she has great devotion to the Eucharist (e.g., 1.10; 2.22); she also possesses the spirit of prophecy (e.g., 3.29–35), and, above all, she experiences rapture and ecstasy, often with strange psychosomatic characteristics (e.g., rolling about like a hoop in 3.35), or for extended periods (e.g., as she approaches death in 5.51). Thomas's *Life of Christina*, while it strains the limits of a modern audience's imagination, was "astonishing" enough to be quite popular with medieval audiences, since it survives in a number of manuscripts and in Dutch and English versions, as well as the original Latin.

Thomas's *Life of Margaret of Ypres*, written ca. 1240–1244, illustrates another aspect of women's mysticism already mentioned, the spiritual friendship (*spiritualis amicitia*) between men and women that was so often a crucial factor in conveying the story of the *mulier religiosa* to posterity, as well as in shaping her access to God. Brian Patrick McGuire has pointed to a shift in the expression of spiritual friendship among late-twelfth-century Cistercian monks. Rather than directing their love to other monks within the community, as had been the case with Aelred of Rievaulx in the twelfth century,³⁵ monks like Adam of Perseigne began to forge bonds of spiritual friendship with the Cistercian nuns, whose numbers were increasing so dramatically around 1200.³⁶ A charming example of this trend is found in a story of the Cistercian raconteur Caesarius of Heisterbach, who tells of a prior of the Cistercian monastery of Villers in Brabant who was a friend of a beguine visionary named Tydela. One Christmas Tydela received a vision in which she physically embraced the Christ-child. But she complained to Christ that she would not be satisfied "unless my friend . . . enjoys you in this way," and so she was miraculously transported inside the cloister at Villers where the prior was offering midnight Mass so that she might physically offer the Divine Child to her friend.³⁷

This movement of mystical friendship between men and women was not restricted to Cistercians, as we have seen in the case of James of Vitry and Mary of Oignies. Thomas of Cantimpré's own friendship with Lutgard (to be considered below) is close to the model found in James and Mary, one in which the learned cleric portrays himself as the disciple inspired by the saint and, through her, is given special graces. In the *Life of Margaret of Ypres,* as John Coakley has shown, we have something different, a more mutual relationship in which the cleric seems to be the guide and protector of the woman as much as he is the admirer and recorder of her mystical graces.[38]

Margaret was born in 1216 and died in 1237, exhausted by her ascetical practices and food deprivation.[39] Thomas of Cantimpré never met her, but gained his information from a fellow friar, Siger of Lille, who was Margaret's friend, guide, and admirer. It was a case of spiritual love at first sight. Although the *Life* paints Margaret with all the traditional colors of precocious piety, it does not hide the fact that at the age of eighteen she fell in love with a young man—something that created an obvious problem for her dedication to the Divine Spouse. In the midst of this crisis, Siger arrived in Ypres to preach and hear confessions. Thomas describes their first encounter:

> While he was looking around at the many women who were present, he chanced to see Margaret, who was dressed in secular clothes. By a kind of divine instinct, through Christ's revelation, he beheld this woman he had never seen before as one who was ready for the reception of God's grace as a "vessel of election" (Acts 9:15). When he called her out and advised her to reject all secular things, she said just what Saul once did without any reluctance, "Lord, what do you want me to do?" (Acts 22:10). . . . At once she abandoned the world totally.[40]

The mutual devotion of the friar and the young beguine is constantly to the fore in the *Life.*[41] Siger guides, instructs, consoles, and even gives her orders (e.g., *Life* chaps. 18, 24, 26, 30, 34, 42),[42] but he allows himself to be corrected by Margaret because he recognizes the divine grace at work in her (e.g., *Life* 18, 45). Siger alone is able to contact Margaret during her extended retreats from normal activities into states that moderns might be inclined to interpret as psychotic withdrawals, but that her hagiographer identified as extended raptures. According to Friar Thomas, there was no one, even among those she loved, that she could bear to listen to for more than a few words, "with the sole exception of her spiritual father through whom she had attained salvation. She used to sit hanging on his words, and her soul would absorb his conversation like the food the body lives upon."[43]

Indeed, the love between Margaret and the friar who had rescued her from the world was so great that the *Life* records her prayer to Jesus asking whether her love for the friar, suspicious in the eyes of some, would compromise her attachment to the Heavenly Spouse. Jesus assured her (and those who might doubt her) that this was not the case (see *Life* 25). Margaret of Ypres's passion-centered asceticism, her eucharistic devotion, and her ecstatic states are standard fare in all the *vitae* of the holy women of thirteenth-century Belgium. What is distinctive of this *Life* is the window it opens upon the intense spiritual bond between religious men and women in the new mysticism.

The portrait that Thomas of Cantimpré gives of his own relation to Lutgard of Aywières in the *Life* he wrote of this Benedictine become Cistercian is not quite so mutual.[44] Although he describes himself as "her most familiar friend" (*familiarissimus ejus* [prol., 234C]), Thomas met Lutgard only late in her life when her reputation for sanctity was well established, so he appears more as a wondering admirer than as a guide and influence. Nevertheless, the careful structure that the Dominican gave to this *Life* (it has been claimed that it is the first *vita* built on the traditional threefold model of beginners, proficient, and perfect),[45] as well as the exemplary and innovative aspects of her mysticism, make this *vita* one of the most important of the thirteenth century.[46]

The first book treats of Lutgard between her birth in 1182 and 1206. It soon becomes clear that the triple pattern of "beginners-proficient-perfect" is not being employed in the traditional way, because Lutgard is portrayed as enjoying mystical visions of Christ from an early age. Her initiating vision, given when she was a boarder at the Benedictine convent of St. Catherine at St. Trond, already centers on the future Cistercian's major contribution to mystical piety—her emphasis on the bleeding heart of Christ.[47] In this tableau Lutgard is portrayed as seated with a noble youth who had been wooing her when Christ appears "in the form of humanity which he once had among humans." Drawing back his garment, he shows her the bloody wound in his side, saying: "Do not seek the deceptions of frivolous love any longer. Here you should ever contemplate what you should love and why you should love. Here are the delights of the total purity I promise you."[48] From that time on, according to Thomas, Lutgard "meditating like a dove at a window looking out upon sunlight, steadfastly gazed upon the clear opening of the symbolic Ark of the Body of Christ."[49]

Lutgard's initial vision of the wound in Christ's side soon took on a more specific relation to the actual heart of the Redeemer. After describing some typical paramystical phenomena experienced by the young woman (e.g., levitation in 1.10), Thomas recounts one of the earliest examples of the motif of the exchange of hearts in medieval mysticism.[50] In response to Jesus' query about what she really wants, Lutgard answers: "I want your heart." Jesus answers, "Rather, it is I who wish your heart." Lutgard then says, "So be it, Lord, as long as you mix in your heart's love with mine, and I own my heart only in you, now being safe for all time under your protection." Thomas explains this "exchange of hearts" (*communicatio cordium*) by referring to traditional motifs of Cistercian mysticism, especially as found in William of St. Thierry, notably the "union of created and uncreated Spirit," which he understands as the *unus spiritus* of 1 Corinthians 6:17.[51]

Such experiences demonstrate Thomas of Cantimpré's desire to show Lutgard's conformity to the Cistercian mystical tradition,[52] but the extent to which she stretched this model is evident in the concrete, pictorial detail found in this vision and in later descriptions of her encounters with Christ recounted in the first book (that is, of Lutgard as a "beginner"!). For example, while she was still an adolescent at St. Catherine's, the crucified Christ appeared to her when she was on her way to Matins and allowed her to drink from the wound at his side (VL 1.13).[53] She also experienced an "eagle vision" in which the bird that is the symbol of John, the "spiritual evangelist," placed its beak in her mouth to fill her with all the secrets of the Godhead (*secreta divinitatis*). As we shall see, female visionaries often picture themselves as enjoying a special relation to John the Evangelist.

Given the potency of the mystical visions described in the first book of the *Life,* Thomas was obviously challenged to describe the advances that took place in Lutgard's mystical career after 1206, when she left St. Catherine's. His solution was to identify the "proficient" stage of book 2 with co-redemptive suffering, and the "perfect" stage of book 3 with public recognition of this exalted status. Lutgard's transfer from the "lax" Benedictine house at St. Trond to the stricter and more private life of a community of *mulieres religiosae* at Awyières, which was incorporated into the Cistercian order in 1210, must therefore be presented as a move to greater penance and interiorization.[54] Her life in this community, where she never learned to speak French adequately enough to be considered for a position of authority, is described as a trying time in which the ecstatic underwent inner trials to enable her to achieve a more perfect identification with Christ. During this Cistercian phase of her career, Lutgard fasted for two seven-year periods (1225–1232 and 1232–1239) in order to participate in the work of redemption effected by the heart of Christ now dwelling within her.[55] Her ongoing miracles, visions, and raptures display a total identification with Christ in the passion (e.g., 2.6, 9, 21, 23) and an intense devotion to the Eucharist (e.g., 2.14).

The third book of Thomas's *Life* concerns the final eleven years of her life. Lutgard, now a blind but powerful patroness and protector, becomes the center of a web of relationships both on earth and in the afterlife through her intercessory prayer. When she died on June 16, 1246, some of the nuns present at the scene are described as becoming aware that "Jesus himself, the Prince of our salvation, along with the immense joy of the supernal spirits, was present and called her soul to the delights of heaven."[56] Thomas of Cantimpré's *Life of Lutgard* is perhaps the crown jewel of the *vitae* that spread the wonders of the holy women of Lotharingia to a wider audience, both in the later Middle Ages and to our own time.

Beatrice of Nazareth: The First Writer

Thomas's *Life of Lutgard* provides us with a picture of the mystical piety of the Belgian Cistercian nuns that is quite similar to that found in the other *vitae* recording the ecstasies and miracles of these holy sisters. There is also little difference between what was written about the Cistercian women and what we find in the hagiography dealing with the beguines. But in passing from these Latin texts written by men, mostly Dominican friars, about women to the vernacular writing of Beatrice of Nazareth (1200–1268), we enter into a related, but rather different world.

Beatrice is arguably the earliest female author of the new mysticism. Though her surviving vernacular work, *The Seven Manners of Loving,* cannot be precisely dated, we know that this beguine-trained Cistercian nun composed a lost mystical journal from probably as early as ca. 1215. Like Athena, who sprang full-grown from the forehead of Zeus, Beatrice and the other female pioneers of the composition of mystical texts by women were not semi-educated (as many of the women in the *vitae* are depicted), nor were they amateur writers. In the sophistication of their literary skill, no less than in the subtlety and profundity of their thought, Beatrice and the women to be considered in the following chapters were the equals of subsequent exponents of vernacular theology in the later Middle Ages, men or women. Although what survives of Beatrice's writing is more restricted than what we have of the three major beguine authors to be treated in chapter 5, if the full text of her journal had been preserved, she might well have proven their equal.

History plays unexpected tricks. While we have a surprising amount of the original writings of Beatrice's contemporary, Hadewijch, we know next to nothing about her life. Although only a fragment of Beatrice's mystical writings remain, we know more about her story than that of many more famous medieval religious women.[57] Beatrice was born into a wealthy middle-class family near Leuven. Her pious father, Bartholomew, founded no fewer than three houses for Cistercian nuns, and most of his children eventually followed him into the Cistercian life. Beatrice, described as a prodigy of learning, became an oblate at the Cistercian convent at Bloemendaal about 1210, after receiving her early education among the beguines. She was well trained in the liberal arts, and although she did not write in Latin, the evidence of *The Seven Manners of Loving* indicates that she read and cited Latin with ease. One place in her *Life* even describes how she gathered books about the Trinity (certainly in Latin) to help her in studying the meaning of the mystery.[58]

The lengthy *Life,* based on the lost spiritual journal Beatrice kept between ca. 1215 and ca. 1235, is both informative and tantalizing. We wish that we had the original—both for itself and to provide a clue about what encouraged her take up the genre of the mystical journal, which had been pioneered by Rupert of Deutz a century before.[59] The *Life* gives us the basic chronology of her career, as well as a detailed account of her mystical experiences, albeit with many interpolations, omissions, and changes made by the chaplain of Nazareth. The fact that an important section of the *Life* contains an adapted translation of *The Seven Manners of Loving* provides the modern student of medieval women's mysticism with the unusual opportunity to compare a woman's own presentation of her mystical consciousness with a male clerical version of the same. Amy Hollywood's careful analysis of the two texts has shown the at times subtle, but still significant, differences demonstrating how the *Life* tends "to translate mystical into paramystical phenomena, or internally apprehended into externally perceptible experiences."[60] What the mystic presented in *The Seven Manners of Loving* as the inner drama of the soul's encounter with God, in the *Life* becomes the manifestation of union through the exterior signs evident in the saint's body.

Beatrice's profession as a Cistercian nun took place in 1216. She was then sent to the convent of Rameya to learn the art of writing liturgical manuscripts. Here she became close friends with Ida of Nivelles—another example of the role of "spiritual friendship," here between two women, in the Cistercian tradition.[61] Her first mystical experience took place not long afterward in January of 1217 (*Life* 1.11). She then returned to Bloemendaal and remained there for some years before moving on to another Cistercian convent at Magdendaal, meanwhile recording the stages of her mystical experiences in what must have been extensive detail. In May of 1236 she transferred to the new Cistercian convent of Nazareth at Lier (funded by her father), where she became prioress. Here she stayed until her death in 1268. Beatrice ceased writing her journal after transferring to Nazareth (this may have something to do with the growing suspicion of women's mysticism that was becoming evident toward the middle of the thirteenth century).[62] We do not know when her surviving brief Dutch text was written, though it may date from her time at Nazareth.[63]

The picture of Beatrice as ecstatic mystic presented in the *Life* is, on the whole, similar to what we have seen in the lives composed by Thomas of Cantimpré, but it is based on a somewhat different perspective. Although the mystical themes are much the same (e.g., penance, devotion to the passion of Christ, visions and mystical experiences associated with the Eucharist, severe temptations that express a form of "dark night," and a wide variety of psychosomatic effects visible in the saint's body),[64] this *Life,* when compared to those analyzed above, provides us with at least some hints of a mystical self-presentation, if only at a second remove, as suggested by Amy Hollywood. At times the *Life* tries to give the impression of speaking from "within" rather than from "without," especially in its concentration on a psychological presentation of the inner torments and indescribable joys of the "vehemence," the "insatiability," and the "insanity" of Divine Love (*caritas/minne*).[65] The asceticism, visions, and ecstasies recounted in the text are unusual by modern standards,[66] but in comparison with Christina the Astonishing, critics might judge Beatrice's actions strange (even pathological) but not impossible. Nevertheless, the *Life* still presents Beatrice in the traditional categories of hagiography, stressing the advance of virtues according to often artificial categories.[67]

Beatrice comes into her own when we turn to *The Seven Manners of Loving,* perhaps the first text written by a woman that can be described as essentially mystagogical, that is, designed to guide others along the path of interior transformation toward direct contact with God, or, in her words, "the fruition of love" (*gebrechen der minne*).[68] Despite its brevity, *The Seven Manners of Loving* is a powerful exploration of the central theme of the women mystics of northern Europe in the thirteenth century—the power of *minne/ fin'amour.*

Minne has many meanings. Though the protean character of *minne* as used by the women mystics has deep connections with the tradition of monastic *caritas,* the word also must be seen in relation to the courtly literature that flourished in Western Europe in the High and Late Middle Ages. From the twelfth century on mystics had made use of courtly themes.[69] This connection has been the subject of considerable literature, but the real character of what has often been called *Minnemystik,* or sometimes "courtly mysticism," still needs further investigation.[70] Barbara Newman has recently utilized the term *la mystique courtoise* for the phenomenon, arguing that this form of mysticism is not just "a pretty new bottle for the same old wine" (i.e., of monastic nuptial mysticism employing the language of the Song of Songs), but a new development. What makes *la mystique courtoise* distinctive, in her view, is how it combines, in a shifting variety of ways, the mysticism of the monastic commentaries on the Song of Songs (in which the mystic adopts the female persona in relation to the male Divine Lover) with the themes of courtly *fin'amour,* which generally assume "a male protagonist and female object of desire," thus allowing for a whole new exploration of the mystery of love between God and the human person.[71]

Newman's observation about the importance of the male voice adopted by some women mystics as contrasted with the traditional gender reversal-language employed by male mystics (who often take on the female role as "soul-bride") shows how gender-identity has often been malleable in the history of Christian mystical discourse.[72] As Saskia Murk-Jansen has suggested, however, such gender reversals were fundamentally intended not so much to reflect preoccupation with gender identity as "to emphasize the fact that the soul's relationship to God was like nothing they [the mystics] had ever experienced."[73] The predication of feminine names (like *minne*) to God, as well as traditional male terms, points in the same direction—God lies beyond all distinctions of gender and the ordinary realms of consciousness.[74] The rich developments displayed in what we might call the "courtly mode" of mystical language (I prefer this term to *Minnemystik,* or even *la mystique courtoise*) are not exhausted by these innovations regarding gender language. We need to examine Beatrice, and especially the three major beguines who will be treated in the following chapter, in order to appreciate the variety and complexity of the possible forms of this courtly mode of mystical language.

The characteristics of the courtly mode of mystical expression were many.[75] Among the most important was the emphasis given to "love from afar" (*amour de lonh*). The mystics did not need the troubadors to inform them about the role of longing for the absent Beloved as integral to the experience of love (witness the importance of such texts as Song of Songs 3:1–2 in the tradition), but for some thirteenth-century women longing seems to become more important than possession; that is to say, in some cases the fruition of love comes to reside in the paradoxical nonfruition of continual yearning for the Beloved. The mystical commentators on the Song, like Bernard and William, conceived of mysticism as an oscillation between lengthy periods of absence and brief experiences of divine presence (both necessary on the mystical path), whereas in a number of the women mystics we shall examine (such as Beatrice) there is a paradoxical fusion of states in which absence is presence and vice versa.

Both the twelfth-century monastic commentators on the Song and the thirteenth-century women were vitally concerned with the purity and disinterestedness of love, though they found different images to express love's "simplicity." Both were also convinced that true love of God involved vehemence or violence (Richard of St. Victor's *violenta caritas*), though the women often surpass the men in the emphasis they give to the devastating effects of love's madness. The spousal love between God and human that Bernard of Clairvaux and others saw as the highest fulfillment of all *affectus* was "mutual" (*amor mutuus*), a love in which Jesus and the soul were equal in the sense that both loved to their fullest extent. But the Cistercian mystic emphasized that one love was infinite while the other remained finite. This understanding of mutuality was challenged and even surpassed in the picture of the stormy relations between human and Divine Lover presented by some of the women, such as Beatrice and Hadewijch. When these authors describe the fruition in which human and divine become truly one, they at times express it as a union of abyssal profundity where the soul becomes completely equal to the Infinite Lover.

As with other examples of the new vernacular theology, Beatrice's brief treatise is initially disconcerting to those who come to it with eyes trained to appreciate the biblical rhetoric of monastic theology or the dialectic skill of the scholastics. The text is also unusual when viewed against the background of the descriptions of the *mulieres religiosae* in contemporary hagiography. *The Seven Manners of Loving* contains no visions, miracles, or ascetical feats. It does not mention the Eucharist, the passion, and scarcely even the name of Christ (only once, in quoting Phil. 1:23). The text concentrates on what Beatrice obviously thought was "the one thing necessary" (*unum est necessarium* of Luke 10:42)—the exploration of the modes of *minne*.

What is *minne?* Or should we rather ask, Who is *minne?* Both questions are appropriate and show why it is virtually impossible to define *minne* in any clear and simple way, either in Beatrice or in the other exponents of the courtly mode of mystical language. Rather than seeing confusion here, it may be more appropriate to realize that the puzzling ambiguity and richness of *minne* are a strong argument for the theological sophistication of Beatrice's treatise.

In this Cistercian nun, as well as in the other women mystics of the thirteenth century who lived in the world of vernacular theology, *minne* functions not unlike the term *esse* in contemporary scholasticism, though with a decidedly more personal and existential import. That is to say (metaphysically speaking), *minne* must be predicated of God, but it also signifies the fundamental reality or power by which all things participate in God and by which they return to him. As used by the women mystics, however, *minne* is much more a phenomenological than a metaphysical term, and hence it has a richly varied range of meanings growing out of the paradox of love experienced as simultaneously both longing and satisfaction. From this perspective, although *minne* can be used as a personification, a power, a person (divine and/or human)—and all three at once—it is perhaps most essentially a form of relational consciousness seeking to find expression. What *minne* means for individual authors can be determined only by close attention to the context of its use based on an appreciation of both the phenomenological and metaphysical dimensions of the term.[76]

In investigating *minne* in the *Seven Manners of Loving*, it is best to begin with *minne*'s various functions, since that is where Beatrice begins: "There are seven manners of loving, which come down from the heights and go back again far above."[77] This pronouncement presents two fundamental aspects of the term. First, *minne* has both cosmic and divine dimensions, not unlike Dionysius's view of *erōs* in *Divine Names* 4, although Beatrice uses these in more existential and personal ways than Dionysius. Second, *minne* manifests itself in a variety of interconnected manners, or ways, which need not be thought of as successive stages in linear progress toward the goal, but more like diverse actuations of the power of love operative throughout the mystic's life.[78] Nevertheless, Beatrice, like so many mystical authors, chose to present her nonlinear teaching in terms of a sevenfold itinerary, so, in order to gain some initial sense of what is new about her presentation, it will be helpful to survey the seven manners briefly.

The first manner of *minne* is described as an "active" longing (*begerte*) that drives the soul to try to regain the "purity, nobility, and freedom" (4.15–17: *puerheit-vriheit-edelheit*) in which it was created. This is Beatrice's adaptation of the monastic mystical insistence on the restoration of the damage done to humanity created "in the image and likeness of God" (Gen. 1:26).[79] The first manner also introduces another of the central themes of the monastic mystical tradition, that is, the imperative to climb to "greater heights of love and nearer knowledge of God" (4.21–22). Both love and knowledge must be involved in the encounter with God, however much the former prevails. Beatrice's second "manner of *minne*" appears to echo Cistercian reflection on the totally disinterested nature of the love of the "maiden who serves her master" (8.7). The third manner describes the torture of *minne* in which the soul cannot satisfy her desire to serve God perfectly because of her created status. "It is above all else the greatest torment to the soul that despite its great longings it cannot do enough for love, and that in loving it comes up so short" (10.17–21). In poetic language Beatrice describes how the soul remains in this hellish condition until our Lord consoles it with "a different manner of loving and longing, when he gives it a closer knowledge of himself" (13.54–56).

The fourth manner of love, though it is announced as involving both "great pleasure" (*groter waelheiden*) and "great sorrow" (*groter welegheiden*), actually deals only with the overwhelming delight, freedom, and sweetness that the soul experiences when "it feels all its senses sanctified in love, its will turned into love and is so deeply immersed and absorbed in the abyss of love that it is made wholly into love."[80] This experience of the *abyssus caritatis*, as the Latin text puts it, establishes Beatrice as one of the first women to utilize this important mystical theme in describing union with God.[81] Here the Cistercian nun seems to be describing the kind of rapture of love involving loss of consciousness that often appears in the accounts of her ecstasies given in the *Life* (4.36–49).

The following three manners also use the language of the abyss, while emphasizing that the "madness of love" (*orewoed van minne*) is by no means left behind.[82] The fifth manner combines a heightened sense of passion and madness in which "love is vehemently excited and rises like a storm with a great uproar and a great frenzy" (5.2–5), along with a resting "in the sweet embrace of love" (5.12–23: *die suete behelsingen van minne*), which gives the soul such great strength of spirit and body that it seems that it can do anything. Nevertheless, the violence of love prevails. Beatrice says that "it seems to the soul that the heart is wounded again and again" (5.36–37). This is the traditional theme of the *vulnus amoris* based on Song of Songs 2:4, but the language with which she explores this motif is far more somatically direct than was customary in the medieval Song of Songs commentaries:

> It seems to the soul that the veins are bursting, the blood spilling, the marrow withering, the bones softening, the heart burning, the throat parching, so that the face and all the members perceive the inward heat, and this is the madness of love. At this time she also feels an arrow piercing through her heart all the way to the throat and beyond to the brain, as if she would lose her mind.[83]

A large part of this torture and madness comes from the fact that *minne* is so high above all understanding (*begripelicheit* [5.61]) that the soul can gain no fruition and cannot maintain measure, moderation, and good judgment (5.62–69).

This conflict between *minne* and all human modes of knowing is over-come in the sixth manner, in which Beatrice describes "the Lord's bride" (the only use of this term in the treatise) as advancing to "another manner of loving in a more exalted form of being and in higher understanding."[84] Here the soul reaches a condition of closeness to God that allows her to experi-ence divine power, purity, sweetness, and freedom, as well as gaining "inti-macy with God" (*nakenisse van gode* [6.24]). Beatrice compares the soul to a housewife (*husurouwen*) who knows how to do all things well because she is ruled by love. She is like a fish swimming in the depths of the sea, or like a bird mounting high in the sky (6.35–42). In a daring manner, the Cistercian nun says that one in whom love has triumphed in this way no longer fears men or demons, angels or saints, not even God himself (6.52–55).

The seventh manner of love, described at greater length than the others (and as being "even higher") is not easily coordinated with the earlier expe-riences.[85] It may represent a summary and recapitulation of the aspects of *minne* studied in the first six manners, one designed to emphasize the dis-tance between all experience of God in this life and the longing the mystic continues to have for the perfect "fruition of love" to come in heaven (*gebruken der minnen* [7.21–22, 44, 60, 87, 113, 144, 155–56, 168]).[86] Here, a half-century before Jacopone of Todi and Angela of Foligno, we find the Flemish mystic employing the language of the abyss: "[The soul is drawn] into the eternity of *minne* and the incomprehensibility and the vastness and the inaccessible sublimity and the deep abyss of the Godhead, which is all in all things, and remains incomprehensible in all things, and which is immu-table, all-existent, all-capable, all-comprehending, and all-powerfully work-ing."[87] In her desire to attain the fruition of *minne,* the soul can find no rest, but as long as she is in this life must undergo increasingly paradoxical expe-riences of pain and pleasure—an epektasis of *minne.*[88] God alone, "the great Godhead and high Trinity" (7.47–48), can satisfy the soul and still leave her yearning for yet greater fruition. Such a lover longs for death and lives in painful hope, refusing all consolation, even from God (7.72–120). The poetic, almost incantatory, style of the last lines of *The Seven Manners of Love* is a powerful expression of the all-embracing role of *minne* as the divine force that draws the soul on to where she finally will "be united with her Bride-groom and will become one spirit with him [1 Cor. 6:17] in inseparable faith-fulness and eternal love."[89]

Only recently has Beatrice of Nazareth begun to take her rightful place among the major women mystics of the later Middle Ages, despite the brevity of what we have from her pen. As a Cistercian, and especially as a member of the female branch of the order, she exemplifies important aspects in the shift from the mysticism of the twelfth century to that of the thirteenth, especially those implied in the move from the language of *caritas* to that of *minne*.

Later Beguine Mystics and a Beguin

The beguine movement had spread throughout northern Europe by the mid-thirteenth century. (Related phenomena of holy women living relatively free forms of religious life, often in a domestic setting, were also known in Italy, often under the names *bizzoche* or *pinzochere.*[90]) During the second half of the century the beguine movement began to face growing criticism that eventually resulted in the condemnation of at least the independent beguines and associated male beghards at the Council of Vienne in 1311.[91] An interesting witness to both the geographical spread and the growing clerical criticism is found in a mid-thirteenth century poem, "The Daughter of Sion," by the Franciscan preacher Lamprecht of Regensburg. This satirizes the claims of illiterate women mystics to higher knowledge of God in the following words:

> This knowledge [*kunst*] has in our own days
> In Brabant and Bavaria
> Risen up among women.
> Lord God, what kind of knowledge is it
> That an old woman knows it better
> Than a learned man?[92]

It is clear, however, that if many clerics were critical of the beguines, others strongly supported them and considered some of the beguine holy women to be miracles of grace, powerful intercessors for the afterlife, and, if not exactly models to be imitated (given their excessive character), at least women worthy of admiration.

The admirers of the later *mulieres religiosae,* like those in Lotharingia in the first decades of the century, came from all ranks of the clergy, though the friars, especially the Dominicans, played a strong role. The career of Thomas of Cantimpré already shows how individual Dominican friars encouraged holy women of different institutional affiliations. The conduct of the *cura animarum* in relation to the beguines was not the subject of general ecclesiastical regulation. The independent beguines, living in the world as they did, were technically always subject to the parish clergy; but from the third decade of the thirteenth century, the mendicants began to establish churches in urban environments, and the higher level of education and often greater fervor of the friars gave them advantages as confessors and spiritual guides for the *mulieres sanctae*.[93] Though some mendicants were suspicious of the freer forms of holy women and called for their regularization and enclosure (e.g., the Franciscan Simon of Tournai at the Second Council of Lyons),[94] others were their greatest champions. The connection between the beguines and the mendicants in Germany can be seen in the case of two contemporaries who also provide good test cases of the unusual, even excessive, character of some beguine visionaries and ecstatics–Christina of Stommeln (1242–1312) and Agnes Blannbekin (ca. 1244–1315).[95]

Christina lived for a time with a beguine community in Cologne, but spent most of her life in her small village northeast of Cologne as an independent house beguine. She was supported by her parish priest, Pastor John (*Johannes Plebanus*), and especially by a group of Dominican admirers including her dearest friend and biographer, Peter of Dacia (ca. 1240–1289). Agnes was also from a farming family, but from about 1260 lived in Vienna as a beguine under the tutelage of the anonymous Franciscan who wrote his account of her *Life and Revelations* shortly after her death.

Christina of Stommeln's story, perhaps even more than the tale of the other Christina, the Astonishing (*admirabilis*), is so bizarre that it has provoked amusement, disgust, and astonishment, as well as attempts to discern what it means for our understanding of medieval religion.[96] Recent evaluations have tried to place the accounts of the beguine's ecstasies and diabolical trials into the wider perspective of the feats ascribed to holy women and the "politics" of saint-making.[97] Here I wish primarily to address the question of the possible significance of Christina for thirteenth-century mysticism.

Two factors make the case of Christina important for evaluating of the limits of the new mysticism. The first is that this strange, in part impossible story was put together not by marginal and semi-educated local clergy, but by a well-trained and learned theologian. Peter of Dacia first met Christina in 1267 when he was a young friar at the Dominican house of studies in Cologne. In 1269 he went on to Paris to study theology with Thomas Aquinas. When he returned to his native Gotland (in modern Sweden, but part of the medieval Dominican province of Dacia, or Denmark) he functioned as lector and prior of the Dominican houses there and seems to have been well respected in the order.[98] Peter, apparently intending to write a *vita* of Christina, gathered a mass of materials about his "dearest" (*carissima*) into a collection that survives in a codex from Jülich and in an abbreviated form in an Einsiedeln manuscript.[99] This mélange in three books consists of: (1) a poem and treatise by Peter on Christina's virtues; (2) a group of materials on her life including [a] the story of her early life, which she dictated to Pastor John, [b] Peter's accounts (constructed as a form of on-the-scene reporting) of his fifteen visits to her over the years, and [c] sixty-three letters he and others wrote to or about her (including fourteen of her letters to him);[100] (3) the narrative of Master John, the village school teacher, about Christina's diabolical trials between 1280 and 1287. The fact that we have material from the beguine herself (even if not written in her own hand),[101] as well the "file cabinet" of texts by a learned theologian, gives the case of Christina particular interest. It demonstrates that any divide between "high" theology and what might be considered popular, or folk, religion is a dubious approach to medieval Christianity.

The second issue involved in studying Christina's role in thirteenth-century mysticism concerns the spiritual friendship between religious men and women that we have seen was often crucial in the development of the new forms of mysticism. The intensity of the love between Peter and Christina (both roughly the same age when they met) is similar to, but arguably more extreme than, other cases we have examined. John Coakley rightly speaks of "Peter's needy fascination with Christina."[102] The feeling certainly seems to have been mutual. Peter visited the beguine thirteen times between December 1267 and July 1269 when he left for Paris.[103] These visits cemented deep love on both sides, as the friar's account of their parting shows:

> When the two of us went along together, sad and downcast about the looming separation, we shared more sighs than words. I said: "Dearest Christina, the time has come for us to be separated. Go in the Lord, dearest." When she heard this she said nothing, but covered her face with her cloak, sat down on the ground and cried most bitterly and abundantly.[104]

Even though the conventions of medieval letters allowed for expressions of love between religious (often between people of the same sex) that moderns may find unusual, few went as far as the Dominican and the beguine.[105] For some examples (among scores) consider Christina's early letters to Peter after he had left for Paris. In her second letter to him (Ep. IV) she recalls how she could tell him things she could never express to others about her experiences because of their mutual love of Christ: "Therefore, I am saddened, because since your departure there is no one with whom I am able or dare to act in this way, since I fear all and I can't be with them the way we are when together."[106] In later letters she says that after their subsequent parting in 1270 she had wept for two whole days (Ep. XVI; 318C), and in another letter she addresses him as "dear, dearer, dearest" (*caro, carior, carissimo* [Ep. XVIII; 320C]). Peter was even more effusive in the language that he used about his love for Christina. Letter xxiv of the second group of epistles gives a good example of his feelings toward the beguine. Written in the early 1280s, this epistle begins with praise for the God who has united Peter to his *dulcissima* in such a "bond of friendship." The major theme, though, is sorrow and pain over the distance that separates them—something that both of them have read in "the same book of experience." Peter confesses he does not know why God has united two such different people "in the one bond of charity," but he assures Christina that if carnal love can make man and woman "one heart and one flesh," spiritual love must be much stronger "in making one heart and soul in the Lord." The letter closes with all the rhetorical stops pulled out:

> O my most beloved! O inner core of my heart! I beg you that we raise up our eyes and lift up our hearts to the Lord in whom all things are one, and that from him and in him we, who in ourselves are divided in many ways, discover ourselves as one. O most beloved, would that I could speak to you mouth to mouth and be with you even in bodily presence.... Every day I pray that God will bring this about before my death, whatever the occasion may be.[107]

Peter, like Aelred of Rievaulx, is too emotionally honest not to express the pain of separation, despite his theology of the ongoing union of those who love each other in Christ.

Both the beguine and the Dominican insisted that their intense love was a bond in and for Christ. In an earlier letter Peter expressed the mutuality of their love in Christ in a form similar to what Aelred had used about spiritual love between male monks:

> If I ask you if you love me, or you ask me if I love you, the response on either side is absolute: "I love and I am loved." Therefore, I will call upon a third person to make the truth of this intention even clearer. If anyone were to ask me if I love Christina, I would answer with total assurance, "I love her." And if he were to go further and ask the reason and cause why I love Christina, with perfect conscience I would say, "Because of Christ."[108]

This love produced a bond so close that Peter and Christina symbolized it as a spiritual marriage, as the ring that the beguine saw Peter wearing in a vision demonstrates.[109]

Given the mass of repetitious, if entertaining, material about Christina and her circle contained in Peter's large collection, here we must be content with a brief survey of her life as background to raising the issue of the extent to which she can be considered a mystic. According to the account of her early life dictated to Pastor John, Christina, like other beguines, began her visionary career quite young. Christ appeared to her when she was ten years old and plighted her his troth. At the age of thirteen she ran away to Cologne to join a beguine house, but she seems to have lasted there only a few years. Her peculiar forms of asceticism, strange eating habits, and the diabolical temptations she was already experiencing, led the other beguines to mock her and she returned home.

Some years later, the fame of her ecstasies and demonic trials had reached the Dominicans in Cologne, prompting the young Peter to travel to Stommeln to see her. (The Franciscans, on the other hand, seem to have opposed her throughout her life.) Peter tells us how he had long wished to find a real saint with the kind of direct line to God that he could experience only vicariously. During his first visit, when he saw Christina receive mysterious nail wounds from the devil, Peter realized that he had found the *mulier sancta* he had been seeking (279D–282B). Later, Christina claimed to have received a special revelation at the same time concerning the importance of Peter in her life.

The young Dominican's reporting of his subsequent visits to the beguine are a mixture of the by now traditional topoi about the ecstatic experiences expected of a *mulier sancta* and a growing emphasis on forms of demonic activity of obvious fascination both to the beguine and her circle of admirers. Traditional mystical experiences occur in many of these visits (e.g., ecstasies, stigmata, *iubilus*),[110] but accompanied by numerous stories of diabolical activity, many resembling modern reports of poltergeist phenomena.[111] The most notorious of these is the account of the ninth visit, during which Christina and those around her were assaulted numerous times with human excrement by diabolical power (291E–294E). The narrative detail of this bizarre incident, which often seems more humorous than frightening, has both puzzled and fascinated historians. Granted the traditional association of the devil with everything noxious, including excrement, what does this account, witnessing to a kind of fecal fixation, add to Peter's attempt to paint Christina as a *mulier sancta?*

Whatever the reason for the inclusion of the incident, it becomes clearer from the later materials found in Peter's dossier that the center of the story is Christina as martyr (*intrepida virgo Christi*), an innocent victim of increasing diabolical assaults, rather than Christina as the mystic rapt into union with Christ.[112] This appears to represent the beguine's own mind, as much as that of her circle. While the descriptions of diabolical activity found in Peter's account of his visits strain credulity, those in Master John's narrative far exceed them, clearly passing into a fictional world something like a medieval version of a horror movie. Peter remained fascinated with these accounts, however fantastic, and included them all in his collection.

The increasing emphasis on the diabolical is matched by a diminution of the mystical elements. Descriptions of Christina's ecstasies, especially after Peter's fifteenth and last visit in 1277, tend to become formulaic. Typically, after lengthy and detailed accounts of nighttime assaults by demons, in many of which Christina is described as torn to pieces and then put back together by angels, or sometimes by Jesus himself, the beguine then quietly goes off to church, receives Communion, and falls into an ecstasy.[113] Little or no description of the content of these ecstatic raptures occurs. Even more significant, as Aviad Kleinberg has noted,[114] is that Christina's letters are scarcely mystical documents, either in a traditional monastic sense, or in the visionary accents encountered in most thirteenth-century female mystics. In her letters Christina often talks about her devotion to Peter, as we have seen, and she also asks him for favors. Her epistles, like the other narratives, emphasize the demonic attacks that torture her so frequently (e.g., Epp. IV, VII, XIII, XVI, XVII, XVIII, XXIV, XXV, XVIII). There are, to be sure, notices of her raptures and visions from time to time in these letters, but they always come from the pens of the scribes.[115] When speaking for herself, Christina does not talk about her visions or conversations with Christ—she scarcely even mentions the Lord. This is not to say that the beguine may not have continued to undergo the catatonic states that Peter himself had once witnessed, but it suggests that her own self-perception was primarily that of a victim of diabolical torture sent to the world to manifest the reality of eternal punishment and the necessity for repentance. Christina mentally lived out the gruesome scenes of hell that medieval believers encountered in sermon and in art. As Peter summarized in one place: "From the ages it has never been heard that a person was so horribly and openly tortured by demons."[116] If Christina *mirabilis*, as I suggested above, can be read as a witness to the gifts of the resurrected body, then Christina of Stommeln testifies to the reality of the sufferings of the damned.

The mystical aspect of Christina's life seems to have come largely from the side of her friend Peter, who wanted (even needed, as he admits) to interpret the beguine's odd behavior as evidence of the mystical graces that would allow him vicarious access to God. In a number of letters (especially Ep. IX, X and XXIV in the first collection of letters and Ep. i in the second) Peter summarizes the mystical theology he had learned in Cologne and Paris for the benefit of his beguine friend, as if he needed to teach her the meaning of what was happening to her during her seizures.[117] It is difficult to think that Christina took in the message; at least none of it appears in her own letters.

Christina of Stommeln, as Peter Dinzelbacher has observed, is one of the earliest examples of an ambivalence that was to continue to haunt later Western women—saint or witch?[118] Many of the mystical descriptions contained in Peter's files—however exaggerated—conform to what can be seen in other female ecstatics of the thirteenth century, but these mystical graces were less important than Christina's obsession with the devil, which seems to have fed a neurosis both in her and in her admirers.[119] Forms of this neurosis, individual and collective, were to spur the infamous witch craze in later centuries.[120] More than a century and a half ago, when Johann Josef von Görres wrote his four-volume *Die christliche Mystik* (1836–42), mysticism was defined primarily in relation to paranormal phenomena and therefore much attention was given to the proper distinction between supernatural and diabolical forms of such activity in determining true mysticism.[121] The roots of this misunderstanding can be seen in the case of Christina of Stommeln, which is one reason why this strange beguine deserves consideration in the history of Western mysticism.

Agnes Blannbekin was also a controversial figure, though she is far more typical of the forms of beguine piety we have seen pioneered by the women of Lotharingia.[122] Agnes was born about 1244 into a peasant family and lived as a beguine in Vienna from about 1260 until her death in 1315. She worshiped at the Franciscan church in that city and was under the tutelage of the Friars Minor, especially of the anonymous confessor who was her spiritual guide and who compiled the account of her *Life and Revelations* in 1318, apparently from notes he had kept over the years.[123] (Agnes was able to read, as a number of references in the text make clear, but, like Christina, could not write in Latin.)[124]

Like many beguines, Agnes was a visionary whose showings often came to her in connection with her participation in the liturgy. Many of the more allegorical visions are given an immediate and explicit explanation for the benefit of the reader. Agnes also experienced auditions in which the voice of God, or other celestial figures, spoke to her within her soul. She was deeply Christocentric, as well as eucharistic, in her piety, taking Communion at the frequent rate of once a week (*Life* chaps. 41 and 219). Indeed, the brief biography of her early life in chapter 39 says that "she hastened more quickly to become a beguine so that she could take Communion more frequently."[125] Although Agnes's visions were sometimes critical of false and evil-living priests and religious, she was solidly loyal in faith and practice to the institutional church.[126] Like Christina, Agnes Blannbekin saw the devil and was sometimes tempted by him and his minions (e.g., *Life* chaps. 66, 97, 125, 143, 188, 200 and 210), but for her the devil was more bothersome than terrifying and there are no demonic tortures or obsessions in her visions. Basically, this Viennese beguine is a good illustration of how the major themes of beguine life and spirituality, pioneered at the beginning of the thirteenth century, were alive and well—even well-respected—in the early fourteenth century.

The character of Agnes's visionary mysticism is evident in the long showing that introduces the *Life and Revelations* (chaps. 1–23). This vision took place in church after mass when the "holy person . . . began to faint away sweetly and be rapt within into an indescribable light," where she saw Christ as someone "more beautiful than the sons of men" with the light emanating from within him. She also witnessed all created things "distinct in brightness" within the divine light (chap. 1; 68). The remainder of the vision (chaps. 2–23), like many of Agnes's manifestations, is primarily didactic—an account of all that she saw in the light vision, including the company of the saved, the ascent or descent of all humans, the wounds of Christ (to which she had a typically beguine devotion),[127] the angels and the various categories of saints. What is most interesting about this vision, however, is the record of the interrogation that the confessor-recorder includes at the end (chap. 23; 90–94). The friar queried the seer about the psychological nature and effects of the showing. The reason for placing this vision at the beginning of the whole collection here becomes clear. Whereas the beguine had experienced previous visions, these were accompanied by feelings of unworthiness and were often difficult for her to recall. In this vision she hears a voice saying "Do not fear!" and this gives her such a sweetness in the soul "that it flows out to the exterior senses and spreads itself through the entire body" (chap. 23; 92), the kind of total embodied experience typical of late medieval female mystics. This vision also marks Agnes's conversion to a life of constant visionary experience:

> She said that after this visitation or revelation she quite frequently has revelations from the Lord and spiritual consolations, at least once a day. . . . She said that when she wishes to be free for contemplation she turns her mind's high intent to whatever she wishes of the things revealed to her in that vision of the Lord. . . . And it very frequently happens that she is there rapt in ecstasy, and with her external senses asleep her heart is at watch within (cf. Song 5:2). . . . And this ecstasy is a sudden one.[128]

Agnes enjoyed a number of other visions of heaven with its ranks of saints and angels and hymns of praise to God (e.g., *Life and Revelations,* 62–64), and there are many visualizations of Mary, the saints, and Christ himself. One form of manifestation of Christ she described was later the subject of controversy—her mystical contact with the foreskin (*praeputium*) of

Jesus. Medieval and baroque devotion to the feast of Christ's circumcision
(Jan. 1) as the first shedding of the sacred blood of the Redeemer was fervent and untroubled by the squeamish suspicions of a post-Freudian age,
though Agnes Blannbekin's fervor and form of the devotion was unprecedented. In chapters 37–38 (116–20) Agnes's confessor tells how from her
youth the beguine wept on this feast "from great compassion of heart at the
pouring out of the blood of Jesus Christ." Once, as she was considering
where the foreskin of Christ was, she tasted on her tongue "a small piece of
skin like the skin of an egg" which gave her the greatest pleasure as often as
she swallowed it (as many as a hundred times!). Nevertheless, Agnes seems
to have felt some hesitancy about this tasting of the foreskin, because she
had to be convinced by divine signs to reveal the incident to her confessor.
The problem was not one involving possible sexual overtones, but rather
involved a theological issue–the revelation the beguine was given said that
the foreskin rose with Christ at the resurrection, but this point was in conflict with the numerous relics of the foreskin honored throughout Europe.[129]
When Pez published the first edition of the *Life and Revelations,* it was
attacked by the Benedictine Hadrianus Pontius precisely on this issue.[130]

While Agnes's visions provide much evidence for her contact with the
heavenly world and its inhabitants, as well as her strong devotion to the
mysteries of Christ's life, there is less attention given to nuptial union or
deeper considerations of the nature of *unio mystica.* Three texts, however,
do treat of the experiences of union the beguine enjoyed. In chapter 70
(172–74) something like an experience of erotic uniting with Jesus is portrayed, but in so brief and allegorical fashion that the account lacks the sexual overtones found in many other beguine narratives. This may be due to
the reticence of her amanuensis, because in chapter 195 there is a description of a Christmas ecstasy that explicitly guards against any sexual content
in recounting the kind of total rapture of soul and body characteristic of so
many other thirteenth-century female ecstatics. In a somewhat convoluted
passage the friar says:

> She felt such great sweetness of spirit, and yet in her whole fleshly nature it
> was not sexual [*libidinosa*], but a chaste melting, that to both forms of delight
> (soul and body) no delight upon earth was comparable–and none under
> heaven–that could please her as much as that joy with which she was plea-
> sured in that sweetness of both soul and flesh.[131]

Finally, in chapter 179 (370) there is a description of a "total rapture in
God" (*totaliter rapta est in deum*) that echoes the language found in many late
medieval accounts of deep union: "And so she felt herself united to God in
God in such a way that whatever she wanted, whatever she desired, what-

ever she was anxious to know, was all immediately present to her."[132] However, in most of the friar's accounts of Agnes's raptures we are merely given standard topoi about mystical union.

A Beguin Mystic

There were many names for the independent forms of female religious common in thirteenth-century Europe, as James of Vitry noted as early as 1230—*beguina, papelarda, humiliata, bizoche,* and the like. The term *beguina* was used not only for northern European female religious but also for a different movement of both women and men found in southern France and Catalonia.[133] Writing in the early 1320s, the Dominican inquisitor Bernard Gui devoted the fourth chapter of his *Inquisitor's Manual* to the "Sect of the Beguins" (*De secta bequinorum*), whom he described as follows:

> The sect of the beguins, who call themselves "Poor Brethren" and say and profess that they hold to the third rule of Saint Francis, arose in recent times in the provinces of Provence and Narbonne and in some parts of the province of Toulouse. . . . By lawful inquisition and through the depositions and confessions of a number of them, . . . the source of their errors and pernicious opinions has been discovered. They have culled these in part from the books and pamphlets of Brother Peter John Olivi, . . . namely from his *Lecture on the Apocalypse* which they have both in Latin and in vernacular translation. . . .[134]

Gui noted that the male and female beguins wore a garb of coarse brown, with or without a cape, according to their self-identity as third order followers of Francis. This identity, however, was accepted neither by the papacy nor by Franciscan authorities.[135]

The beguins were a lay form of religious life growing out of the radical wing of the Franciscan Spirituals. Although different from the beguines in many ways, their unstructured form of life, as well as the difficulties they encountered with ecclesiastical authorities, display a number of analogies. A fundamental difference, however, is that the *beguines* of the north began as a positive experiment in religious life, encouraged by many ranking clerics, whereas the *beguins* of the south from the outset were colored with the tincture of heresy.

The visionary mysticism found among the beguines was not unknown among the beguins, though naturally little survives, given the zeal of the inquisitors and the destruction of the movement. At least one document, known only in a late and corrupt copy, gives us information about a beguin female mystic whose claims to visionary contact with God produced a more dangerous message than anything found among the northern beguines. Na (short for *domina*) Prous Boneta was born about 1295 and was executed for heresy probably in 1328. A resident of Montpellier, she was arrested in 1325 and questioned by the inquisition to whom she responded quite freely about her visions and teachings.[136] Na Prous's message amounts to a rejection of the present state of the church as an instrument of salvation. She based this radical teaching on visionary claims to immediate contact with Christ similar to those found in many other women mystics.[137]

At her trial the beguin described how four years before, when she was praying after mass on Good Friday in the Franciscan church at Montpellier:

> Our Lord Jesus Christ transported her in spirit (i.e., in soul) to the first heaven. And when she was there she saw Jesus Christ in human form and in his divinity, and he appeared to her (the woman speaking). He showed her his pierced heart as if it were the window of a little lantern from which came forth the rays of the sun.

When Na Prous protested her unworthiness, Christ reassured her, so she then approached him and "placed her head below Christ's body [presumably bowing down], and she saw nothing but that brightness which Christ gave her in the rays."[138] This was the beginning of a series of experiences in which celestial light and heavenly figures appeared to the beguin, culminating in a vision of God the Father during the liturgy on Holy Saturday. In this experience she was given "high contemplation and the grace of contemplating heaven and seeing Our Lord Jesus Christ, along with constant prayer and feeling of our Savior."[139] In the course of these experiences Christ spoke to her, saying that he had given himself to her as he once did to the Virgin Mary. Na Prous went on to tell her inquisitors that she often enjoyed face-to-face vision of Christ in human form, and that she also heard him giving her the fateful commission: "St. John the Baptist was the herald of the coming of Jesus Christ's holy baptism; and you are the herald of the coming of the Holy Spirit" (*tu es praeco adventus Spiritus Sancti*).

The visionary recital that follows these initial experiences is fairly confusing, but it is important for providing further confirmation of Na Prous's special status in the history of salvation. She goes into ecstasy while praying for the salvation of all; then Christ assures her that despite her protestations of unworthiness he is transforming her soul into him as fire transforms what it burns. She also enjoys a vision in which she is given all three Persons of the Trinity—"She says," according to the court record, "that from that time on the whole Holy Trinity was with her in spirit."[140] The Franciscan Spiritual connection also comes to the fore here, as the beguin tells her investigators how the conception in the Holy Spirit that God gave her took place years ago when she visited the tomb of Peter John Olivi at Narbonne.[141] The claim the beguin makes at this point must have astonished and horrified her examiners:

> God himself completely gave her the whole divinity in spirit as completely as he gave it to his Virgin Mother and to her Son. All human nature was not sufficient for seeking this truth unless God were to give it the Holy Spirit. That divinity that God gave to her formed for itself one spiritual body of a more precious and pure intellect than she had possessed. . . . And God said to her: "The blessed Virgin Mary was she who gave the Son of God; you will be she who will give the Holy Spirit."[142]

As Barbara Newman suggests, this passage indicates that Na Prous believed that she had been in some way transubstantiated from her physical existence to a higher divine body.[143]

The remainder of the report consists of an account of Na Prous's teaching, along with frequent references to her authority as the *donatrix Spiritus Sancti*. The beguin's message is a rather obscure theology of history based on aspects of the Joachitism of the Franciscan Spirituals and a quasi-dualistic view of the conflict between good and evil that seems to be related to Cather teaching (e.g., the roles played by *Lucibel/Lucifer* and Adam and Eve). Na Prous often uses parallels between events in biblical history and current and/or imminent divine actions that are vaguely reminiscent of Joachim's *concordiae*. The picture that emerges could serve only to confirm her heresy in the eyes of her judges. Christ's passion, she says, had begun the work of the restoration of fallen souls to the terrestrial paradise from which Adam and Eve had been excluded. This terrestrial paradise is the church with its seven sacraments. The coming of the friars represented a new stage in the restoration process, with St. Francis and Olivi set up in the "paradise of the church" as Enoch and Elijah, the prophets of the last days. Olivi's writings are a new scripture, the *scriptura Spiritus Sancti*, so Pope John XXII's condemnation of these writings is a new "Fall," as great as that of Adam, one which also recapitulates the evil of the other major sinners of the Bible (e.g., Cain, Herod, Caiaphas, etc.). Because of the action of this papal Antichrist, the sacraments of the church have completely lost their saving power;[144] the only source of salvation now is to believe in the message of the Holy Spirit conveyed through Na Prous. At the end of the account she speaks about the "new age of the church" (*novus status ecclesiae* [ed., 27]) inaugurated by Olivi and reaching culmination in her. Her claims here become even more extreme, as when she says that "she sees God in the spirit every day and night and every hour." She accords herself the status of a co-redeemer:

The Lord said to her that just as Eve, the first woman, was the beginning and cause of the damnation of the whole of humanity or of the human race through Adam's sin, so too, "You will be the beginning and cause of the salvation of the whole of humanity or of the human race through the words which I am making you say, if they are believed."[145]

It is significant that another female mystic who claimed a similar co-redemptive status, namely Marguerite Porete, was also condemned to death.[146]

Mysticism among Anchoresses (*Reclusae*)

The beguine style of life created in Lotharingia was an innovation that was central to the growth of the new mysticism of the later Middle Ages. Just as this new mysticism did not mark the end of the monastic mysticism that had dominated Western Europe before 1200, but rather interacted with it, so too older forms of religious life (*religio*) for women that were not subject to a single approved rule continued to provide a basis for mystical spirituality. Among these was the life of the *reclusa/inclusa*, or anchoress.

Christians who, for ascetic reasons, deliberately died to the world by voluntary enclosure in a small room or cell had existed for many centuries as a special form of the life of solitude.[147] Though originally the terms *eremita* (hermit) and *anchorita* (anchorite) had been used interchangeably, the anchorite and anchoress (from the Greek *anachōrein* meaning "to withdraw or depart") later acquired a distinctive character because of their stability of place and total separation from the world, usually until death. A thirteenth-century anchoritic rule originally from England expressed the distinctiveness in this way: "The whole life of anchorites is comparable to the life of monks and hermits—he sits alone like a hermit in the desert and he ought to live in the silence of monks, and no one has as hard a life as a good anchorite."[148] Always popular in Eastern Christianity, the life of the recluse was known in sixth-century Gaul and Italy and was also found among Irish and Anglo-Saxon monastics from an early period. The ninth-century *Rule of Grimlaic*, often referred to as a rule for hermits, is really the first Western legislation for the anchoritic life.[149] Although a number of rules and handbooks for anchorites were drawn up,[150] the life of the recluse by definition took many forms and no legislation could cover all of them. Most early medieval anchorites were monastics, and among them women as well as men were to be found.[151]

The revival of the eremitical ideal among monastics of the eleventh and twelfth centuries also spurred renewed interest in the life of the recluse, as important texts from Peter Damian, Peter the Venerable, and others show.[152] Women outnumbered men in the movement, doubtless because medieval society made it difficult, if not impossible, for women to adopt the wandering life of the hermit, but did allow them this rigorous type of stable enclosure. The most noted witness to the life of enclosed women in the twelfth century is the *Rule of Life for Recluses (De institutione inclusarum)* that the Cistercian Aelred of Rievaulx wrote for his sister, probably in the 1150s. The work is divided into three parts—regulations for daily life; an ascetical treatise; and a meditation on the past, present, and future designed to deepen the recluse's devotion to Christ. Aelred's treatise was mined by many later clerics who wrote works of instruction and encouragement for recluses.

The life of the *reclusa* was necessarily more varied, more local, and more individual than that of the established communities for women who followed a single approved rule. The anchoritic commitment could be lived both by individuals and by small goups. It was often practiced within a monastery as a higher form of dedication, although in the late Middle Ages most anchorites were not monastics. Most forms of "reclusion," initiated by a celebration of the liturgy of the dead wherein the recluse was "buried to the world," were intended as life imprisonment in a tiny cell, but some reclusions were temporary, or at least capable of termination for specific reasons. While the anchoritic ideal was certainly strong in medieval England,[153] it would be a mistake to think that it was not widespread elsewhere. For example, a catalogue of the churches of Rome dating from ca. 1320 notes: "The total of all the female recluses or *incarceratae* of the city is 260."[154]

As one of the traditional forms of life in which women could express their total devotion to God, the life of the anchoress was also affected by the currents of change, both social and religious, of thirteenth-century Europe. Increasing urbanization and the desire for a life of heroic sanctity were at the root of the spread of new forms of urban reclusion. Most often the recluse lived in a cell connected with a local church, but other forms were known. These religious laywomen, often widows, gravitated to the mendicants for spiritual advice and other support.

Some of the thirteenth-century changes in the anchoritic life for women are evident in the first major body of spiritual literature written for women in English, the collection often referred to as the "Katherine Group," because in some manuscripts a vernacular version of the popular Latin *Life of St. Katherine* is featured. Though not mystical treatises as such, these six works, composed by one or more male advisors for a group of anchoresses between about 1200 and 1230, contain reflections on mystical themes, as well as important evidence concerning the transition of spiritual literature from Latin into a surprisingly sophisticated vernacular (nothing comparable survives in English for the next century).

Given their role in the development of English prose, these works have been the subject of a number of editions and considerable literature, though investigations of the spiritual and mystical dimensions of the texts have lagged behind the philological ones.[155] The most important and longest of the texts is the *Ancrene Wisse* (also known as the *Ancrene Riwle*), a guide for anchoresses containing regulations for daily living and mostly pragmatic spiritual direction. It is in part dependent on Aelred's book for his sister, but mines a rich range of other spiritual literature, testifying to the learning and literary skill of its author. Closely associated with this work are two brief treatises: *Sawles Warde* (*The Soul's Keeping*), a meditation on heaven and hell; and *Hali Meidhad* (*Holy Virginity*), a letter in praise of virginity (one of the most extreme of the Middle Ages). Two other groups of texts accompany these in some of the manuscripts, arguing to a complicated process of composition, revision and translation over some decades. In order to provide spiritual paradigms for the anchoresses, some manuscripts contain adapted translations of three lives (i.e., *passiones*) of female martyrs: Katherine, Margaret (not the Magdalene), and Julian. (The popular, often humorous, character of these lives once again demonstrates that medieval religious life was lived on many different levels.) Finally, there is a series of prayers and meditations in the style of Anselm that approach more standard genres of mystical literature. The most important of these is *The Wohunge of Ure Lauerd* (*The Wooing of Our Lord*). Discussion of the dating, context, and authorship of these texts continues. The most recent view is that they were composed by a learned Augustinian canon (or canons) of Wigmore Abbey in Herefordshire in the first quarter of the thirteenth century for a group of aristocratic anchoresses living in a nearby rural retreat.

The spirituality found in the works confirms this view. In many ways it is old-fashioned in relation to the paradigm of the new mysticism—but not totally. The works are old-fashioned in their lack of interest in visionary experience and also in the fact that these women were not encouraged to write, although they were able to read both English and at least some Latin.[156] However, the "Katherine Group" does have an affinity with aspects of the spirituality of contemporary female mystics on the Continent in at least two areas: the use of graphic meditation as a means to intense participation in Christ's passion; and expressions of erotic union with Christ that are more direct and more embodied than those typical of male monastic nuptial mysticism.[157]

The *Ancrene Wisse* comprises an introduction and eight parts: the first and last dealing with the "outer rule" of the anchoress's daily life and the other six dealing with the more important "inner rule." While the bridal, or nuptial, motif is by no means a central concern, it occurs in several places and receives two lengthy treatments. The first is in part II dealing with the outer senses, where the author encourages the anchoress to guard her senses from all worldly contact as befitting her position as "God's dear spouse" and "beloved" and "mirror" of Christ (*godes deore spuse/leofman/schawere*), so that she may enjoy the delights of the kiss of her Divine Spouse:

> *Osculetur me osculo oris sui* (Song 1:1), that is, "Let my Lover kiss me with the kiss of his mouth, the sweetest of mouths." This kiss, dear sisters, is a sweetness and delight of the heart so immeasurably sweet that every taste of the world is bitter compared to it. But our Lord kisses no soul with this kiss who loves anything but him, and those things it helps to have for his sake.[158]

A longer development of the nuptial theme is found in part VII, the section devoted to love as the culmination of the inner rule. Here we find a long *exemplum* likening Christ to a knightly ruler who rescues the besieged soul from her enemies through his death on the cross.[159] Such meditation on the passion becomes the main motif for the anchoress's total devotion to her Lover, even to the point of hinting at the exchange-of-hearts motif that was to prove so popular with other female mystics of the thirteenth century.[160] Christ's knightly shield is his body, covering his divinity, which is pierced in death for his lover: "His beloved should see by it how he bought her love, letting his shield be pierced, his side opened to show her his heart, to show her openly how deeply he loved her, and to draw out her heart."[161] In showing the superiority of the love of Christ to all human loves, the *Ancrene Wisse* is not afraid to describe the Lord's wooing in concrete terms of embracing and kissing, bidding the recluse, "Reach out for him with as much love as you sometimes have for some man. He is yours to do all that you want with."[162]

These intertwined motifs of participation in the passion and concrete descriptions of the wooing of the Lord appear elsewhere in these texts, especially in *Holy Virginity* and *The Soul's Keeping*.[163] They are also powerful in *The Wooing of Our Lord*, a prayer surviving in only one manuscript that appears to be among the latest of the texts. Although forms of devout meditation on the passion were pioneered by Anselm and developed by the Cistercians (who also said so much about the soul's nuptial union with Christ), there is a literalness to the language here that does not occur in twelfth-century texts. The anchoress is invited to woo Christ exactly the way a woman would woo any male lover, with sweet words and loving gazes on his beautiful face and white body.[164] Jesus, of course, is infinitely nobler than any human lover, not only because he is the ruler of the world, but especially because he demonstrated his supreme love for the soul by his death on the cross. Therefore, the bride's loving response should be to be crucified with him through poverty, shame, and the suffering unto death that is the life of the anchoress. A vivid meditation on the incidents of the passion, not unlike what later became popular among the Franciscans, leads to union with Christ on the cross in the living death of the cell:

> My body will hang with your body, nailed on the cross, fastened, transfixed within four walls. And I will hang with you and nevermore come from my cross until I die—for then I shall leap from the cross into rest, from grief into joy and eternal happiness. Ah Jesus, so sweet it is to hang with you.[165]

This passion-centered mysticism of hanging with Jesus on the cross also appears in other anchoresses of the thirteenth and fourteenth centuries.[166]

On the Continent, the lives of women recluses of the thirteenth century incorporate many of the visionary and ecstatic aspects of the new mysticism. Three anchoresses can serve to illustrate these developments: Juette of Huy (d. 1226) from Lotharingia, Umiliana dei Cerchi of Tuscany (d. 1246), and Margaret the Cripple (*Margarita contracta*) of Magdeburg (d. ca. 1265).[167] Unlike the rural, presumably aristocratic, anchoresses to whom the "Katherine Group" was directed, these mystical women lived within an urban environment and appear to have been from a mercantile, or middle-class, background. They witness to the growth of the new urban anchoritic life noted above.

Juette of Huy was a pioneer among the urban recluses, playing a role for her successors not unlike Mary of Oignies' position as the archetypal beguine saint.[168] Born in the commercial town of Huy near Liège in 1158, she was forced to marry, but was left a widow with two children at age eighteen. Resisting a second marriage, like Mary of Oignies she devoted herself to caring for lepers between 1181 and 1191 (see *Life* 10), leading a mendicant style of life. Eventually, she decided to adopt the "ultimate" form of religious life, that of the recluse. And so in 1194, with the permission of the Cistercian abbot of Orval, she was walled up in a cell built by her father "alongside the church" near the leprosarium where she had served in her town (*Life* 14).[169] Here she lived until 1228.

Juette's life as an urban lay saint (*vidua reclusa*) was written by the Premonstratensian Hugh of Floreffe. As in most male accounts of the female saints that proliferated in Lotharingia at the time, there is much emphasis on Juette's visionary and ecstatic experiences.[170] Despite prodding by Hugh, however, Juette refused to say much about the content of her raptures, especially those that she enjoyed of the Trinity (*Life* 23). Hugh describes her union with Christ in his humanity in the language of human love, though adhering to the traditional insistence that such uniting with Christ must always be brief. When she was compelled to "come down" from union, he says that she acted:

> As if she refused to be snatched from her Beloved's arms, she used to become swollen, and she cried out; she was distressed as though she were in pain; like a woman in childbirth she was tossed about hither and yon, and she sighed like a woman impatient for love.[171]

These depictions of her raptures were already standard fare when Hugh penned the work.

Such ecstatic states, however, were not just for Juette's own enjoyment; they were meant for the whole Christian community, especially for her clerical friends and those described as her *familiares et mulieres honestae*. Although Juette had abandoned the life of Martha when she gave up her active service of lepers to take up the higher contemplative task of Mary (see *Life* 11), her experiences of God increased her love for all and gave her supernatural knowledge that allowed her to correct, guide, and encourage scores of people, clergy and laity. According to Hugh,

> It was there [i.e., in her mystical experiences] that she without doubt conceived the feeling of love that she had for the salvation of all. It was so strong that her speech had great power for giving congratulation, compassion, consolation, correction, and edification for all who saw or heard her. Her love prevailed.[172]

Juette, a pious laywomen, was a strong critic of the unreformed local clergy who controlled the religious life of Huy (e.g., *Life* 26–27), but her concern was not so much to call down divine wrath as to lead sinners to repentance (e.g., chap. 32). Although Hugh mentions that there were many who doubted the visions of such "old women and poor little females," scoffing at them as "total dreams or jokes" (*somnia prorsus esse aut truffas* [*Life* 41: 883]), she found many supporters, especially among the Cistercians and Premonstrations, who at this period were the main confessors and guides of the *mulieres sanctae*. Nevertheless, as we have seen in the case of her contemporary Mary of Oignies, Juette is more the leader than the follower—a quite different relation from that witnessed to in the English texts discussed above. Her relation to those who came to her for counsel and intercession is described as that of "a most wise mother of the household" (*sapientissima materfamilias* [*Life* 30]). Like Angela of Foligno at the end of the thirteenth century, here at its outset we meet a woman who is characterized as both *mater* and *magistra*.[173]

The spread of the urban anchoresses and the significant religious role they played—often *because of* rather than despite their withdrawal into the anchoritic cell—is evident in a number of other women in the century after Juette's death. Some of these women also attained fame as mystics. The phenomenon was especially widespread in Italy, where the Florentine Umiliana dei Cerchi provides an illuminating example.[174] Umiliana was born into a wealthy mercantile family in 1219. Like Juette, she was married against her will and left a widow with small children in 1241. She refused to remarry, was dispossesed by her family, and took up a life of service to the poor. Umiliana was much influenced by Franciscans, especially her confessor, Michael Alberti, but she was refused entry into the Poor Clares (perhaps because she now lacked a dowry). Although she desired to go off "into the desert" to live as a rural anchoress, Friar Michael seems to have convinced her that she could provide an *exemplum* of a life of perfect asceticism in the midst of the city by leaving behind her active charity and withdrawing into the tower of her family mansion to live as a *reclusa*.[175] She spent only five years there, however, dying young in 1246.

Umiliana's withdrawal into solitude was paradoxically also a public manifestation to the citizens of Florence of how to live a perfect life. According to the *vita*, Umiliana's desire to follow Christ in all things was so complete that "God did not wish the lighted lamp to be hidden under a bushel (see Matt. 5:15) any longer and therefore placed her on the candlestick in a height of life and example so that she might light up all in the house, that is, in the church militant."[176] Although she is described as taking the cord of the third order of Franciscans,[177] Vito hails Umiliana as the "marvelous founder of a new life and holy form of conduct" (*novae vitae ac sanctae conversationis mirabilem Fundatricem*), one equal to all earlier forms of religious life—to monks in silence, to hermits in solitude, to Poor Clares in asceticism, and to Franciscans in following the Gospel (389E). Umiliana is portrayed as a classic example of the public, secular, and democratized form of mystical life which became so powerful in the thirteenth century. She "preaches" to all perpetually by work rather than word "with her dead body, . . . so that no one from the least to the greatest could have an excuse that they were not able to serve God as far as they can in their own house and in secular garb."[178] Like Juette, she is described as a teacher who instructs others in words, as well as in her life, giving each a fitting message (*Life* 3). She moved some city dwellers toward their own form of solitary life, saying, "Think of your house as the solitude of the forest and your family as wild animals and you will live among them as if you were in the forest, keeping silence and intent on constant prayer."[179] Even more, Umiliana is described as being able to make public places the equivalent of the cell of contemplation and mystical ecstasy. When she had to go out to church to receive Communion, she hurried through the streets of Florence with downcast eyes, telling her companion: "Do not bother me with words, because often when I'm going through the street, and in the midst of creatures and hearing sermons and things about God, I find my Lord just as fully as in my cell when I'm intent on prayers and devotion."[180] Friar Vito observed that "she was often ecstatically rapt into God in a marvellous way" in such circumstances.

Umiliana's mode of life parallels much of what we have seen in other ecstatic *mulieres sanctae*. She is praised for her humility and asceticism, though the *Life* notes that Friar Michael made her moderate some of her more severe practices. She suffers attacks from the devil designed to interrupt her nightly prayers (*Life* 2, 390E–392A); she prophesies, performs miracles, and even levitates, like Douceline de Digne and others (396DE). Like many holy women, she had a particular devotion to Christ's passion (see *Life* 3 and 4; 394AB and 395A).

Umiliana's ecstasies and raptures are also similar to those encountered among contemporary *mulieres sanctae* in Lotharingia and elsewhere. She had already received visions during her marital life (*Life* 1; 388B), but naturally these moved into a higher gear when she adopted the anchoritic lifestyle.[181] The Franciscan hagiographer was anxious to defend the saint against her detractors, not only those who considered her way of life useless (389F) but also those who felt that some of her more extreme visions were dreams rather than waking experiences (397F). Like many of the beguines, Umiliana is described as going into ecstatic states more frequently (every day) and longer (often three whole days) than had been seen as possible in earlier mystical accounts—"There scarcely or ever was a day in which she did not have a rapture of this sort; and at times for two days, or for a whole day and night, or the greater part of a day, or of a night, she rested in ecstasy in this way, as God afforded her."[182] The recluse experienced a *iubilus* like those given to other women mystics (394F), and also an unusual vision and conversation with Jesus as a four-year-old child that is so detailed and concrete that it must reflect the recluse's own account and not the mystical *topoi* of her biographer (397B–398A).

Given the relation between ecstatic women and the male guides that was so marked a feature of thirteenth-century mysticism, one of the most interesting features of Umiliana's ecstasies is the sharing of mystical experiences

she enjoyed with some of the holy men she admired. One of these was a
Camaldolese hermit named Simon whom she loved by report, never having
met him. Umiliana prayed to have a vision of him, which God granted,
showing her the holy hermit accompanied by two angels. This showing raptured her for three days "in the sweetness of the beloved Jesus" (395CD). The
recluse enjoyed another form of shared experience with her confessor Friar
Michael, one that is characteristic of the mystical conversations between
men and women in this century. One day, when the friar was praying in her
presence, he could feel no devotion, and so cried out: "My daughter, pray
for me, because I'm totally dry!" Umiliana then lifted up her eyes and
prayed, and the text continues: "At once she was given so much grace that it
was clearly apparent that she could not take in such fullness of grace and so
the holy woman was raptured in these gifts."[183] Thus Friar Michael, like
Peter of Dacia, found in Umiliana a channel of grace to relieve his own dry-
ness and doubts about the possibility of immediate contact with God.

The final mystical *inclusa* to be considered here, Margaret the Cripple,
demonstrates the variety of both lifestyle and message of the urban
anchoresses. Juette's anchoritic life was a formal lifelong enclosure (Abbot
John of Floreffe had her enclosure wall broken down so he could give her
the last rites after thirty-six years in her anchorhold). Umiliana's five-year
enclosure was more informal, if no less effective for her circle of adherents.
Both women existed within the context of powerful support groups, Cistercian and Premonstratensian for Juette and Franciscan for Umiliana.
Margaret's style of enclosure appears as a middle option, one closely connected to the Dominican order and offering its own distinctive mystical
message.

All we know about Margaret comes from the hints given in the *Life* composed by her confessor and friend, the also otherwise unknown Dominican
friar John of Magdeburg.[184] Margaret was born in that city about 1235,
apparently of well-to-do parents, and was crippled by disease as an infant.
In her early teens, "she desired to withdraw from the world and serve the
Lord in some solitary place, but she feared to lose the contempt [*despectus*]
that she had received from people, relatives and friends, if she were to
locate in a cloister or anchorhold."[185] But she finally decided to undertake
the life of a recluse, approaching it initially with fear, because while she
might appear to be an anchoress, she could not perform the manual labor
required of such women (e.g., weaving). Nevertheless, she felt that through
this strict form of life God might allow her to regain internally what she had
lost externally by her physical defects. Margaret therefore began an anchoritic life connected to an unidentified church in Madgeburg.[186]

The notion of contempt mentioned in the above passage concerning her entry into the anchoritic life provides a central clue to Margaret's religious physiognomy. At the outset of the work Friar John announces three forms of *despectus* that serve as the key to her mysticism. Commenting on her physical impairment as a sign of divine election, he says, "God acted like someone who wishes to hide a precious treasure in a contemptible sack to keep it safe. . . . The God who chose her . . . gave her three things in abundance, that is, pain, abjection and poverty."[187] *Pena-abiectio-paupertas* were familiar to many mystics, male and female, of the thirteenth century, but few if any ever lived them as totally as John portrays Margaret doing. The recluse's crippled body and headaches apparently caused her terrible physical suffering throughout her life (see, e.g., *Life* 4, 18–19, 44, 49, 64). But Margaret went beyond this by internalizing her pain, abjection, and poverty to make them the core of her experience of God. Like some other women mystics, her most severe pain (*pena*) was her realization of the constant sin and imperfection of this life and her inability ever to be able to love and praise God as fully as he should be loved and praised (*Life* 16). Margaret also internalized abjection and poverty into the inner state she referred to as the *abissus humilitatis* (e.g., *Life* 4, 24) or *abissus paupertatis* (e.g., *Life* 36–37, 56), a condition of total self-emptying which paradoxically brings the soul so close to God, the *abissus bonitatis,* that he is forced to come down, fill her with himself and act directly in and through her.[188] As she puts it, "Hence, because the soul here distanced herself from God by considering her own unworthiness, by that very fact she will be closer to God."[189] Margaret's mysticism is above all a mysticism of suffering rooted in the paradox of the cross.

In reading *The Life of Margaret* we enter quite a different world from that of the *mulieres religiosae* of Brabant, despite Friar John's comparison of his friend to the holy women he had seen there (*Life* 66). There are no outward miracles and wonders; even her sufferings are more internal than external, manifested only by the contortions of her body.[190] She does not receive visions. Given her desire for abjection and humility, she even begs God *not* to give her the visions of angels that others were granted (*Life* 60). She does, however, see the meaning of divine mysteries with "spiritual eyes" in her heart (e.g., chap. 9) and she frequently has conversations with God "in her heart" (e.g., chap. 55)–the *Life* is filled with these.[191] Finally, there is no erotic element in John's account of her relation to Christ. Even the late chapters in which she is at times described as a *sponsa* are in no way erotic or courtly in nature.

Margaret's mysticism of suffering is set forth through frequent repetition of a number of interrelated themes: the necessity for absolute dedication to God's will alone; the willingness to love God even if he were to consign her to hell; the choice of desolation not consolation; and the anchoritic life conceived of as hanging on the cross with Christ.[192] Many mystics have stressed the necessity for doing all for God alone and nothing for self. Margaret obsessed about this from the beginning of her career. For example, in speaking about her desire to experience pain greater than that given to anyone else for the sake of Christ, Friar John assures us that this was not done out of any hope of reward: "She did not desire such pain in order to have greater joy after this life. . . . She didn't want to make bargains or arrangements with Christ, but only [to show] that the grace of God which he would create in her in heaven would be more pleasing and acceptable to her."[193] This form of total dedication to the will of God, whatever it may bring, is often expressed in terms of the traditional theme of the *resignatio ad infernum* (see Rom. 9:2-3), that is, the willingness to endure damnation if such should be God's will. This appears more frequently in Margaret than perhaps any other thirteenth-century mystic.[194]

There is no denying that many passages in the *Life of Margaret* take on the flavor of a kind of spiritual masochism (e.g., chap. 62), but somehow the basic theological conviction of the text—namely, that the paradox of the cross has reversed all selfish human values through the example of divine humiliation and suffering—gives the account a nobility of tone that also contains an overt critique of the fixation on spiritual delights found in many late medieval mystical texts.[195] Margaret's message is that suffering not sweetness, desolation not consolation is the real way to God. As God tells her in one place, "If solace were solace to you, then I would not have given you that kind of solace; but because your solace is desolation, I have consoled you in this fashion."[196] Hence, like *The Wooing of Our Lord,* the conception of the anchoritic life that Friar John scripts out of her experience is that of being crucified along with Christ—"Then she was on the cross with Christ and she desired the church's salvation and God's praise above all things."[197]

The consequences of this for the public aspects of her vocation as an anchorite are both touching and daring. Her choice to embrace "suffering, abjection, and humility" to the fullest meant that she felt herself bound to love and console all others, especially sinners and the afflicted.[198] Even the attacks of her detractors could bring nothing but joy to her because they were a further form of humiliation. But, since the deepest humiliation and suffering, as shown in Christ, is the only way to redemption, by embracing the cross in a total fashion Margaret must, like Christ, become the redeemer of all. A lengthy section in the *Life* contains some of the most extreme formulations of the mystic as co-redemptor in the literature of the Middle Ages.

In chapters 55–56 of the *Life* God conveys a message to Margaret that is presented as being troubling both to her and to her confessor and biographer. At carnival time before Lent, when the anchoress was especially troubled because of the many sins being committed, she begins to understand something the Lord had told her in an earlier conversation about how she would someday begin to "suffer his will." "At that time," the text continues, "he illumined her in a marvellous fashion, and showed himself to her in her heart in an unaccustomed manner which was such that heart could not conceive nor tongue express it without having learned it through experience."[199] Christ tells her that he had specially chosen her in the same way as he had chosen his mother:

> At the time when I willed to become man, I elected you beforehand in a special way in your mother's womb, [just as] the greatest thing that I have ever done for a person was that I chose a virgin mother. In the last time you are now the greatest thing that has ever happened to a person in your time–this happens in you.[200]

Christ has chosen her as his special instrument of praise in the last times; everything that he once chose to do for his mother he now chooses to do for Margaret. The recluse's position as higher than any other saint is carefully spelled out in terms of Christ's promise to fulfill four desires she had expressed concerning her powers of intercession for others. In effect, Margaret here becomes a kind of co-redeemer with Christ–"Except for me alone," Christ tells her, "no one has ever atoned for the world in his heart as you have."[201]

Naturally, Margaret trembles at this unusual message and asks God to confer the gift on someone else. In chapter 57, when she tells Friar John of the revelation, he finds it "so great and unheard of" that he exhibits a certain reluctance about it; he knows that after this unveiling of the secret to him the devil will tempt Margaret to disbelieve the message. This indeed happens. From Tuesday to Saturday Margaret struggles with temptations to doubt her special position, temptations brought on both by her own weakness and by the devil's deceptive arguments. Finally, divine intervention banishes doubt and helps her to counter the devil's wiles.[202] As subsequent texts make clear, from that time on Margaret was able to accept her role as a co-redemptrix.[203]

During the course of her life as a recluse, Margaret's mode of union with God was based on uniting her suffering with that of Christ, or, as one extended treatment puts it, achieving a perfect union of wills with God (*Life*

58). The final stage of her pilgrimage, after she entered the Cistercian convent of St. Agnes, brought a new form of experience, one closer to that of the other *mulieres religiosae*. Chapters 67–69 of the *Life* provide a picture of this final stage, during which Margaret attained a union that is described in spousal terms. Margaret's role as a *sponsa,* however, is couched not in erotic images but in terms of the perfect conformity of will and mutual security that spouses learn "from the habit of living together." Here, "the heart of God is united to the soul, as if it were the soul's own heart," and, in language that hints at that to be found later in mystics like Meister Eckhart, such souls "see into themselves as if they see themselves in God's eyes, because their eyes are God's eyes."[204] The grace of this union is described as thousands of times beyond that found in the divine locutions recounted previously; it belongs only to those souls "who have been reduced to nothing" (*que in nichilum est reducta*). In this union, which can only last a brief time, Margaret's soul reaches equilibrium, so that even the ongoing struggle between her fear over her own unworthiness and her trust in God adds to rather than detracts from her joy. Her ongoing desire to help others, especially her friends and followers, no longer brings anxiety. She loses the pains that had troubled her and, like a bride, is adorned with such security and liberty that "it is as if she already possessed the home that had long ago been promised her."[205] This description of a mystical union that finally brought peace to the suffering soul of Margaret the crippled recluse is one of the longest and most moving of the thirteenth century.

Conclusion

The foregoing analysis of some of the forms of mysticism found among the women of the thirteenth century and the first part of the fourteenth provides considerable evidence for the creativity of the era. The women studied here, with the exception of Beatrice of Nazareth and Christina of Stommeln, are known to us only through the hagiographical texts that their clerical advisors composed to spread their fame. It is difficult to know how accurate a picture we get from these male texts about such original women. Nevertheless, this mass of evidence certainly tells us something about the nature and power of the new women's mysticism, and not just about the ways in which it was perceived and presented by the clerics who took it so seriously. With this evidence in mind, we can now turn to the three major beguine mystics of the thirteenth century, who speak to us (to a greater or lesser extent) in their own words.

CHAPTER 5

Three Great Beguine Mystics: Hadewijch, Mechthild, and Marguerite

IN TREATING ANGELA OF FOLIGNO in chapter 3, I used the term the "Four Female Evangelists" of thirteenth-century mysticism (pp. 141–42) to describe Angela and the three women to be treated in this chapter.[1] This is, of course, not a medieval denomination. I am employing the term to indicate not only the central role that these four women had in the new mysticism of the thirteenth century but also to underline the ways in which they sought to give their writings a status comparable to that of the Bible itself. There were, to be sure, other significant women mystical authors during the thirteenth century, such as Beatrice of Nazareth and Clare of Assisi; there were also female mystics who wrote more, such as the Cistercian nuns of Helfta to be treated in the next chapter. Still, Angela and the three beguines stand out for the originality of their views and the profundity of their theological vision. It is no accident that all four of these women lived independent forms of religious lives, though Angela's had a Franciscan character. Angela was also different in having no connection with the courtly motifs employed by the three northern *mulieres religiosae*.

Each of these three beguines had much to say on the themes identified at the beginning of the last chapter as characteristic of the new mysticism of the thirteenth century—the problem of authority, the role of visions, the relation of soul and body in consciousness of God, the excess of love, and the annihilation that leads to indistinct union (see pp. 154–57). Each also expressed aspects of the "courtly mode" of mystical language discussed in the previous chapter (pp. 168–70). Their teachings regarding these issues and modes of expression were far from uniform, however, and were sometimes even opposed. But a synthetic consideration of the three great beguines will show why these once-forgotten women now occupy so important a rank in the history of Christian mysticism.[2]

Hadewijch of Antwerp

Hadewijch remains a mystery, as much for the paradoxes and perplexity of her writings as for her life.[3] She was obviously learned, being familiar with Augustine, Richard of St. Victor, Bernard of Clairvaux, and especially William of St. Thierry.[4] If Marguerite Porete can be considered the most speculatively difficult of the three great beguine mystics, and Mechthild the most dramatic, Hadewijch remains the most difficult to summarize. The variety of her literary remains and the inner tensions of her thought challenge, even defeat, attempts to provide a general introduction to her mystical theology.

Hadewijch lived as a beguine in the first half of the thirteenth century, probably in the vicinity of Antwerp. She came from noble stock as her learning and knowledge of French courtly poetry suggest. Her *Letters* (*Brieven*, hereafter cited as L with number and line indications) show that she functioned as the head of a beguine house, but that she had experienced opposition that drove her to a wandering life (L 29—unless this is a literary topos). Hadewijch's writings were not widely known. Her works do not appear to have been collected and published until the middle of the fourteenth century, and only five manuscripts survive. Although she was read by John Ruusbroec and religious groups associated with the Brethren of the Common Life, it is only during the past century that one of the greatest medieval mystics has begun to be appreciated.

Hadewijch's literary mastery surpasses that of any other medieval woman mystic, not least because of the variety of genres in which she expressed her message.[5] Her forty-five *Poems in Stanzas* (*Strophische Gedichten*, hereafter cited PS with number) are modeled on the songs of the northern French *trouvères* and demonstrate a subtle transposition of the motifs and language of secular love poetry into the field of mystical discourse.[6] As compared with the highly stylized, often indirect, language of the *Poems in Stanzas,* the sixteen authentic *Poems in Couplets* (*Mengeldichten*, hereafter PC) are composed in rhyming couplets and generally assume a more direct and didactic mode as letters in verse.[7] Hadewijch's *Book of Visions* (*Visioenenboek,* hereafter V), the earliest vernacular collection of such revelations, appears to have been composed in the 1240s. Following Joseph Van Mierlo, most scholars think that the author arranged her rich and often strange visions according to a form of mystical itinerary, with V1 (a tree allegory) providing the introduction, V2–12 illustrating the seer's growth in mystical graces, and V13–14 constituting a summary and conclusion.[8] If the beguine's visions often recall those of John of the Apocalypse, Hadewijch's thirty letters are part of the long tradition of Christian didactic epistolography going back to Paul.[9] Though the letters have a deeply personal character, they are also doctrinal in their explanations of the motifs that are presented in a more symbolic way in the Visions. Kurt Ruh stresses that the relation between the two prose genres used by Hadewijch is a complementary one: "God's love as the central and (almost) only theme has different dimensions in the Letters than it has in the Visions; one could say that the view *in patria* stands over against that *in via*, in such a way, however, that the perspective always remains open to the other realm."[10]

Hadewijch's earthy and highly embodied descriptions of her encounters with Christ, the Divine Bridegroom (*brudegom*), especially in her visions, contain accounts of excessive ecstasy to rival those ascribed to other women of Lotharingia (see, e.g., V 7).[11] Her poems and letters ring the changes on the power and problems of *minne* in a way second to none among the women writers of the late Middle Ages.[12] Nevertheless, as Paul Mommaers has pointed out,[13] the beguine's works actually go far beyond the often simplistic picture of late medieval excessive women mystics presented by their male admirers then and now, serving as a valuable critique for those who overemphasize the delights of the ecstasy of love. For Hadewijch ecstasy, joy, and melting into the arms of Christ are decidedly *not* the end of the mature mystical life,[14] but rather the youthful beginning. As she put it in one poem: "They who love their love perfectly to the end are noble, and not only old but wise. . . ."[15] The theme of the old and wise lover, one who, like Jacob, wrestles with God (see Gen. 32:23–32 as treated in L 12), is central to Hadewijch's teaching. In what follows I will present the beguine's mystical message under three interdependent headings dealing with (1) the nature and activity of *minne*, (2) the relation of God and the soul in *minne*, and (3) the exemplary role of Jesus in living true *minne*.

The Nature and Activity of Minne[16]

Minne is Hadewijch's all-embracing theme.[17] "*Minne* is everything" (*De Minne es al* [L 25.39]), as she put once put it.[18] Love is meant to be explored and experienced in all its many moods and forms rather than defined and categorized. As the beguine says in PS 22:

> The power which I come to know in the nature of *minne*
> Throws my mind into bewilderment:
> The thing has no form, no manner, no outward appearance.
> Yet it can be tasted as something actual:
>   It is the substance of my joy. . . .[19]

Although *minne* is mysterious for Hadewijch, it is absolutely necessary—the very meaning of existence. "I will tell you without beating around the bush," she says, "be satisfied with nothing less than *minne*."[20] *Minne* is the air that she breathes: "I have nothing else: I must live on *minne*."[21]

Following the text from 1 John 4:16 (*Deus caritas est*), Hadewijch identifies *minne* with God himself in many passages, sometimes in a general way (e.g., V 3 and L 19.27–36), and sometimes explicitly as either the Son (PS 29.41–43) or the Holy Spirit (V 2). But *minne* is also the divine power that pervades the created universe—"*Minne* itself is the divine power that must have priority and does so in me" (*minne selue dats godlike moghentheit die moet vore gaen also doetse hier ane mi* [V 11.233–35]). As such, *minne* is capable of being personified and addressed as Lady and Queen (e.g., PS 2, V 13).[22] The fierce strength (*cracht*) and madness (*orewoet*) of *minne* fascinated Hadewijch:

> O powerful, wonderful minne,
> You who can conquer all with wonder!
> Conquer me, so that I may conquer you,
> In your unconquered power.[23]

From the human perspective, *minne* is both the experience of being subjected to this overpowering force and our response to it, the power of our own activity of loving that brings us to God. As L 12 puts it: "May God be God for you, and may you be *minne* for him. May he grant you to experience the work of *minne* in all things that belong to *minne*."[24] In PC 15 the same message repeats the word *minne* in almost mantric fashion:

> O *minne*, were I *minne*,
> And with *minne, minne,* to *minne* you,
> O *minne* for *minne* give that *minne*
> Which *minne* fully recognizes as *minne*.[25]

Given the omnipresence of *minne* in Hadewijch's writings, any complete summary would need to be book-length. Here, I can only try to suggest the richness of her teaching by an analysis of four key discussions, one from each of the genres of her oeuvre. We can begin with PC 16, which treats of the seven names of *minne*.[26]

The seven names that Hadewijch ascribes to *minne* do not constitute an itinerary of seven distinct stages, but rather an exploration of different manifestations of love's power in two "registers," the first consisting of four names, the second of three. Hadewijch ties these names to biblical texts (PC 16.8–11), just as Dionysius based his positive theology on the names found in scripture. (Like the other women mystics, Hadewijch could not be a *doctor scripturae*, but scripture was an essential resource for her mystical teaching.[27]) In the first register, her description of love as a bond (*bant*), or chain (PC 16.17–50), recalls not only Paul (see Col. 3:14) but also the *amor ligans* of Richard of St. Victor's *Four Degrees of Violent Charity*.[28] But what is striking about the beguine's treatment of this theme is how she employs it to express her personal experience of being enchained by love, as well as the cosmic bonds that form the foundation for all the delights and the tortures of the experience of *minne:*

> But her chains conjoin all things
> In a single fruition (*ghebruken*) and a single delight.
> This is the chain that binds all in union
> So that each one knows the other through and through
> In the anguish or the repose of the madness of love
> And eats his flesh and drinks his blood. . . .[29]

Like Richard, Hadewijch is comparing the madness (*orewoet*) of both profane and sacred love here—manifestations (though in opposed ways) of the *minne* that powers the universe.[30] The mention of how all lovers desire to eat and drink the beloved allows her to make a brilliant, and typical, move of much beguine piety—that is, the invocation of a eucharistic model. In the *Confessions,* Augustine (one of Hadewijch's heroes—see V 11, L 22 and 26) had said that when we think we eat or consume God it is actually he who consumes us, though the bishop had not explicitly invoked the Eucharist in this connection.[31] Here Hadewijch boldly proclaims that the madness of love is best manifested in the sacrament where Christ gives himself to be eaten by us, but in which he really incorporates those who receive him. Christ can never be consumed—the mystery of his divinity exceeds all absorption. But those enchained by *minne* must continue to feed on both "the God and the man" (another favorite theme of Hadewijch) in order to grasp the meaning of the text from the Song of Songs: "I to my Beloved and my Beloved to me" (Song 2:16).[32]

Light (*licht*), the second name of *minne* (16.51–58), seems to represent the "enlightened reason" (*verlichte redene*) that Hadewijch often treats as necessary to the proper understanding of "how we shall love the God-Man in his Godhead and in his Manhood." Live coal (*cole;* see Isa. 6:6), the third name, symbolizes the paradoxes of *minne* in which all contradictory behavior is "set afire and extinguished by the madness of love" (16.59–86).[33] The next name of love, fire (16.87–102), carries this fusing of opposites even further into a realm where love and hate, gain or loss, even heaven and hell have no more meaning:

> But once this fire gains control,
> It is all the same to him what it devours: . . .
> Consolation at being with God in heaven
> Or in the torture of hell:
> This fire makes no distinction.
> It burns to death everything it ever touches:
> Damnation or blessing no longer matters,
> This I can confess.[34]

The final three names of *minne* seem to represent a second "register," that is, a deeper penetration into the experience of love. In treating love as dew (16.103–26; see Dan. 3:49–50) Hadewijch begins by noting that this action comes after the fire of love has burned up everything in its violence. The gentle dew signifies the loving union between God and the soul, the kisses by which the soul eats the flesh and drinks the blood of *minne*. This is to experience "the indivisible Kiss which fully unites the three Persons in one being."[35] Here the beguine shows the influence of William of St. Thierry's Spirit-centered view of mystical union. The sixth name, living spring (16.127–48; see John 4:10 for the scriptural source), describes the metaphysical foundation of the experience of the unitive kiss—"This flowing forth and this reflux of one into the other."[36] *Minne,* like a great river, is the "sweet living life" that ceaselessly flows out from God and draws all things back into the divine source. But lest we think that names 5 and 6 indicate that we can ever attain a state of perfect fruition of love in this life, Hadewijch caps her analysis with a seventh name—a name of terror:

> Hell is the seventh name
> Of this love wherein I suffer.
> For there is nothing that love does not engulf and damn . . .
> As hell turns everything to ruin,
> In love nothing else is acquired
> But disquiet and torture without pity. . . .
> To be wholly devoured and engulfed
> In her unfathomable nature,
> To founder unceasingly in heat and cold,
> In the depths of love, its high darkness,
> This outdoes the work of hell.[37]

We should not be surprised that hell is "the highest name of *minne*." Perhaps even more powerfully than Angela of Foligno, Hadewijch taught that the mystical encounter with God in this life maintains, rather, even heightens, the sense of *tremendum,* the terror of those who are "lost in the storms of love" so deeply that they are totally "lovers lost in hell" (16.203–5).

Similar teaching can be found scattered throughout the Letters, such as in L 20, which provides an analysis of "perfect love" (*gherechte minne*) through a description of the twelve nameless hours "which fling love forth from herself and carry her back again into herself."[38] Here, however, I will make use of L 30, which expands on the trinitarian dimensions of the paradoxical fusion of fruition and fear in the experience of *minne.* L 30 is not as lengthy as some of the other epistolary treatises of Hadewijch, but it yields to none in its theological presentation of how *minne* establishes a bond between the human lover and the Trinity.[39]

The letter begins with the foundation of "perfect Love" in the love with which God loves himself, emphasizing that in selfless dedication to *minne* the lover must be prepared equally for sweetness or torment (30.22–48). This conforms to what we have seen in PC 16, but when Hadewijch insists that it is in the torment of love that we first begin to experience the true meaning of the phrase that "*minne* demands *minne*" (30.47–48), she is able to ground her teaching not just in human experience, but in the inner relations of the Trinity. In a difficult passage (30.49–67), she speaks of the relations of the Three Persons in terms of the "demand" (*maninghe*) of love that the Father, as source, makes of the Son and the Holy Spirit, and the "debt" (*scout*) that the Son and Spirit demand of the Father within the same "fruition of the Holy Trinity."[40] This demand of love is the source of both creation and redemption; it is in turn demanded of us. Our "noble reason" must "recognize its just debt and follow love's leading into her land."[41]

The remainder of L 30 lays out the requirements of living the demand of *minne* in order to attain the Unity that is also Trinity. Following one of the central themes of her teaching, Hadewijch first notes that anyone who wishes to reach the Godhead must practice all the virtues found in God when he lived on earth as an unexalted man (30.84–99). In living the demands of this form of *minne* we actually live the very life of the Trinity. By desiring *minne* under the guidance of reason one "lives the Son of God" (*leuet men den sone gods* [30.113]). In willing "love's will," and in exercising the virtues and enlightening all creatures, one "lives the Holy Spirit" (30.122). Finally, with unconquered power (i.e., *cracht/potentia* as an attribute of the Father) to strive "to grow up as loved one in the Beloved in every respect," especially by tasting "the unheard-of sweetness he merited by his sufferings," and to be certain that one is "wholly in the unity of *minne*," is *to be* the Father, according to Hadewijch (*Met desen wesene es men den vader* [30.144]).

Those who pay the debt that the Trinity demands in order to ascend to the Unity "in the Beloved with the Beloved" (30.149) eventually "are gathered there where the great light, the brilliant lightning, has flashed and the loud thunder has resounded."[42] Here Hadewijch employs the language of the Sinai theophany (Exod. 19:16–20) to symbolize the positive and negative aspects of experiencing union with God. Lightning is the "light of *minne*" which reveals who *minne* is and how she gives and receives in the embrace and kiss where she herself exclaims, "I am the one who has embraced you. This is I! I am the all! I give the all!" (30.161–62). Thunder, on the other hand, is the fearful voice of "enlightened reason" which tells us the truth about our failure and smallness in comparison with the greatness of *minne* (30.162–66). When the soul is drawn into union and "becomes all that that [i.e., *minne*] is," the divine Unity finally attains what it has demanded and the soul reaches fruition through the Trinity. "Then shall the three Persons forever demand and eternally render—at one and the same time—one being in one will, one possession, and one fruition."[43] Hadewijch concludes her letter by admitting that she cannot explain this because her love is still too small (30.177–78), and then she closes with a lengthy passage (30.179–248) criticizing herself and her audience for the self-will and cowardice that prevents them from being "united to the Unity of the Godhead" (*enicheit der godheit*).

Minne as hell, the suffering that every fruition of love brings with it, is omnipresent in the *Poems in Stanzas*—"More multitudinous than the stars of heaven are the griefs of love" (PS 17.17–18). Here, and elsewhere in her oeuvre, the beguine makes use of the traditional image of the "wound of love."[44] But Hadewijch always locates the courtly theme of suffering for love within the framework of her wider teaching about *minne* as the divine force whose mysterious being and acting demand the utmost. This is well brought out in PS 43. As with most of the poems inspired by the courtly genre, Hadewijch begins the piece by setting it within the course of the seasons, here the winter that brings on fear and a heavy heart rather than the spring that announces the coming of love. The harshness of winter matches the fear in the poet's heart that she will not be able to attain love (43.1–7). But because *minne* also grants understanding, Hadewijch knows, intellectually at least, that "whether I lose or win, *minne* shall be my gain" (43.12–13). Nevertheless, the following stanzas consist of a series of complaints and laments about the suffering that *minne* has brought upon the beguine. Although she was never willingly without *minne*, "the need of all needs" (*Want dat es alre node noet* [43.37]), she recognizes that the loving soul must not act cowardly toward love, but rather boldly claim what is due to it, namely, total transformation in the fire of *minne:*

> O sublime nature, noble love (*minne fine,* i.e., *fin'amours*),
> When will you make my nature so fair
> That it will be wholly conformed to your nature?
> For I wish to be wholly conformed.
> If all that is other in me were yours,
> Everything that is yours would be altogether mine:
> I should burn to ashes in your fire![45]

In order to belong to the nature of love, we must practice the humility that ascribes all success not to self but to *minne.* We must also be prepared to choose the misfortunes which *minne* brings to her followers. Reason (note, not "enlightened reason") counsels patience and promises great rewards, but the lover knows that the brave must seek the "depths of love" (*minnen grond*). Just when we seem on the point of knowing *minne,* however, she hides in her groundless nature, so that Hadewijch reaches the final wisdom which the suffering of *minne* bestows–the paradox of giving up love for love's sake:

> We must wholly forsake love for love;
> He who forsakes love for love is wise.
> It is all one whether we die or live:
> To die for love's sake is to have lived enough.
> Alas, love! You have long driven me to extremity;
> But in this very extremity to which you have driven me,
> I will keep vigil, love, in service of your love.[46]

This sober, even somber, expectancy characterizes those that Hadewijch elsewhere describes as mature lovers.

Finally, we can look at the role of *minne* in the last two visions of the beguine's *Book of Visions* (these actually constitute a single revelation). In this showing Hadewijch relates an encounter with divine love appearing as a seraph-countenance with six wings and then adds a meditation and letter on how this experience of the madness of love enabled her to be conformed to the humanity of God.[47] Hadewijch's vision took place on the Sunday before Pentecost when she was raised up "in the spirit" (*inden gheeste* [V13.2]), an expression she often used for the first stage of an experience of rapture.[48] Here the beguine experienced a totally new revelation of love and the seraphim singing "Alleluja" in a new secret heaven, "which is closed to all those who never were God's mother with perfect motherhood."[49] In this heaven Hadewijch sees "the countenance of God" (*dat anschijn van gode* [13.30f.]) with which he will satisfy the saints for all eternity, a countenance with six ceaselessly flying wings, like the seraph vision of Isaiah 6:2.[50]

Seeing the divine countenance was a major issue for mystics, both Jewish and Christian.[51] Exodus 33 confusingly has Moses both speaking to God "face to face" (33:10) and also being forbidden to see God's face (33:20–23). In the New Testament, John's Gospel insists, "No one has ever seen God; it is only the Son . . . who has made him known" (John 1:18), and Paul restricts face-to-face vision to heaven (1 Cor. 13:12). But in Apocalypse 1:12–16 the prophet John sees the face of the one "like the Son of Man." Among the mystics known to Hadewijch, William of St. Thierry was noted for his concern with the *facies Dei*, though he followed Paul in restricting any direct vision of the divine countenance to heaven.[52] Hadewijch, however, often speaks of seeing the "countenance of love," as well as the "countenance of God," especially in her visions with their similarities to the Apocalypse.[53] For her, *anschijn* seems to be a particularly potent way to describe the direct presence of God.[54]

Hadewijch's visual imagination is second to none among the medieval mystics, though its very originality often makes it difficult to interpret. In this vision, the six-winged divine countenance has both locks (*slote*), which are immediately opened so that the seer can behold the three directions of the flight of divine *minne*, and also seals (*seghele*) closed over the countenance and signifying the divine attributes in which no one can share without living the life of the God-man (13.46–53). Hadewijch's showing centers on the opening of these six seals to reveal the meaning of *minne*, an obvious parallel to the opening of the seven seals in Apocalypse 6:1–8:1. First, the host of the seraphim lead forward the "glorified spirits," who, like Jacob, have reached maturity in love (13.53–68). They then use the seals in their hands to unlock the middle set of wings of the countenance. Hadewijch continues: "The seraph who belonged to me and who had brought me there lifted me up, and instantly I saw in the eyes of the countenance a seat. Upon it sat *minne*, richly arrayed, in the form of a queen."[55] In the lengthy allegorical description of *minne* and her accoutrements that follows (13.84–150), Hadewijch, who is given a throne opposite *minne* and addressed as "mother of love" by her seraph (*moeder der minnen* [13:133–34]), is accorded extravagant praise for her reception of a vision of love surpassing that given to any created being, including Mary prior to her Assumption! She has truly become the perfected soul, higher even than the seraphim.[56]

Now that Hadewijch has realized her perfected status, she is in a position to command the seraph to open the other seals on the wings of the divine countenance. The opening of the two highest seals reveals the spirits who are totally annihilated in humility and who are therefore capable of sounding a new heavenly melody and enkindling "an eternally new conflagration" (13.150–77). To the accompaniment of a new song in the "depth of love" these souls are adorned with the "same form of love" that Hadewijch had been given. The opening of the two lowest seals brings forth a small number of souls of even higher perfection. "These were they who, in the liberty of love (*bi vriheiden van minnen*) between them and their Beloved had cast off humility and had placed knowledge between them and their God."[57] Such souls have knowledge of the divine attributes through their possession of the seven gifts of the Holy Spirit, the signs of love that Hadewijch had seen under the feet of *minne* seated on the throne. But they also have a further gift–"the eighth is the divine touch giving fruition, which does away with everything that pertains to reason so that the loved one becomes one with the Beloved."[58] These souls have attained this final gift through what Hadewijch calls "unfaith" or "mistrust" (*ontrouwe*), one of the most original and difficult aspects of her mystical teaching.

Unfaith may be described as the soul's hard-won response to the torture and suffering that *minne* inflicts on her in the game of love. As described here and elsewhere, this mysterious state occurs when the soul's frustrated desire passes beyond humility and knowledge to a consciousness in which she ceases to believe in the faithfulness of *minne*. This indifference to, even hatred of, love's consolations allows her to engage in a far deeper struggle with love on love's own grounds. Abandoning *minne* for the sake of *minne* compels *minne* to surrender herself to the soul. Of such souls, Hadewijch says:

> They called continually for fruition and did not believe in the love of their Beloved; it rather appeared to them that they alone were loving and that love did not help them. Unfaith made them so deep that they wholly engulfed *minne* and dared to fight her with sweet and bitter.[59]

By giving up not only present consolation, but even all hope of consolation, by ceasing to have faith in love at the same time that one remains totally dedicated to love, the soul finally attains the maturity of true love. As Hadewijch puts it slightly later: "The denial of love with humility is the highest voice of love" (*Want loechenen der minnen met oetmoede dat es die hoechste stemme der minnen* [13.283–84]).

The remainder of the first part of the vision (13.241–322) includes a discussion of the enigmatic number of these perfected souls (107 all together, of whom 29 are already in heaven). This prepares the way for Hadewijch's "List of Perfected" that accompanies the vision in the manuscripts.[60] Mary, who is the highest of the perfect in heaven, addresses Hadewijch in a lengthy speech (13.271–314), praising her for attaining mature union with *minne* through "highest unfaith" (*hoechster ontrouwen*). The Virgin Mother tells her that the only possible fuller fruition would be by leaving the body through death, but reminds her that her duty to lead others to perfection, especially those she loves, requires her to defer this final enjoyment. This is reminiscent of the command that Hadewijch received from the divine voice in V 8: "Lead all the unled according to their worthiness in which they are loved by me."[61] Hadewijch, like all Christian mystics, is restrained by the bonds of active love from following the path to a literal *mors mystica*.[62] At the end of this part of the vision, the beguine again beholds all things in the divine countenance, and then concludes by emphasizing the novelty of this stage of her experience of God: "Then fruition overcame me as before, and I sank into the fathomless depth and came out of the spirit in that hour—of which one can never speak at all."[63] This comment suggests that the entire experience, though having begun "in the spirit," involved a passage "beyond the spirit" in its lofty character.

Hadewijch's theological meditation on the vision of the countenance that follows confirms this (V 14.1–223). Here she connects the vision with other major themes of her teaching on love, particularly its relation to our imitation of Christ, the God-man. The beguine reflects that before the vision she had been in such great desire, insanity (*orewoede*), and disturbance (*ongheduricheit*) that she thought she could no longer live (compare this with the account of her physical and psychical distress in V 7.3–29). Through her reception of her own throne in this vision, however, God has given her "the strength of his own being to be God with my sufferings according to his example and in union with him, as he was for me when he lived for me as man."[64] Hadewijch thanks him for the throne of the height of love that he has given her,[65] marveling that he has preferred her to all the creatures she ever saw (!). The beguine recognizes that this preference means not pleasure but more suffering for the sake of her likeness to Christ. She now can see all her works and all her suffering—"with the madness" (*orewoet*) and "great horror" (*groten gruwele*)—as taken up in God himself (14.26–74).

The second part of this theological meditation is a letter addressed to an unknown young beguine, one of the group for whom Hadewijch composed her mystagogical collection of visions.[66] Here Hadewijch summarizes the meaning of the vision of the countenance, as well as other visions not recounted in the surviving *Book of Visions*. God's countenance is invisible for "those who have never tasted human and divine love in one being," the flowing out and back of all things in God (14.102–8). Though Hadewijch refers to having seen God previously in a Transfiguration-like experience (not recorded in the *Book of Visions*), she again asserts the novelty of the countenance-vision. The rather confusing account of other visions of the divine countenance that she gives also mentions the interesting fact that she once lay for three days and nights "in rapture of spirit at the countenance of our Beloved" (*in opghenomenheiden van gheeste in dat anschijn one lieues* [14.183–85]). She also claims to have been "entirely out of the spirit" (*altemale buten den gheeste* [187–88]) for a similar length of time. These notices mirror the lengthy ecstatic experiences we have seen in the case of other thirteenth-century women mystics. But Hadewijch once again is original in her conclusion to this lengthy visionary recital, as she leaves us with the picture of God sitting on the new throne "which was I myself," addressing her in extraordinary terms as "the strongest of all warriors" and "greatest heroine," who has deserved to know him perfectly (V 14.206–24).[67] Because Hadewijch has become united to *minne* in her ongoing struggle, she has attained the level of the perfected ones.

The Relation of God and Soul in Minne: The Mutual Abyss (afgront)

Minne brings God to the mystic and the mystic to God. But what kind of God does the mystic find in *minne?* And what kind of a person or subject does God seek through the "demand of *minne*"? Hadewijch's teaching about the mutual abyss of God and the human person, founded upon her own version of exemplaristic Christian Platonism, is no less original than her subtle and complex presentation of the meaning of love.

Especially in her letters and visions, the beguine advances a teaching concerning the divine Uni-Trinity (often through original symbolic presentations) that ranks among the most intriguing of the medieval period. We have already mentioned her fascination with the "divine countenence" as seen in V 13–14; other basic symbolic images that represent the Trinity, such as those found in V 1, 4, 11 and 12, include the depth/abyss (*diepheit/ afgront*), the wheel/disk (*sciue*), and the whirlpool (*wiel*). To be sure, Hadewijch's vernacular theology is not restricted to symbolic presentations. L 22, for example, stands out as an example of a more speculative analysis, both for its treatment of four fundamental paradoxes involved in thinking about God, as well as for its description of five ways to union with him.[68]

The four paradoxes of the divine nature taken up by Hadewijch are based on the trinitarian hymn, "Alpha et Omega, magne Deus," ascribed both to Abelard and to Hildebert of Lavardin. This speaks of God as,

> Above all things, below all things;
> Outside all things, within all things;
> Within all things, but not included;
> Outside all things, but not excluded;
> Above all things, not elevated;
> Below all things, not subjugated.[69]

Hadewijch's exploration of these paradoxes is no abstract exercise, but is designed to remind her readers "to demand unity with him in the three Persons" (*wi so weder manen sine einicheit in drien personen* [22:49–50]).

In her consideration of the third paradox, namely, that God is within all things, but not included (i.e., "uncircumscribed" in traditional theological terms), Hadewijch sets out the foundations for her exemplaristic view of the relation of the human subject to the three persons of the Trinity. As she puts it, "God has fruition of his blessed wonders in all persons who were, who are, and who shall be, in the state that is their due in the plenitude of glory."[70] Just as God "pours forth his Unity in Persons," he also "inclines" the persons of the Trinity toward us through four gifts that form the basis of our return to union with him. In the first mysterious and incommunicable gift, Hadewijch says that God gives us the "eternal time" that is himself in "a way beyond being," one that can only be understood by those who have become one spirit with him (see 1 Cor. 6:17). In the second way he gives his nature to the soul, imprinting in it "the enlightened reason" corresponding to the Son's love of the Father, the "memory" that matches the Father's love for the Son, and the "high flaming will" of the Holy Spirit that is the mutual love of both (22.137–42).[71] If the first gift is a participation in eternity, and the second our creation in time, then the third gift is the path of recreation or redemption by which God-man delivered up his substance to death and left us himself to be consumed in the Eucharist. Finally, in the fourth donation, God "relaxes time"; that is, he waits for us to embrace him during the course of our lives.

Hadewijch discusses how these gifts are the foundation for various ways of returning to God's "inmost reality" (*alre binnenste*). The first way penetrates the depths of God in an indescribable manner. Those who follow the gift by which he gave us a share in his nature, what Hadewijch calls the "way of heaven," "apply themselves to *minne* without great woe" (22.166–67). Those who go to God by the "way of hell," that is, by following Christ's cross (see 22.169–82 and 228–36), are led "very deep into God, for their great despair (*onthope*) leads them above all the ramparts and through all the passageways and into all places where the truth is."[72] Those who follow the fourth way, which is described as the "way of purgatory" (see 22.183–212 and 237–46), burn ceaselessly for God in such a manner that the depths of their souls can never be filled. They live in a land of "holy anger" (*heilich toren*) where they "consume without being satisfied" (*dese sijn int teren sonder voeden* [22.212]). It is obvious that Hadewijch's own mystical path primarily combined elements from the way of hell and the way of purgatory.[73]

In her lengthy treatment of the fourth paradox (God as outside all things, but not excluded) Hadewijch returns to a treatment of the inner dynamism of the Trinity. God is outside all things because "he rests in nothing but the tempestuous nature of his profusely overflowing flood which flows back and forth over all."[74] Hadewijch's expression of trinitarian emanation here through the language of flood and flowing is comparable to that of David of Augsburg (see chap. 3, p. 116), but it is also a testimony to the creative role of women in vernacular theology, because her formulations may actually predate those of the Franciscan.[75] Taking a cue from the text of Song of Songs 1:2 ("Your name is as oil poured out"), the beguine introduces a discussion of how the "pouring out of the name" of the Father (*dat vloyen van sinen name*), as well as that of the Son and of the Holy Spirit in the works appropriate to each, allows us access to their unique names in the properties of the persons. Without following the details of this rich theology of the Trinity, it is interesting to note that Hadewijch, like Bonaventure, insists on the priority of the Father as the person "who includes (*omgriptene*) the Godhead in justice, in his own right" (22.363–65), and thus also comprises the justice of the Son and the Holy Spirit, as well as the "justice in all spirits whom he has inspirited in jubilation and the full fruition of *minne*" (22.368–71). In concluding this letter, Hadewijch seems to refer to a vision not included in the *Book of Visions*, describing how the four paradoxical attributes, or "modes of being of God" (*wesene van gode*), meet in a "totality that sits in the midst of a circle with four creatures," the four "living creatures" of Ezekiel and the Apocalypse (cf. Ezek. 1:5–25; Apocalypse 5–6).

This dynamic theology of the inner life of the Trinity, ceaselessly and stormily flowing, is presented in a similar fashion in the *Book of Visions*. In V 1, for example, after an allegory of trees representing virtues, the seer is given a manifestation of God and an inaugural series of commands concerning her mystical vocation (V 1.278–551). Looking through a cross like a crystal, she beholds a great space. Before it there is a "seat like a disk" representing eternity; beneath the disk are three pillars of precious stones that

signify the names by which the persons of the Trinity are commonly
known. Under the disk "a whirlpool revolved in such a frightful manner
and was so terrible to see that heaven and earth might have been astonished and made fearful by it." This dark whirlpool is "divine fruition in its
hidden storms."[76] On the disk Hadewijch sees the divine countenance (the
description is based on Apoc. 1:12–18) in such a concrete way that she says
that God gave himself to her "both in spiritual understanding of himself
and in feeling" (V 1.334–36). When she falls at his feet, she hears the significant command: "Stand up (cf. Ezek. 2:1)! For you are standing in me from
all eternity, entirely free and without fall. For you have desired to be one
with me."[77] The "eternal standing in God" that Hadewijch is reminded of
here highlights an important theme of the new mysticism of the thirteenth
century—its emphasis on the exemplary or virtual preexistence of the soul
in God, a notion that served as at least part of the foundation for new
modes of conceiving *unio mystica.*[78]

In order to grasp the import of this it is necessary to take a brief historical
detour. The first-century Jewish mystic and philosopher Philo of Alexandria
is the earliest witness to the incorporation of the Platonic ideas, the forms of
all reality, into the mind of God. This "intradeical" interpretation of the
ideas was taken up by Christians beginning with Origen;[79] it was important
to Augustine of Hippo, who insisted that the Word of God from all eternity
contains the exemplars of all created things (*rationes aeternae*) and through
them has direct knowledge of all particulars.[80] Stress on this eternal, exemplary, and virtual (i.e., in divine power, or *virtus*) preexistence was developed by John Scottus Eriugena and also appears in William of St. Thierry.[81]
When William and other twelfth-century mystics called on the soul to recognize her dignity and honor as made in the *imago Dei,* however, they did
not make *direct* appeal to her precreational and eternal status in the Word.
This form of address, often cast in a highly personal tone (as above with
Hadewijch), first appears in the thirteenth century with the three beguine
mystics under consideration here. For Hadewijch it seems to have been
central to the claims she made for her writings. When we ask on what
authority the beguine advances her rich and unusual theology and directs
those under her along the mystical path, her consciousness of speaking out
of her precreational self in God provides the central clue.

Hadewijch's letters contain several treatments of the exemplary existence
of the human subject in the eternal *wesene* of God,[82] but it is primarily in the
visions that the mystical implications of exemplarism are spelled out. In
V 4 Hadewijch sees two equally splendid kingdoms. A fiery seraph appears,
who stills the whole universe with seven claps of his wings and asks the

beguine to choose one of the two heavenly kingdoms she beholds. She then addresses the seraph, telling him that she now understands the meaning of the two heavens. The one represents her eternal self or exemplar; the other that of her Beloved, "and each of them equally powerful, in the same service, the same glory, the same omnipotence, and the same long-suffering mercy in all eternal being."[83] The seraph next makes a remarkable statement, addressed to the exemplary Hadewijch, referring to the earthly Hadewijch in the third person:

> Now see me united in unity with your Beloved [i.e., the seraph form is really Christ]. You are my loved one, loved with me. These heavens, which you beheld, are wholly hers [i.e., the earthly Hadewijch's] and mine; and these that you saw as two kingdoms that were separated were our two humanities before they attained full growth. I was full grown before [i.e., through my life on earth]; and nevertheless we remained equal. And I came into my kingdom yesterday [i.e., when Christ's humanity ascended to heaven]; and you became full grown afterwards; nevertheless, we remained equal. And she shall become full-grown today and come tomorrow with you into her kingdom; and nevertheless shall remain equal with me.[84]

Although this speech is obscure, the general import is clear: Hadewijch's exemplary self and her historical self are growing together in love to attain the fullness of their primordially given equality with the Beloved.

Another significant treatment of the relation between the exemplary and the historical "persons" named Hadewijch is found in V 11. On a Christmas night the beguine is taken up in spirit and beholds "a very deep whirlpool" containing all things. Here she sees an infant being born in "the souls hidden from their own eyes in the depth of which I speak, and to whom nothing is lacking but that they should lose themselves in it."[85] Then the seer beholds a phoenix symbolizing "the Unity within which the Trinity dwells" devour a young eagle with grey feathers and an old yellow eagle with new feathers. A divine voice reveals to Hadewijch that one of the eagles stands for St. Augustine, the other for herself. Hadewijch is the young eagle, because she is still attaining perfection, but her feathers are grey and old. The explanation of this is that "[t]he old age that I had was in the perfect nature of eternal being, even though I was youthful in created nature."[86] Although Hadewijch confesses to the pleasure that this union with Augustine conveyed, she asks her Beloved to grant her wish to remain only "in his deepest abyss, alone in fruition" (*in sine dipste afgront allene in ghe-brukeleecheiden* [V 11.116–17]).[87]

The relationship between the mystery of the Trinity and the soul's mystery, with its dual modes of existence, that is, exemplary existence in God and historical existence in space and time, is also the theme of V 12. During Mass on the feast of the Epiphany Hadewijch is taken up in spirit to behold the now familiar disk of divinity ceaselessly spinning in the immeasurably deep and dark whirlpool.[88] On the disk sits the figure bearing the divine countenance whose breast is inscribed with the words, "The Most Loved of all Beloveds" (*ghelieue lief* [cf. Apoc. 19:16]). As in V 1, Hadewijch falls down in adoration, but four eagles arrive who command her to stand, because those who stand up to contemplate the countenance will be able to "fathom the deep abysses" (*bekinne die diepte afgronde* [12.60]). Then the seer is raised up to behold twelve virtues conducting her as a bride to union with her Beloved. The last three virtues form the culmination of her journey to union. Wisdom summarizes all the previous virtues and gives Hadewijch knowledge of the Trinity in Unity (12.125–34). "Unanimity" (*vredeleecheit*) expresses her perfect conformity to all the mysteries of the life of Christ, including his ascension back to heaven and the acknowledgment of the three persons in the divine Unity (12.134–62). Finally, patience shows her as "godlike in one being and in one work" (*godeleec in enen wesene ende in enen werke* [12.167–68]). Hadewijch is now ready for total union:

> And in that very instant, I saw myself received in union by the One who sat there in the whirlpool upon the circling disk, and there I became one with him in the certainty of union. . . . In that depth I saw myself swallowed up. Then I received the certainty of being received, in this form, in my Beloved, and my Beloved also in me.[89]

This unification of the "all-powerful, perfect" (*alweldeghe, volcomenleke*) bride with the Beloved Lord suggests a union of indistinction that goes beyond traditional Western understandings of a loving union of wills with God. Hadewijch's teaching on this "deep" union is also evident in her use of the language of the abyss.[90]

The term *abyssus* (Greek *a-byssos,* "without ground") occurs frequently in the Bible, usually to signify the underworld or the depth of the divine judgments (e.g., Ps. 35:7). The word was used by Bernard of Clairvaux in reference to God (e.g., *abyssus luminis,* or *abyssus aeternitatis*). The abbot also employed a passage from Psalm 41:8, "Abyss calls out to abyss (*abyssus abyssum invocat*)" to express the way in which the Abyss of divine light calls out to the dark abyss of the sinful human heart;[91] William of St. Thierry used this text to signify how the embrace we receive from the Holy Spirit in this life "calls out to" the perfect embrace reserved for heaven.[92] This form of abyss language within a mystical context, pioneered by the Cistercians in the twelfth century, flowered in the thirteenth century, especially among the women mystics (we have already seen examples in Angela and Beatrice).

Hadewijch was particularly fond of such language. Where the beguine moves beyond other uses of abyss terminology is the way in which she conceives of God *and* the mystic as mutual abysses, equally bottomless in the power of *minne*. This is most evident in a remarkable passage from L 18:

> The soul is a bottomlessness in which God suffices to himself; and his own self-sufficiency ever finds fruition to the full in this soul, as the soul, for its part, ever does in him. Soul is a way for the passage of God from the depths of his liberty, that is, into his inmost depths, and God is a way for the passage of the soul into its liberty, that is, into his ground that cannot be touched without contact with the soul's depth. As long as God does not belong to the soul in his totality, he does not truly satisfy it.[93]

Another passage, this time from L 12, speaks of those who are "ready to content *minne*" as being "as unfathomable as God is" so that they are "never attained by the depths of *minne*."[94]

But how can there be two infinite abysses? The perfect Oneness (*enecheit*) of human bride and Divine Bridegroom described in V 12 and elsewhere implies that there is only one infinite abyss, as a passage from the twelfth of the PC poems makes clear:

> And that kiss will be with one single mouth,
> And that fathoming will be of one single ground,
> And with a single gaze will be the vision of all
> That is, and was, and shall be.[95]

Such texts indicate that in Hadewijch we find one of the earliest witnesses for a major turning point in Western mysticism. The Dutch beguine moves beyond conceiving of union with God as a loving union of finite spirit with Infinite Spirit (*unitas spiritus*) to a deeper and more daring treatment of union involving something similar to the *unitas indistinctionis* (union of indistinction) found in Eckhart and other late-thirteenth- and fourteenth-century mystics.[96] We should not seek in Hadewijch any systematic account of such a theology of union (this would involve the dubious category of *Wesenmystik* that has sometimes been applied to her).[97] What we do find, however, is a variety of formulations indicating that the goal of the mystic's quest includes a realization of the indistinct unity that the preexistent, or exemplary, self has always enjoyed in the depths of the Trinity.

In analyzing L 30 above, we saw Hadewijch claiming that she "lives" the Son and the Holy Spirit, and even that she "is" the Father (L 30.144). In the same letter she becomes all that *minne* is (30.167–68). In L 17 the beguine says that in the fruition of *minne* "a person becomes God, mighty and just" (*es men god worden moghende ende gherecht* [17.98–99]). Hadewijch illustrates this by the account of her own reception of a kiss from the Son during Mass which united her to the second person in such a way that "the Father took the Son to himself with me and took me to himself with the Son." In this unity she understands the divine "being" (*wesen*), though she admits that there are neither "words enough nor Dutch enough" to express this mystery (L 17.101–22). This is reminiscent of the Pentecost experience described in V 7, where the beguine recounts her erotic union with Christ in the Eucharist, typical of what we find with many other beguines (see V 7.75–105).[98] But after her initial embrace of the God-man, she says that the vision of Christ's form faded so that she could no longer perceive him outside her or distinguish him within her. "Then it was to me," she says, using one of the later technical terms for such union, "as if we were one without distinction" (*wie een waren sonder differencie* [7.114–15]). These and other texts clearly move beyond twelfth-century expressions of mystical union toward the indistinct union favored by some late-thirteenth-century mystics like Marguerite Porete and Meister Eckhart.[99]

It is true that Hadewijch often uses the traditional language of "becoming one spirit with Christ," based on 1 Corinthians 6:17 and other formulations associated with the *unitas spiritus* conception of mystical union.[100] Like many other late-medieval mystics, Hadewijch apparently saw both forms of union-language as quite compatible. In L 9 she describes how the loved one and the Divine Lover dwell in each other in such a way "that neither of the two distinguishes himself from the other, . . . while one sweet divine nature flows through them both, and they are both one thing through each other, but at the same time both remain—yes, and remain so forever."[101] This text is an effective summary of the beguine's view of the "fruition," or "enjoyment of love" (*ghebrukken van minne*), which is the goal of her message. It emphasizes the absolute mutuality of the experience of loving in a way that goes beyond traditional distinctions between God and the human person. Such a view of union is implied also in the passages noted above which affirm the infinite character of the soul's abyss, a teaching that seems rooted in the beguine's new "personalized" form of Christian Platonic exemplarism.

Hadewijch's tentative expressions of a union of identity, or indistinction, also imply that in the abyss of *minne* the soul "affects" or attracts God, just as much as God draws the soul to himself. Nevertheless, Hadewijch views loving fruition from multiple angles. Though her mysticism is in many ways different from that advanced by Meister Eckhart and his followers half a century later, she insisted that if, from one aspect, union is "without difference" (*sonder differencie* [V 7.115]), from another, "both [subjects] remain" (*beide bluien* [L 9.80]). Eckhart would have agreed.

The Exemplary Role of Jesus in Minne

Hadewijch's mysticism is no less christological than that of Angela of Foligno, or of the beguines described in the previous chapter. Nevertheless, the form in which she expresses her mystical devotion to Christ is distinctive. The key theme, already seen in a number of the texts analyzed above, is that no one can participate in perfection "unless he/she wishes to live God and man" (*gode ende mensche pleghen* [V 13.53]). In the tenth vision, when Hadewijch is proclaimed the perfect Bride by the Divine Voice, this message is highlighted:

> "Behold, this is my bride, who has passed through all your honors with perfect love, and whose love is so strong that through it all attain growth!" And he said: "Behold, bride and mother, you like no one have been able to live me as God and man!"[102]

This "living God and man" means that one must follow the example of the Savior, especially in suffering. In L 6, for instance, Hadewijch says that we all wish "to be God with God," but that there are few who want to live as humans according to the model of suffering humanity found in Christ.[103] Jesus is our only way to God, as the beguine explains by joining together two of her favorite scriptural texts:

> He [Jesus] worked with vigilant charity (*caritate*), and he gave to *minne* all his heart, and all his soul, and all his strength [cf. Deut. 6:5]. This is the way that Jesus teaches, and that he himself is [cf. John 14:6], and that he himself went, and wherein are found eternal life and the fruition of the truth of the Father's glory.[104]

It is crucial to recognize that "living Jesus as God and man," especially through sharing in his sufferings, is not a preparatory stage for a higher goal of purely spiritual enjoyment of God, at least in this life. The paradoxical message of *vercrighen in ontbliuen*–that is, of "receiving [joy, bliss, fruition] in lack [absence, suffering]"–is, on the contrary, the wisdom that mature lovers are taught through the pedagogy of *minne*.[105] As Paul Mommaers has shown, this means that, for Hadewijch, the common experience of being human, with all its suffering, especially the pain of God's absence, is integral to true mystical consciousness.[106] In L 29, for example, "enlightened reason" shows her the true height of *minne*, so that she comes to understand that "I might no longer have joy or grief in anything, great or small, except in this, that I

was a human being, and that I experienced *minne* with a loving heart. . . ."[107]
All that human life involves save sin has been taken into God by Jesus—not
negated or rejected. Hadewijch, despite the ecstatic experiences she describes
with such ardor, insists that these are not the goal. What is essential to mystical consciousness is the recognition of God's presence in absence, the realization of the joy that can be found in the midst of suffering, and the adherence
to the faith hidden in the midst of "unfaith." The combination of fruition and
frustration in the experience of *minne* implies what Gregory of Nyssa called
epektasis, constant progress in unfulfilled-fulfillment, at least here if not hereafter. She puts it this way:

> Inseparable satiety and hunger
> Are the appanage of lavish *minne,*
> As is ever well known by those
> Whom *minne* has touched by herself.[108]

Hadewijch's teaching on the mystical character of common human experience, especially the painful experience that seems far from God, was to
have many analogues among later medieval mystics. It also provides a key
for understanding how her following of the way of Jesus led her to a life of
responsibility for others. The beguine agrees with most Christian mystics
that it is not feelings of sweetness but rather the practice of the virtues that
proves true adherence to *minne* (L 10.1–50). Living exclusively "for holy
minne out of pure *minne,*" as she explains in L 23, involves a life of humble
moderation, devoid of eccentricities, in a bond of common love with those
pledged to serve love alone—"Live in the same fervor as we; and let us live
in sweet love. Live for God; let his life be yours, and let yours be ours."[109]

This practical and communal aspect to Hadewijch's view of mysticism
has been rightly underlined by recent investigators.[110] The beguine's works,
especially her letters, are full of discussions of the necessity of serving others in love and humility.[111] In L 2 she adopts the Pauline language (see
Rom. 9:3) of being willing to "be deprived of the Beloved" if this would be
of assistance to the salvation of others (the *resignatio ad infernum* motif).[112]
But the obligations of active charity (*caritate*) encounter a problem in one of
her more difficult texts, L 17.[113] This letter takes as its theme the role of the
Trinity in the Christian life. Hadewijch begins by exegeting one of her own
poems for the instruction of her beguine charges, showing how generosity
toward every virtue, persistence in a multitude of works, and compassion-
ate good will allow one to share in the attributes of the Holy Spirit, the
Father, and the Son. She continues: "And you have heard this continually,
for I always recommended it above all; and I also experienced it above all,
and rendered service accordingly and worked chivalrously until the day it

was forbidden me."[114] This "forbidding" of the works of active love, which Hadewijch says was commanded her by the Father four years previously in a eucharistic union, is puzzling. It may reflect the dual aspects of the divine nature–simultaneous in God but successive to the mystic on earth (at least at this stage of her development). Just as the three divine persons reveal the "pouring out" (*vte gheuen* [17.22]) of the pure nature of *minne* and are the model for all active love, so too "the holding back" (*op houden*), or "engulfing," of the Son and the Holy Spirit in the mystery of the Father's unity reveals that "in that fruition of *minne* there never was and never can be any other work than that one fruition in which the one almighty deity is *minne*."[115] In other words, God's forbidding Hadewijch to exercise active love, which she expressly notes was only temporary (17.88–100), was meant to express the self-contained, or "holding back," aspect of the mystery of the Trinity.

In conclusion, we can say that the boldness of Hadewijch's theological vision, evident both in the problems of interpreting L 17 and throughout her works,[116] raises the question of her relation to the emerging tensions over mysticism, especially female mysticism, in the thirteenth century. Hadewijch lived in a time of growing suspicion of the beguine movement, although systematic persecution was not to come until later.[117] In the beguine's "List of the Perfect," the twenty-ninth person is "A beguine killed by Master Robert because of her true love" (*Een beghine die meester robbaert doedde om hare gherechte minne*). This note provides us with one of the few possibly secure dates in Hadewijch's life, because it is likely that it refers to the former heretic turned Inquisitor, Robert le Bougre, who headed the investigation of heresy in northern France and Flanders between 1235 and 1245, and who was instrumental in the execution of a beguine named Aeleis in Cambrai in 1236.[118] Obviously, Hadewijch disagreed with this verdict–and it is characteristic of her forthrightness to list a condemned heretic among the perfect.

Older discussions of Hadewijch's relation to the "Heresy of the Free Spirit" produced no proof of substantive links, especially because during her lifetime one can scarcely speak of any such heresy.[119] The beguine certainly wrote for an elite group of those dedicated to the service of *minne*,[120] separated from the "strangers" who could not appreciate such devotion. But, unlike Mechthild of Magdeburg and Marguerite Porete, she did not often criticize the clergy and the institutional church. Though her mystical theology is among the most daring of the medieval period, as far as we can tell, it does not seem to have come under suspicion of heresy. The Flemish beguine's account of the misunderstandings she experienced (see L 29) does not seem to be tied to inquisitorial activity, but rather to interpersonal tensions that we can no longer recover. Nevertheless, Hadewijch, because of her beguine status and the challenge implied in her original mystical theology, was bound to be controversial, both in the thirteenth century and today. Controversy, however, never dissuaded her from her single-hearted devotion to *minne*. As she put it in her second letter:

> Serve nobly, wish for nothing else, and fear nothing else: and let *minne* freely take care of herself! For *minne* rewards to the full, even though she often comes late.[121]

Mechthild of Magdeburg[122]

Like Hadewijch, Mechthild is known only through her writings, the seven books that constitute *The Flowing Light of the Godhead* (*Das fliessende Lichte der Gottheit*) composed between 1250 and 1280.[123] As with Angela of Foligno, modern views of what can be known of Mechthild's life waver between the Scylla of uncritical acceptance of the literal truth of the supposed autobiographical passages found in *The Flowing Light* and the Charybdis of positions that see these descriptions as an imaginative presentation of an ideal female religious.[124] Though we should recognize that aspects of the text's presentation of the beguine's life are colored by traditional topoi, there is no good reason to doubt the basic historicity of the picture we are given in *The Flowing Light*.

According to this view, Mechthild was born about 1208. She began to receive mystical experiences in the form of divine "greetings" (*gruos*) and visions from the age of twelve (FL 4.2). About 1230 she fled to Magdeburg to become a beguine (FL 4.2), where, like Hadewijch, she appears to have exercised a position of authority in a beguine community (FL 6.7). In the manner of many beguines, she came under the influence of the Dominicans—*The Flowing Light* offers much evidence of her contacts with the friars (e.g., FL 4.20–22).[125] She may have known the Premonstratensian turned Dominican, Wichmann of Arnstein (ca. 1180–1274), who wrote a group of *Collations* containing mystical materials.[126] It was her Dominican confessor, Henry of Halle, who was instrumental in encouraging and helping Mechthild with the composition of her mystical book (FL 4.2).[127]

The Flowing Light, as it has come down to us, comprises seven books with chapters of varying length and genre: a miniature mystical and literary cosmos. There appear to have been three stages in the evolution of the work. The first five books were finished by about 1260.[128] During the next decade Mechthild added a sixth book. About 1272, aged and in ill health, she

joined the community of Cistercian nuns at Helfta, one of the most important centers for female spiritual writing of the later Middle Ages.[129] Here a
seventh book was composed, rather different in tone from the previous six
in its concern for dogmatic and community issues. Mechthild probably died
about 1282, though some scholars have her surviving into the last decade of
the thirteenth century.

The original version of *The Flowing Light of the Godhead,* written in
Mechthild's Middle Low German (i.e., the dialect of northern Germany), is
lost. The text survives in two later versions. About 1290, Dominican friars
of the Halle community made a translation of the first six books into Latin,
thus giving Mechthild's work the privilege of being one of the first major
vernacular texts to be rendered into the universal language of theology and
spirituality—another example of the conversational model of late medieval
mysticism.[130] In the mid-fourteenth century the secular priest Henry of
Nördlingen, confessor and advisor to the religious and secular "Friends of
God" in southern Germany, translated *The Flowing Light* into the Alemannic
dialect of Middle High German and recommended it highly to his spiritual
charges, such as Margaret Ebner. This version survives complete in one
manuscript and in fragmentary form in three others. Mechthild's work had
a more restricted circulation than the writings of the other Helfta nuns, perhaps in part due to the originality of its mystical teaching.[131]

Hadewijch composed her mystical works for her spiritual community in
a variety of genres and with her own hand. Mechthild's *Flowing Light* displays an equally rich mixture of prose and verse forms, but in mixed forms
within each book of her work.[132] Though the German beguine had the assistance of Friar Henry, it is difficult to discern what his contribution was from
the text that comes down to us. He may have filled in some theological
details, but could a scholastically trained friar have been responsible for the
idiosyncratic literary inventiveness of the book? Mechthild appears to have
been an auto-didact of sorts, though this does not mean that *The Flowing
Light* was in any sense intended to be a private, restricted, or esoteric work.
Quite the contrary, it presents itself as a new "vernacular" Bible intended
for public reading and discussion, and not just among beguines and other
"friends of God,"[133] but for all Christians, as the beguine often insisted.

Given the way in which her text advances a case for the "gospel truth" of
The Flowing Light, Mechthild might not have been totally uncomfortable
with my designation of her as an "evangelist." The strength of her claim is
evident already in the prologue to *The Flowing Light,* a text that has been the
subject of some discussion in recent Mechthild literature.[134] Here is the passage, including the captions, which may be from a later hand:

One should receive this book eagerly, for it is God himself who speaks the words.

This book I hereby send as a messenger to all religious people, both the bad and the good, for if the pillars fall [i.e., the prelates; see Gal. 2:9], the building cannot remain standing; and it signifies me alone and proclaims in praise-worthy fashion my inner life. All who wish to understand this book should read it nine times.

This book is called a flowing light of the Godhead.

"Ah, Lord God, who made this book?"

"I made it in my powerlessness, for I cannot restrain myself as to my gifts."

"Well then, Lord, what shall the title of the book be, which is to your glory alone?"

"It shall be called the flowing light of my Godhead into all hearts that live free of falseness."[135]

Two problems emerge from this text: First, is the passage from Mechthild or was it added by a redactor? Second, who is speaking, Mechthild or God? It is probably impossible to be sure that the text is authentically Mech-thild's. The fact that it uses material from two later authentic discussions in the book (FL 2.26 and 5.34) can be an argument in favor of either side. An analysis of these texts indicates that while Mechthild certainly sees herself as an instrument for the public dissemination of God's message, the speaker here is God himself, asserting that the book signifies him *alone* (Mechthild would scarcely want to claim that much for herself!) and that God cannot "restrain" himself in the sense that the divine goodness of its very nature must overflow not only in the inner life of the Trinity, but also in the flow-ing light that forms the universe and that is contained in the book itself—a version of the traditional theological axiom *bonum est diffusivum sui*.[136] If God cannot help but reveal his message of love, of course, it is equally impossible for Mechthild to resist the divine imperative to transmit the mes-sage despite the dangers it involves for a woman: "Now I fear God if I keep silent and I fear uncomprehending people if I write. Dear people, what can I do about it that this happens to me, and happened often?"[137]

Mechthild, therefore, saw herself as a special instrument of God, as is made clear in other discussions of the combined divine and human author-ship. For example, in FL 2.26 she responds to those who warned her that her book might be burned (no idle threat given what happened to Mar-guerite Porete some decades later) by complaining to God that it was he who commanded her to write. God then appears to her holding the book in his right hand, proclaiming: "No one can burn up the truth. If anyone were to take this book out of my hand, he would have to be stronger than I am.

The book is trinitarian and portrays me alone."[138] Especially noteworthy here is the way in which Mechthild has adapted the traditional portrayal of the *maiestas Domini*, in which Christ appears in a mandola holding the book of the Gospels, in order to defend the scriptural character of her own book.[139]

Like the Gospels, Mechthild's *Flowing Light* explicitly reveals the Trinity. The white parchment signifies the humanity of the second person, the written words signify the "wonderful Godhead," that is, the Father as flowing into Mechthild's soul, and the sound of the words indicates the Living Spirit (a reflection on the importance of reading the text aloud). But why was Mechthild, triply disadvantaged as she was ("Ah, Lord, if I were a *learned religious man . . .*), chosen to be the instrument to convey the book that is the Trinity? Her answer employs the traditional topos of humble reversal used by so many women authors ("The weak things of the world God has chosen to put to shame the strong" [1 Cor. 1:27]), but daringly roots this in the very nature of God as overflowing light, life, and truth. "The highest mountains on earth cannot receive the revelations of my favors, because the flood of my Holy Spirit flows by nature downhill."[140] Thus, the essence of God as "flowing" (which I will argue is her central symbol) *demands* that the new "gospel" be revealed to a woman rather than a man. So it comes as no surprise when God goes on to declare that many a wise master of scripture (*wisen meister an der schrift*) is really a fool (*tore*) in his eyes. But Christianity is much strengthened by the divine imperative "that the unlearned mouth teaches the learned tongue through my Holy Spirit" (*das der ungelerhte munt die gelerte zungen von minem heligen geiste leret*).[141] The praise that God gives to the book in concluding this passage (and even to the scribes who will later write it down!) underlines its quasi-scriptural status.[142]

If Mechthild presents her book as scripture, it is significant that she finds a special affinity with the final book of the Bible, John's Apocalypse, filled as it is with heavenly visions, dialogues with Christ and other revealers, and warnings about the imminent end. The apocalyptic dimensions of Mechthild's *Flowing Light* also help us understand the universality of its message. For example, in FL 5.34, the Lord announces:

> I hereby send this book as a messenger to all religious people, both the good and the bad; for if the pillars fall, the building cannot remain standing. Truly, I say to you, . . . in this book my heart's blood is written which I shall shed again in the last times.[143]

To the best of my knowledge, no medieval male mystics ever made quite the same claims for the divine authorization of their texts that we see advanced by the female evangelists of the thirteenth century. Mechthild, Hadewijch, Angela of Foligno, and Marguerite Porete each worked out her own strategies of authorization in the face of a common dilemma—ecclesiastical strictures against women taking on a public teaching role. The strength of the barriers created by the church's opposition to women's writing helps explain the ingenuity and boldness these four women displayed in the claims they made to be given a hearing.

There is evidence that there were many, even among the male masters "wise in scripture," who accepted the claims of these women. In the case of Mechthild, the prologue to the Latin translation of *The Flowing Light,* as Nigel Palmer has pointed out, introduces the work by means of an analysis of the four headings (author, matter, mode of procedure, and goal) that contemporary *magistri* employed in their prefaces to biblical expositions. This suggests that at least some friars were not beyond accepting the beguine's claim for the similarity, if not equality, of her book with the biblical text.[144]

What *kind* of a book is *The Flowing Light of the Godhead?* Few, if any, mystical texts of the Middle Ages make this question more difficult to answer. Though recent scholarship has cast considerable light on some aspects of this sometimes confusing collection, even scholars who have made *The Flowing Light* a central focus of their research (and therefore have presumably read it at least nine times) continue to disagree about its genre.[145]

The Flowing Light contains numerous accounts of visions, "showings," or visualizations of considerable complexity in both presentation and content. From this perspective, Mechthild takes her place in the shift to a greater emphasis on visionary narratives found in the new mysticism.[146] Most of Mechthild's visions fall into the traditional category of what Augustine would call spiritual, or symbolic, visions;[147] but, like many other late medieval mystics, she often does not clearly distinguish between spiritual visions and purely intellectual ones.[148] This conforms to an essential characteristic of her style, that is, the way in which she fuses symbolization and conceptualization, personal mystical experience and the objective events of salvation history into a seamless whole.[149] Despite the important role that visions play, however, the seven books that constitute *The Flowing Light of the Godhead* can scarcely be described as a visionary recital or just a collection of visions, such as we find in Hadewijch's *Book of Visions.*[150]

Most investigators agree that no single genre is adequate to capture the literary variety of *The Flowing Light.* As Frank Tobin puts it, Mechthild "wrote a book whose paradoxical nature is that its unity consists, in part, in its diversity of forms."[151] In introducing Mechthild's book, then, it may be helpful to describe three of the fundamental strategies or techniques she employs to convey her message throughout the work. The first strategy concerns its "confessional" character. Rather than conceiving of the text as autobiographical in the modern sense, or even as forming a "journal of the soul" (e.g., Wolfgang Mohr's "fragments of an inner biography"),[152] it seems more helpful to think of *The Flowing Light* as a theological reflection upon– or a reactualization, if you will–of the meaning of Mechthild's life and mystical experiences as a guide for all Christians, but especially "the friends of God." In this sense *The Flowing Light,* for all its many differences, has interesting affinities with Augustine's *Confessions.*[153] Like Augustine's *Confessions,* Mechthild's *confessio* expresses both praise for the goodness of God and a sense of her own poverty and sinfulness. Also like Augustine's work, Mechthild's confession of the greatness of God's love for her is not a private message but tells the story of one person in order to provide a message for all. The major differences in genre between Augustine and Mechthild are based in part on what we may identify as other key "strategies" of her text: the roles of dialogue and poetry.

It is not that dialogue is totally lacking in the *Confessions.* Augustine often speaks to God in his book, but God speaks to him only in the words of scripture, which, however, are often incorporated in the bishop's prayers and petitions, thus forming a kind of implied conversation. The second major stylistic aspect or strategy of *The Flowing Light,* however, is its overtly dialogic character. God often speaks directly, both to Mechthild and to the reader, and a whole variety of voices address God. It is sometimes difficult to know who is actually speaking and to whom.[154] Furthermore, as Walter Haug has shown, the complex temporal dimensions or levels of the dialogical character of the work are integral to the way in which it presents and - re-presents mystical consciousness, inviting the reader to imagine the possibility of entering into a realm beyond temporal past and present through unexpected manipulations of their usual relations. "Writing down and reading, that is, the literary existence of *The Flowing Light,* is therefore the release that connects the previous experience and the re-entry into the mystical process."[155]

Dialogical chapters are strongest in the early books, though present throughout *The Flowing Light.* Of the forty-six chapters contained in book 1, for example, only eight relatively brief ones are totally in the third person. Six chapters mix teaching with dialogue, including the lengthy mystical drama contained in 1.44. No fewer than thirty-two chapters are totally dialogic and of these twenty-five are arranged into shorter or longer series in which God and the soul converse in forms often close to those employed in courtly poetry (FL 7–8, 12–20, 23–24, 31–34, 35–37, and 39–43).

An analysis of Mechthild's dialogic practice in key chapters of book 1 will illustrate some of the techniques she employs, which may be broadly described as comprising reversals, dislocations, and fragmentations, along with ambiguities and mergings of voices. In chapter 1, for instance, the dialogue between the soul, addressed as *frouwe kúniginne,* and personified Love addressed as *frouwe minne* reverses the ontological dependence of the soul on Love by having *minne* address the soul as its superior, or queen, at the same time that the soul's voice complains of the suffering that *minne* has inflicted upon it (implying the soul's subservience to all-powerful Love).[156] The soul's claim to superiority suggests that she is speaking from the perspective of her union with God through total surrender to love; that is, indeed, what is described in chapter 2 where the soul leaves the body after receiving the divine greeting (*gruos*). She then enters into a secret place to play a game of love with God that is totally hidden to everyone else—even to Mary! Mechthild continues: "Then *she* soars further to a blissful place of which *I* neither will nor can speak"—the first entry of Mechthild's "own" voice.[157] But if the beguine seems to split herself off from her soul at this point, the last part of the chapter appears to identify both soul and self as the maiden (*juncfrou*) who conducts a double dialogue: one of love-language with God based in part on the Song of Songs, and a second of contention with the body because it hinders and shortens her ecstatic moments of union. The conclusion returns to the theme of *gruos,* the gift of mystical grace, and once more leaves the speaking voice ambiguous:

> No one can or should receive this greeting unless one has gone beyond oneself and become nothing. In this greeting I want to die while living. The blind holy people can never ruin this for me. These are those who love and do not know.[158]

The conflict between body and soul introduced in FL 1.2 is heightened in chapter 5, which begins with the body in "great torment" (*langer qwale*) and the soul in the bliss of erotic union and contains another quarrel (*Streitgedicht*) between body and soul. But again, things are not so simple. The soul's surrender to the Divine Lover and her willingness to be sent into hell if that would be to his praise (the *resignatio in infernum* theme going back to Rom. 9:3) means that her bliss is actually itself a form of torment—"I am his joy, he is my torment" (*Ich bin sin vroede, er ist min qwale* [11.13–14]). Therefore, soul and body may not be quite so opposed, as Mechthild was to reemphasize strongly in her later books. This chapter closes with the first direct address to the reader in the second person in the couplet:

> This torment must you endure,
> No escaping it you must assure!"[159]

Subsequent chapters in book 1 add to the complexity of the various forms of dialogue. The distinction between the "I," or self-voice, and the higher soul-voice in chapter 2 is undercut in chapter 28, for example, where the "I" so delights in loving God that she encourages the soul to deeper love and even says to her, "You can no longer teach me anything."[160] In the next chapter Christ speaks directly to his bride, addressed as the concrete self, or "you," who is invited to participate in the physical sufferings of the *imitatio Christi*. Later, in the chapter entitled "The Desert has Twelve Things" (1.35), the unnamed speaker is presumably God, while the "you" addressed is both the reader and Mechthild's soul responding to her Lover, as suggested in neighboring chapters of this extended dialogue (see 1.33 and 37). Thus, Mechthild's strategies of both splitting and merging the participants in her dialogues (God and soul/God and self/self and soul/self and body/self and senses) underline the ambiguous nature and function of the "I" in *The Flowing Light of the Godhead*–essentially God, but often Mechthild, and aspects of Mechthild too. The complexities of the dialogical structure of the work would become even more dense were we to attempt to integrate the shifting voices with the diverse temporal levels as studied by Walter Haug, but this investigation cannot be pursued here.

The third literary characteristic or strategy of *The Flowing Light* is its use of poetry. Though Hadewijch's mystical poems are earlier in date, and although Jacopone of Todi was the only thirteenth-century mystic to make poetry the central form of his mystical communication, Mechthild must be ranked along with these two in the triumvirate of major mystical poets of the thirteenth century.[161] The relationship between mysticism and poetry, a topic often addressed in modern literature, is too large a question to be taken up here.[162] For the mystic, poetic inspiration is not the same as mystical inspiration, however much some mystics find in poetry a more adequate way of conveying their message than prose.[163] The reason that certain mystics choose poetry for their mode of expression, at least in part, has to do with the ways in which poetry tests and subverts ordinary language–overcoming language within the realm of language being also one of the essential tasks of mystical discourse.

Mechthild employs a variety of poetic forms. The German beguine's poems often have a popular flavor, sometimes sounding like dances, spells, riddles, and the like,[164] but this should not be taken to mean that Mechthild was unskilled or unoriginal as a poet. Hans-Georg Kemper has argued, for example, that Mechthild made a major contribution to a mixed form of allegory in both her verse and the more deeply imagistic sections of her prose. This form, which he calls "allegorical allegorizing" (*allegorische Alle-*

gorese), takes traditional biblical images that were usually allegorized in the commentary tradition and gives them a new "direct" application to the mystic's life.[165]

The ways in which Mechthild employs poetry throughout *The Flowing Light* are multiple. The transition from prose to poetry often indicates a moment of heightened emotion or a closure, such as in FL 4.12, where, at the conclusion of a powerful, even troubling, exposition of "blessed estrangement from God" (*selige gottes vroemdunge*) by which the soul sinks "away" from the Divine Lover in humility, she places a simple couplet as a form of summary:

> Rather, the deeper I sink,
> The sweeter I drink.[166]

At other times poetry seems to be employed in a more pedestrian manner for didactic purposes and possible memorization (e.g., 3.24, 4.4, 6.12). Sometimes, entire chapters or large portions thereof, representing her most challenging teaching, are given a poetic form (e.g., 1.35, 2.2, 2.5, 2.6, 2.21, 2.25, 3.10). Some chapters are striking examples of the power of poetry to express the mystery of the encounter with God. For example, the brief poem that comprises FL 2.15:

> Whoever there is who at some hour
> Has felt true love's wounding power,
> His health will never again flower,
> Unless he kisses those same lips
> From which his soul its wound sips.[167]

Mechthild's employment of a complex "quilting of images" (to use a phrase suggested by Ulrike Wiethaus)[168] in her deeply dialogic and poetic book presents a strongly cataphatic, or positive, form of mystical awareness of God.[169] Although she recognizes that all speech about God must end in silence, the German beguine shows little interest in the usual forms of apophatic theology. (Mechthild was scarcely "theological" in the sense of scholastic or monastic theologies, far less so than Hadewijch.) Nevertheless, the power of her "vernacular theology" creates its own type of negation of customary views of God. To speak of God, and in God's voice, with such novelty and variety confuses and overwhelms accepted expectations of how God is and how he/she relates to humans. Such a practice is perhaps just as apophatic in the long run as the great game of constructing intricate structures of negative predications employed by other mystics.

Image Complexes of The Flowing Light

Even more than in the case of the other thirteenth-century female evangelists, Mechthild resists a presentation according to scholastic doctrinal headings, though there are few articles of belief of the medieval church that she does not at least touch on. To try to give something of the flavor and message of her mystical teaching, I will study three key images–those of "flowing" (*vliessen*), "courting" or "playing at love" (*minne spielen*), and "sinking" (*sinken*).

The Platonic master paradigm of *exitus* and *reditus*, the flowing out of all things from the First Principle and their eventual return to it, had been incorporated into Christian mysticism as early as the time of Origen. This central motif also appeared in the thought of Dionysius and through him influenced mystics in both Eastern and Western Christianity. Mechthild's contemporary, Bonaventure, used *exitus/reditus* as a basic theme for his influential mystical theology, as we saw in chapter 2. The "flowing forth" of all things from God was employed by earlier mystics primarily to express the ontological foundation for their major concern, that is, the exploration of the soul's ascent to God. Although Mechthild often speaks of how the soul "soars" (*sweben*) above itself in returning to God, she insists that this must be understood in conjunction with the soul's downward, or "sinking" (*sinkend*), movement, which is in turn based on its participation in the divine flowing (*vliessen*).[170] God "flows" within as Trinity; God also "flows" down to create the world and to bestow his mystical greeting (*gruos*) on the soul. In response, the soul may soar for a time, but it must finally sink down and utterly expend itself to reach the deepest union with the out-flowing God. A chapter from book 7 summarizes thus:

> I shall greet (*gruos*) the sublimity . . . and the wondrous oneness of the Holy Trinity. Out of it has flowed forth immaculate all that was, that is, that ever shall be. There I must one day enter again. How shall that happen? I must crawl back, for I am sinful. . . . I must fly with the feathers of doves. . . . I must soar in all things above myself. *When I am utterly spent, then I shall enter.* . . . Glory to you, Trinity![171]

The trinitarian basis for Mechthild's mystical teaching found in this important text will be evident in each of the image complexes to which we now turn.

Flowing

Mechthild might be described as the "flowing mystic"; indeed, the language of flowing is omnipresent in her book, as the title itself suggests. The beguine often uses such symbols as light, fire, and spring (*brunne*) to describe God (see 1.28, 3.24, 4.21, 6.29, and 7.32 for examples), but what particularly fascinated her is the flowing movement suggested by these images as a way of symbolizing the ceaseless activity of the Trinity.[172] Flowing begins within the three persons themselves. Mechthild speaks from time to time of the inner life of the three divine persons, as in FL 5.26, entitled "How God praises himself and celebrates himself in song." In this chapter the Father's voice sings: "I am an *overflowing spring* that no one can block, but a person can easily block up his heart with an idle thought, so that the never-resting Godhead that continually toils without toil cannot *flow* into his soul."[173] The Son sings: "I am constantly recurring richness that no one can contain except the boundlessness which always *flowed* and shall ever *flow* from God, and which comes again into its fullness with his Son." The Holy Spirit sings: "I am an insuperable power of truth. . . ." Finally, the entire Trinity concludes: "I am so strong in my undividedness that no one can ever divide me or shatter me in all my eternity."[174] But, as this passage suggests, Mechthild more frequently employs flowing language to depict the mutual relationship between the Trinity and creation, especially created spirits.[175]

The "flowing" of light and sight into and from a mirror provides a good example of how Mechthild understands this reciprocity.[176] Toward the end of book 6 she complains that she cannot say anything further because she is overwhelmed by divine glory, but then she adds:

> A mirror was seen in heaven before the breast of each soul and body. In it shines the mirror of the Holy Trinity, giving truth and knowledge of all virtues which the body had ever practiced and of all the gifts which the soul had ever received on earth. From here the glorious reflection of each and every person shines forth back again into the sublime majesty from which it flowed forth.[177]

Flowing as implying participation and reciprocal relation is a frequent motif. Christ's created soul and his entire humanity flow out of the Trinity as its perfect image (see, e.g., 6.16 and 7.1). FL 1.22 says: "The sweet dew of the Eternal Trinity gushed forth from the fountain of the everlasting Godhead into the flower of the chosen maid," that is, the Virgin Mary.[178] Mechthild's soul, and by extension, the souls and even the bodies of all humans, as suggested above, flow forth from the depths of God as *imago Trinitatis* and have as their high destiny a return to where they were created and, in deepest reality, always remain.[179]

Mechthild, like a number of the other women mystics of the thirteenth century such as Hadewijch, emphasized the exemplary, or preexistent, reality of the soul in the Trinity. At times the beguine even takes the reader into the inner life of the three persons in order to overhear the *consilium Trinitatis,* that is, the joyful decision by which God elects to make all things and to establish his plan for salvation history.[180] This eternal plan centers on the preexistent soul's status as the bride of the Trinity, as we are told in FL 1.22. To the question "Where did the Redeemer become the Bridegroom?" comes the response, "In the *iubilus* of the Holy Trinity, when God could no longer hold himself within, he created the soul and gave himself to her as her own from the greatest love." When the soul is then asked what it is made of that it can dare to mingle (*mengest*) with the Trinity, she responds: "You spoke about my beginning, so now I say to you truly, I was made in that same place [i.e., the Trinity] by *minne*."[181] Here the soul is identical with Mary who was chosen to be "the bride of the Holy Trinity and mother of orphans" (*alleine brut der heligen drivaltikeit und muoter der weisen* [ed., 18.48–49]) in order to restore the damage done to the joy of the Trinity by Adam's fall. Through her giving birth to the Savior and suckling both "Holy Christianity" and all redeemed souls Mary thus takes on an essential role in the *consilium Trinitatis.*[182] Insofar as other souls return to their divine source, however, they are scarcely to be distinguished from Mary. In a later text God says that "the least soul . . . is a bride of the Holy Trinity," just as Mary was (FL 2.22; ed. 55.14–15; cf. 2.9), and while Mary is daringly called a "goddess" (*goetinne*) in FL 1.22 (ed., 75.78), the same language is addressed to the soul in FL 3.9: "I am the God of gods; you are the goddess of all creatures, and I give you my solemn assurance that I will never reject you."[183]

Mechthild's stress on the exemplary, or virtual, existence of the soul in the Trinity parallels that found in other women mystics. In *The Flowing Light* 4.14, however, she adds to this in important ways. Although this chapter is in some places obscure, two important points seem clear. First, it was part of the eternal divine plan that the second person of the Trinity take on flesh—the incarnation was not merely the consequence of Adam's sin.[184] Closely allied to this is Mechthild's claim that "[t]he human (*der mensche*) has a complete nature in the Holy Trinity and God saw fit to fashion it with his own divine hands."[185] What this means is that it is not just the soul, but the entire person, body and soul, that has existed in the power (*virtus*) of the Creator from all eternity.[186] Two reasons are given for this. If the human person had a single nature (*einig nature*), that is, a purely spiritual being like Lucifer, there would have been no possibility of restoration after sin. More significantly, since the divine nature itself through the Incarnate Word now includes "bone and flesh, body and soul," the soul with its flesh gets to share the highest union with God, superior to that of the angels who remain pure spirit: "There eye shines into eye, there spirit flows in spirit, there hand touches hand, there mouth speaks to mouth, and there heart greets heart. Thus does the Master honor the mistress at his side."[187] Mechthild's understanding of the precreational status and heavenly reward of the body led her to a profoundly optimistic view of corporeal existence, despite the presence of some of the negative language about the body to be expected in any medieval religious author.[188]

Mechthild's emphasis on humanity's eternal existence in and of the Trinity, not surprisingly, did not go unchallenged. It was apparently a line from the love drama found in FL 1.44 in which God tells the soul: "You are now so ennatured (*genatûrt*) in me that the least thing cannot be between you and me," which got her into trouble. She responded to her critics in an important chapter found in book 6.[189] To the objection that everything that God has done for us comes from grace, not nature, Mechthild judiciously answered: "You are right, but I am also right." The loving soul has one eye that peers into the Godhead and sees how the Father has "formed her according to himself" (*hat si gebildet nach im selber* [ed. 239.12]), just as the body has its value from its relationship with the suffering humanity of Christ, and the grace of the Holy Spirit provides us with all the gifts we have received. To this somewhat unclear trinitarian analogy, Mechthild joins a reflection, which we may suggest comes from the perspective of the soul's other eye (i.e., knowledge, or *bekantnisse*). Before creation, God "was in himself and all things were as present and manifest to him as they are today." His form was "exactly like a sphere (*clot*) . . . without a lock and a door." In an unusually scholastic-sounding passage she continues: "The lowest part of the sphere is a bottomless foundation beneath all abysses; the highest part of the sphere is a height above which there is nothing. The circumference of the sphere is an immeasurable circle."[190] When God creates, the sphere does not open, because God must remain whole in himself and hidden forever. Rather, "all creatures become manifest in themselves" (*do wurden alle creaturen an in selben offenbar*) in order to live the form of being that God has determined for them.

The full understanding of the "flowing" of the Trinity outside itself into created reality and of the divine decision about salvation grounds Mechthild's view of the saving mysteries of Christ's life and of her attitude, often quite critical, toward the contemporary church and its clergy. It also forms the basis for the beguine's unique apocalyptic theology.[191] All these issues are integral to her thought, but cannot be allowed to distract us from this attempt to describe the essential symbolic matrices of *The Flowing Light of the Godhead*.

Playing (and Leaving) the Game of Love

Wenne das spil allerbest ist, so muos man 'es lassen.
Just when the game is at its best, one has to leave it. (FL 1.2)

Mechthild of Madgeburg has most often been treated as a preeminent representative of *Minnemystik* or *la mystique courtoise*.[192] There is no reason to deny a strong element of what I have called the "courtly mode" in the beguine's mysticism, but there are also good reasons to put the claim in perspective, as suggested by the opening quotation. It is not only that one *has* to leave the "game of love" because of the human spirit's inability to enjoy more than brief moments of ecstatic contact with God (as the twelfth-century mystics taught), but also because one *should* leave ecstasy in "sinking love" (to be discussed in the final section) that Mechthild's employment of the courtly mode is a qualified one.

While Mechthild may not use the term *minne* as often as Hadewijch did, it is still pervasive in *The Flowing Light*.[193] Like Beatrice and Hadewijch, the German beguine uses *minne* in a rich variety of ways–the term can refer to God (e.g., FL 1.24), to the personification Lady Love (e.g., FL 1.1, 1.3, 5.4, 7.48), and also, most often, to love as the active force by which we participate in and return to God. Distinctive of her view of *minne* is a fondness for lists of the kinds of love or its powers and purposes (e.g., FL 1.30, 2.11, 3.13, 3.24, 4.15, 5.30, 5.31, 6.30, 7.61). As a lover, Mechthild herself can assume a variety of roles. In FL 2.19, Lady Knowledge (*vrovwe bekantnisse*) tells the soul: "You are of threefold nature in yourself in order to be indeed God's image. You are a virile man in your battle; you are a well-dressed maiden in the palace before your Lord; you are an eager bride in your and God's love-bed."[194]

There is no doubt that Mechthild preferred the third role, as her direct and unashamed use of erotic descriptions demonstrates.[195] Although she knew the Song of Songs and even quotes it at times (e.g., FL 3.3 and 3.20), her erotic experience of God is filtered not through the biblical text but through her presentation of the "book of experience."[196] In FL 2.22, Lady Contemplation (*vrowe beschowunge*) asks the soul if it would rather be a human or an angel of the order of the seraphim. She almost disdainfully replies that she is a bride of the Holy Trinity and that her Lover is "the noblest angel, Jesus Christ, who soars above the seraphim, who is undivided with his Father." Then she becomes more direct in typical fashion:

Him shall I, the least of souls, take in my arms, eat him and drink him and have my way with him. This can never happen to the angels. No matter how high he dwells above me, his Godhead shall never be so distant that I cannot constantly entwine my limbs with him. And so I shall never cool off.[197]

The Trinity itself speaks a similar language of erotic desire and surrender in many passages. For example, in *Flowing Light* 5.25 God says:

I cannot be completely intimate with her unless she is willing to lay herself in utter repose and nakedness in my divine arms, so that I can play with her. For it was for this that I surrendered myself into her power. . . . And she shall ever more in soul and body soar about and play to her heart's content in my Holy Trinity and drink herself full like a fish in the sea.[198]

Thus, mutuality of desire is central to Mechthild's experience of the game of love. When she complains to the Lord that she cannot contain her desire, he answers: "I longed for you before the beginning of the world. I long for you and you long for me. Where two burning desires meet, there love is perfect."[199] Embracing, kissing, wounding hearts,[200] exchanging hearts,[201] lying together on the bed of love[202]—*The Flowing Light of the Godhead* contains a host of these and like images of the erotic encounter with God.

It would be easy, but scarcely necessary, to multiply examples of Mechthild's use of erotic language. One classic text, the forty-fourth chapter of the first book, can indicate something of the range of the beguine's "spiritual sexuality," as it has been called.[203] Few texts in the history of Christian erotic mysticism are more striking.[204] The chapter is constructed as a courtly love drama in five acts with a cast of speakers and an extended description of the location and action.

In Act One (27.1–13), the Holy Spirit names seven stages which the loving soul (*minnendú sele*) must traverse before she can call out in longing for the Fair Youth (*schoener jungeling*), her Divine Lover.[205] The Youth then responds to her call, promising to hurry to "one who bears sorrow and love together" (*kumber und minne*). In the Second Act (27.13–28.25), which begins in the morning dew, signifying the soul's interiority, the five senses (the soul's chamberlains) instruct her to put on the garments of the virtues to prepare herself for the approach of her Lover.[206] She goes into the forest to wait for her Lover where the personified virtues of the saints perform "a beautiful dance of praise" (*ein schoener loptanz*). In Act Three (28.25–29.43) the Youth appears and invites her to dance. The two dance to the following love duet:

And the Youth has to sing thus:
"Through me into you

> And through you from me."
> [The soul]:
> "Willingly with you,
> Woefully from you."²⁰⁷

After the dance, the Youth invites her in her weariness to come "at noon-time to the shady spring into the bed of love," but the soul at this point demurs, proclaiming her unworthiness—another example of the mutual playfulness involved in the game of love.

The long Act Four (29.43–31.78) contains a dialogue between the soul and the five senses in which they invite her to refresh herself with the virtues and religious experiences of the saints, but she refuses, proclaiming: "I am a fullgrown bride; I want to go to my Lover!" (*Ich bin ein vollewahsen brut, ich will gan nach minem trut* [30.63–64]). The senses complain that the blazing heat of the Godhead will blind them, but Mechthild, using images for the affinity of the mystic with God that we have also seen in Beatrice of Nazareth, announces:

> A fish in water does not drown,
> A bird in the air does not sink down,
> Gold in fire does not perish. . . .
> How, then, am I to resist my nature?
> I must go from all things to God,
> Who is my Father by nature,
> My Brother by his humanity,
> My Bridegroom by love,
> And I his Bride without beginning.²⁰⁸

Finally, in Act Five (31.78–32.95) the soul goes into the "secret chamber of the invisible Godhead," where she finds the "bed and abode of love." The Lord bids her to take off her clothes, saying "Lady Soul, you are so enna-tured in me (*genatúrt in mich*) that the least thing cannot be between you and me." External virtues must go; only interior virtues of "noble longing" (*edele begerunge*) and "bottomless desire" (*grundelose girheit*) can remain. Mechthild, now as a "naked soul" (*nakent sele*), that is, one who has attained her pre-creational status in God, is finally ready for union with the "richly clothed God" (*wolgezieret got*). Their uniting is portrayed with a simple but powerful allusion to sexual intercourse:

> Then a blessed stillness
> That both desire comes over them.
> He gives himself to her,
> And she gives herself to him.

What happens to her then—she knows—
And that is fine with me.[209]

Mechthild the courting maiden and the fullgrown bride had considerable experience of the ecstatic union ascribed to so many women in thirteenth-century hagiography. The language that she uses for ecstatic states involves terms that are familiar in contemporary mystical literature, such as *iubilus* (e.g., FL 4.23), *übertrunken* (drunkenness; e.g., FL 2.3), and various forms of "drawing out" (*zuge-ziehen;* e.g., FL 1.5, 4.18, 5.5, 5.28).[210] She also has her unique vocabulary of the "divine greeting," as we have seen.[211] Mechthild's presentations of mystical union are varied and complex. It would be a mistake to try to discern a coherent theology of the nature of union from *The Flowing Light,* whether of the older *unitas spiritus* understanding, or of newer presentations of a union without difference or distinction; but the beguine's numerous discussions of union (*einunge*) are still among the richest of her era.[212]

Language drawn from human sexual experience, as we have seen, is Mechthild's dominant motif for union. Whereas many male interpreters of the Song of Songs, like Bernard of Clairvaux and William of St. Thierry, tended to emphasize the unitive connotations of kissing and embracing, Mechthild often suggests, if indirectly, sexual intercourse itself as the most appropriate symbol. She employs some of the traditional metaphors for union with God, such as the mingling of water and wine (FL 1.4), and the mixing of air and sunlight (FL 7.55),[213] and she also emphasizes, as we have seen, the mutuality of union (e.g., FL 4.15, 5.25, etc.), though without explicitly employing the language of mutual infinity that appeared in Hadewijch. At times, however, her expressions of merging in love are so strongly put that they might suggest total identity (see, e.g., FL 3.5). There are also a number of passages in *The Flowing Light* that hint at the kind of language that in later, more metaphysically minded mystics would indicate an indistinct oneness with God of a permanent nature, but it would be a mistake to press these too far.[214]

If the most widespread form of language Mechthild employs to picture union with God is erotic, we must remember that the God with whom she unites is the Trinity, not just Christ, although obviously erotic imagery is more easily and frequently used in relation to the God-man. Mechthild, like Mary, is the "bride of the Holy Trinity." We have already noted a number of texts that present the unconditionally trinitarian character of Mechthild's notion of union, many of which do not have erotic content. For example, in FL 6.1, a lengthy chapter in which the beguine instructs a prior or prioress on the proper way to behave toward their charges, Mechthild suddenly breaks in with a "true message" (*ware rede*) that she saw in the Holy Trinity while she was alone in prayer. The message is about how the practices of the Christian life, both contemplative and active, lead to inner uniting with the Trinity. Prayer that is offered in absolute humility and complete detachment from all save God enables a person to realize the state of "a divine god with the heavenly Father."[215] Active love unites with the Son and the Holy Spirit. "When a person toils for a correct purpose through real need with the same love with which he prayed, then he is a human god with Christ." Further: "When for God's love and not for earthly reward a person instructs the ignorant, converts sinners, consoles the troubled, and brings those in despair back to God, then he is a spiritual god with the Holy Spirit." Finally, the blessed person who tries to do everything in life from love of God and with a good intention "is one whole person with the Holy Trinity," who, despite the dust of sin becomes "one god with God, so that whatever he wills she wills and they can be united in complete union in no other way."[216] This presentation of trinitarian union, though lacking any erotic motifs or metaphysical speculation, joins with those found in other late medieval mystics, like Meister Eckhart, in insisting that the deepest form of union is realized not just in ecstatic contemplation but in a totally God-centered life.

Sinking

Mechthild's mastery of the language of love marks her out as one of the premier voices in the history of erotic mysticism in Christianity. Her description of forms of ecstatic consciousness in which she "soars into God" provides ample testimony of the importance of ecstasy among thirteenth-century women. But the German beguine does not consider ecstatic union to be the ultimate goal. Several texts in the last books of *The Flowing Light* speak of three stages in the mystical life, stages realized in Mechthild's own life (at least in an idealized way) and meant to be applicable to all who seek God. In FL 7.3 God tells her: "Your childhood was a playmate of my Holy Spirit; your youth was a bride of my humanity; your old age is now a housewife of my Godhead."[217] Similarly, in FL 6.20 Mechthild reflects on the nature of her book as a threefold divine gift:

> God bestowed upon me the favor that is written down in this book in a three-fold manner. First of all with great tenderness; then with high intimacy; now with intense suffering. I much prefer to remain in this state than in the other

two. . . . But the nature of love is such that it first of all flows in sweetness; then it becomes rich in knowledge; in the third place it becomes desirous in rejection.[218]

Returning to the central image of *vliessen* will help to set the context for this third important aspect of the experience of God. We come to know and love God because of the "playful flood of love that flows intimately from God into the soul and through his power flows back again according to her power."[219] God must flow down to us in the cosmic outpouring of creation and the humble taking on of flesh in order for the mystic (body and soul) to begin to flow with love and to soar upward. But the closest form of union with God in this life, paradoxical as it may seem, will be through imitating God and Christ in "flowing down," or "sinking" away from ecstasy into pain, humility, and even into estrangement from God (*gotesvremedunge/ verworfenheit*).[220] As she puts it in one place, "If you want to have love, you must leave love" (*Wiltu liep haben, so muostu liep lassen* [FL 2.23; ed. 58.55–56]). This message appears in a number of places in *The Flowing Light*, especially in the twelfth chapter of the fourth book.[221]

It is important to note that in this chapter, as well as in related passages such as FL 5.4 describing "sinking humility," Mechthild insists on the dual roles of body and soul in the experience of estrangement. Although she recognized a real tension between body and soul in our present existence,[222] the beguine insisted that sinking and estrangement are embodied modes of finding God, experiences intimately connected with actual physical suffering, though not exhausted by it.[223] Mechthild's sense of the necessity of estrangement recalls Hadewijch's teaching on the role of "unfaith" and the need for "living Jesus as God and man." The German beguine's teaching also taps into traditional themes of the "resignation to hell" and literal imitation of Christ's desolation on the cross. But her evocation of why "flowing farthest down" is paradoxically the most intimate form of union is very much her own creation.

FL 4.12 is among the more complex chapters in *The Flowing Light of the Godhead*, an intricate mixture of dialogue, poetry, and description. In the initial dialogue (123.1–18) the soul as bride, disturbed from her rest in the Trinity by the departure of the Beloved, refuses consolation from all creatures in a manner similar to that seen in FL 1.44. In a beautiful poem (123.18–124.29) the soul declares that its "nobility" (*edelkeit*, that is, its precreational status in God) can be satisfied only by being drawn into the Trinity so that "[n]othing tastes good to me but God alone; I am wondrously dead."[224] She also avers, however, that she is willing to give up even the "taste of God" as long as he can continue to be praised in all the creatures he has created. This sets the stage for the second part of the chapter, which the beguine introduces with a dialogue between her and God that took place after eight years of consolation (124.34–125.71). In this section Mechthild learns the consolation of giving up all consolation.

First, God consoles her "*beyond* [her] soul's nobility" by allowing her to fall down to the level of those suspended in purgatory and rejected in hell, though he then rewards her with another experience of heavenly joy. Mechthild's response is to request a more ultimate form of descent: "Then our Lord said: "How long do you want to be here?" The bride said: "Oh, leave me, dear Lord, and let me sink further for your honor."[225] Now soul and body enter into a great darkness without light and knowledge within which Mechthild loses all sense of intimacy with God. She holds converse with good and bad personified forces (Trust, Disbelief, Constancy), and even with the three persons of the Trinity, who encourage her to be strong in memory of their former gifts. The final personification encountered is that of Estrangement itself:

> After this came Constant Estrangement from God and enveloped the soul so completely that the blessed soul said: "Welcome, very blessed Estrangement. Fortunate am I that I was born–that you, Lady, shall now be my chambermaid, for you bring me unusual joy and incomprehensible marvels and unbearable delight as well. But, Lord, you should take delight from me and let me have Estrangment from you."[226]

God's honor is now fulfilled in her and he is "strangely with her" (*nu ist got wunderlich mit mir*)–"Now his estrangement from me is more welcome to me than he himself is."[227] Mechthild's easy acceptance of estrangement may itself seem a bit strange, and it contrasts with the sense of tortured despair found in Hadewijch, Ubertino, and Angela of Foligno. But the German beguine closes her account with a description of how she entered a great darkness in which "her body sweated and writhed in painful cramping." Here "Lady Pain" holds dialogue with the Lord, who reminds her that, although she is the devil's minion, she was Christ's closest garment while he was on earth and that she is now Mechthild's messenger to remind others that humility, pain, and God-estrangement are actually the way to God:

> *Mere ie ich tieffer sinke,*
> *Ie ich suesser trinke.*

In chapter 4 of book 5 (ed. 156–59) Mechthild provides another account of the descent of love, this time with a stress on the role of "sinking humility" (*sinkende diemuetekeit*). Lady *Minne* is praised for her power to make the soul flow and to raise it to God, and also for the way in which she dissolves into the senses and helps the body put all things in order. But when Love has ascended the mountain,[228] like a pilgrim, she must climb down the other side. After the experience of the embrace of the Holy Trinity, the soul and the body both begin to sink and cool (*so beginnet si ze sinkende und ze kuolende* [ed. 157.30]). Mechthild describes the sinking as follows:

> The love-rich soul sinks downward under the pull of profound humility and constantly retreats from what God does to her out of love. . . . The body, too, sinks far down when it serves its enemy [i.e., the soul]. . . . The soul sinks deeper still because she has more strength than the body. She sinks with great zeal to the lowest place God holds in his power. Oh, how dare I name this place for those who know nothing of sinking humility![229]

But Mechthild does go on to name it. The place is called "under Lucifer's tail" (*under Lucifers zagel* [ed. 158.52]),[230] that is, it is the experience of being trapped in hell where the "poor love-rich soul" may feel no shame or fear but where the body quakes because it has not yet been transformed through death. Mechthild concludes by saying that both forms of experience are necessary for full holiness—ascent to the highest heights and descent to deepest depths, the abyss of hell.[231]

While Mechthild delights in the joys of being a bride of the Trinity, playing the game of love with the *schoener jungeling* who is Christ, it is clear from this emphasis on the necessity for accepting pain and even estrangement from God that it is the kenotic Christ on the cross, suffering, dying, and emptying himself of all things, who is her deepest love. As with many of her contemporaries, especially in the Franciscan tradition, Mechthild's visions involved concrete meditations on all the saving mysteries of Christ's life (see, e.g., FL 1.45, 5.9, 5.23, 7.21, and 7.60), but her sense of participation in Christ's saving action centered on the passion. In the moving poem found in FL 3.10 Mechthild's "loving soul" (*minnende sele*), although initially captured "in the first experience when God kisses her with sweet union,"[232] expresses the union she has reached in Christ not by her own enjoyment, but by living out in her daily trials all the details of his passion.

> She carries her cross on a sweet path
> When she truly surrenders herself to God in all sufferings.
> Her head is struck with a reed
> When one compares her great holiness to a fool.
> With the hammer of the strong love-pursuit she is nailed so
>   fast to the cross

> That all creatures cannot call her back again. . . .
> She hangs on the cross of sublime love,
> High in the air of the Holy Spirit,
> Facing the eternal sun of the living Godhead
> So that she becomes completely dry and bare of all earthly
> things.[233]

It is true that the poem goes on to portray the soul's participation in the mysteries of the resurrection and ascension as well, but the chapter closes with a prose note emphasizing that this *passion* must be suffered by every soul that is filled with love of God. Several powerful chapters in book 7 (e.g., FL 7.18, 7.21, and 7.27) indicate that such passion-centered imitation of Christ grew even stronger in Mechthild's last years, although recognition that the cross is the key in Christ's hand that opens heaven to sinners (FL 6.16; ed. 227.41–47) is found throughout *The Flowing Light of the Godhead*.[234]

Mechthild's conviction that identity with the kenotic Christ presents the ultimate form of union, far less pleasant but ultimately more necessary than the delights of erotic encounter, had important consequences for her sense of her own mission. Earlier beguines, like Mary of Oignies, had been portrayed by their hagiographers as combining both contemplative prayer and active good works; Mechthild lives out and brings to personal expression the union of these loves in a distinctive way. Like other beguines, her experience as loving bride allows her to serve as an intercessor powerful with God, someone able to rescue souls from purgatory, perhaps even from hell itself. Her union with the Savior and her visionary gifts provide her with a prophetic responsibility for the welfare of the church both now and for all ages to come, especially in the crisis of the last days. The beguine's sense of service was scarcely an abstract one. Her solidarity with the dead and empty Christ led her to the "true desert" (*waren wuestenunge*) of everyday life, where the Divine Lover is met in emptiness and humble service of others. She summarizes this in a noted poem from FL 1.35:

> You should love the nothing,
> You should flee the something,
> You should stand alone
> And should go to no one.
> You should not be too busy
> And you should be free of all things.
> You should unbind the captives
> And compel the free.
> You should refresh the sick
> And should still have nothing for yourself.

You should drink the water of pain
And ignite the fire of love with the wood of virtue.
Then you are living in the true desert.[235]

Marguerite Porete

Her Book and Trial

No medieval woman mystic challenged her contemporaries—and still challenges us—more than the northern French beguine Marguerite Porete.[236] Her bold and uncompromising spirituality led to her execution as a heretic on June 1, 1310. After centuries of misattribution, Porete's book, *The Mirror of Simple Souls,* has been finally reunited with its author and in recent years has become the subject of a growing literature.[237] Contemporary interest has less to do with the evaluation of whether or not she was a heretic, though the debate continues,[238] than with the problems involved in interpreting a text as elusive as it is profound. As the translator of the book into Middle English put it: "For the boke is of high divine maters, and of high goostli felynges, and kernyngli and ful mystili it is spoken."[239] If the questioning, and even the subversion, of religious stereotypes is among the tasks of the mystics, few have been so ambiguously successful as Marguerite Porete.

Like her book, Marguerite presents us with many mysteries. Because of her execution, we have considerable external information about the last years of her life; but, as with Hadewijch and Mechthild, everything else about her remains hidden. Though she was said to have come from Hainaut in northern France, we have no idea when she was born. Her high level of education argues for an upper-class origin.[240] In one text, she includes "beguines" among those who attack her (chap. 122), but it is likely that she was referring to the enclosed beguines, who felt uncomfortable with the wandering and mendicant beguine lifestyle that she appears to have practiced.

Marguerite's trial, condemnation, and execution must be seen as a critical moment in the history of Christian mysticism, one equivalent to the execution of Al-Hallaj in the story of Islamic mystical traditions.[241] Although Hadewijch recorded a beguine killed by another Dominican Inquisitor "for her great love," as we have seen, Marguerite is the first documented case of an execution for mystical heresy in Western Christianity. Unfortunately, it was not to be the last. Her death was not just an individual tragedy; it also provided critical ammunition for an ongoing struggle between the mystical and the institutional elements of Christianity that has continued almost down to the present day.

Marguerite, called a "phony-woman," *pseudo-mulier,* by her inquisitors (apparently because her religious claims undermined traditional categories so radically), appears to have written the first version of her book in the 1290s. Sometime between 1296 and 1306 it was condemned to be burned in her presence at Valenciennes by Bishop Guy II of Cambrai. It may well have been at this point that she sought out three theologians (a Franciscan Friar John, a Cistercian named Dom Franco from Villiers, and the well-known secular Paris Master Godfrey of Fontaines) to certify the orthodoxy of the work.[242] She continued to disseminate the text, however, and even sent it to John of Castro Villani, Bishop of Chalons. In 1308 Marguerite was arrested and handed over to William Humbert, the Dominican Inquisitor of Paris, for continuing to spread her condemned text. She refused to speak to him or to any of her inquisitors during her imprisonment and trial. In 1310 a commission of twenty-one theologians investigated a series of fifteen propositions drawn from the book (only three of which are securely identifiable today),[243] judging them heretical. Their major opposition to her teaching seems to have centered on fears that she advocated antinomian freedom from the virtues and the moral law, as well as a form of "quietism," or indifference to the ecclesiastically mediated means of salvation.[244] Since Marguerite refused to recant, or even to make a formal statement to the inquisitors, she was condemned as a relapsed heretic and handed over for execution. Despite the negative view taken toward the beguine in the sources, the *Chronicle of Nanges* records that "[s]he showed many noble and devout signs of penance at her death by which the feelings of many were moved to heartfelt compassion for her and even to tears, as eyewitnesses who saw it testified."[245]

Though we know a good deal about the details of the trial, the motivation behind the process remains elusive. The beguine movement had attracted critics from the outset, though it also had powerful supporters. The conciliar bans against new religious orders (1215 and 1274), the increasing competition among existing orders, suspicions concerning the proliferation of heresy, and especially the deeply ingrained medieval fear of women who stepped outside the carefully controlled roles prescribed for them by the church and society, all contributed to growing opposition to the beguines in the second half of the thirteenth century.[246] Much has been made of a possible political dimension to the trial and execution of Marguerite Porete in the context of the tensions between Philip IV of France and the papacy. Was the pursuit of Porete engineered, at least in part, by the Capetian court as another expression of "the most Christian king's" zeal for the defense of orthodoxy at the time of the highly controversial destruction of the Templar Order under the guise of their "heretical depravity"?[247] Circumstantial evidence points in this direction, but we must not forget the important role of the growing fear of heresy, especially mystical heresy, at the time. In the early 1270s the Dominican teacher Albert the Great had put together a list of ninety-seven erroneous articles culled from material sent him about a group of heretics of the Swabian Ries in southwest Germany. This *Compilation concerning the New Spirit* already heralds the kinds of errors concerning deification, antinomianism, and anti-ecclesiasticism that the "Free Spirit" heretics were to be accused of in the early years of the fourteenth century. (It also seems that the errors are primarily ascribed to women.)[248] The bull *Ad nostrum*, issued at the Council of Vienne in 1311 as the document that first identified and condemned "the sect of the Free Spirit," made use of some of the articles drawn from Porete's *Mirror*, and also may have employed Albert's *Compilation*.[249] The same council also issued a disciplinary decree *Cum de quibusdam*, which condemned at least some groups of beguines, although the notion that it was a blanket condemnation cannot be sustained.[250]

Despite *Ad nostrum* and the fact that Marguerite's book was burned along with her, *The Mirror of Simple Souls* survives in no fewer than six versions in four languages with thirteen manuscripts, making it among the more widely disseminated of the vernacular mystical texts of the Middle Ages.[251] But the book continued to provoke controversy.[252] The French beguine's text was almost certainly known and used by Meister Eckhart,[253] and in recent years considerable attention has been given to the relation between the two premier apophatic theologians of the late thirteenth century.[254]

What kind of a book is *The Mirror of Simple Annihilated Souls and Those Who Remain Only in Will and Desire of Love* (to give the text its full title)? A direct answer is not easy. *The Mirror* is more overtly didactic than the texts of the other major thirteenth-century women mystics, though it shares with Hadewijch and Mechthild a strong affinity for the language and themes of courtly love, such as its inherent elitism, its use of personification allegory, and the interpersonal dynamics of generosity/meanness, distance/nearness, worthiness/unworthiness, yearning/fulfillment that the courtly ideal employed to portray the relations between lover and beloved.[255] *The Mirror* does not display a mixing of genres comparable to that found in Mechthild's *Flowing Light*, but it is like the German beguine's work in its fundamentally dialogical form and in the complexity of voices it presents. Although it is relatively clear *who* is speaking in the dialogues that constitute the bulk of *The Mirror*,[256] it is often difficult to determine who the speakers represent and what their conversation means, especially in light of the problems of determining who the purported "author" is and for whom the text was written.

These issues center on the authority, implied and explicit, upon which the message of *The Mirror* is based. Most texts composed by or about medieval female mystics anchor their authority, at least in part, on the reception of divinely given visions. *The Mirror* contains no visionary recitals; indeed, it is hostile to visions, even of the highest kind.[257] Most medieval women, including such hardy souls as Hildegard of Bingen and Mechthild of Magdeburg (though not Hadewijch), make use of the topos of female weakness–God's chooses the weak (female) things of the world to confound the strong (male) ones. Marguerite Porete never apologizes for being a woman. Like the texts of the other "female evangelists" of the thirteenth century, *The Mirror* gives itself the authority of a "new form of the gospel," though *The Mirror* does this in a different way from anything else found in the Middle Ages.

The very title *Mirouer (Speculum) des simples ames anienties* introduces us to the ambiguities of the book's authority. A mirror in medieval literature traditionally indicates a text that represents or images some reality or state of affairs.[258] But if souls are truly annihilated, how can they be represented? Furthermore, is the "mirror" a possessive or an objective genitive? That is, are the Annihilated Souls themselves the mirror or does it only represent them? In the first chapter Marguerite uses the story of the princess Candace's love for the far-off Alexander the Great which caused her to have an image painted to remind her of him as an *exemplum* of her book's ambiguous representational status. The "Soul who had this book written" here claims:

> He was so far from me and I from him that I was not able to receive any consolation from myself. For the sake of my memory of him [Latin: For the sake of giving me peace], he gave me this book which represents in some ways his love. Although I have his image with me, this does not mean that I am not in a foreign land and far from that peace [French: palace] where the very noble friends of that Lord dwell. . . .[259]

"This book" (*ce livre*), as *The Mirror* often speaks of itself in a self-referential way, initially is a divine image inscribed within the Soul (hinting at the Soul's nature as *imago Dei*), and is then externally written down as a book-image by the Soul herself. The fact that both God and the Soul are authors of *ce livre* compares with what we have seen in some of the other women, but the ambiguities of the mode of representation are distinctive in Porete.

Throughout *The Mirror,* as Amy Hollywood has noted, the Soul is both
one of the interlocutors and also the arena of the drama in the sense that the
transformation of consciousness that is the subject of the book is taking place
within her.[260] This process might be described as the creation of a mystical
identity, though it paradoxically takes place through the "decreation" of the
self in annihilation, the final goal being what Paul Mommaers has referred to
as the emergence of "un 'je' sans moi"–"An 'I' without a me."[261] The strange-
ness of the geography of the land within which this journey of transformation occurs is heightened by the absence of a narrative voice describing
where the speakers are and where they are going, although some chapters
do provide more sense of direction and location.[262] It is not so much that *The
Mirror* lacks structures detailing the process of mystical transformation (e.g.,
the seven stages to union in chap. 118), but that these structures are necessarily secondary in a treatise whose whole purpose is to negate structure. To
introduce strong doses of confusion and vertigo in the reader is central to
the mystical therapy of *The Mirror of Simple Souls.*

It is essential for reading *The Mirror,* then, to allow oneself to be caught
up in a dialogue that is at times pedestrian, sometimes parodic and humorous, often obscure, and frequently moving and profound. Marguerite drew
on at least three predecessors in her use of dialogue–the biblical dialogue of
the Song of Songs, the philosophical dialogue available in the West through
Cicero and Boethius, and the interiorized personification dialogue found in
Old French courtly romances.[263] This richness makes her form of mystical
dialogue rank with Mechthild's as among the most original of the thirteenth
century.

The three main discussants of *The Mirror* are the Soul (*L'Ame*), Love or
"Lady Love" (*Dame Amour*), and Reason (*Raison*), though scores of others
join in from time to time. The Soul, who is sometimes said to be the author
of the book (chaps. 1, 96, 119), is not to be thought of as identical with the
historical Marguerite Porete, though she often speaks for her. In the final
part of the book (chaps. 123–39, after the first *explicit*) the voice of the Soul
and that of Marguerite as author do seem to merge in a way not found earlier.[264] Lady Love, who likewise is described as the author of the book
(chaps. 2, 32, 37, 60, 84, 119) is, of course, God (see the explicit identifica-
tions in chaps. 21 and 112); but she is also the power in the Soul which par-
ticipates in (and even becomes) God through annihilation (chaps. 39 and
133). Reason is overtly Love's opponent, the faculty that must be overcome
and die if the Soul is to reach the goal of annihilation. But Reason is also
essential to the transformational process. Reason both dies (chap. 87) and
does not die. Not only do Love and Soul have to take over what Reason

would have said had she remained alive (chaps. 87–88)–what we may take to be Marguerite's version of the traditional mystical theme of *amor ipse intellectus est*–but Reason mysteriously comes back to life later in the text to continue her part in the dialogue (chaps. 98, 101, 106).[265] The grounds for Reason's refusal to disappear are multiple, involving not only the necessity for the continuing presence of the rational faculty to highlight the paradoxes of annihilating union, but also Reason's ambiguous role as at least a partial subject of the transformational process described in *The Mirror*.[266]

Among the other participants in the dialogue, "Holy Church the Little" and "Holy Church the Great," as institutional manifestations of Reason and Love, play a significant role. Most of the other characters (e.g., "Intellect of Reason," "Height of Intellect of Love," "Light of Faith," "Truth," "Divine Righteousness," etc.) are personifications of the powers of the Soul or divine attributes. However, God himself also enters into the discussion, speaking as the Holy Trinity (chap. 121), or sometimes in the person of the Holy Spirit (chaps. 42–43, 57) and once in the person of the Father (chap. 50). (Significantly, Christ himself never speaks.)[267]

The ambiguities and paradoxes evident in the genre of *The Mirror* are important for understanding the form of evangelical authority advanced and the audience addressed by this claim. As befits a work whose central theme is annihilation,[268] Marguerite's gospel is one that continually strives to negate itself–a vanishing gospel written for secret free souls who really do not need it.[269] This inner contradiction introduces tensions, puzzles, and paradoxes into *The Mirror* of an unusual character, even among medieval mystical texts. Whereas the appeal to a divine source for the book's teaching, as we have seen with Mechthild of Magdeburg, usually is meant to put security and confidence into the text, even the fact that *Dame Amour*, who is God, is the major teaching voice in *The Mirror*, does little to alleviate the instability of the book upon which Marguerite literally staked her life. *The Mirror* presents itself as a book that was both necessary and impossible to write.

The two main interlocutors, Love and Reason, often discuss and gloss "this book" in a way analogous to how scholastic theologians glossed and debated the biblical text.[270] Indeed, Marguerite seems to want to claim a reciprocal relationship between her text and the Bible. In one passage Holy Church the Little says that "this word [about the Annihilated Soul] opens the scriptures and we are not able to grasp through Reason what she [Love] says."[271] Because *The Mirror* was an internal "Bible" before it was externalized as a written text, and especially because its main purpose is to lead the soul to annihilation, the authority and even the existence of the text begin to waver and collapse at key points. Similarly, the role of the "Mendicant

Creature" (*mendiant creature*) in whom the book was written and who lost her life in disseminating it, becomes ambivalent.

Three passages from chapters 96–98 reflecting on the author and purpose of the work illustrate this process. The first speaks of how the Mendicant Creature long sought God in this life but was not able to find him. Then she sought him "at the depth of the core of the intellect of the purity of her sublime thought." The passage continues:

> And so this Mendicant Creature wrote what you hear. And she desired that her neighbors might find God in her, through writings and words; that is to say and mean, that she wished her neighbors become the perfect ones she described (at least all those to whom she desired to say this).[272]

This stress on finding God in the text of the book, which is actually the externalized text of the annihilated soul of Marguerite, also appears in chapter 98, which asks the "Ladies to whom God has abundantly given this life" to recognize their practice in the book (272.13–17). But the book's role as a true and necessary divine text is undercut by a passage from chapter 97 sandwiched between these two. Here the Mendicant Creature reflects on the fact that she wrote the book "to vindicate herself" (or "to be repaid"– *revenger/reuindicare*), and that although it was necessary both for herself and for other perfect souls that creatures learn "to beg" (or "to be poor"–*mendiassent/mendicarent*) from other creatures in order to attain the state of freeness, she was foolish at the time she wrote the book because she did not realize that she had undertaken something "which one could neither do, nor think, nor say, any more than someone could desire to enclose the sea in his eye. . . ."[273]

In chapter 119 the Soul who causes the book to be written goes even further, excusing herself to the "Ladies never known" (*dames nient cognues*) for having made the book "very large through words, though it seems to you very small, if I have ever been able to understand you." Thus the book "is more like lying than speaking the truth," and "very small even though it seemed large at the beginning of the demonstration. . . ."[274] Porete's text, then, is designed to implode—first back into the soul, and finally, when the soul is truly annihilated, back into the Divine Abyss. The first implosion is described in chapter 66, when *Amour* says, "This lesson is not placed in writing by human hand, but by the Holy Spirit, who writes this lesson in a marvellous way, and the Soul is the precious parchment."[275] The second implosion is the final purpose of *The Mirror* and appears in many guises in the text. An important summary in chapter 101 highlights both the necessity and the impossibility of the book. The book is necessary because it reveals the message that the ultimate meaning of Love is annihilation; it is impossible because both the text and the Soul who fulfills its teaching vanish in attaining their joint purpose. As the Soul puts it:

> The opening of this book has made me see so clearly that it made me give back what is his and receive what is mine–that is, that he is, . . . and I am not, and so it is indeed right that I do not possess myself. And the light of the opening (*ouverture/apertura*) of this book has made me find what is mine and to remain in it. Thus I have only as much being as he is able to be of himself in me. Thus, what is right has rightly restored what is mine to me and nakedly shown that I do not exist.[276]

Here Porete describes the book as an opening or aperture, using technical language that she elsewhere employed for the "chink of contemplation," or "opening of the moment of glory" by which the Soul passes from the fifth to the sixth and final stage of complete annihilation.[277] In this transition everything disappears into primordial oneness with God. "It is thus with this book and me, says this Soul, as it was with God and creatures when he created them."[278]

Who is the audience for whom this strange, disappearing book was written?[279] Here, too, nothing is simple about *The Mirror of Simple Annihilated Souls*. As the title indicates, the book is about and for the Simple Souls who have reached annihilation, but it does not exclude some role for those Sad Souls who still dwell in the land of will and desire. The audience is often addressed as "hearers of the book" or "hearers who read" (e.g., chaps. 13, 19, 37, 58, 82), an indication of the mode of presentation by oral delivery that Marguerite seems to have employed. There are a number of passages, such as that found in the prologue, where Love addresses both "actives and contemplatives" pointing to the beguine's desire to disseminate her work to a broad audience.[280] Nonetheless, Porete's *Mirror* is fundamentally an esoteric work, as the book insists in at least a score of its chapters.[281] In chapter 76, for example, Soul says that the examples she has just given of annihilated saints are sufficient for those who have the intellect to grasp the point, and that "[t]his book is not written for others" (212.25). In chapter 84 Love says that unless one has attained annihilation in God, one will suffer in vain to understand the book (238.20–27), while in chapter 132 Soul declares: "If you do not understand, I cannot help you. This is a miraculous book, of which one can tell you nothing, unless it is a lie."[282]

The esoteric and elitist nature of *The Mirror* grounds its attacks on the clergy, Reason's servants, who are representative of those who will never be able to grasp the message that Love teaches the Simple Soul (see the introductory poem and chaps. 5, 9, 53, and 122). Late in the work the Holy Trinity praises the Soul in poetic form in chapter 121 as follows:

O heavenly rock,
   says the Holy Trinity,
I pray you, dear daughter,
   let this be.
There is not so great a cleric in the world
   who knows how to speak to you about it.[283]

The Trinity goes on to advise the Soul that she "no longer desire to tell the secrets which you know" so that those who cannot understand might be condemned for their lack of knowledge (340.55–65). This same elitism, even disdain for the ignorant, is at the root of the passage in chapter 85 in which Love says of the Simple Soul: "She responds to no one if she does not wish to, if he is not of her lineage. For a gentleman would not deign to respond to a peasant, even if such a one would call him or attack him in a battlefield. . . . Her enemies have no longer any response from her."[284] This is exactly the course of action that Marguerite Porete followed during her trial.

If Porete's *Mirror of Simple Souls* can be considered a new "gospel" of some sort, it is clear that it is more like the Gnostic gospels of the second century than the traditional four Gospels of the New Testament. At times it even displays affinities with themes frequent in Gnostic texts, such as in chapter 117, where there is an obscure passage about the descent and ascent of perfect souls. However, the quasi-Gnostic esotericism of *The Mirror* (something considered suspect in the history of Christian mysticism)[285] is modified in two important ways. First, Marguerite continued to preach and spread her book to the "whole Holy Church" (chap. 19 [74.6–9]), even to the point of endangering her life, because she was convinced that the message would help some to recognize their true lineage as Simple-Souls-in-the-making. In chapter 59 she says that the book is written "not for sake of those who are this [i.e., the already-arrived], but for those who are not, who yet will be. . . ."[286] Perhaps we could say that although she knew her book was esoteric, she wished that it were not. Second, Porete (in a manner oddly reminiscent of John Scottus Eriugena) believed in two forms or levels of salvation, though perhaps not, like the Irishman, in the universal redemption of all humanity.[287] According to Porete, even the crass merchant souls who do nothing more than fulfill the commandments, as well as the Lost and Sad Souls who have attained higher stages of love without reaching freedom, will be saved, as Love insists to the astonishment of the Simple Annihilated Soul.[288] This concept of salvation in an "uncourtly way" (*mal courtoisement/incurialiter* [chap. 62; 180–81]) is typical of the qualifications that

Maguerite often introduces into her teaching to show that it does not contra-dict the doctrines of Holy Church the Little.

Annihilation and Apophaticism

Marguerite Porete's message about annihilation cannot be easily sepa-rated from the form and style of her book. Nevertheless, in order to gain a deeper appreciation of the subtlety and depth of her teaching, it will be helpful now to approach the text from a thematic point of view by investi-gating three topics: (A) binary dynamics; (B) the soul and its itinerary; and (C) annihilating union.

Binary Dynamics

Mystical theology expresses itself in many ways, not least through the invocation of binary terms of many kinds—correlative binaries, opposed binaries, dialectical binaries. These forms of language are evident through-out Marguerite's *Mirror*. The book seems to exist on the border between the opposition of orthodoxy and heterodoxy, flaunting its extreme statements at the same time that it often seeks to qualify them and to protect its essen-tial orthodoxy. Although the beguine frames the soul's transformation in terms of traditional enumerations of 3s, 7s and 9s, binary personifications and terms are more essential to her message. Many of these binaries are immediately obvious, such as Love and Reason, Holy Church the Great and Holy Church the Little, or the contrast between the works-salvation involved in serving the virtues and the free-salvation that comes from faith alone (at times Marguerite sounds almost like Luther, e.g., chap. 11). So too, the transition of the Soul from a state of being "encumbered" (*encumber/ impeditus*) to one of "disencumberence" (*disencumber/expeditus*) and liberty (*enfranchie/libera*) is based on what first looks like simple binary opposi-tion.[289] Things get more complicated, however, when we consider the role of ascent and descent and sin and salvation in *The Mirror*. Here, binaries that seem initially opposed begin to appear as correlative, and even to fuse into something like a dialectical *coincidentia oppositorum*. The correlation of opposed terms, moving forward at times to a dialectical fusion, helps us to understand why the beguine felt it necessary to create a new name for God—the *Loingprés*, or "FarNigh," as the Middle English translation nicely renders it.

A brief consideration of the relation of some opposed terms and personi-fications will help to illustrate Marguerite's strategies of correlation and fusion. Reason dies, as we have seen, but has to come back to life because the mystical transformation of the Soul demands both Reason and Love. Holy Church the Great, the realm of Love and freedom, despite her superiority, does not break off her dialogue with Holy Church the Little, where Reason rules.[290] Although the Annihilated Soul bids farewell to the virtues insofar as they are external forces of domination, they also remain as connatural expressions of her new being.[291] This tendency to bring together opposites is more daringly expressed in how Porete suggests that "descent" into sin is necessary for "ascent" to union. Here, as Michael Sells has pointed out, the beguine inverts the Christian language of the Fall,[292] though it is necessary to add that the model she employs has important christological implications in the descent and emptying (*kenōsis*) of the second person of the Trinity into human nature and his sacrifice on the cross.

In chapter 40 Love speaks of the person who is "abyssed in humility," using both feminine and masculine language. Such a one "has injustice in nothing and nevertheless knows that he has justice in nothing. He who exists in this knowledge of his injustice, sees so clearly that he sees himself beneath every creature in the mire [Fr.: sea] of sin." As a slave to sin, such a soul is beneath even the demons, and yet by recognizing her total sinfulness "this soul has become nothing and less than nothing in all respects." The chapter concludes: "She has heard it said by the Holy Spirit for a long time that God will place the least and lowest in the higher [Fr.: highest] place by his goodness alone" (cf. Luke 14:10).[293] This message concerning the necessity of descending to the depths by recognition of one's total sinfulness in order to gain the annihilating humility that places one on the heights is expanded upon later in *The Mirror* in a series of rich texts.

Chapters 102 to 109 contain a long and difficult discussion of bodiliness, sin, annihilation, and the fall that is necessary for ascent.[294] Although God created both body and soul as good, Adam's Fall introduced humanity to the "prison of correction," where, even after baptism, our continuing defects, however small, displease him (chap. 102). Some try to ameliorate this fact by citing Proverbs 24:16 ("The just man shall fall seven times and rise again"), but Porete emphasizes that no one sins without free will, so that the seven falls in the biblical verse cannot be forced acts of the will but must refer to that weakness of the fallen body which hinders "contemplation of divine goodness without any impediment" (chap. 105; 286.5–6). This recognition of what can be described as a necessary human condition prompts a further reflection on the blessedness of the annihilated soul who is reminded of her high station by the "fall" of the wretched body (chap. 105) and then leads on to a deeper meditation on the nature of sin and fall (chaps. 106–9). The truly Annihilated Soul cannot ask for anything of herself, but she says that God, "of whom and from whom I am, who is himself in me," can make such petitions in her (chap. 106). The petitions are twofold: that the soul see herself where she was before she was made, and that she see the significance of sin as a removal of the will from God (chap. 107). Sin now is redefined as *any act* in which the soul does not strive to do what is best, so that it must be viewed as a constant condition until the will is totally annihilated:

> As long as I have had will, I have not stopped [removing it from him], until I totally lost the will and nakedly restored it to him who gave it to me freely of his goodness. [This is] because a person who does well and recognizes some other better thing that he could do, if he is called to do it and does not do it, he sins.[295]

When the soul was nothing (i.e., before its creation) it could owe God nothing. When it becomes a thing or creature, it begins to owe God something because of the constant defects of its will. Hence, the soul must again become nothing in order to be acquitted of even *one* of its sins ("Not more! Not more! Not more!" as Marguerite passionately exclaims–chap. 109; 296.10). It is significant that the extended treatment of sin in chapters 102–109 ends with the invocation of the incarnate Son of God as what Marguerite calls "my mirror of this," namely, the exemplar of total obedience to the will to the Father.

This Christocentric turn helps us to understand one of the most striking texts in the entire *Mirror,* chapter 117, which in a sense summarizes the core of Marguerite's dialogical presentation of her message, allowing her then to spell out in more linear fashion the seven stages of the soul's progress in the lengthy chapter 118. In chapter 117 the "Superexalted Spirit" (*supersublimatus Spiritus*), who has emptied herself totally so that divine goodness must dwell in her, exclaims:

> And through this I am an exemplar of salvation, and even more the salvation itself of every creature and the glory of God. And I will tell you how, why, and in what. First, because I am the height of all evil, for I contain of my own nature what is wretched, and therefore I am total wretchedness. And he ... is the height of all goodness. . . . Now God cannot do what is unjust, for then he would destroy himself. . . . Since I am total wretchedness and he is total goodness, it is necessary for me to have the totality of his goodness before my wretchedness can be terminated.[296]

The soul that has recognized her complete sinfulness and thus become divine goodness and the salvation of the human race does so after the model of Christ, who, by dying on the cross, first revealed the totality of divine goodness. For Porete, salvation consists in grasping the meaning of divine goodness, and thus the Superexalted Spirit boldly claims that she is the cause of this realization for others, not because of any good work that she does but precisely in her wretchedness—"Thus I can never lose his goodness, for I cannot lose my wretchedness" (*Sa bonté aussi jamais ne puis je perdre, car je ne puis perdre ma mauvaistié* [314.58–59]). Marguerite's understanding of union with God rests on this fusion of wretchedness and goodness. "Since I possess his total goodness, I am necessarily what he is through the transformation of love."[297] In a quasi-Gnostic conclusion, she refers to such Superexalted Souls as "those who are planted by the Father" and who come into this world descending from perfection to imperfection in order to attain higher perfection. The christological dimension remains present, but these fully humbled souls are now presented as co-redeemers with Christ: "They have carried Christ's cross through good works; now they are carrying their own cross" (cf. Matt. 16:24).[298]

The fusion of the height of goodness and the depth of wretched alienation in one and the same Soul and at one and the same time helps us to understand the French beguine's distinctive teaching about God. Marguerite was well versed in traditional trinitarian theology, as is evident in many places in her book (e.g., chaps. 11, 14, 33, 42, 67, 108, 110, 115, 130), but it was her sense of the centrality of the fusion of opposites in the Soul's immediate consciousness of God that was the source for her new name for the Trinity, the *Loingprés*.[299] The term involves the combining of two qualifiers without a substantive, thus suggesting that God is not a thing but is better seen as a dialectical "relationship," or "presence," one both infinitely distant and unknown and for that very reason more "here" in its absence.[300] Porete does not try to describe or define FarNigh, but she does talk about its effect on (or better "in") the Annihilated Soul. FarNigh is both "ravishing" (*ravissable*) and *gentil/nobile* in the courtly sense. He (the word is masculine) is "very sweet" (*tres doulx*) in the peace and "unencumbering" he brings to the soul. In chapter 84 Love describes what happens to the Soul after she has been freed in four aspects:

> Then she falls from this into an astonishment, which one calls "pondering nothing about the nearness of the FarNigh," who is her nearest one. Then such a soul, says Love, lives not by the life of grace, or by the life of the spirit, but only by the divine life, freely not gloriously, because she is not yet glorified.[301]

The action of FarNigh brings the Soul to the ultimate identification of created nothingness with divine goodness and being, the place where she was "before she flowed out from the Goodness of God," as a remarkable passage from the end of *The Mirror* describes:

> The farness of this [Goodness] is greater nearness, because she [Soul] knows that farness in itself more in its nearness, which [knowing] always makes her to be in union with his will without the hindrance of anything else that might happen to her. All is one for her, without a why, and she is nothing in such a One. Then she has nothing more to do for God than God has to do for her. Why? Because he is and she is not.[302]

This is "the land of the Forgotten Ones, the Naked Annihilated Ones, the Clarified Ones," as chapter 95 puts it, where God "is neither known, nor loved, nor praised by such creatures, except only in this, that one cannot know, nor love, nor praise him."[303]

Apophatic language, as Michael Sells has shown, strives not to create systems or express ontologies but rather to break down systems and to subvert ontologies that threaten to make God another "reality."[304] Like all apophatic mystics, Marguerite insists that there is no coming to terms with God, but only the constant effort, the performance, of the process of negating the works of intellect and will in order to attain the annihilation in which God and the Soul become absolutely one once more.[305] Therefore, nothingness (*nihil*) is central to Marguerite Porete. Her mystical thought may be said to be founded on two apophatic pillars: (1) God is totally incomprehensible and therefore "nothing" from the perspective of human categories;[306] (2) the Soul must become nothing by willing nothing in order to attain the God who is nothing and therefore all.

The Soul and Its Itinerary

The fusion of binaries in Porete's thought gives us a new perspective on her description of the soul's path to such annihilating union, "the nothing that gives her everything" (chap. 81; 230.11–12). Porete provides several clear mystical itineraries in her book (notably chap. 118), but we are not always sure how to correlate them with the rest of the text. For example, any first-time reader of the book must wonder why, after a brief mention of the seven stages of the soul's progression in chapter 1 and some hints in chapters 58, 61, and 91, we have to wait until what seems to be the end of the original version of the treatise (the lengthy chapter 118) for a full account. It is also not always clear how the seven-stage itinerary relates to two other patterns of mystical transformation—that of the three kinds of souls (see chaps. 55–58, 95, 133),[307] and the analysis of the three kinds of death needed for annihilation (see chaps. 54, 60–64, 73, 87, 131).[308]

Based on an analysis of chapter 118, we can integrate the seven stages or states (*estaz/gradus-status*) with the types of souls and deaths as follows. The first stage (chap. 118; 318.8–25; cf. chap. 62–63) involves the first death, that is, the death to sin by which the soul begins to keep the commandments. The Freed Soul remembers being in such a state, but describes its practitioners as cowardly and slothful. The second stage (318.26–320.36) strives to mortify nature (i.e., the second death, or death to nature) by practicing the evangelical counsels, of which Jesus Christ is the exemplar. In the third stage (320.39–322.64) the soul continues to strive for the works of perfection in trying "to conquer the works of the will of the spirit" (322.59–60) by giving herself over to religious obedience. This is a continuation of the second death (i.e., it puts the natural will to death), but since this stage involves the *will* willing such activity, it is still far from true annihilation. The fourth stage (322.66–324.92) marks the traditional height of the mystical path in the classic twelfth-century patterns of ascent, such as those of the Cistercians and Victorines. Here the soul is drawn into the "height of contemplation" (*haultesse de contemplacion*), where she enjoys "the touch of the pure delight of love." Love totally satisfies her so that she becomes completely inebriated and cannot see the possibility of any higher state on earth. "But," as the Freed Soul reminds the reader, "love has deceived many souls by the sweetness of the pleasure of her love" (324.88–89)–a remarkable critique of most previous Christian understandings of mystical consciousness.

It seems to be on this high, but still incomplete, level that Porete begins her distinction between the three kinds of souls–the Lost, the Sad, and the Free or Annihilated. The Lost Souls are those who are so content to remain in the land of desire and in the enjoyment of the experience of bliss that they are blind to any other possibility (see chaps. 55–56). The Sad Souls, on the other hand, "maintain that there is a being better than theirs," and so they are "miserable and sad" and often ask direction from Lady Understanding, who teaches them "the right royal road that runs through the land of willing nothing."[309] (It is for these, we can assume, that *The Mirror of Simple Annihilated Souls* was primarily written.)

True annihilation commences with the fifth stage (324.94–330.173), where the third death, the death of the spirit, takes place. Here the overflowing of divine light into the soul shows "the will of the soul the rightness of that which is and the understanding of that which is not, in order to move the will of the soul from the place where it is, where it ought not to be, and to place it where it is not, but from which it nevertheless comes and where it ought to be."[310] The soul's recognition of the coincidence of her wretchedness and divine goodness means the disappearance of the will precisely as a created *something*. In this long discussion Marguerite rings the changes on dialectical language experiments exploring how the soul sinks into a bottomless abyss of wretchedness under the "flood of sin" in order to be able to see the Divine Goodness which transforms her into the nature of Love—no longer created, desiring love, but Divine Love itself. "Now she is All, and so she is Nothing, for her Beloved makes her one."[311]

The death of the spirit that makes possible the passage into the fifth state is described in three other places. The first is a general account in chapter 73 (204–7). There is also a description of the death of Reason recounted in chapter 87 (246–49), which may be described as the preliminary stage of annihilation of the spirit. To the Soul's assertion that she is now identical with Love and therefore without beginning, end, or limit, Reason (who has had to put up with a lot) finally succumbs. Her heart fails and Soul rejoices that she is now ready to receive her inheritance freely. But there is an even more startling death of the spirit toward the end of *The Mirror* in chapter 131. Here the Soul, speaking in an "I" voice that brings her closer to Marguerite as author than to a personification, first addresses God in a series of eleven statements testing love based on a genre familiar in the courtly tradition.[312] These are designed to prove the absolute disinterestedness, the nothingness in a sense, of her devotion to the divine will. But the demands, despite their purity of intention, still represent a created will willing to be pure. In other words, they are expressions of what chapter 118 would see as love of a Sad Soul on level 4. The transition to levels 5 and 6 is not possible until God intervenes (as he does in the fifth stage in chap. 118) with three demands of his own (384.77–92). First, he asks Soul how she would fare "if I [Soul] knew that he could be better pleased that I should love another better than him." Next, he asks how she would fare if he loved someone better than he loved her; and finally, God asks what she would do if he willed that someone else love her better than he does. The test is a fatal one. "And there I fainted, for I could respond nothing to these three things, nor refuse, nor deny" (384.96–386.98). The tests have demonstrated to Soul-Marguerite that her prior love was imperfect because it still involved a "self." Will and love need to be martyred and die for the "her" who is not a "she" to depart from her infancy (388.129–35).[313]

Once the spirit has died and attained the fifth stage, there is no slipping back to lower levels,[314] but there is a difference between two forms of annihilated (un)consciousness. In the fifth state, Marguerite still seems to speak mostly from the perspective of the effaced "I," while in the sixth state (330.175–332.203) the divine perspective predominates, that of the "Ravishing FarNigh" (see chaps. 58–61). Here the French beguine comes close to expressions employed by Meister Eckhart about the paradoxical seeing by which "the eye in which I see God is the same eye in which God sees me."[315] The Soul no longer sees (i.e., knows) either herself or God, but as she says:

> God sees himself of himself in her, for her, without her. God shows to her that there is nothing except him. And thus this Soul understands nothing except him, for there is nothing except him. . . . And so nothing is, except He Who Is [cf. Exod. 3:14], who sees himself in such a being by his divine majesty through the transformation of love. . . .[316]

There is a seventh stage, that of glorification—as distinct from the brief moment of "aperture," or clarification, of the sixth stage. But this is reserved to heaven, and Marguerite says nothing about it.

Many previous Christian mystical itineraries made use of saintly figures, scriptural and nonscriptural (e.g., Moses, Paul, the Virgin Mary, Mary Magdalene, and Francis), to provide models for the ascent to God. Most were also deeply christological in the sense that they were explicitly tied to love of Jesus, the God-man, as both the way and the goal of mystical union. In the thirteenth century the christological core of Christian mysticism began to take on an increasingly passion-oriented tinge. How does Marguerite Porete stand in relation to these mystical themes?

It is obvious that Porete constitutues an exception, though not a total one. Biblical prototypes play a role for her, especially the Blessed Virgin, who is seen as a special model of the Annihilated Soul.[317] There is also a significant christological dimension to annihilation, though it does not depend on the usual meditative presentation of the suffering Christ so prevalent in Franciscans, such as Angela of Foligno, and found also in Hadewijch and Mechthild.

Significant discussion of the role of Christ occurs in over twenty chapters of *The Mirror.* Jesus is not the Divine Bridegroom for Marguerite, as he was for the monastic commentators on the Song of Songs or for so many of the women mystics.[318] Marguerite herself is described as a bride in several places, notably chapter 82, which speaks of how the Soul that flows back into God "is perfectly transformed, that is, into the love of the Bridegroom of her youth, who has completely transformed the bride into himself."[319] But the Annihilated Soul (such as Marguerite) is the bride of the Holy Spirit (e.g., chaps. 96, 115, and 122), or of the entire Trinity (e.g., chap. 68), rather than of Christ. Marguerite Porete, as Barbara Newman has shown,[320] is passionately erotic, but in the courtly rather than the bridal sense so that direct sexual imagery is largely absent from her text.

The role of Christ (as noted above in discussing chapters 109 and 117) is that of the exemplar, or first manifestation, of the descent into wretchedness and sin as the only way to come to knowledge of the saving goodness of God. This is not to say that Marguerite does not reflect on Christ's suffering for her and for all in his "sweet humanity" (chap. 34; cf. chaps. 5, 50, 126, 128), nor on the necessity for us to take Christ as the model for all our works and suffering (e.g., chaps. 13, 39, 62, 69, 94, 118), but we should understand this not as a fixation on the bloody wounds of the dying Lord but rather as the theophany of the true *kenōsis,* the emptying of the will by annihilation. It is perhaps surprising that the beguine does not make explicit use of the famous *kenōsis* text from Philippians 2:7 ("He emptied himself taking the form of a slave . . .), but she does employ the evangelical notion of Christ's descent and ascent in obedience to the Father's *will* as the model for our annihilating obedience (e.g., John 3:13 and Matt 12:50 as cited in chap. 128; 370.23–29). The Soul's ascent to God is possible only because of "the worthy indwelling of human creation by the sweet humanity of the Son of God our Savior" (chap. 122; 340.3–4), but the considerations of the incarnation and the passion found in chapters 127–28 (366–74) show that the mystery of the Word's descent is meant to "amaze" the Soul into loss of self and perfect obedience to the Father's will. Thus, Marguerite Porete's radical understanding of mystical annihilation has a definite christological dimension, but a rather different one from that found in most medieval women mystics.

Annihilating Union

Finally, we turn to a consideration of what kind of union *The Mirror of Simple Annihilated Souls* teaches. As noted in chapter 4 (p. 157), an important shift took place in the thirteenth century in Western Christian views concerning the union possible between created spirit and Uncreated Spirit. Unprecedented emphasis upon returning to, or growing into, the mystic's virtual preexistence in God before creation, or the necessity of annihilation in order to sink into a bottomless abyss where God and the soul are one abyss, or modes of expression emphasizing union without distinction or mediation, all argue for a radical new sense of the oneness with God that can be attained in this life. Even where these new forms of expression coexist with more traditional language about the loving union of wills between God and human that maintains the distinction of substances, we can sense the onset of a new and more challenging notion of *unio mystica.* For example, Marguerite, like William of St. Thierry, saw the Holy Spirit, the Love uniting Father and Son in the Trinity, as the power drawing the soul to the deepest union with God–"The Goodness of the Holy Spirit unites her to the love of the Father and the Son" (chap. 115; 308.16–17). But she goes further than the Cistercian mystic by following this statement with an apophatic paradox undercutting any stable description of such union: "This union places the Soul in the being without being that is being" (306.16–17). Although her teaching on union may not have given rise to any of the explicit articles excerpted from *The Mirror* for condemnation as heretical, it cannot be doubted that the beguine's view of union was the ground for some of the most controversial aspects of her teaching.

We have already seen the importance of union as a return to preexistence in God in Hadewijch and Mechthild of Magdeburg. The Dutch beguine was the first Western mystic to speak from her precreational, ideal existence in God as a way of expressing the authority of her message. Marguerite, on the other hand, employs virtual existence in God in order to emphasize the necessity for the annihilation of her created will and being. In his great *The Trinity,* Augustine had reflected on the preexistence of the soul and its will in God, the supreme Good, noting that in its created state the soul can either will to be converted to the source from which it came or to turn away from it and cease being a good will, but that "the soul which could wish to be before it was did not as yet exist." All that then existed (i.e., before time) was "our Good wherein we see whether the thing ought to have been or ought to be. . . ."[321] Marguerite Porete's need to return to that precreation in which there is no good save God went beyond Augustine and previous Western theologians in finding in the very notion of a created will and its *possibility* of not willing the good a separation or fault that tortures the loving soul until it is negated through annihilation. The beguine's stress on the Soul's eternal preexistence in God is found throughout her book, but it becomes especially insistent in the final chapters 135–38.[322] The description of the union found in awareness of the FarNigh in chapter 135, as noted above, strips the Soul "of all things because she is without existence, where she was before she was."[323] In chapter 137 the Annihilated Soul's "professed religious life" (*religio professa*) "is that she is dissolved by annihilation into that first being where Love has received her."[324] Finally, chapter 138 summarizes:

> Now she is in the being of her primordial being which is her being. And she has left the three [deaths] behind and made the two [natures] one. When is that One? That One is when the Soul is melted into the Simple Divinity which is one simple being of spread out and diffused fruition in full knowing

without feeling above the mind. That simple being does in the Soul from charity whatever the Soul does because the will has been made simple.[325]

The Mirror uses many metaphors for suggesting the nature of this primordial *unum simplex esse* in which there is no longer any distinction between God and Soul. We have already noted the growing popularity of the language of the abyss in the thirteenth century, especially among some of the women mystics, like Hadewijch and Angela of Foligno.[326] The abyss is also a favored term in Marguerite's *Mirror,* appearing more than a dozen times.[327] Reason can address Soul as "O most sweet abyssed one at the bottom without bottom of total humility" (chap. 53) because to be "abyssed in humility and poverty" (see chaps. 23, 38 and 40) is just another way of expressing the annihilation that comes from the Soul's recognition of her total sinfulness. The abyss language is strongest in the description of the fifth and sixth stages of the Soul's journey in chapter 118. Of the fifth stage she says:

> Now such a Soul is nothing. . . . And so she is all things, for she sees by means of the depth of understanding of her wretchedness, which is so deep and so great that she finds there neither beginning nor middle nor end, only an abyssal abyss without bottom. There she finds herself, without finding and without bottom.[328]

Unlike Hadewijch, Marguerite does not explicitly speak of God as abyss, but her mystical discourse in which the soul attains its own abyss through humility effectively comes down to the same thing insofar as the *anima abyssata* no longer exists but is the nothingness where "she sees neither herself nor him and thus God himself sees only himself by his divine Goodness" (chap. 91; 259.14–15).

The union expressed as a return to primordial being, or found by being submerged in an abyss without bottom, is called a union without intermediary (*sans moyen*),[329] even a union without difference (*nulle différence* [chap. 23; 86.32]). These are categories that will be developed with scholastic finesse by Meister Eckhart and John Ruusbroec among others, but it is significant that we find them first put forth by the female vernacular theologians. Like Eckhart and Ruusbroec, Marguerite also introduces qualifications about the proper understanding of this lack of mediation and difference. For example, she at times uses the traditional formula of attaining union through God's grace and not by nature (e.g., "I am what I am, says this Soul, by the grace of God").[330] In terms of the beguine's understanding of union this can be taken to mean that the Soul must lose *her* own nature as a created something through the grace, or gift, of Divine Love in order to return to the abyss of primordial being where there is no mediation or difference between the Soul and God.[331]

When we ask *The Mirror* to tell us more about how the Soul conducts herself in this union, the answer the text gives centers on another mystical theme that first appeared among the female mystics of the thirteenth century and was subsequently taken over by male mystics such as Meister Eckhart. As Marguerite succinctly puts it in chapter 134, "Perfect freedom has no why" (*parfaicte franchise n'a nul pourquoy/perfecta libertas non habet aliquod propter quid* [394.15/395.12–13]). Beatrice of Nazareth is the earliest textual witness to the theme of the perfect soul living "without a why," but Marguerite Porete develops the notion more richly than any of her predecessors.[332] Living without a why is loving with the pure spontaneity of a child (see chap. 29). In chapter 81 Marguerite provides us with a more detailed discussion of what this entails. The Soul that has been reduced to nothingness has no concern for herself, for her neighbors, or even for God. In the nothing that gives her everything she "swims and bobs and floats" in divine peace and fruition "without any movement in her interior and without any exterior work." If she does any exterior work, "it is always without herself," because the work is God's work "in her, without herself, for her sake." No work can encumber or bind her. "For she has nothing of herself; she has given all freely without a why, for she is the Lady of the Bridegroom of her youth."[333] It was, of course, this form of statement which raised the suspicions of the French beguine's inquisitors.

The appeal to the language of the sea and water as a metaphor for the indistinct union of living without a why in this chapter is found in other places in *The Mirror*. The most noted is in the following chapter, where Love recounts how the Soul is unencumbered in four things to the extent that "she loses her name in the One in whom she is melted and dissolved through himself and in himself."[334] The example given is of a river, such as the Aisne or Seine, which has a name as long as it flows by itself, but when it returns to the sea loses its name and all its labor.[335] Another metaphor for union, also favored by many mystics, is that of self-consuming fire. In chapter 25 Love says, "Such a Soul is so enflamed in the furnace of the fire of Love that she has become properly fire, which is why she feels no fire, for she is fire in herself. . . ."[336] Chapter 85 combines the two images in a striking example of Porete's gift for language: "Such a Soul, says Love, is scorched through mortification and burned through the ardor of the fire of charity, and her ashes are thrown into the open sea through the nothingness of the will."[337]

We may also ask about the stability and duration of Marguerite Porete's understanding of union, especially in light of the traditional monastic insistence that loving union of wills (*unitas spiritus*) was necessarily a rare and brief phenomenon. Is union a more permanent phenomenon for Marguerite Porete? The answer appears to be a paradoxical yes and no. The Annihilated Soul does say that she is "confirmed in nothingness" (*confermee en nient* [chap. 80; 228.48]), and we have already noted that Marguerite insists that once a soul reaches the fifth stage or level there is no slipping back to the lower stages. In that sense, union is permanent. Nevertheless, it is clear that the highest earthly stage, the flash of the aperture or opening of the trinitarian abyss itself, is brief and rare and thus the height of union is not an achieved state here on earth but has a moving, epektetic character like that found in many Christian mystics.[338] It is in speaking about these flashes of glory from the divine life, as in chapters 58, 61, 80, 117, and 136, where Marguerite comes closest to what some would describe as autobiographical accounts of mystical consciousness,[339] but the rigor of her apophaticism undercuts all attempts to describe "what" merging into the abyss is like, precisely because it is not a what!

Marguerite Porete's extraordinary book and tragic fate give her a position in the history of mysticism that modern scholarship is just beginning to appreciate. Given the boldness of *The Mirror*'s teaching, it is possible to appreciate why the book was attacked, while not losing admiration for the insight, the passion, and the fortitude of its author. Porete's book and body were burned, but her message, "cast into the open sea of the nothingness of the will," has continued to be heard and pondered. One of the best summaries of Porete's teaching comes from the pen of a mystic who had not read her but perhaps tried to re-create her, another Frenchwoman, Simone Weil, who once said: "God created me as a non-being which has the appearance of existing, in order that through love I should renounce this apparent existence and be annihilated by the plenitude of being."[340]

Sub Regula: Women Mystics in Religious Orders

THE WOMEN MYSTICS CONSIDERED in the previous two chapters
shared many interests and modes of expression. Most of them,
with the exception of the early Cistercians of Lotharingia, followed forms of religious life whose rules, even if they existed, had not
received ecclesiastical approbation from the papacy. The majority of
beguines appear to have lived under no rule at all. To be sure, many
of these women followed regimens of rigid asceticism, and some of
them, notably the anchoresses (*inclusae*), were separated from the
world in the discipline of the cell. Others, however, adhered to styles
of life that allowed considerable contact with the world. Simple labels
separating approved and nonapproved forms of religious life for
women are misleading; still, there are differences between those
women who chose to live more on the margins of ecclesiastical approbation and those who joined orders that had been accorded some
form of official recognition by Rome and (often more grudgingly) by
their male counterparts.[1] Did the more regulated instititional life of
the latter holy women, especially their enclosure in full cloister, produce a different form of mysticism from that of the women considered in the two previous chapters? The answer is not simple or easily
generalizable.

Once again, the wealth of the contribution of women to mysticism
in the thirteenth and early fourteenth centuries requires selection in
pursuing this question. In this chapter I will concentrate on women
mystical authors rather than on the accounts of ecstatics and visionaries written by male hagiographers, though some of these will be
included. I will examine the women living under approved rules
according to three groups. First, the nuns of the remarkable Cistercian

convent at Helfta in Saxony in the late thirteenth century; second, three women representing other established forms of monastic life: Premonstratensian, Vallombrosan, and Carthusian; and finally, the Dominican female mystics, especially the German women described in the *Sister Books* and mystical autohagiographies of the first half of the fourteenth century. Common themes and concerns, especially about visionary and ecstatic experience, will be evident, not only among these women but also in relation to those considered in the two preceding chapters. Nevertheless, there were elements distinctive of the mystics considered here, some of which appear to have been dependent on the rules and spiritual traditions to which they belonged.

Cistercians: The Women of Helfta[2]

Chronologically, the earliest group to be considered in this chapter is that of the German Cistercians of Helfta. In 1229 Count Burkhard of Mansfeld and his wife Elisabeth founded a convent for Cisterician nuns near their castle in Thuringia in Saxony. Unfortunately, the Cistercian General Chapter in the previous year had forbidden further foundation or incorporation of houses for women into the order and thus Burkhard's house remained technically a Benedictine convent, though one that used the gray habit of Cistercian nuns and followed their usages. In 1234 the convent was moved to Rodarsdorf and then in 1258 to Helfta not far from the town of Eisleben.[3] Strongly supported by the nobility of Saxony, the convent flourished, especially under the forty-year rule of Abbess Gertrude, daughter of the baron of Hackeborn (1251–1291). Though Abbess Gertrude herself did not leave any writings, she was a patroness of learning as well as an effective leader. Concerning her learning we are told:

> She would read sacred scripture very eagerly and with great delight whenever she could, requiring her subjects to love sacred readings and often recite them from memory. Hence, she bought all the good books she could for her church or made her sisters transcribe them. She eagerly promoted the girls to learn the liberal arts, saying that if the pursuit of knowledge were lost they would no longer understand sacred scripture and the religious life would also perish.[4]

The ancient monastic ideal of combining the love of learning and the desire for God was alive and well at Helfta and reaped a rich reward.

In 1247 Abbess Gertrude's younger sister, Mechthild of Hackeborn (1240–1298), entered the convent, growing up to become the chantress of the house and a teacher and spiritual guide for the younger nuns. In 1261 a five-year-old girl of unknown parentage also named Gertrude entered

Helfta, eventually to emerge as its most famous holy woman, known to history as Gertrude the Great (1256–1301). About 1270, as we have seen, the
aged beguine Mechthild of Magdeburg also joined the community, apparently surviving there for a decade or more and composing the seventh and
final book of her *Flowing Light of the Godhead.* Many other members of the
community were literate; indeed, its most prolific writer was the unnamed
nun (she calls herself the *compilatrix*) who collaborated with Gertrude and
Mechthild in producing the two lengthy collections that summarize the
mysticism of the Cistercian women of Helfta, the books called *The Herald of
Divine Love* and *The Book of Special Grace.*[5]

The presence of Mechthild of Magdeburg, already a mystical author for
some time, must have had an influence on the outpouring of mystical literature at Helfta in the last two decades of the thirteenth century. Nevertheless,
the character of the writings associated with Gertrude and Mechthild of
Hackeborn are in many ways different from the work of the former beguine.
First, their writings are in Latin, not in the vernacular, and they are deeply
rooted in the traditions of monastic theology and liturgy.[6] Second, the form
of mysticism advanced by Gertrude, Mechthild of Hackeborn, and their
nameless collaborator combines older themes of monastic mysticism with
elements of the new mysticism of the thirteenth century in a highly distinctive way, one quite different from that of the older Mechthild. Finally, as
Caroline Walker Bynum has shown, the socialization of these women within
the stable and protected intellectual environment of the Cistercian cloister
gave them a sense of security and authority unusual among medieval
women mystics. In Bynum's words: "In contrast to twelfth-century women
and to many of their thirteenth-century predecessors (including Mechthild of
Magdeburg), Gertrude and Mechthild of Hackeborn are serene about the
implications of both their learning and their contact with Christ."[7]

The composition of the major texts illustrating this mysticism of Helfta—
"the largest single body of women's mystical writing of the period"[8]—is
complicated. In 1281 Gertrude experienced a vision of Christ that she
described as marking her conversion to a deeper life of mystical piety. In
1289, urged on by God and her superiors, she began to write an account of
her experiences. She describes how, while she was waiting with the community for the Eucharist to be carried to a sick nun, "moved by a very violent impulse of the Holy Spirit, she snatched the tablet hanging at her side
and with overflowing gratitude wrote with her own hand in his praise what
she had felt in her heart in her secret conversation with her Beloved."[9] This
account became the second book of the longer compilation whose full title
is *Legatus memorialis abundantiae divinae pietatis,* that is, *The Memorial Herald*

of the Abundance of Divine Love (the title is based on Ps. 144:7). Books 3–5 of *The Herald*, written by the anonymous *compilatrix* (possibly with collaborators), detail Gertrude's visions and revelations and were completed in 1301 shortly before her death. Though obviously based on the seer's own accounts, they represent an editorial reworking, as well as a hagiographical process that eventually culminated in book 1, a standard *vita* of the saint composed most likely by the same anonymous nun after Gertrude's death.[10] One other important work that comes directly from Gertrude's hand is the relatively brief text perhaps originally called *Documenta spiritualium exercitionum* (*Teachings of Spiritual Exercises*), which consists of seven liturgically based exercises for prayer and meditation designed to lead the soul to mystical union.[11]

The *Liber specialis gratiae* that presents the mysticism of Mechthild of Hackeborn was not written down by her. Though Mechthild is described as the author of numerous prayers (see 5.30), none of these survives and only one chapter of the lengthy *Book of Special Grace* is from her hand (that containing letters to a laywoman found in 4.59). It was in 1291, during a serious illness, that this Mechthild first began to reveal her visions and experiences of God to two confidants, Gertrude herself and the same mystery nun who finished *The Herald*.[12] These two nuns wrote the seven parts of the work during Mechthild's last years, ending it with a section devoted to "the most joyful time of her most blessed passing over" (*jucundissimo tempore beatissimi transitus ipsius* [7.5]). This compilatory work, known in both its original form and in an abbreviated version, was the most widely known of the Helfta treatises in the Middle Ages and was translated into both Middle Dutch and Middle English. In the sixteenth century it was also made available in German and Italian.[13]

This large body of material (well over one thousand pages of Latin text) can be characterized as containing a distinctive form of visionary-liturgical mysticism. Despite its production by three close spiritual friends within the same convent and the many common themes throughout these books, there are some significant differences between what is presented in *The Book of Special Grace* and the two works relating to Gertrude, as Bynum has demonstrated.[14] Nevertheless, what ties the Helfta mystics together is more important than what distinguishes them, so we can begin with some general remarks about Helfta mysticism before passing on to a study of Gertrude, primarily based on her own writings (i.e., *The Exercises* and book 2 of *The Herald*), and a briefer treatment of Mechthild concentrating on her teaching on the central theme of the "heart of God" (*cor Dei*).

What was the character of Helfta mysticism? Traditional Christian mysticism, as has been insisted upon throughout this history, was never individualistic, but rather attempted to root its immediate consciousness of God's presence within the liturgical and sacramental life of the total *ecclesia*. Few Christian mystical texts are more overtly liturgical, however, than those from Helfta, although their use of the liturgy is different from what one finds in the patristic or medieval monastic sources.[15] The nuns of Helfta combine the liturgical basis for Christian mysticism found in monastic traditions with the new visionary mysticism of the thirteenth century. Like the writings of beguines such as Hadewijch and Mechthild of Magdeburg, their works are filled with visions, often of an allegorical character; but these visions tend to be more explicitly and systematically based on the liturgy than were those of the beguines. Given the biblical-liturgical character of most of their accounts, it might be better to speak of them as "visualizations" rather than visions, in order to stress the fact that they are imaginative creations "seen" by the mystic as she strives to appropriate the inner meaning of the action of the liturgy.[16] At the heart of both *The Herald* and *The Book of Special Grace* are lengthy narratives of such visualizations (book 4 and part 1 respectively). These are structured according to the course of the liturgical year and can be considered visionary commentaries on the mystical significance of the annual liturgical cycle.[17]

Even more than the beguines and earlier women mystics of the century, the Helfta writers center their unitive encounter with Christ in the reception of the Eucharist. Receiving Communion (which they apparently did quite frequently, often more than once a week) was the source of their vivid experiences of the heavenly world and especially of their union with Jesus, the Divine Bridegroom. "To the nuns of Helfta," as Caroline Bynum puts it, "the Eucharist was the equivalent of and the occasion for ecstasy."[18]

Helfta mysticism is primarily nuptial in expression. Christ is the *sponsus* who embraces his bride and bestows the kiss of union on her. Nevertheless, there is no insane yearning or erotic frenzy in this form of nuptial imagery, such as we encounter in many of the beguines,[19] nor is there much that could be described as overtly sexual in the manner of some of the imagery found in Mechthild of Magdeburg. Gertrude and Mechthild of Hackeborn are regal figures: queens welcomed into the stately embrace of the King of Heaven.

The union of bride and Bridegroom centers on the uniting of their hearts. Fixation on the *cor Jesu* or *cor Dei* is one of the most common themes throughout the Helfta texts, and the role of these women in the growth of the devotion to the Sacred Heart has long been appreciated.[20] Though earlier Christian theologians and mystics had also seen the heart of Jesus as the source of salvation and place of access to God (especially as opened in death through the piercing of his side on the cross; cf. John 7:37–39 and 19:31–37), no one had spoken as insistently, as personally, and as dramatically about the heart of Jesus as the Helfta nuns. Mystical union, for both Gertrude and Mechthild, is a fusing of the human heart with the heart of Jesus. In book 2 of *The Herald,* for example, Gertrude tells Christ: "In addition to all these favors, you have granted me the priceless gift of your familiar friendship, giving me in various ways, to my indescribable delight, the noblest treasure of the divinity, your divine heart, now bestowing it freely, now as a sign of our mutual familiarity, exchanging it with mine."[21] In a vision on the Octave of Easter, Christ appears to Mechthild and allows her to enter into the wound in his side, where he bestows the Holy Spirit on her as he had once done upon the apostles. The account concludes, "And when she had communicated her heart with the heart of God she saw it as a mass of gold melted into one and heard the Lord saying to her, 'Your heart will adhere in this manner forever according to your every desire and delight.'"[22] Loving fixation on what Gertrude speaks of as "Your most sweet heart broken on the cross through love" was central to her and the other mystics of Helfta.[23] As the revelation of the redemptive love of God, the Helfta Cistercians present the heart of Jesus as "the 'sacrament' of union with God," in the phrase of Hugues Minguet.[24] This emphasis on the love of God revealed in the heart of Jesus is at the root of the optimism about salvation that is one of the most winning aspects of Helfta mysticism.[25]

Gertrude and Mechthild are ecstatics, making use of the traditional monastic language of *excessus mentis, ecstasis, inebriatio,* and *unus spiritus,* as well as the ecstatic song to God, the *iubilus* characteristic of thirteenth-century women. But their visions and ecstasies take place in and for the entire community. All the sisters are brides of Christ, and while not all may experience this directly, both Gertrude and Mechthild describe visions of the heavenly liturgy in which they see the whole community united with God. Their visions and ecstasies, then, are meant as manifestations, even guarantees, of the status of the community. Traditionally monastic too is the stress that true contemplation and union will only be realized at death when the brief and partial encounters with God possible in this life will yield to the final embrace in the *mors mystica.* This is why the descriptions of the deaths and reception into heaven of both Gertrude and Mechthild, as well as Abbess Gertrude, Mechthild of Magdeburg, and other unnamed nuns and associates of the convent, receive such a prominent place in *The Herald* (see book 5) and *The Book of Special Grace* (parts 6–7).

Although both Gertrude and her mentor Mechthild of Hackeborn were powerful visionaries, unlike other seers (at least as described by male hagiographers), miracles and excessive asceticism play a minor role in the accounts written by and about them, as noted by Bynum.[26] The Helfta nuns, well-educated as they were, had an easy familiarity with basic patristic sources and especially the Cistercian authors,[27] but in contrast with beguines like Hadewijch and Marguerite Porete, they were not interested in theological speculation about such issues as the Trinity or the nature of the soul.[28] Their theology is fundamentally concerned with redemption, conceived of not in a juridical way but as the manifestation of divine love.[29] In their appropriation of this great saving act, both Gertrude and Mechthild are presented as mediators of divine power and, more forcefully, almost as priests with the power to bind and loose. Nevertheless, their position in no way contains the kinds of threat to the status of the clergy and the role of the sacramental church found in the writings of Marguerite Porete. Their mysticism, as Bynum puts it, is "an alternative to the authority of office" that should be seen as "a complement to, not a contradiction of, the clerical role."[30]

This attitude helps explain why the Helfta mystics rarely use the topos of the "weak woman" (for one exception, see *The Herald* 3.15) or a consistent gender language contrasting male positivity and female negativity. This did not mean, however, that the authors of these two large works were unaware of the temerity of women writing, since a defense of this appears in both *The Herald* and *The Book of Special Grace*. The final four chapters of *The Herald of Divine Love* contain a strong apologia for the work, in which Christ appears to Gertrude with the book impressed on his own heart to indicate that it partakes of the sweetness of divinity. An even stronger claim is then made as he signs the book with the sign of the cross, saying: "By the same effectiveness with which in this mass I have transubstantiated bread and wine for the salvation of all, I have now sanctified everything written in this book for all with my heavenly blessing. . . ."[31] In the next chapter the mysterious *compilatrix hujus libri* secretly carries the book with her to Communion intending to offer it to Christ. Another nun sees Christ appearing to the *compilatrix* at this juncture, making a speech in which he promises that whoever comes to him with a humble heart to read the book, "I will truly show him point-by-point in my bosom whatever is useful for him with my own finger."[32] Here the book has daringly merged with the *cor Jesu* itself. This vision is followed by the compiler's magnificent prayer (the literary high point of the Helfta writings) offering the book to Christ (5.35) and a final, more sober conclusion explaining the usefulness of the book for all, both beginners and more advanced souls, through an invocation of the traditional monastic practices of *lectio, meditatio,* and *contemplatio.*[33]

The Book of Spiritual Grace has a more complicated presentation of its divine authorization, if only because Gertrude and the *compilatrix* began it without Mechthild's knowledge and the chantress was obviously ambivalent about having her mystical gifts recorded.[34] Two chapters at the end of part 2 tell how knowledge of its existence came to Mechthild from divine revelation. To quiet her doubts, the Lord appeared to her. "Holding this book above his heart in his right hand, he kissed her and said: 'Everything which is written in this book has flowed out from my divine heart and flows back into it.'" When Mechthild asks him if she should cease revealing the mystical gifts she has received, Christ commands her, "Give me in the generosity of my overflowing heart, and give me in my goodness not in yours." He then assigns the name of the book.[35] The image of Christ holding the book as a sign of its authenticity, previously used by Mechthild of Magdeburg (*Flowing Light* 2.26), has been significantly heightened here by the invocation of the divine heart.[36]

Although the main lines of the Helfta mysticism were shared by the three Cistercians, there are certainly distinctive mystical personalities that emerge from their writings. For a better appreciation of this it will be helpful to investigate in more detail Gertrude's teaching as reflected primarily in the writings we know come from her hand alone (this constitutes about a quarter of the *Herald* and the whole of the *Exercises*).[37]

Gertrude shows no interest in the standard itineraries of the soul's journey to God or in a description of the various types of contemplation, let alone in their introspective examination. Nevertheless, there is a kind of liturgical itinerary found in the cycle of the seven exemplary practices that make up her *Exercises.* These were written for the members of the community of Helfta as a week-long practice to help refocus themselves on the goal of the monastic life, especially during the Easter season. Composed in the characteristically lush style of Helfta (*dulcis* is their favorite adjective), the *Exercises* are marked by liberal use of biblical quotations and reminiscences that recall the writings of the twelfth-century male Cistercians, especially Bernard of Clairvaux. They also feature the rich profusion of images, such as light and fire, singing and dancing, vegetation, precious clothing and gems, found in the writings of the Helfta nuns.

The first exercise begins where the Christian life does, with the rebirth of baptism and confirmation (see I:56-78). Gertrude invites her sisters to follow the liturgical action in an interior conversion that eventually will lead to union with the Divine Lover and the face-to-face vision of God.[38] The invocation of the assistance of the Blessed Virgin (*mater et commater tua*) and each nun's guardian angel, and especially the role assigned to "the most sweet heart of Jesus Christ, the Son of God," in the closing meditations on receiving Communion, announce major themes that pervade the mysticism of Gertrude and her associates.[39] The second exercise is based on reliving the rite of clothing the nun with the monastic habit as a sign of progress in the "school of love" (I:80–90). The third concentrates on spiritual marriage through a reappropriation of the ritual of the consecration of the virgin during a pontifical Mass (I:92–122). This section features an extensive development of traditional monastic nuptial language, often invoking the images of the Song of Songs, such as the kiss, the embrace, and the "wound of love" seen as the mutual wounding of the hearts of the two lovers (I:96, 106). The goal is an indissoluble union of hearts that leads to the desire to die and be with Christ forever:

> Make me to be so indissolubly joined to you by the most burning love that I may wish to die by reason of the force of the love of being with you. May the pact that you have begun with me take my heart from me so that it may no longer be mine but dwell with you in an indivisible love.[40]

The next three exercises bring out different aspects of the nuptial union to which the nun was introduced at her consecration. The fourth deals with the theme of following Christ which the nun promised at the time of her profession (chronologically preceding the consecration, but designed to be the beginning of a lifelong effort). Only through such an effort can the soul be led deeper into the union which Gertrude here describes in the language of the abyss so popular with many thirteenth-century mystical women:

> Let me be submerged in the abyss of the sea of your most merciful goodness. Let me perish in the deluge of your living love, as a drop of the sea dies in the depth of its fullness. Let me die, let me die, in the outpouring of your immense mercy, as dies the spark of flame in the irresistible force of the flood.[41]

The sensuousness of the Cistercian's language, evident throughout her writings, closes off this exercise with an appeal to the five spiritual senses, as the nun asks Christ to console her eventually "there" (*ibi*, i.e., in heaven) with "the sight of your honeylike presence," to recreate her with "the taste of your dear ransom," to call her with "the voice of your beautiful love," to receive her "in the embrace of your most indulgent pardon," and finally "to attract, to inhale, and to imbibe me there to you yourself in the sweet breath of your pleasant-flowing Spirit."[42]

The fifth and sixth exercises, the culmination of the work, contain a lyrical "Exercise of Divine Love" (II:156–98) and an "Exercise of Praise and Thanksgiving" that centers on the *iubilus* (II:200–256). The "Exercise of Divine Love" is an evocation of the nature of *unio mystica* employing all the traditional vocabulary of standard Cistercian teaching on the *unitas spiritus* motif originating in 1 Corinthians 6:17.[43] Characteristically, however, Gertrude puts an exercise concerning the meaning of the seven canonical hours at the center of her treatment (I:178–92), thus underlining that union is realized in and through the daily liturgical life of the community. In the sixth exercise Gertrude in a sense creates her own liturgy, weaving together the themes of nuptial mysticism with the musical ecstasy of the *iubilus* in a series of petitions and hymns that anticipate the heavenly liturgy. This text may be considered to be among the saint's most poetically successful, though it is interesting that the term *iubilus* does not play a large part elsewhere in *The Exercises* or in *The Herald*. Still, Gertrude's sense of belonging to heaven while still on earth indicates that the "praise, joy, and awareness of glory"[44] so characteristic of her mysticism finds a summation in this exercise in which all things, the powers and virtues of her soul and body, as well as the divine attributes and all creation, are called upon to offer jubilation to God.[45]

After the fervid rhetoric of the sixth exercise, the seventh exercise on "Reparation for Sins and Preparation for Death" (II:258–306), also based on the liturgy of the canonical hours, may seem a bit of a letdown. Still, Gertrude's "Hymn to Death" (I:282–84) shows that the mystical theology of the Helfta nuns insisted that final union was attained only through the *mors mystica* by which the nun underwent her *transitus* to complete enjoyment of nuptial union. Hence, the final spiritual exercise of this week-long course in mystical renewal is a preparation for the end of the nun's itinerary when she will need to summon all her remaining powers for the difficult final stage of the journey to God. The poetic power and cosmic inclusivity of Gertrude's vision of the mystical life are immediately evident in her *Exercises*.[46] Nevertheless, it may not be an accident that a work like the *Exercises*, bound as it was to the life of an enclosed community and its full-scale liturgical life, has no surviving medieval manuscripts. In a sense, Helfta's spirituality went against the grain of much late medieval mysticism which attempted to address a wider audience than those contained in cloisters.

The second book of *The Herald*, Gertrude's mystical autobiography, offers comment and expansion on the themes put forth in the *Exercises*.[47] One of the characteristics of much monastic mysticism was insistent repetition of the fundamental message of loving union with God from a variety of biblical perspectives. An analogous style is found throughout *The Herald,* both in book 2 and the later books, though here the exegetical variations common in male commentaries on the Bible are replaced by a variety of presentations of the mystic's visionary recitals, often tied to the liturgy. Because of this repetition, it is not necessary to give a detailed exegesis of the entire *Herald* here, but it will be helpful to highlight what book 2 says about the role of Christ in Gertrude's mysticism.

The first five chapters of book 2 form a coherent narrative of Gertrude's progress as a visionary between 1281 and 1289. They also indicate, as Kurt Ruh has pointed out, that it was under the influence of Mechthild of Hacke-born that the younger nun developed her devotion to the heart of Christ.[48] Gertrude's conversion to a deeper life began in January of 1281 with a vision of Christ as a beautiful youth who pledged his troth to her. The unifying visions that she subsequently enjoyed, always given on days when she received the Eucharist (2.2; II:234), were connected with her devotion to the wounds of Christ. During the winter of 1282–1283 she repeated a prayer asking Christ to inscribe his wounds on her heart with his own blood. (It was at this time that she began to reveal the secrets of her visions to Mechthild.) As a result of this form of petition, Gertrude says, "Through the Spirit I knew that there had been impressed internally in my heart, as if in the various places of the body, those worthy and adorable marks (*stigmata*) of your most holy wounds."[49] Gertrude's reception of the internal stigmata, of course, had been claimed for St. Francis as early as his vision at San Damiano (1208), and a number of other medieval women mystics also received purely interior signs of the passion.[50]

A shift occurred seven years later (ca. 1289), when, through the intercession of Mechthild, Gertrude received the mystical grace of the piercing of her heart directly from the heart of Christ. Her devotion to the wounds of Christ now centers on the wound in the side which gives access to the divine heart, as her interesting account reveals. According to this:

> After I had received the life-giving sacrament, on returning to my place to pray, it seemed to me as if, on the right side of the Crucified One painted in the page, that is to say, in the wound in the side, a ray of sunlight like a sharp arrow came forth and spread itself out for a moment, drew back, and then spread out again. It continued like this for a while, tenderly drawing my love.[51]

Three days later, Christ suddenly appeared to her and inflicted a wound on her heart. Mechthild then advised her to meditate constantly on "the love of your heart hanging on the cross."

Gertrude's visions of Christ came to focus on his heart as the visible image and source of his overflowing love for humanity, but this love continued to be manifested in all the mysteries of salvation. Hence, the second part of book 2 begins with a vision of the Christ child on the feast of the Nativity (2.6; cf. 2.16). But Gertrude keeps returning to the image of the breast of Christ, its wound, and the heart made accessible by it. During the feast of the Purification she experienced a vision of her soul placed against Christ's breast and melting like wax to be drawn within to the "treasury . . . of all fullness of divinity" (2.7). In the middle of Lent, Christ appeared to the sick Gertrude and showed her "a stream of flowing water as pure and solid as crystal coming from his left side as though from the innermost depths of his blessed heart" (2.9). As book 2 progresses the concentration on the heart of Jesus and Gertrude's own heart as the place of his solace increases until it culminates in two remarkable passages. In *The Herald* 2.20 (II:308–20) Gertrude recounts seven extraordinary gifts, both for herself and for others, that divine grace has given her, but she remains unsatisfied that God has not confirmed the perpetuity of these gifts by the feudal ritual of a clasping of hands. Christ then appears to her, saying, "Stop complaining and come and receive the confirmation of my pact." Gertrude continues:

> Immediately (in my nothingness) I saw you opening with both hands the tabernacle of your divine faithfulness and infallible truth, your deified heart, and bidding me in my perversity (like the Jews seeking signs), to put in my right hand.[52]

Gertrude places her right hand in the side wound, which then closes on it as the Lord repeats a solemn pledge to keep her gifts intact. When she withdraws her hand, it is adorned with seven golden rings as a sign of his fidelity.

This vivid showing (an example of what the Augustinian tradition would call a *visio spiritualis*) is followed by quite a different account in which Gertrude, quoting Genesis 32:30, says that she saw the Lord "face to face" in a "flash of marvelous and priceless brightness." This is a true *visio intellectualis*, one that cannot be recounted in images, but only as light, or better, following Bernard of Clairvaux, in terms of its effect on the heart of the recipient.[53] Nevertheless, Gertrude tries to find "some similitude" that will provide a distant hint of this indescribable experience in the picture of an ineffable light passing from Christ's eyes into her that dissolves her bones and flesh until only divine splendor remains.[54] This prompts an important discussion of the nature of visions, embraces, kisses, and other gifts of God's love, which, as Gertrude says "[God] always adapts with the greatest fittingness to the place, the time, and the person, as I have frequently experienced."[55] The notion of the accommodation of mystical graces to the recipient, the time, and the place, is a sign of the subtlety of Gertrude's appreciation of the necessity and also the limits of the highly detailed pictorial visualizations that were the staple of the Helfta literature. The point is often repeated by the *compilatrix* in the subsequent books of *The Herald*.[56]

In the great prayer of thanksgiving that concludes book 2 (another "spiritual exercise"), Gertrude expresses one final major theme of her christological piety, one also found among the other mystics of Helfta, the notion of *suppletio*.[57] All goodness comes from God; of ourselves we have only sin and failure. Hence, Gertrude offers God the Father the whole life of Christ from his infancy through his passion, as "recompense for all my negligences" (*in suppletionem omnium neglegentiarum mearum* [2.23.3, II:332]). Christ's infinite redemptive love both supplies for our failings and completes his own sapiential plan. Recalling all the mystical graces she has received, from the first vision of Christ betrothing her, through the joy of his constant inner presence, down to the two particular favors of the inner stigmata and the piercing of her heart, Gertrude rejoices that she has been thus privileged to exchange hearts with Christ himself (2.23.7–8). Even if sin and lack still remain with her, she knows that the fount of the mercy of Jesus will never dry up. The essential optimism of Gertrude is founded on her liturgical picture of the universe as one great act of praise–"May that eternal praise be given to you which comes forth from uncreated Love and always flows back into yourself."[58]

Mechthild of Hackeborn was Gertrude's mentor and spiritual friend, while the younger nun, along with the *compilatrix*, was the recorder of the older nun's revelations in *The Book of Special Grace*.[59] Any extended comparison of Gertrude and Mechthild is fraught with problems about the influence each had upon the other and how this is reflected in the Helfta literature. While it would be valuable to compare what they have to say about many issues, especially the nature of mystical union, here I wish to dwell only on the central image for Helfta mysticism, that of the heart of Christ, in reference especially to *The Book of Special Grace*. The book contains the full-blown evolution of this symbol of divine love, which Mechthild had introduced to Gertrude.[60]

The *cor Iesu* or *cor Dei* can be seen as a master symbol in the sense that its use among the Helfta mystics functioned as a magnet that drew to itself a range of mystical imagery both new and old. We have already considered how the interior stigmatization, building upon traditional devotional and mystical themes, such as the five wounds of Christ and the *vulnus amoris*, became central to Gertrude's mysticism in *The Exercises* and *The Herald*. The mystical "exchange of hearts" noted above was not new, but this, as well as many other aspects of how Gertrude and the *compilatrix* presented the heart of Jesus in recording Mechthild's visions, was unprecedented in the richness of its development. As Alois Haas puts it, "The heart of God clearly became the medium of sensation for her [Mechthilds's] mystical experience of God."[61]

The *cor Iesu,* like all great symbolic matrices, allows for polyvalent development in different dimensions. Three of these are of central importance in Mechthild: the heart as the source of nourishment (featuring a wide variety of images); the heart as the place of entry and incorporation into God; and finally, the heart as vital connection, the living engine that works to unify God and human.

The sheer variety of images used for the divine heart in *The Book of Special Grace* is a tribute to the power of the pictorial imagination of the Helfta mystics. Many of these images are relatively common, such as the heart as a flame or fire (3.10, 3.36, 4.15, 5.30), the heart as a lamp (1.46, 2.21, 3.17), or the well-known *vulnus amoris* (1.18, 1.19, 2.25, 2.32). Others are more unusual—the divine heart is described as a vineyard (2.2), a book (4.40), a mirror (3.15), a psaltery (2.35), a lyre (7.14),[62] a rose (3.2), and even a pharmacy from which three healing unguents of water, wine, and divine sweetness are distributed to humans (3.25). Perhaps the most common image complex relating to the divine heart deals with how it nourishes and refreshes all who turn to it in love.[63] The heart is described as a wine cup (*scyphus*) or a drinking vessel (*poculum*) in many places (e.g., 1.1, 1.14, 1.21, 1.25, 4.59), and the picture of drinking or sucking nourishment from the wounded heart of Christ is common. In one vision love leads Mechthild's soul to the Lord and then,

> She bent over to the wound of the honeyed heart of her only Savior, drawing from it draughts of all delight and very full of pleasure. There all her bitterness was turned to sweetness and her fear to trust. And there she sucked the sweetest fruit from the most pleasing heart of Christ, which she drew from the heart of God and put in her mouth. This signified that eternal praise which comes from the heart of God.[64]

The *cor Dei* is frequently described as a fountain, flood, or river from which cleansing and refreshment proceed (e.g., 1.22, 2.1, 2.22, 2.27, 2.29, 3.8, 3.10, 5.22, 5.25). Many of these same images are found in Gertrude, but the younger nun has one symbol of nourishment and growth connected to the divine heart that is lacking in Mechthild—that of the tree, especially as portrayed in the vision of "the tree of marvelous beauty" that grows out of the united hearts of the mystic and her Lord as she is on her deathbed.[65]

Another form of these images of nourishment and participation in God, one especially characteristic of Mechthild, comprises visions of the divine heart as connected to one or more persons by rays of light (1.11, 2.42, 5.22, 7.16), by tubes (2.1, 4.40, 6.9), or by cords or ropes (1.10, 1.13, 1.31, 2.21). In 4.20 (277), for example, the seer beholds Jesus with a person standing in front of him. In the heart of God there is a continually turning wheel connected to a similar wheel in the heart of the person by a long cord. The person signifies all humanity, the revolving wheel our participation in divine freedom of will, and the cord "the will of God which always draws a person to good and not to evil." The nourishment aspect appears more clearly in the places where straws (*fistulae*) connect the divine heart to our hearts. In book 4, chapter 1, after receiving Communion, Mechthild sees Christ enthroned and is given to understand how he administers his heart to the Helfta community in three ways (citing Luke 22:28–30). She sees the divine heart as a chalice with three straws coming from it signifying his three dispositions–love and reverence toward the Father, mercy and charity toward humans, and humility and abjection toward himself. "Then she saw that to all those who drew near the Lord offered a drink from the three straws of his heart, saying at the same time: 'Drink and be inebriated, most beloved ones'" (Song 5:1). . . . When this was done, the Lord said: 'I will drink from the hearts of all those who drink from my heart.'"[66]

Mechthild sometimes describes the divine heart as a door or entry (*janua*) into the depths of God, and more frequently as a house (*domus*) in which the bride of Christ can rest safely and comfortably. (This image was later to receive pictorial expression).[67] Again, a note of mutuality is present in some of these descriptions of incorporation, as in that found in 1.19:

> After this the Lord showed her a very beautiful house, quite tall and wide. Inside she saw another little house made of cedar and decorated on the inside with gleaming silver plates in whose midst the Lord resided. The first house she easily recognized as the heart of God, because she had often seen it in that form. The little house within symbolized the soul which is immortal and eternal, just as cedar does not corrupt.

The allegorical image continues with a description of the golden bolt of the door of the little house, which is connected to the heart of God by a little golden chain, so that when the door is opened the chain moves the divine heart. The door is desire, the bolt the will, and the chain yearning for God. The Lord tells Mechthild:

> Thus, your soul is always in my heart and I am in your soul's heart. Although you contain me in your deepest parts so that I am deeper in you than your every depth, nonetheless, my divine heart so excells and surpasses your soul that it seems completely unattainable, which is denoted by the height and breadth of the house.[68]

Another text compares the *domus cordis Dei* with a kitchen, because it is open and used by all (2.33), while other descriptions give its various parts (2.18), or note the bedchamber and bed it contains (2.27 and 2.20).[69]

The final major dimension of the symbol of the heart of Christ is how it is employed to present the living union of Christ and the mystic. These portrayals concentrate on the heart's vital action of beating and the related activity of breathing. Early in *The Book of Special Grace* Mechthild is embraced by Christ so tightly that she can hear his unusual heartbeat consisting of three strong beats and one weak one. Christ tells her, "The beats of my heart are not like those of other men, but I have always had such heartbeats from my infancy to my death and they are the reason why I would die on the cross so quickly." The first beat comes from omnipotent love that conquers all adversity; the second from the wise love that orders all things. The third strong beat of sweet love makes all bitter things pleasant, while the weak fourth best "symbolizes the kindness of my humanity which made me lovable, accessible, and imitable by all."[70] In another vision the nun is "rapt above herself on high" to see the King of Glory and listen to the beating of his "sweetly flowing heart." Here the four beats proclaim a more personal message—"Come to do penance; come to be reconciled; come to be consoled; come to be made blessed."[71]

Hearing the beating heart of Christ and interpreting the beats as indications of aspects of his loving invitation to union appears several other times in *The Book of Special Grace* (e.g., 2.20 and 5.32) and is also is found in Gertrude's *Herald*.[72] However, just as both Mechthild and Gertrude saw the exchange or merging of their own hearts with the *cor Dei* as a fitting image for loving union (see, e.g., *Book* 1.19, 2.3, 2.21, 2.34, 3.27, 3.29, 3.32, 4.59, 5.22, 7.11), so too the beating and breathing activity of both hearts must also be joined to indicate the vitality of mystical union. This is most forcefully described in the account of Mechthild's death in part seven of *The Book of Special Grace*. One of the visionaries, most probably Gertrude, sees Christ himself taking the place of the priest as Mechthild is being anointed on her deathbed. "Having completed the anointing, the Lord took her most lovingly into his arms and supported her in this way for two days so that the wound of his most beloved heart was open to the mouth of the sick one. It seemed that every breath she took was drawn from it and sent back into the heart."[73] As Mechthild enters her death agony, Gertrude sees her soul as a very delicate girl standing before God, "and every breath she drew was breathed into his honey-flowing heart through the wound of his most sacred side." Here the mystic has been so united to Christ in love that her breathing into him becomes the source of the beating-breathing action of his love poured out upon the world and especially the Helfta community. Gertrude continues:

> From this, the deified heart was moved by the unrestrained power of its own goodness and sweetness, so that as often as it received her breath breathed into it, boiling over from the abundance of love, it scattered forth drops of grace through the breadth of the whole church and especially on those present there.[74]

Here Mechthild's living union with her divine lover makes her into something like a co-redemptrix. This visualization, with its characteristic picture of divine saving love centering on the image of the beating heart of Christ, serves as an admirable summation of the mysticism of the nuns of Helfta.

Other Female Monastic Mystics[75]

There were many forms of traditional monastic life open to women in the thirteenth century. These orders also profited from the flowering of female mysticism of the era. Among the cloistered women of the late thirteenth century and early fourteenth who enjoyed mystical contact with God, three stand out, each representing a different order—Premonstratensian, Vallombrosan, and Carthusian.

A Premonstratensian Canoness

The Premonstratensian order was founded in 1120 as a result of the activities of Norbert of Xanten (ca. 1080–1134), one of the most successful itinerant preachers of the early twelfth century. Norbert's preaching attracted both men and women to the *vita apostolica* and many of his first foundations were double monasteries. The Premonstratensians (or Norbertines) were canons, following an austere form of the *Rule of St. Augustine,* though they soon came to live more like enclosed monastics, eschewing the public role of some of the other canonical reforms of the time.[76] Though they were among the most important reform movements of the twelfth century, the Premonstratensians did not produce many notable mystical authors or ecstatic saints.[77] The Scotsman Adam (d. ca. 1210), briefly treated in *The Growth of Mysticism* for his work *The Fourfold Exercise of the Cell,* left the Premonstratensians for the Carthusians before he wrote the book.[78] Herman Joseph, abbot of Steinfeld (ca. 1160–1241), author of some moving Latin sequences, is portrayed as an ecstatic and visionary in a contemporary *Vita* and has been claimed for the ranks of medieval mystics, though his contribution was scarcely a major one.[79]

Although initially encouraging female participation, the Norbertines, like the Cistercians, reacted against the obligation of care for women's houses in the later twelfth century. A struggle ensued over the relation between the male and female branches of the order. About 1240 the male branch issued regulations concerning women's houses that were approved by Innocent IV in 1247, and the latter half of the thirteenth century witnessed a flourishing of Premonstratensian canonesses (*sorores cantantes*), especially in Frisia and Germany. The female Premonstratenisians usually had close ties to male houses, as we can see in the case of Christina of Hane (1269–1292), the most noted mystic among the Premonstratensian women.[80]

Christina was born of a noble family. She entered the Norbertine house at Hane in the Pfalz area of the Rhineland at the age of six and was educated in the monastery, making her profession at any early age.[81] The Middle High German account of her life and ecstasies found in a single manuscript from the mid-fifteenth century appears to incorporate documents composed by her confessor and other Norbertines of the monastery of Rodenkirchen, who were responsible for the spiritual and physical oversight of the Hane community.[82] Christina's short life combined extremes of asceticism and mysticism echoing much that we have already seen. This Christina (like the other two examined in chapter 4) was nothing if not excessive.

The first part of the Strassburg *Description of Her Life* (*Lebensbeschreibung*) (also reflected in another version in Latin) is essentially a traditional *vita* giving a general account of her life and piety, concentrating on the seven-year battle (ca. 1282–1289) during her adolescent years in which she overcame the seven deadly sins (see 17.234–39). Her combat against lust is especially noteworthy. Christina's biographer describes the virgin performing a series of self-inflicted tortures on her sexual organs that are so extreme that even he doubted their appropriateness, describing them as a "terrible hard thing" (*eyn grusselich swere dynge* [17.235]). (Christ eventually appears and commands Christina to cease; cf. 17.236.) Unlike the miracles ascribed to Christina the Astonishing, however, it is conceivable that these ascetic feats (or something like them) actually happened and that they help explain the nun's short life.

After seven years of excessive asceticism, Christina is portrayed as reaching the state of a perfected soul who enjoys total and frequent access to God during the rest of her brief life (ca. 1288/89–1292). As befitted an enclosed woman whose life centered on the liturgical calender (like the Helfta nuns), the *Description*'s accounts of the Premonstratensian's colloquies and unions with Jesus follow the yearly feasts. They appear to fall into three groups or layers: (1) largely third-person reports of her ecstasies, which occasionally give Christ's words to her and more rarely hers to him (17.239–51 and 18.203–7); (2) a series of reports based on contemporary witnesses recounting Christ's speeches to her (18.207–32); and (3) a number of mostly theological questions she addresses to Christ (18.232–38).[83]

Little or nothing in the descriptions of these ecstasies or in the colloquies of part (2) can be described as original. Indeed, it is precisely the repetitiveness of the account that makes it interesting as a sign of how widely known and used the motifs of strong forms of bridal and union language were by the end of the thirteenth century. There is also no mystical itinerary laid out in the text. Christina is obviously not a model for imitation, or a teacher of the path to God. She is an icon of the extraordinary, meant for awe and admiration. After the description of the seven years of ascesis, Christina always appears as the perfected soul to whom Christ offers effusive praise in formulaic speeches as "my most beloved soul," or "the chosen bride of my heart."[84] The central section of the *Description,* focusing on these addresses, refers to sixty-two mystical encounters organized by feast days, many quite short. A standard formula is (a) mention of the feast and sometimes a description of the circumstances (often in relation to the reception of the Eucharist); (b) Christ's praise-address to his beloved bride (God the Father speaks once); and (3) sometimes a notice of the number of souls released from purgatory by Christina's intercession.

The language of bridal love is omnipresent in these accounts. But if Christina is a bride, she is scarcely a longing bride—Christ is always there ready to welcome her as his most beloved. The other dominant forms of mystical language used in the text are also positive and cataphatic. Christina has special access to heavenly light, the divine brilliance into which Christ welcomes his bride. Like some of the beguines, she is described as enjoying the sweetness, or fruition, of her Beloved. Once Christ tells her, in an expression that mirrors what we have seen in Hadewijch: "Then you flow out into God with an unexpressible fruition of the sweet Godhead and the lovely humanity."[85]

Many of the images, themes, and terms found in other women mystics of the thirteenth century also make an appearance in the *Description*'s account of Christina's ecstasies. For example, the language of "flowing" (*flussen*) and "melting" (*versmiltzen*) into God, or of "being swept up" (*swebet*) and "raptured" (*gezucket*), characteristic of mystics like Mechthild of Magdeburg, is frequent.[86] Like the beguine, Christina even speaks of the "divine flow of love" (*gotliche mynnen flusse* [18.220]) into the soul. The expressions used to characterize the canoness's mode of union with Christ were all traditional by the late thirteenth century. For example, Christ often tells her that she has achieved "oneness of spirit" with him, using the formula drawn from 1 Corinthians 6:17. In the account of the rapture she experienced on the feast of the Three Kings in 1291, speaking in her own voice, Christina says:

> The divine shining and light poured itself into me and mixed itself so much with me that it made one spirit from two things, that is, from my soul and from God. And my soul became God with God and was totally united with God.[87]

Equally traditional is Christ's reminder to her that "You have by grace what I have by nature";[88] or the references to the soul as the image of the Trinity (e.g., 18.225, 229). The verb "unified" (*vereynigt*), used in a rather generic way, is one of the more common terms in these accounts.[89] There are, however, also a few expressions that reflect some of the more daring themes of thirteenth-century mysticism, including descriptions of union utilizing the deep union suggested in the Gospel of John. In an appearance on the feast of the Ascension in 1290, Christ says to Christina, "My Father is in me and I am in him and you are in us; everything that I have is yours and what you have is mine."[90] Christina's Christ also speaks to her of the divine abyss (*abgront*) several times,[91] though there is no merging of God's abyss and the soul's abyss, probably because the theme of annihilation is absent from the *Description*. When Christ invites Christina to "leave God through God" (*Du salt got durch got laissen* [18.213]), or when he tells her that "All your work and life is a divine work that God works in you" (18.228), we may even detect motifs reminiscent of the mysticism of Marguerite Porete or Meister Eckhart. Nevertheless, the divine addresses in the *Description* present a mélanges of motifs rather than a coherent theology of mysticism.

A Vallombrosan Abbess

The Vallombrosan order's roots go back to the activity of John Gualbert and his foundation of an abbey at Vallombrosa east of Florence about 1036. This mixture of coenobitic and eremitical life, whose rule was approved by Victor II in 1055, was mostly found in Italy.[92] The origins of the Vallombrosan nuns is obscure, though female houses appear to have begun in the twelfth century. The major figure in the development of the female branch of the order, however, is Umiltà (*Humilitas*) of Faenza (1226–1310), who also distinguished herself by leaving Latin texts, traditionally called *sermones*, which contain a form of mystical teaching.[93]

Umiltà's life story illustrates the multiple forms of religious life that many thirteenth-century women explored.[94] She was born Rosanese Negusanti of a noble family in Faenza. Married against her will to a local nobleman, she bore several children, but her desire to embrace the religious life led her to pray to God for her freedom from family obligations (like Angela of Foligno). Her children died and her husband was stricken with disease and gave his permission for her departure to the Cluniac monastery of Santa Perpetua, where she was given the name *Humilitas*. Cluniac monasticism was obviously not ascetic enough for her, however, and after some time she effected a miraculous "escape" from Santa Perpetua and fled to a community of Poor Clares. This too was unsatisfacory and so, like Umiliana dei Cerchi, she took up the life of a *reclusa* in the home of an uncle. After considerable negotiation, as well as demonstration of her miraculous and prophetic powers, about 1254 she was allowed to build a cell attached to the Vallombrosan monastery of Sant' Apollinare in Faenza, where she spent a dozen years in isolation and the severest asceticism, accompanied only by her pet weasel. Although Umiltà expressed regrets over leaving the life of a recluse,[95] it was apparently under the impulse of a command from God that she took on the role of a religious founder in building a house for nuns (Santa Maria Novella), following the Vallombrosan way of life. About 1280, her special patron St. John the Evangelist, commanded her to abandon this house and with only two companions make the dangerous journey across the Apennines to Florence to found a monastery in his honor. This foundation flourished and it was there that the aged Umiltà died in 1310.[96]

The fifteen surviving "sermons" of Umiltà appear to date from her last years in Florence. Though they are often of a didactic character and some are tied to the liturgical calender, like those for the Nativity and in honor of the apostles John and James, they are scarcely sermons in the ordinary sense. Written in a strange form of Latin, sometimes close to biblical and liturgical language, but often idiosyncratic and obscure, they represent a distinctive vernacular theology influenced by Umiltà's native speech.[97] The Vallombrosan abbess's sermons are quite unlike the visionary narratives in which so many thirteenth-century women expressed their encounter with God. She does not speak as a visionary, though at times she seems to refer to appearances of heavenly beings and various allegorical figures. She is clearest when she speaks objectively in a quasi-liturgical manner; when she appears to be trying to recount her own experiences, she often becomes obscure and evasive. Formulae of reticence, secrecy, and inexpressibility dot her texts.[98] Above all, as Adele Simonetti has shown, Umiltà hides herself behind her favorite saints, especially John the Evangelist, describing her own consciousness of God's presence through hymns and reflections on the beloved disciple's intimate contact with Jesus–a kind of surrogate mysticism.[99] A good example of her reticence appears in Sermon VI, where it introduces a brief summary of the strange imagistic message she conveyed to the audience she often described as comprised of both brothers and sisters (*O sanctissimi fratres necnon sorores* [*Sermo* IX.50]):

> I assert this to you only through an example, as if stammering with a likeness. No one could be born, or has been born, who would be able to comprehend the situation well save the Lord who was wounded, who placed the rivers in the lance and the scourge, and who bore that pain that was so bitter. From it the saints make a glorious new shoot for themselves which is always renewed in sweetness, and in the sweet love of the "little house," [that is], in that blessed humanity which bore the scourge in its body. And they always exult with joy to see the beautiful flesh.[100]

This passage illustrates central images of Umiltà's devotion to the crucified Christ that appear especially in Sermons IV–VI. These images are rooted in texts from the Gospel of her *alter ego* John, specifically the proclamation of Christ in John 7:37–38 ("Let anyone who is thirsty come to me! Let anyone who believes in me come and drink!") and the account of the piercing of Christ's side on the cross (John 19:34–37). Umiltà pictures five regal rivers larger than any ocean flowing from the throne of God (*Sermo* IV.80–109). It soon becomes clear that these five rivers are the five wounds of the crucified flesh of Christ which she identifies with a feminine image, the *domicella abundans luminis,* "the little house abounding in light." Umiltà invites the reader to embrace and kiss the *domicella* in a highly rhetorical and erotic passage (IV.136–58). The remainder of Sermon IV, the longest of her texts, furthers explains the *domicella* and the *flumines* by commenting on Christ's humility in taking on flesh and saving humanity through his conflict with the devil and victory on the cross.

Umiltà's use of a female image for the humanity of Christ, a feature of much women's piety in the later Middle Ages as Caroline Bynum has shown,[101] is heightened in Sermon V, which emphasizes the devout soul's drinking both the milk of charity and the milk coagulated as blood that flowed from Christ as he was scourged during the passion.[102] To the five rivers seen in Sermon IV, the abbess now adds a sixth, the wounded head of Christ pouring blood: "And this river is more exalted and dominates the other five–that glorious human flesh, the sweet little house about which I have spoken to you" (*Sermo* V.115–17; ed., 66). Umiltà then, like so many other women mystics, though in her own way, fastens her attention on the cross of Christ as the only ladder by which we can ascend to God (*Sermones*

IV.115–16 and 512–13; VI.20–33). The seventh and eighth sermons, which are described as forming a brief "Treatise on Divine Matters," contain a series of more personal appropriations of the objective picture of salvation found in the previous three pieces. Here Umiltà makes use of some traditional mystical themes, such as the language of contemplation, the vision of God as Trinity, identification with Christ in the Eucharist, and the mystical marriage. Occasionally, she even breaks into the kind of personal and passionate language found in many of her contemporaries (e.g., the Hymn to Jesus in *Sermo* VIII.179–85). These more direct expressions of her mystical devotion to Christ are especially prevalent in Sermon XI (e.g., *Sermo* XI.1–23, 36–56).

There can be no question of the Vallombrosan abbess's deep desire for Christ—"If I had this whole world in my hands, I would give it over for the love of Christ."[103] Nevertheless, Umiltà's basic tendency is to hide her own experiences behind those of her favorite patrons, including her two guardian angels, the Blessed Virgin, Mary Magdalene, and most especially John the Beloved (see *Sermones* XII–XIII). She does, however, tell her audience that through, with, and in these patrons she has enjoyed direct contact with God:

> And you know, brothers, [I have received celestial gifts] sent down not only by vision, but also by familiar and friendly address, and gentle speech and most welcome response to all our questions and petitions, granted by divine power. . . . And you know that these [her patrons] are the appropriate, the first, and the best for our aid and great support. They have opened up for us many of the secrets of heaven.[104]

A Carthusian Prioress

The early traditions of Carthusian mysticism have been discussed in *The Growth of Mysticism*.[105] As with the Cistercians, the first fathers of Le Grand Chartreuse had not envisaged a female branch, but the attraction of their austere way of life led the nuns of Prébayon in Provence to request a customary (*consuetudines*) based on the Carthusian way of life as early as the 1140s.[106] Although the Carthusian nuns were not able to adopt the quasi-eremitical style of their male counterparts, their asceticism and devotion to learning were modeled on the much larger male branch of the order (only seventeen female houses are known from the medieval period). Carthusian nuns enjoyed a double consecration, both as virgins and as deaconesses able to read the epistle at Mass and gospel in the divine office—a fact that argues for their general literacy.

The Carthusian convent of Poletains was founded near Lyons in 1230. The fourth prioress of the house, Marguerite d'Oingt, who came from a wealthy Lyonnais family, began her writing career with a work in Latin, the *Page of Meditations* (*Pagina meditationum*) in 1286. In 1294, Hugh, prior of the Charterhouse of Valbonne, presented a book she had written in her native Franco-Provençal entitled the *Mirror* (*Speculum*) to the Carthusian General Chapter, where it received approval. After her death in 1310, these two works, along with a vernacular *Life of Beatrice the Virgin of Ornaciu,* several letter-extracts and accounts of three miracles, were collected. This brief corpus survives in three manuscripts.[107]

Marguerite d'Oingt has not been well studied. Despite the brevity of her writings, however, she is a distinctive voice in the new female mysticism and an interesting adaptation of Carthusian motifs, especially those relating to the role of sacred reading (*lectio divina*) and writing (*scriptio*), in attaining a more intense consciousness of God.[108] Marguerite would have been familiar with Guigo II's *Ladder of Monks,* with its fourfold "spiritual exercise" of *lectio-meditatio-oratio-contemplatio.* As Stephanie Paulsell has shown, this form of monastic practice represents the subtext of her two main works, the *Page of Meditations* and the *Mirror;* but Marguerite modifies the traditional program by the way in which she gives *explicit* attention to the mystical significance of the book and the act of writing as necessary to an ever-deepening experience of God.[109] In this she provides another variation on the ways in which the women mystics of the period created new strategies for understanding and defending their taking up the pens usually reserved for male ecclesiastics.

There is a strong interaction between Marguerite's two main texts. The *Page of Meditations,* though written in learned Latin, is composed in the first person as a therapy for Marguerite's own struggle with the temptation to despair, while the vernacular *Mirror* speaks of Marguerite in the third person, using her as an exemplar for the spiritual exercise of her community and her other readers.[110] In both cases, the act of writing is crucial to the process of attaining God. Exterior writing down of the experience that God inwardly writes on the heart provides a constant source for ever-new penetration of the message of divine love.

On Septuagesima Sunday in 1286, as the *Page of Meditations* informs us, while she listened to the lugubrious chant of the Introit, "The laments of death surrounded me" (Ps. 17:5),

> I began to think about the misery to which we have been handed over by the sin of our first parents. In that thought I began to experience such fear and

pain that my heart seemed to fail me utterly; because of this I did not know if I were worthy of salvation or not.[111]

Although she is immediately reassured by the versicle of the same Introit ("I will love you, O Lord, my strength" [Ps. 17:2]), remembering God's promise in Proverbs 8:17 ("I will love those who love me"), Marguerite's spiritual crisis needed to be worked out in greater detail through a lengthy meditation on the divine love realized in creation and salvation. This is what God writes in her heart so that she may write it down for future *lectio divina*. But for Marguerite there was no choice whether to write or not—she *must* write, both for herself and eventually for others. What "she feels in her heart from her most sweet Creator" is so overpowering that she can neither sleep nor eat. Because she recognizes the instability of the human heart, "I put down in writing the thoughts that God had ordered in my heart so that I would not lose them when I removed them from my heart and would be able to think about them little by little when God would give me his grace."[112] Marguerite admits to having neither understanding (*sensum*) nor clerical education, but she still defends the necessity of her act of writing because the *exemplar* from which she copies her book (as a good monastic scribe) is God's grace working within her. The Carthusian needed to externalize the inner message she had been given by God in order to make it a message she could continue to rely upon.[113]

The meditations that make up Marguerite's book have a liturgical starting point, but they evolve as a consideration of the love that compelled the ineffable Creator to lower himself to take on flesh to save humanity. Marguerite's presentation delights in paradoxes contrasting divine omnipotence and the weakness and suffering of the God-man, especially in the passion. She speaks of the Lord as Father (n. 7) and Brother (n. 8), but it is her discussion of Christ as the Mother who bore us through the painful birth of the cross that is distinctive of her view of salvation (see nn. 30–46) —"Ah, sweet Lord Jesus Christ, who has ever seen any mother suffer such a birth!" (n. 36).

The *Page of Meditations,* like many earlier Carthusian documents, is rooted in a deep sense of the *mysterium Christi,* but is perhaps not an overtly mystical document. That Marguerite had a mystical goal in mind (i.e., one aimed at an immediate consciousness of God) becomes more evident in the text's companion piece, the *Mirror.* Speaking in the third person, this mystagogical work holds up the experience of "this creature" (*citi creatura,* i.e., Marguerite as the visionary who sees and writes down what she sees) as the model for her monastic readers. The first chapter describes how "this creature" had the life of Jesus so written into her heart that he seemed present within her with a book in his hand. The exterior of the book, with letters in white, black, and red, and two golden clasps, is given an allegorical explanation relating to Christ's life and virtues.[114] In the second chapter, as she was praying after matins, Marguerite saw the book open to reveal two pages that were like a "beautiful mirror" revealing the ineffable "place" of the Trinity, which she describes in terms of the effect it has on the spiritual senses (nn. 14–17). When the angels and saints contemplate the beauty of the Savior in this place they break out into "a totally new song" (see Apoc. 5:9). Using a watery image found in other women mystics (e.g., Beatrice of Nazareth, Mechthild of Magdeburg, and Marguerite Porete), the Carthusian nun describes the life of the saints in heaven thus:

> The saints will be in their Creator as fish are in the sea; every day they will drink as much as they want without tiring and without diminishing the water. The saints will be like that, because they will drink and eat the great sweetness of God. The more they will get, the greater their hunger.[115]

Finally, the third book of Marguerite's *Mirror* describes another vision of what is clearly an illuminated book, one also given at matins. Here she sees the body of Christ:

> This glorious body was so noble and so transparent that one saw clearly the soul within. The body was so noble that one could see oneself there more clearly than in a mirror. This body was so beautiful that one could see the angels and saints there as if they were painted on him.[116]

Marguerite, like many other late medieval women mystics, had a strong pictorial imagination, one shaped by meditation on sacred images. The point of the vision of Christ's body, however, is as much aspiration as it is admiration—he gives to the saints who are members of his body the gift "of being as brilliant as the sun" (n. 26). The *Mirror* closes with a hymn or litany praising the splendors of the resurrected bodies of the saints which themselves become mirrors so that each can see the Trinity within the self (n. 35), while God looks upon them "as a good master likes to look at a beautiful panel when he has done it well" (n. 36). This is true deification (Marguerite cites here the Latin of Psalm 81:6, *Ego dixi dii estis*) and the face-to-face vision of God promised to the pure of heart (cf. 1 Cor. 13:12 and Matt. 5:8).

In the manner of monastic mystics since the time of Gregory the Great, Marguerite fixes her attention on the perfect vision of heaven, but this does not mean that her internal vision of Christ as the *liber vitae* which she externalizes for the benefit of her community should be described as less than mystical. Two of her letters provide further information on the relation between seeing God and writing God.[117] In Letter 2, addressed to an unnamed priest, she once again defends her writing by insisting that it was a physical necessity for her to unburden herself of what Christ had written on her heart by writing it down for her own future use. Here, however, she uses the technical language of ecstasy—"I do not know whether what is written in the book is in sacred scripture, but I know that she who put these things in writing was ravished (*si esleve*) in Our Lord one night so that it seemed that she saw all these things."[118] More fascinating for the personal symbolism of her mysticism is the strange account, or parable, in Letter 4 of the woman (i.e., Marguerite) who had the word "vehement" (*vehemens*) so deeply driven into her heart that she could get no relief until she prayed to God to teach her its meaning. The Lord then granted her a vision of a dried-out tree (i.e., herself) with five faded branches representing the five senses. A nearby high mountain, however, gave forth a "great stream which descended with such a great force that it seemed to be a sea." This image of what twelfth-century mystics like Bernard of Clairvaux would have called divine "vehement love" (*amor vehemens*) turned the tree upside down so that its top was stuck in the earth, while its roots and revived branches pointed to the sky. Marguerite does not exegete the parable, but this vision of an *arbor eversa* is a kind of structural analogue to the internalized book that grace causes to be externalized both for the author herself and for her audience.[119] Vehemence in love, originating in God, causes Marguerite to flourish into God, not only in soul but also in her bodily senses.

Dominican Women Mystics

Women were a part of the Dominican movement from its inception.[120] As noted in the first chapter (pp. 35–36), when Bishop Diego and Dominic began their preaching against the heretics in southern France in the early years of the thirteenth century, they quickly realized the necessity of winning the women who had joined the heresy back to the fold of the church. Dominic founded a house for women at Prouille in 1206, his first such venture. Documentation is too sparse to settle the modern debates about Prouille—for example: Was it just for converted heretics? Were the women involved in an active ministry that included some form of preaching as well as teaching? Prouille does indicate that Dominic, like Francis, was concerned that women, no less than men, should play a role in the form of the apostolic life he envisaged.

Dominic's opening to a role for women is evident in the founder's subsequent efforts in creating convents in Toulouse (1215–1217), Madrid (ca. 1220),[121] and Rome (San Sisto, ca. 1221, whose regulations became a model for many later houses of Dominican women). He also supported the young Bolognese noblewoman Diana d'Andalò, who attempted to establish a house for religious women in her native city in 1219, but was rebuffed by her family and bishop.[122] It was not until 1223 that she was able to establish the convent of S. Agnese at Bologna with the support of Jordan of Saxony, Dominic's successor as General of the order (1222–1237). The close ties between this pious woman and the early leaders of the preaching friars are a good illustration of the cooperation between men and women in the spread of new forms of the *vita apostolica* in the thirteenth century.

Although there is ample evidence that both women and men responded to the evangelical impetus of the Dominicans within the first two decades of the movement (ca. 1206–1226), the Friar Preachers, no less than the Friars Minor and older reformed orders, subsequently had a difficult job incorporating women's houses into their growing international movements in the decades from 1227 to 1257.[123] In addition to misogyny and administrative myopia, there were also serious institutional and spiritual reasons for the hesitation of the friars about the involvement of women. The male religious felt that taking on full responsibility for the rapidly expanding women's houses would compromise the human, financial, and spiritual resources at their disposal to fulfill their primary mission of the wider *cura animarum*, especially through preaching and teaching. The thirteenth-century popes, however, tended to side with the women in their desire to attain recognition as members of the mendicants, though it is difficult to know if the curia was inspired more by a conviction of the importance of female houses for the good of the church or by the importunate appeals of the women and their powerful relatives. Whatever the weight of motivation, one cannot but admire how successive popes labored to work out compromises between female efforts at incorporation and male resistance.

At the General Chapter of 1228 held at Paris, the Dominicans, like the Cistercians in the same year, forbade the acceptance of new houses of women, but this rule appears to have had little effect. In 1239, Gregory IX issued a bull that supported the ban. The Dominicans, however, continued to attract women, especially in Germany,[124] so it is not surprising that the friars of the province of *Teutonia* seem to have felt particularly overwhelmed. It was the German Master General, John of Wildeshausen (1241–1252), who became the standard-bearer of opposition to the incorporation of women. But for every effort the general or the chapters made to exclude new female houses, and even to free themselves from obligations to the convents that had been accepted by the founders, they soon discovered how difficult it was for them to abandon the *cura monialium*. The women were there to stay.

After much to-ing and fro-ing, a solution that allowed the women access was worked out between 1257 and 1259 during the pontificate of Alexander IV, largely through the efforts of Hugh of St. Cher, a Dominican theologian-become-papal-legate and troubleshooter, and the new General Humbert of Romans (1254–1263). Humbert imposed standard *Constitutions* on the women in 1259.

From the perspective of the desire for religious women to gain affiliation with the order of preachers, the story follows general patterns, despite the details of individual houses. Most of the convents for which we have records began as free associations of devoted women—beguines, even if the term was not in use in Germany until later in the thirteenth century. At a certain point in their development, often after being given grants of land and buildings, they sought more official and stable status. The preaching and pastoral activity of the Dominicans, especially in the southwest of Germany, made the new order attractive to these communities and fostered forms of association that the women sought to regularize, doubtless often with the cooperation of local friars, despite the opposition of generals and chapters.[125] As Herbert Grundmann put it:

> Such close cooperation between religious women and Dominicans in Germany arose directly from the encounter between the two religious movements, each pollinating and enlivening the other. No one planned this result, yet the course of history created a situation which was neither consciously registered nor foreseen by anyone. . . . Nothing could demonstrate more clearly the autonomous dynamism of the women's religious movement.[126]

A brief look at the history of one German Dominican convent, Engelthal near Nuremberg in Franconia, can illustrate the process.[127] The Engelthal *Sister Book* (a later account of the history of the house and lives of its famous nuns), as well as contemporary archival documents, inform us that when Elizabeth of Hungary passed through Nuremberg in 1211 one of her entourage, a harpist named Alheit, converted to a life of penance and stayed behind in the city. Alheit soon became the center of a small gathering of beguines who were known as the *sorores Rottarinne* ("Sisters of the Harpist"). In 1240 when Nuremberg was placed under interdict by Innocent IV for supporting Frederick II, they fled the city and were given a donation of land at Engelthal ("Angel Valley") by an imperial official, Ulrich of Königstein. Now financially well established, the sisters were courted by the Cistercians (despite their 1228 ban on receiving women), but with the encouragement of Bishop Frederick of Eichstätt they adopted the statutes of the nuns of S. Sisto in 1244 and sought incorporation into the Dominicans, which they received from Innocent IV in 1248. In the fourteenth century Engelthal was to become a center of female mysticism with two important authors, Christine Ebner and Adelheid Langmann.

The role of mysticism in the Dominican order took a rather different course from what we have seen in the Franciscans. The first Dominicans were devoted to a form of *vita apostolica* which concentrated on apostolic preaching of faith and morals.[128] This emphasis on learned preaching gave the order a more academic and pragmatic orientation than the Franciscans. While Dominic is portrayed in the hagiographical accounts as a man of intense prayer, even these texts did not accord him the kinds of mystical graces and visions that the lives of Francis ascribed to *Il Poverello*.

If Dominic remains a shadowy figure, his successor Jordan of Saxony, "the second founder of the order," is accessible through a number of writings, especially his letters. Like Dominic, Jordan was also described as being devoted to prayer, even when traveling; but he is not pictured as an ecstatic endowed with mystical visions. However, Jordan's fifty surviving letters to Diana d'Andalò (out of fifty-six in his corpus) provide ample evidence for the depth of spiritual friendship between men and women that helped shape the new mysticism of the thirteenth century.[129] His fluid and sensitive style and the delicacy of his love-language toward this impetuous young aristocrat are evident throughout the corpus. Unfortunately, Diana's side of the correspondence does not survive, and it is difficult to know from Jordan's letters to what extent she may have experienced states of consciousness of God similar to those found among her contemporaries, like Beatrice of Nazareth.

Jordan's letters deal primarily with the doctrinal foundations for mysticism that are characteristic of traditional monastic teaching on *contemplatio* (a word he rarely uses). They should not be characterized as essentially mystical in content or tone. Most of what he says about longing for heaven (see Letters 9, 13, 16, 18, 22, 35, 46, 51), the identity of the nun as the spouse of Christ (e.g., Letters 1, 17, 18, 22, 23, 24, 31, 32, 34, 44, 48, 51, 54, 55), reliance upon the inner action of the Holy Spirit (e.g., Letters 12, 19, 36, 44), and even devotion to Christ, is general in tone. Jordan uses these themes as part of a program of spiritual teaching that is presented without any analysis of the stages of contemplative ascent to God. In harmony with this perspective, he shows considerable hesitancy about the more extreme aspects of the burgeoning women's piety, as his frequent warnings to Diana and her sister about the dangers of excessive and unusual ascetical practices indicate (see Letters 1, 11, 16, 18, 23, 24, 27, 31, 39).

Friar Jordan's love of friends in the love they all share in Christ was expressed primarily to Diana, but also to others. Letter 52, written to an unknown nun about the death of his beloved friend, Friar Henry, gives an apt summary of this aspect of his theology. He expresses it this way:

> What am I prepared to say about that greatest good by which I love you so much in the love of Christ our mediator? He is the mediator not only of those who love each other in Christ, but also of God and human beings, whom he makes one. He makes them one so that God might become human and humans become God, and so that a human might love God in another human and another human in God.[130]

This pregnant passage not only enshrines an ancient formula about divinization common to Eastern and Western theology since Irenaeus but also integrates this into a typically twelfth- and thirteenth-century expression of the redemptive character of *spiritualis amicitia*.

On the basis of his traditional theology, Jordan's notion of being one with Christ is expressed more in terms of the mystery of all believers' incorporation with Jesus through baptism than of individual mystical union.[131] Diana and her sisters, to be sure, are called to be brides of Christ through the dedication of their lives, as Jordan often says (e.g., Letter 28).[132] At times, the General even employs the language of intimate devotion to the infant Jesus, or of gazing upon Christ on the cross as the "book of life" (*liber vitae*) in which the nun will have revealed to her the meaning of her present exercises.[133] Nor did he exclude the possibility of brief experiences of "seeing Christ" in this life. In writing to the Dominican community at Paris in 1233 at Easter, he reminded his brethren that as long as they maintain mutual charity, do penance for their sins, and long for Christ, like the disciples, they too may have some "vision" of the Risen Savior in their lives: ". . . certainly they will not be deprived of some appearance of Jesus when the fat of devotion begins to boil and they immediately exclaim with wonder, 'Wasn't our heart burning within us when he spoke with us on the way?' (Lk. 24:32)."[134] But for Jordan the real reward lies beyond this life—not in present ecstatic experience but in constant yearning for the ultimate ecstasy of heaven.

Jordan's stress on balance in the ascetic life and his reticence about ecstatic experience were not typical of all friars, as we have seen in considering Thomas of Cantimpré and the other Dominicans who during the same years that Jordan was corresponding with Diana were writing about the women mystics of Lotharingia. Rather, Jordan and succeeding masters of the order, like Humbert of Romans, seem to be exceptions to the enthusiasm with which many friars on the local level became propagandists for the more extreme examples of female mystics (e.g., Peter of Dacia and Christina of Stommeln). During the second half of the thirteenth century the growing involvement of the preachers as guardians and chaplains of houses of cloistered women devoted to prayer and contemplation cemented this link between them and women whose feats of asceticism and mystical raptures followed the models set down by the early beguines.

The Dominican contribution to the mysticism of this period of ca. 1250–1350 falls into two broad camps, only one of which, that relating to ecstatic women, will be pursued here. The other tradition, the speculative and apophatic mysticism characteristic of Meister Eckhart and his followers, was primarily a male phenomenon.[135] Despite Eckhart's preaching and teaching in many Dominican convents, "Rhineland mysticism," as it has been called, did not have a major impact on the mysticism of most later Dominican women, even in Germany.[136] In a sense, as Herbert Grundmann argued, the influence moved more in the other direction, that is, the growth of female mysticism, both of the beguines and of Dominican women, was a part of the historical and spiritual matrix for Eckhart's teaching.[137] As a result, there are affinities between Eckhart and the writings of some of the beguines, such as Mechthild of Magdeburg and especially Marguerite Porete,[138] and the *cura monialium* was an important context for the development of his vernacular preaching. While it is true that some of Eckhart's followers, especially Henry Suso (d. 1366) and John Tauler (d. 1361), show closer bonds with the mystical themes found in the nuns whom they advised, guided, and befriended, the story of Dominican women's mysticism can be understood largely on its own terms.

Like the Franciscans, the Dominicans inspired "third orders" of penitents, lay men and women who strove to live the life of the friars as far as possible without taking orders in the case of the men or entering a cloistered house in the case of women.[139] These movements were especially popular in Italy. Among the Dominican female penitents of the thirteenth and early fourteenth centuries, several achieved fame for sanctity and visionary experiences. Benevenuta of Cividale (1255–1295), who lived for the most part in a house of Dominican nuns without taking vows, is described in her *Vita* written by a sympathetic friar as enjoying numerous revelations from Christ, Mary, and the angels and saints. According to the friar, she was also frequently raptured for an hour or more.[140] Like many holy women, Benevenuta had a special attachment to one friar, her confessor Conrad, whom St. Dominic revealed to her had been chosen by divine providence to enter the order to take special care of her.[141] Vanna (Johanna) of Orvieto (1264–1306) and the blind and crippled Margaret of Città Castello (1287–1320) also left similar reputations.[142] The greatest of these Italian tertiaries, one of the premier Christian mystics, Catherine of Siena (1347–1380), will be treated in the next volume.

It was in the German cloisters of the first half of the fourteenth century that female mystical writers first became abundant among the Dominicans. The extensive literature that gives us access to this chapter in the contribution of women to the new mysticism falls into two groups: the *Sister Books* that survive from at least nine different Dominican houses; and the related mystical autohagiographies (often called *Revelations*) written down by at least four nuns and even one priest who served as a chaplain to one of the houses.[143]

The *Sister Books* (German *Schwesternbücher,* or *Nonnenleben*) are among the most interesting products of the explosion of writing by and about women in the later Middle Ages. As described by Gertrud Jaron Lewis in her survey of the surviving examples:

> Thirteenth- and fourteenth-century women *are* the subject, they *are* the authors, compilers, editors, and copyists, and they *are* the audience. The end result is a complex literary narrative in praise of successful and saintly women's communities.[144]

The tendency to emphasize the role of the holy community, already observed with regard to the mystics of Helfta, is here taken a step further as individual lives, miracles, and mystical graces are employed as proofs of God's special love for the monastery itself. Although the *Sister Books* have links with the earlier *Lives of the Brethren* compiled by Gerard of Frachette at the command of the Dominican Chapter between ca. 1260 and 1270, as well as with the ancient *Lives of the Fathers* (*Vitae Patrum*) that were read in medieval convents, they constitute an original genre. They can be described as a form of "community hagiography," legends whose intent is to demonstrate God's approval of the monastery through recording the virtues, asceticism, and especially the mystical graces granted to the convent's members. At times these mystical graces are portrayed as poured out upon the entire community. For example, on Pentecost, as the community of Unterlinden was singing the *Veni Creator,* Sister Gertrude,

> suddenly saw the divine fire in a visible way coming down from heaven with a loud sound upon the holy convent of nuns as they sang to God. And it filled the whole choir where the sisters were gathered in praise of God, illuminating them to such a degree with divine splendors that they all looked like flames.[145]

Though these books often give the appearance of spontaneous recording of events, the research of Siegfried Ringler, Otto Langer, and Ruth Meyer has shown the literary art with which they were composed. Part history, part hagiography, and part mystical narratives, the *Sister Books* reveal just how deeply ecstatic mysticism had become rooted in the German female monasteries.[146]

The nine known *Sister Books* were produced between ca. 1310 and 1350 in southern German monasteries that had been accepted into the order in 1245–1248 during the flood of entries under Innocent IV. These cloisters, typical of the German women's houses, had all begun life as communities of beguine women. In some cases the name of the nun or nuns who put the materials together is known (e.g., Christine Ebner at Engelthal ca. 1340); in other cases the authors are anonymous. Most of the texts were composed in Middle High German, though the longest, the book for Unterlinden (ca. 1320), is in Latin. While there are individual tendencies expressed in each collection, the similarities among the books allows them to be described as constituting a single form of mystical literature.[147] They are, as Siegfried Ringler puts it, "grace-lives" (*Gnaden-viten*), that is, a form of narrative theology that presents model lives reduced to core accounts of mystical graces, such as auditions, visions, and descriptions of union with God.[148]

The *Sister Books* generally begin with or contain an account of the founding of the monastery, often stressing the difficulties the sisters encountered in gaining incorporation into the Dominican order—a sign both of their persistence and of the grudging acceptance they eventually won from the friars who were their counselors, confessors, and often their friends.[149] Still, the *Sister Books* are remarkable, as Lewis has pointed out, not only for the female context in which they were composed but also for the audience of women to which they were directed. The fact that hundreds of other women's religious houses existed across Europe in the early fourteenth century, many of which contained highly literate nuns, only adds to the achievement of these south German Dominicans in creating a new form of literature.

The *Sister Books* are not mystical texts in the traditional sense of either monastic commentaries on the mystical meaning of the scriptures or mystagogical guides. They are close to the hagiographies devoted to mystical beguines and other women, but differ from these in their concentration on experiences of grace rather than a whole life story and in their corporate character demonstrating the holiness of the form of life lived in a particular convent. Many notices are short, though others approach the length of mini-lives. Accounts of visions, ecstasies, and union with Christ are omnipresent in the *Sister Books*. As Sister Katharine tells us at the beginning of the Unterlinden book, she undertook her efforts in old age, "lest such excellent sisters at some time fall into oblivion, and to bring notice to present and future folk of their glorious deeds and wonderful works of great holiness, as well as with what great glory and devotion this holy monastery was founded."[150]

In terms of content, the *Sister Books* did not initiate anything new in the mysticism of the later Middle Ages. The accounts often begin with, or contain, the story of the sister's conversion (*kêr*) to a deeper form of spiritual life.[151] Their main purpose, though, is to recount "the revelations and special graces" (*revelationes et karismatum gratiae*) or "consolations" (*consolationes*) of the holy nuns, as Katherine of Unterlinden states it. The descriptions of auditions (i.e., hearing heavenly voices), and the visions of Christ, especially of the infant Jesus and the suffering Savior, are typical of what we have already seen in many thirteenth-century women. Standard too is their emphasis on the role of the Eucharist and the frequent descriptions of Christ appearing in the host. The ascetical feats of some of the nuns, along with the efficacy of their prayers in delivering souls from purgatory, are also common. The special mystical graces recounted (light experiences; stigmata, sometimes self-induced; levitation; *iubilus;*[152] etc.), as well as the language, often nuptial, used to describe rapture and union, are traditional.[153] Although we know that Meister Eckhart visited at least two of these convents,[154] it is surprising that the mysticism represented in the *Sister Books* has so few resonances with that of Eckhart and his followers.[155]

The mystical experiences of the nuns recounted in the *Sister Books* were based on a cloistered life devoted to liturgy and prayer, often severe penance, as well as practice of the virtues, especially obedience. Many of the sisters are described as great ascetics, although the accounts in the *Sister Books* do not generally feature the physically impossible feats that some male Dominicans told about the early beguines.[156] Sleep deprivation, silence, rigid fasting, frequent use of the "discipline" (i.e., the scourge), also girding oneself with painful cords and chains that cut into the flesh, are found throughout the stories.[157] Traditionally, asceticism was seen as a necessary but not sufficient condition for the reception of mystical graces. In some cases, however, the nuns seem to have confused the relationship, as when Gertrude of Girsperc, unhappy over the loss of her usual "divine illuminations," scourged herself severely "until the Lord was merciful and she suddenly felt a very great abundance of divine grace poured into the depths of her heart."[158]

Along with self-induced pain, illness played a role in the mystical life of these nuns. Given the state of medieval medicine, most thirteenth- and fourteenth-century people lived with a good deal more physical suffering and illness than modern folk usually do, at least those in the developed world. Sickness as an opportunity to suffer with Christ had a long history in

Christianity,[159] but the relation between sickness and forms of mystical experience seems to have become stronger in the later Middle Ages, particularly among women. For patristic mystical authors, illness was just one of the many trials of common human experience that reminds us of the fall and of our need for God. Even Gregory the Great, whose ill health drew him to sympathize with Job as the type of Christ suffering in both head and body, did not make illness a special factor in one's access to consciousness of God. Bernard of Clairvaux, who ruined his health by early excessive fasting, knew that suffering was an essential part of Christian living, but did not dwell on the role of his own illness.

This relatively neutral attitude toward the place of illness in the mystical itinerary began to change in the thirteenth century.[160] In the new mysticism, especially that pioneered by women, we often find serious physical ailments portrayed as an integral part of the story, even as an initiating factor or central element in the mystic's encounter with God—a special form of the *imitatio passionis* that has always been a part of Christian mysticism. The story of Margaret the Cripple, as well as those of some of the other *mulieres sanctae* given above, provide illustrations of this. Mechthild of Magdeburg spoke of the role of suffering and illness in her life, as we have seen. Later, German male mystics, including Eckhart, Suso, and Tauler, also reflected on suffering's place in the way to God. In the *Sister Books,* as well as in the autohagiographies composed by some of the nuns of these south German Dominican houses, severe and prolonged illness was frequently connected with the nun's reception of mystical graces. For example, as Sister Kungund of Engelthal approached death, a loud divine voice announced to her: "Pain is a good word, pain is a sweet word, pain is word rich in grace."[161] Many of the nuns saw suffering as a sign of special election. Else of Neustatt, a nun of Adelhausen, prayed that God might strike her best friend with great suffering because that was the quickest way to him (A 181). At the beginning of the life of Anne of Ramschwag the author says, "Our Lord gave her much suffering in her life so that she was quite sick and ill for many years. . . . And by her suffering she was made ready to receive great grace."[162] Stories like this could easily be multiplied.[163] At times, the inner suffering of distance from God is seen as the best way to find him, in a way comparable to Mechthild of Magdeburg's notion of alienation. Sister Gepe of Adelhausen noted that when she lost God "in all my senses and in all my mind so that I did not know where he is" was when she had the truest experience of him.[164] All these texts point to the fact that a new relationship between suffering and illness (physical and psychological), on the one hand, and mystical states, on the other, was developing, one that would grow more complex as time went on. The histories of such noted mystics as Catherine of Siena, Julian of Norwich, and Teresa of Avila demonstrate this.

Another characteristic of the mysticism of the later Middle Ages, touched on from time to time in this volume, was also highly developed in the *Sister Books*. This is the relation between religious images and mysticism. Sacred images played a role in Christianity almost from the beginning. The icon, taken in the broad sense of a religious image thought to have special contact with the heavenly world and used within the context of Christian worship and devotion, although most highly developed in Eastern Christianity, was also present in the West.[165] Such images doubtless contributed not only to the preparation of early medieval monastic mystics' encounter with God but also to the form in which the encounter was realized and communicated. However, prior to 1200 we do not have much explicit reflection in mystical texts themselves on the role that such images took. Connections can be made, but mostly of an indirect nature. Direct descriptions of the role of images begin to appear in the thirteenth century and to grow more frequent in the later medieval period.

The visionary character of much late medieval mysticism seems to have been an important factor in encouraging more explicit attention to images in mystical texts.[166] Consider, for example, the part that pictures of Francis's stigmata played in shaping the received view of him as mystic and also in encouraging the spread of the stigmata, received and self-induced, as a sign of mystical identification with the suffering Christ.[167] The illustrations that accompanied the *Meditations on the Life of Jesus Christ* (see chap. 3, p. 119), allowing the user to focus on the inner depth of each mystery of the redemption through both eye and ear, were a part of the popularity of this pseudo-Bonaventurean work. The power of visualization noted in many of the mystical women, such as Hadewijch, Mechthild, and Angela of Foligno, although it can rarely be tied to specific images (but see FL 2.26 discussed on p. 225), also suggests the importance of the growing relation between sacred art and states of immediate consciousness of God. As noted earlier in this chapter, the visions of the Cistercian nuns of Helfta in the last decades of the thirteenth century were related both to liturgy and sometimes to sacred images. The fourteenth- and fifteenth-century explosion of images for private devotion has recently become the subject of studies indicating rich interconnections between mysticism and art.[168] Especially significant here, as the work of Jeffrey Hamburger among others has shown, is the role of nuns as patrons, artists, and users of sacred images.[169] The integration of visual evidence into the history of mysticism, particularly after 1200, has certainly begun, but much still remains to do.

The importance of images in the spiritual life of the Dominican nuns is evident throughout the *Sister Books*. Later texts from these convents even provide us with information about some of the particular images that were treasured by the nuns.[170] Not only is there a host of direct references to the use of images as a part of the sisters' prayer life, but in many cases the descriptions of the heavenly figures who appear to the nuns are modeled on pictures and statues we know existed in the convents (e.g., A 170, D 108, E 36, G 138, T 88, U 403, 413, 431). Sometimes the accounts even make explicit note of this (e.g., U 363). The two primary modes of Christ's appearance, as a child (often in Mary's arms) and as the "Man of Suffering" (*Schmerzensmann*) in his passion, were among the most common images found in late medieval convents.

Gazing at images often induced visionary experience, as, for example, in the case of Sister Elisa of Engelthal as she meditated on a window depicting the last judgment (E 39). Concerning Sister Hilti Brúmsin of Diessenhofen we have the following story:

> She prayed one day before a picture of our Lord as he stood at the pillar [i.e., being scourged] and she begged with all her heart that our Lord would give her the pain and bitterness in which he was when he stood at the pillar. Our Lord granted her this, and all her innards and limbs were filled with such great suffering and bitterness that she compassionately felt the passion our Lord suffered when he stood at the pillar, as much as she was able to bear.[171]

One common experience was having a picture or statue of Christ or Mary come to life as one prayed before it. Thus, Anne of Constance, a nun of Diessenhofen, grasped the foot of the infant Jesus and felt it "become flesh and blood in her hand" (D 107; cf. D 133). At Unterlinden Gertrude of Brugge experienced a vision in which a statue of Jesus in Mary's arms came to life and addressed her (U 414). Experiencing the embrace of the crucified Christ is a form of mystical contact reported about Bernard of Clairvaux and many thirteenth-century women mystics, but in the *Sister Books* it was often connected to an actual crucifix. Thus, Adelheit, the prioress of Diessenhofen, and two other sisters stood before "our large crucifix" and heard Christ say to them, "Avete!" (the "Hail" given by Christ to the three women after his resurrection). "And then," the report continues, "our Lord moved his right arm from the cross and embraced them and pressed them against him."[172] In another account, also from Diessenhofen, one holy nun sees another transformed into a shining crystal as she prays before an image of St. John resting on Christ's breast, one of the standard portrayals of mystical union.[173] Other stories leave the exact manner of the experience of God's presence conveyed through the sacred image ambiguous, but it is clear that the image as concrete object was important to the mystical experience of many of these nuns.

The auditions and visions recounted in the *Sister Books* are not essentially different from many that we have already seen in this volume. Rather than trying to give a detailed treatment of the kinds of visions and the language used to describe union, we can get a sense of the mysticism of the *Sister Books* through brief presentations of the lives of four nuns noted for their mystical experiences drawn from four different books: Hedwig of Laufenburg from Unterlinden; Anne of Ramschwag from Diessenhofen; Alheit of Trochaw from Engelthal; and Sophie of Klingenow from Töss.

Hedwig of Laufenburg's life is among the longest in the Unterlinden book.[174] She is described as one of the first nuns of the monastery (one of her visions can be dated to ca. 1253) and as someone who suffered from many illnesses throughout her life. The Lord sent her "many and frequent divine consolations," revealing heavenly mysteries to her "often while she was awake with a sensible vision or in an ecstasy of mind" (U 439.14–17). The account records about a dozen visions. Once, shortly after she entered the monastery, Hedwig went to the choir after supper and was transported "in ecstasy of mind" (*in mentis excessum*) to heaven to view the blessed (440.1–23). At Christmas she had a corporeal vision of Christ's holy ancestors, and when she was called to choir for matins she heard a divine voice and was rapt in ecstasy (*extra se in extasim rapta fuit*) to contemplate hidden divine mysteries, presumably in a noncorporeal fashion (440.33–441.34). Perhaps the most interesting of Hedwig's experiences took place at the moment of consecration in the Mass when she was once again raptured and "saw the deepest mysteries of the undivided Trinity through rays of interior light" (441.36–39). The account says that everything that the "remarkable doctor St. Augustine" wrote in all his books could not be compared to "one moment of the purest understanding by which she was incomparably illuminated into a divine way of knowing in that hour" (442.7–13). Upon her return to herself, Hedwig said that she was able to preach about the essence of the ineffable Trinity to the whole world—the kind of claim for superior infused knowledge made by a number of visionaries.[175] Hedwig also had a vision of Christ giving Communion to the whole convent (442.30–34), as well as showings of Mary, St. Peter Martyr (the recently canonized Dominican), John the Baptist, and the angels. Like other holy nuns, she was also a powerful intercessor. When she prayed to the Lord for Count Gottfried of Hapsburg, Christ appeared to her, showing the count within the wounds in his hands, feet, and side (447.11–448.12). Hedwig's mysticism was certainly passion-centered, even to extent of the self-inflicted sharing in the passion that remains one of the most troubling aspects of medieval mysticism. For many years she continually scratched a deep cross-shaped wound on her breast with a sharpened stick, "in order to keep the memory of the passion and cross of our Lord Jesus Christ always in mind and body" (449.28–30).

Anne of Ramschwag, referred to several times above, was another noted visionary, one given a relatively long entry in the Diessenhofen book (D 128–33).[176] Anne was a contemporary of the visionary author, so we have not only accounts of her visions but also quotations of some of her sayings (e.g., 129.16–24). Offered to the monastery as a child, she learned her letters in the convent, at one time being given a vision of the Christ child appearing in her schoolbook to encourage her progress. Anne's intercessory prayers, as in the case of her petitions for her dead father, were realized through her deep devotion to the crucified Christ (129.20–130.1). On one occasion Christ appeared as a child of about seven years, holding three red roses symbolizing the love and suffering with which he had pierced her heart (the *transverberatio cordis* theme) and citing an invitation to union based on secular love poetry: "Give me what is yours and I will give you what is mine."[177] The first rose she receives with "pure knowledge, with burning love and with enflamed desire"; in the second rose she "has pure knowledge of God and sees everything she wants in God."[178] The third rose, unnamed, appears to represent the promise of heavenly glory.

Devotion to the Christ child is widespread in the *Sister Books,* but Anne's mystical contact with the divine infant was special in some respects. Sitting in her choir stall on Christmas eve, she "was raptured [*gezogen*] in a divine light"[179] and beheld her body separately so that she could see two children within her who embraced in a loving manner (131.80–84). "And in this showing she recognized that one child was our Lord and the other was her soul and how she and God were united [*vereinet*]."[180] As mentioned above, Anne consulted with Meister Eckhart when he visited Diessenhofen concerning her mystical experiences, but she was reticent about letting the author of the *Sister Book* know anything of what he said to her. Anne did, however, reveal to the writer three special inner experiences before she died (132.107–133.129). The first was an identification with Christ in his passion; the second was her request of the risen Christ that he give her the power that the Father had granted to him over all things (see Matt. 28:18)! The third is more mysterious. One day in May as Anne gazed at the flowers and considered "how all things have flowed out from God and how every creature has received its being and life from God," she was given knowledge of "high incomprehensible matters" (*hohen vnbegrifflichen dingen* [132.116–27]). These revelations, which the author declines to describe, troubled her so much that after Anne's death she approached the mystic's relative, the Dominican Hugh of Stoffenberg, who assured the writer that he could find no error in what Anne had told him. This testifies that fourteenth-century suspicions about the orthodoxy of mystical visions had also entered the Dominican convents.

The longest life in *The Engenthal Sisters' Little Book of the Excess of Grace* is devoted to Sister Alheit of Trochaw, who is portrayed as an ecstatic, a seer— and a person not always easy to get along with. Some of the stories told about her have a humorous side that show that the *Sister Books* were meant to entertain as well as instruct.[181] As is common in this literature, Alheit has a great devotion to the passion, especially Christ's scourging. "She was raptured," says the account, "from Wednesday of Holy Week until Easter eve and saw all the things that our Lord underwent, and she perceived that when he was scourged at the pillar he began to bleed at the third stroke."[182] While she was still young, Christ appeared to her and promised that he would make her the greatest prioress that the convent had ever seen, but that this would mean depriving her of "my game" (*meins spils*), that is, the game of love. Alheit refused and underwent many trials from the convent authorities, including not being accepted into the community by one prioress because her father had contracted leprosy (often thought to be the result of personal sin).

Many of the stories about Alheit concentrate on her abilities as a seer to read the hearts of others (e.g., 14.25–32) and her at times humorous relations with her friend Friar Conrad of Eystet, who was the guardian of Engelthal (see 13.1–16 and 14.8–24). Alheit is described as receiving miraculous knowledge of books, at least for a time (13.29–31), as well as possessing the gift of being so totally rapt in love of God that she was without her "bodily senses" (*leiplich sinne*), even in the ordinary daily tasks of work, recreation, and the like (13.32–14.7). Along with these special graces, Alheit is sometimes depicted in comic fashion. For example, one day in choir she sang the verses of both choirs and the prioress upbraided her, "You are acting like a goose; sing in your choir and let the other one be." "Then," the account continues, "she fluttered her arms and imagined she was a goose until the prioress said, 'You are not a goose!'"[183] This story may be a topos about obedience, but the writer also characterizes it as an example of "unruliness" (*ungeperde*). Nevertheless, we are told little about the content and meaning of Alheit's visions; she appears as an object of wonder, even of amusement, more than as a teacher or guide.

In contrast to the rather folkloric and externalized portrait of Alheit, the account of Sophie of Klingenow in the *Sister Book* from Töss (roughly equivalent in length) is a remarkable exploration of an inner relation to God, containing a perceptive account of a prolonged mystical experience. Sophie entered the monastery after some time in the world, and her path to God reflects the serious sorrow for sin that was part of convent life, at least as an ideal. According to the *vita,* she spent an entire year in constant tears over her sins as preparation for the extraordinary tale of what took place on Christmas night after matins, which she revealed to another sister only on her deathbed.[184]

Sophie went alone into the chapel after matins and began to pray. She was overcome by remembrance of her sins to such an extent that she felt as if her heart had received a physical wound and that it would break in two.[185] She imagined a pit opening before her with a stake stretching from heaven down into the abyss upon which she would gladly be impaled until Judgment Day for the ways in which she had angered God. Her pain and disturbance were so great that she fainted three times. Afraid that the other sisters would find her, Sophie then offered an impassioned prayer to Christ confessing her complete sinfulness and managed to make her way back to the dormitory to go to sleep. Here, as she made the sign of the cross before retiring and dedicated herself to God with the versicle "Into your hands, O Lord, I commend my spirit," the nun's penance and spiritual death were suddenly transformed:

> Then I saw a light coming from heaven that was beautiful and wonderful beyond measure. It surrounded me and shone and blazed in me, through and through. My heart was totally altered and was filled with an unspeakable and unaccustomed joy, so that I completely forgot all the distress and pain that I had previously had.[186]

Sophie then underwent a series of mystical experiences that lasted for eight days (i.e., the Octave of the Feast of Christmas). During this extended rapture, she first experienced what today we would call an "out of body" experience, seeing her soul drawn out of her heart and exiting from her mouth so that she could look at it just as she saw things with her physical eyes (57.19–24). Prefacing the customary warning that no word can describe what she then beheld, Sophie went on to give a description of the nature of the soul and of its union with God. Pressed by her deathbed inquirer to say more, she described how the soul was created as a "completely spiritual being" (*gar gaistlich ding*) whose form is pure light like the sun that illuminates the whole world; but she also recounted how in seeing the light that was her soul she also was able to see God united with it:

And in this light that was my soul I saw God shining in a marvelous way, as a beautiful light shines out from a beautiful light-giving lamp. And I saw that he so fit himself in with my soul in love and goodness that he was truly united with her and her with him. And in this loving union my soul received assurance that all my sins were freely forgiven.[187]

This union with God transformed Sister Sophie into an effective intercessor for a soul in purgatory (58.9–17), and it also provided her with a series of vivid experiences during her out-of-body state. She first heard heavenly voices calling her upward to supernal joy, but then she descended to observe the lifeless and corruptible body she had left behind. Nevertheless, when her soul is reunited with her body ("How I know not"), for the following eight days she remained in ecstasy: "And when she returned to her body she was not deprived of this joyful vision, because while she was still dwelling in the body she beheld both herself and God so purely and truly that it were as if she had been raptured from the body."[188] During the eight days of this experience Sophie was filled with joy and enjoyed perfect health (like Adam in paradise). When God withdrew this mystical grace, "then she first discovered that she had a body" (*und do befand ich erst das ich ainen lib hat* [59.15]). Although the section devoted to Sophie in the Töss book contains several other tales of her experiences of divine consolations, these are footnotes to what is among the most detailed and interesting of all the mystical descriptions in the *Gnadenviten*. Although these books broke no new theological ground, the fascinating presentation of Sophie's eight-day ecstasy, as well as a number of other stories found in this literature, demonstrate that this new genre made its own contribution to the story the new mysticism.

The mysticism that flourished in the German Dominican convents in the first half of the fourteenth century left a second body of literature, autobiographical—or, better, autohagiographical—accounts of visions and other mystical experiences written down by individual ecstatics. These texts have similarities to the literature produced by the Cistercian nuns of Helfta in the last decade of the thirteenth century, but also differences involving not only language (the shift to the vernacular) but also modes of expression and content, as we shall see in what follows.

The most noted of these Dominican authors is Margaret Ebner (ca. 1291–1351), a nun of the convent of Maria Medingen. Although Maria Medingen did not produce a *Sister Book*, the kind of mystical piety found in these works is reflected in the *Revelations* that Margaret composed with the encouragement of her spiritual advisor and close friend, Henry of Nördlingen, recounting the special graces she received between 1312 and 1348.[189]

Margaret came from a patrician family of Donauwörth and entered the convent about 1305. The *Revelations* (not written down until 1344–1348) are one of the major autohagiographies of the fourteenth century. Margaret presents herself as a mediocre nun until she experienced a serious illness beginning in 1312. For three years, she "had no control over herself" (*daz ich min selbs ungeweltig was* [ed., 2.7]), laughing or crying continuously for days at a time. This illness, which lasted until 1315, was the occasion, even the stimulus, for her conversion to a deeper mystical life of devotion, as we have seen in the case of other Dominican nuns. Under the guidance of an older sister, she gradually learned to use the illness to teach her to depend on God alone. Even when she partially recovered, for the next thirteen years Margaret had to remain in bed for six months each year and she was subject to further bouts of sickness for the rest of her life. She is a good example of the growing number of ill, or invalid, mystics whose very sicknesses were part of the mystical favors they were given.[190]

Although Margaret's mystical life began about 1315, it was many years before she began to record her *Revelations* in a kind of mystical journal, or autohagiographical narrative. The impetus for this is to be found in a situation by now quite familiar to us—Margaret's intimate relation with a male spiritual advisor and friend, the secular priest Henry of Nördlingen. Henry remains a shadowy figure, despite his importance for the history of mysticism in the first half of the fourteenth century.[191] Margaret first met him on October 29, 1332, during one of his visits to Maria Medingen (ed., 16; trans., 93). She soon came to trust him totally as a "the most faithful friend of our Lord" (*aller getriwest friund unsers herren*), and "true friend of God" (*got sinem warhaften friund*), or "our Lord's friend and mine" (*friund unsers herren und min*). Although Henry's peripatetic life meant that he visited the convent only seven other times recorded in the *Revelations,* he was a constant presence for Margaret. The fifty-six letters he wrote to her (only one of hers to him survives) illustrate their deep devotion. While the priest may have begun as her confessor and guide, he soon recognized Margaret's special divine gifts and came to praise them in terms both affectionate and excessive.[192] Henry, in the manner of many clerics since the time of James of Vitry, came to see in Margaret a miracle of grace with a message for the whole church that he felt it was his vocation to communicate. As he put it in one letter: "God sent you to me once. I trust him, . . . that he wants to grant me and the whole church a special blessing from you and by you."[193] When she is drawn within herself to loving union with Christ, Henry knows that he and all created things must withdraw from her, but he is confident (employing a motif used by Bernard of Clairvaux) that Margaret's "chaste breasts will be full and overflowing, so they will not only be mine, your unworthy servant, but will also be sweet nourishment for the whole church."[194] Hence, it comes as no surprise that Henry—again like other clerics—was willing to speak of Margaret's writings as a "holy writing" (*hailig geschrift*), though he does not explore how its authority relates to the Bible.[195] If Margaret's *Revelations* have God as their direct source, they also have Henry as their instrument. It was he who convinced the nun to begin to write her account down, rather late in life.[196] The composition of the book, as with Marguerite d'Oingt, was itself an act of grace. "When I wished to write all this down," she says, "it was made present to me with the very same inner grace as when it had first happened."[197] Given their interchanges, by letter and during Henry's visits, he certainly had some hand in the text as it comes down to us—how much is difficult to know.[198]

Henry of Nördlingen needed the *Revelations,* it seems, for the same reason that he saw to the translation of Mechthild of Magdeburg's *Flowing Light of the Godhead* (which he also sent on to Margaret).[199] Henry was a central figure in a circle of pious south German clergy and laity who had been inspired to seek a higher life of devotion, and even mystical union, with God—the "Friends of God." For these devotees, vernacular accounts of special mystical graces, such as those of Mechthild, and even more a contemporary like Margaret, were proof that divine gifts were not the province of the few, or known only in the distant past, but were available to all Christians.

The denomination "friends of God" (*amici Dei/gottes vrunt*) is as old as Christianity, rooted in texts of the Old and New Testaments (e.g., Ps. 138:17, John 15:13–15). As a description for the devout, it had been employed for centuries.[200] In thirteenth- and fourteenth-century German-speaking lands, however, this general term seems to have acquired a more specific social connotation, describing actual circles of people who met together, conversed, prayed, and wrote each other about their desire for loving union with God. Even more amorphous than the early beguines, the "Friends of God" movement was, nevertheless, a force in the democratization of mysticism that has been one of the themes of this volume.[201] Mechthild's *Flowing Light,* as noted in the previous chapter (p. 223), already used the term in what seems to be a fairly concrete way to describe those interested in her teaching. In the case of Henry and Margaret, we not only have the numerous references to the "friends of God" contained in their texts, but we also have other proof of the existence and some of the members of these circles.[202] Thus, we can agree with Leonard Hindsley and Margot Schmidt that Henry's encouragement of Margaret's writing career had, as its main purpose, his desire "to acquire written testimony from an authentic source on the course of a rapturous spiritual life . . . in order to promote mysticism in the framework of his activity in the circle of the Friends of God."[203]

Margaret Ebner's *Revelations,* like the *Description* of Christina of Hane, is a day-book or journal that allows us to give precise dates for scores of ecstatic experiences.[204] Unlike the account of Christina, however, the *Revelations* takes us inside the mystic's consciousness in a manner that has few equals in its time. The literary art displayed in these first-person accounts of the presence of God gives the text a convincing appearance of actuality. For example, a year after the death of a sister who had been very close to her, Margaret visited her grave and then returned to church. She recounts:

> As I went into choir a sweet fragrance surrounded me and penetrated through my heart and into all my limbs and the name *Jesus Christus* was given to me so powerfully that I could pay attention to nothing else. And it seemed to me that I was really in his presence. I experienced such great grace that I could not pull myself away.[205]

This experience of being given the name of Jesus, as well as the overwhelming force of the divine action, is characteristic of the text.

Feeling the "presence of God"—especially in a totally embodied way—is one of the constant themes of the *Revelations.* Again a single case will have to suffice: the account of how Margaret experienced the presence of Jesus through devotion to a statue of the Christ child in the manger. In this incident Jesus demanded to be taken out of the manger and suckled by Margaret. When she complied and placed the image against her "naked heart," she received such a strong sense of the presence of God that she wondered how the Blessed Virgin could ever have endured it for long. Mary was given the aid of the Holy Spirit (Luke 1:35 is cited), "but my desire and my delight," Margaret says,

> are in the suckling through which I am purified by his pure humanity. I am set afire by the ardent love coming from him and am filled up by his presence and by his sweet grace so that I am drawn into the true enjoyment of his divine essence with all loving souls who have lived in the truth.[206]

Such embodied experience of the physical presence of Christ through a sacred image was not restricted to the divine infant. Margaret also recounts how she repeated this action with a "large crucifix," pressing it as hard as she could against her naked heart, so that she "received death spots on her heart and on my body" (*daz mir totmal werdent an minem herzen und an minem libe* [ed., 88.25–26]). This sensation of the divine presence also overpowered her–"Delight and desire are so strong and powerful in me that they strongly compel me, whether I wish it or not, and I cannot break off the whole time I suffer the divine presence with such powerful and sweet grace."[207]

The physical intensity of Margaret's experiences is yet more evidence for the embodied character of much of the mysticism of late medieval women. With Margaret the role of the senses in mystical experience even became a thematic issue. She tells us how the irresistibility of her experiences led her to wonder what was happening to her and to fear for her senses when the experiences grew especially strong. "But I was answered by the presence of God with sweet delight, 'I am no robber of the senses, I am the enlightener of the senses.'"[208] She says that Christ often used these words to her at other times when she feared for her senses.[209] Christ himself, then, assured the nun that the physical reaction to his visits was both appropriate and bearable, despite its ecstatic force.[210]

Margaret Ebner's mystical experiences of the Christ child and of Christ's passion, as well as her eucharistic ecstasies, were common to the other female mystics of her era. She desired to receive the stigmata, just as Francis had (ed., 46 and 78). Like other Dominican nuns, when she was at prayer before a crucifix, the image of Christ bent down "and let me kiss his open heart and gave me to drink of the blood flowing from his heart."[211] Like the nuns of Helfta, Margaret had a great devotion to the heart of Jesus; but she concentrates more on how *her* heart is wounded, pierced, and grasped in the love union than on creating a wealth of symbols to reveal the mysteries of the Divine Heart. These descriptions of the wounding, piercing, and embracing of her heart are interwoven with what is perhaps most characteristic of Margaret's experiences of Christ–the ongoing oscillation between times of "bound silence" (*gebundene swige*) and irresistible speaking, either of repeating the name of Jesus (*rede*) or of wordless "loud outcries" (*luten rüefe*).

On February 28, 1335, Margaret first experienced the "grasp of love in the heart" (*minnegrif in daz hertz* [ed., 28.18]) in which "the sweetest name of Jesus Christ was given to me with such great love that by the interior divine power of God I could pray only with continuous 'speaking'; I could not resist it."[212] This impelled the nun to repeat over and over again the name of Jesus even when she wanted to say her *Pater Noster* (a special doctrinal formula she used throughout her life),[213] or when she was supposed to join the community to recite the office. Sometimes this compulsive speaking (*rede*) brought great delight and sweetness, at other times pain. The experience of repetition of the name *Jesus Christus* with "loud speaking," sometimes "more than a thousand times," became frequent after that. But compulsive divine speaking is soon portrayed as alternating with a commitment to inner silence that goes far beyond the typical monastic practice of refraining from speech (ed., 45). Margaret initially seems to have chosen this commitment, as if she were attempting to find God through silence while he found her through ecstatic glossalalia; but soon the "binding silence," as she calls it, became just as irresistible as the loud repetition of the name of Jesus.[214] On Passion Sunday in 1339, for instance, Margaret has silence imposed on her during Mass until the Gospel of the passion is read, whereupon she breaks out into loud cries of, "Oh no! Oh no! My Lord Jesus Christ!" (ed., 50-51). Margaret also begins to speak of "being grasped by the usual silence" (*gefangen mit der gewonlichen swige* [ed., 89.15]), as well as being forced into "loud outcries" because of how she sees Christ's passion in her heart.[215] At one point in 1347, she even reflects on the four causes, or occasions, when the binding silence overcomes her before going on to give a detailed description of the physical paralysis which it involves:

> The binding silence came upon me with great pain every day at noon lasting until matins, so that I could not bear to place one hand upon the other, nor could I open my eyes. My teeth were closed shut and I could not make a fist with my hand.[216]

The stronger the binding silence, the more forceful the outcries when they arrive. During the week of Laetare Sunday in Lent of the same year, "The loud outcries commenced and lasted for a long time. And I exclaimed in a loud voice, 'Oh no! Oh no!' This screaming was so loud that it could be heard everywhere in the monastery and the courtyard."[217]

Both the binding silence and the loud cries were forms of sharing in the passion and both involved physically painful wounding of her heart. In this same Lenten outcry, for example, Margaret describes how the superhuman sounds she made seven times that day were the result of "strong thrusts" (*starken stössen*) hitting against her heart so forcefully that they harmed her insides and she swelled up like a pregnant women. These "strong thrusts" appear elsewhere in her accounts, as do the motifs of the "splitting heart" (*hercze zerspalten* [ed., 75.23]) and the wounding of her heart by a "sharp arrow" (*sagitta acuta* [ed., 131.17]). Margaret, then, is a prime witness for the mystical *transverberatio cordis,* known among other female mystics, both in the late medieval period and later.[218]

The suffering involved in these encounters with divine love is described mostly in terms of physical, somatic effects. In only one place does Margaret echo the inner spiritual suffering of estrangement from God that we have seen in Angela of Foligno and Mechthild of Magdeburg. On March 16,

1347, she experienced "loud outcries" ten times and became so ill that she could not respond with her usual speaking. "The same night, before matins," she says, "my Lord Jesus Christ placed me in such indescribable misery and a feeling of abandonment that it seemed as if I had never experienced the grace of our Lord in my whole life. I had completely lost trust in his mercy."[219] Margaret's experience of doubt, like the illness that marked the beginning of her mystical career, led her to deeper humility and the desire to suffer willingly and patiently for his sake alone. She goes on:

> He came like a friend after matins . . . and gave me his true help. . . . And in his holy suffering he gave me the sweetest delight and the greatest pain and the most incomparably severe sorrow. And his suffering was as present to me as if it had happened that day before my very own eyes. And then, compelled by the power of God working in me, I broke out crying in lamentation, . . . "Oh dear, my Lord Jesus Christ! Oh dear, my Lord Jesus Christ!"[220]

Other Dominican nuns of the south German houses also wrote of the experience of God's coming into their lives. Elsbeth Stagel (d. ca. 1360), who composed part of the Töss *Sister Book,* was a learned and skillful author. Because of her role in the production of Henry Suso's *Exemplar* she will be considered in the following volume. Two of her contemporaries left significant mystical writings, but because these are still unedited they will only be mentioned here.

Elsbeth of Oye (ca. 1290–1340) was a nun at Oetenbach, one of the south German convents that had produced a *Sister Book.* Peter Ochsenbein, who is at work on an edition of Elsbeth's text, *The Little Book of the Life and Revelation of Elsbeth of Oye* (*Puchlein des lebens und offenbarung Elsbethen von Oye*), has argued that this nun was original in joining the themes characteristic of Dominican women mystics, such as pictorial visions and concrete forms of sharing in the passion of Christ, with important motifs taken from the teaching of Meister Eckhart about the divine ground and the birth of the Word in the soul.[221] The publication of this text may well lead to qualifications concerning our current state of knowledge about the relationship between these two strands of Dominican mysticism in the fourteenth century.

The convent of Engelthal in many ways was a special center of the production of mystical texts among the female Dominican houses of the fourteenth century.[222] Christine Ebner (1277–1356)–no relative of Margaret Ebner–entered this house in 1289 and spent the remainder of her life there. We have already seen her as the author of *The Engelthal Sister's Little Book of the Excess of Grace* considered above, but she also composed two extensive accounts of her own mystical experiences. The first is a chronological description of her visions from 1344 to about 1351, one that, like the Helfta texts described earlier in this chapter and the *Sister Books,* concentrates on presenting the visionary within the context of the spiritual life of the entire community. Another manuscript, today in the library at Maria Medingen, contains an autohagiography, a *Grace-Life (Gnaden-Vita)* that began to be put in writing as early as 1317. These texts are now being edited by Ursula Peters.[223] Christine corresponded with John Tauler, and in 1338 she became acquainted with Henry of Nördlingen. Henry may have sent her Mechthild's *Flowing Light of the Godhead,* as he had to Margaret; we do know that he visited her in 1351 for a period of three weeks. In the absence of a critical edition, I will refrain from any substantive comments on the content of Christine's writings, but the discussions by Peters and Ringler indicate that they generally adhere to the major themes that we have seen in our investigation of the *Sister Books* and Margaret Ebner's *Revelations.*

The Engelthal literature also shows that however much the form of mysticism of the German Dominican nuns was primarily created by and for and about women, it was not restricted to them. This is not only because we must always remember the role of male confessors, advisors, editors, and spiritual friends in the production of these texts but also because of the autohagiography of Frederick Sunder (1254–1328), the secular priest who was chaplain at Engelthal for many years. Sunder's book, *The Grace-Life of Frederick Sunder, Chaplain of the Convent of Engelthal (Das Gnaden-Leben des Friedrich Sunder, Klosterkaplan zu Engelthal),* completed in 1351, has been published by Siegfried Ringler with an extensive commentary.[224] A detailed presentation cannot be pursued here. Suffice it to say that the work utilizes many of the mystical themes of the *Sister Books* and revelations of the other Dominican sisters of this creative era in the history of mysticism. Particularly significant is the way in which Sunder used highly erotic language to describe the encounters between his soul (feminine) and Jesus, the Divine Bridegroom.

Engelthal produced another mystical author, one whose life span goes beyond the chronological limits of this volume, but whose mystical *Revelations* were composed before 1350. Adelheid Langmann (1312–1375) was born into a noble family in Nuremberg and became a nun sometime between 1325 and 1330. She began the *Revelations* about 1330 at the request of an unnamed Dominican priest and continued to write until 1344.[225] In comparison with Margaret Ebner's book, this is the work of young nun writing over an extended period of time.

Adelheid's book is not well known, surviving in only three manuscripts. The *Revelations* is interesting from a literary point of view, especially because of its variety of genres—direct and rather naive visions, longer allegorical ones, moral exempla (e.g., the story of the knight Eberhard Schutz of Hohenstein in ed., 53–61), and even courtly dialogues (ed., 26–28). It is scarcely the most striking or profound of the texts produced by the south German Dominicans. In some ways, however, it can form a fitting conclusion to this chapter, because it reflects many of the best, as well as some of the worst, aspects of the mysticism of these monastic women. Above all, it is typical.

Among the less attractive features of the account is the concern with extreme asceticism (ed., 37, 53), as well as the celestial arithmetic by which Adelheid's prayers and sufferings are calculated to release hundreds of thousands of souls from purgatory.[226] The nun's visions are often naive and folkloric, as, for instance, the story of how Christ forces her into the monastery by making the Communion wafer stick in her mouth (ed., 2-3), or the account of the temptation by devils at the time of her monastic profession, who are routed by the appearance of an angelic orchestra.[227] Adelheid's mystical path is typical of the German Dominican women, from its close connection with illness (a five-year sickness in which she lay in "immeasurable suffering" is described in ed., 42–44) to the details of her auditions, visions, and forms of ecstasy. Many of her experiences are tied to reception of the Eucharist (e.g., visions of the Christ child when she receives Communion; see ed., 18–19, 33–35). One night she even experiences the infant Jesus sucking milk from her breast (ed., 66–67). Adelheid is equally devoted to Christ as the "Man of Sorrows"–he speaks to her from the cross (ed., 4, 7–8, 60–61); she kisses his five wounds (ed., 69–70), and also drinks from his side (ed., 68). She is also on familiar terms with the Trinity. Father, Son, and Holy Spirit visit her, speak with her, clothe her with virtues, and unite themselves with her (ed., 6–7, 15, 19–20, 30–32, 35, 50, 81). These encounters often involve lengthy ecstatic experiences, times when "she goes out of herself" (e.g., *si kam so gar von ir selben* [ed., 35.30– 36.1]), or when she is "drawn" (*gezogen/verzogen*) or "raptured" (*enzüket*) in God.

Adelheid's relation to Christ is a nuptial one centering on the hearts of the two lovers. She rests upon Christ's heart, as did John the Beloved (ed., 23 and 28); Christ writes his name on her heart (ed., 21–22), and he presses her into his heart (ed., 39, 67). Her spiritual friend, the Cistercian prior Ulrich of Kaisheim, receives a message from Christ declaring the exchange of hearts promised her–"I will pour my heart into her heart and her heart into my heart, and I will join them together and protect them both."[228] Adelheid knew the Song of Songs well and cites it in some of her descriptions of erotic union. For example, in one conversation Christ says to her: "'Sit down, my love, I will marry you.' And he said, 'My beloved, my darling, my beautiful, my love-sweet dear, honey is under your tongue' (Song 4:11)." In another place, he addresses her as "My sugarsweet and honey-sweet love, my darling, my pure one, you are mine and I am yours (see Song 2:16); we are united and shall be united forever."[229] It is interesting, however, that the most direct erotic language in the *Revelations* comes not from the nun herself, but from her friend Ulrich in a letter included in the text in which he describes the "love-play" (*minnenspil*) that she enjoys with her Divine Lover (ed., 93.11–36).

The spiritual friendship between the Dominican nun and the Cistercian monk also introduces us to one of the places in the *Revelations* that expresses an understanding of mystical union that involves a deep uniting in the Trinity and in the divine essence itself. Christ tells Adelheid that he has united her and Ulrich in the very unity of the Trinity (see John 17:21). "I have made you of one mind in the unanimity of the Holy Trinity; you will be given the gift of the Holy Trinity."[230] In two earlier places Adelheid used more Eckhartian language of being drawn into the depths of God. On March 25, 1334, for example, Adelheid went into ecstasy after receiving Communion and only returned to herself at midday. Christ tells her: "I want to tell you that I drew your soul away from all your limbs and all your powers and that it was raptured and drawn into the divine wilderness and into the desert of my Godhead."[231] In describing a later experience, similar language is combined with the nun's more usual nuptial themes. This lengthy erotic vision has the allegorical figures of Hope and Charity lead Adelheid to the consummation of her marriage to Christ. After a lengthy voyage through the events of salvation history, they finally place her on a bed where she sees her Lover approaching with a beauty a thousand times greater than she had imagined. As he kneels down beside the bed and turns his face toward her, he addresses her, "My Beloved!" (*mein geminte*). She continues:

> With the same word that so sweetly came out of his mouth, he drew my poor sinful soul into the Godhead–a vision that I can never talk about, save for the fact that I know very well that it began when compline was being sung and lasted until the next day when mass was sung.[232]

It was this kind of experience of divine love that led Adelheid to exclaim in gratitude in another place, "Oh, you living God, who could deserve something like this, if you did not give it from the freedom of love!" (*ach du lebentiger got, wer kond diseu dink verdinen, gebstu si niht von freier minne* [ed., 67.5–7]). This was something that all the women mystics studied in this chapter would have agreed with.

Postscript

T HE READER WHO HAS FOLLOWED this lengthy account deserves some form of summary of the new mysticism (as I have called it) that began about the year 1200. Unfortunately, as pointed out in the preface, these pages have not given the whole story, but only two-thirds of it. The last part dealing with another aspect of the new mysticism, the speculative search for God associated primarily with Meister Eckhart that appeared in the late thirteenth century, will be part of the next volume of *The Presence of God*. Still, a few words should be said in concluding.

Some of the figures surveyed here, especially Francis of Assisi, have always been central to the Christian tradition. For theologians at least, Bonaventure has also played a major role as one of the premier investigators of the meaning of Christian belief, not least concerning its goal of union with God. Of the many women studied in these pages only Clare of Assisi, and to a lesser extent Gertrude the Great, have enjoyed a constant reputation in later tradition. Many of the mystics and the texts of the new mysticism, even those once famous, faded from view after the medieval period. A number of them, like Marguerite Porete, have been resurrected only in this century. If mysticism, as has been claimed throughout this history, is an ongoing element within Western Christianity, it may seem that too much time and too many pages have been devoted here to mystics who did not have a major impact on this broad historical stream in the way that Augustine of Hippo, Gregory the Great, Bernard of Clairvaux, and others studied in the previous two volumes did. Further, it cannot be denied that some of the *vitae* and the other mystical texts discussed in this volume are strange, even bizarre, by the standards of sober theology and even of common sense. Trying to be fair to the intent of these texts does not mean that one has to approve of everything in their message or its effect in later centuries, as I have tried to suggest in a number of places. Given these limitations to the new mysticism, one may be again inclined to question how much attention it really deserves.

Historical theology is as much about the recovery of tradition as about the preservation of its sometimes faulty memory. A number of the mystics and mystical texts studied in this volume, such as the pseudo-Bonaventurean treatises, were so widely used for centuries in helping Christians to find God that to neglect their role would be to fail to do justice to important parts of the story of Western mysticism. While none of the texts about women, or written by them, attained a similar broad audience, we have seen how some female mystics achieved repute through their *vitae,* while others (against considerable odds) became noted teachers who produced works that were read, translated, and treasured by many. But it is not so much their past fame (or lack of it) that makes these texts worthy of investigation today. It is their content—what they still have to tell us about that loving, direct consciousness of God's presence that is the goal of the mystical life.

This volume has tried to show, as best it can, why many of these texts deserve to rank among the classics of Western mysticism and why they are a significant part of a tradition that is constantly renewing itself. If it invites contemporary seekers after God to find resources in the men and women whose conversations created the new mysticism, it will have more than fulfilled its task.

Notes

Preface

1. For a brief presentation of this case, see Bernard McGinn, "Mysticism," in *The Oxford Encyclopedia of the Reformation*, Hans J. Hillerbrand, Editor-in-Chief, 4 vols. (New York/Oxford: Oxford University Press, 1996), 3:119–24.

2. Without my intending it, the division between volumes 3 and 4 of *The Presence of God* has parallels to that adopted by Kurt Ruh in the second two volumes of his excellent *Geschichte der abendländische Mystik*. Ruh's second volume, *Frauenmystik und Franziskanische Mystik der Frühzeit* (Munich: Beck, 1993), treats many of the figures dealt with here, while his third volume, *Die Mystik des deutschen Predigerordens und ihre Grundlegung durch die Hochscholastik* (Munich: Beck, 1996), considers much of the third tradition, which will form the starting point of my next volume. Naturally, there are also significant differences in perspective, as well as in the case of some of the figures treated (e.g., I consider Thomas Gallus in this volume, because of his role in the formation of Franciscan mysticism, whereas Ruh treats him in his third volume).

3. To quote from *The Foundations of Mysticism:* "the mystical element of Christianity is that part of its beliefs and practices that concerns the preparation for, the consciousness of, and the reaction to what can be described as the immediate or direct presence of God" (p. xvii).

4. *Mechthild von Magdeburg 'Das fliessende Licht der Gottheit,'* ed. Hans Neumann, 2 vols. (Munich: Artemis, 1990), book 4, chap. 4 (1:117.7–8).

5. To be sure, this does not preclude ongoing discussion about how far some twelfth-century women, especially Hildegard of Bingen and Elisabeth of Schönau, briefly treated in *The Growth of Mysticism* (pp. 333–37), might or might not be accorded a more significant role.

6. See especially Bynum's seminal paper "Jesus as Mother and Abbot as Mother: Some Themes in Twelfth-Century Cistercian Writing," which was first published in the *Harvard Theological Review* in 1977 and was subsequently reissued in an expanded form in Bynum's *Jesus as Mother: Studies in the Spirituality of the High Middle Ages* (Berkeley/Los Angeles: University of California Press, 1982), pp. 110–69.

7. Again, the significance of hagiography cannot be restricted to the *vitae* of women, as the role of the lives of Francis alone indicates.

8. One of the first to recognize the importance of this literature for mysticism was Karl Bihlmeyer, "Die Selbstbiographie in der deutschen Mystik des Mittelalters," *Theologische Quartalschrift* 114 (1933): 504–44. The term was developed by Richard Kieckhefer, *Unquiet Souls: Fourteenth-Century Saints in Their Religious Milieu* (Chicago: University of Chicago Press, 1984), introduction; see also Kate Greenspan, "Autohagiography and Medieval Women's Spiritual Autobiography," in *Gender and Text in the Later Middle Ages*, ed. Jane Chance (Gainesville: University Press of Florida, 1996), pp. 217–36.

9. The point has recently been made by Amy Hollywood, *The Soul as Virgin Wife: Mechthild of Magdeburg, Marguerite Porete, and Meister Eckhart* (Notre Dame: University of Notre Dame Press, 1995), especially chap. 2.

10. Augustine, *Enarratio in Ps. 146* 11 (PL 37:1906).

Introduction

1. Ernst Kitzinger, *Early Medieval Art* (Bloomington/London: Indiana University Press, 1966), p. 16.

2. A classic study of the role of the twelfth century, broadly defined, in the formation of medieval culture is R. W. Southern, *The Making of the Middle Ages* (New Haven/London: Yale University Press, 1953). For a broader chronological perspective, see Robert Bartlett, *The Making of Europe: Conquest, Colonization and Cultural Change, 950–1350* (Princeton: Princeton University Press, 1993). On the early part of the period covered in this volume, see John H. Mundy, *Europe in the High Middle Ages, 1150–1309* (London: Longman, 1973).

3. There is no single work that provides an adequate introduction to the history of Christianity during the whole of the period covered in this volume (1200–1350). Though it begins closer to 1300, Francis Oakley's *The Western Church in the Later Middle Ages* (Ithaca: Cornell University Press, 1979) is a judicious survey, one that can be complemented by the rather different perspective found in Steven Ozment, *The Age of Reform, 1250–1550: An Intellectual and Religious History of Late Medieval and Reformation Europe* (New Haven: Yale University Press, 1980). On the general history of spirituality, we have the older survey of François Vandenbroucke, "New Milieux, New Problems from the Twelfth to the Sixteenth Centuries," in *The Spirituality of the Middle Ages*, ed. Jean Leclercq, François Vandenbroucke, and Louis Bouyer (New York: Seabury, 1982), pp. 221–543; and, more recently, the essays available in *Christian Spirituality II: High Middle Ages and Reformation*, ed. Jill Raitt in collaboration with Bernard McGinn and John Meyendorff (New York: Crossroad, 1987), as well as the recent survey of R. N. Swanson, *Religion and Devotion in Europe, c. 1215–c. 1515* (Cambridge: Cambridge University Press, 1995).

4. See Joseph R. Strayer, *On the Medieval Origins of the Modern State* (Princeton: Princeton University Press, 1970).

5. R. S. Lopez coined the term "commercial revolution" for this movement; see *The Commercial Revolution of the Middle Ages, 950–1350* (Cambridge: Cambridge University Press, 1976).

6. For an attempt to analyze these developments, see Bernard McGinn, *The Growth of Mysticism: Gregory the Great through the Twelfth Century* (New York: Crossroad, 1994), chap. 1.

7. On the development of the "new urban system," see Leonardo Benevolo, *The European City* (Oxford: Blackwell, 1995), chap. 2.

8. See the analysis of Lester K. Little, *Religious Poverty and the Profit Economy in Medieval Europe* (Ithaca: Cornell University Press, 1978).

9. For a brief characterization, see *Growth of Mysticism*, pp. 367–74.

10. See Gordon Leff, *Paris and Oxford Universities in the Thirteenth and Fourteenth Centuries* (London: John Wiley, 1968).

11. On medieval literacy in general, see M. B. Parkes, "The Literacy of the Laity," in *Literature and Western Civilization: The Medieval World*, ed. David Daiches and Anthony Thorlby (London: Aldus, 1973), pp. 555–77; Robert E. Lerner, "Literacy and Learning," in *One Thousand Years*, ed. Richard L. DeMolen (Boston: Houghton Mifflin, 1974), pp. 165–233; and Harvey J. Graff, *The Legacies of Literacy: Continuities and Contradictions in Western Culture and Society* (Bloomington: Indiana University Press, 1987), chaps. 3–4. There are important methodological observations in Franz H. Bäuml, "Varieties and Consequences of Medieval Literacy and Illiteracy," *Speculum* 55 (1980): 237–65.

12. Generally speaking, throughout the Middle Ages a *literatus* was a person who could read Latin. Hence, all who could read only the vernacular remained *illiterati*. M. B. Parkes suggests three kinds of medieval literacy–"that of the professional reader, which is the literacy of the scholar or the professional man of letters; that of the cultivated reader, which is the literacy of recreation; and that of the pragmatic reader, which is the literacy of one who has to read and write in the course of transacting any kind of business" ("Literacy of the Laity," p. 555). Only the first of these would be *literatus* in the medieval sense. Franz Bäuml, noting that the function of an "illiterate" person is different in a literate than a preliterate society, suggests a different division: "the fully literate, that of the individual who must rely on the literacy of another for access to written transmission [quasi-literate, as he calls them], and that of the illiterate without need or means of such reliance" ("Medieval Literacy and Illiteracy," p. 246).

13. Some helpful evidence for the growing literacy of women is to be found in Susan Groag Bell, "Medieval Women Book Owners: Arbiters of Lay Piety and Ambassadors of Popular Culture," in *Sisters and Workers in the Middle Ages*, ed. Judith M. Bennett et al. (Chicago: University of Chicago Press, 1989), pp. 135–61. According to her figures, of 242 laywomen identified as owning books before 1500, 75 percent of these owned books of piety (60 percent written in the vernacular). Some recent work on female literacy in late medieval England also suggests a larger percentage of reading women than previously suspected; see Anne Clark Bartlett, *Male Authors, Female Readers: Representation and Subjectivity in Middle English Devotional Literature* (Ithaca: Cornell University Press, 1995), chap. 1; and David Bell, *What Nuns Read: Books and Libraries in Medieval English Nunneries* (Kalamazoo: Cistercian Publications, 1995).

14. Parkes, "Literacy of the Laity," p. 572. According to Bäuml, "Beginning with the last half of the twelfth century, the increase of the use of writing in the vernacular, both for literary and documentary purposes, breached the link between literacy and Latin, and vernacular literature from the oral tradition made its appearance in written form" ("Medieval Literacy and Illiteracy," p. 244).

15. Beryl Smalley, "Ecclesiastical Attitudes to Novelty c. 1100–c. 1250," in *Church Society and Politics: Papers Read at the Thirteenth Summer Meeting and Fourteenth Winter Meeting of the Ecclesiastical History Society*, ed. Derek Baker (Oxford: Blackwell, 1975), p. 115.

16. For a brief survey, see Jane Sayers, *Innocent III: Leader of Europe 1198–1216* (London/New York: Longman, 1994).

17. For a survey of Innocent's attitude toward religious life, see Michele Maccarrone, "Riforma e sviluppo della vita religiosa con Innocenzo III," *Rivista della Storia della Chiesa in Italia* 16 (1962): 29–72.

18. Much has been written on the history of the term *vita apostolica* in the twelfth and thirteenth centuries. Classic accounts are two chapters in M.-D. Chenu, "Monks, Canons, and Laymen in Search of the Apostolic Life," and "The Evangelical Awakening," in *Nature, Man,*

and Society in the Twelfth Century (Chicago: University of Chicago Press, 1968), pp. 202–69; and Herbert Grundmann, *Religious Movements in the Middle Ages*, trans. Steven Rowan with an introduction by Robert E. Lerner (Notre Dame: University of Notre Dame Press, 1995), chaps. 1 and 2. On the role of the *vita apostolica* in twelfth-century reform, see also Giles Constable, *The Reformation of the Twelfth Century* (Cambridge: Cambridge University Press, 1996). On the history of the term, see L. M. Dewailly, "Notes sur l'histoire de l'adjectif 'apostolique,'" *Mélanges de science religieuse* 5 (1948): 141–52.

19. On the role of the laity, see André Vauchez, *The Laity in the Middle Ages: Religious Beliefs and Devotional Practices* (Notre Dame: University of Notre Dame Press, 1993), especially chaps. 7–8.

20. The key opening sentence of the Constitution *De novis religionibus prohibitis* demonstrates this negative attitude: Ne nimia religionum diversitas gravem in ecclesia Dei confusionem inducat, firmiter prohibemus, ne quis de caetero novam religionem inveniat, sed quicumque voluerit ad religionem converti, unam de approbatis assumat (see *Conciliorum Oecumenicorum Decreta*, curantibus Josepho Alberigo et al. [3rd ed.; Bologna: Istituto per le Scienze Religiose, 1973], p. 242). Subsequent history, as well as the necessity of repeating the prohibition at later councils, shows how controversial a decision it was.

21. Ernest W. McDonnell summarizes the three components of this understanding of the *vita apostolica* as: "imitation of the primitive church, poor, simple, and humble . . . , a passionate love for souls at home and far afield . . . , and finally, evangelical poverty and the common life, frequently mitigated, however, by the work of one's own hands" (*The Beguines and Beghards in Medieval Culture: With special reference on the Belgian scene* [New Brunswick: Rutgers University Press, 1954], p. 141).

22. See Bernold of Constance, *Chronicon* (PL 148:1407–8). The passage is discussed and translated in Chenu, *Nature, Man, and Society*, pp. 220–21.

23. Two useful general studies of this issue are R. I. Moore, *The Origins of European Dissent* (New York: St. Martin's Press, 1977); and Malcolm Lambert, *Medieval Heresy: Popular Movements from the Gregorian Reform to the Reformation* (2nd ed.; Oxford: Blackwell, 1992), part 2.

24. *Chronicon universale anonymi Laudunensis*, under 1177. I use the translation of Walter L. Wakefield and Austin P. Evans, *Heresies of the High Middle Ages* (New York: Columbia University Press, 1969), p. 202. This volume contains an excellent selection of the sources for Valdez (pp. 200–213). For a recent summary of Valdez and his followers, see Lambert, *Medieval Heresy*, chap. 5.

25. *Chronicon Laudunensis*, under 1177, as translated in *Heresies of the High Middle Ages*, p. 203.

26. Stephen of Bourbon, *Tractatus de diversis materialibus praedicabilis* IV.vii.342, as translated in *Heresies of the High Middle Ages*, p. 210.

27. *Dialogus duorum monachorum* 2.49, as edited by R. B. C. Huygens, "Le moine Idung et ses deux ouvrages: 'Argumentum super quatuor quaestionibus' et 'Dialogus duorum monachorum,'" *Studi Medievali*, 3a serie, 13 (1972): 430–31. There is a translation and discussion of this text in *Cistercians and Cluniacs: The Case for Cîteaux* (Kalamazoo: Cistercian Publications, 1977).

28. Chenu has a brief discussion (*Nature, Man, and Society*, pp. 259–61). For more detail on the issue of lay preaching, see Rolph Zerfass, *Die Streit um die Laienpredigt: Eine pastoralgeschichtliche Untersuchung zum Verständnis des Predigtamtes und zu seiner Entwicklung im 12. und 13. Jahrhundert* (Freiburg/Basel/Vienna: Herder, 1974).

29. For a brief sketch of religious poverty, see Chenu, *Nature, Man, and Society*, 240–46. An overview of the social context can be found in Karl Bosl, *Armut Christi: Ideal der Mönche und Ketzer, Ideologie der aufsteigenden Gesellschaftsschichten vom 11. bis 13. Jahrhundert* (Munich:

Bayerische Akademie der Wissenschaften. Philosophisch-historische Klasse, Jahrgang 1981, Heft 1). See also the various collections of essays on the topic, such as *La concezione della povertà nel Medioevo*, ed. Ovidio Capitani (Bologna: Pàtron Editore, 1974); and *Études sur l'histoire de la pauvreté*, ed. Michel Mollat, 2 vols. (Paris: Publications de la Sorbonne, 1974).

30. Chenu, *Nature, Man, and Society*, 242.

31. For a survey, see Leonard E. Boyle, "The Inter-Conciliar Period 1179–1215 and the Beginnings of the Pastoral Manuals," in *Miscellanea Rolando Bandinelli, Papa Alessandro III*, ed. Filippo Liotta (Siena: Accademia Senese degli Intronati, 1986), pp. 43–56.

32. See Beryl Smalley, *The Study of the Bible in the Middle Ages* (2nd ed.; Notre Dame: University of Notre Dame Press, 1964), chap. 5.

33. Peter Cantor, *Verbum abbreviatum* 62 and 65 (PL 205:191D–192A and 198A–199D). On Peter, see John W. Baldwin, *Masters, Princes and Merchants: The Social Views of Peter the Chanter and his Circle*, 2 vols. (Princeton: Princeton University Press, 1970).

34. Peter Cantor, *Verbum abbreviatum* 65 (PL 205:199c): Et respondit Alexander in vulgari suo dicens: Si scirem, "Bien jujar, et bien predicar, et penitense donar, je seroie boene pape." Et ita his tribus expressit totum officium prelati.

35. Richard Kieckhefer has observed that "the religious culture of the later Middle Ages was in large measure a preached culture" ("Major Currents in Late Medieval Devotion," in *Christian Spirituality II*, p. 77).

36. There is a growing literature devoted to the history of medieval preaching. For a general survey, see Jean Longère, *La prédication médiévale* (Paris: Études Augustiniennes, 1983). A major resource for the study of late medieval preaching is J. B. Schneyer, *Repertorium der lateinischen Sermones des Mittelalters für die Zeit von 1155–1350*, 9 vols. (Münster: Aschendorff, 1969–80).

37. C. A. Robson, *Maurice de Sully and the Medieval Vernacular Homily, with the Text of Maurice's French Homilies from a Sens Cathedral Chapter MS* (Oxford: Blackwell, 1952).

38. Alan of Lille, *Summa de arte praedicatoria*, praef. (PL 210:111). See *Alan of Lille: The Art of Preaching*, trans. Gillian R. Evans (Kalamazoo: Cistercian Publications, 1981).

39. *Summa de arte praedicatoria*, chap. 1 (PL 210:111D): Praedicatio est manifesta et publica instructio morum et fidei, informationi hominum deserviens, ex rationum semita, et auctoritatum fonte proveniens.

40. Concilium Lateranse IV, Constit. 10 (*Conciliorum Oecumenicorum Decreta*, 239–40): Inter caetera quae ad salutem spectant populi christiani, pabulum verbi Dei permaxime sibi noscitur esse necessarium, quia sicut corpus materiali sic anima spirituali cibo nutritur, eo quod *non in solo pane vivit homo, sed in omni verbo quod procedit de ore Dei* . . . Unde praecipimus tam in cathedralibus quam in aliis conventualibus ecclesiis viros idoneos ordinari, quos episcopi possint coadjutores et cooperatores habere, non solum in praedicationis officio verum etiam in audiendis confessionibus et poenitentiis iniungendis ac caeteris, quae ad salutem pertinent animarum.

41. The Dominicans were founded as an order of preachers (*ordo praedicatorum*). A good sense of the role of preaching in the Dominican life can be found in *Early Dominicans: Selected Writings*, ed. with an introduction by Simon Tugwell (New York: Paulist Press, 1982). On the debates over the image of the apostolic preacher at the time of the origins of the mendicants, see Roberto Rusconi, "'Forma apostolorum': l'immagine del predicatore nei movimenti religiosi francesi ed italiani dei secc. XII e XIII," *Cristianesimo nella Storia* 6 (1985): 513–42. For the Franciscans and preaching, see Zelina Zafarana, "La predicazione francescana," in *Francescanesimo e vita religiosa dei laici nel '200* (Assisi: Università degli Studi di Perugia, 1981), pp. 203–50; Roberto Rusconi, "La predicazione minoritica in Europa nei secoli XIII-XV," in *Francesco, Francescanesimo e la cultura della nuova Europa*, ed. Ignazio Baldelli and Angiola

Maria Romanini (Rome: Istituto della Enciclopedia Italiana, 1986), pp. 141–65. See also David L. d'Avry, *The Preaching of the Friars: Sermons diffused from Paris before 1300* (Oxford: Oxford University Press, 1985).

42. Lateran IV, Const. 1 (*Conciliorum Oecumenicorum Decreta,* 230).

43. For general observations, see J. C. Payen, "La Pénitence dans la contexte culturel des xiie et xiiie siècles," *Revue des sciences philosophiques et théologiques* 61 (1977): 399–428; Alexander Murray, "Confession as an historical source in the thirteenth century," in *The Writing of History in the Middle Ages: Essays presented to Richard William Southern,* ed. R. H. C. Davis and J. M. Wallace-Hadrill (Oxford: Clarendon Press, 1981), pp. 275–322; and Nicole Bériou, "Autour de Latran IV (1215): La naissance de la confession moderne et sa diffusion," in *Pratique de la confession: Des pères du désert à Vatican II. Quinze études d'histoire* (Paris: Cerf, 1983), pp. 73–93.

44. This is not the forum to enter into the debate over how far this positive aspect did or did not last throughout the Middle Ages. See especially Thomas N. Tentler, *Sin and Confession on the Eve of the Reformation* (Princeton: Princeton University Press, 1977).

45. *Alanus de Insulis: Liber poenitentialis,* ed. Jean Longère, 2 vols. (Louvain-Lille: Nauwelaerts, 1965).

46. For Franciscan attitudes toward the sacrament, see Roberto Rusconi, "I francescani e la confessione nel secolo XIII," in *Francescanesimo e vita religiosa dei laici nel '200,* pp. 251–309.

47. Miri Rubin, *Corpus Christi: The Eucharist in Late Medieval Culture* (Cambridge: Cambridge University Press, 1991), p. 348.

48. James F. McCue, "Liturgy and Eucharist: II, The West," *Christian Spirituality II,* p. 430. For a brief introduction to the development of the theology of the Eucharist, see Gary Macy, *The Banquet's Wisdom: A Short History of the Theologies of the Lord's Supper* (Mahwah, N.J.: Paulist Press, 1992).

49. See Caroline Walker Bynum, *Holy Feast and Holy Fast: The Religious Significance of Food to Medieval Women* (Berkeley/Los Angeles: University of California Press, 1987), especially chap. 5.

50. For the history of the feast, see Rubin, *Corpus Christi,* chaps. 3 and 4.

51. Richard Kieckhefer, "Major Currents in Late Medieval Devotion," in *Christian Spirituality II,* pp. 75–108. The quotation is from p. 75; see also his summary of the major trends on pp. 100–102. Still useful among older works is Louis Gougaud, *Devotional and Ascetic Practices in the Middle Ages* (London: Burns, Oates & Washbourne, 1927).

52. For introductions to these forms of devotion, see Ewert Cousins, "The Humanity and Passion of Christ," and Elizabeth A. Johnson, "Marian Devotion in the Western Church," in *Christian Spirituality II,* pp. 375–414.

53. Parts of this section have appeared as "The Changing Shape of Late Medieval Mysticism," *Church History* 65 (1996): 197–219. For further reflection on the role of visions, see also my forthcoming essay, "Visions and Critiques of Visions in Late Medieval Mysticism," in *Rending the Veil,* ed. Elliot R. Wolfson.

54. For Ambrose and Augustine on the universality of the call to mystical contact with God, see *Foundations of Mysticism,* pp. 211–13, and 255–57. For Gregory's views on the matter, see *Growth of Mysticism,* pp. 74–76.

55. Bernard of Clairvaux, *Sermones super Cantica* 83.1, as cited and discussed in *Growth of Mysticism,* pp. 181–82.

56. Obviously, flight from the world was always a highly ambiguous notion. Many of the great monastic mystics, such as Bernard, were deeply engaged in activities outside the cloister. My point is that they always saw such activity as constituting a barrier to the mystical quest.

57. *Vita B. Idae Lewensis* 1.6 (AA.SS. Oct. 29:109D).

58. For a brief review of this debate, see *Foundations of Mysticism,* pp. 277–81 and 288–90.

59. *Sacrum Commercium sancti Francisci cum domina Paupertate,* ed. Stefano Brufani (Assisi: Edizioni Porziuncola, 1990), chap. 30 (ed. 173): Illa vero, quietissimo somno ac sobria dormiens, surrexit festinanter, petens sibi claustrum ostendi. Adducentes eam in quodam colle ostenderunt ei totum orbem quem respicere poterant, dicentes: "Hoc est claustrum nostrum, domina."

60. *Sacrum Commercium,* chap. 31 (ed. 174): . . . ut visum sit mihi hodie esse vobiscum tamquam *in paradiso Dei.* . . . quoniam illis sum coniuncta in terris, qui mihi imaginem representant eius cui sum desponsata in celis.

61. Meister Eckhart, Predigt 5b, in *Meister Eckhart: Die deutschen und lateinischen Werke* (Stuttgart/Berlin: Kohlhammer, 1936–), *Deutsche Werke* 1:91.10–16. The translation is from *Meister Eckhart: The Essential Sermons, Commentaries, Treatises, and Defense,* translation and introduction by Edmund Colledge, O.S.A., and Bernard McGinn (New York: Paulist Press, 1981), p. 183.

62. Eckhart, Predigt 66 (*Deutsche Werke* 3:113–14). Translation from *Meister Eckhart: Sermons and Treatises,* trans. and ed. M. O'C. Walshe, 3 vols. (London/Dulverton: Watkins, 1981) 2:91.

63. Reiner Schürmann, *Meister Eckhart: Mystic and Philosopher* (Bloomington: Indiana University Press, 1978), pp. 15, 47, 109–10.

64. Karen Scott, "St. Catherine of Siena, 'Apostola,'" *Church History* 61 (1992): 34–46; and "Urban Spaces, Women's Networks, and the Lay Apostolate in the Siena of Catherine Benincasa," in *Creative Women in Medieval and Early Modern Italy: A Religious and Artistic Renaissance,* ed. E. Ann Matter and John Coakley (Philadelphia: University of Pennsylvania Press, 1994), 105–19.

65. Raymond of Capua, *Legenda Major Sanctae Catherinae* 2.6 (AA.SS. April 3:898D): Coepit enim Dominus ex tunc non tantum in locis secretis, ut prius consueverat, sed etiam in patentibus, palam et familiariter se ostendere sponsae suae, tam eunti quam stanti. . . .

66. See "Subject Indices," under "Contemplation (contemplation and action)" in *Foundations of Mysticism* and *Growth of Mysticism.*

67. See the discussion of Hildegard of Bingen and *A Teaching of the Loving Knowledge of God* in *Growth of Mysticism,* pp. 333–36 and 347–52.

68. Many recent studies and anthologies have uncovered much about the role of women writers in the Christian tradition. See especially Peter Dronke, *Women Writers of the Middle Ages: A Critical Study of Texts from Perpetua (d. 203) to Marguerite Porete (d. 1310)* (Cambridge: Cambridge University Press, 1984); Elizabeth Alvida Petroff, *Medieval Women's Visionary Literature* (New York: Oxford University Press, 1986); and Elizabeth A. Clark, trans., *Women in the Early Church* (Collegeville, Minn.: Liturgical Press, 1990). For a bibliographical survey, see Andrew Kadel, *Matrology: A Bibliography of Writings by Christian Women from the First to the Fifteenth Centuries* (New York: Continuum, 1995).

69. The large and constantly growing literature on women's spirituality and mysticism in the later Middle Ages cannot be surveyed here. For the German-language realm, there is a helpful bibliography, though only of works up to 1980. See Gertrud Jaron Lewis, *Bibliographie zur deutschen Frauenmystik des Mittelalters: Mit ein Anhang zu Beatrijs van Nazareth und Hadewijch,* by Frank Willaert and Marie-José Govers (Berlin: Erich Schmidt, 1989). For Italy, see the bibliography in *Scrittrici mistiche italiane,* ed. Giovanni Pozzi and Claudio Leonardi (Genoa: Marietti, 1988), pp. 701–38. There is no comparable bibliography in English.

70. For all its many merits, Bynum's *Holy Feast and Holy Fast* seems to me at times to move from perceptive analysis of particular patterns to more questionable generalizations about the

differences between male and female spirituality and mysticism. See especially *Holy Feast and Holy Fast*, pp. 238–44 and 290–94, as discussed in my review in *History of Religions* 28 (1988): 90–92.

71. Bynum, "Religious Women in the Later Middle Ages," *Christian Spirituality II*, p. 137.

72. For an overview of thirteenth-century lives of female saints, see Michael Goodich, "The Contours of Female Piety in Later Medieval Hagiography," *Church History* 50 (1981): 20–32.

73. For an insightful illustration of the difference between a female mystic's own presentation of her message and its revision by a male advisor, see the analysis of the two forms of Beatrice of Nazareth's *Seuen manieren van minne* in Amy Hollywood's *The Soul as Virgin Wife*, pp. 29–37 (see also the discussion below, pp. 166–73).

74. E.g., Bynum, "Religious Women," pp. 136–37; and Rubin, *Corpus Christi*, p. 169.

75. For two overviews of the role of women in thirteenth-century religious movements, see Jean Leclercq, "Women's Monasticism in the 12th and 13th Centuries," *Greyfriars Review* 7 (1993): 167–92 (a paper first published in Italian in 1980, and one that deliberately excludes the Franciscan women); and Raoul Manselli, "La donna nella vita della chiesa tra duecento e trecento," in *Il movimento religiose femminile in Umbria nei secoli XIII–XIV*, ed. Roberto Rusconi (Florence: La Nuova Italia Editrice, 1984), pp. 243–55.

76. Kurt Ruh claims that the cooperation between Elisabeth of Schönau and her brother Ekbert in the 1160s provides the earliest example of the interchange between a female visionary and a male theologian that marks the new *Frauenmystik* (*Geschichte der abendländische Mystik* 2, p. 66). This is certainly true of the mode of interaction, though I do not consider their joint product, the *Libri Visionum*, an essentially mystical text, at least in the same sense as the thirteenth-century examples cited above. See *Growth of Mysticism*, p. 337.

77. Marguerite Yourcenar, *That Mighty Sculptor, Time* (New York: Noonday Press, 1992), p. 4.

78. *Leben und Offenbarungen der Wiener Begine Agnes Blannbekin (d. 1315)*, ed. and trans. by Peter Dinzelbacher and Renate Vogeler (Göppingen: Kümmerle, 1994). Chapter 127 (ed., 284) provides evidence for Agnes's literacy.

79. *Leben und Offenbarungen*, chap. 118 (ed., 262): Quadam die legeram ei quaedam beati Bernhardi super cantica, quomodo anima sponsa cunctis affectionibus renuncians aliis soli et tota incumbat amori. Hoc ipsa mente pertractans mirabatur, quomodo honori non intenderet, quia hoc etiam ex dictis beati Bernhardi habetur, quod deus, in quantum sponsus, non exigit nisi amari. Cumque ista mente volveret, audivit vocem intra se dicentem sibi: "Anima devota in thalamo contemplationis ut sponsa non intendit nisi amori."

80. Danielle Régnier-Bohler, "Literary and Mystical Voices," in *A History of Women:* Vol. 2, *Silences of the Middle Ages*, ed. Christiane Klapisch-Zuber (Cambridge, Mass.: Belknap Press, 1992), pp. 447–48. Régnier-Bohler, of course, does not deny the specific character of women's voices. As she puts it, "They [women] aspired not to speak the language of men but a language that was at once less and more" (p. 466).

81. Fuller proof for this will emerge in the course of this volume. Here I only note that a number of recent studies have illustrated aspects of this conversation in diverse linguistic and historical contexts. For a general overview, see Ursula Peters, *Religiöse Erfahrung als literarisches Faktum: Zur Vorgeschichte und Genese frauenmystischer Texte des 13. und 14. Jahrhunderts* (Tübingen: Niemeyer, 1988), especially chap. 3; as well as her article "Vita religiosa und spirituelles Erleben: Frauenmystik und frauenmystische Literatur im 13. und 14. Jahrhundert," in *Deutsche Literatur von Frauen:* Erster Band, *Vom Mittelalter bis zum Ende des 18. Jahrhundert*, ed. Gisela Brinker-Gabler (Munich: Beck, 1987), pp. 88–109. For France, Nicole Bériou has shown how the sermons that Pierre Limoges gave to the Paris beguines were worked out together with the *magistra* of the house; see "Le prédication au béguinage de Paris pendant l'année liturgique

1272–73," *Recherches augustiniennes* 13 (1978): 105–229, especially pp. 121–22, 194. Miri Rubin has given a good description of the roles of women and men in Liège in the Low Countries in fostering the feast of Corpus Christi (*Corpus Christi,* pp. 164–76). With regard to Germany, John Coakley has published two studies on the cooperation between the friars and the *mulieres sanctae:* "Friars as Confidants of Holy Women in Medieval Dominican Hagiography," in *Images of Sainthood in Medieval Europe,* ed. Renate Blumenfeld-Kosinski and Timea Szell (Ithaca: Cornell University Press, 1991), pp. 222–46; and "Gender and the Authority of the Friars: The Significance of Holy Women for Thirteenth-Century Franciscans and Dominicans," *Church History* 60 (1991): 445–60. For Italy, see Katherine Gill, "Women and the Production of Religious Literature in the Vernacular, 1300–1500," in *Creative Women in Medieval and Early Modern Italy,* pp. 64–104.

82. On "reading" a picture as an essential part of medieval literacy, see Michael Camille, "Seeing and Reading: Some Implications of Medieval Literacy and Illiteracy," *Art History* 8 (1985): 26–49.

83. The importance of vernacularization, and especially the role of women in this, is no new discovery. Among the first to stress its significance was Herbert Grundmann, both in his *Religious Movements in the Middle Ages,* first published in 1935, and his essay, "Die Frauen und die Literatur im Mittelalter," *Archiv für Kulturgeschichte* 26 (1936): 129–61.

84. I am happy to acknowledge a debt here to the contrast suggested by Barbara Newman in her review article of *Growth of Mysticism,* published as "The Mozartian Moment: Reflections on Medieval Mysticism," *Christian Spirituality Bulletin* 3.1 (Spring 1995): 1–5.

85. See Bernard McGinn, "Meister Eckhart and the Beguines in the Context of Vernacular Theology," in *Meister Eckhart and the Beguine Mystics: Hadewijch of Brabant, Mechthild of Magdeburg, and Marguerite Porete,* ed. Bernard McGinn (New York: Continuum, 1994), pp. 4–14.

86. Erich Auerbach, "The Western Public and Its Language," in *Literary Language & Its Public in Late Latin Antiquity and in the Middle Ages* (New York: Pantheon, 1965), pp. 312–13.

87. Erich Auerbach, *Mimesis: The Representation of Reality in Western Literature* (Garden City, N.Y.: Doubleday, 1957), p. 134 (see also pp. 63–66). On the *sermo humilis* as characteristic of the Christian Middle Ages, see especially the essay *"Sermo Humilis,"* in *Literary Language and Its Public,* pp. 27–81.

88. For a survey of these genres, see *Growth of Mysticism,* pp. 367–74.

89. Of the large literature regarding hagiography, especially in the later Middle Ages, I cite only a few important studies. See especially André Vauchez, *Sainthood in the Later Middle Ages* (Cambridge: Cambridge University Press, 1997; French original edition, 1981). See also Donald Weinstein and Rudolph M. Bell, *Saints and Society: The Two Worlds of Western Christendom, 1000–1700* (Chicago: University of Chicago Press, 1982); *Images of Sainthood in Medieval Europe,* ed. Renate Blumenfeld-Kosinski and Timea Szell (Ithaca: Cornell University Press, 1991); and Michael E. Goodich, *Violence and Miracle in the Fourteenth Century: Private Grief and Public Salvation* (Chicago: University of Chicago Press, 1995). For the investigation of mystical saints, see, e.g., Richard Kieckhefer, *Unquiet Souls;* Aviad M. Kleinberg, *Prophets in Their Own Country: Living Saints and the Making of Sainthood in the Later Middle Ages* (Chicago: University of Chicago Press, 1992); and Peter Dinzelbacher, *Heilige oder Hexen? Schicksale auffälliger Frauen in mittelalter und Frühneuzeit* (Zurich: Artemis & Winkler, 1995).

90. I borrow the term from Kieckhefer, *Unquiet Souls,* p. 6. See also Frank Tobin, "Introduction," in *Henry Suso: The Exemplar, with Two German Sermons* (Mahwah, N.J.: Paulist Press, 1989), pp. 38–50.

91. For the influence of courtly motifs on thirteenth-century women, see, e.g., Julius Schwietering, *Mystik und Höfische Dichtung im Mittelalter* (Tübingen: Max Niemeyer, 1960); Elizabeth Wainwright-deKadt, "Courtly Literature and Mysticism: Some Aspects of Their

Interaction," *Acta Germanica* 12 (1980): 41–60; and the perceptive analysis of Barbara New-man, "*La mystique courtoise:* Thirteenth-Century Beguines and the Art of Love," in *From Virile Woman to WomanChrist: Studies in Medieval Religion and Literature* (Philadelphia: University of Pennsylvania Press, 1995), pp. 137–67.

92. On the sacral character of medieval Latin, especially liturgical Latin, see Christine Mohrmann, *Liturgical Latin: Its Origins and Character* (Washington, D.C.: Catholic University Press, 1957).

93. For the interaction between Latin and the vernacular literatures in the medieval period, a still insightful sketch is Auerbach's "The Western Public and Its Language," in *Literary Language and Its Public,* pp. 237–338.

94. On the importance of the religious element in the rise of the vernaculars to literary status, see Auerbach, "Western Public and Its Language," pp. 281–87. This has not been recognized by all medievalists. When a respected scholar of medieval literature can say of the new vernacular literatures that "their fields of reference remained predominantly secular" (Bäuml, "Varieties and Consequences of Medieval Literacy and Illiteracy," 263), one recognizes that vernacular theology has been as disregarded by literary students as it was by neoscholastic thinkers.

95. This tradition had been given legal force in Gratian's *Decretum,* dist. 23, can. 29: Mulier quamvis docta et sancta, viros in conventu docere non praesumat. Laicus autem praesentibus clericis (nisi ipsis rogantibus) docere non audeat.

96. Henry of Ghent, *Summa Quaestionum Ordinarium,* vol. 1 (Paris: Badius Ascensius, 1520; reprint, St. Bonaventure: Franciscan Institute, 1953), Art. XI, q. 11, f. 78r: Loquendo autem de docere ex beneficio et charitatis fervore, bene licet mulierem docere sicut et quemlibet alium si sanam doctrinam habeat. . . .

97. "Parla per carità e parlerai per teologia. Sensa grammatica se intende la Scriptura, cioè per uno certo lume di Dio. La grammatica non è altro se no uno lenguaggio." I cite from the text and translation found in Katherine Gill, "Women and the Production of Religious Literature in the Vernacular, 1300–1500," in *Creative Women in Medieval and Early Modern Italy,* p. 77.

98. Nicholas Watson, *Richard Rolle and the Invention of Authority* (Cambridge: Cambridge University Press, 1991).

99. See the analysis of Francis's style by Erich Auerbach in *Mimesis,* pp. 141–51, which concludes with the judgment: "It would perhaps be rash to maintain that Italian literature owed this freedom of dramatic expression to Saint Francis, for it was doubtless implicit in the character of the people; but it cannot be denied that, a great poet, an instinctive master of the art of acting out his own being, he was the first to awaken the dramatic powers of the Italian feeling and of the Italian language."

100. See the discussion by Catherine M. Mooney, "The Authorial Role of Brother A. in the Composition of Angela of Foligno's Revelations," in *Creative Women in Medieval and Early Modern Italy,* pp. 34–63.

101. On these two forms of Latin and their revival in the twelfth century, see Auerbach, "Western Public and Its Language," pp. 272–77.

102. Dante Alighieri, *Il Convivio,* ed. Maria Simonelli (Bologna: Pàtron, 1966). See the English version, *Dante's Il Convivio (The Banquet),* trans. Richard H. Lansing (New York/London: Garland, 1990).

103. *De vulgari eloquentia,* book 1, especially chaps. 16–19. See Warman Welliver, *Dante in Hell: The 'De Vulgari Eloquentia'. Introduction, Text, Translation, Commentary* (Ravenna: Longo Editore, 1981), pp. 78–87. Welliver's "Appendix A: Latin and Italian" (pp. 237–42) discusses the "complementary contradictions" (p. 238) of Dante's view of the relations between Latin and Italian.

104. Welliver, noting how in the *De vulgari eloquentia* Dante shades his language toward a "vulgar" Latin, while in the *Convivio* he adapts a latinizing form of Italian, asks: "Has not Dante balanced his sharp separation of the two languages in the argument and his consistent use of the wrong one by writing in a blend of both? A favorite theme and technique of the *stilnuovo* poet of love is the subtle combination and reconciliation of opposites" (p. 240)–also one of the dominant themes of mystical language.

105. Thus, I think that Kurt Ruh's claim that "Mystik . . . kommt erst in den Volkssprachen eigentlich zu sich selbst" (*Geschichte der abendländische Mystik*, 1:17; cf. 2:18–20) overemphasizes the role of the vernacular (see my review in *Journal of Religion* 74 [1994]: 94–96). Also questionable is Peter Dinzelbacher's use of the distinction between *Mystologie*, or reflection on mysticism, and the *Erlebnismystik* that represents the core of mysticism, as set forth in his *Christliche Mystik im Abendland: Ihrer Geschichte von den Anfängen bis zum Ende des Mittelalters* (Paderborn: Schöningh, 1994), pp. 9–22. Dinzelbacher's distinction leads to an unfortunate exclusion of key mystics from his account, as well as to confusion about the differences between mystical consciousness and visionary experience in general (see my review in *Cahiers de civilisation médiévale* 39 [1996]: 121–23). See also Dinzelbacher's essay "Zur Interpretation erlebnismystischer Texte des Mittelalters," *Zeitschrift für deutsches Altertum und deutsche Literatur* 117 (1988): 1–23.

106. In this context Seamus Heaney's recent remarks about tradition and change in poetry may be helpful. As Heaney puts it: "Writers have to start out as readers, and before they put pen to paper, even the most disaffected of them will have internalized the norms and forms of the tradition from which they wish to secede" (*The Redress of Poetry* [New York: Farrar, Straus & Giroux, 1995], p. 6).

107. See the discussion in *Growth of Mysticism, pp.* 166, 185–90, 192–93, 207–10, etc. Bernard asked his monks to compare what they found in the *liber experientiae* with what they read in the Bible. The subsequent shift toward giving the book of experience a preponderant role is evident, for example, in the prologue to the *Vita Venerabilis Beatricis,* who, according to her confessor and hagiographer, *totum in experientie libro legit et didicit.* See *The Life of Beatrice of Nazareth, 1200–1268,* trans. and annotated by Roger De Ganck (Kalamazoo: Cistercian Publications, 1991), p. 4.

108. See the treatments of Rupert and Joachim in *Growth of Mysticism,* pp. 328–33 and 337–41.

109. *Growth of Mysticism,* pp. 333–36.

110. See *The Life of Christina of Markyate: A Twelfth Century Recluse,* ed. C. H. Talbot (2nd ed.; Oxford: Clarendon Press, 1987), especially the visions of the Christ found on pp. 118, 154, and 168–70.

111. On the "bodily" character of these descriptions, see, e.g., Caroline Walker Bynum, *Fragmentation and Redemption: Essays on Gender and the Human Body in Medieval Religion* (New York: Zone Books, 1992), chaps. 3–7 (especially pp. 223–25); and her *The Resurrection of the Body in Western Christianity, 200–1336* (New York: Columbia University Press, 1995), pp. 182–83. For another analysis, see John Giles Milhaven, *Hadewijch and Her Sisters: Other Ways of Loving and Knowing* (Albany: State University of New York Press, 1993).

112. The negative evaluation of the new visionary mysticism associated with women is evident, for example, in Cuthbert Butler's *Western Mysticism* (New York: Dutton, 1923), pp. 179–92. For a collection of similar evaluations in German authors, see Dinzelbacher, "Zur Interpretation erlebnismystischer Texte," p. 7. To say that such texts should not be automatically dismissed as an inferior form of mysticism, of course, does not mean that one need refrain from all forms of judgment about their theological value. On this, see Ewert Cousins, "The Humanity and Passion of Christ," *Christian Spirituality II,* pp. 386–89.

113. On this point, see *Growth of Mysticism,* pp. 326–27.

114. Alois M. Haas, "Mystik als Theologie," *Zeitschrift für Katholische Theologie* 116 (1994): 48: "Es ist nicht Unsorgfalt, wenn die christlichen Mystiker die Unterscheidung zwischen mystischer Erfahrung und Deutung oder Lehre von dieser Erfahrung nicht machen wollen, sondern Absicht."

115. Antoine Vergote, *Guilt and Desire: Religious Attitudes and Their Pathological Derivative* (New Haven/London: Yale University Press, 1988), p. 180. Vergote begins his treatment of mystical visions with the reminder (often forgotten today): "It is not an accident that visions, which are properly speaking ecstatic phenomena, and mystical ecstasies are frequently confused." Vergote's approach is not unlike that taken by Karl Rahner, who wrote one of the few modern theological attempts to deal with the issue of visions. Rahner distinguishes between that contact with God that takes place in the core of the person and the modalities of its sense reception, insisting that "the imaginative vision . . . is only the radiation and reflex of contemplation in the sphere of the senses, the incarnation of the mystical process of the spirit" (*Visions and Prophecies* [London: Burns-Oates, 1963], p. 57).

116. See *Il Libro della Beata Angela da Folingo,* ed. Ludger Thier and Abele Calufetti (Grottaferrata: Collegii S. Bonaventurae ad Claras Aquas, 1985), e.g., Instructiones XIV and XXXI (564 and 660). Julian of Norwich, *A Book of Showings to the Anchoress Julian of Norwich,* ed. Edmund Colledge and James Walsh (Toronto: PIMS, 1978), Long Text, chap. 9 (vol. 2:321–22).

117. C. J. Holdsworth, "Visions and Visionaries in the Middle Ages," *History* 48 (1963): 144.

118. Peter Dinzelbacher terms the latter category *erlebte Visionen* (experienced visions); see his *Vision- und Visionsliteratur im Mittelalter* (Stuttgart: Hiersemann, 1981), which explores this distinction in chaps. 5–7. Dinzelbacher provides lists of both "Erlebte Visionen" (pp. 13–23) and "Literarische Visionen" (pp. 25–28). An updated version of the former list appears in Dinzelbacher's handbook *"Revelationes,"* Typologie des sources du moyen âge occidental 57 (Turnhout: Brepols, 1991), pp. 88–108.

119. Dinzelbacher, *Vision und Visionsliteratur,* p. 29, for a definition. See chaps. 12–16 for a detailed discussion.

120. In *De genesi ad litteram* 12, Augustine had distinguished three forms of visions—corporeal, spiritual (i.e., imaginative), and intellectual. See the discussion in *Foundations of Mysticism,* pp. 253–56. In his *In Apocalypsim* 1.1 (PL 196:686B–687C), Richard of St. Victor distinguished four types of visions: two external (corporeal vision, and seeing hidden signification in a bodily object); and two internal (divine interior illuminations in the likeness of visible things, and anagogic visions that raise one to divine contemplation without such likenesses).

121. For a psychological investigation of such mystical visions and their erotic content, see Vergote, *Guilt and Desire,* chaps. 7–9.

122. For an overview, see Frank Tobin, *Mechthild of Magdeburg: A Medieval Mystic in Modern Eyes* (Columbia, S.C.: Camden House, 1995), pp. 115–22.

123. Siegfried Ringler, *Viten- und Offenbarungsliteratur in Frauenklöstern des Mittelalters: Quellen und Studien* (Munich: Artemis, 1980), especially pp. 375–80.

124. Dinzelbacher, review of S. Ringler's *Viten- und Offenbarungsliteratur,* in *Anzeiger für deutsches Altertum und deutsche Literatur* 39 (1982): 63–71.

125. See especially Siegfried Ringler, "Die Rezeption mittelalterlicher Frauenmystik als wissenschaftlicher Problem, dargestellt am Werk der Christine Ebner," *Frauenmystik im Mittelalter,* ed. Peter Dinzelbacher and Dieter R. Bauer (Stuttgart: Bauernverlag, 1985), pp. 178–200.

126. Ringler, "Die Rezeption," p. 192: "'Wirklich' ist nicht nur das historische Substrat, das der literarischen Darstellung zugrunde liegt; wirklich ist oft in einem weit höheren Mass die literarische Darstellung selbst, und zwar auch in ihren fiktiven Teilen: insofern sie ein

Produkt geschichtlich wirksamer Kräfte ist, und vor allem, insofern sie selbst geschichtlich 'wirk-sam' wird."

127. Dinzelbacher, "Zur Interpretation erlebnismysticher Texte," p. 5: "Ohne das ihnen zugrundliegende Erleben aber wurde diese Textsorte nicht existieren!"

128. This point has been discussed in the recent Anglo-American debate between so-called constructivists and perennialists on the nature of mysticism. It is also reflected by some of the proponents of *Erlebnismystik* (e.g., Dinzelbacher, "Zur Interpretation," pp. 17–18).

129. Concilium Lateranse IV, Constit. 2 (*Conciliorum Oecumenicorum Decreta*, 232): . . . inter creatorem et creaturam non potest tanta similitudo notari, quin inter eos maior sit dissimilitudo notanda.

130. Bäuml, "Varieties and Consequences of Medieval Literacy and Illiteracy," p. 262, commenting on the new "realistic" tendency in post-Romanesque art and written vernacular narrative. In the same vein, note the comments of Roger Chartier in *Cultural History: Between Practices and Representations* (Ithaca: Cornell University Press, 1988): "It is clear from the outset that no text, even the most apparently documentary, even the most 'objective' . . . maintains a transparent relationship with the reality that it apprehends. . . . What is real, in fact, is not (or is not only) the reality that the text aims at, but the very manner in which it aims at it in the historic setting of its own production and the strategy used in its writing" (pp. 43–44).

131. Among the many theoretical discussions of this approach I note only the classic account of Hans-Georg Gadamer, "The Concept of Experience and the Essence of the Hermeneutical Experience," in *Truth and Method* (New York: Seabury, 1975), pp. 310–25.

132. Michael Camille, *Gothic Art: Glorious Visions* (New York: Harry M. Abrams, 1996), especially chap. 1. See also Barbara Nolan, *The Gothic Visionary Perspective* (Princeton: Princeton University Press, 1977) for the visionary perspective in literature.

133. Camille, *Gothic Art*, pp. 124–25.

134. For example, Felix Vernet, *Medieval Spirituality* (London/St. Louis: Sands & Herder, 1930), pp. 220–23. See also Ann Marie Caron, "Taste and See the Goodness of the Lord: Mechthild of Hackeborn," in *Hidden Springs: Cistercian Monastic Women*, ed. John A. Nichols and Lillian Thomas Shank (Kalamazoo: Cistercian Publications, 1995), book 2, pp. 512–13.

135. Gadamer, *Truth and Method*, p. 324.

Chapter 1

1. These connections have been noted before, e.g., by Alcantera Mens, *L'Ombrie italienne et l'Ombrie brabançonne: Deux courants religieux parallèles d'inspiration commune*, Études Franciscaines, Supplement 17 (Paris, 1967). See also Romana Guarnieri, "Beguines beyond the Alps and Italian Bizzoche between the 14th and 15th Centuries," *Greyfriars Review* 5 (1991): 93–104.

2. A somewhat similar picture of the role of men and women can also be seen in the beginnings of the Dominican order in Languedoc, though there was no central female figure in this case (see chap. 6, pp. 292–93 below).

3. The literature on the beguines, and the associated male beghards, is extensive. Two helpful introductions are Alcantara Mens, "Beghine, Begardi, Beghinaggi," DIP 1:1165–80; and Robert E. Lerner, "Beguines and Beghards," *Dictionary of the Middle Ages* (New York: Charles Scribner's Sons, 1982–89) 2:157–62. See also the brief survey in R. W. Southern, *Western Society and the Church in the Middle Ages* (Baltimore: Penguin, 1970), pp. 318–31. The most extensive account in English (still a mine of information despite its poor organization) remains that of Ernest W. McDonnell, *The Beguines and Beghards in Medieval Culture*, on which

see the important review of A. Mens, "Les béguines et les bégards dans le cadre de la culture médiévale," *Le moyen âge* 64 (1958): 303–15. Also of fundamental significance is A. Mens, *Oorsprong en betekenis van de Nederlandse begijnen-en begardenbeweging: Vergelijkende studie: XIIde-XIIIde eeuw*, Letteren en Schone Kunsten van Belgie. Klasse der Letteren, IX/7 (Antwerp: Verhandelingen van de Koninklijke Vlaamse Academie voor Wetenschappen, 1947). Among older works, see also Joseph Van Mierlo, "Béguinages," *Dictionnaire d'histoire et de géographie ecclesiastique* (Paris: Letouzey et Ané, 1912–) 7:457–73; Herbert Grundmann, *Religious Movements in the Middle Ages* (Notre Dame: University of Notre Dame Press, 1995), especially chap. 6; and Eva Gertrud Neumann, *Rheinisches Beginen- und Begardenwesen: Ein mainzer Beitrag zur religiösen Bewegung am Rhein*, Mainzer Abhandlungen zur mittleren und neueren Geschichte 4 (Meisenheim-am-Glan: 1960). In English, consult Brenda Bolton: "Mulieres Sanctae," in *Sanctity and Secularity: The Church and the World*, ed. Derek Baker (New York: Barnes & Noble, 1973), pp. 77–95; eadem, "*Vitae Matrum:* A Further Aspect of the *Frauenfrage*," in *Medieval Women*, ed. Derek Baker (Oxford: Blackwell, 1978), pp. 253–73; and "Some Thirteenth Century Women in the Low Countries: *A Special Case?*" *Nederlands Archief voor Kerkgeschiedenis* 61 (1981): 2–29. For more recent surveys of the *status quaestionis*, see Joanna E. Ziegler, "The *curtis* beguinage in the Southern Low Countries and art patronage: interpretation and historiography," *Bulletin de l'Institut historique Belge de Rome* 57 (1987): 31–70; and Walter Simons, "The Beguine Movement in the Southern Low Countries: A Reassessment," *Bulletin de l'Institut historique Belge de Rome* 59 (1989): 63–105.

4. These have been stressed by Carol Neel, "The Origins of the Beguines," in *Sisters and Workers in the Middle Ages*, ed. Judith M. Bennett et al. (Chicago: University of Chicago Press, 1989), pp. 240–60.

5. For a general sketch of the religious context of the world in which the beguine life came to birth, see Adriaan Bredero, "Religious Life in the Low Countries (ca. 1050–1384)," in *Christendom and Christianity in the Middle Ages* (Grand Rapids: Eerdmans, 1994), pp. 319–75. Despite historians' best efforts, there is still no agreement on the etymology of the term *beguina*. The most common view is that it is derived from *Al-bigen-ses*, the Latin for the Cathar heretics whom the new *mulieres religiosae* were accused of resembling. For a discussion, see Joseph Van Mierlo, "Béguine, béguines, béguinages," DS 1:1341–43. The Lowland and Rhineland beguines show considerable similarity to pious women living a free form of religious life in other parts of Europe, as James of Vitry noted in a sermon he preached to them (*Secundus Sermo ad Virgines*) probably in the 1230s: Sapientes autem Egypti, id est sapientes huius seculi, prelati scilicet seculares et alii maliciosi homines, volunt eam [the Beguine he is speaking of and using as an *exemplum*] interficere et a bono proposito retrahere dicentes: Hec vult esse Beguina–sic enim nominantur in Flandria et Brabancia–vel Papelarda–sic enim appellantur in Francia–vel Humiliata–sicut dicitur in Lumbardia–vel Bizoke–secundum quod dicitur in Ytalia–vel Coquennunne–ut dicitur in Theotonia; . . . (Joseph Greven, "Der Ursprung des Beginenwesens: Eine Auseinandersetzung mit Godefried Kurth," *Historisches Jahrbuch* 35 [1914]: 44–45).

6. See Simons, "Beguine Movement," pp. 68–78.

7. These four stages were first identified by L. J. M. Philippen, *De Begijnhoven, Oorsprong, geschiednis, inrichting* (Antwerp: n.p., 1918), pp. 40–126.

8. Simons, "Beguine Movement," pp. 85–92.

9. On Lambert, see the accounts in McDonnell, *Beguines and Beghards*, pp. 71–77 and 388–91; and R. I. Moore, *The Origins of European Dissent* (New York: St. Martin's Press, 1977), pp. 191–94. Most of what we know about him comes from his surviving letters, which are edited in Paul Fredericq, *Corpus Documentorum Inquisitionis Haereticae Pravitatis Neerlandicae*, 2 vols. (Gent: Vuylseke, 1889), 2:9–32.

10. On the geographic extent of the diocese of Liège, see Mens, *L'Ombrie italienne et l'Ombrie brabançonne*, pp. v–viii.

11. Alberic of Trois-Fontaines, *Chronica* (MGH.SS. 23:855): Nove religionis que fervet in Leodio et circa partes illas ferventissimus praedicator.

12. In this connection, it is worthwhile to quote one passage from Lambert's lengthy *apologia* contained in Document 16 in Fredericq's *Corpus Documentorum Inquisitionis* (30): Unde et ego, bonis eorum studiis cooperans, virginibus vitam et passionem beate Virginis et Christi matris agnitis, omnibus vero generaliter actus apostolorum rithmicis concrepantes modulis ad linguam sibi notiorem a Latina transfuderem, multis loco congruo insertis exhortationibus, ut videlicet haberent et diebus festis, mundo in rebus pessimis exultante, a venenanto ipsius melle sese revocare potuissent.

13. The essential source for Mary's life is James of Vitry's *Vita Beatae Mariae Oigniacensis* found in AA.SS. Junius 23:636–66 (here abbreviated as VMO and cited by book, chapter, section, and page in the AA.SS. edition). About 1230 the Dominican Thomas of Cantimpré wrote a *Supplementum* to this found in AA.SS. Junius 23:666–78 (abbreviated as VMOS and cited hereafter by chapter, section, and page). These have been translated in the series *Matrologia Latina* by Margot H. King and Hugh Feiss respectively, but I will use my own versions here. On the *Vita*, see especially Michel Lauwers, "Expérience Béguinale et récit hagiographique: A propos de la 'Vita Mariae Oigniacensis' de Jacques de Vitry (vers 1215)," *Journal des Savants* (année 1989): 61–103; and the same author's "Entre Beguinisme et Mysticisme: La Vie de Marie d'Oignies (d. 1213) de Jacques de Vitry ou la définition d'une sainteté féminine," *Ons geestelijk Erf* 66 (1992): 46–69. The most recent monograph on Mary is Iris Geyer, *Maria von Oignies: Eine hochmittelalterliche Mystikerin zwischen Ketzerei und Rechtgläubigkeit* (Frankfurt: Peter Lang, 1992). Most treatments of the beguines and studies of medieval mysticism contain discussions of Mary and her relation to James of Vitry. See especially McDonnell, *Beguines and Beghards*, pp. 8–58, 120–21, 149–50, and 237; Peter Dinzelbacher, *Christliche Mystik im Abendland*, pp. 199–200; Ursula Peters, *Religiöse Erfahrung als literarisches Faktum*, pp. 111–16; Kurt Ruh, *Geschichte*, 2:85–90. Part of the account that follows has already appeared in Bernard McGinn, "Marie d'Oignies and the New Mysticism," *Svensk Teologisk Kvartalskrift* 72 (1996): 97–109.

14. VMO 1.3.14 (640C): . . . imo sese pro Domino penitus abjicientes, leprosis quibusdam juxta Nivellam, in loco qui dicitur Willambroc, pro Domino aliquanto tempore servierunt.

15. VMO 1.6.19 (641C): . . . cum tanta contritione ostendebat se Sacerdoti, quod plerumque ex vehementi cordis anxietate, more parturientium cogebatur proclamare.

16. VMO 2.9.93 (661D): . . . frequentiam hominum, ad eam ex devotione concurrentium, quae soli Deo vacare cupiebat, jam non poterat sustinere.

17. VMOS 4.25 (675E): . . . in humili loco de Oignies inter oves Beghinarum, quas utique abhominantur Aegyptii. . . .

18. VMO 2.3.50 (650AC).

19. McDonnell gives a detailed account (*Beguines and Beghards*, pp. 8–19 and 40–58).

20. The most complete treatment of James of Vitry is that of Philipp Funk, *Jakob von Vitry: Leben und Werke* (Leipzig/Berlin: Teubner, 1909). See also McDonnell, *Beguines and Beghards*, pp. 20–39. There are modern editions of two of James's major works: *The Historia Occidentalis of Jacques de Vitry: A Critical Edition*, ed. John Frederick Hinnebusch, O.P., Spicilegium Friburgense 17 (Fribourg: University Press, 1972); and *Lettres de Jacques de Vitry (1160/1170–1240)*, *Eveque de Saint-Jean-d'Acre*, ed. R. B. C. Huygens (Leiden: Brill, 1960). There are no modern editions of his sermons or the *Vita Mariae Oigniacensis*.

21. This is the account given by Thomas of Cantimpré in VMOS 1.2 (667DE). Though it has been doubted by Funk (*Jakob von Vitry*, pp. 15–30), most authorities find Thomas's witness quite plausible (e.g., McDonnell, *Beguines and Beghards*, p. 22).

22. James describes how Mary was miraculously present in spirit during his ordination in Paris in VMO 2.7.86 (659AB). For Mary's greeting of the newly ordained James at his return, see VMOS 1 (667EF). There can be no question about James's tender devotion to Mary; see, for example, his touching description of the relics of her clothing that she gave him on her deathbed in 2.10.96 (662D).

23. VMO 2.8.79 (657BD).

24. VMO 2.11.101 (663D). See also 2.7.69 (654F–655A): . . . ut meritum et officium praedicationis quod in se actualiter exercere non poterat, in aliqua alia persona Dominus ei recompensaret: et quod sibi Dominus pro magno munere unum Praedicatorem daret.

25. On Fulk, see Brenda Bolton, "Fulk of Toulouse: The Escape that Failed," in *Church, Society and Politics,* ed. Derek Baker (Oxford: Blackwell, 1975), pp. 83–93. The background to Fulk's activities in Toulouse is described in John Hine Mundy, *Liberty and Political Power in Toulouse, 1050–1230* (New York: Columbia University Press, 1954), chap. 6.

26. See Christine Thouzellier, "La pauvreté, arme contre l'Albigéisme, en 1206," *Revue de l'histoire des religions* 151 (1957): 79–92.

27. The most complete account of the struggle against heresy in southern France during this time is Christine Thouzellier, *Catharisme et Valdéisme en Languedoc à la fin du XIIe et au début du XIIIe siècle* (2nd ed.; Louvain: Nauwelaerts, 1969). See also Walter L. Wakefield, *Heresy, Crusade and Inquisition in Southern France, 1100–1250* (Berkeley/Los Angeles: University of California Press, 1974).

28. VMO, Prol. 2 (636D): . . . et tandem usque in Episcopatum Leodii, quasi tractus odore et fama quorumdam, Deo in vera humilitate militantium, descendisset; non cessabat admirari fidem et devotionem, maxime sanctarum mulierum, quae summo desiderio et reverentia Christi Ecclesiam et sanctae Eccelsiae Sacramenta venerabantur: quae in partibus suis fere ab omnibus vel penitus abjiciebantur, vel parvipendebantur. For an account of Fulk's meeting with Mary, see 1.13.41 (647CD).

29. On the house at Prouille, see M.-H. Vicaire, O.P., *Saint Dominic and His Times* (New York: McGraw-Hill, 1964), pp. 115–36.

30. According to VMO 2.12.104 (664D), Fulk was present during Mary's final illness and said mass for her.

31. James's encomium begins with praise for the holiness of all the classes of women that Fulk had seen on his visit–virgins, widows, and married women (VMO, Prol. 3 [636E–637A]), but when he goes on to single out ten different individuals or groups of women (Prol. 6–8 [637D–638C]) he seems to have only the virgins in mind. Although these women are not named, some of them can be identified and will be treated below (e.g., Lutgard of Aywières and Christina of St. Trond; see pp. 160–66).

32. On the importance of Gregory's teaching on the seven gifts, see *Growth of Mysticism,* pp. 54–56; for other treatments of the gifts in the tradition, see pp. 349–50, 360, 396.

33. The antiheretical intent of the *vita* has been emphasized in recent research; see, e.g., Geyer, *Maria von Oignies,* pp. 221–24.

34. VMO Prol. 9 (638D): Licet autem tu diceris valde tibi et aliis multis esse commodum, si contra haereticos provinciae tuae, ea quae Deus in Sanctis modernis in diebus nostris operatur, in publicum posses praedicare. . . .

35. Prol. 9 (638C): Sed quid opus est in diversis diversas et mirabiles gratiarum varietates enarrare? cum in una pretiosa et praeexcellente margarita omnium fere gratiarum inveniam plenitudinem. . . .

36. VMO 1.7.22 (641F): Fervore enim spiritus quasi inebriata, prae dulcedine Agni Paschalis carnes suas fastidiens; frustra non modica cum cultello resecavit, quae prae verecundia in terra abscondit: et quia nimio amoris incendio inflammata carnis dolorem superavit, unum de Seraphin in hoc mentis excessu sibi adstantem aspexit. I take the *frustra* here

not in the classical sense of "vainly, mistakenly," but in the medieval sense of "with impunity, i.e., with no undesirable effect," as James of Vitry makes clear in the remainder of the passage. Though James does not recommend that others follow Mary's example, and even does not "commend her excess" (*Nec hoc dixero ut excessum commendam* [1.1.12 (639F)]), he ordinarily treats her unusual behavior as a mysterious and miraculous manifestation of divine power. For another story of Mary cutting herself, this time because of the sins of others, see 2.4.67 (654E).

37. The most detailed gathering of materials about such activity remains Herbert Thurston's *The Physical Phenomena of Mysticism* (Chicago: Henry Regnery, 1952). Thurston discusses Mary's fasting on pp. 332–34, but not her self-mutilation.

38. See especially VMOS 2.12 (670F–671B), where her mother, who has been damned because of usury, appears to the saint.

39. VMO 2.8.92 (661A): . . . hoc erat ei mori, quod ab hoc Sacramento diutius oportebat abstinendo separari.

40. VMO 1.8.25 (642DE): Aliquando etiam in suavi et beato silentio triginta quinque diebus cum Domino suaviter requiescens, nullo corporali usa est cibo, nullumque verbum per dies aliquot penitus proferre poterat, nisi istud solummodo: Volo Corpus Domini nostri Jesu Christi: quo recepto, in silentio suo singulis diebus cum Domino permanebat. Sentiebat autem in diebus illis spiritum suum, quasi a corpore separatum. . . . Sic enim a sensibilibus abstracta, et super se in quodam excessu rapta. Tandem vero post quinque hebdomadas ad se revertens, aperuit os suum: et mirantibus circumstantibus locuta est, cibumque corporalem recepit. This thirty-five-day fast was surpassed by the fifty-three-day period before her death when the only food she could receive was the Eucharist, as James and others tested by attempting to give her an unconsecrated host (2.12.105 [664EF]).

41. The role of food and fasting in late medieval women has been illuminated by Caroline Walker Bynum, *Holy Feast and Holy Fast*, especially chaps. 2–4 (on Mary on the other early beguines, see pp. 115–24). A different, and less successful, "anorexic" explanation of prolonged fasts by medieval women saints, appears in Rudolph M. Bell, *Holy Anorexia* (Chicago: University of Chicago Press, 1985).

42. See *Growth of Mysticism*, pp. 63–70, 190–93, and 208–13.

43. See VMO 1.5.16 (640DE) in relation to the passion of Christ; 1.6.20 (641D); 1.7.22 (641F), the flesh-cutting incident cited above; 1.8.24 (642D); 2.2.48 (649CE) using the theme of mystical inebriation from the Song of Songs (Song 2:4); and a series of texts from the latter part of book 2 now to be considered–2.4.63 (654AC); 2.7.81 (658AB); 2.8.87–88 (659D–660A); 2.8.90 (660CE); 2.10.95 (662AC); and the descriptions of her deathbed *iubilus* in 2.11.98–99 (662E–663C) and 2.12.107 (665DE). Several of these texts are discussed in Geyer, *Maria von Oignies*, chap. 8.

44. VMO 2.4.65 (654AB): Aliquando autem cum dulcius et suavius, quasi unus spiritus cum Domino facta, timoris glutino eidem Domino adhaereret. . . . Ipsa vero, audito extraneorum adventu, ne forte aliquem scandalizaret, a suavi illa contemplationis jucunditate, ab amplexibus Sponsi sui, vim sibimet inferens, spiritum suum tanto dolore avellebat; quod quandoque, quasi ruptis visceribus, sanguinem purum in magna quantitate evomebat vel conspuebat; malens hoc affligi martyrio, quam Fratrum, et maxime peregrinorum pacem turbare.

45. VMO 2.7.81 (658A): . . . dum volaret sublimius per diem integrum, . . . [non] reverberata radiis solis ad inferiora, solem justitiae velut aquila intuebatur. . . . [A]bsque omni phantasia vel imaginatione, formas simplices et divinas quasi in puro speculo suscipiebat in anima. The comparison of Mary to the eagle signifying contemplation uses the language of Gregory the Great (cf. *Hom. in Ez.* 1.4.2) On the mystical understanding of *suspendium*, see the teaching of Hugh of St. Victor, discussed in *Growth of Mysticism*, pp. 389–90.

46. VMOS 2.11 (670EF).

47. VMO 2.10.95 (662AC): . . . ex cordis plenitudine fere tota disrumpi videbatur in copore. . . . et quod mirabilius est, dum esset in illo mentis excessu, irreverberatis oculorum radiis, rotam solis materialis valebat intueri. . . . Cumque ad se revertens miraretur, quod vehementius solito supra se raperetur. . . .

48. For references to discussions by Gregory the Great and Richard of St. Victor, see *Growth of Mysticism*, pp. 64–65 and 413.

49. VMO 2.11.98 (662F): Incepit enim alta voce et clara cantare, nec cessavit spatio trium dierum et noctium Deum laudare, gratias agere. . . . The whole account occupies 2.11.98–101 (662E–663E).

50. On the history *iubilum/iubilus* from its roots in scripture through to the Reformation, see Herbert Grundmann, "Jubel," *Ausgewählte Aufsätze*, 3 vols. (2nd ed.; Stuttgart: Hierse-mann, 1978), 3:130–62. Grundmann notes that it was in the twelfth century that the term began to be used to indicate a subjective experience as well as an objective singing, noting the distinction introduced by Richard of St. Victor between the *iubilus oris* of the liturgy and the *iubilus cordis* of inner mystical experience (pp. 150–51). While not every use of *iubilus* need be thought of as a mystical grace, it is clear that James thought that Mary's deathbed song was a special gift from God.

51. VMO 2.11.99 (663B): Quaedam etiam de divinis Scripturis, novo et mirabili modo exponens; de Euangelio, de Psalmis, de novo et de veteri Testamento quae numquam audierat, multa et subtiliter disserens.

52. VMO 2.12.107 (665E): . . . dulci voce coepit Alleluia cantare: et fere tota nocte illa, quasi ad epulas invitata, fuit in jubilo et exultatione.

53. James's praise of her poverty is found especially in VMO 2.2.45–46 (648D–649B), where he uses some of the traditional biblical texts associated with the evangelical under-standing of the *vita apostolica* (e.g., Matt. 8:20; Luke 2:7), as well as the famous expression originating with Jerome, *ut nudum Christum nuda sequeretur* (648D). On this tag, which Bonaventure was to apply to St. Francis, see Matthäus Bernards, "Nudus nudum Christum sequi," *Wissenschaft und Weisheit* 14 (1951): 148–51; Réginald Grégoire, "L'adage ascétique 'Nudus nudum Christum sequi,'" in *Studi storici in onore de Ottorino Bertolini* (Pisa: Pacini, 1972), 1:395–409; and especially Jean Châtillon, "Nudum Christum Nudus Sequere: Note sur les origines et la signification du thème de la nudité spirituelle dans les écrits de Saint Bonaventure," in *S. Bonaventura. 1274–1974*, 5 vols. (Rome: Collegio S. Bonaventura, 1974) 4:719–72. The description of Mary's clothing and appearance in 1.11.37-13.39 (646A–647A) also emphasizes her poverty of life.

54. Key examples of her apostolic service through works of mercy are portrayed in the section devoted to her *spiritus pietatis* in VMO 2.3.50–63.

55. VMO 1.13.39 (646E): Capite inclinato vultuque in terram dimisso, tardo maturoque gressu humiliter incedebat. Adeo autem ex plenitudine cordis ejus in facie illius Spiritus sancti gratia resultabat, quod multi ex eius aspectu spiritualiter refecti ad devotionem et lacry-mas provocabantur; et in vultu ejus, quasi in libro unctionem Spiritus sancti legentes, vir-tutem ex ea procedere cognoscebant.

56. A number of passages speak of how Mary is instrumental in empowering others to learn divine truth by experience; see, e.g., 1.5.17 (640F–641A), 1.13.39 (647A), and VMOS 1.5 (668DF).

57. On her devotion to preachers, see, as noted above, 2.4.68–69 (654E–655A) and 2.6.79 (657CD). For comments, see Lauwers, "Entre Béguinisme," pp. 61–62 and 67–68.

58. For Mary's love for scripture, see VMO 2.4.71 (655BC), 2.6.76 (656E), 2.11.99 (663B), and 2.12.102 (664AB).

59. VMO 1.1.12 (639F): Nec hoc dixero ut excessum commendam, sed ut fervorem ostendam. In iis autem et multis aliis, quae privilegio gratiae operata est, attendat lector dis-

cretus, quod paucorum privilegia non faciunt legem communem. Ejus virtutes imitemur; opera vero virutum ejus, sine privato privilegio non possumus.

60. See VMO 2.4.66 (654CD), where James says of Mary's mode of action *rationem humanam ejus vita excederet* and she is described as fasting on Sunday and eating on Friday!

61. Parts of the following treatment of Francis have appeared in Bernard McGinn, "Was St. Francis a Mystic?" in *Doors of Understanding: Conversations on Global Spirituality in Honor of Ewert Cousins*, ed. Steven Chase (Quincy, Ill.: Franciscan Press, 1997), pp. 145–74. I wish to thank Paul Lachance for his valuable help in this section, not only in keeping me apprised of recent Franciscan scholarship, but especially for his insightful comments and suggestions.

62. For the passage in which James reports the Pope's approval, see Huygens, *Lettres de Jacques de Vitry*, 74.76–81.

63. VMOS 3.15–17 (672D–673C).

64. *The Historia Occidentalis of Jacques de Vitry*, chap. 11 (ed. Hinnebusch, 107.3–5): Singulis autem diebus status occidentalis ecclesie reformabatur in melius, et illuminabantur per uerbum domini qui diu sederant in tenebris et in umbra mortis.

65. *Historia Occidentalis*, chap. 32 (ed. Hinnebusch, 158.19–20): Hec est religio vere pauperum crucifixi et ordo predicatorum quos fratres minores appellamus. On James's witness to the early Franciscans, see R. B. C. Huygens, "Les passages des lettres de Jacques de Vitry rélatifs à S. François d'Assise et à ses premiers disciples," in *Hommages à Léon Herrman*, ed. R. B. C. Huygens (Brussels: Collection Latomus, 1960), pp. 446–53.

66. *Historia Occidentalis*, chap. 32 (ed. Hinnebusch, 161.13–162.2): Vidimus primum huius ordinis fundatorem et magistrum, cui tamquam summo priori suo omnes alii obediunt, uirum simplicem et illiteratum, dilectum deo et hominibus, fratrem Francinum [sic] nominatum, ad tantum ebrietatis excessum et feruorem spiritus raptum fuissse....

67. Few, if any figures in medieval religious history have had more written about them than Francis of Assisi. Regarding the life of the saint, a detailed study can be found in Arnaldo Fortini, *Francis of Assisi* (New York: Crossroad, 1981; Italian original, 1959), but a more stimulating interpretation is that of Raoul Manselli, *St. Francis of Assisi* (Chicago: Franciscan Herald Press, 1988; Italian original, 1980). For a theological interpretation, see Leonardo Boff, *St. Francis: A Model for Human Liberation* (New York: Crossroad, 1982). Other works relating to Francis, especially as theologian, will be listed below.

68. For some recent discussions of the problems and perspectives on the historical Francis, see Luigi Pelligrini, "A Century Reading the Sources for the Life of Francis of Assisi," *Greyfriars Review* 7 (1993): 323–46; and Carlo Dolicini, "Francesco d'Assisi e la storiografia degli ultimi vent'anni: problemi di metodo," in *Frate Francesco d'Assisi: Atti del XXI Convegno internazionale* (Spoleto: Centro Italiano di Studi sull'alto Medioevo, 1994), pp. 3–35. For a recent survey of the issues, consult the studies in *Francesco d'Assisi e il primo secolo di storia francescana* (Turin: Einaudi, 1997). Contemporary scholarly investigation of Francis and the beginnings of the mendicants stretches back a generation, to the appearance in 1965 of the important revisionist work of Kajetan Esser available in English as *Origins of the Franciscan Order* (Chicago: Franciscan Herald Press, 1970). Among significant subsequent contributions, see especially Raoul Manselli, *NOS QUI CUM EO FUIMUS: Contributo alla questione francescana* (Rome: Istituto Storico dei Cappuccini, 1980); David Flood, *Francis of Assisi and the Franciscan Movement* (Quezon City, Philippines: FIA Publications, 1989); Giovanni Miccoli, *Francesco d'Assisi: Realtà e memoria di un'esperienza cristiana* (Turin: Einaudi, 1991); and Thaddée Matura, *François d'Assise: Auteur spirituel. Le message de ses écrits* (Paris: Cerf, 1996; Eng. trans., *Francis of Assisi: The Message in His Writings* [St. Bonaventure: Franciscan Institute, 1997]).

69. The century of confusion about the sources relating to the saint has only recently been put on firm (if not uncontested) ground by the publication of the massive volume *Fontes Franciscani*, ed. Enrico Menestò, Stefano Brufani et al. (Assisi: Edizioni Porziuncola, 1995), which

includes the latest critical editions of the writings of Francis and Clare, as well as editions of all the early materials about them (in over 2500 pages!). For initial reactions, see Felice Accrocca, "Nodi problematici delle fonti francescane a proposito di due recenti edizioni," *Collectanea Francescana* 6 (1996): 563–96. In this chapter and the next I shall cite Francis's authentic works according to this edition. The best English translation of Francis's writings (from an earlier but not substantially different edition) is by Regis J. Armstrong in *Francis and Clare: The Complete Works* (New York: Paulist Press, 1982), though I shall use my own translations unless otherwise noted. Most of the texts relating to Francis (also translated from earlier editions) are available in *St. Francis of Assisi: Writings and Early Biographies. English Omnibus of Sources for the Life of St. Francis,* ed. Marion A. Habig (Chicago: Franciscan Herald Press, 1983; a new edition is planned). Also important for research on the texts of Francis is the concordance to early Franciscan sources produced by Georges Mailleux, Jean-François Godet and Pierre Beguin, *Corpus des Sources Franciscaines,* 6 vols. (Louvain: Centre de Traitement Electronique des Documents del'Université de Louvain, 1974-87).

70. At the risk of some oversimplification, we can divide the major Franciscan sources concerning Francis (there were others produced outside the order) into two groups: the more-or-less official lives written at the behest of the Franciscan authorities; and the unofficial hagiographical collections of stories about Francis, especially those going back to his first companions (*nos qui cum eo fuimus*). A list of major texts of the two groups follows, along with the abbreviations used in the *Fontes Franciscani* that will also be employed here. All translations are my own unless otherwise noted.

A. Official Sources

1. Thomas of Celano, *Vita Prima s. Francisci* (1Cel; *Fontes,* pp. 275–424), written 1228–29.

2. Thomas of Celano, *Vita Secunda s. Francisci* (2Cel; *Fontes,* pp. 443–639), finished in 1247.

3. Thomas of Celano, *Tractatus de miraculis b. Francisci* (3Cel; *Fontes,* pp. 643–754), written about 1250–53.

4. St. Bonaventure, *Legenda major s. Francisci* (1Bon; *Fontes,* pp. 777–961), written 1260–63.

5. St. Bonaventure, *Legenda minor s. Francisci* (2Bon; *Fontes,* pp. 965–1013), written ca. 1266.

B. Hagiographical Collections and Other Writings

1. *Sacrum Commercium* (SCom; *Fontes,* pp. 1705–32), probably written in 1227 (though some argue it is later).

2. *Legenda trium sociorum* (3Soc; *Fontes,* pp. 1373–1445), based on the compilation of materials sent to the minister general Crescentius of Jesi in 1246, if the introductory letter is to be believed.

3. *Compilatio Assisiensis (Legenda Perusina)* (CAss; *Fontes,* pp. 1471–1690), sometimes called the *Scripta Leonis, Rufini et Angeli sociorum s. Francisci.* There is considerable debate about the relationship of this text to the preceding one.

4. *Speculum Perfectionis* (existing in two forms, the shorter 1Spe in *Fontes,* pp. 1745–1825; and the longer 2Spe in *Fontes,* pp. 1849–2053). This is a fourteenth-century document, but it uses earlier materials.

5. *Actus b. Francisci et sociorum eius* (Actus; *Fontes,* pp. 2085–2219). This was composed ca. 1330, mostly by Ugolino di Monte Santa Maria, and is the source of the popular Italian *Fioretti,* which dates to ca. 1375 (first printed in 1476).

71. *Testamentum* 1–4 (*Fontes,* pp. 227): Dominus ita dedit mihi fratri Francisco incipere faciendi poenitentiam: quia cum essem in peccatis nimis mihi videbatur amarum videre leprosos. Et ipse Dominus conduxit me inter illos et feci misericordiam cum illis. Et recedente me ab ipsis, id quod videbatur mihi amarum, conversum fuit mihi in dulcedinem animi et corporis; et postea parum steti et exivi de saeculo. I translate as literally as possible to try to give some flavor of Francis's own voice. For later hagiographical references to Francis and

lepers, see, e.g., 1Cel 17, 2Cel 9, CAss 64 and 3Soc 4.11. The standard abbreviations for Francis's own writings (over thirty in all) that will be used in the following account include (in alphabetical order): Adms (Admonitions); BLeo (Blessing for Brother Leo); CSol (Canticle of Brother Sun); ECle (Letter to the Clergy); 1EFi (First Version of Letter to Faithful); 2EFi (Second Version of Letter to Faithful); ELeo (Letter to Brother Leo); EMin (Letter to Minister); EOrd (Letter to Entire Order); ExhL (Exhortation to Praise of God); FOff (Office of the Passion); FoVi (Form of Life for Clare); LDei (Praises of God Most High); ReBu (*Regula Bullata*, or Later Rule); ReEr (Rule for Hermitages); RnBu (*Regula non Bullata*, or Earlier Rule); SVig (Salutation of Blessed Virgin Mary); SVit (Salutation of the Virtues); Test (Testament).

72. Manselli, *St. Francis of Assisi*, pp. 33–39, 52, 125. See also Flood, *Francis of Assisi and the Franciscan Movement*, pp. 28–32. For an analysis of the role of the Test as a summary of Francis's religious experience, see Giovanni Miccoli, "Francis of Assisi's Christian Proposal," *Greyfriars Review* 2 (1989): 132–42.

73. Francis died on October 4, 1226, and was canonized on July 16, 1228. Francis welcomed the title of "crazy man," as can be seen from a noted text in CAss 19 (*Fontes*, p. 1498): Et dixit Dominus michi, quod volebat, quod ego essem unus novellus pazzus in mundo.... Here *Il Poverello* joins himself with the ancient tradition of "fools for Christ sake" (see 1 Cor. 4:10), on which see François Vandenbroucke, "Fous pour le Christ," DS 5:752–70 (cc. 764–65 on Francis).

74. RnBu 1 begins: In nomine Patris et Filii et Spiritus Sancti! Haec est vita evangelii Jesu Christi, quam frater Franciscus petiit a domino papa concedi et confirmari sibi ... (*Fontes*, p. 185). Francis never used the popular term *vita apostolica*. See the discussion in Matura, *François d'Assise*, pp. 236–39.

75. It is precisely this note of witness *in the world* that underlines the significance of Francis for the new mysticism. Miccoli puts it well: "On the one hand, there is a way of being which is radically at odds with standards of the world. Yet at the same time, only by completely inserting ourselves into the world and accepting its many facets can we present a radically different alternative. The apparent contradiction can be overcome through a deeper understanding of Christ's Incarnation, which makes no sense except in the world where it takes place" ("Francis of Assisi's Christian Proposal," pp. 146–47). On the economic opposition of the early Franciscan *fraternitas* to the systems of domination in the world of Assisi and like-minded urban centers, see Flood, *Francis of Assisi and the Franciscan Movement*, chaps. 1-2.

76. 3Soc 5.13 (*Fontes*, p. 1386): Quam ingressus coepit orare ferventer coram quadam imagine Crucifixi, quae pie ac benigne locuta est ei dicens: "Francisce, nonne vides quod domus mea destruitur? Vade igitur et repara illam mihi." Et tremens ac stupens ait: "Libenter faciam, Domine." Intellexit enim de illa ecclesia sibi dici, quae prae nimia vetustate casum proximum minabatur (for parallel accounts, see 2Cel 10-11 and 1Bon 2.1). There is some question about how far the *Legenda trium sociorum* can be considered a primitive source, one reflecting the views of the saint's fellow citizens and his early companions, because its manuscript witness is late. Following Manselli, I take it as an important witness to early traditions, though obviously reflecting the fame of Francis after 1230. According to the theological interpretation found in 3Soc 5.14 (*Fontes*, p. 386), it was from this experience that Francis conceived his special devotion to Christ crucified that was to culminate in his reception of the stigmata: Ab illa itaque hora ita vulneratum et liquefactum est cor eius ad memoriam Dominicae passionis quod semper dum vixit stigmata Domini Iesu in corde suo portavit, sicut postea luculenter apparuit ex renovatione eorumdem stigmatum in corpore ipsius mirabiliter facta et clarissime demonstrata.

77. The classic accounts of Francis's struggle with his family and the scene with the bishop are 1Cel 10-15 and 1Bon 2.2-4. The phrase *nudus nudum sequi* was first applied to the whole order of *fratres minores* by James of Vitry in his *Historia Occidentalis*, chap. 32 (ed. Hinnebusch,

159.9–10). (We noted above how James had also used it of Mary of Oignies [see n. 53].) The expression was often used of Francis in hagiography, e.g., in an implied sense in 3Soc 7.22 (*Fontes*, p. 1395), as well as explicitly by Bonaventure in 1Bon 2.4 (*Fontes*, p. 790) and in his theological treatises.

78. For introductions to the rich literature on the subject, see "Érémitisme," DS 4:936–82; and especially *L'eremitismo in Occidente nei secoli XI e XII: Atti della seconda Settimana internazionale di studio* (Milan: Società editrice vita e pensiero, 1965).

79. See, e.g., 1Cel 71, 2Cel 59 and 94–95, 3Soc 3.8. On Franciscan eremitism, see Octavian Schmucki, "A Place of Solitude: An Essay on the External Circumstances of the Prayer Life of St. Francis of Assisi," *Greyfriars Review* 1 (1988): 77–132; and the papers collected in *Franciscan Solitude*, ed. by André Cirino and Josef Raischl (St. Bonaventure: Franciscan Institute, 1995). On the Franciscans and the tradition of the Desert Fathers, consult Jacques Paul, "L'érémitisme et la survivance de la spiritualité du désert chez les Franciscaines," in *La mystiques de désert dans l'Islam, le Judaisme et le Christianisme* (n.p.: Association des Amis de Sénanque, 1974), pp. 133–45.

80. For the ReEr see *Fontes*, pp. 215–16.

81. It cannot be denied that a certain tension remained in Francis's life between contemplative withdrawal and apostolic engagement. The issue surfaces in later theological treatments, especially 1Bon 12.1.

82. 3Soc 8.25 (*Fontes*, p. 1398): . . . indicibili repletus gaudio: "Hoc, inquit, est quod cupio totis viribus adimplere." For parallels, see 1Cel 22 and 1Bon 3.1.

83. 3Soc 8.25 (*Fontes*, pp. 1398–99): . . . coepit, instinctu divino, evangelicae perfectionis annunciator existere poenitentiamque simpliciter in publicum praedicare.

84. The most recent summary of the development of the early *fraternitas* is Luigi Pellegrini, "La prima *Fraternitas* francescana: una rilettura delle fonti," in *Frate Francesco d'Assisi*, pp. 37–70. See also Flood, *Francis of Assisi and the Franciscan Movement*, who emphasizes the corporate role of the *fraternitas* in developing the new way of life, a dimension often neglected in the hagiographical concentration on Francis himself.

85. The *sortes apostolicae* are recounted in only two of the sources, 3Soc 8.28–29; and 2Cel 10.15, possibly because other writers were embarrassed by the story.

86. Test 15 (*Fontes*, p. 228): Et postquam Dominus dedit mihi de fratribus, nemo ostendebat mihi, quid deberem facere, sed ipse Altissimus revelavit mihi, quod deberem vivere secundum formam sancti Evangelii.

87. Flood, *Francis of Assisi and the Franciscan Movement*, p. 21. Flood's analysis of RnBu 1–17 in the first two chapters of his book convincingly demonstrates the originality of the *fraternitas* as a challenge to the social injustice of the time.

88. On the importance of the concept of mission in Francis and his followers, see E. Randolph Daniel, *The Franciscan Concept of Mission in the High Middle Ages* (Lexington: University of Kentucky Press, 1975).

89. Test 10 (*Fontes*, p. 228): Et propter hoc facio, quia nihil video corporaliter in hoc saeculo de ipso altissimo Filio Dei, nisi sanctissimum corpus et sanctissimum sanguinem suum, quod ipsi recipiunt et ipsi soli aliis ministrant. The necessity for respect for the clergy occurs throughout Francis's writings, see, e.g., Adms 26, EOrd 14–25, 2 EFi 22 and 32–36, RnBu 17 and 19.3, and ReBu 9 and 12.

90. For Francis's devotion to the Eucharist as one of the hallmarks of his spirituality, see, e.g., Adms 1.8–22; ECle; EOrd 12–22 and 26–37; 1EFi 1.3 and 2.1; 2EFi 22–36; and RnBu 20.5. His devotion is also stressed in the hagiographical sources, e.g., 2Spe 65. See the discussions in Manselli, *St. Francis of Assisi*, pp. 290–97 and 303–4; and Matura, *François d'Assise*, pp. 115–21 and 192–94.

91. 3Soc 12.51 (*Fontes*, p. 1424). On the importance of this permission, as well as Francis's relations with the hierarchy in general, see Roberto Rusconi, "*Clerici secundum alios clericos*: Francesco d'Assisi e l'istituzione ecclesiastica," in *Frate Francesco d'Assisi*, pp. 71–100.

92. Elements of this lost rule may survive in chap. 1 of the RnBu.

93. *Historia Occidentalis* 32 (ed. Hinnebusch, 158.13–15): Si tamen ecclesie primitiue statum et ordinem diligenter attendamus, non tam nouam addidit regulam quam ueterem renouauit. This was not a totally new idea. In the early twelfth century, Stephen of Muret had told his followers that they should describe themselves as belonging to the order of the Gospel (see M. D. Chenu, *Nature, Man, and Society in the Twelfth Century*,p. 239).

94. Considerable recent literature has been devoted to Clare and will be discussed below. Her own writings and the documents relating to her life can be found in the *Fontes Franciscani*, pp. 2223–2507, and are available in English in *Clare of Assisi: Early Documents*, ed. and trans. Regis J. Armstrong (New York: Paulist Press, 1988).

95. The story of Francis's prophecy in 1206 about the coming of the women to San Damiano, contained in some of the hagiographical literature (e.g., 3Soc 7.24), seems too good to be true, though it also appears in Clare's own *Testament*.

96. On the exclusion of women from the *fraternitas* itself, see RnBu 12. The statement with which Francis is supposed to have subsequently greeted the idea of having "sisters" (*sorores*) as a part of the structure of the order, though only found in late witnesses, has a ring of authenticity: "God has taken away our wives, and now the devil gives us sisters" (Dominus a nobis uxores abstulit, dyabolus autem nobis procurat sorores; see *Archivum Franciscanum Historicum* 12 [1919]: 383). On the complexity of Francis's view of the role of women in the developing Franciscan family, see Grundmann, *Religious Movements*, pp. 109–24 and 130–37; and Bolton, "*Mulieres Sanctae*," pp. 87–95. For a brief introduction to the origins of the female Franciscans, see John Moorman, *A History of the Franciscan Order: From its Origins to the Year 1517* (Oxford: Clarendon Press, 1968), pp. 32–39. For the wider picture of Francis's view of women, as well as their role in early Franciscanism, see Jacques Dalarun, *Francesco: un passagio: Donna e donne negli scritti e nelle legende di Francesco d'Assisi* (Rome: Viella, 1994).

97. *Legenda sanctae Clarae* 5 (*Fontes*, p. 2418): Hortatur eam pater Franciscus ad mundi contemptum: spem saeculi aridam et speciem deceptivam vivo sermone demonstrans: instillat auribus eius dulcia connubia Christi, suadens virginalis pudicitiae margaritam beato illi sponso, quem amor humanavit, fore servandam (using the translation of Regis Armstrong, *Clare of Assisi: Early Documents*, p. 194).

98. On the meaning of Francis's gesture, see Luigi Padovese, "Clare's Tonsure: Act of Consecration or Sign of Penance?" *Greyfriars Review* 6 (1992): 67–80.

99. James of Vitry, *Epistola* 1 (ed. Huygens, 75–76): Mulieres vero iuxta civitates in diversis hospiciis simul commorantur, nichil accipiunt, sed de labore manuum <suarum> vivunt, valde autem dolent et turbantur quod a clericis et laicis plus quam vellent honorantur. For a translation and discussion, see *Clare of Assisi: Early Documents*, pp. 245–46.

100. The "Privilege of Poverty" is translated in Armstrong, *Clare of Assisi: Early Documents*, pp. 83–84. See the discussion in Marco Bartoli, *Chiara d'Assisi* (Rome: Istituto Storico dei Cappuccini, 1989), chap. 3, especially pp. 99–100. (There is now an English translation of this work, *Clare of Assisi* [Quincy, Ill.: Franciscan Press, 1993].) The most recent discussion is that of Werner Maleczek, *Das 'Privilegium Paupertatis' Innocenz III. und das Testament der Klara von Assisi: Überlegungen zur Frage ihrer Echtheit* (Rome: Istituto storico dei Cappuccini, 1995)

101. This text, citing Francis's original FoVi, is from Clare's *Regula* 6.2–4 (*Fontes*, p. 2299): Attendens autem beatus pater quod nullam paupertatem, laborem, tribulationem, vilitatem et contemptum saeculi timeremus, immo pro magnis deliciis haberemus, pietate motus scripsit nobis formam vivendi in hunc modum: Quia divina inspiratione fecisti vos filias et ancillas altissimi summi Regis, Patris caelestis, et Spiritui Sancto vos desponsastis eligendo vivere

secundum perfectionem sancti Evangelii, volo et promitto per me et fratres meos semper habere de vobis tamquam de ipsis curam diligentem et sollicitudinem specialem. . . . Especially noteworthy here is Francis's use of the novel identification of the *dominae* as "espoused to the Holy Spirit," a term he had applied to Mary in the Marian antiphon in FOff, pars 1 (*Fontes,* p. 146).

102. On Francis's challenge to traditional social and religious divisions, see Manselli, *St. Francis of Assisi,* pp. 337–38; and especially Flood, *Francis of Assisi and the Franciscan Movement.* Nevertheless (and perhaps paradoxically), the movement begun by Francis has also been seen as a typical expression of the changing society of the time, as Jacques Le Goff has shown in "Franciscanisme et modèles culturels du XIIIe siècle," in *Francescanismo e vita religiosa dei laici nel'200: Atti dell'VIII Convegno Internazionale* (Assisi: Università degli Studi di Perugia, 1981), pp. 83–128, who summarizes: "Peu de mouvements religieux ont été mieux insérés que celui des Mineurs, . . . dans l'actualité profonde de leurs temps, s'adaptant à une societé nouvelle dans ses progrès comme dans ses refus . . . (p. 128).

103. For the text of these letters, see *Fontes,* pp. 73–86, and the translation in *Francis and Clare,* pp. 62–73. On the role of the penitents, see Flood, *Francis of Assisi and the Franciscan Order,* pp. 108–14. The history of the origins of the Third Order of the Franciscan family is murky to say the least. For an introduction, see Moorman, *A History of the Franciscan Order,* pp. 40–45; and, more recently, Octavian Schmucki, "The Third Order in the Biographies of St. Francis," *Greyfriars Review* 6 (1992): 81–107. For studies of the wider influence of Francis and the Franciscans on European society, besides the papers in *Francescanismo e vita religiosa dei laici nel'200,* see Etienne Delaruelle, "L'influence de Saint François d'Assise sur la piété populaire," in *Third International Congress of Historical Studies* (Florence, 1955), pp. 449–66; and Jacques Paul, "La signification sociale du franciscanisme," in *Mouvements Franciscains et Societé Française XIIe-XIIIe siècles,* ed. André Vauchez (Paris: Beauchesne, 1983), pp. 9–25.

104. This is the meditation on the mystery of Jesus found in 2 EFi 2-15 (*Fontes,* pp. 79–80). The other text is the trinitarian *credo* found in RnBu 23.1-6 (*Fontes,* pp. 209–10). For Matura's case for the centrality of these texts, see *François d'Assise,* part 1, chap. 2.

105. CAss 108 (*Fontes,* pp. 1656–57): . . . eligo provinciam Francie, in qua est catholica gens, maxime quia inter alios catholicos sancte Ecclesie reverentiam magnam exibent Corpori Christi: quod michi plurimum gratum est. Propter quod libentius cum illis conuersabor. For parallels, see 2Cel 201 and 2Spe 65.

106. On Francis's illnesses, see Octavian Schmucki, "The Illnesses of St. Francis before his Stigmatization," *Greyfriars Review* 4 (1990): 31–61.

107. For the text of these *regulae,* see *Fontes,* pp. 171–212; and the translation in *Francis and Clare,* pp. 107–45. For an introduction, see Octavian Schmucki, "Gli Scritti Legislativi di San Francesco," in *Approccio Storico-Critico alle Fonti Francescane* (Rome: Editiones Antonianum, 1979), pp. 73–98. For a study of the RnBu, see Flood, *Francis of Assisi and the Franciscan Movement.*

108. Manselli has nuanced, though scarcely final, discussions of this problem; see, e.g., *St. Francis of Assisi,* pp. 101, 176, 181, 198–99, 204–5, 272, 286, 311, 337–38, 345, and 361. See also Miccoli, "Francis of Assisi's Christian Proposal," pp. 153–61.

109. Francis's famous saying on "true joy" (*Fontes,* pp. 241–42) may reflect his frame of mind during this time of trial; see André Jansen, "The Story of True Joy: An Autobiographical Reading," *Greyfriars Review* 5 (1991): 367–87.

110. Test 39 (*Fontes,* 231): Sed sicut dedit mihi Dominus simpliciter et pure dicere et scribere regulam et ista verba, ita simpliciter et sine glossa intelligatis et cum sancta operatione observetis usque ad finem.

111. On being laid naked on the naked ground, see 2Cel 214 and 217, and 1Bon 14.3–4; and on the quasi-eucharistic supper, see 1Cel 110 and 2Cel 217.

112. 1Cel 112 (*Fontes,* p. 390): Resultabat revera in eo forma crucis et passionis Agni immaculati, qui lavit crimina mundi, dum quasi recenter e cruce depositus videretur. . . . Intuebantur namque carnem illius, quae nigra fuit prius, candore nimio renitentem, et ex sui pulchritudine beatae resurrectionis praemia pollicentem.

113. It is worthwhile distinguishing between the writings that belong to Francis as source (dictated and "written" in some form of collaboration with others) and those that actually come from the pen of Francis, who had rudimentary scribal training (another interesting aspect of the new vernacular theology). The most noted of the latter are the LDei and the BLeo. For observations, see Attilio Bartoli Langeli, "Gli Scritti da Francesco: L'autografia di un *illitteratus,*" in *Frate Francesco d'Assisi,* pp. 101–59.

114. For a survey of the ideological conflicts evident in the developing hagiographical portraits of the saint, see Roberto Lambertini and Andrea Tabarroni, *Dopo Francesco: l'Eredità difficile* (Turin: Edizioni Gruppo Abele, 1989). On the role of the hagiography in spreading Francis's reputation as a saint, see Aviad Kleinberg, *Prophets in their Own Country,* chap. 6. For observations on some theological aspects of the developing legend, see, e.g., Ewert Cousins, "Francis of Assisi and Bonaventure: Mysticism and Theological Interpretation," in *The Other Side of God: A Polarity in World Religion,* ed. Peter Berger (Garden City, N.Y.: Doubleday, Anchor, 1981), pp. 74–103; and Bernard McGinn, "The Influence of St. Francis on the Theology of the Middle Ages: The Testimony of St. Bonaventure," in *Bonaventuriana: Miscellanea in onore di Jacques Guy Bougerol, ofm,* ed. Francisco de Asis Chavero Blanco, 2 vols. (Rome: Edizioni Antonianum, 1988), 1:97–117.

115. Some of the hagiographical sources refer to Francis as a theologian, e.g., 2Cel 102 and 2Spe 53. Among the older discussions of Francis's theology, the most complete is Éphrem Longpré, "Frères mineurs: I, Saint François d'Assise," DS 5:1271–1303, which treats Francis's mysticism on 1292-1303. For recent approaches to his theology, see, e.g., Matura, *François d'Assise,* especially pp. 57, 139–43, and 273–75, as well the same author's "Introduction," in *François d'Assise: Écrits,* SC 285 (Paris: Cerf, 1981), pp. 49–81; and his article, "'Mi Pater Sancte': Dieu come père dans les écrits de François," in *L'esperienza di Dio in Francesco d'Assisi,* ed. Ettore Covi (Rome: Editrice Laurentianum, 1982), pp. 102–32. Other recent contributions of note include Octavian Schmucki, "Fundamental Characteristics of the Franciscan 'Form of Life,'" *Greyfriars Review* 3 (1991): 325–66; Norbert Nguyen-Van-Khanh, O.F.M., *The Teaching of His Heart: Jesus Christ in the Thought and Writings of St. Francis* (St. Bonaventure: Franciscan Institute, 1994; French original, 1984); Pierre Brunette, O.F.M., *Essai d'analyse symbolique des Admonitions de François d'Assise* (Montréal: Pontificia Universitas Gregoriana, 1989).

116. From the perspective of their mode of production, Francis's writings can be divided into two classes, twenty-seven "works" and seven "small dictated works." Most of the prior category, with the exception of the two versions of the *Regula* and the *Officium Passionis,* are quite short. Matura suggests a threefold division in terms of context: (1) works setting out the evangelical way of life; (2) prayers; and (3) letters (*François d'Assise,* pp. 26–35).

117. With regard to identifying Francis as a mystic *on the basis of his own writings alone,* I would agree with Matura (*François d'Assise,* p. 57), who puts it this way: "Tout en étant connu comme une parmi les plus grands figures de la sainteté chrétienne, François n'est jamais considéré ni comme mystique, ni comme théologien. Or, si ces deux mots sont compris dans leur sens originaire, utilisé à l'époque patristique: *mystique* est celui qui découvre et pénètre spirituellement le mystère de Dieu et de son oeuvre; *théologien,* celui que scrute et contemple la profondeur du réel visible et invisible, François est l'un et l'autre." My position here is different from that of Kurt Ruh, who argues (*Geschichte der abendländische Mystik,* 2:380) that while Francis never thought of himself as a mystic, the spirituality revealed in his writings must be understood on the basis of mystical experience. My claim is that we cannot penetrate to what

Francis chose not to speak of, but that we can show that what he did express and what was said about him became the basis for new forms of mystical expression.

118. On the differences between Francis's own writings and the hagiographical picture, even in the earliest strata, see the succinct remarks of Matura, "Introduction," in *François d'Assise*, pp. 80–81.

119. Matura, "Introduction," *Claire d'Assise: Écrits*, SC 325 (Paris: Cerf, 1985), p. 64.

120. For a summary, see Nguyên-Van-Khanh, *Teacher of His Heart*, pp. 78–89.

121. RnBu 23.9 (*Fontes*, p. 211): Nihil ergo aliquid aliud desideremus, nihil aliud velimus, nihil aliud placeat et delectet nos nisi Creator et Redemptor et Salvator noster, solus verus Deus, qui est plenum bonum, omne bonum, totum bonum, verum et summum bonum. . . .

122. E.g., BLeo 3; EOrd 1, 33, 52; 1 EFi 1.5–13; 2 EFi 48–62; RnBu 16.7, 21, and 23; SVig 2; Test 40. For a good summary of the trinitarian basis of Francis's theology, see Matura, *François d'Assise*, part 2, chap. 1.

123. For a study of these titles of Christ in Francis's writings, see Nguyên-Van-Kanh, *Teacher of His Heart*, chaps. 1–5.

124. Adms 7.4 (*Fontes*, p. 29): Et illi sunt vivificati a spiritu divinae litterae, qui omnem litteram, quam sciunt et cupiunt scire, non attribuunt corpori, sed verbo et exemplo reddunt ea altissimo Domino Deo, cuius est omne bonum. The importance of living in the Spirit as central for the Franciscan life appears in RnBu 17.14–16 and ReBu 10.8. For more on the *Spiritus Domini*, see, e.g., Adms 12.1, FoVi 1, EOrd 51, 2 EFi 48, RnBu 5, and SVig 6. Note also that 2Cel 193 testifies to Francis's conviction that it was the Holy Spirit who was the true minister general of the order. For surveys of Francis's teaching on the Holy Spirit, see Optatus Van Asseldonk, "The Spirit of the Lord and Its Holy Activity in the Writings of St. Francis," *Greyfriars Review* 5 (1991): 105–58; and Matura, *François d'Assise*, pp. 130–39.

125. Francis speaks not of "imitating Christ" but rather of "following Christ" (see Matt. 16:24; 19:21; and 1 Pet. 2:21), as is made clear in texts like Adms 6.2 (where the title *De Imitatione Domini* is a later addition), ELeo 3, EOrd 51, 2 EFi 13, FOff, RnBu 1.1 and 22.1. Of course, as Augustine once put it: "Quid est enim sequi nisi imitari?" (*De sancta virginitate* 27 [PL 40:411]).

126. 2EFi 49–53 (*Fontes*, p. 83): Et erunt filii Patris caelestis, cuius opera faciunt. Et sunt sponsi, fratres et matres Domini nostri Jesu Christi. Sponsi sumus, quando Spiritu Sancto coniungitur fidelis anima Jesu Christo. Fratres enim sumus, quando facimus voluntatem Patris eius, qui est in caelo; matres, quando portamus eum in corde et corpore nostro per amorem et puram et sinceram conscientiam; parturimus eum per sanctam operationem, quae lucere debet aliis in exemplum. A similar passage is found in 1EFi 1.5–10. The notion of being a living example to others appears both in the saint's own writings and in the stories about him (e.g., 2Spe 45 and 85).

127. Matura (*François d'Assise*, pp. 31, 45, 72, 83–85, and 125–27) cites this passage as "parmi les plus mystiques de François" (p. 31) and notes how it is immediately followed (2 EFi 54–60) by a passage expressing ecstatic joy that is rare in Francis's writings.

128. *Obedientia* and its forms occur fifty-nine times in his writings, while *pauper, paupertas* and the like occur thirty-three times. For Francis *obedientia* was more than just ecclesiastical deference to superiors; it was rather a fundamental commitment to the gospel as a way of life, one rooted in the Johannine conception of Christ's obedience to the Father. For key texts on obedience, see Adms 2.2–3; Adms 3; EOrd 10 and 36; 2 EFi 4–44; RnBu prol., 1.1, 2.9–10, 5.2 and 16–17; ReBu 1.1, 2; SVit 14–15; Test 25–28, 32–33, and 35–38. Important texts on poverty are to be found in ELeo 3; 2 EFi 5; RnBu 1.1, 2, 8–9, 14; ReBu 2, 4–6; SVit 11; Test 16–17 and 24. The literature on Francis's notion of poverty is extensive. There is a useful summary in Malcolm Lambert, *Franciscan Poverty* (London: SPCK, 1961), chaps. 1–2.

129. For a translation, see *Francis and Clare*, pp. 165–66. The theme of willingness to suffer for Christ in this text is close to Adms 5.

130. According to a story found in several later accounts (e.g., 2Spe 87), on his deathbed the saint left three commands to his brethren: love one another, love Lady Holy Poverty–and be faithful and submissive to prelates and the church.

131. For a review of such studies, see Octavian Schmucki, "The Mysticism of St. Francis in the Light of His Writings," *Greyfriars Review* 3 (1989; from the German original of 1986): 241–66, especially 241–46. A recent similarly undifferentiated approach is found in Dinzel-bacher, *Christliche Mystik im Abendland*, pp. 161–68.

132. See Ewert Cousins, "Francis of Assisi and Bonaventure"; as well as "Francis of Assisi: Christian Mysticism at the Crossroads," in *Mysticism and Religious Traditions*, ed. Steven T. Katz (Oxford/London: Oxford University Press, 1983), pp. 163–90; idem, "Francis of Assisi: Nature, Poverty, and the Humanity of Christ," in *Mystics of the Book: Themes, Topics, and Typologies*, edited with an Introduction by R. A. Herrera (New York: Peter Lang, 1993), pp. 203–17.

133. Schmucki, "Mysticism of St. Francis."

134. Ibid., 248–59. Ruh also stresses the importance of the indwelling theme in Francis's writings (*Geschichte der abendländische Mystik*, 2:382–83).

135. See the edition in *Fontes*, pp. 39–41. On the historical context of the CSol, see 1Cel 81; CAss 84; 2Spe 101, 118–20, and 123. The *Canticum* was meant to be sung, for Francis was devoted to music all his life. By composing this song in the vernacular, Francis seems to have intended it for a wider audience than the *fraternitas*–another argument for the new "democratized" mysticism.

136. Among the older studies, see Eloi Leclercq, *The Canticle of Creatures: Symbols of Union* (Chicago: Franciscan Herald Press, 1978). More recently, see Schmucki, "Mysticism of St. Francis," pp. 259–63; and Cousins, "Francis of Assisi and Bonaventure," pp. 79–88. An important recent interpretation is that of Giovanni Pozzi, "The Canticle of Brother Sun: From Grammar to Prayer," *Greyfriars Review* 4 (1992): 1–21 (Italian original, 1985). It is worth noting that aspects of the mystical meaning of the canticle may also be found in the BLeo (*Fontes*, pp. 45–48), which Francis composed on Monte Alverna, as well as in the ExhL and the *Laudes ad omnes horas dicendae* (*Fontes*, pp. 111–12 and 141–42).

137. The nature stories appear throughout the hagiographical texts, but there is a useful collection in 2Cel 165–71. On Francis's attitude toward nature, a good introduction can be found in Roger D. Sorrell, *St. Francis of Assisi and Nature: Tradition and Innovation in Western Christian Attitudes toward the Environment* (New York/Oxford: Oxford University Press, 1988), which treats the CSol in chaps. 5–7 (on "enfraternization," see pp. 127–30). Less successful is Edward A. Armstrong, *Saint Francis: Nature Mystic. The Derivation and Significance of the Nature Stories in the Franciscan Legend* (Berkeley/Los Angeles: University of California Press, 1973).

138. Much analysis has been given to the significance of praising God "with" (*cun*) and "through" (*per*) creatures, especially the various senses borne by the ambiguous particle *per*. Though the sun is given a certain priority, all the creatures mentioned (moon and stars, wind and related airy phenomena, water, fire, and mother earth) are associated with *both* modes of praise in strophe 3.

139. See Pozzi, "Canticle of Brother Sun," pp. 7–18, a number of whose insights are utilized in these comments. For other discussions, consult Schmucki, "Mysticism of St. Francis," pp. 260–61; Cousins, "Francis of Assisi and Bonaventure," pp. 85–88; and Sorrell, *St. Francis of Assisi*, pp. 118–24.

140. Schmucki notes that *frater* is the second most popular term in Francis's vocabulary (306 occurrences), second only to *dominus* (410 occurrences) ("The Mysticism of St. Francis," 262).

141. Richard Jeffries, *The Story of My Heart: My Autobiography*, the classic of this genre, was first published in 1883.

142. Augustine, *De civitate Dei* 22.29.6 (PL 41:800): ... sic nos esse visuros mundana tunc corpora coeli novi et terrae novae, ut Deum ubique praesentem et universa etiam corporalia gubernantem....

143. R. C. Zaehner, in his discussion of nature mysticism in *Mysticism Sacred and Profane* (New York: Oxford University Press, 1961), chaps. 3 and 4, does not mention Francis, probably because he wanted to see nature mysticism as restricted to panenhenic integration with the universe, and not as a possible form of theistic mysticism.

144. Pozzi, "Canticle of Brother Son," p. 21.

145. For Francis this reticence was not a matter of choice but one of command, as he expressed it in Adms 21.2 (*Fontes*, p. 34): Vae illi religioso, qui bona, quae Deus sibi ostendit, non retinet in corde suo et aliis non ostendit per operationem, sed sub specie mercedis magis hominibus verbis cupit ostendere.

146. 3Soc 2.4–6 (*Fontes*, pp. 1376–79).

147. Francis is often depicted in the hagiographical sources as being married to *Domina Paupertas*. See the discussion in Ruh, *Geschichte der abendländische Mystik*, 2:383–92.

148. 3Soc 3.7–4.11 (*Fontes*, pp. 1379–84).

149. 3Soc 5.13–14 (*Fontes*, pp. 1385–87). See p. 44 above.

150. These are: (1) a vision when Pope Innocent was approving the rule in which Francis sees himself as a "little poor woman in the desert" (3Soc 12.50); (2) a vision on the way back from the Roman encounter with the pope (12.53); and finally, (3) a dream given sometime in 1220 or later in which the saint sees himself as a "little black hen" (*gallina statura pusillus nigerque natura*) who needs to put his chicks under the protection of the Roman Church (16.63). The fascination of the author of the *Legenda* with dream visions is displayed also by his accounts of the confirmatory manifestations given to other figures in the narrative, such as the famous vision of Innocent III in which Francis upholds the collapsing Lateran basilica representing the contemporary state of the church (3Soc 12.51 [*Fontes*, pp. 1423–24]), and the vision of a *frater ... adhuc existens in saeculo* predicting the future glories of the church of the Portiuncula (13.56 [*Fontes*, pp. 1427–28]). The tendentious political character of some of these showings gives an indication of the difficulties facing modern scholars who try to extract the "real" Francis from the many sources that tell us about the *Franciscus legendus*.

151. For dream visions, see, e.g., 1Cel 5 and 33; 2Cel 6, 24, 82 (vision of Lady Poverty) and 209.

152. For a summary of the texts, see Octavian Schmucki, *The Stigmata of St. Francis of Assisi: A Critical Investigation in the Light of the Thirteenth-Century Sources* (St. Bonaventure: The Franciscan Institute, 1991), pp. 124–41.

153. 1Cel 26 (*Fontes*, p. 301): Raptus est deinde supra se, atque in quodam lumine totus absorptus, dilatato mentis sinu, quae futura erant luculenter inspexit. This ecstasy later appears in 1Bon 3.6. It is interesting to note that while Benedict's experience of the divine light described in Gregory the Great's *Dialogi* 2.35 (see *Growth of Mysticism*, pp. 71–74) provided him with a cosmological vision of the whole world, St. Francis's light vision gives him historical knowledge of the future of his order.

154. See, e.g., 2Cel 7, 9, 10 (the San Damiano incident), 27 (his spirit of prophecy), 95, 98 (an important summary text on his frequent ecstasies), 127 (a musical ecstasy), 158, 159, 178 and 213.

155. Cousins, "Francis of Assisi: Christian Mysticism at the Crossroads," pp. 166–69; and "Humanity and Passion of Christ," in *Christian Spirituality II*, pp. 381–86.

156. 1Cel 112 (*Fontes*, p. 390): ... revera in eo forma crucis et passionis Agni immaculati ...; and 1Cel 90 (*Fontes*, p. 366): ... salutaris evidentia documenta....

157. For the slogan "the proclaimer became the proclaimed," see Rudolf Bultmann, *Theology of the New Testament* (New York: Scribner, 1951), p. 33. The phrase *verus imitator et discipulus Salvatoris* is from SCom, prol. (*Fontes*, p. 1706). For more on this transition, see my article "The Influence of St. Francis on the Theology of the High Middle Ages," pp. 102–5.

158. In Adms 7 he counsels *religiosi* to "follow the spirit of the divine letter" (*spiritum divinae litterae... sequi*). On this basis, André Vauchez speaks of him as advising "une observance 'spirituellement' littérale" ("François d'Assise entre littéralisme évangelique et renouveau spirituel," in *Frate Francesco d'Assisi*, p. 194). Matura also questions the emphasis on Francis's literalism (*François d'Assise*, 218 and 264).

159. Cousins analyzes the mysticism of the historical event as follows—"one recalls a significant event in the past, enters into its drama and draws from it spiritual energy, eventually moving beyond the event to union with God" ("Francis of Assisi," p. 166). This is not, however, mere recalling, but a transcending of present time to enter into real unity with a past event (p. 167). The concept has been utilized by others, e.g., Giles Constable, "The Ideal of the Imitation of Christ," in *Three Studies in Medieval Religious and Social Thought* (Cambridge: Cambridge University Press, 1995), pp. 203ff.

160. On the Greccio Christmas crib, see 1Cel 84–87 (*Fontes*, pp. 359–63), which summarizes Francis's attitude by saying that his desire was "to recall Christ's words through persistent meditation and bring to mind his deeds through the most penetrating consideration" (*Recordabatur assidua meditatione verborum eius et sagacissima consideratione ispsius opera recolabat* [1Cel 84]). The Greccio incident also appears in 1Bon 10.7. Cousins notes the importance of the emphasis on the birth and death of Christ as central to devotion to the humanity of Christ—"because it is precisely birth and death that establish the historicity of the human situation" ("Humanity and Passion of Christ," p. 382).

161. These earlier developments have been discussed by Cousins, "Humanity and Passion of Christ," pp. 377–80; and especially by Giles Constable, *Three Studies*, pp. 194–217. For comments on this form of imitation as it relates to mysticism, see *Growth of Mysticism*, pp. 141–42, 174–77, 235, 315–16.

162. Matura, for example, believes that emphasis on reproducing the events of Christ's life is not the center of Francis's theology: "Il ressort de ces texts que 'suivre les traces du Christ' ne signifie pas, en premier lieu, reproduire les faits et les gestes de la vie terrestre de Jésus. Il s'agit plutôt de 'suivre' ou recevoir le globalité de l'Évangile..." (*François d'Assise*, p. 218; cf. pp. 104–6, 140).

163. A considerable literature has been devoted to Francis's stigmata and to the broader history of the phenomenon. For the general history of stigmata, see Thurston, *Physical Phenomena of Mysticism*, chap. 2; Pierre Adnès, "Stigmates," DS 14:1211–43; and F. A. Whitlock and J. V. Hynes, "Religious stigmatization: an historical and psychophysiological enquiry," *Psychological Medicine* 8 (1978): 185–202. On the wider phenomenon of imitation of the suffering body of Christ, including stigmata, see Giles Constable, "The Imitation of the Body of Christ" and "The Late Middle Ages," in *Three Studies*, pp. 194–248. The large literature on Francis's stigmata (at least 372 items published between 1850 and 1985), as well as the relevant sources, have been summarized in Schmucki's *Stigmata of St. Francis*, though not all will be convinced by his historical reconstruction. The most recent important survey is that of Chiara Frugoni, *Francesco e l'invenzione delle stimmate: Una storia per parole e immagini fino a Bonaventura e Giotto* (Turin: Einaudi, 1993). For a treatment of the stigmata in relation to Francis's claims as mystic, see Ruh, *Geschichte der abendländische Mystik*, 2:392–95.

164. This passage is not without its textual problems with some Vg manuscripts using *insuper* ("on") and many adding *Domini*. Related ideas are expressed in Gal. 2:19 and 5:24.

165. See the account in Thurston, *Physical Phenomena of Mysticism*, pp. 33–38.

166. These include Dauphin Robert of Auvergne and the Premonstratensian Dodo of Hascha; see Thurston, *Physical Phenomena of Mysticism*, pp. 38–40. Women do not seem to have participated in self-stigmatization prior to 1225, *pace* the claims of Bynum and Constable (see *Holy Feast and Holy Fast*, p. 119; and *Three Studies*, pp. 216–17) concerning Mary of Oignies, for which I find no direct evidence in the VMO.

167. Figures for the number of stigmatics reported since Francis vary between fifty and sixty authenticated cases, and vague estimates of three hundred to five hundred often repeated in the popular literature.

168. Dante, *Divina Commedia*, Paradiso XI.106–11.

169. Adnès outlines five forms of explanation for stigmata: (1) mutilation artificially produced; (2) nervous hysteria; (3) natural psychophysiological mechanism; (4) supernatural intervention; and (5) the collaboration of nature and divine intervention ("Stigmates," cc. 1229–39).

170. On this, see especially Thurston, *Physical Phenomena of Mysticism*, pp. 70–83, 100, 104, etc.

171. *Vida y Obras de San Juan de la Cruz*, ed. Crisogono de Jesus, Matias del Nino Jesus, and Lucinio del SS. Sacramento (Madrid: BAC, 1964), *Llama de amor viva*, Canc. 2.10 (p. 855): ... en lo cual parece al alma que todo el universo es un mar de amor en que ella está engolfada ... ; and 2.13 (p. 856): ... como acaeció cuando el serafín hirió al sancto Francisco, que llagándole el alma de amor en las cinco llagas, también salía en aquella manera el efecto de ellas al cuerpo, imprimiéndolas también en él y llagándole, como también las había impreso en su alma llagándola de amor.

172. Ibid.: "As a rule, God gives no favors to the body without bestowing them first and foremost on the soul" (Porque Dios, ordinariamente, ninguna merced hace al cuerpo que primero y principalmente no la haga en el alma ...).

173. A similar interpretation of Francis appears in Francis de Sales; see his *Treatise on the Love of God* 6.15.

174. The essential sources are available in the *Fontes Franciscani*. They include: (1) the Encyclical of Elias; (2) 1Cel 91–96, the account of the vision, and 112–15 dealing with the observation and theological meditation on the stigmata at the time of Francis's death; (3) the Parchment given to Brother Leo by St. Francis with Leo's later brief account of the stigmata (BLeo); (4) 2Cel 135–38; (5) 3Cel 2; (6) 1Bon 13 and 15.2; (7) 2Bon 6; (8) 3Soc 17.69–70; (9) Actus 65. In addition, there were other notices, such as the account found in the English Franciscan Thomas of Eccleston (see Schmucki, *Stigmata of St. Francis*, pp. 186–90), as well as no fewer than three papal encylicals, two by Gregory IX and one by Alexander IV, devoted to the stigmata (see Schmucki, *Stigmata of St. Francis*, pp. 273–76).

175. Frugoni, *Francesco e l'invenzione delle stimmate*, pp. 149, 155, 162, etc.

176. Schmucki, *Stigmata of St. Francis*, pp. 312–17.

177. See J. A. Wayne Hellmann, "The Seraph in Thomas of Celano's *Vita Prima*," in *That Others May Know and Love: Essays in Honor of Zachary Hayes, OFM*, ed. Michael F. Cusato and F. Edward Coughlin (St. Bonaventure: Franciscan Institute, 1997), pp. 23–41.

178. For the attacks on the stigmata, see André Vauchez, "Les stigmates de Saint François et leurs détracteurs dans les derniers siècles du moyen âge," *Mélanges d'archéologie et d'histoire* 80 (1968): 595–625. I leave to one side here the numerous studies of the iconography of the stigmata, important as these are for subsequent theological elaborations. See the extensive account in Frugoni, *Francesco e l'invenzione delle stimmate*, chaps. 5–10.

179. Epistola Encyclica de Transitu sancti Francisci (*Fontes*, p. 254): ... annuntio vobis gaudium magnum et miraculi novitatem. A saeculo non est auditum tale signum, praeterquam in Filio Dei, qui est Christus Dominus. Non diu ante mortem Frater et Pater noster apparuit crucifixus, quinque plagas, quae vere sunt stigmata Christi, portans in corpore suo.

Nam manus eius et pedes quasi puncturas clavorum habuerunt, ex utraque parte confixas, reservantes cicatrices et clavorum nigredinem ostendentes. Latus vero eius lanceatum apparuit et saepe sanguinem evaporavit. Hellmann dismisses the evidence of the encyclical, because it survives only in a late printed source, but we can suppose that Elias's fall from grace may have led to loss of the manuscripts ("The Seraph in Thomas of Celano's *Vita Prima*," pp. 23–27).

180. E.g., the case of Domenica Lazzari discussed in Thurston, *Physical Phenomena of Mysticism*, pp. 49–51.

181. The FOff can be found in *Fontes*, pp. 145–63. For other mentions of the cross in Francis's writings, see Adms 5.8, Adms 6, 2 EFi 6–25, RnBu 22, Test 5, etc. For a study, see Octavian Schmucki, "The Passion of Christ in the Life of St. Francis of Assisi: A Comparative Study of the Sources in the Light of the Devotion to the Passion Practiced in his Time," *Greyfriars Review* 4 (1990, Supplement): 1–101. Francis's devotion to the cross is stressed in the lives, e.g., the account of the San Damiano incident in 3Soc 5.14 cited above, as well as the emphasis on the memory of Christ's wounds mentioned in the account of the same vision in 2Cel 10–11 (cf. 2Cel 203). Similar accounts of Francis's devotion to the passion are found elsewhere, e.g., 2Spe 91–93. For the term "crucifixion complex," see Thurston, *Physical Phenomena of Mysticism*, p. 122, who uses it of Theresa Neumann, a far more dubious stigmatic, but there should be no problem in applying it to Francis as long as we are willing to discriminate between more and less healthy and transformative aspects of such fixations.

182. 1Cel 94 (*Fontes*, p. 370): Cumque ista videret beatus servus Altissimi, admiratione permaxima replebatur, sed quid sibi vellet haec visio advertere nesciebat. . . . coeperunt in manibus eius et pedibus apparere signa clavorum, quemadmodum paulo ante virum supra se viderat crucifixum.

183. The identification of the seraph figure with Christ is not evident before Bonaventure; e.g., 1Bon 13.3. See Frugoni, *Francesco e l'invenzione delle stimmate*, pp. 174–79.

184. For background on the seraph figure, see Schmucki, *Stigmata of St. Francis*, chap. 3; Hellmann, "Seraph in Thomas of Celano's *Vita Prima*," pp. 32–41; and "The Seraph in the Legends of Thomas of Celano and St. Bonaventure: The Victorine Transition," in *Bonaventuriana*, 1:347–56; and Frugoni, *Francesco e l'invenzione delle stimmate*, chap. 4.

185. This identification was made by Origen in order to give a trinitarian dimension to the Isaiah 6 vision, so that the Seated Lord is the Father and the two seraphim are the Son and Holy Spirit. Though attacked by Jerome, the interpretation was mentioned in the *Glossa ordinaria*, sub Is. 6:1.

186. Dionysius (*De caelesti hierarchia* 7.1) characterized the seraphim as "fiery," but their identification with burning love of God is a twelfth-century development, found both among Cistercians (e.g., Bernard, *Sermo super Cantica* 19.5) and Victorines (e.g., Hugh of St. Victor, *De arca Noe morali* 1.9).

187. See Frugoni, *Francesco e l'invenzione delle stimmate*, especially p. 148: Il cardine della meditazione di Francesco . . . non è l'umanità sofferente di Cristo, ma l'amore del Padre. La croce a Tau scelta da Francesco . . . è un altro sintomo che conferma come il santo orientasse la sua meditazione verso il significato dell'incarnazione piuttosto che verso le fasi del supplizio.

188. The BLeo can be found in *Fontes*, pp. 45–48 (see *Francis and Clare: The Complete Works*, pp. 99–100, for a translation). For the argument about the relation of this text to the Seraph vision, see Frugoni, *Francesco e l'invenzione delle stimmate*, pp. 139–42 and 144–48; and Miccoli, "Francis of Assisi's Christian Proposal," pp. 160–61.

189. Hellmann gives a good account of this ("The Seraph in Thomas of Celano's *Vita Prima*, pp. 32–41). I differ from Hellmann in thinking that the seraph vision was not Celano's

creation, but that it quite possibly goes back to Francis himself, or at least the witness of those who were with him on Alverna.

190. On the early development of the house at San Damiano, see Clara Gennaro, "Clare, Agnes, and Their Earliest Followers: From the Poor Ladies of San Damiano to the Poor Clares," in *Women and Religion in Medieval and Renaissance Italy,* ed. Daniel Bornstein and Roberto Rusconi (Chicago: University of Chicago Press, 1996), pp. 39–55. At the time of Clare's death, there were 110 houses following her rule. The article "Francescane" in DIP 4:174–445 lists no fewer than 394 groups of Franciscan women today. There is a growing literature on Clare. The most helpful recent monograph is that of Marco Bartoli, *Chiara d'Assisi* (Rome: Istituto Storico dei Cappuccini, 1989), now available in English as *Clare of Assisi* (Quincy, Ill.: Franciscan Press, 1993). See also Ingrid J. Peterson, *Clare of Assisi: A Biographical Study* (Quincy, Ill.: Franciscan Press, 1993); and Margaret Carney, *The First Franciscan Woman: Clare of Assisi and Her Form of Life* (Quincy, Ill.: Franciscan Press, 1993). For recent English summaries, consult Lázaro Iriarte, "Clare of Assisi: Her Place in Female Hagiography," *Greyfriars Review* 3 (1989): 173–206; and Ingrid Peterson, "Clare of Assisi's Mysticism of the Poor Crucified," *Studies in Spirituality* 4 (1994): 51–78. A recent collection of Italian essays is found in *Dialoghi con Chiara de Assisi: Atti delle Giornate di studio e riflessione per l'VIII Centenario di Santa Chiara,* ed. Luigi Giacometti (Assisi: Edizioni Porziuncola, 1995).

191. Testament of Clare 5 (*Fontes,* p. 2311): Factus est nobis Filius Dei *via,* quam *verbo* et *exemplo* ostendit et docuit nos beatissimus pater noster Franciscus, verus amator et imitator ipsius. I will use the abbreviations for Clare's writings found in the *Fontes Franciscani:* Testament of Clare (TeCl); Four Letters to Agnes (1–4ECl); Rule of Clare (ReCl); Blessing of Clare (BeCl).

192. See the story ascribed to Brother Stephan as found in Livarius Oliger, "Descriptio Codicis S. Antonii de Urbe," *Archivum Franciscanum Historicum* 12 (1920): 383.

193. Among Francis's own writings, we have the witness not only of the *forma vitae* (FoVi) given to Clare in 1215 and cited in ReCl 6, but also the "Last Will," which Francis wrote for her as he was dying and which is included in the same part of her Rule (*Fontes,* p. 235). The vernacular "Canticle of Exhortation" that Francis composed for Clare and the Poor Ladies shortly after the "Canticle of Brother Sun" was not discovered until 1976. For an edition, translation, and study, see Octavian Schmucki, "The Rediscovery of the Canticle of Exhortation *Audite* of St. Francis for the Poor Ladies of San Damiano," *Greyfriars Review* 3 (1989): 115–26 (the text can also be found in *Fontes,* p. 245). A full account of all the references to Clare in the hagiography about Francis is not needed here, but for some key passages, see, e.g., 1Cel 18–20, 78, and 116–18; 2Cel 204–5 and 207; 1Bon 4.6, 12.2, 13.8, and 15.5; 3Soc 7.24 and 14.60.

194. See, e.g., Margaret Carney, "Francis and Clare: A Critical Examination of the Sources," *Greyfriars Review* 3 (1989): 15–43; Pierre Brunette, "Une amitié spirituelle: François et Claire d'Assise vue par les symboles de leur itinéraire," in *La vie des communautés religieuses* 47 (1989): 26–48; Jean-François Godet, "Claire et la vie au féminin: Symboles de la femme dans ses écrits," *Laurentianum* 31 (1990): 148–75 (a revised version of this appeared in English as *Clare of Assisi: A Woman's Life* [Chicago: Haversack, 1991]); and Pierre Brunette, "François et Claire," in *Sainte Claire d'Assise et sa posterité: VIIIe Centenaire de Sainte Claire* (Paris-Montréal: Actes du Colloque de l'UNESCO, 1994), pp. 87–100. According to Godet: "Claire et François s'appellent l'un l'autre parce que, dans l'échange qu'il y avait antre eux, dans l'amour qu'ils partageaient, Claire est devenue vraiment femme 'mâle et femelle' et François est devenu vraiment homme 'mâle et femelle.'"

195. Although Francis's RnBu cautions the friars about their contacts with women (see 12.3–4; cf. 2Cel 112–14), he was deeply attached not only to Clare, but also to the Roman

noble woman Jacoba of Settesoli, who visited him on his deathbed and who later joined the third order (see 3Cel 37–39).

196. See Matura, "Introduction," in *Claire d'Assise: Écrits,* pp. 29–30.

197. The *Legenda s. Clarae Assisiensis* can be found in *Fontes,* pp. 2401–49. The *Processus* survives only in a fourteenth-century Italian translation (*Fontes,* pp. 2453–2507; hereafter this text will be abbreviated as Proc with appropriate section and number). On the *Legenda,* see the important paper of Frederic Raurell, "La Bibbia nella visione sponsale della *Legenda sanctae Clarae Virginis,*" in *Dialoghi con Chiara d'Assisi,* pp. 67–150.

198. The shared vision of Francis and Clare did not, of course, prevent some differences of viewpoint between the two. For example, in 1215 Francis was instrumental in making Clare adopt the title of abbess according to the Benedictine model, but the *Legenda Clarae* 12 (cf. Proc. 1.6) indicates her resistance to this, and she never used the title to describe herself. It is also well known (see Proc. 1.8, 2.8, 4.5, and 10.7, as well as *Legenda* 17–18) that Francis and Guido, the bishop of Assisi, twice intervened to compel Clare to moderate her ascetical practices, especially her fasting. On the tensions between Clare and Francis, see Optatus Van Asseldonk, "'Sorores Minores': Una nuova impostazione del Problema," *Collectanea Franciscana* 62 (1992): 595–633; and "Sorores Minores e Chaira d'Assisi a San Damiano: Una scelta tra clausura e lebbrosi?" *Collectanea Franciscana* 63 (1993): 399–421.

199. Clare refers to Francis twenty-four times in the TeCl, mostly under the title *pater,* as compared with eight references in the ReCl and only two in the letters.

200. See Caroline Walker Bynum, "Jesus as Mother and Abbot as Mother: Some Themes in Twelfth-Century Cistercian Writing," in *Jesus as Mother,* pp. 110–69.

201. Proc 3.29 (*Fontes,* p. 2473): Et essendo pervenuta ad sancto Francesco, epso sancto trasse del suo seno una mammilla et disse ad esse vergine Chiara: "Viene, receve et sugge": Et avendo lei succhato, epso sancto la admoniva che suggesse un'altra volta; et epsa suggendo, quello che di li suggeva, era tanto dolce et delectevole, che per nesuno modo lo poteria explicare. Et havendo succhato, quella rotondità overo boccha de la poppa dondo escie lo lacte remase intra li labri de epsa beata Chiara; et pigliando epsa con le mane quello che li era remaso nella boccha, li pareva che fusse oro così chiaro et lucido, che ce se vedeva tucta, come quasi in uno specchio. For an analysis of this vision, see Marco Bartoli, "Analisi storica e interpretazione psicanalitica di una visione di S. Chiara d'Assisi," *Archivum Franciscanum historicum* 73 (1980): 449–72, which is largely repeated in his *Chiara d'Assisi,* pp. 186–99. Other witnesses in the Proc also refer to this vision (see 4.16, 6.13, and 7.10).

202. Francis spoke of himself as a *mater* in ELeo 2 (*Ita dico tibi fili mei sicut mater . . . , Fontes,* p. 89), and he encouraged the brethren to love as mothers in RnBu 9.11 and ReBu 6.8. In the *Regula pro eremitoriis* 1ff. (*Fontes,* pp. 215–16) the superiors in the hermitages are described as mothers who take the part of Martha. Many early witnesses refer to Francis as a mother; see Bynum, *Holy Feast and Holy Fast,* p. 341 n. 139.

203. To be sure, Clare also spoke of herself as *mater* in relation to her community; see 4 ECl 33, TeCl 79, and BeCl 6.

204. The foundational work for the study of the Rule remains Livarius Oliger, "De origine regularum ordinis S. Clarae," *Archivum Franciscanum Historicum* 5 (1912): 181–209 and 413–47. For a recent summary, see Fernando Uribe, "L'iter storico della Regola di S. Chiara: una prova di fedeltà al Vangelo," in *Dialoghi con Chiara d'Assisi,* pp. 211–40.

205. See Bartoli, *Chiara d'Assisi,* chaps. 3–4; cf. Matura, "Introduction," in *Claire d'Assise: Écrits,* pp. 41–47), who notes a more "democratic" conception of community life in relation to the rules composed by Francis; see also Jean François Godet, "A New Look at Clare's Gospel Plan of Life," *Greyfriars Review* 5 (1991, Supplement).

206. Several accounts note that although she was an *illiterata,* she delighted in listening to learned sermons, cf. Proc 10.3. Anyone who studies her letters cannot fail to be impressed with the extent of Clare's theological education.

207. It is true that the fourth witness of the Proc mentions two other visions (4.16 and 4.19), but the absence of other testimonies gives one pause. There are also accounts of several witnesses who claim that *they* saw the Christ child appearing to or in the arms of Clare (cf. 9.4, 9.10 and 10.8), or the heavenly court appearing at her deathbed (e.g., 11.4).

208. See Proc 3.25, an account much expanded upon in *Legenda* 1.31.

209. The ReCl 3.14 (*Fontes,* p. 2296) legislates reception of the Eucharist only seven times per year. In one famous miracle, Clare routs the Saracens threatening Assisi by having the Eucharist carried in procession (see Proc 9.2, and *Legenda* 21), but it is worth noting that other accounts of this miracle do not mention the Eucharist at all (see Proc 2.20, 3.18, 4.14, 6.10, 7.6, 10.9, 12.8 and 18.6). Otherwise, the Eucharist makes a relatively rare appearance in the Proc (e.g., 2.11 and 3.7) and in *Legenda* 28.

210. This occurs in 1ECl 12 and 24 (*Fontes,* pp. 2264–65) and obviously reflects Francis's understanding of the threefold relation to God in terms of *sponsi-fratres-matres* in 1 EFi 1.7–9, 2 EFi 50–52 (*Fontes,* pp. 73–74, 83). For the development of the theme in Clare, see Marianne Schlosser, "Mother, Sister, Bride: The Spirituality of St. Clare," *Greyfriars Review* 5 (1991): 233–49.

211. 3ECl 21–22 (*Fontes,* p. 2276): Ecce iam liquet per Dei gratiam dignissimam creaturarum fidelis hominis animam maiorem esse caelum, cum caeli cum creaturis ceteris capere nequeant Creatorem, et sola fidelis anima ipsius mansio sit et sedes, et hoc solum per caritatem qua carent impii. . . .

212. For other texts on the role of Mary in Clare, particularly Mary as a model of poverty, see ReCl 2.24, 8.5–6, 12.13; and TeCl 46.

213. Like Francis, Clare emphasizes the importance of mutual love for all, especially as realized in the community. See, e.g., 4ECl 37–38; ReCl 4.16–17 and 10.5; TeCl 18.

214. See 1ECl 6–11; 2ECl 1–7 and 18–20; 3ECl 5–28; 4ECl 7–27 and 28–32. Clare also refers to Agnes often in the Letters as a *sponsa Christi.* For a survey, see Elena Marchitielli, "L'alleanza sponsale con Cristo nelle lettere di S. Chiara a S. Agnese di Praga," in *Dialoghi con Chiara d'Assisi,* pp. 309–22. References to Clare as the *sponsa Christi* are, as might be expected, frequent in the *Legenda;* see, e.g., 6, 8, 9, 11, 13, 24, and 32. The papal documents concerning the community of San Damiano also make use of Song of Songs language, both in the *Privilegium paupertatis* of Innocent III and its confirmation by Gregory IX in 1228 (see Armstrong, *Clare of Assisi: Early Documents,* 84 and 99–100).

215. See especially 1ECl 6–11, 2ECl 1–7, and 4ECl 28–32, which cites Sg. 1:3, 2:4, 2:6 and 1:1. On Clare's use of the language of the Song of Songs, see Frederic Raurell, "El 'Càntic dels Càntics' en els segles XII–XIII: Lectura de Clara d'Assis," *Estudios Franciscanos* 91 (1990): 421–559.

216. 2ECl 18–20 (*Fontes,* pp. 2270–71): . . . sed pauperem Christum, virgo pauper, amplectere. . . . Sponsum tuum *prae filiis hominum speciosum,* pro salute tua factum virorum vilissimum, despectum, percussum et toto corpore multipliciter flagellatum, inter ipsas crucis angustias morientem, regina praenobilis, intuere, considera, contemplare, desiderans imitari. Clare's devotion to the crucified Christ can be found both in her authentic writings (e.g., 1ECl 13–14; 2ECl 20–21; 4ECl 23–24), as well as in the hagiographical accounts (e.g., Proc 1.30–35; 3.25; 10.3 and 10; 11.2; 14.8; *Legenda* 30; etc.). See Ingrid Peterson, "Images of the Crucified Christ in Clare of Assisi and Angela of Foligno," in *That Others May Know and Love,* pp. 171–76. The hagiography (e.g., Proc 10.10) speaks of her devotion to a "Prayer to the Five Wounds of Christ," which survives only in a late medieval (and doubtful) version. See

Zefferino Lazzeri, "L'Orazione delle cinque piaghe recitata da S. Chiara," *Archivum Franciscanum Historicum* 16 (1923): 246–49.

217. This motif was popular among the Cistercians, as in Aelred's *Speculum caritatis,* as well as in a number of other mystics. See *Growth of Mysticism,* pp. 40, 279–80, 347–48, 384, 404. Cf. Margot Schmidt, "Miroir," DS 10:1290–1303; and Ritamary Bradley, "Backgrounds of the Title *speculum* in Mediaeval Literature," *Speculum* 29 (1954): 100–115. The motif was to be used by a number of later mystics to be discussed in this volume, such as Marguerite Porete and Marguerite d'Oingt.

218. 3ECl 12–14 (*Fontes,* p. 2276): . . . pone mentem tuam in speculo aeternitatis, pone animam tuam in *splendore gloriae,* pone cor tuum in *figura* divinae *substantiae* et *transforma* te ipsam totam per contemplationem *in imagine* divinitatis ipsius, ut et ipsa sentias quod sentiunt amici gustando *absconditam dulcedinem,* quam ipse Deus ab initio suis amatoribus reservavit. The term *contemplatio,* absent in Francis, occurs six times in Clare (3ECl 13; 4ECl 11, 18, 23, 28, 33).

219. See Timothy J. Johnson, "Visual Imagery and Contemplation in Clare of Assisi's 'Letters to Agnes of Prague,'" *Mystics Quarterly* 19 (1993): 161–72. Clare's visual emphasis, of course, is also mirrored in her name, Chiara, "light or clear." Both Alexander IV's Bull of Canonization of 1255 and the *Legenda* (e.g., 1.1, 2.49 and 62) contain wordplays on this.

220. 4ECl 14–16 (*Fontes,* p. 2282): . . . quae *cum sit splendor* aeternae *gloriae, candor lucis aeternae et speculum sine macula,* hoc speculum quotidie intuere, o regina, sponsa Jesu Christi, et in eo faciem tuam iugiter speculare, ut sic totam interius et exterius te adornes amictam *circumdatam* que *varietatibus.* . . .

221. 4ECl 23 (*Fontes,* p. 2283): In fine vero eiusdem speculi contemplare ineffabilem caritatem, qua pati voluit in crucis stipite et in eodem mori omni mortis genere turpiori.

222. TeCl 19–20 (*Fontes,* p. 2313): Ipse enim Dominus non solum nos posuit et formam aliis in exemplum et speculum, sed etiam sororibus nostris, quas ad vocationem nostram Dominus advocabit, ut et ipsae sint conversantibus in mundo in speculum et exemplum.

223. Bartoli, *Chiara d'Assisi,* chap. 4, has a good discussion.

224. Godet, "Claire et la vie au féminin," 151. The same point is made by Bartoli, *Chiara d'Assisi,* pp. 115–29, who speaks of her model as a "communità aperta."

225. Bull of Canonization (*Clara claris praeclara*) of Alexander IV (*Fontes,* 2332): . . . servabatur intra, et extra manebat. Latebat namque Clara, sed eius via patebat; silebat Clara, sed sua fama clamabat; celabatur in cella, et in urbibus docebatur. Nec mirum; quia *lucerna* tam *accensa,* tam *lucens, abscondi non poterat* quin splenderet et clarum *in domo* Domini daret lucem. . . .

Chapter 2

1. Again, I wish to extend a special word of thanks to Paul Lachance for the numerous helpful suggestions which he contributed to this chapter. My gratitude also to Ewert Cousins for commenting on the section devoted to Bonaventure.

2. On *Cum inter nonnullos,* see L. Duval-Arnould, "La Constitution 'Cum inter nonnullos' de Jean XXII sur le pauvreté du Christ et les Apotres: Redaction préparatoire et rédaction définitive," *Archivum Franciscanum Historicum* 77 (1984): 406–20.

3. Both John Moorman (*A History of the Franciscan Order from its Origins to the Year 1517*) and Duncan Nimmo (*Reform and Division in the Franciscan Order: From St. Francis to the Foundation of the Capuchins* [Rome: Capuchin Historical Institute, 1987]) provide general accounts and bibliographical resources. More recently, see Roberto Lambertini and Andrea Tabarroni, *Dopo Francesco: L'Eredità Difficile.* For more detail on institutional development, see

Rosalind B. Brooke, *Early Franciscan Government* (Cambridge: Cambridge University Press, 1959). On the question of poverty, see M. D. Lambert, *Franciscan Poverty: The Doctrine of the Absolute Poverty of Christ and the Apostles in the Franciscan Order 1210–1323* (London: SPCK, 1961); Gordon Leff, *Heresy in the Later Middle Ages,* 2 vols. (New York: Barnes & Noble, 1967), vol. 1, part 1; and the essays in *Dalla sequela Christi di Francesco d'Assisi all'apologia della povertà,* Atti del XVIII Convegno Internazionale Assisi della Società Internazionale di Studi Francescani (Spoleto: Centro Italiano di Studi sull'Alto Medioevo, 1992).

4. For an introduction to Franciscan theology, see Kenan B. Osborne, ed., *The History of Franciscan Theology* (St. Bonaventure: Franciscan Institute, 1994); and Damian McElrath, ed., *Franciscan Christology: Selected Texts, Translations and Introductory Essays* (St. Bonaventure: Franciscan Institute, 1980). No single work provides an adequate overview of Franciscan spirituality, but see Antonio Blasucci, "Frères Mineurs: III, Spiritualité Franciscaine: 1226–1517," DS 5:1315–47. A survey of the varying genres of Franciscan writing can be found in John V. Fleming, *An Introduction to the Franciscan Literature of the Middle Ages* (Chicago: Franciscan Herald Press, 1977).

5. On Franciscan mysticism the most recent extensive treatment is that of Ruh, *Geschichte der abendländische Mystik,* 2:374–537. The first volume of a major collection of translated sources has recently appeared in Italy, *Dizionario Francescano,* Vol. 1, *I Mistici: Scritti dei Mistici Francescani Secolo XIII* (Assisi: Editrici Francescane, 1995). For an older survey, see Moorman, "Franciscan Literature, 1: Mysticism, Poetry, and Preaching," in *History of the Franciscan Order,* pp. 256–77.

6. The central role of *Domina Paupertas* in the course of salvation history already appears in the *Sacrum commercium* (SCom), a text that may have been written as early as 1227. See Engelbert Grau, "Das 'Sacrum commercium sancti Francisci cum domina paupertate': Seine Bedeutung für die franziskanische Mystik," in *Abendländische Mystik im Mittelalter: Symposium Kloster Engelberg 1984,* ed. Kurt Ruh (Stuttgart: Metzler, 1986), pp. 269–85, as well as the comments in Ruh, *Geschichte,* 2:386–91.

7. ReBu 10.9 (*Fontes,* p. 179): . . . sed attendant, quod super omnia desiderare debent habere Spiritum Domini et sanctam eius operationem. . . .

8. Test 35–39 (*Fontes,* p. 231): Et generalis minister et omnes alii ministri et custodes per obedientiam teneantur, in istis verbis non *addere* vel *minuere.* . . . Et omnibus fratribus meis clericis et laicis praecipio firmiter per obedientiam, ut non mittant glossas in regula neque in istis verbis dicendo: Ita volunt intelligi. Sed sicut dedit mihi Dominus simpliciter et pure dicere et scribere regulam et ista verba, ita simpliciter et sine glossa intelligatis et cum sancta operatione observetis usque in finem.

9. Moorman, *History of the Franciscan Order,* p. 90.

10. Francis's own attitude toward learning was ambivalent. He insisted that an educated clergy was necessary for the church, but he also felt that the role of the brethren as witnesses to the gospel precluded the possession of books and prolonged study. Francis was obviously concerned that learning might lessen the spirit of prayer among the brethren or be used as a form of domination, but among his own writings the letter he wrote to Anthony of Padua (*Epistola ad s. Antonium* [*Fontes,* p. 55]) provides a clue to his position. The movement of the friars into the world of the universities, however, seems to have been generally accepted after ca. 1230, even by those who disagreed about the proper meaning and practice of poverty.

11. For Joachim's thought, see Bernard McGinn, *The Calabrian Abbot: Joachim of Fiore in the History of Western Thought* (New York: Macmillan, 1985). On the *viri spirituales,* see also McGinn, "Apocalyptic Traditions and Spiritual Identity in Thirteenth-Century Religious Life," in *The Roots of the Modern Christian Tradition,* ed. E. Rozanne Elder (Kalamazoo: Cistercian Publications, 1984), pp. 1–26 and 293–300. The most complete account of the identifica-

tion of Francis with the angel of Apoc. 7:2 is that of Stanislao da Campagnola, *L'Angelo del sesto sigillo e l'alter Christus* (Rome: Laurentianum, 1971).

12. Though the Paris masters, led by William of St. Amour, were also condemned, their attacks on the friars mark the beginning of a long tradition of criticism of the mendicants in medieval theology and literature. See Penn R. Szittya, *The Antifraternal Tradition in Medieval Literature* (Princeton: Princeton University Press, 1986).

13. The most complete statement of Bonaventure's theology of poverty is found in his *Apologia pauperum* of 1269.

14. For a discussion, see Lambert, *Franciscan Poverty*, pp. 141–48, as well as Brian Tierney, *Origins of Papal Infallibility: A Study of the Concepts of Infallibility, Sovereignty and Tradition in the Middle Ages* (Leiden: Brill, 1972), pp. 97–100.

15. The text of the bull can be found in the *Bullarium Franciscanum*, ed. J. H. Sbaralea and A. de Latera, 5 vols. (Rome, 1759–80), 5:128–30. The passage cited is found on p. 130: Magna quidem paupertas, sed major integritas; bonum est obedientia maximum, si custodiatur illaesa.

16. For a survey, see Ruh, *Geschichte*, 2:400–402. Many of the stories about the ecstasies of these early Franciscans occur in the late witness of the *Actus/Fioretti* and are therefore to be used with caution. On the companions of Francis, see *I compagni di Francesco e la prima generazione minoritica*, Atti del XIX Convegno Internazionale, Società Internazionale di Studi Francescani (Spoleto: Centro Italiano di Studi sull'Alto Medioevo, 1992).

17. For studies, see Jacques Campbell, "Gilles d'Assise," DS 6:379–82; and Stefano Brufani, "Egidio d'Assisi: Una santità feriale," in *I compagni di Francesco e la prima generazione minoritica*, pp. 285–311.

18. From the viewpoint of mysticism, the most important of the three lives is that probably written by Brother Leo, the *Vita Beati Fratris Egidii,* ed. Rosalind B. Brooke in *Scripta Leonis, Rufini et Angeli Sociorum S. Francisci* (Oxford: Clarendon Press, 1970), pp. 304–49. An edition of two versions of the *Dicta* is to be found in the *Dicta B. Aegidii Assisiensis,* Bibliotheca Franciscana Ascetica Medii Aevi 3 (Quaracchi: Collegium S. Bonaventurae, 1905). For a translation, see *Golden Words: The Sayings of Brother Giles of Assisi with a Biography by Nello Vian,* trans. Ivo O'Sullivan (Chicago: Franciscan Herald Press, 1966). Stories about Giles are also found in the literature about Francis; see, e.g., 1Cel 25 and 30; 3Soc 32-34; 1Bon 3.4.

19. For examples of this, see *Vita* 12 and 14 (ed., 336, 340).

20. *Vita* 6 (ed., 326).

21. *Vita* 8 (ed., 330): . . . apparuit sibi Dominus uisibiliter eum uidens oculis corporeis, in qua apparitione frater Egidius pre nimio odore uoces emittebat immensas, eique uidebatur humanitate deficere, quia talia non poterat substinere. . . . The same emphasis on "heavenly odor" appears below: . . . subito enim fuit ineffabili odore repletus et dulcedine cordis immensa. . . .

22. *Vita* 9 (ed., 332): Fuit enim in tanta et tali dulcedine indicibili et iubilo tam suaui et odore tribus diebus ante Natiuitatem Domini usque ad Epiphaniam, non tamen continue, sed interpolate die et nocte; non enim poterat substinere humanitas, cum apparebat immensa claritas.

23. The *Vita* often mentions Giles's reticence in describing his experiences to his inquisitive *socii:* (1) to the friar who asks him about a brilliant light that passed between them, he replies *dimitte ire* (9, ed. 332); (2) he warns the brethren: Cum magno timore et cautela oportet custodire secreta Domini et thesaurum suum (11, ed. 336); (3) in response to those who question him about his Cetona visions in *Vita* 13 (338–40), he avoids any detailed description, concluding, *non fuit in illo facto mea culpa;* (3) to the friar who queries him about a manifestation made to him on *mons Pesulanus,* he says: Si ego glorifico meipsum, gloria mea

nichil est, et addidit: Non dicamus plus de ista materia (14, ed. 340). This matches the general tone of the *Dicta*, which, like the *Meditationes* of the Carthusian Guigo I (see *Growth of Mysticism*, pp. 356–57), are primarily concerned with ascetic virtue and religious life rather than with analysis of the higher stages of contemplation. Giles's insistence on the impossibility of speaking adequately about God, even in the Bible, comes through in *Dicta* 2 (ed., 6–7).

24. See *Vita* 9 (ed., 330–32): Vsque modo ibam, quo uolebam, et quod uolebam facere, faciebam laborans manibus meis; nunc autem et deinceps non ita, sicut consueui, facere possum, sed sentio in me oportet me facere. Super quo ualde timeo, ne aliqui querant a me de me, quod eis dare non possum.

25. *Vita* 13 (ed., 338): Verum est, quod illa magna fuerunt, sed aliud sunt opera Domini, aliud ipse. . . . There is a passage close to this in *Dicta* XV (ed., 54): Homo fingit Deum qualem vult, sed ipse semper est talis, qualis ipse est.

26. *Vita* 19 (ed., 346): Ego, inquid, nolo mori meliori morte quam de contemplatione.

27. 1Bon 3.4 (*Fontes*, p. 797): . . . ad excelsae contemplationis sublimatus est verticem.

28. *Chronica XXIV Generalium*, edited in *Analecta Franciscana* 3 (1897): 101: Et frater Aegidius ait: Potest idiota tantum deum diligere sicut litteratus? Respondit Generalis: Potest una vetula plus etiam quam magister in theologia. Tunc frater Aegidius in fervore surrexit, vadens in hortum versus partem quae respicit civitatem et clamavit: Vetula paupercula, simplex et idiota, diligas Dominum Deum et poteris esse maior quam frater Bonaventura.

29. This story appears in *Vita fratris Aegidii*, which was inserted into the *Chronica XXIV Generalium;* see *Analecta Franciscana*, pp. 104–5.

30. *Dicta* XIII (ed., 48–49): *Ignis,* dico, id est quaedam lux, quae antecedit ad illuminandam animam. Deinde *unctio* unguentorum; unde oritur odor quidam mirabilis, qui subsequitur illam lucem, de quo in Canticis: *In odorem unguentorum tuorum* etc. Postea *ecstasis;* sentito enim odore, rapitur anima et abstrahitur a sensu corporis. Hinc sequitur *contemplatio;* postquam enim est sic abstracta a sensibus corporalibis, mire contemplatur Deum. Postea sequitur *gustus;* in contemplatione enim illa sentit dulcedinem mirabilem, de qua in psalmo: *Gustate et videte* etc. Deinde *requies;* quia dulcorato palato spirituali requiescit anima in illa dulcedine. Ultimo sequitur *gloria;* quia in tanta requie anima gloriatur et ingenti gaudio reficitur; unde psalmus: *Satiabor, cum apparuerit gloria tua.* The importance of *odor* in stages 2 and 3 reflects Giles's raptures at Cetona.

31. Bonaventure's earlier discussion is found in his 1248 *Commentarium in Evangelium Lucae* Chap. IX.48 (*Sancti Bonaventurae Opera Omnia*, 10 vols. [Quaracchi: Collegium S. Bonaventurae, 1882–1902], 7:231–32; hereafter abbreviated as *Opera*). A more extended discussion is found in his Sermo I de Sabbato Sancto, preached in 1267 (*Opera*, 9:269) where he expands the stages to eight by placing *amplexus* between *gustus* and *requies.*

32. The *De septem gradibus contemplationis* is known in three different versions and exists in seventy manuscripts. One version is printed in *S. Bonaventurae Opera Omnia*, ed. A. C. Peltier, 15 vols. (Paris, 1864–71), 12:183–86. Gabriel Théry first demonstrated the connection with Gallus in his article "Thomas Gallus et Egide d'Assise: Le traité 'De septem gradibus contemplationis,'" *Revue Néoscholastique de Philosophie* 36 (1934): 180–90. See also Ruh, *Geschichte*, 2:403–5; and Balduinus Distelbrink, *Bonaventurae Scripta: Authentica dubia vel spuria critice recensita* (Rome: Istituto Storico Cappuccini, 1975), p. 123.

33. An expanded version of this section will appear under the title "The Role of Thomas Gallus in the History of Dionysian Mysticism," *Studies in Spirituality* 8 (1998).

34. On the connections between Antony and Gallus, see Gabriel Théry, "Saint Antoine de Padoue et Thomas Gallus," *La vie spirituelle, Supplement* 37 (1933): 94–115; and Jean Châtillon, "Saint Anthony of Padua and the Victorines," *Greyfriars Review* 8 (1994): 347–80. The career of Antony represents an early connection between the friars and the world of theological education that was to increase dramatically after Francis's death. See Antonio Rigon, "San

Antonio e la cultura universitaria nell'ordine francescano delle origini," in *Francescanesimo e cultura universitaria*, Atti del XVI Convegno Internazionale (Perugia: Centro di Studi Francescani, 1990), pp. 67–92. Antony's *Sermones dominicales et festivi* show considerable acquaintance with the themes of monastic contemplation found in Augustine, Gregory the Great, and Bernard, and even some knowledge of the writings of Richard of St. Victor that probably came to him from Gallus, but they demonstrate no direct contact with the Dionysianism of his Victorine friend. On Antony's use of mystical themes, see Jacques Heerinckx, "S. Antoninus Patavinus auctor mysticus," *Antonianum* 7 (1932): 39–76 and 167–200; and "Les sources de la théologie mystique de S. Antoine de Padoue," *Revue d'ascetique et de mystique* 13 (1932): 225–56.

35. For an introduction to these two strands in late-medieval Dionysianism, see Paul Rorem, *Pseudo Dionysius: A Commentary on the Texts and an Introduction to Their Influence* (New York/Oxford: Oxford University Press, 1993), pp. 216–26. The Dionysian corpus will be referenced according to the new critical edition of Beate Suchla, Gunter Heil, and A. M. Ritter, *Corpus Dionysiacum*, 2 vols., Patristische Texte und Studien 33, 36 (Berlin/New York: Walter de Gruyter, 1990–91), superseding the old edition of Balthasar Corderius first published in 1634 and reprinted in J. P. Migne's *Patrologia Graeca* 3:119–1122 (references to the Migne text will appear in brackets.) The corpus will be cited according to the following abbreviations MT (*De mystica theologia*), DN (*De divinis nominibus*), CH (*De caelesti hierarchia*) and EH (*De ecclesiastica hierarchia*).

36. For a summary of Gallus's life and thought, see Jeanne Barbet, "Thomas Gallus," DS 15:800–816; cf. Gabriel Théry, "Thomas Gallus: Aperçu biographique," *Archives d'histoire doctrinale et littéraire du moyen age* 12 (1939): 141–208. See also Ruh, *Geschichte*, 3:59–81.

37. Gallus's earliest work, written in 1218 while he was still at Paris, was a *Commentum super Isaiam 6*. A surviving fragment was edited by G. Théry, "Commentaire sur Isaïe de Thomas de Saint-Victor," *La vie spirituelle, Supplement* 47 (1936): 146–62. Gallus wrote three commentaries on the Song of Songs: (1) an early lost work of 1224; (2) *Commentarium II* written at Vercelli 1237–38 covering Song 1:1–5:8; (3) and *Commentarium III* written at Ivrea in 1243, which is a more extensive gloss on the entire Song. These texts, which one ms. aptly named *Cantica Canticorum ierarchice exposita*, have been edited by Jeanne Barbet, *Thomas Gallus: Commentaires du Cantique des Cantiques* (Paris: Vrin, 1967), pp. 65–104 and 105–232. There is a partial English translation of *Comm. II* in Denys Turner, *Eros and Allegory: Medieval Exegesis of the Song of Songs* (Kalamazoo: Cistercian Publications, 1995), pp. 317–39. Gallus's work as an exponent of Dionysius comprises two parts. (1) The *Extractio*, finished in 1238, which was an attempt to render a more comprehensible text of the Dionysian writings, part translation and part paraphrase, using the versions of Eriugena and of John Sarrazin. (It was incorporated into the Paris *corpus dionysiacum* and can be found in part in Philippe Chevalier, *Dionysiaca*, 2 vols. [Paris: Desclée, 1937], 1:673–717.) (2) The *Explanatio* (1241–43), a full commentary on the whole Dionysian corpus. Most of this has not been given a modern edition. There are also two mystical treatises: the *De septem gradibus contemplationis* (ca. 1224–26) referred to above; and the *Spectacula contemplationis* (ca. 1243, unedited). The *Glossae in Mysticam Theologiam* found in PL 122:267–84, under the name of Eriugena, have been claimed for Gallus, but the attribution is contested and I will not employ them here. The commentary on the Song of Songs beginning *Deiformis animae gemitus*, once ascribed to Gallus, does not appear to be by him, but may be of Franciscan provenance. See Jeanne Barbet, *Un Commentaire du Cantique attribué a Thomas Gallus* (Paris-Louvain: Béatrice-Nauwelaerts, 1972).

38. On the relation between Richard and Gallus, see Robert Javelet, "Thomas Gallus et Richard de Saint-Victor mystiques," *Recherches de théologie ancienne et médiévale* 29 (1962): 205–33; and 30 (1963): 88–121, as well as Barbet's comments in DS 15:813–14.

39. This was first recognized by Endre von Ivánka in a series of articles published

1950–55 that were subsequently included in his book *Plato Christianus: Übernahme und Umgestaltung der Platonismus durch die Väter* (Einsiedeln: Johannes Verlag, 1964), pp. 315–63. For the broad context of how the relations between love and knowledge interact with conceptions of mystical union, see Bernard McGinn, "Love, Knowledge and *Unio Mystica* in the Western Christian Tradition," in *Mystical Union in Judaism, Christianity, and Islam: An Ecumenical Dialogue*, ed. Moshe Idel and Bernard McGinn (New York: Continuum, 1996), pp. 59–86, with comments on Gallus on pp. 68–69.

40. Gallus, Prologus, *Comm. II* (ed., 65–66): Duplex hic designatur Dei cognitio, una intellectualis que operatur per considerationem in Ecclesiastice, secundum expositionem venerabilis doctoris magistri Hugoni, quondam canonici ecclesie nostre Sancti Victoris Parisius. . . . Alia autem est Dei cognitio que istam incomparabiliter excedit, quam sic describit magnus Dionysius, *De div. nom.* 7. . . . Hec enim sapientia superior est corde hominis. . . . Et, ex doctrina Apostoli, magnus Dionysius Areopagita theoricam huius superintellectualis sapientie scribit, sicut possibile est eam scribi, in libello suo de Mystica theologia. . . . In hoc autem libro, Solomon tradit practicam eiusdem mystice theologie, ut patet per totius libri seriem. For similar comments on the *theorica* and the *practica* of the *superintellectualis cognitio Dei,* see *Comm. III* (ed., 107, 114, 122 and 128).

41. *Comm. II* uses phrases referring to the Bride's personal experience sixteen times in thirty-nine pages. *Comm. III* speaks of the *verba experientialia* of the Song (ed., 130).

42. *Comm. II* (ed., 102): VOX DILECTI MEI PULSANTIS, et dum sic exerceor, sonat superintellectualiter in auribus experientie mee vox, id est influitio dilecti, que aliter designare non valeam pulsantis. Non dicit loquentis, vel suadentis, quia non intelligentie, sed affectionis, summum ostium pulsat radii incendio.

43. MT 1.3 (Suchla ed., 2:144 [1001A]), using the translation of Colm Luibheid, *Pseudo-Dionysius: The Complete Works* (New York: Paulist Press, 1987), p. 137. On this text, see *Foundations of Mysticism*, p. 175.

44. Thomas Gallus, *Extractio in MT 1 (Dionysiaca* 1:710 n. 578): . . . et ab omnibus et quasi a se ipso segregatur, et per unitionem dilectionis (quae effectiva est verae cognitionis) unitur Deo intellectualiter ignoto, cognitione multo meliori quam sit cognitio intellectualis, et in eo quod intellectualem cognitionem derelinquit super intellectum et mentem deum cognoscit.

45. Rorem, *Pseudo-Dionysius,* pp. 218–19.

46. *Comm. super Isaiam* (ed. Théry, 156): . . . affectum inestimabiliter profundius et sublimius a Domino in ipsum Dominum trahi quam intellectum, quia videlicet plus diligunt quam investigare vel intelligere sufficiunt. In typical fashion, Gallus goes to demonstrate this by appealing to experience (*eciam experimento discere possumus*).

47. See Bernard McGinn, "God as Eros: Metaphysical Foundations of Christian Mysticism," in *New Perspectives on Historical Theology: Essays in Memory of John Meyendorff,* ed. Bradley Nassif (Grand Rapids: Eerdmans, 1995), pp. 189–209, especially 199–202 on Dionysius. For even more universal claims for the influence of Dionysian cosmic eros on the medieval monastic tradition of Song of Songs exegesis, see Turner, *Eros and Allegory,* pp. 47–81.

48. DN 4.14 (Suchla ed., 1:160 [712CD]). I have slightly modified the translation of Luibheid, *Pseudo-Dionysius,* pp. 82–83.

49. See *Comm. III,* where in treating of Song 1:3: *trahe me post te,* he explains how "the love of God draws him to minds and minds to him" by introducing a lengthy quotation from his *Extractio* of DN 4.17 (ed. Barbet, 125–26, using *Extractio in Dionysiaca,* 1:685 nn. 220–24). Given his usual practice of citing only a line or two when referencing Dionysius, this twenty-line citation is remarkable.

50. See the passage from the *Explanatio* as cited by Javelet, "Thomas Gallus et Richard de Saint-Victor," p. 93: Et ipsa est scintilla synderesis, que sola unibilis est Spiritui divino. . . .

51. *Comm. III,* prologus (ed., 111): Scintilla siquidem apicis affectualis, que est principalis et pura participatio divine bonitatis que fluit de veritate in imaginem. . . . (cf. 218; and the *Comm. in Is.,* 152). Gallus's terminolgy for this high point of the soul varies: *scintilla synderesis-affectio principalis-apex affectionis,* etc., but the meaning seems to remain the same. The term *synderesis/synteresis* goes back to Jerome's *Commentarium in Hiezechielem* as a corrupt reading for the Greek *syneidēsin* meaning "conscience." Thomas Gallus seems to have been the first to use the term in a mystical sense. For introductions to the complex history of this terminology and Gallus's role (still insufficiently investigated), see the two articles by Aimé Solignac, "'NOYS' et 'MENS',", DS 11:459–69, and "'SYNDERESIS,'" DS 14:1407–12. There is also a discussion in Javelet, "Thomas Gallus et Richard de Saint-Victor," pp. 93–97. Cf. "Contemplation," DS 2:374–76.

52. On the relation between love and knowledge in Gregory, see *Growth of Mysticism,* pp. 58 and 62–63. For treatments of Bernard, William, and Richard, see ibid., 200–203, 250–60, and 411–12 respectively.

53. William of St. Thierry, *Expositio super Cantica Canticorum* 92 (*Guillaume de Saint-Thierry: Exposé sur la Cantique des Cantiques,* ed. J.-M. Déchanet, SC 82 [Paris: Cerf, 1962], p. 212): . . . cum in contemplatione Dei, in qua maxime amor operatur, ratio transit in amorem et in quendam spiritualem vel divinum formatur intellectum, qui omnem superat et absorbet rationem.

54. For examples of this kind of language, see *Comm. II* (ed., 102): EXPOLIAVI ME TUNICA, id est *dereliqui* omnes intellectuales operationes . . . ; *Comm. III* (ed., 111): Scintilla siquidem apicis affectualis, . . . *ab omni inferioritate ineffabiliter separata; Comm. III* (ed., 173): Mens autem sponse *secans suas intellectuales operationes* per suum seraphim ad supersubstantialem radium transiens secundum quod fas est. . . . The language of leaving behind and cutting off was suggested to Gallus by MT 1.1 (Suchla ed., 2:142 [997B]), which he interpreted in one passage thus: Quotiens ergo superintellectualiter exercemur ad divinum radium, totiens opus est *ut resecemus intellectuales operationes, Myst. theol.* 1b (ed., 158).

55. See, e.g., *Comm. II* (ed., 93–94 and 101).

56. See, e.g., *Comm. III* (ed., 153 and 225), and the texts from the *Explanatio super Mysticam Theologiam* cited by Robert Javelet, "Thomas Gallus ou les écritures dans une dialectique mystique," in *L'homme devant Dieu: Mélanges offerts au Père Henri de Lubac,* 3 vols (Paris: Aubier, 1964) 2:108–10. Gallus also uses such phrases as *cognitio unitiva* (ed., 158) and *cognitio extatica* (ed., 225).

57. The evolution of Gallus's views on the interpretation of Exod. 3:14 has been studied by Francis Ruello, "La mystique de l'Exode (Exode 3:14 selon Thomas Gallus, commentateur dionysien, d. 1246)," *Dieu et l'Être: Exégèses d'Exode 3,14 et de Coran 20, 11–24* (Paris: Études Augustiniennes, 1978), pp. 213–43.

58. *Comm. III* (ed., 123): Hoc nomen unitivum non cognoscunt nisi uniti. Unde Moysi unito interroganti hoc nomen pro ipso dixit: *sum qui sum,* id est esse in se reflexum, vel entitas. Gallus's identification of *ego sum qui sum* bears an analogy to Eckhart's comments on Exod. 3:14, though I have not found direct evidence that the Dominican knew the Victorine's commentaries on the Song of Songs.

59. Ibid.: . . . sed summo apici affectionis principalis rectissime imprimitur, nec descendit inferius.

60. See von Ivánka, *Plato Christianus,* especially pp. 352–73.

61. CH 3.1–2 (Suchla ed., 2:17–18 [164D–165B]; translation of Luibheid, *Pseudo-Dionysius,* pp. 153–54).

62. See, e.g., CH 15.1 (Suchla ed., 2:50–51 [328A]).

63. Richard of St. Victor, *De arca mystica* (also known as the *Benjamin major*) 4.4 (PL

196:140C): . . . in se coelestium et pennatorum animalium figuram transformet, et humanus animus in eorum se imaginem transfiguret. See Steven Chase, *Angelic Wisdom: The Cherubim and the Grace of Contemplation in Richard of St. Victor* (Notre Dame: University of Notre Dame Press, 1995), chap. 6, from whom I take the term "angelization." As Chase points out (pp. 115–16), angelization does not mean the person grows less human; it is rather a theological category for analyzing the meeting of God and human in the process of divinization. For a treatment of Richard's *De arca mystica,* see *Growth of Mysticism,* pp. 405–13.

64. Hugh of St. Victor, *Commentarium in Caelestem Hierarchiam* 6.7 (PL 175:1038D): . . . dilectio supereminet scientiae et major est intelligentia. Plus enim diligitur, quam intelligitur, et intrat dilectio, et approprinquet, ubi scientia foris est. Hugh's discussion is to be found in cc. 1036–39. On this text and Hugh's shift, see Rorem, *Pseudo-Dionysius,* p. 217. I am indebted to Prof. Rorem for correcting my discussion of this text in *Growth of Mysticism,* p. 390, where I suggest that the love language was actually present in the Dionysian text.

65. *De septem gradibus contemplationis* (*Sancti Bonaventurae Opera Omnia,* ed. A. C. Peltier) 12:184: Felix nimis qui hujus gradus collem attingit: hic plane angelificatus in praesenti, futuram jam inchoavit vitam. On the following page he speaks of *de hominibus in quodammodo angelos transformari.*

66. For discussions of Gallus's account of the hierarchy of ascent, see Barbet, "Introduction," in *Commentaires du Cantique des Cantiques,* pp. 43–61; and James Walsh, "Thomas Gallus et l'effort contemplatif," *Revue d'Histoire de Spiritualité* 51 (1975): 17–42.

67. This passage is taken from the *Explanatio* on CH 1, as cited from manuscript in Walsh, "Thomas Gallus et l'effort contemplatif," p. 20: "Intencio ierarchie est assimilacio et unicio ad Deum": idest, assimilare plenos habitus et operaciones Deo et uniri ei. . . . Gallus has a wide range of qualifying terms for *hierarchia;* see "Table idéologique des principaux mots," in Barbet, *Commentaires de Cantiques des Cantiques,* 262.

68. Gallus often cites this text from CH 10.3 (Suchla ed., 2:41 [273C]); e.g., *Comm. III,* prologue (ed., 107–8). For a list of citations and discussion, see DS 15:812–13.

69. *Comm. III,* prologus (ed., 108): . . . eo quod sponsa nunc in una hierarchia mentis sue loquitur, nunc in altera, nunc in uno ordine, nunc in altera.

70. This chart is based on the discussions found in *Comm. in Is. 6* (ed. Théry, 153-57), and the prologues to *Comm. II* and *Comm. III* (ed., 66-67, 108-09). For similar diagrams, see Barbet, *Commentaire des Cantique des Cantiques,* p. 60; and Walsh, "Thomas Gallus et l'effort contemplatif," p. 24. In likening the nine orders of angels to the ascent of the powers of the soul to God, Gallus had a predecessor in Isaac of Stella, though the Cistercian's ascent pattern culminates in the higher knowing power called *intelligentia.* See Isaac's *Epistola de anima* 8 (PL 194:1880AB) and the discussion in *Growth of Mysticism,* pp. 289–90.

71. A summary statement can be found in *Comm. II* (ed., 100): Tota siquidem contemplativa mentis exercitatio in hiis tribus consistit: haurire superius, hausta reponere, de repositis influere. Thomas also often mentions the threefold distinction of *purgatio-illuminatio-perfectio,* but he does not use it as his organizing principle, save insofar as it is expressed in the distinction of the three basic orders of angels.

72. *Excessus mentis* appears eight times, *ecstasis* four, and various forms of *rapere-raptus* three times in the two Song commentaries. Also present are such traditional terms as *inebriatio* (seven times) and *somnus contemplativus* (four times). For a study of his terminology on ecstasy, see Javelet, "Thomas Gallus et Richard de Saint-Victor mystiques," pp. 88–93. Like Richard, who stressed the necessity for Rachel (= *ratio*) to die in order for Benjamin (= *excessus mentis*) to be born, Gallus makes use of the notion of mystical death; e.g., *Comm. II* (ed., 71–72, 79); *Comm. III* (ed., 130–31, 139–40, 148 and 199). The language of *deificatio* also appears at times; e.g., *Comm. III* (ed., 111, 191).

73. See, e.g., *Comm. III* (ed., 141–42).

74. See, e.g., *Comm. II* (ed., 102); *Comm. III* (ed., 110, 118, 214, 223–24).

75. See, e.g., *Comm. II,* (ed., 68), and *Comm. III* (ed., 204–6 and 210).

76. See David Knowles, "The Influence of Pseudo-Dionysius on Western Mysticism," in *Christian Spirituality: Essays in Honour of Gordon Rupp* (London: SCM, 1975), pp. 79–94, who discusses Gallus on p. 91. Cf. Bernard McGinn, "Pseudo-Dionysius and the Early Cistercians," in *One Yet Two: Monastic Tradition East and West,* ed. M. Basil Pennington (Kalamazoo: Cistercian Publications, 1976), pp. 200–241.

77. The term "Dionysius renaissance" is found in Joseph Ratzinger, *The Theology of History in St. Bonaventure* (Chicago: Franciscan Herald Press, 1971), pp. 87–91. Despite previous research (e.g., "Denys l'Aréopagite: En Occident," DS 3:340–58 on the thirteenth century), there is no really adequate account of this significant aspect of late medieval thought. Of special significance was the creation of the standard *corpus dionysiacum* used at Paris by roughly the middle of the century; see H. F. Dondaine, *Le corpus dionysien de l'Université de Paris au xiiie siècle* (Rome: Edizioni di Storia e Letteratura, 1953).

78. *Comm. III* (ed., 129): Ipsa ergo in sui incontemplabilitate eis loquitur inferioribus: NIGRA SUM, id est superlucenti divine incomprehensibilitatis caligine inclusa. Cf. *Comm. II* (ed., 71).

79. E.g., *Comm. II* (ed., 87–88).

80. *Comm. III* (ed., 154): Desertum est invia et singularis eterne Trinitatis supersubstantialis solitudo . . . (here Gallus uses two of his favorite proof texts for this theme, Exod. 3:1 and 5:3). Other references to God as desert can be found on pp. 127, 133, and 169, while reference to the soul as a desert (Song 8:5) can be found on p. 225.

81. For a more extended discussion, see Bernard McGinn, "Ocean and Desert as Symbols of Mystical Absorption in the Christian Tradition," *The Journal of Religion* 74 (1994): 155–81.

82. DN 4.13 (Suchla ed., 1:159 [712AB]; translation of Luibheid, *Pseudo-Dionysius,* p. 82).

83. This text from the *Explanatio* on DN 4.14 is cited in Javelet, "Thomas Gallus et Richard de Saint-Victor," p. 99: Tante autem virtutis est dileccio ut non tantum hominem extra se ad Deum, sed, si fas est dicere, quasi Deum extra se trahit ad hominem, ut infinitum distantes uniat. See also the *Extractio* text in *Dionysiaca,* 1:685 nn. 217–18. Contrast Gallus's acceptance of reciprocal ecstasy, with the treatment of Thomas Aquinas of this passage as analyzed in my essay "God as Eros," pp. 204–7.

84. *Explanatio* (*Dionysiaca* 1:cix): . . . sensum, quem in ipsis libris (quibus vigiliis, quo labore) per annos viginti conceperam, stylo communi exprimere. . . .

85. The literature on Bonaventure is large. A bibliography compiled by Jacques Guy Bougerol listing 4,842 items published between ca. 1850 and 1973 appeared as the fifth volume of the important collection of studies *San Bonaventura 1274–1974,* 5 vols. (Grottaferrata/Rome: Collegio S. Bonaventura, 1974). Numerous monographs and hundreds of articles have been published since then. There are a number of volumes devoted to aspects of Bonaventure's life and thought, such as *S. Bonaventura Francescano,* Convegni del Centro di Studi sulla Spiritualità Medievale 14 (Todi: L'Accademia Tudertina, 1974), and the two-volume collection *Bonaventuriana* already noted. Among the general attempts to present Bonaventure's thought, I have found the following especially helpful: Etienne Gilson, *The Philosophy of St. Bonaventure* (Paterson: St. Anthony Guild Press, 1965; French original, 1924); Hans Urs von Balthasar, *The Glory of the Lord: A Theological Aesthetics,* Vol. II, *Studies in Theological Style: Clerical Styles* (San Francisco: Ignatius, 1984; German original, 1962), pp. 260–362; Ewert H. Cousins, *Bonaventure and the Coincidence of Opposites* (Chicago: Franciscan Herald Press, 1978); and Zachary Hayes, *The Hidden Center: Spirituality and Speculative Christology in St. Bonaventure* (New York: Paulist Press, 1981). For an introductory sketch of Bonaventure's theology, see Zachary Hayes, "Bonaventure: Mystery of the Triune God," in *History of Franciscan Theology,* pp. 39–125.

86. Bonaventure's writings appear in the standard edition of the Quaracchi fathers, *Sancti Bonaventurae Opera Omnia,* which will be cited with appropriate volume, page, and column in parentheses. The following abbreviations will be employed for the most frequently cited works: *I, II, III, and IV Sent.* = *Commentarius in Libros Sententiarum (Opera* 1–4); *Sc. Chr.* = *Quaestiones disputatae de scientia Christi* (5:3–43); *M. Trin.* = *Quaestiones disputatae de mysterio Trinitatis* (5:45–115); *Brevil.* = *Breviloquium* (5:201–91); *Itin.* = *Itinerarium mentis in Deum* (5:295–313); *Red. art.* = *De reductione artium ad theologiam* (5:319–25); *Hexaem.* = *Collationes in Hexaemeron* (5:329–449); *Comm. Jn.* = *Commentarius in Evangelium S. Ioannes* (6:239–634); *Tripl. via* = *De triplici via* (8:3–18); *Solil.* = *Soliloquium de quatuor mentalibus exercitiis* (8:28–67); *Lign. vit.* = *Lignum vitae* (8:68–86); *Vit. myst.* = *Vitis mystica seu tractatus de passione Domini* (8:159–229); *Leg. maj.* = *Legenda major* (8:504–64); *Serm.* = *Sermones (Opera* 9). For an overview of Bonaventure's works and their context, see Jacques Guy Bougerol, *Introduction to the Works of Bonaventure* (Paterson: St. Anthony Guild Press, 1963).

87. Gilson, *Philosophy,* 436.

88. Gilson (see *Philosophy,* chap. 15) argued that it is precisely the mysticism that provides the key to the synthesis.

89. Pope Leo XIII, from an audience given to the Franciscans in 1890, as cited in *Opera* 10:34b.

90. *Hexaem.* 1.17 (5:332ab): Verbum ergo exprimit Patrem et res, quae per ipsum factae sunt, et principaliter ducit nos ad Patris congregantis unitatem; et secundum hoc est lignum vitae, quia per hoc medium redimus et vivificamur in ipso fonte vitae. . . . Hoc est medium metaphysicum reducens, et haec est tota nostra metaphysica: de emanatione, de exemplaritate, de consummatione, scilicet illuminari per radios spirituales et reduci ad summum. Et sic eris verus metaphysicus. Bonaventure did not live to finish the last three "illuminations" of the seven announced at the outset of the work—those of the soul sublimated by prophecy, absorbed by rapture, and consummated in glory. Had he done so, some of the problems discussed below might have been clarified.

91. For a presentation of the relations between the two forms of metaphysics in Bonaventure, see Zachary Hayes, "Christology and Metaphysics in the Thought of Bonaventure," in *Celebrating the Medieval Heritage: A Colloquy on the Thought of Aquinas and Bonaventure,* ed. David Tracy, *The Journal of Religion, Supplement* 58 (1978): S82–S96, along with the "Response" by Ewert Cousins (S97–S104). For a more detailed treatment of the dual metaphysics, consult John Quinn, *The Historical Constitution of Saint Bonaventure's Philosophy* (Toronto: PIMS, 1973). On Bonaventure's view of theology, see G. H. Tavard, *Transiency and Permanence: The Nature of Theology According to St. Bonaventure* (St. Bonaventure: Franciscan Institute, 1954).

92. *M. Trin.,* q. 8, sed contra 2 (5:113a): . . . quanto aliquid prius, tanto potentius et actualius [*Liber de causis,* prop. 1]: ergo primum principium necessarium fuit actualissimum et potentissimum. See also ad 7 (5:115b): Secundum autem quod dicit privationem originis personalis, sic competit soli personae innascibili, scilicet Patri, in qua est plenitudo fontalitatis ad productionem Filii et Spiritus sancti. Haec autem fontalitas quodam modo origo est alterius fontalitatis.

93. *I Sent.* d.27, p.1, a.un., q.2 (1:471a): . . . primitas in prima persona est ratio producendi alias; et quia innascibilis dicit primitatem, hinc est, quod dicit fontalem plenitudinem respectu productionis personalis. See also *I Sent.* d.2, a.un., q.2 (1:53–54). On *fontalis plenitudo,* see Alejandro Villamonte, "El Padre Plenitud fontal de la Deidad," in *San Bonaventura 1274–1974,* 4:221–42.

94. *M. Trin.* q.8, conc. (5:114a): Quoniam ergo perfecta productio, emanatio et pullulatio attenditur secundum duos modos intrinsecos, scilicet per modum naturae et per modum voluntatis, verbi scilicet et amoris. . . . Cf. q.3, a.2, conc., on the different forms of personal dis-

tinction, and q.4, a.2, conc., on the principle that there can be only two perfect forms of emanation (5:75–76, 85–86).

95. This is evident from a consideration not only of the *M. Trin.*, but also of such texts as *I Sent.* d.2, q.un., qq.2–4 (1:53-58); and *Itin.* 6 (5:310–12). Bonaventure's use of Richard of St. Victor, as well as Dionysius and Augustine, is obvious, but his synthesis is his own. For a good summary in English, see the "Introduction" by Zachary Hayes in *Works of St. Bonaventure:* III, *Disputed Questions on the Mystery of the Trinity* (St. Bonaventure: Franciscan Institute, 1979), pp. 13–103. See also Konrad Fischer, *De Deo trino et uno: Das Verhältnis von productio und reductio in seiner Bedeutung für die Gotteslehre Bonaventuras* (Göttingen: Vandenhoeck & Ruprecht, 1978).

96. Much has been written on Bonaventure's Christology. For useful surveys, besides the work of Hayes, *Hidden Center,* cited above, see especially Alexander Gerken, *Theologie des Wortes: Das Verhältnis von Schöpfung und Inkarnation bei Bonaventura* (Düsseldorf: Patmos, 1963).

97. On Bonaventurean exemplarism, see the classic accounts of J.-M. Bissen, *L'exemplarisme divin selon Saint Bonaventure* (Paris: Vrin, 1929); Gilson, *Philosophy,* chap. 4; and von Balthasar, *Glory of the Lord,* 2:282–308 and 335–43.

98. See Ewert Cousins, "Bonaventure's Mysticism of Language," in *Mysticism and Language,* ed. Steven T. Katz (New York: Oxford, 1992), pp. 236–57.

99. *I Sent.* d.27, p.2, a.un., q.3 (1:488a): Verbum autem non est aliud quam similitudo expressa et expressiva, concepta vi spiritus intelligentis, secundum quod se vel aliud intuetur.

100. *Sc. Chr.* q.2, conc. (5:9a): . . . similitudo exemplativa, et sic in Creatore ratio exemplaris est similitudo creaturae. Cf. *I Sent.* d.35, a.un., q.1 (1:601–2).

101. *Comm. Jo.* chap. 1.6 (6:247b): Dicendum, quod filius solum dicit comparationem ad patrem, verbum vero dicit comparationem ad dicentem, dicit comparationem ad id quod per verbum dicitur, dicit comparationem ad vocem, quam induit, dicit etiam comparationem ad doctrinam, quae mediante verbo in altero efficitur. . . . Cf. *I Sent.* d.27, p.2, a.un., q.4 (1:488–90).

102. For other reflections on the denominations *filius-verbum-imago,* see, e.g., *Brevil.* I.3 (5:212a); *I Sent.* d.31, p.1, a.1, q. 2, conc.; *III Sent.* d.1, a.2, q.3, conc. (1:542b; 3:29b). Bonaventure often reduces the four relations implied in *verbum* to the triple formula *verbum increatum-verbum incarnatum-verbum inspiratum* (see n. 106 following).

103. See *Sc. Chr.* q.3, conc. (5:13–14).

104. *M. Trin.* q.4, a.2, ad 8 (5:87a): Nam eodem Verbo, quo Pater dicit se, dicit quaecumque dicit. . . .

105. *I Sent.* d.27, p.2, a.un., q.2, conc. (1:485b): . . . Verbum, quod est similitudo Patris imitativa et similitudo rerum exemplativa et similitudo operativa; et ita tenet quasi medium, et dicitur Pater operari per Verbum. . . . Cf. *Hexaem.* 1.14 and 38 (5:331–32 and 335). On this theme, see Werner Dettloff, "'Christus tenens medium in omnibus': Sinn und Funktion der Theologie bei Bonaventura," *Wissenschaft und Weisheit* 20 (1957): 28–42 and 120–40.

106. *Hexaem.* 3.2 (5:343a): Clavis ergo contemplationis est intellectus triplex, scilicet intellectus Verbi increati, per quod omnia producuntur; intellectus verbi incarnati, per quod omnia reparantur; intellectus Verbi inspirati, per quod omnia revelantur. For other appearances of the three states of the *verbum,* see, e.g., *Hexaem.* 9.1–8, *Itin.* 4.3, *Brevil.* 4.1, *Collationes de septem donis Spiritus sancti* 1.5–7 (5:372–74, 306b, 242a, 458); and *Lign. vit.* 12 (8:84–85). For a consideration of this theme in the context of a comparative study of Bonaventure's doctrine of revelation, see David Carpenter, *Revelation, History, and the Dialogue of Religions: A Study of Bhartṛhari and Bonaventure* (Maryknoll, N.Y.: Orbis, 1995), chap. 5.

107. Bonaventure loved the symbolism of the book, as is evident from his references to "the book written within and without" (Apoc. 5:1) as indicating the Word and the created

universe (e.g., *Itin.* 6.7), or the soul and the world (e.g., *Hexaem.* 12.14–16), as well as his discussion of the threefold book that gives testimony to the Trinity: the book of creation, the book of scripture and the book of life (*M.Trin.* q.1, a.2, conc.). See Grover A. Zinn, "Book and Word: The Victorine Background of Bonaventure's Use of Symbols," in *San Bonaventura 1274–1974*, 2:143–69; and Winthir Rauch, *Das Buch Gottes: Eine systematische Untersuchung des Buchbegriffes bei Bonaventura* (Munich: Hueber, 1961).

108. Bonaventure's emphasis on the necessary historical mediation of the *verbum incarnatum* and the *verbum inspiratum* is the foundation for his theology of history, on which see Joseph Ratzinger, *The Theology of History in St. Bonaventure;* and Bernard McGinn, "The Significance of Bonaventure's Theology of History," in *Celebrating the Medieval Heritage: A Colloquy on the Thought of Aquinas and Bonaventure, The Journal of Religion, Supplement* 58 (1978): S64–S81.

109. *III Sent.* d.19, a.2, q.2, sol.1 (3:411a): Non enim est idem dicere esse mediatorem et esse medium; verumtamen mediator esse non potest, nisi esset medius.

110. For a survey, see Guy-H. Allard, "La technique de la 'reductio' chez Bonaventure," in *San Bonaventura 1274–1974*, 2:395–416.

111. See *II Sent.* d.24, p.1, a.2, q.1, ad 8 (2:562–63). For other discussions, see, e.g., *I Sent.* proem., q.1, conc.; d.8, p.2, a.un., q.2, sed contra 4; d.28, dub.1 (1:7, 167b, 504).

112. Bougerol, *Introduction to Bonaventure,* p. 76.

113. On analogy in Bonaventure, see Gilson, *Philosophy,* chap. 9; and Bougerol, *Introduction to Bonaventure,* pp. 77–79.

114. Alexander Gerken, "Identity and Freedom: Bonaventure's Position and Method," *Greyfriars Review* 4 (1990): 91–105 (quotation on p. 94)—an excellent brief presentation of the centrality of *reductio* in Bonaventure's thought.

115. *Red. art.* 23 (5:325a): Necesse est etiam ponere medium in egressu et regressu rerum; sed medium in egressu necesse est, quod plus teneat se a parte producentis, medium vero in regressu, plus a parte redeuntis: sicut ergo res exierunt a Deo per Verbum Dei, sic ad completum reditum necesse est, Mediatorem Dei et hominum non tantum Deum esse, sed etiam hominem, ut homines reducat ad Deum. This is a constant theme in the *Red. art.;* cf. 8, 12, 16 and 18. It is well summarized in *I Sent.* d.31, p.2, dub.6 (1:552a): Sed Pater quoniam caput non habet, cum sit innascibilis, est caput omnium; et idea dicitur *fontale principium,* a quo omnia et in quem omnia per Filium reducuntur.

116. See *I Sent.* d.27, p.2, a.un., q.2 (1:486b).

117. On Bonaventure's theology of the Holy Spirit, see especially *I Sent.* d.10, and d.32, q.1 (1:194–207, 555–61). For studies, consult Jean François Bonnefoy, *Le Saint-Esprit et ses dons selon Saint Bonaventure* (Paris: Vrin, 1929); and Walter H. Principe, "St. Bonaventure's Theology of the Holy Spirit with Reference to the Expression 'Pater et Filius Diligunt Se Spiritu Sancto,'" in *San Bonaventura 1274–1974*, 4:243–69.

118. On this see Gerken, "Identity and Freedom," pp. 96–103.

119. See, e.g., *Tripl. via* 3.1 and 6 (8:12a and 14a) for the Holy Spirit as Spouse, and *Brevil.* 5.1 (5:253A) for Christ as Spouse. On the threefold pattern of becoming temple, child, and bride of God, see *II Sent.* d.29, a.1, q.1 (2:695b–696a).

120. *Solil.* prol. (8:28a): Unde non immerito in omni boni operis initio ille est invocandus, a quo omne bonum originaliter progreditur, per quem omne bonum exemplariter producitur, et ad quem omne bonum finaliter reducitur. Haec est illa ineffabilis Trinitas, Pater, Filius, et Spiritus sanctus. . . .

121. For a good introduction, see Hans Mercker, *Schriftauslegung als Weltauslegung: Untersuchungen zur Stellung der Schrift in der Theologie Bonaventuras* (Munich: Schöningh, 1971).

122. On Bonaventure's sources, see especially the papers collected in Jacques Guy Bougerol, *Saint Bonaventure: Études sur les sources de sa pensée* (Northhampton: Variorum Reprints, 1989).

123. *Leg. maj.* 15.1 (8:547a): . . . sanctitatis speculum et totius evangelicae perfectionis exemplar. . . . The importance of Francis in Bonaventure's thought has been investigated by almost all the major writers on the Seraphic Doctor. For two classic accounts, see Gilson, *Philosophy*, pp. 59–78; and von Balthasar, *Glory of the Lord*, pp. 2:270–76 and 352–63.

124. *Itin.* prol. 2 (5:295b): In cuius consideratione statim visum est mihi, quod visio illa praetenderet ipsius patris suspensionem in contemplando et viam, per quam pervenitur ad eam.

125. *Itin.* 7.3 (5:312b): Quod etiam ostensum est beato Francisco, cum in excessu contemplationis in monte excelso . . . ; ubi in Deum transiit per contemplationis excessum; et positus est in exemplum perfectae contemplationis, sicut prius fuerat actionis tamquam alter Iacob et Israel, ut omnes viros vere spirituales Deus per eum invitaret ad huiusmodi transitum et mentis excessum magis exemplo quam verbo. Francis, then, combined action and contemplation and provided a model for the traditional teaching that both forms of life are necessary for the Christian. In other places Bonaventure has some sparse and fairly traditional comments on this issue, e.g., *III Sent.* d.27, a.2, q.4 (3:610b); *Commentarius in Evangelium Lucae* 9.62 (8:236b); and *Serm. VI in Dom. XXIV post Pent.* (9:457a).

126. Francis is described as the *vir hierarchicus* in *Leg. maj.* prol. 1 (8:504b). The term *vir angelicus* is found in *Leg. maj.* 13.1 and 5 (8:542a and 543b), where Francis is also characterized as inspired by *seraphicis desideriorum ardoribus* (13.3; cf. 14.1). Bonaventure's considerations of how perfect souls, like that of Francis, are "hierarchized" (to be treated below) can be seen in such texts as *Itin.* 4.4–8 and *Hexaem.* 22.

127. No full study of the influence of Thomas Gallus on Bonaventure exists, but see Bougerol, *Introduction to Bonaventure*, pp. 39–48 and 123–25; as well as his articles "Saint Bonaventure et le Pseudo-Denys l'Aréopagite," and "Saint Bonaventure et la Hiérarchie dionysienne" in *Saint Bonaventure: Études sur les sources de sa pensée.* See also Robert Javelet, "Reflections sur l'exemplarisme bonaventurien," in *San Bonaventura 1274–1974,* 4:349–70.

128. The identification of Francis as the angel of Apoc. 7:2 may have been first made by John of Parma. Bonaventure employs it in *Leg. maj.* prol. 1, 4.11, and 13.10 (8:504b, 516b, 545b); *Hexaem.* 16.16 and 29, 23.3 and 23.14 (5.405b, 408b, 445b, 447a); cf. also 22.21–23 (5:440b–441a), which does not cite the Apocalypse passage but describes Francis's seraphic activity. It also appears in *Serm. IV* (9.587a).

129. There is a rich literature, so I will cite only some contemporary discussions, mostly in English. See especially E. R. Daniel, "St. Bonaventure A Faithful Disciple of St. Francis? A Reexamination of the Question," and "St. Bonaventure: Defender of Franciscan Eschatology," in *San Bonaventura 1274–1974,* 2:171–87 and 4:793–806; as well as his "Symbol or Model? St. Bonaventure's Use of St. Francis," in *Bonaventuriana,* 1:55–62. See also Ewert Cousins, "Francis of Assisi: Christian Mysticism at the Crossroads," in *Mysticism and Religious Traditions,* pp. 163–90; and "The Image of St. Francis in Bonaventure's *Legenda Major,*" in *Bonaventuriana,* 1:311–21; Bernard McGinn, "The Influence of St. Francis on the Theology of the High Middle Ages: The Testimony of St. Bonaventure," in *Bonaventuriana,* 1:97–117; and Richard K. Emmerson and Ronald B. Herzman, *The Apocalyptic Imagination in Medieval Literature* (Philadelphia: University of Pennsylvania, 1992), chap. 2: "The *Legenda major:* Bonaventure's apocalyptic Francis" (pp. 36–75). On the role of Bonaventure's *Leg. maj.* in the developing Franciscan treatment of Francis's life as a *vita mystica,* see Ruh, *Geschichte,* 2:377–98. Although the theological aspects of the *Leg. maj.* have been rightly stressed, we must also remember that the text was intended to be a form of history as the thirteenth century understood this, as well as to serve a crucial role in the development of the order. On this, see Giovanni Miccoli, "Bonaventura e Francesco," in *S. Bonaventura Francescano,* pp. 49–73.

130. On Francis as a book to be read, see Emmerson and Herzman, *Apocalyptic Imagination,* pp. 48, 52, 70–72.

368 *Notes to Pages 95–98*

131. *Leg. maj.* prol. 1 (8:504b): . . . incendioque seraphico totus ignitus et ut vir hierarchicus curru igneo sursum vectus, sicut ex ipsius vitae decursu luculenter apparet, rationabiliter comprobatur venisse in spiritu et virtute Eliae. Ideoque alterius amici Sponsi, Apostoli et Evangelistae Ioannis vaticinatione veridica sub similitudine Angeli ascendentis ab ortu solis signumque Dei vivi habentis astruitur non immerito designatus.

132. The comments that follow are largely based on the analysis of Emmerson and Herzman, *Apocalyptic Imagination,* pp. 52–75, as well on the "Introduction" of Ewert Cousins in *Bonaventure: The Soul's Journey into God. The Tree of Life. The Life of St. Francis* (New York: Paulist, 1978), pp. 42–46.

133. The combination of the ascensional and historical dimensions is also evident in the comments in *Leg. maj.* 2.8 (8:509b–510a).

134. *Apologia pauperum* 3.10 (8:247a): Digne proinde huic pauperculo sacro, qui perfectionem Evangelii perfecte servavit et docuit, in apparitione seraphica stigmata sua tamquam sigillum approbativum Christus impressit, ut contra finalium temporum periculosam caliginem manifestum nobis in via perfectionis ostenderet signum, quo reducemur in Christum perfectae virtutis exemplar et finem. . . .

135. Cousins, "The Image of St. Francis in Bonaventure's *Legenda major,*" p. 312.

136. *De perfectione vitae ad sorores* 3.1 (8:112): Est etiam paupertas virtus ad perfectionis integritatem necessaria ad tantum, ut nullius omnino sine ea possit esse perfectus, teste Domino . . . (citing Matt. 19:21). This important discussion of poverty goes on to analyze three aspects of Christ's exemplary poverty: *nascendo-conversando in mundo-pauperrimus moriendo.*

137. See Zachary Hayes, "The Theological Image of St. Francis in the Sermons of St. Bonaventure," in *Bonaventuriana,* 1:333–34, on the four aspects of the stigmata revealed in the sermons (esp. *Serm. IV* in 9:585–90)–(a) a supreme experience, (b) ecstatic-contemplative, (c) eschatological, and (d) a vindication of Francis's life.

138. Bonaventure associates three apocalyptic texts with the signing: Apoc. 7:2 on the Angel with the seal; Ezek. 9:4 concerning the man clothed in linen who signs the elect with the *TAU*; and Matt. 24:30, the sign of the Son of Man appearing in the heavens at the end. The first two texts appear together in *Leg. maj.* prol. 1–2, while *Serm. IV* (9:585–90) uses all three.

139. See the discussion in *Growth of Mysticism,* pp. 340–41.

140. Since the publication of Joseph Ratzinger's seminal work, *The Theology of History in St. Bonaventure* (German original, 1959), there has been an extensive literature devoted to Bonaventure's theology of history. In what follows, I will largely depend on my earlier writings on the topic, especially, "The Significance of Bonaventure's Theology of History"; and chapter 7, entitled "The Abbot and the Doctors: Joachim, Aquinas, and Bonaventure," in *The Calabrian Abbot: Joachim of Fiore in the History of Western Thought,* pp. 207–34.

141. See *Growth of Mysticism,* pp. 50–52.

142. For a survey of views, see Luchesius Smits, "Die Utopie des mystischen Zeitalters bei Bonaventura (1217-1274)," *Franziskanische Studien* 67 (1985): 114–33.

143. It is still controverted how well Bonaventure may have known the abbot of Fiore's authentic works and how much he depends on the writings of the abbot's followers. See E. Randolph Daniel, "St. Bonaventure's Debt to Joachim," *Mediaevalia et Humanistica* n.s. 11 (1982): 61–75.

144. *Hexaem.* 16.2 (5:403b): Post novum testamentum non erit aliud, nec aliquod sacramentum novae legis subtrahi potest, quia illud testamentum aeternum est.

145. *Hexaem.* 16.16 (5:405b): Dies humanae formationis, tempus vocis propheticae, tempus clarae doctrinae, in quo esset vita prophetica. Et necesse fuit, ut in hoc tempore veniret

unus ordo, scilicet habitus propheticus, similis ordini Iesu Christi, cuius caput esset *Angelus, ascendens ab ortu solis habens signum Dei vivi*, et conformis Christo. Et dixit, quod iam venerat.

146. Gallus is specifically cited in *Hexaem.* 22.24 (5:441a), and the whole section on the *anima hierarchizata* (22.24-42) is deeply under his influence.

147. For a chart laying out the various comparisons, see Ratzinger, *Theology of History*, p. 47.

148. *Hexaem.* 22.22 (5:440b–441a): Tertius ordo est vacantium Deo secundum modum sursumactivum, scilicet ecstaticum seu excessivum.... Iste est ordo seraphicus. De isto videtur fuisse Franciscus.... Et in his consummabitur Ecclesia. Quis autem ordo iste futurus sit, vel iam sit, non est facile scire.

149. See *Hexaem.* 16.29 (5:408b). For other passages on the characteristics of the coming age of contemplation, see, e.g., 13.7, 16.30, 20.15, 20.30, and 23.4 (5:389a, 408b, 428a, 430b–31b, 445b).

150. *Hexaem.* 22.23 (5:441a) concludes by stressing: ... comparatio autem est secundum status, non secundum personas; quia una persona laica aliquando est perfectior quam religiosa. For helpful remarks on this inclusive aspect, see Emmerson and Herzman, *Apocalyptic Imagination*, pp. 43–46 and 49, and Hayes, "Theological Image of St. Francis in the Sermons of St. Bonaventure," pp. 344–45.

151. *Leg. maj.* 14.4 (8:346b): O vere christianissimum virum, qui et vivens Christo viventi et moriens morienti et mortuus mortuo perfecta esse studuit imitatione conformis et expressa promeruit similitudine decorari!

152. See Hayes, *Hidden Center.*

153. *I Sent.* proem (1:2a): ... dicitur fluvius Filii Dei incarnatio, quoniam, sicut in circulo ultimum coniungitur principio, sic in incarnatione supremum coniungitur imo....

154. The role of the various mysteries is well brought out in the discussion of the seven ways in which Christ functions as *medium* in *Hexaem.* 1.11–39 (5:331–35). Christ is the *medium metaphysicum* in the order of essence expressed in the three metaphysical principles discussed above on pp. 88–90 (*Hexaem.* 1.12–17). He is the *medium physicum* in the order of nature through the mystery of the incarnation (1.18–20) and the *medium mathematicum* in the order of distance as found in the mystery of the crucifixion (1.21–24). He is also the *medium logicum* in the order of doctrine in the resurrection (1.25–30), and the *medium ethicum* in the order of moderation in his ascension (1.31–33). Finally, he is the *medium politicum* in the order of justice through the last judgment (1.34–36) and the *medium theologicum* in the order of concord through the eternal beatitude of heaven (1.37–38). On this issue, see Justo L. Gonzalez, "The Work of Christ in Bonaventure's Systematic Works," in *San Bonaventura 1274–1974*, 4:371–85. The devotional treatise *The Tree of Life* is also organized around a treatment of the mysteries of Christ's life divided into *origo, passio*, and *glorificatio*.

155. *Serm. I in Vigilia Nativitatis* (9:91a): Et iste fidelissimus mediator, ut posset pacem perfectam facere, primo dedit se totum homini in nativitate, et postmodum obtulit et dedit se totum Deo pro homine in passione....

156. For general surveys, see Flavio di Bernardo, "Passion (Mystique de la)," DS 12:313–38; and Cousins, "Humanity and Passion of Christ," *Christian Spirituality II*, pp. 375–91.

157. See *III Sent.* d.19, a.1, q.2, conc (3:400b–401a).

158. This is well brought out by, among others, von Balthasar, *Glory of the Lord*, 2:356–62; and Cousins, "Image of St. Francis in Bonaventure's *Legenda major*," pp. 319–20.

159. *Vit. myst.* 4.5 (6:168b): Vinculis enim caritatis ipse devinctus, ad suscipienda vincula passionis de caelo tractus fuit in terram, et e contrario, qui de terris trahi desideramus ad caelum prius passionis vinculis nostro capiti colligemur, ut per hoc ad caritatis vincula pervenientes, unum cum ipso efficiamur.

160. For a collection of Bonaventurean texts on the *imitatio Christi*, see Ephrem Longpré, "Bonaventure," DS 1:1806–9; see also the discussion in Hayes, *Hidden Center,* chap. 2.

161. For a list of Bonaventure's most important passages on meditation on the cross, see Longpré, "Bonaventure," DS 1:803. For more detailed treatment of his theology of the cross, consult Werner Hüsbusch, *Elemente einer Kreuzestheologie in den Spätschriften Bonaventuras* (Düsseldorf: Patmos, 1968).

162. *Lign. vit.* prol. (8:68a). Bernard of Clairvaux had identified the "little bundle of myrrh" with the memory of the sufferings of Christ, especially in the passion, in *Super Cantica* 43 (*Sancti Bernardi Opera,* 2:41–44).

163. On sharing and entering into the *vulnera Christi*, see, e.g., *Lign. vit.* 7.26, 28, and 30; and *Vit. myst.* 3.2–6 (using Song 4:9 and 2:5), 15.1, 24.2–3 (8:78a, 79a, 79b–80a; and 162b–165b, 180ab, 188a–189b). There is also a noted passage on this theme in the *De perfectione vitae ad sorores* 6.2 (8:120): Accede ergo, tu, o famula, pedibus affectionum tuarum ad Iesum vulneratum, . . . et cum beato Thoma Apostolo non solum intuere in manibus eius fixuram clavorum . . . , sed totaliter per ostium lateris ingredere usque ad cor ipsius Iesu, ibique ardentissimo Crucifixi amore in Christum transformata, . . . nihil aliud quaeras, . . . quam ut cum Christo tu possis in cruce mori. Although Bonaventure is not usually listed among the exponents of erotic language in mysticism, this dimension is at least suggested in his writings.

164. *Vit. myst.* 8.2 (8:174b): Accedimus ad te, o benigne Jesu, mente, qua possumus, sedentem in *throno maiestatis,* orantes, ut illuc ad te et a te introduci mereamur, quo ingressus est latro, te confitens in *throno crucis.* The example of the good thief from Luke 23:43 is also used in *Itin.* 7.2.

165. *Vit. myst.* 24.3 (8:189ab): Nam propterea homo visibilis factus sum, ut a te visus amarer, qui in Deitate mea invisus et invisibilis quodam modo non amabar. Da ergo praemium incarnationi meae et passioni te, pro quo incarnatus simul sum et passus. Dedi me tibi, da te mihi. Bonaventure's argument here is close to Bernard's theology of the *cur Deus homo?* as found in *Super Cantica* 6 (*Opera Sancti Bernardi* 1:27–28), on which see *Growth of Mysticism,* pp. 166–68.

166. It is clear from Bonaventure's discussion of the *ordo seraphicus* in *Hexaem.* 22.23 discussed above (p. 99) that he did not believe that mystical contact with God was to be limited to religious orders, let alone to Franciscans. Francis and his true followers were models for the Christian values that all must practice who set forth on the *itinerarium mentis in Deum.* His *Sermo V de Patre nostro Francisco* (9:594a) declares: Quamvis autem non omnium sit, esse Fratrem Minorem habitu et professione, omnes tamen oportet esse mites et humiles, praescribente illa sententia Domini, Matthaei decimo octavo: *Nisi efficiamini sicut parvuli, non intrabitis in regnum caelorum.* For other texts that demonstrate the universality of the call to mystical consciousness, see, e.g., *II Sent.* d.33, a.2, q.3 (2:546a); *De quinque festivitatibus pueri Iesu,* fest. 1.6–7 (8:90–91); and *Serm. I de Sabbato sancto* (9:269b).

167. Bonaventure's mysticism has been the subject of many discussions. Among the most important: Ephrem Longpré, "La théologie mystique de Saint Bonaventure," *Archivum Franciscanum Historicum* 14 (1921): 36–108, and the same author's "Bonaventure (Saint)," DS 1:1768–1843; Gilson, *Philosophy,* chap. 14; Karl Rahner, "Der Begriff der ecstasis bei Bonaventura," *Zeitschrift für Aszese und Mystik* 9 (1934): 1–19; George Tavard, *Transiency and Permanence,* chap. 12; Bernardino Garcia, "Bonaventura da Bagnoregio:Introduzione," *Dizionario Francescano: I Mistici . . . Secolo XIII,* pp. 289–337; Ruh, *Geschichte,* 2:406–38; as well as the various books and articles of E. Cousins and Z. Hayes mentioned below.

168. *Red. art.* 5 (5:321b). The discussion of how the other five forms of human illumination all teach union can be found in nn. 10, 14, 18, 22, and 25–26.

169. While Bonaventure appealed to his own life experience at the beginning of the *Itin.* and the *Leg. maj.,* as noted above, he never gave any autobiographical accounts of ecstasy or

union. Indeed, in the dialogue of *Solil.* 2.15 (8:50a) *anima* advises *homo* that it is legitimate to speak of deep matters that we do not know from experience but only from the knowledge of others. Several places (e.g., *Sc. Chr.* epil. [5:42b-43b], and *Lign. vit.* 32 [8:80b]) contain prayers begging for a share in the experience of God in Christ that the saints have enjoyed. If the history of mysticism were to be restricted to autobiographical witness to direct consciousness of the divine presence, Bonaventure would clearly play no large role in it.

170. My concentration on these two treatises, necessary in this brief account, precludes discussion of the *Soliloquium* of ca. 1259–60, whose form as a mystical handbook with extensive quotations of classical texts was important for the growth of this genre in the later Middle Ages.

171. The Quaracchi editors list 138 manuscripts of the *Itin.* and no fewer than 299 manuscripts of the *Tripl. via.* The classic study of this work remains Jean-François Bonnefoy, "Une somme bonaventurienne de théologie mystique," *La France Franciscaine* 15 (1932): 77–86, 227–64, 311–59; and 16 (1933): 259–326 (reprinted in 1934 in book form). See also J.-G. Bougerol, "La perfection chrétienne et la structuration des trois vies de la vie spirituelle dans la pensée de saint Bonaventure," *Études Franciscaines* 19 (1969): 397–409.

172. For the development of the triple pattern in Origen and Dionysius, see *Foundations of Mysticism,* pp. 117 and 172–73.

173. Bonaventure uses the the classic three ways throughout his writings. An important text in *III Sent.* d.34, p.1, a.1, q.1, conc. (3:737a) ties the three forms of grace-given habits–i.e., the seven virtues (four cardinal and three theological), the seven gifts of the Holy Spirit, and the seven beatitudes–to the three stages of the spiritual life: *rectificatio-expeditio-perfectio.* This theme is expanded upon in *Brevil.* 5.4–6 (5:256–60), and has been treated by Longpré, "Bonaventure," DS 1:1779–91, as constituting the essential form of Bonaventure's spiritual teaching.

174. *Tripl. via* 3.1 (8:11a–12a): Postquam diximus, qualiter ad sapientiam nos exercere debeamus per meditationem et orationem, nunc breviter tangamus, qualiter contemplando ad veram sapientiam pervenitur. Per contemplationem namque transit mens nostra in supernam Ierusalem, ad cuius instar est formata Ecclesia. . . . Necesse est enim, Ecclesiam militantem conformari triumphanti, ... In gloria autem triplex est dos, in qua consistit perfectio praemii, scilicet summae pacis aeternalis tentio, summae veritatis manifesta visio, summae bonitatis vel caritatis plena fruitio.

175. The point is put more succinctly in *Hexaem.* 20.28 (5:430b): Nec enim est anima contemplativa, nisi per Ecclesiam sustentata quasi super basim.

176. *Commentarius in Evangelium Lucae* chap. 13, n. 46 (7:349b): Nam, sicut dicit Dionysius, tota mystica theologia, . . . ipsa tota consistit in dilectione excessiva secundum triplicem vim hierarchicam: purgativam, illuminativam et perfectivam. Bonaventure has in mind here *De cael hier.* 7.3, but the reference to ecstatic love (not found in Dionysius) is taken from Gallus. A similar text is also indicative of the characteristics of Bonaventure's Dionysianism in tying the three ways to the passion: . . . passio Christi habet in nobis triplicem effectum secundum triplicem actum hierarchicum, . . . scilicet effectum purgandi, illuminandi et perficiendi (*Serm. II Dom. 2 post Pascha* in 9:296b). For a brief summary of the role of hierarchy in Bonaventure's thought, see Bougerol, "Le perfection chrétienne et la structuration des trois voies," pp. 400–409.

177. *Tripl. via* 1.18 (8:7b): Et hic stare debet omnis meditatio nostra, quia hic est finis omnis cognitionis et operationis, et est sapientia vera, in qua est cognitio per veram experientiam.

178. *III Sent.* d.35, a.1, q.1 (3:774ab): Et quoniam ad gustum interiorem, in quo est delectatio, necessario requiritur actus affectionis ad coniungendum et actus cognitionis ad apprehendendum, . . . ita quid in cognitione inchoatur et in affectione consummatur, secundum

quod ipse gustus vel saporatio est experimentalis boni et dulcis cognitio. . . . Secundum quod patet in viris sanctis et contemplativis, qui prae nimia dulcedine modo elevantur in ecstasim, modo sublevantur usque ad raptum, licet hoc contingat paucissimis. Bonaventure composed a series of *Collationes de septem donis Spiritus sancti* in 1268 (5:457–503), which treat the gift of *sapientia* in a more general way (5:499–503).

179. For a treatment of Bonaventure's doctrine on private prayer, see *De sex alis Seraphim* 7.10 (8:149b). A broad consideration of his teaching can be found in Timothy Johnson, *Iste Pauper Clamavit: Saint Bonaventure's Mendicant Theology of Prayer* (Frankfurt/Bern/New York/Paris: Peter Lang, 1990); as well as the same author's "Poverty and Prayer in the Theology of Saint Bonaventure," *Miscellanea Francescana* 90 (1990): 19–60.

180. The latter half of the second chapter of *Tripl. via* (8:9a–11a) contains a discussion of how we offer *benevolentia* to God in prayer and concludes with a treatment of the three forms of *complacentia* and six stages *dilectio* on the path to God.

181. For some important discussions of *contemplatio*, see: (1) *II Sent.* d.23, a.2, q.3, conc. et ad 6 (2:545a–546a); (2) *III Sent.* d.24, dub.4 (3:530b–531b); (3) *III Sent.* d. 35, a.1, q.3 (3:778a–779b); (4) *Brevil.* 5.6 (5:258b–260b); (5) *Commentarius in Evangelium Lucae* chap. 9, nn.43–70 (7:230–39); (6) *Sc. Chr.* q.7, conc. (5:39b–40b); (7) *Itin.* 7 (5:312a–313b); (8) *Serm. Christus unus omnium magister* 11–19 (5:570a–572b); (9) *Serm. IV de Epiphania* (9:162b–163a); (10) *Serm. II ad Dom. 3 in Quad.* (9:228b–229b); (11) *Serm. I de Sabbato Sancto* (9:268b–269b); (12) *Serm. II de Sancta Agnete* (9:509b–510b); (13) *Hexaem.* 2.28–34 (5:340b–342b); (14) *Hexaem.* 3.30 (5:347b–348a); and (15) *Hexaem.* 20–22 passim (5:425–49). Jean-Marie Bisson's five articles on aspects of contemplation in Bonaventure published in *La France Franciscaine* between 1931 and 1936 remain the most extensive treatment (see 14 [1931]: 175–92; 15 [1932]: 87–105 and 437–54; 17 [1934]: 387–404; 19 [1936]: 20–29). See also Longpré, "Bonaventure," DS 1:1796–99, 1805–6, and especially 1814–40.

182. *Affectus/affectio* is one of the richest terms in Bonaventure's vocabulary, as is true of many other mystical authors. For a study with special reference to the *Tripl. via* and *Itin.*, see Elizabeth Ann Dreyer, "'*Affectus*' in St. Bonaventure's Description of the Journey of the Soul to God" (Ph.D diss., Marquette University, 1982).

183. *Tripl. via* 3.7 (8:15a): Vigiliantia enim consideret, quam honestum, quam conferens, quam delectabile, sit diligere Deum; et ex hoc quasi nata fiducia parit concupiscentiam, et illa excedentiam, quousque perveniatur ad copulam et osculum et amplexum. . . .

184. As we have seen above, Bonaventure describes Francis as the *vir hierarchicus* in *Leg. maj.* prol. 1 (cf. *De plantatione paradisi* 10 in 5:577b). The theme of the *anima hierarchizata*, based on the Dionysianism of Gallus, is also found in the *Itin.* 4.4–8, and discussed in detail in *Hexaem.* 20.22–29, 21.16–33, 22.24–42 and 23.1–31. Bonaventure defends the theological legitimacy of such "angelization" in *II Sent.* d.9. a.1, q.5 (2:250a–251b). For a summary of his teaching, see Longpré, "Bonaventure," DS 1:1816–18.

185. Bonaventure's understanding of the relationship between love and knowledge, always one of the central themes of Christian mysticism, has been treated by Marianne Schlosser, *Cognitio et amor: Zum kognitiven und voluntativen Grund der Gotteserfahrung nach Bonaventura* (Paderborn: Schöningh, 1990).

186. *Tripl. via* 3.13 (8:17b): Et hic est nobilissimus elevationis modus; sed tamen ad hoc, quod sit perfectus, praeexigit alium, sicut perfectio illuminationem, et sicut negatio affirmationem. Hic autem modus ascendendi tanto est vigorosior, quanto vis ascendens est intimior; tanto fructuosior, quanto affectio proximior.

187. For a classic account of the *Itin.*, see Gilson, *Philosophy*, chaps. 12 and 14. Other useful general surveys include Jacques Guy Bougerol, "L'aspect original de *l'Itinerarium mentis in deum* et son influence sur la spiritualité de son temps," *Antonianum* 52 (1977): 309–25; Ruh, *Geschichte*, 2:412–28; and, for the relation to Neoplatonism, Werner Beierwaltes, "Aufstieg

und Einung in Bonaventuras mysticher Schrift 'Itinerarium mentis in Deum,'" *Denken des Einen* (Franfurt: Klostermann, 1984), pp. 385–423. See also the recent account of Denys Turner, *The Darkness of God: Negativity in Christian Mysticism* (Cambridge: Cambridge University Press, 1995), chap. 5, "Hierarchy interiorised: Bonaventure's *Itinerarium Mentis in Deum*."

188. The seraph symbol is introduced in *Itin.* prol. 2 and is omnipresent in the text (e.g., prol. 3, 2.11, 4.7, 7.1, 7.3). The tabernacle symbol enters in 3.1 and is strongly developed in chapters 5 and 6. Other important symbols include the mirror (prol. 4, 1.5, 2.1, 3.1, 3.5, 4.7), the ladder (prol. 2, 1.3, 1.9, 4.1, 7.1) and the book (1.14, 2.1, 2.12). On Bonaventure's use of the symbolism of the Temple and its relation to previous mystical interpretations, such as that of Richard of St. Victor, see Sister Lilian Turner, "The Symbolism of the Temple in St. Bonaventure's '*Itinerarium mentis in Deum*'" (Ph.D. diss., Fordham University, 1968).

189. *II Sent.* d.8, p.2, a.1, q.2, conc. (2:226b–227a): In anima namque humana idem est intimum et supremum; et hoc patet, quia secundum sui supremum maxime approximat Deo, similiter secundum sui intimum; unde quanto magis redit ad interiora, tanto magis ascendit et unitur aeternis. For more on this theme and Bonaventure's symbolic mentality, see Bernard McGinn, "Ascension and Introversion in the *Itinerarium mentis in Deum*," in *San Bonaventura 1274–1974*, 3:535–52.

190. Bonaventure makes an interesting comment on why the Bible resorts to symbols and metaphors in *Serm. I de Sanctis Apostolis Petro et Paulo* (9:547a): . . . quia sub una metaphora saepe concluditur quod multis dictionibus non exprimeretur. Ewert Cousins in his article "Mandala Symbolism in the Theology of Bonaventure," *University of Toronto Quarterly* 40 (1971): 185–201, compares the seraph and the tabernacle to mandala symbols, that is, sacred circular diagrams that are simultaneously "a picture of the cosmos, of the inner world, and of the spiritual journey" (p. 195). Another treatment of the role of symbols in the *Itin.* can be found in Nguyen Van Si, "Les symboles de l'itinéraire dans l'*Itinerarium mentis in deum* de Bonaventure," *Antonianum* 68 (1993): 327–47.

191. *Itin.* 1.2 (5:297a): . . . ipsa rerum universitas sit scala ad ascendendum in Deum; et in rebus quaedam sint vestigium, quaedam imago . . . : ad hoc, quod perveniamus ad primum principium considerandum, . . . oportet nos transire per vestigium, quod est corporale et temporale et extra nos . . . ; oportet, nos intrare in mentem nostram, quae est imago Dei aeviterna, spiritualis et intra nos . . . ; oportet, nos transcendere ad aeternum, spiritualissimum, et supra nos, aspiciendo ad primum principium. . . .

192. *Itin.* 1.5 (5:297b): . . . sic minor mundus sex gradibus illuminationum sibi succedentium ad quietem contemplationis ordinatissime perducatur.

193. This was first shown by Friedrich Andres, "Die Stufen der Contemplatio in Bonaventuras *Itinerarium mentis in Deum* und im *Benjamin maior* des Richard von St. Viktor," *Franziskanische Studien* 8 (1921): 189–200. For the background, see J.-A. Robillaird, "Les six genres de contemplation chez Richard de Saint-Victor et leur origine platonicienne," *Revue des sciences philosophiques et théologiques* 28 (1939): 229–33.

194. See my paper, "Ascension and Introversion," pp. 545–49; and the discussion of Isaac in *Growth of Mysticism*, pp. 288–91.

195. In *Serm. V de Epiphania* (9:162b) Bonaventure defines the term as follows: . . . apex mentis, quod est summum ipsius animae et quasi centrum, in quo recolliguntur omnes aliae vires.

196. Bonaventure includes a brief discussion of how the Trinity is revealed in creatures on the natural level in 2.7–8; but the Augustinian analysis of the three powers of the souls as the *imago* occurs in 3.2–5. Both chapters contain accounts of how all true knowledge depends on our contact with the exemplary ideas in the Divine Art, that is, Augustinian illumination theory (see 2.9–10; 3.3–4 and 7). On the illumination theory in *Itin.*, see Beierwaltes, "Aufstieg und Einung," pp. 403–6.

197. *Itin.* 4.2 (5:306a): . . . non potuit anima nostra perfecte ab his sensibilibus relevari ad contuitum sui et aeternae Veritatis in se ipsa, nisi Veritas, assumpta forma humana in Christo, fieret sibi scala reparans scalam, quae fracta fuerat in Adam.

198. Bonaventure is one of the major exponents of the classical teaching concerning the spiritual senses, as is evident not only from this summary text but also from such other treatments as *III Sent.* d.13, dub.1 (3:291a–292a); *De plantatione paradisi* 16 (5:578b–579b); *Brevil.* 5.6 (5:258b–260a) and *Red. art.* 10 (5:322b). For a discussion, see Karl Rahner, "The Doctrine of the Spiritual Senses in the Middle Ages," in *Theological Investigations XVI* (New York: Crossroad, 1979), 109–28. While the spiritual senses for Bonaventure are activated and belong primarily to the second or illuminative stage of the journey into God, the Franciscan's conviction regarding the dynamic co-presence of all the stages does not restrict their operation to that level and hence the sense of *tactus* is particularly associated with the ecstatic love of union.

199. The terms that Bonaventure employs to describe the activities of the nine angelic orders (*Itin.* 4.4; 5:307a) are taken directly from Gallus (see chart 1): *nuntiatio, dictatio, ductio, ordinatio, roboratio, imperatio, susceptio, revelatio, unitio* (*unctio* in some mss.). For the importance of this interiorization of the hierarchies, see Turner, *Darkness of God*, chap. 5.

200. For the coincidence of opposites, see, e.g., *Itin.* 6.3 (5:311a): Nam ibi est summa communicabilitas cum personarum proprietate, summa consubstantialitas cum hypostasum pluralitate, summa configurabilitas cum discreta personalitate, summa coaequalitas cum ordine, summa coaeternitas cum emanatione, summa cointimitas cum emissione. Bonaventure, unlike Nicholas of Cusa, does not explicitly employ the term *coincidentia oppositorum* to describe this form of argumentation, and therefore some have contended that it should not be applied to the Franciscan. Nevertheless, Ewert Cousins makes a good case for the helpfulness of the *coincidentia oppositorum* in understanding Bonaventure; see especially his *Bonaventure and the Coincidence of Opposites*, chaps. 1 and 7, and the discussion of the *Itin.* in chap. 3. Other scholars have also been willing to use this language in relation to the final chapters of the work. e.g., Hayes, *Hidden Center*, pp. 89–90; and Beierwaltes, "Aufstieg und Einung," pp. 409–10, 413.

201. *Itin.* 3.2 (310b): . . . summum igitur bonum summe diffusivum est sui. . . . Bonaventure also uses the axiom in *M. Trin.* q.2, a.1, opp.7 (5:60b), and *Serm. de regno Dei* 43 (5:551b).

202. This is also stressed in the analysis of contemplation in Bonaventure's exegesis of the transfiguration account, *Commentarius in Evangelium Lucae* 9.64 (7:237b): Ex hoc eriudiuntur contemplativi, ut non tantum erigant oculos ad lucem Deitatis radiantem, sed etiam ad nubem humanitatis obumbrantem.

203. *Itin.* 6.7 (5:312a): In hac autem consideratione est perfecta illuminationis mentis . . . . in sexto gradu quasi in sexta die perveniat; nec aliquid iam amplius restet nisi dies requiei, in qua per mentis excessum requiescat humanae mentis perspicacitas ab omni opere, quod patraret (cf. Gen. 2:2).

204. Etymologically, *contuitus* can be translated as "concomitant gaze, insight, or grasp." The most important discussion of the teaching that the divine reason is "contuited by us" along with created reason in every act of certain knowledge is found in *Sc. Chr.* q.4, conc. (5:22b–24b). See also *Red. art.* 18 (5:324a), *Sermo Christus unus omnium magister* 7–19 (5:569a–572a), and *III Sent.* d.35, a.1, q.3, conc. (3:778). For a succinct presentation of the significance of *contuitio* in Bonaventure's mysticism, see Cousins, "Bonaventure's Mysticism of Language," pp. 248–52, who summarizes: "This innate awareness of God can be awakened by the exercise of contuition through the technique of contemplative *reductio,* and it can be brought to ecstatic awareness by divine grace."

205. *Itin.* 7.1 (5:312ab): . . . postquam mens nostra contuita est Deum extra se per vestigia et in vestigiis, intra se per imaginem et in imagine, supra se per divinae lucis similitudinem

supra nos relucentuem et in ipsa luce . . . ; cum tandem in sexto gradu ad hoc pervenerit, ut speculetur in principio primo et summo et mediatore dei et hominum, Iesu Christo, ea quorum similia in creaturis nullatenus reperiri possunt . . . : restat, ut haec speculando transcendat et transeat non solum mundum istum sensibilem, verum etiam semetipsam. . . . In 4.2, as noted above, Bonaventure had insisted that after the Fall it is Christ alone who restores to us the possibility of such *contuitio sui et aeternae Veritatis.* The grounds for this are expressed in *Red. art.* 20 (5:324b), where Bonaventure argues that the highest perfection can be found in the world only if a nature in which the *rationes seminales* are found (i.e., a body), and the nature in which the *rationes intellectuales* are found (i.e., human nature), are united with the *rationes ideales* present in the person of the Son.

206. On the notion of *transitus* in Bonaventure, see Werner Hülsbusch, "Die Theologie des Transitus bei Bonaventura," and André Ménard, "Spiritualité du Transitus," both in *San Bonaventura 1274–1974*, 4:533–65 and 607–35.

207. *Itin.* 7.4 (312b): In hoc autem transitu, si sit perfectus, oportet quod reliquantur omnes intellectuales operationes, et apex affectus totus transferetur et transformetur in Deum. Hoc autem est mysticum et secretissimum, quod nemo novit, nisi qui accipit. . . . A verbal parallel to this passage can be found in the discussion of mystical wisdom in *Hexaem.* 2.29 (5:341a): Et ibi est operatio transcendens omnem intellectum, secretissima: quod nemo scit, nisi qui experitur. Another passage close to *Itin.* 7 occurs in *Hexaem.* 2.32–34 (342ab), with its quotations from Dionysius's *De mystica theologia,* its insistence that *ibi non intrat intellectus sed affectus,* and its emphasis on the death of Christ.

208. In two other places Bonaventure speaks of it as *docta ignorantia;* cf. *II Sent.* d.33, a.2, q.2, ad 6 (2:546a), and *Brevil.* 5.6 (5:260a). On the significance of the apophatic conclusion of Bonaventure's presentation of the journey into God, see Tavard, *Transiency and Permanence,* pp. 238–40; and Rahner, "Spiritual Senses," pp. 125–26. For a survey of Bonaventure's negative theology, see Marianne Schlosser, "Lux Inaccessibilis: Zur negativen Theologie bei Bonaventura," *Franziskanische Studien* 68 (1986): 1–140.

209. *Itin.* 7.6 (313b): Moriamur igitur et ingrediamur in caliginem . . . ; transeamus cum Christo crucifixo ex hoc mundo ad Patrem. For other texts on the *mors mystica,* see *Hexaem.* 2.31 (5:341b), and *Comm. Jo.* 42.13–14 (6:590b). In the *Commentarius in Evangelium Lucae* 9.54 (7:234a) Bonaventure analyzes four ways in which the passion can be spoken of as an *excessus.* On Bonaventure's view of the *mors mystica,* see Longpré, "Bonaventure," DS 1:1833–35; and Alois M. Haas, "Mors mystica: Ein mystologisches Motif," in *Sermo Mysticus: Studien zu Theologie und Sprache der deutschen Mystik* (Freiburg: Universitätsverlag, 1979), 406–9.

210. Turner, *Darkness of God,* 132. On ecstasy's relation to the cross, see von Balthasar, *Glory of the Lord,* 2:268–72.

211. On the distinction of the two forms of contemplation, see Longpré, "Bonaventure," DS 1:1819–40, especially the texts he gathers under the headings, "Extase de l'enseignement" (1823–25) and "Extase de la volonté" (1828–30).

212. Bonaventure has a rich and fluid range of terms for this passing over into God in love: *excessus mentis, alienatio mentis, ecstasis, excessus anagogicus, amor ecstaticus, anagogica unitio, intima unio, amplexus, caligo, docta ignorantia, sursumactio, arcanum spiritualis connubii, sapientia nulliformis, cognitio excellentissima in ecstatico amore, cognitio in caligine, sapientia vera in qua est cognitio per veram experientiam,* etc.

213. Some authors, like Ratzinger (*Theology of History,* p. 90), speak of it as "fully free of knowledge." Others, such as Gilson (*Philosophy,* pp. 417–21), Rahner ("Spiritual Senses," pp. 123–25; and "Der Begriff der ecstasis," pp. 12–16), and Tavard (*Transiency and Permanence,* pp. 245–46) hold that the culmination takes place in love alone, but try to express some relationship between this love and the soul's powers of cognition. On the other side, Longpré ("Bonaventure," DS 1:1835–38) insists that there is always an intellectual element in the

ecstasy of love, as do Titus Szabó ("Extase IV: Chez les théologiens du XIIIe siècle," DS 4:2120–26) and Johannes Beumer ("Zwei schwierige Begriffe in der mystischen Theologie Bonaventuras ['raptus' und 'ecstasis']," *Franziskanische Studien* 56 [1974]: 259–61). Different interpretations tend to appeal to different texts, or at least to weight them differently. It is obvious that there is no single systematic statement in the Franciscan's corpus–and perhaps there is some ambiguity as well. Also important in discussing this issue is the large literature devoted to Bonaventure's doctrine of love, on which see especially the classic work of Zoltan Alszeghy, *Grundformen der Liebe: Die Theorie der Gottesliebe bei dem Hl. Bonaventura* (Rome: Gregorian University, 1946).

214. For expressions of tasting and touching, see, e.g., *Itin.* 4.3 (5:306b). Touch is given the highest value in *Brevil.* 5.6 (259b): . . . astringitur [some manuscripts read amplectitur] summa suavitas sub ratione Verbi incarnati, inter nos habitantis corporaliter et reddentis se nobis palpabile, osculabile, amplexabile per ardentissimam caritatem, quae mentem nostram per ecstasim et raptum transire facit ex hoc mundo ad Patrem. Cf. *III Sent.* d.27, a.2, q.1, ad 6 (3:604b).

215. *Sc. Chr.* q.7, ad 19–21 (5:43a): . . . excessus est ultimus modus cognoscendi et nobilissimus. He goes on to say: . . . istum cognoscendi modum vix aut nunquam intelligit nisi expertus, nec expertus, nisi qui est in caritate radicatus et fundatus, ut possit comprehendere cum omnibus sanctis, quod sit longitudo, latitudo, etc. (Eph. 3:17–18); in quo etiam experimentalis et vera consistit sapientia, quae inchoatur in via et consummatur in patria. . . . See, e.g., the comments on *cognitio in ecstatico amore* in *III Sent.,* d.24, dub.4 (3:531b).

216. Not just theological knowing but all human knowing aims at *ecstasis,* as is clear from *Red. art.* 26 (5:325b). It is in this sense that I think that Bonaventure is closer to the mystics of the twelfth century than he is to Thomas Gallus.

217. Bonaventure seems to try to express this interaction in several texts, e.g., *III Sent.* d.34, p.1, a.2, q.2, ad 2 (3:748b–49a): Cognitio experimentalis de divina suavitate amplificat cognitionem speculativam de divina veritate: secreta enim Dei amicis et familiaribus consueverunt revelari. The primary argument, however, rests on the exemplary function of St. Francis.

218. See, e.g., *I Sent.* d.1, a.3, q.2, conc. (1:40b–41a); and *III Sent.* d.23, a.2, q.3, ad 7 (3:546b).

219. *Comm. Jn.* 1.43 (6:256a): . . . et sublimiter contemplantes, in quorum aspectu nulla figitur imago creaturae. Et tunc revera magis sentiunt, quam cognoscunt.

220. *Sc. Chr.* q. 7, conc. (5:40ab): . . . in comprehensivo [modo] cognoscens capit cognitum, in excessivo vero cognitum capit cognoscentem. Here I agree with Rahner ("Spiritual Senses," pp. 118–21) against Longpré ("Bonaventure," DS 1:1829 n. 2) that the contact in ecstatic love takes place without an *effectus interior.* The basis for this is found in the discussions in *II Sent.* d.23, a.2, q.3, conc., and ad 5 and 6 (2:545a–546b); and *III Sent.* d. 24 (3:531b). Joseph Maréchal (*Études sur la psychologie des mystiques,* 2 vols. [Bruges: Beyaert-Desclée, 1924–37], 2:25–27) sides with Rahner, while Beumer ("Zwei schwierige Begriffe," pp. 257–59) tends to side with Longpré but admits that Bonaventure may be ambiguous.

221. *III Sent.* d.9, a.1, q.6 (3:21a): Unde tales apparitiones potius sunt formidandae quam desiderandae. Cf. *Hexaem.* 22.42 (5:414), *Commentarius in Evangelium Lucae* 9.62 and 10.32 (7:236b and 262b).

222. The trinitarian aspect of the experience is suggested in *Itin.* 7.6 and *Sc. Chr.* q. 7, conc., and is clearly expressed in *Brevil.* prol. (5:202b): . . . et per hanc notitiam [of the fullness of scripture] pervenire ad plenissimam notitiam et excessivum amorem beatissimae Trinitatis, quo Sanctorum desideria tendunt, in quo est status et complementum omnis veri et boni.

223. For a study of the two terms, see Johannes Beumer, "Zwei schwierige Begriffe, pp.

249–62; cf. Longpré, "Bonaventure," DS 1:1838–40. It is interesting to note that Bonaventure's teacher, Alexander of Hales, devoted a *quaestio* to the issue of the mode of rapture enjoyed by Paul; see Quaestio LXVIII, "De Raptu Pauli," in *Magistri Alexandri de Hales: Quaestiones Disputatae 'Antequam esset Frater,'* 3 vols. (Quaracchi: Collegium S. Bonaventurae, 1960) 3:1345–63.

224. *Hexaem.* 3.30 (5:348a): Haec enim sublevatio facit animam Deo simillimam, quoniam potest in statu viae–nec est idem ecstasis et raptus–unde, ut dicunt, non habent habitum gloriae, sed actum. For other texts that discuss *raptus,* see, e.g., *II Sent.* d.23, a.2, q.3, ad 6 (2:546a); *III Sent.* d.35, a.1, q.1, conc. (3:774b); *IV Sent.* d.6, a.3, q.2, dub.1 (4:160a); *Sc. Chr.* q.4, conc. (5:24b); *Brevil.* 5.6 (5:259b); *Serm. III in Dom. III in Quad.* (9:229b).

225. *Hexaem.* 22.22 (5:441a) speaks of Francis being raptured: Et dicebat, quod etiam antequam haberet habitum, raptus fuit et inventus iuxta quandam sepem. It is significant that this language does not occur in the *Itin.,* though it used in three places in the *Leg. maj.* (3.6, 9.2, and 10.2).

226. Bonaventure explicitly says in *II Sent.* d.23, a.2, q.3, ad 6 (2:546a) that ecstasy is open to all: Hunc modum cognoscendi arbitror cuilibet viro iusto in via ista esse quaerendum; quodsi Deus aliquid ultra faciet, hoc privilegium est speciale, non legis communis.

227. See *III Sent.* d.32, a.1, q.3, ad 3; cf. d.27, a.2, q.1, conc. (3:701b and 604a).

228. E.g., *III Sent.* d.6, a.2, q.2, conc. (3:161a–62b). Cf. *Brevil.* 6.13 (5:279b).

229. *Sc. Chr.* q.7, epil. (5:43b): . . . ad cuius experientiam plus valet internum silentium quam exterius verbum. Et ideo hic finis verbi habendus est, et orandus Dominus, ut experiri donet quod loquimur.

Chapter 3

1. The pseudonymous writings at one time or another ascribed to Bonaventure number 184 in the catalogue compiled by Balduinus Distelbrink, *Bonaventurae Scripta: Authentica dubia vel spuria critice recensita.* This is probably a greater number than for any other medieval author, and it includes some of the most popular ascetical and mystical treatises of the later Middle Ages.

2. The best recent treatment is that of Kurt Ruh in *Geschichte,* 2:524–37. See also Dagobert Stöckerl, *Bruder David von Augsburg: Ein deutscher Mystiker aus dem Franziskanerorden* (Munich: Lentner, 1914); André Rayez, "David d'Augsbourg," DS 3:42–44; Taddeo Bargiel, "Davide d'Augusta: Introduzione," in *Dizionario Francescano,* Vol. 1, *I Mistici: Scritti dei Mistici Francescani Secolo XIII,* pp. 177–80; and in English J. V. Fleming, *An Introduction to the Franciscan Literature of the Middle Ages,* pp. 216–25. On David's mysticism, see Jacques Heerinckx, "Theologia mystica in scriptis fratris David ab Augusta," *Antonianum* 8 (1933): 49–83 and 161–92. The importance of David's vernacular works (twenty-four are known, fourteen still unedited) has been stressed by Kurt Ruh, "David von Augsburg und die Entstehung eines franziskanisches Schrifttums in deutscher Sprache," in *Kleine Schriften:* Band II, *Scholastik und Mystik im Spätmittelalter* (Berlin: Walter de Gruyter, 1984), pp. 46–67. Many of David's vernacular works were also translated into Middle Dutch and had a significant influence on the *Devotio moderna.*

3. *Fr. David ab Augusta: De exterioris et interioris hominis compositione secundum triplicem statum incipientium, proficientium et perfectorum* (Quaracchi: Collegium S. Bonaventurae, 1899). There is an English translation, *Spiritual Life and Progress by David of Augsburg,* trans. Dominic Devas, 2 vols. (London: Burns Oates & Washbourne, 1937). I will cite the *De compositione* by book, chapter, and section (where required), with the page of the edition in parentheses–e.g., 1.10.2 (15).

4. St. Francis is mentioned in only three places: 1.6.3 (10), 3.43.3 (267), and 3.44.1 (269). Poverty is encouraged but not singled out; see 2.33.1 (120), 3.44–45 and 49 (268–76 and 284–86). There is no special concentration on the passion, though there is some devotion to the *amor carnalis Christi* as manifested in the cross, see, e.g., 3.2.4 (165) and 3.65.1 (352-53). Franciscan elements are stronger in some of David's vernacular works; see Ruh, *Geschichte*, 2:528–29.

5. See *De comp.* 2.10.4 (94): Appetitus honoris datus ei fuerat, ut altissimum honorem desideraret, scilicet Deo placere, amicum Dei esse et filium et heredem . . . ; item, unus cum Deo fieri spiritus et aequalis Angelis fieri et nulli subesse nisi summo Domino omnium. . . . Of course, David's presentation is not totally cloistral in the way a twelfth-century monastic treatise would have been since he also includes instructions for friars regarding their conduct outside the house, e.g., 1.22-24 (28-34).

6. This section comprises *De comp.* 3.63-68 (338-67).

7. *De comp.* 3.62.2 (338): Omnis igitur orationis fructus et finis est Deo adhaerere et unus cum eo spiritus fieri per liquefactionem purissimi amoris et speculationem serenissimae cognitionis et absconsionem in Dei vultu ab omni mundanorum strepitu per excessum quietissimae fruitionis. . . .

8. *De comp.* 3.63.8 (346): . . . liquet, quod istorum perfecta inchoatio est perfectio viae in hac vita.

9. *De comp.* 3.6.64. In typically eclectic fashion, David then adds a discussion of seven kinds of devotion based on different affections in 3.6.65, another itinerary culminating in what is clearly a mystical state of "rapture of admiration." David's discussion of *iubilus* was noted by Herbert Grundmann, "Jubel," *Ausgewählte Aufsätze*, 3:154.

10. *De comp.* 3.66.1 (356): His autem tanto minus immorandum est, quanto frequentius eis innitentes decipiunt.

11. *De comp.* 3.66.5 (359–60): . . . quidam, decepti a seductoribus spiritibus, vel propriis falsis opinionibus, putant, sibi apparere in visione vel ipsum Christum vel eius gloriossimam Genitricem et non solum amplexibus et osculis, sed etiam aliis indecentioribus gestibus et actibus ab eis demulceri, ut, sicut spiritus ipsorum interius ab ipsis consolatur spiritualiter, ita et caro exterius sibi congruo oblectationis sensu sensibiliter demulceatur et carnaliter consoletur.

12. *De comp.* 3.67.1 (361): . . . multifariis vaticiniis iam usque ad fastidium repleti sumus de antichristi adventu. . . .

13. Herbert Grundmann (*Religious Movements in the Middle Ages,* p. 199) argued that David himself probably wrote nothing in German; but Ruh ("David von Augsburg und die Entstehung eines franziskanisches Schrifttums," pp. 58–61) effectively demonstrates the authenticity of at least three treatises.

14. Ruh, "David von Augsburg," p. 64.

15. The Latin text was edited by Jacques Heerinckx, "Le 'Septem Gradus Orationis' de David d'Augsbourg," *Revue d'ascetique et de mystique* 14 (1933): 146–70. Kurt Ruh edited David's own German version in *David von Augsburg: Die sieben Staffeln des Gebetes* (Munich: Fink, 1965). In addition, there is a later German translation of the Latin found in Franz Pfeiffer, *Deutsche Mystiker des vierzehnten Jahrhunderts,* 2 vols. (Aalen: Scientia, 1962; reprint of Leipzig 1845 ed.), 1:387–97; as well as two unedited Middle Dutch versions.

16. *Dei sieben Staffeln,* lines 435–40 (ed. Ruh, 65): Da wirt dv sele also vereinet mit gotte, das si ist, das got ist, swie si doch got niht ist, doch ein herce, ein wile, ein minne, ein geist mit gotte, nit allein mit der einvnge, das si iesa niht anders welle, denne das got wil, mer das si niht anders mac wellen denne got (the Latin text can be found in Heerinckx, "Le 'Septem Gradus Orationis,'" p. 167). The quotation is from William of St. Thierry, *Epistola aurea* 262 (see SC 223:352-54), on which see *Growth of Mysticism*, p. 265. The teaching on the higher

mystical states in David's treatise was first discussed by Joseph Maréchal in his *Études sur la psychologie des mystiques,* 2 vols. (Bruges: Beyaert-Desclée, 1924–37), 2:272–75.

17. The treatise was published by Franz Pfeiffer in his article "Bruder David von Augsburg," *Zeitschrift für Deutsches Alterthum* 9 (1853): 8–55. The trinitarian section can be found on pp. 48–51. For the importance of this treatise, see Kurt Ruh, "Die trinitarische Spekulation in deutscher Mystik und Scholastik," in *Kleine Schriften: Band II, Scholastik und Mystik im Spätmittelalter,* pp. 14–45 (especially pp. 19–21, 30–32, and 40–41).

18. See the discussion in *Growth of Mysticism,* pp. 347–52, noting the trinitarian teaching on p. 349.

19. *Von der Offenbarung* (49–50): der vater ist der brunne unde der ursprunc des götelîchen fluzzes; der sun ist alse daz rivier unde der bach der von dem brunnen fluizet; der heilige geist ist also der sê der von dem brunnen unde von dem riviere fluizet. der vater ist daz anegenge, der sun daz mittel, der heilige geist daz zil des götelîchen fluzzes, wan daz oberste guot mac niht an stete gestân alsô, ez enteile sich und erbiete sich ze niezende unde ze würkende daz beste. The analogy of fountain-brook-sea first appears in Anselm, *Epistola de Incarnatione Verbi* (PL 158:280), but David's expression of the analogy depends on the Dionysian understanding of the Father as "fountain of superessential deity" (*pēgē tēs hyperousiou theotētos* [DN 2.5]), who flows forth into the Son and Spirit as the highest expression of the principle *bonum est diffusivum sui* (for appearances of this axiom in David's vernacular works, see Pfeiffer, *Deutsche Mystiker,* 310.2–3, 363.5–7, 365.30–33, and 376.33–35). The final sentence reflects the famous first axiom of the Proclean *Liber de causis,* summarized by Bonaventure as *quanto aliquid prius, tanto potentius et actualius* (*M. Trin.* q.7, sed contra 2).

20. The German materials have been analyzed by Kurt Ruh, *Bonaventura deutsch: Ein Beitrag zur deutschen Franziskaner-Mystik und-Scholastik* (Bern: Francke, 1956).

21. It is not possible to treat all the Franciscans who composed mystical texts during the second half of the thirteenth century. Among those not considered here are Gilbert of Tournai (d. 1284), the author of the *Tractatus de pace,* and John Pecham (d. 1292) whose poem *Philomena* is one of the most charming examples of what has been called the Franciscan "mysticism of the historical event." Also not treated is the anonymous *Meditatio pauperis in solitudine,* a learned ascetical-mystical treatise that appears to have been composed in the 1280s.

22. The Latin text, edited by A. C. Peltier among the works of Bonaventure, has been reprinted with some corrections and apparatus in *Rudolph von Biberach: De septem itineribus aeternitatis,* ed. Margot Schmidt (Stuttgart/Bad Canstatt: frommann-holzboog, 1985. (Of the 109 known manuscripts, thirteen ascribe the text to Bonaventure and only eight to Rudolph.) The German text was edited by Margot Schmidt, *Rudolph von Biberach: Die sieben strassen zu got: Revidierte hochalemannische Übertragung nach der Handschrift Einsiedeln 278 mit hochdeutscher Übersetzung* (Stuttgart/Bad Canstatt: frommann-holzboog, 1985).

23. The *septem itinera,* which Rudolph treats as successive, are (1) *recta intentio,* (2) *studiosa meditatio,* (3) *limpida contemplatio,* (4) *caritativa affectio* (the longest section), (5) *occulta revelatio,* (6) *experimentalis praegustatio* (the highest stage, containing a rich teaching on the spiritual senses, as well as an emphasis on the role of the Eucharist), and (7) *deiformis operatio,* the standard return to the active life incumbent upon all true mystics. For a sketch of Rudolph's teaching and further literature, see Margot Schmidt, "Rodolphe de Biberach," DS 13:846–50. Rudolph was not alone among Franciscans in composing handbooks on mysticism based on recognized authorities, especially Dionysius. Another example can be found in the *De laude Domini novi saeculi* written by Bertram of Ahlen about 1315. See Michael Bihl, "Fr. Bertramus von Ahlen, O.F.M.: Ein Mystiker und Scholastiker, c. 1315," *Archivum Franciscanum Historicum* 40 (1947): 3–48, especially the discussion of the possibility of the vision of God (pp. 41–46).

24. The Latin and German versions have been edited by Urs Kamber, *Arbor Amoris: Der Minnebaum. Ein Pseudo-Bonaventura-Traktat herausgegeben nach lateinischen und deutschen Handschriften des XIV. und XV. Jahrhunderts* (Berlin: Schmidt, 1964). Of the seventeen Latin manuscripts, three bear the name of Bonaventure. Ten manuscripts of the German version are known. Kamber has interesting remarks on the structural and linguistic changes the text underwent in being translated into the vernacular (pp. 93–94, 100–106, 157–58).

25. Only five of these characteristics are actually found in the text of CH 7.2, which in Hugh of St. Victor's *Expositio in Hierarchiam Caelestem* (PL 175:1031C) reads: Mobile enim semper eorum [i.e., seraphim] eorum circa divina, et incessabile, et calidum, et acutum, et superfervidum intentae. . . . The addition of *fervidum* and *inaccessabile* in the *Arbor Amoris* seems to be the author's own invention. Rudolph of Biberach, *De septem itineraribus,* dist. 5, art. 3 (ed., 452–56) discusses seraphic love using only the five Dionysian predicates. On the relation of the *Arbor Amoris* to Hugh and the Dionysian tradition, see Kambers, *Arbor Amoris,* pp. 80–91.

26. *Arbor Amoris* (ed., 51.171–72): Calidum ergo ponitur in amore, ut sensum viuificet, incitet et inflammet. Each distinction is divided into two branches: *risus et suspiria* for the *distinccio mobile; continuacio et perseuerancia* for the *distinccio incessabile;* and *ardor et lacrime* for the *distinccio calidum.*

27. These four stages are treated in *Arbor Amoris* (ed., 53.212–59.331). The passage cited is at 58.315–18: Nam si inaccessabilem iubilum amoris dicerem, et ramos eius mentis alienacionem uel excessum et racionis omnis excecacionem, ita quod ab affectu trahatur sicut cecus a catello, multorum obiecciones pertimesco.

28. At least six forms of the Latin text are known (see Distelbrink, *Bonaventura Scripta,* pp. 194–97). The original *forma brevis* with the incipit "Ad te levavi animam meam" was written by Friar James of Milan toward the end of the thirteenth century. The most popular version of the text, however, was the *forma longa* of the "Currite" version, which is found complete in 221 manuscripts and partially in another 147! This text uses all of James's original twenty-three chapters but adds considerable material from Bonaventure and other authors, especially on devotion to the passsion. Here I will use the original version as edited by the Quaracchi Fathers, *Stimulus Amoris Fr. Iacobi Mediolanensis,* Bibliotheca Franciscana Ascetica Medii Aevi 4 (Quaracchi: Collegium S. Bonaventurae, 1905). Hilton's translation has been edited by Harold Kane, *The Prickynge of Love,* 2 vols. (Salzburg: Institut für Anglistik und Amerikanistik, 1983). For surveys of the text and its versions, see Pierre Péano, "Jacques de Milan," DS 8:48–49; and Clare Kirchberger, "Introduction," in *Walter Hilton, The Goad of Love: An Unpublished Translation of the Stimulus Amoris* (London: Faber & Faber, 1952), pp. 13–44. See also Stephen E. Wessley, "James of Milan and the Guglielmites: Franciscan spirituality and popular heresy in late thirteenth-century Milan," *Collectanea Francescana* 54 (1984): 5–20; Celestino Piana, "Il 'Fr. Iacobus de Mediolano Lector' autore dello Pseudo-Bonaventurino *Stimulus Amoris* ed un convento del suo insegnamento," *Antonianum* 61 (1986): 329–39; and Ruh, *Geschichte,* 2:442–45.

29. The original version by James contains two full chapters devoted to meditation on the passion, though the theme also occurs eleswhere; the full version from the later fourteenth century has fifteen chapters on the passion.

30. E.g., the summary in chap. 13 (ed., 64), or the meditation on the passion and nativity in chap. 14 (70–72). James's mixing of the milk he sucks from the Virgin with the blood he drinks from Christ's side is an almost baroque mystical conceit: Et non solum apparebo cum suo Filio crucifixus, sed etiam ad praesepe rediens ibi cum eo iacebo parvulus, ut ibidem cum suo Filio suis uberibus merear adlactari. Miscebo ergo lac matris cum sanguine Filii et mihi faciam unam dulcissimam potionem (ed., 71).

31. *Stimulus Amoris,* prologus (ed., 3-4): Transfige, dulcissime Domine Iesu Christe, medullas animae meae suavissimo ac saluberrimo vulnere amoris tui. Vulnera viscera animae meae vera et fraterna et apostolica caritate, ut vere ardeat et langueat, liquefiat anima mea solo semper amore et desiderio tui. The wounding theme occurs often, e.g., caps. 1, 3, 6, 7, 14, 15, 16, 23 (ed., 13, 17, 29–30, 32–35, 71–75, 78–81, 93, 129).

32. *Stimulus Amoris* chap. 9 (ed., 40–43) distinguishes between an *inebriatio . . . in intensione laetitiae* achieved through compassion with Christ on the cross, which is primarily in the heart but which also finds external expression, and an *inebriatio . . . in intensione dulcedinis,* which reduces the soul to sleep or quiet in which all sense activity is taken away. Given the fact that the devil can imitate the latter, James warns contemplatives to beware of pride and always to be sure to fix the *acies mentis* on God alone in such experiences.

33. *Stimulus Amoris,* chap. 23 (ed., 126–29); cf. chap. 8 (ed., 39).

34. The one hundred chapters of the Latin version of the *Meditationes Vitae Christi* can be found in *Opera Omnia Sancti Bonaventurae,* ed. A. C. Peltier (Paris: Vives, 1868) 12:509–630. An improved edition of the key chapters on the passion (chaps. 73–85) was prepared by Sister M. Jordan Stallings, *Meditaciones de Passione Christi olim Sancto Bonaventurae attributae* (Washington, D.C.: Catholic University, 1965). Isa Ragusa and Rosalie B. Green, in their *Meditations on the Life of Christ: An Illustrated Manuscript of the Fourteenth Century* (Princeton: Princeton University Press, 1961), provide a translation of the whole text (partly from an Italian manuscript and completed from the Latin text). This volume gives the surviving 193 illustrations found in Paris, Bibliothèque Nationale, MS ital. 115 (this manuscript, despite its incomplete text, had room for 297 pictures).

35. For surveys of the complex authorship question, see Distelbrink, *Bonaventura Scripta,* pp. 157–58; and Jacques-Guy Bougerol, "Jean 'de Caulibus,'" DS 8:324–26.

36. Columba Fischer, "Die 'Meditationes Vitae Christi': Ihre handschriftliche Ueberlieferung und die Verfasserfrage," *Archivum Franciscanum Historicum* 25 (1932): 3–35, 175–209, 305–48, and 449–83, lists 217 manuscripts–132 Latin, 51 Italian, 26 English and 24 French. The most important English version was completed by the Carthusian Nicholas Love in 1410. See Elizabeth Salter, *Nicholas Love's "Myrrour of the Blessed Lyf of Jesu Christ,"* Analecta Carthusiana 10 (Salzburg: Institut für Englische Sprache und Literatur, 1974).

37. For example, Ruh concludes: "Die 'Meditationes vitae Christi' sind ein Erbauungs-, kein Mystikbuch. Sie wollen indes und können zur mystischen Erfahrung hinführen" (*Geschichte,* 2:441).

38. For some comments on this aspect, see Fleming, *Introduction to Franciscan Literature,* pp. 242–51.

39. See the discussion in chap. 51 (Peltier, 578), which admits: Et ideo ista de humanitate Christi rectius et proprius meditatio, quam contemplatio nominari debet.

40. The three forms of contemplation are introduced in chap. 50 and discussed in chaps. 51–53. The lengthy treatise on action and contemplation in chaps. 45–58 (Peltier, 569–88), of which this discussion forms the center, shows that although the author concentrated on the contemplation of the humanity of Christ, he intended his doctrine to be seen within the broader Bernardine picture of the transition from carnal to spiritual love.

41. *Meditationes* 50 (Peltier, 577): Scire autem debes, quod in qualibet harum duo sunt mentis excessus, intellectualis, et affectualis. The passage from Bernard can be found in SC 49.4 (*Sancti Bernardi Opera,* 2:75.20–24). Despite the mention of affectivity here, the *Meditationes,* like David of Augsburg, are free of the affective Dionysian emphasis found in Bonaventure and many other Franciscan writers.

42. *Meditationes* 99 (Peltier, 628): Vides quomodo etiam carnalis est haec meditatio, respectu spiritualis. Hoc non accipias, ut minuatur devotio; sed ut fervor crescat ad majora,

ad quae tamen per haec transeundo, te venire oporteat; .... Haec ergo meditari sit tota et una intentio tua, requies tua, cibus tuus, studium tuum.... Non enim qui ad majorem contemplationem ascendunt, hanc dimittere debent pro loco et tempore.... Unde recordare, quod habuisti supra in tractatu hujusmodi contemplationis, scilicet de humanitate Christi, quam beatus Bernardus, qui fuit altissimus contemplator, nunquam dimissit.

43. *Meditationes,* prol. (Peltier, 510): Propterea sic ardenter afficiebatur ad ipsam, ut quasi sua pictura fieret. Nam in cunctis virtutibus, quam perfectius poterat, imitabatur eamdem, ut tandem complente ac perficiente Jesu per impressionem sacrorum stigmatum, fuit in eum transformatus totaliter.

44. The nativity cycle takes up chaps. 4–12, while the passion cycle, which is arranged according to the hours of the liturgical day, is found in chaps. 73–85.

45. The most ringing defense of poverty is found in chap. 44 (Peltier, 564–69), but it is given special praise in many places; e.g., chaps. 5, 9, 12, 13, 14, 16, 21, 24, 28. On the Spiritual tendency of the text, see Michael Thomas ("Zum religionsgeschichtlichen Standort der 'Meditationes vitae Christi,'" *Zeitschrift für Religions- und Geistesgeschichte* 24 [1972]: 209–26), who even detects possible knowledge of Joachim of Fiore in the prologue.

46. In this and the following section I wish once again to acknowledge my indebtedness to Paul Lachance for bibliographic help and a number of suggestions.

47. Angelo of Clareno (ca. 1255–1337), a leader of the Spirituals in the Italian Marche, was among the group that Pope Celestine V allowed to break off from the Franciscans to live Francis's true ideal of poverty as the new order of Poor Hermits of Celestine. This permission was revoked under Boniface VIII. Angelo was imprisoned for a time under John XXII, but was eventually freed to lead a life of exile. His *Chronicon seu Historia Septem Tribulationum Ordinis Minorum,* written during this period, considers Bonaventure's "persecution" of John of Parma as the fourth of the seven apocalyptic tribulations to face the true followers of Francis before their expected triumph at the end of the age. For a study of his life and works, see Lydia von Auw, *Angelo Clareno et les spirituels italiens* (Rome: Edizioni di Storia e Letteratura, 1979), and the brief survey of Pierre Péano, "Pierre de Fossombrone (Angelo Clareno)," DS 12:1582–88.

48. The drama of the history of the Spirituals has attracted considerable literature. Among the older accounts, see Livarius Oliger, "Spirituels," *Dictionnaire de théologie catholique,* ed. A. Vacant and E. Mangenot, 16 vols. (Paris: Letouzey et Ané, 1903–50) 14:2522–49; and Decima L. Douie, *The Nature and Effect of the Heresy of the Fraticelli* (Manchester: Manchester University Press, 1932). Among more recent studies, consult Raoul Manselli, *La "Lectura super Apocalipsim" di Pietro di Giovanni Olivi* (Rome: Istituto Storico Italiano per il Medio Evo, 1955) and *Spirituali e Beghini in Provenza* (Rome: Istituto Storico Italiano per il Medio Evo. 1959); Gordon Leff, *Heresy in the Later Middle Ages,* Vol. 1, Part 1, *Franciscains d'Oc: Les Spirituels ca. 1280–1324,* Cahiers de Fanjeaux 10 (Toulouse: Privat, 1976); *Chi erano Gli Spirituali?* (Assisi: Società Internazionale di Studi Francescani, 1976); and *Fin du monde et signes des temps: Visionnaires et prophètes en France méridionale (fin XIIIe–début XVe siècle),* Cahiers de Fanjeaux 27 (Toulouse: Privat, 1992). On the relation of the Spirituals to Bonaventure, see the historiographical discussion of Edith Pásztor, "Gli Spirituali di fronte a San Bonaventura," *S. Bonaventura Francescano,* pp. 161–79.

49. For a brief introduction that discusses his spiritual writings, see Pierre Péano, "Olieu (Olivi; Pierre Jean)," DS 11:751–62. In English, the numerous works of David Burr over more than twenty years have done much to reveal the importance of Olivi's theology; see especially *The Persecution of Peter Olivi* (Philadelphia: American Philosophical Society, 1976); *Olivi and Franciscan Poverty* (Philadelphia: University of Pennsylvania Press, 1989); and *Olivi's Peaceable Kingdom: A Reading of the Apocalypse Commentary* (Philadelphia: University of Pennsylvania Press, 1993). We still lack any complete survey of this major theological voice.

50. See especially the first four of his *Quaestiones XVII de perfectione evangelica*, ed. A. Emmen and F. Simoncioli in *Studi Francescani* 60 (1963): 382–445; 61 (1964): 108–67. There is also a discussion of the nature of contemplation in the *Quaestiones in secundum Librum Sententiarum*, ed. Bernard Jansen (Quaracchi: Collegium S. Bonaventurae, 1924), q. 54 (pp. 281–82).

51. This manual on the role of suffering in the Christian life was edited by Franz Ehrle in the *Archiv für Literatur- und Kirchengeschichte* 3 (1887): 534–40, and is translated in *Apocalyptic Spirituality*, translation and introduction by Bernard McGinn (New York: Paulist Press, 1979), pp. 173–81. See also the four brief treatises edited by Manselli, *Spirituali e beghini in Provenza*, pp. 267–90. These treatises were translated into Provençal for reading among the communities of beguins, that is, the lay supporters of the Spiritual Franciscans found in Languedoc and Catalonia. See Robert E. Lerner, "Writing and resistance among Beguins of Languedoc and Catalonia," in *Heresy and Literacy, 1000–1530*, ed. Peter Biller and Anne Hudson (Cambridge: Cambridge University Press, 1994), pp. 186–204.

52. *Remedia contra temptationes spirituales*, ed. Manselli in *Spirituali e Beghini in Provenza*, pp. 282–87.

53. This is available in the *Sancti Bonaventurae Operum Supplementum*, ed. Benedict Bonelli, 3 vols. (Trent: J. B. Monauni, 1772–74) 1:50–281. For a recent study, see J. Schlageter, "Die Bedeutung des Hoheliedkommentar des Franziskanertheologen Petrus Johannis Olivi (d. 1298): Argumente für eine neue Edition," *Wissenschaft und Weisheit* 58 (1995): 137–51.

54. Gallus is explicitly mentioned, e.g., *Expositio*, chap. 1.7 (Bonelli, 72).

55. *Expositio* 1.40 (Bonelli, 92–93): Optimus ergo modus quaerendi Deum est recte sursum superintellectualiter extendi, donec mentis apex ab omni ente separatus super omnia exsistentem supersubstantialem intelligat, et per plenam ignorantiam superignota cognoscat. Perfecta ignorantia cognitio est ejus, qui est super omnia, quae cognoscuntur. Hoc est cum Moyse ingredi caliginem, seu nebulam.

56. E.g., *Expositio* 1.42 (Bonelli, 94), which speaks of how the tension between carnal and contemplative minds, found in every age, grows greater "around the beginning of contemplative times" (*circa initiationem contemplativorum statuum*).

57. This vision is reported in several sources, e.g., the *De obitu dicti fratris Petri* edited by Albanus Heysse, "Descriptio Codicis Bibliothecae Laurentianae Florentinae S. Crucis, Plut. 31 sin., Cod. 3," *Archivum Franciscanum Historicum* 11 (1918): 267. Most modern scholars doubt its authenticity. On Joachim's vision, see *Growth of Mysticism*, pp. 337–38.

58. See David Burr, "Olivi, Apocalyptic Expectation, and Visionary Experience," *Traditio* 41 (1985): 273–88. On the role of visions among the Spirituals in general, see Robert E. Lerner, "Ecstatic Dissent," *Speculum* 67 (1992): 52–55.

59. The best account is Burr, *Olivi's Peaceable Kingdom*, especially chaps. 5 and 8 on the coming age. See also Burr, "Olivi, Apocalyptic Expectation, and Visionary Experience."

60. *Lectura super Ioannem* (MS Florence Bibl. Laur. Plut 10 dext. 8, f.73vb), commenting on John 16:25, as cited and translated by Burr, *Olivi's Peaceable Kingdom*, p. 114 (Latin text, 129 n. 46): Christus secundum primum modum vult dicere quod tota doctrina sua exterior secundum quam eos ut homo de divinis usque nunc docuit est quasi parabolica et enigmatica seu similitudinaria et obscura respectu illius quam paulo post faciet per spiritum suum. The other brief quotations in this paragraph are drawn from texts in the unpublished *Lectura super Apocalypsim* quoted by Burr. Burr has also shown how Olivi attempted to construct a general theory of divine communication to humans that embraced prophecy, mystical *gustus* and spiritual exegesis; see his essay "Olivi on Prophecy," in *Lo statuto della profezia nel Medioevo*, ed. G. L. Potestà and Roberto Rusconi as a special issue of *Cristianesimo nella storia* 17.2 (1996): 369–91.

61. For introductions to Ubertino's mystical teaching, see especially Gian-Luca Potestà, "Ubertin de Casale," DS 16:3–25, and his article "Aspetti e implicazioni della mistica cristo-

centrica di Ubertino da Casale," *Abendländischer Mystik im Mittelalter*, pp. 286–99. Also helpful is the summary in Ruh, *Geschichte*, 2:485–95. The fullest account in English remains that of Douie, *Heresy of the Fraticelli*, chap. 5.

62. There is no modern edition, but the work is available in a reprint of the 1485 incunable, *Ubertinus de Casali: Arbor Vitae Crucifixae Jesu*, with an introduction and bibliography by Charles T. Davis (Turin: Bottega d'Erasmo, 1961). The structure, following the popular tree (= cross) image, is as follows: two prologues containing Ubertino's spiritual autobiography; book 1 (11 chapters) deals with the roots of the tree, that is, the Trinity and the Word prior to the incarnation; book 2 is the trunk, containing 8 chapters on the life of Jesus from infancy to baptism; book 3 (23 chapters) is devoted to Christ's miracles and forms the branches; book 4 is the summit of the tree, with 41 chapters on the mysteries of the passion, resurrection, and ascension of the Savior; book 5 is the fruit of the tree (18 chapters on history of the church in the form of a commentary on the Apocalypse). For a survey of scholarship, see G.-L. Potestà, "Un secolo di studi sull'*Arbor Vitae*: Chiesa ed escatologia in Ubertino da Casale," *Collectanea Francescana* 47 (1977): 217–67.

63. For a summary of the speculations of the Spirituals on Antichrist, see Bernard McGinn, *Antichrist: Two Thousand Years of the Human Fascination with Evil* (San Francisco: HarperSanFrancisco, 1994), pp. 157–66.

64. The revival of interest in Ubertino's work can be seen in Gian-Luca Potestà, *Storia ed Escatologia in Ubertino da Casale* (Milan: Università Cattolica del Sacro Cuore, 1980); and Mariano Damiata, *Pietà e Storia nell'Arbor Vitae di Ubertino da Casale* (Florence: Edizioni 'Studi Francescani,' 1988).

65. Ubertino's understanding of the historical and mystical role of Francis is summarized in *Arbor* 5.3, *Iesus Franciscum generans* (26 columns), and 5.4, *Iesus seraph alatus* (18 columns).

66. See E. Randolph Daniel, "Spirituality and Poverty: Angelo da Clareno and Ubertino da Casale," *Medievalia et Humanistica* n.s. 4 (1973): 89–98.

67. See especially *Arbor* 4.7 (304ab). For a collection of texts, see Potestà, "Mistica cristocentrica," pp. 294–95.

68. See the texts cited in Potestà, "Mistica cristocentrica," pp. 296–97.

69. Jean Gerson, however, criticized it as heretical. For the dissemination of the work, see Frédégand Callaey, "L'influence et diffusion de l'*Arbor Vitae* de Ubertin de Casale," *Revue d'histoire ecclésiastique* 17 (1921): 533–46.

70. *Arbor Vitae*, prol.1 (4b): Nam prefata virgo que nunc simul cum prefato Petro regnat in celis totum processum superioris contemplationis de vita Iesu et arcana cordis mei et alia multa de paruuli Iesu sepissime me instruxit. . . . Nam docuit [frater Iohannes Olivi] me: prius interius docente Iesu: in omni lumine cuiuscumque scientie quam maxime in altis ueritatibus theologie et in omni aspectu cuiuscumque create nature quasi ubique intueri dilectum: et meipsum semper sentire cum Iesu mente et corpore crucifixum.

71. Later in the *prologus* he gives equal praise to the Dominican tertiary, Margaret of Città di Castello (1287–1320), for her help as he was composing the *Arbor Vitae* (6b). For a note on this mystic, see chap. 6 (n. 142).

72. *Arbor Vitae*, prol. 2 (8a): Exstasis autem est dicta extra se faciens: unde uiri spirituales dicuntur exstatici, id est, extra se facti Deum considerantes in omnibus non semetipsos. . . . In quo intelligitur ungens Pater: unctio Spiritus Sanctus: unctus Christus homo.

73. *Arbor* 2.4 (97a): Nam non te Christus inuitat ad facienda miracula, sed ad eius sequenda uestigia et ad ruminanda et amplexanda crucis sue opprobria.

74. *Arbor* 4.37 (381a–397a). Also important for the mystical content of the *Arbor* are 2.5 (*Iesus redemptus paruulus* [113b–130b]), where Ubertino treats Simeon's prophecy (Luke 2:29–32), and 4.7 (*Iesus dilecto stratus* [304a–305b]), which discusses John as a contemplative (see John 13:25).

75. The latter three crosses are Ubertino's version of the three traditional stages of spiritual advance found, for example, in Bonaventure's *Tripl. via.* Ubertino uses a number of different itineraries in the *Arbor,* on which see Potestà, "Mistica cristocentrica," pp. 290–91. The cross of the *perfecti* is treated in eighteen columns (382a–391a), the cross of the *proficientes* in a bit more than five (391a–393b), and the cross of beginners in seven columns (393b–397a).

76. *Arbor* 4.37 (381a): Attende quod crux prout a Christo sumitur et filiis dispensatur dicit dolorem et gaudium in proportionata mensura a Spiritus Sancti amore procedentia utrumque equaliter dispensante.

77. *Arbor* (382b): Sic sic nimirum opportet in te fieri anima que uis ad istius crucis perfectionem attingere: ut quia uniri debes deo unione amoris: et uoluntatis: et per abnegationem perfectam tui deficiat amor proprius et reciprocus tui: et omnis complacentia et appetitus uoluntatis tue. . . . quod ipse spiritus sanctus quasi videatur esse tua uoluntas et amor: ut nichil propter te uelis: sed solum propter iesum: immo nihil uelis nisi ipsum: et quod ipse. For Ruh's comments on this text, see *Geschichte,* 2:393–94.

78. See the list of texts given in Potestà, "Mistica cristocentrica," p. 290.

79. *Arbor* 4.37 (389b): Aut quommodo cadit supra spiritum libertatis in illa anima incompassio ad proximum in tribulationibus: . . . . unde ista anima optime fugit pestem illius uenenati erroris: spiritus libertatis: imo potius malignitatis. On the "Free Spirit" heretics in Italy, see Romana Guarnieri, "Il movimento del Libero Spiritu: dalle origini al secolo XVI," *Archivio Italiano per la Storia della Pietà* 4 (1965): 351–708 (see pp. 404–5 for discussion of Ubertino). The "Free Spirit" will be treated in more detail below (pp. 150 and 221–22) and in chap. 5 in our consideration of Marguerite Porete (pp. 245–46).

80. *Arbor* 4.7 (305a): Sed nihilominus omnia mala que uidet uel sentit fortissime in se recipiat cum dolore et compassione dei iniurie et angustie proximi: et tanto plus quiescit quanto plenius ista sentit: et hanc suam reputet quietem omnia hec sustinere: ut quies augeatur ex angustia, et angustia ex quiete voluntaria: et hoc est participium soporis dilecti. See the discussion of *quies* in Potestà, "Mistica cristocentrica," pp. 292–94.

81. Jacopone was introduced to English readers through the biography of the indefatigable student of mysticism Evelyn Underhill, *Jacopone da Todi, Poet and Mystic 1228–1306: A Spiritual Biography* (London: Dent, 1919). A more up-to-date account of his life can be found in George T. Peck, *The Fool of God: Jacopone da Todi* (n.p.: University of Alabama Press, 1980). For a survey of some of the literature on Jacopone, see V. Louise Katainen, "Jacopone da Todi, Poet and Mystic: A Review of the History of Criticism," *Mystics Quarterly* 22 (1996): 46–57. Giacomo Sabatelli, "Jacopone da Todi," DS 8:20–26, is a rather disappointing survey.

82. Among these are three poems addressed to Boniface VIII asking for pardon (*Laude* 56–58, and the wonderful self-satire of *Lauda* 55). Two modern editions of the *Laude* exist: *Iacopone da Todi: Laudi, Trattato e Detti,* ed. Franca Ageno (Florence: Le Monnier, 1953); and *Iacopone da Todi: Laude,* ed. Franco Mancini (Rome: Laterza, 1974). I have generally used Ageno's edition since it keeps the standard numeration provided by the first printed edition of 1490, but for all passages cited I have also checked Mancini. On the *Laude,* see Enrico Menestò, "Le Laude drammatiche di Iacopone da Todi: Fonti e struttura," in *Le laudi drammatiche umbre delle origini,* Atti del V Convegno di Studio (Viterbo: Centro di Studi sul Teatro Medioevale e Rinascimentale Viterbo, 1981), 105–40.

83. Enrico Menestò (*Le prose latine attribuite a Jacopone da Todi* [Bologna: Pàtron, 1979], pp. 77–86) has edited the *Tractatus utilissimus,* a brief mystical treatise which some have claimed for the early friar Rizzerio of Muccia (d. 1236), but which seems more likely to be Jacopone's. This volume also contains Jacopone's *Dicta.* Modern scholarship has rejected the traditional ascription to Jacopone of the famous hymn *Stabat mater dolorosa.*

84. Elémire Zolla, "Preface," in *Jacopone da Todi: The Lauds,* trans. Serge and Elizabeth Hughes (New York: Paulist Press, 1982), p. xiii. This volume is the only complete translation

of the *Lauds.* While it does a good job of catching the spirit of these often difficult poems, because of its tendency to paraphrase, I will make my own translations unless otherwise noted.

85. See Arsenio Frugoni, "Iacopone Francescano," in *Iacopone e il suo tempo,* Convegni del Centro di Studi sulla Spiritualità Medievale (Todi: L'Accademia Tudertina, 1959), pp. 73–102.

86. *Lauda* 40.36 and 42–44 (ed., 142–43): Eo ensegno amare, e questa è l'arte mia,/. . . Eo so libro de vita, segnato de sette signi;/ puoi ch'eo siraio aperto, trovarai cinque migni,/ so de sangue vermigni, ove porran studiare. The mystery of redemption is the major theme in many of the *Laude,* e.g., 39, 40–42, 61, 65, 73, 75, 82–83, 85, 90, and 93. On the role of the cross in Jacopone, see Alvaro Cacciotti, "The Cross: Where, according to Jacopone da Todi, God and Humanity are Defined," in *Studies in Spirituality* 2 (1992): 59–98.

87. *Lauda* 61.71–74 and 83–86 (ed., 249): L'amor divino altissimo con Cristo l'abbracciao:/ l'affetto suo ardentissimo sì lo ce 'ncorporao/ lo cor li stemerao como cera a segello:/ empremettece quello ov'era trasformato. . . . Nullo trovamo santo che tal signa portasse;/ misterio sì alto, si Deo non revelasse,/ bono è che lo passe, non ne saccio parlare;/ quilli el porron trattare che l'averò gustato. On Francis, see also *Lauda* 62.

88. See *Laude* 59–60 (ed., 233–43). The latter concludes with a note reminiscent of Eckhart and Marguerite Porete: Povertate è nulla avere e nulla cosa puoi volere,/ e onne cosa possedere en spirito de libertate.

89. *Laude* 69 and 88 (ed., 283–95, and 350–59).

90. Given the power of Jacopone's teaching on love, it is surprising that so little literature has been devoted to it. See Alvaro Bizziccari, "L'amore mistico di Jacopone da Todi," *Italica* 45 (1968): 1–27; and Alvaro Cacciotti, *Amor sacro e amor profano in Jacopone da Todi* (Rome: Bibliotheca Pontificii Athenaei Antoniani, 1989).

91. Much of the recent literature about Jacopone has concentrated on the non-mystical aspects of his life and poetry. See the two collections of conference papers, *Iacopone e il suo tempo;* and *Atti del convengo storico iacoponico in occasione del 750 anniversario della nascità di Iacopone da Todi, 29–30 novembre 1980,* ed. Enrico Menestò (Florence: La Nuova Italia, 1981). The best recent account of his mysticism is that of Ruh, *Geschichte,* 2:473–85.

92. Ruh (*Geschichte,* 2:477–85) comments on *Lauda* 90. Peck (*Fool of God,* 174–84) treats all three poems.

93. *Lauda* 90.99–100 and 105–6 (ed., 370): En Cristo trasformata, quasi è Cristo, / con Dio congiunta, tutta sta divina. / . . . Nulla c'è più sentina, dove trovi peccato: / lo vecchio n'è mozato, purgato onne fetore.

94. *Lauda* 90.139–46 (ed., 372): Sappi parlare, ora so fatto muto; / vedea, mo so cieco deventato. / Sì grande abisso non fo mai veduto: / tacendo parlo, fugo e so legato, / scendendo salgo, tengo e so tenuto, / de for se dentro, caccio e so cacciato. / Amor esmesurato, perché me fai empazire, / en fornace morire de sì forte calore? (using the Hughes translation, *Jacopone da Todi,* p. 261).

95. See *Growth of Mysticism,* pp. 203–4, and 413–18.

96. *Lauda* 90.283–90 (ed., 378): Amor, amor Iesù desideroso, / amor, voglio morire te abbracciando; / amor, amor Iesù, dolce mio sposo, / amor, amor, la morte t'addemando; / amor, amor Iesù sì delettoso, / tu me t'arrendi en te me trasformando; / pensa ch'io vo pasmando, Amor, non so o' me sia: / Iesù, speranza mia, abissame en amore.

97. For a discussion of the relation of Jacopone to the Free Spirit, see Guarnieri, "Il movimento del libero spirito," pp. 400–403, who notes that *Lauda* 60.28–34 and 60–61 also express such themes.

98. The bridal language is particularly strong in *Lauda* 71. See also *Laude* 41, 65, 81–83, 85, 87, and 89.

99. Nevertheless, one could argue from Jacopone's insistence on severe asceticism and the necessity for virtuous practice found in so many of the *Lauds* that he did not wish his lines about sinlessness to be taken to indicate that all actions become lawful to some mystical adepts. Like Marguerite Porete, he may rather be suggesting that in certain cases a person could become so united to God that sinful action of any kind becomes impossible. A number of perfectly orthodox mystics, for example, Bernard of Clairvaux, expressed similar teachings (see *Growth of Mysticism*, p. 189).

100. These three passages are (1) *Lauda* 91.33–34 (ed., 381): De tutto prende sorte; tanto ha per unione / de trasformazione, che dice: "Tutto e mio." (2) 91.157–58 (ed., 386): la forma che gli è data tanto sì l'ha absorto, / che vive stando morto, è vinto ed è vittore. (3) 91.195–98 and 204 (ed., 388–89): Possedi posseduta en tanta unione, / non c'è divisione che te da lui retragga; / tu bevi e se' bevuta en trasformazione; / da tal perfezione non è chi te distragga; / . . . en Dio fatta enfinita, non è chi te contenda.

101. *Lauda* 91.185 (ed., 388): volere e non volere en te sì è annegato. See also lines 99–104 and 165.

102. *Lauda* 91.169–72 (ed., 387): Questa sì somma alteza en nichilo è fondata, / nichilata, formata, messa ne lo Signore. / Alta nichilitate, tuo atto è tanto forte, / c'apre tutte le porte, entra ne lo'nfinito. I take the second line to mean that the hidden divine Nothingness takes on a "formed" shape in the Word Incarnate that allows us access to the mystery. The second passage is 91.207–10 (ed., 389): Tua profonda basseza sì alto è sublimata, / en sedia collocata con Dio sempre regnare, / en quella somma alteza en tanto è nabissata, / che già non è trovata, ed en sé non appare. References to *nichil* and annihilation can be found in other *Laude*, e.g., 39.57–60, 60.44–45, 61.17, 73.44–45, 85.37–38, 87.35–36, 92.18 (ed., 139–40, 241, 245, 308, 345, 349, 392). The language of the divine abyss or abyss of love, as distinct from the abyss of hell, is also found in *Laude* 60.54, 75.35–38, 85.21–22 (ed., 248, 316, 344).

103. For an exploration of this theme, see Bernard McGinn, "The Abyss of Love," in *The Joy of Learning and the Love of God: Studies in Honor of Jean Leclercq*, ed. E. Rozanne Elder (Kalamazoo: Cistercian Publications, 1995), pp. 95–120.

104. This is discussed in a number of *Laude*, e.g., 73, 79, 87, and 88.

105. *Lauda* 92.75–80 (ed., 394–95): L'autunni son quadrati, / son stabiliti, non posson voltare; / li cieli son stainiti, / lo lor silere me face gridare: / o profondata mare, altura del tuo abisso / m'ha cercostritto a volerme annegare! In the final part of this poem (lines 87–116) Jacopone returns to themes found in *Lauda* 91, such as the soul's dominion over all things (lines 86–98) and its passage to a sinless state (lines 111–16).

106. The ongoing interest in visions is reflected, for example, in the vernacular treatise of Friar Hugh Panziera (d. ca. 1330) written in 1319, *Trattato contro i falsi mistici*. Hugh also wrote *Laude* in the style of Jacopone and other mystical treatises. See the translations into modern Italian in Arrigo Levasti, *Mistici del duecento e del trecento* (Milan/Rome: Rizzoli, 1935), pp. 273–316.

107. For a brief account, see Ruh, *Geschichte*, 2:468–69.

108. On John, see Ruh, *Geschichte*, 2:470–72; and Giacomo V. Sabatelli, "Jean della Verna (de l'Alverne)," DS 8:782–84.

109. *Actus beati Francisci et sociorum eius* 49.38 (*Fontes Franciscani*, ed. Enrico Menestò, Stefano Brufani et al., p. 2186): Et in hoc amplexu et odore ac luminibus, in ipso beato pectore Ihesu Cristi fuit raptus fr. Iohannes et totaliter consolatus et mirabiliter illustratus. The materials on John of Alverna are found in chaps. 49–57 (*Fontes*, pp. 2182–98).

110. On the triple kiss, see Bernard of Clairvaux, *Sermo super Cantica* 3 (*Sancti Bernardi Opera*, 1:14–17); on the transition from carnal to spiritual love, see, e.g., *Sermo de diversis* 101 (*Opera*, 6:368). For discussions, see *Growth of Mysticism*, pp. 175–77 and 183–85.

111. See *Actus* 56.9–10 (*Fontes,* p. 2195). On Benedict's vision as recounted in Gregory the Great's *Dialogi* 2.34, see *Growth of Mysticism,* pp. 71–74.

112. Roger's *Meditationes* were published in the *Analecta Francescana* 3 (1897): 393–406. The *Vita* can be found in the *Catalogus Codicum Hagiographicorum Bibliothecae Regiae Bruxellensis: Pars I, Codices Latini Membranei* (Brussels: Polleunis, 1886), 1:347–62. On this interesting mystic, see Claude Carozzi, "Extases et visions chez frère Roger de Provence," in *Fin du monde et signes des temps,* pp. 81–105.

113. In *Vita* 7 (ed., 352), Raymond reports that he once praised Friar Giles's reputation for ecstasy and Roger replied that it was an easy thing (*facillimum quid*) to be raptured and continued: Scio, inquit, homo quo aliquando centies in uno Matutino fuit raptus ad altissimos intellectus divinorum et forte in quolibet versu. Et ille, inquit, infinities restitit raptui, et aliquando tantam vim oportet et facere ut recedat a Deo suo et fugiat, quantum aliquis fecit ut appropinquet ei.

114. This phrase, first used by John of Fécamp, was employed by Bernard in *Sermo Super Cantica* 23.15 (*Opera,* 1:148.20). Cf. *Super Cantica* 18.6 and 85.13 for other texts. On monastic insistence on the brevity of ecstasy, see *Growth of Mysticism,* pp. 142–43, 190–93, 211–12.

115. E.g., *Vita* 7, 11–12 (ed., 353, 355).

116. *Vita* 10 (ed., 354): . . . occurrit et ipse mihi tamquam homo qui esset ebrius, totam faciem habens adeo rubeam et inflammatam quod quasi videbatur ignis exire de facie ejus, et oculos habens quasi alienatos, et sic terribilis in facie quod non fui ausus loqui sibi nec etiam in faciem respicere. . . . A similar description occurs at the beginning of 11 (ed., 355).

117. *Vita* 15–16 (ed., 357–59). The quoted phrase (358): . . . et clauso ostio respiciens semper in coelum coepit, ac si legeret in libro, ita alta et profunda mysteria a seculo inaudita disserere, manifeste ex divina infusione, quod non credo quod vivat sub coelo qui illa posset plene retinere vel etiam intelligere. Raymond quotes Roger's later comment–. . . et dicebat mihi: Quid dicerent modo fratres, si audirent ista verba? Dicerent quod graecum loquor.

118. This is especially true of the final consideration (ed., 403.20–404.21), which closes with a strange kind of *iubilus:* Taliter ergo clarificati facies dicat Deo, scilicet Deus, scilicet creatura, scilicet Christus, scilicet populus christianus, bonus scilicet in hoc mundo: O qui es! O qui non es! O qui non es, es! O qui non es, es! O qui nondum es! O qui iam es!, scilicet sanctus in patria! O qui es! (404.45–48).

119. *Meditationes* (ed., 402.5–8): Vide, homo, quia verba, quae audisti, proxima sunt silentio et sic proxima, ut extra silentium audiri nequeant, quia audiri non possunt, nisi ubi sunt, et quia infra silentium sunt. Intra igitur intimum tuum, intra silentium proprium, ut de tuo venias ad divinum et eius inexcogitabile silentium hoc tibi loquatur.

120. A good survey of Llull's system can be found in Anthony Bonner and Charles Lohr, "Raymond Lulle," DS 13:171–87. The basic principles of Llull's theology are laid out in R. D. F. Pring-Mill, "The Trinitarian World Picture of Ramon Lull," in *Romanistische Jahrbuch* 7 (1955–56): 229–56. Though old, there is still value in Ephrem Longpré's "Lulle, Raymond (Le Bienheureux)," *Dictionnaire de théologie catholique* 9:1072–1141 (cols. 1128–32 on his mysticism, an overly Bonaventurean reading). Among more recent works, see especially Mark D. Johnston, *The Spiritual Logic of Ramon Llull* (Oxford: Clarendon Press, 1987), and *The Evangelical Rhetoric of Ramon Llull: Lay Learning and Piety in the Christian West around 1300* (New York/Oxford: Oxford University Press, 1996). Kurt Ruh does not discuss Llull in volume 2 of his *Geschichte der abendländische Mystik,* though Llull is treated in the section devoted to Conventual Franciscans in Peter Dinzelbacher, *Christliche Mystik im Abendland,* pp. 185–90.

121. Knowledge of Llull's life is mostly dependent on the remarkable *Vita coaetanea,* which Llull recounted to the Carthusian monks in Paris. This has been translated with a commentary in *Selected Works of Ramon Llull (1232–1316),* ed. and trans. Anthony Bonner, 2 vols.

(Princeton: Princeton University Press, 1985), 1:12–52 (the phrase quoted comes from #6, p. 15). On Llull's conversion, see Mark D. Johnston, "Ramon Lull's Conversion to Penitence," *Mystics Quarterly* 16 (1990): 179–92.

122. For a survey of the contents, see E. Allison Peers, *Ramon Lull: A Biography* (London: Jarrold's, 1929), pp. 43–81.

123. For a brief description of the *ars generalis* and the various stages of its evolution, see Bonner, *Selected Works of Ramon Llull*, 1:56–70.

124. The whole *Blaquerna* was edited in four volumes by Salvador Galmés in the series *Els nostres classics* (Barcelona, 1935–54). For the *Book of the Lover and Beloved* I will use the edition and translation of the Latin and Old Catalan of Mark D. Johnston, *Ramon Llull: The Book of the Lover and Beloved* (Warminster: Aries & Phillips, 1995).

125. On his contacts with the Spirituals, see Jocelyn N. Hillgarth, *Ramon Lull and Lullism in Fourteenth Century France* (Oxford: Oxford University Press, 1971), 52–56; and Dominique Urvoy, *Penser d'Islam: le présupposés islamiques de l'"Art" de Lull* (Paris: Vrin, 1980), pp. 124–29.

126. Among these are the *Art amativa* (Montpellier, 1290), the *Flors d'amor e flors d'intel·ligència* (Naples, 1294), the *Contemplatio Raymundi* (Paris, 1297), *Oracions de Ramon* (Barcelona, 1299), *Liber de ascensu et descensu intellectus* (Montpellier, 1305), *Ars mystica theologiae et philosophiae* (Paris, 1309), and *Liber de compendiosa contemplatione* (Messina, 1313).

127. The work has been translated in Bonner, *Selected Works of Ramon Llull*, 2:1223–56.

128. These treatises have appeared in the ongoing edition of the Latin works of Llull, *Raimundi Lulli Opera Omnia*, ed. F. Stegmüller et al. (35 volumes projected), under the auspices of the CCCM. See *Liber de ascensu et descensu intellectus*, ed. Aloisius Madre, *Opera Omnia*, vol. 9, CCCM 35 (Turnholt: Brepols, 1981), pp. 20–199; and *De contemplatione Raymundi*, ed. M. Pereira and T. Pindl-Büchel, *Opera Omnia*, vol. 17, CCCM 89 (Turnholt: Brepols, 1984), pp. 20–61.

129. I wish to thank Gordon Rudy, whose unpublished paper "The Contemplation of God in Ramon Llull's *Liber de ascensu et descensu intellectus*" clarified this aspect of Lllul for me. Note also that Llull's intellectual program has no room for apophatic knowing–the proper operation of the mind is affirming; all negation is a mark of failure.

130. For a good expression of this superiority of intellect, see *The Art of Contemplation* 6.4 in *Blaquerna*, pp. 493–94. Many texts in *The Art of Contemplation* (e.g., 9.6 on 508) and generally throughout the *Blaquerna* indicate that in this early work Llull teaches an ongoing interaction between the three powers of memory, intellect, and will.

131. In *The Book of the Lover and Beloved*, for example, although the Beloved is clearly the Divine Word, only 14 of the 366 aphorisms concern Christ's earthly life directly (nn. 15, 30, 67, *101, 135, 153, 217,* 273, *276, 316–17,* 321, 328, and *337*–italicized texts mention the passion explicitly). In *The Art of Contemplation* meditation on the passion occurs only in 8.9 and 11.15.

132. *The Book of the Lover and Beloved,* chap. 99.3 (ed., 4): . . . son unes gents qui han nom sufies E aquells han paraules damor e exemplis abreuyats e qui donen a home gran devocio. . . . Like all of Llull's works dealing with mysticism, *The Book of the Lover and Beloved* is unusual in being almost totally unscriptural–the Bible is hardly ever cited.

133. *The Book,* nn. 26, 235, 350 (ed., 14, 90, 134): 26. Cantaven los auçells lalba e despertas lamich qui es lalba e los auçells feniren lur cant el amich muri per lamat en lalba./ 235. Amor es mar tribulada de ondes e de vents qui no ha port ni ribatge pereix lamich en la mar e en son perill perexen sos turments e nexen sos complimens./ 350. Esguardava lamich si mateix per ço que fos mirall on vees son amat e esguardava son amat per ço que li fos mirayll on agues conexença de si meteix e es questio a qual des dos miralls era son enteniment pus acostat.

134. *The Book* n. 131 (ed., 50): Nuavençe les amors del amich e lamat ab membrança enteniment volentat per ço quel amich el amat nos partissen e la corda en que les dues amors se nuaven era de pensaments languiments suspirs e plors. In some texts intellect seems higher (e.g., n. 19), but generally the language is one of interaction (e.g., nn. 92, 103, 107, 112, 138, 184, 189, 193, 197, 226, 314, 331, 335, 348, 364). The same teaching appears throughout *The Art of Contemplation,* e.g., 1.7–9, 2.10, 5.2, 6.4 and 7, although 9.2–6 agains seems to exalt the superiority of intellect.

135. Much has recently been written on the role of women in late medieval Italy. Two helpful collections in English, already referred to above, are *Creative Women in Medieval and Early Modern Italy: A Religious and Artistic Renaissance,* ed. E. Ann Matter and John Coakley; and *Women and Religion in Medieval and Renaissance Italy,* ed. Daniel Bornstein and Roberto Rusconi. See especially the overview of Bornstein, "Women and Religion in Late Medieval Italy: History and Historiography" (pp. 1–27). For Franciscan women, consult *Movimento religioso femminile e Francescanesimo nel secolo XIII* (Assisi: Società Internazionale di Studi Francescani, 1980), especially the essays by Giovanni Gonnet and Roberto Rusconi. Also helpful is André Vauchez, *The Laity in the Middle Ages: Religious Beliefs and Devotional Practices,* chap. 14, "Female Sanctity in the Franciscan Movement."

136. The majority of these Franciscan women were Italian. Excerpts from the *vitae* or writings of many can be found in *Scrittrici mistiche italiane,* ed. Giovanni Pozzi and Claudio Leonardi.

137. Among these are Agnes of Assisi (ca. 1197–1253), who was Clare's younger sister; Elena Enselmini (1207–1231), a friend of Antony of Padua; and Rose of Viterbo (ca. 1233–1251).

138. For a study of these siblings, along with an edition of Hugh's writings, see Alessandra Sisto, *Figure del primo francescanesimo in Provenza: Ugo e Douceline di Digne* (Florence: Olschki, 1971). On Douceline, Claude Carozzi has published two important articles, though his psychoanalytic interpretation is sometimes forced: "Une béguine joachimite: Douceline, soeur d'Hugues de Digne," *Franciscains d'Oc,* pp. 169–201; and "Douceline et les autres," in *La religion en Languedoc du XIIIe siècle à la moitié du XIVe siècle,* Cahiers de Fanjeaux 11 (Toulouse: Privat, 1957), pp. 251–67. More recently, see the accounts of Geneviève Brunel-Lobrichon, "Existe-t-il un christianisme méridional? L'exemple de Douceline: Le béguinage provençal," *Heresis* 11 (1988): 41–51; Ruh, *Geschichte,* 2:497–501; and Aviad Kleinberg, *Prophets in Their Own Country,* pp. 121–25.

139. The work was apparently first composed in 1297 and then reworked in 1312 after the condemnation of the free beguines at the Council of Vienne in order to defend the community of Roubaut. (It was apparently successful since the community survived until 1414.) The *Vida* survives in only one manuscript and was first edited by J.-H. Albanès, *La vie de sainte Douceline, fondatrice des béguines de Marseilles* (Marseilles: Camoin, 1879).

140. *Vida* 1.6 (ed., 8): Filla, non aias vergonha de mi, qu'iue non aurai vergonha de manifestar tu al paire.

141. *Vida,* 8.6–9 (ed., 66–68). Albanés and later scholars (e.g., Brunel-Lobrichon, "Existe-t-il un christianisme méridional?" pp. 48–49) have demonstrated the dependence of the structure of the *Vida* on Bonaventure's *Leg. maj.,* but it is not known if Phelipa read this in Latin or in translation.

142. The incident is recounted in *Vida* 2.4–6 (ed., 14–16), The quotation comes from 2.11 (ed., 20): El sancta maire[s] volc esser apellada beguina, per amor de Nostra Dona quez era totz sos caps; qu'illi dizia que Nostra Dona fon li premiera beguina.... The convent on the river Roubaud near Hyères does not appear to have come into being until ca. 1244. It was the first beguine house in southern France. A second house was later founded in Marseilles.

Since it was Hugh of Digne who received the temporary vows of chastity of the nuns and was considered its "father" (Douceline alone took a vow of absolute poverty), the community was a new mode of adoption of the Franciscan way of life for women. On the relation to the other forms of Franciscans, see Sisto, *Figure del primo Francescanesimo in Provenza,* pp. 31–47.

143. See Carozzi, "Une Béguine Joachimite," pp. 194–96, 200–201; and Brunel-Lobrichon, "Existe-t-il un christianisme méridional?" pp. 50–51. Given the brevity of this statement (*Vida* 9.42–43, ed., 98; cf. also 9.57, ed. 108–10), this is possible but not certain.

144. See *Vida* 4.10–12, 9.33–34 and 11.4–9 (ed., 34–36, 154–58), and the comments in Brunel-Lobrichon, "Existe-t-il un christianisme méridional?" pp. 49 and 51.

145. *Vida* 93 (ed., 72): Car jassiaisso qu'illi fos sempla femena, e ses letras, a las sobeiranas autezas de contemplacion la levet Nostre Seinnhers. Car per motz cors e espazis de temps, continuamens entenduda els celestials fagz, tan soven era ab Dieu en los autz raubimens, aissi cant presentmens estant ab ell, que mais semblava menes vida d'angel entre las gens, que non fazia femena.

146. Salimbene de Adamo, *Cronica* (MGH.SS. 32:554): Hec a Deo obtinuit gratiam specialem, ut in extasim raperetur, sicut fratres Minores viderunt mille vicibus in ecclesia sua; et si elevabant ei brachium, ita elevatum tenebat illud a mane usque ad vesperam, eo quod in Deum totaliter esset absorta.

147. See *Vida* 9.6–9, 12–13 (ed., 74–78). Levitation appears to be first associated with ecstatic states in the thirteenth century. Both Francis and Dominic, at least in late thirteenth-century accounts, are said to have levitated. See Herbert Thurston, *The Physical Phenomena of Mysticism,* chap. 1; and Isaias Rodriguez, "Lévitation," DS 9:738–41 (neither of which notes the example of Douceline).

148. *Vida* 9.59–63 (ed., 110–14).

149. An interesting comparison might be made between these two third-order Franciscans and their contemporary, the Augustinian recluse Clare of Montefalco (1268–1320). Clare, who was much influenced by Franciscans, was an ecstatic with a strong devotion to the passion. See the papers collected in *S. Chiara da Montefalco e il suo tempo,* ed. Claudio Leonardi and Enrico Menestò (Florence: La Nuova Italia, 1985). A growing literature has been devoted to these and the other *sante* of late medieval Umbria in recent decades. See especially *Il movimento religioso femminile in Umbria nei secoli XIII–XIV,* ed. Roberto Rusconi (Florence: La Nuova Italia, 1984); and Enrico Menestò and Roberto Rusconi, *Umbria sacra e civile* (Turin: Nuova Eri Edizioni Rai, 1989).

150. Our major source for Margaret is the *Legenda de vita et miracolis Margaritae de Cortona* (AA.SS. Feb. 22:298–357), in which Christ addresses her thus: Iam te in exemplum praebui peccatorum, ut in te certissime videant, quod si se ad gratiam praeparare voluerint, sum paratus eis misericordiam elargiri, sicut misericors fui tecum (2.21; 303F). On Margaret, see Enrico Menestò, "La mistica di Margherita da Cortona," in *Temi e problemi nella mistica femminile trecentesca* (Todi: Convegni del Centro di Studi sulla Spiritualità Medievale XX, 1983), pp. 183–206; Roberto Rusconi, "Margherita da Cortona: Peccatrice redenta e patrona cittadina," in *Umbria sacra e civile,* pp. 89–104; Daniel Bornstein, "The Uses of the Body: The Church and the Cult of Santa Margherita da Cortona," *Church History* 62 (1993): 163–77; Fortunato Iozzelli, "I miracoli nella 'Legenda' di Santa Margherita da Cortona," *Archivum Franciscanum Historicum* 86 (1993): 217–61; Ruh, *Geschichte,* 2:501–9; and Dinzelbacher, *Christliche Mystik im Abendland,* pp. 240–42.

151. *Vita* 11.267 (353EF): . . . quia tu es tertia lux in ordine dilecti mei Francisci concessa. Nam in ordine Fratrum Minorum ipse prima lux, in ordine monialium B. Clara secunda, et tu in ordine Poenitentium tertia.

152. This topos of medieval women mystics, also to be seen in the case of Angela of

Foligno, has been studied by Barbara Newman, *From Virile Woman to WomanChrist: Studies in Medieval Religion and Literature* (Philadelphia: University of Pennsylvania Press, 1995), pp. 84–96.

153. *Vita* 2.27 (305A): Cur petis, o Margarita, meas incessanter gustare dulcedines, et amaritudines disponentes ad ipsas praegustare non vis? Cur postulas, ut te in cella recludam? . . . Vade, inquit, ad locum B. Francisci Patris tui, ut ibi audias Missas: et ibi me reverenter adora, et vide me manibus sacerdotum. Vade, et non te recludas, quousque te abscondere volam.

154. Like Mary of Oignies, Margaret conceived a hatred for her beauty as a source of sin to the extent that her confessor had to forbid her to cut off her nose and upper lip lest she bleed to death (*Vita* 2.40 [307BC]).

155. For brief comments on this development and how it affected her relations with the friars, see Bornstein, "Margherita da Cortona," 166-70.

156. The event is described in *Vita* 5.83–84 (315F–316C), the passage cited is at 316B: Hoc tam novum et compassione plenum spectaculum ita Cortonenses omnes commovit, quod relictis officiis suis et artibus, homines et mulieres, infantibus et languidis et in cunis decumbentibus, pluries illa die oratorium nostri loci, . . . in fletu et planctu repleverunt. Videbant namque non iuxta Crucem, sed quasi Cruce positam Margaritam, diris confectam doloribus, . . . Prae nimio enim vehementique dolore stridebat dentibus, torquebatur ut vermis et torques, discolorabatur ad instar cineris, perdebat pulsum, amittebat loquelum, et glaciabatur totaliter, et ita sunt effectae raucae fauces eius, ut vix posset intelligi cum redibat ad sensum.

157. Ruh, *Geschichte*, 2:508–9.

158. *Vita* 6.152 (330CD): Tunc se Christus ei ostendit, veluti crucifixum, dicens: Pone palmas super locis clavorum manuum mearum. Et cum Margarita ob reverentiam diceret, Non Domini mi, subito patuit vulnus lateris amantis Iesu, et in caverna illa cor sui est intuitia Salvatoris. In quo excessu amplectens Dominum crucifixum sursum ab eo ferebatur in caelum et audivit eum dicentem sibi: Filia, de istis vulneribus trahes illa, quae queunt preadicatores referre.

159. Angela's *Book* consisting of the *Memoriale* and the subsequent *Instructiones* has recently been given a critical edition, *Il libro della Beata Angela da Foligno*, ed. Ludger Thier and Abele Calufetti (Rome: Editiones Collegii S. Bonaventurae, 1985). Twenty-eight manuscripts are known, in two Latin versions and a vernacular translation. There is an English translation with excellent introduction and notes by Paul Lachance, *Angela of Foligno: Complete Works* (New York: Paulist Press, 1993). This introduction expands upon Paul Lachance, *The Spiritual Journey of the Blessed Angela of Foligno according to the Memorial of Brother A.* (Rome: Pontificium Athenaeum Antonianum, 1984). See also the papers collected in *Vita e Spiritualità della Beata Angela da Foligno*, ed. Clément Schmitt (Perugia: Serafica Provincia di San Francisco, 1987); and *Angela da Foligno Terziaria Francescana*, ed. Enrico Menestò (Spoleto: Centro Italiano di Studi sull'Alto Medioevo, 1992). Most histories of medieval spirituality and mysticism contain extensive accounts of Angela; see especially Ruh, *Geschichte*, 2:509–23; and Dinzelbacher, *Christliche Mystik im Abendland*, pp. 245–52.

160. The other three women, Hadewijch of Antwerp, Mechthild of Magdeburg, and Marguerite Porete, will be treated in chapter 5.

161. For Angela's relation to the wider phenomenon of women's mysticism in the thirteenth century (including remarks on the other three "evangelists"), see Romana Guarnieri, "Angela, mistica europea," in *Angela da Foligno Terziaria Francescana*, pp. 39–82.

162. See Barbara Newman, "Hildegard of Bingen: Visions and Validation," *Church History* 54 (1985): 163–75.

163. Nicholas Watson, *Richard Rolle and the Invention of Authority* (Cambridge: Cambridge University Press, 1991).

164. See *Memoriale* chap. 2 (ed., 168–74).

165. Jacques Dalarun, "Angèle de Foligno a-t-elle existé," in *Alla Signoria: Mélanges offerts à Noëlle de la Blanchardière* (Rome: École Française, 1995), pp. 59–97 (see pp. 94–95 especially). Dalarun builds upon the textual difficulties noted in the essays of Mario Sensi and Mauro Donnini in *Angela da Foligno Terziaria Francescana*, pp. 127–59 and 181–213, but extends these in more radical directions.

166. The issue of the contribution of Brother A. in relation to Angela's dictation is fueled in part by the numerous accounts he gives of the process of the construction of the text; see, e.g., *Memoriale* 1 (ed., 134, 156); 2 (ed., 158, 166–69, and especially 168–74); and the Epil. (ed. 398–400). The phrase "co-protagonist" I take from Lachance ("Introduction," *Angela of Foligno*, 51), whose discussion of this issue (pp. 47–54) is helpful. Recently, Catherine M. Mooney in "The Authorial Role of Brother A. in the Composition of Angela of Foligno's Revelations," has stressed the friar's collaborative role (see *Creative Women in Medieval and Early Modern Italy*, pp. 34–63). See also Ruh, *Geschichte*, 2:512–13.

167. Angela's attitude toward the death of her family seems ambivalent. In *Memoriale* 1 (ed., 138) she prays for their death and receives great consolation from it in a manner not untypical of other mystics. In chapter 3 (ed., 186), however, she refers to the pain and sorrow she felt at the demise of her mother and sons (not her husband). See Newman, *From Virile Woman to WomanChrist*, pp. 88–89.

168. The seven supplementary stages are outlined in *Memoriale* 2 (ed., 160–66). Each stage is then given a chapter of its own in chaps. 3–9 (ed., 176–400).

169. James of Colonna (d. 1308) was one of the Cardinals opposed to Boniface VIII and a supporter of the Franciscan Spirituals. It is possible, but unproven, that Ubertino of Casale was one of the Franciscans deputed by him to examine the work and that his acquaintance with Angela dates from this time. Though Angela does not polemicize in relation to the poverty question, and though she has nothing of the apocalyptic rhetoric of the male Spiritual authors, there is good reason to believe that she was closely linked with their party, something that would help explain why her book had a largely clandestine history until it was revived by the Observantine Franciscan reformers in the late fifteenth century. On this question, see the remarks in Lachance, "Introduction," *Angela of Foligno*, pp. 43–45, 96–97, 110–12; and Stefano Brufani, "Angela da Foligno e gli Spirituali," in *Angela da Foligno Terziaria Francescana*, pp. 83–104.

170. *Instructiones* 2 (ed., 412.34–414.41): Prima transformatio est quando anima conatur imitari opera istius Dei hominis passionati, quia in ipsis manifestatur et est manifestata voluntas Dei. Secunda transformatio est quando anima unitur Deo et habet magna sentimenta et magnas de Deo dulcedines, sed tamen possunt exprimi verbis et cogitari. Tertia transformatio est quando anima unione perfectissima est transformata intra Deum et Deus intra animam et alitissima de Deo sentit et gustat, in tantum quod nullo modo possunt exprimi verbis nec cogitari.

171. *Memoriale* 1 (ed. 138.80): . . . et nuda irem ad crucem. Cf. chap. 3 (ed., 178.19–21) for the specific Franciscan context.

172. These stages include some unusual ascetical practices, such as in #8 (ed., 136), where Angela strips herself naked before a crucifix (like Francis) to indicate her desire to follow Christ perfectly. They also describe traditional mystical experiences, such as in #14, where Christ appears to Angela and lets her drink from his side (ed., 142–44).

173. The marks of this collaboration are evident throughout the text. To provide just two examples from the first supplementary step (#20, ed., 176–98): (1) note how Brother A. asks

Angela for a further explanation of what she saw at Assisi (ed., 184.104–5); and (2) see the manner in which the text adds a subsequent theological elaboration (composed by Brother A., one presumes) to explain the rather confusing original references to the manifestations of the Holy Spirit and Christ to Angela on the way to Assisi (ed., 190.181–192.206). If this is all a literary fiction, it may be one of the most elaborate ever attempted in the Middle Ages.

174. *Memoriale* 3 (ed., 178–80).

175. *Instructiones* 21 (ed., 598.33–34): Et tunc dixit mihi verba secretissima et altissima. Et postea dixit: Tu es sola nata de me.

176. On these aspects of her thought, see the summary in Lachance, "Introduction," *Angela of Foligno,* pp. 87–90 and 99–100. For some examples of the role of Mary, see, e.g., *Memoriale* 4, 6, 7 (ed., 222–26, 258, 292, 304).

177. *Memoriale* 3 (ed., 180.45–46): Et saepissime dicebat: Filia et sponsa dulcis mihi. Et dixit: Ego diligo te plus quam aliquam quae sit in valle Spoletina.

178. *Memoriale* 3 (ed., 184.96–101): Ita te astrictam tenebo et multo plus quam possit considerari cum oculis corporis. Et modo est hora quod te, filia dulcis, templum meum, delectum meum, adimpleo quod dixi tibi. . . . The growing role of holy images in late medieval mysticism is highlighted by this event. The window in question, which has been interpreted as an illustration of the spiritual motherhood of Christ, perfectly fits the theological significance of the experience. See Jerome Poulenc, "Saint François dans le 'vitrail des anges' de l'église supérieure de la basilique d'Assise," *Archivum Franciscanum Historicum* 76 (1983): 701–13.

179. *Memoriale* 3 (ed., 184.110–13): Amor non cognitus, et quare scilicet me dimittis? . . . Amor non cognitus, et quare et quare et quare? Reference to God as the "All Good" (*omne bonum,* based on Exod. 33:19), found in Francis and others, is frequent with Angela (the passage here at 184.106, and see such other mentions as 210.130 and 212.141 in the next stage). For a full list of references, see the "Indice tematico" in the critical edition.

180. On the role of abjection in Angela there are some interesting reflections in Karmie Lochrie, "The Language of Transgression: Body, Flesh, and Word in Mystical Discourse," in *Speaking Two Languages: Traditional Disciplines and Contemporary Theory in Medieval Studies,* ed. Allen J. Frantzen (Albany: SUNY Press, 1991), pp. 129–39, though I do not agree with the interpretive framework of her study, especially the analysis of Bernard of Clairvaux.

181. *Memoriale* 5 (ed., 242.134–36): Et tantam dulcedinem sensimus, quod per totam viam venimus in magna suavitate ac si communicavissemus. This eating of "abject food" (a phrase I owe to Aden Kumler), found also in Francis (see *CAss* 64 in *Fontes,* pp. 1560–62) and in several women mystics, like Catherine of Siena and Catherine of Genoa, has been noted by Caroline Walker Bynum, "The Female Body and Religious Practice in the Later Middle Ages," in *Fragments for a History of the Human Body: Part One,* ed. Michel Feher (New York: Zone, 1989), p. 163.

182. *Memoriale* 6 (ed., 278.254): Et tota laetitia est modo in isto Deo homine passionato. The vision continues with a description of entering into Christ's wounded side similar to what we have seen in Margaret of Cortona above (p. 141).

183. *Memoriale* 7 (ed., 296.106–298.111): . . . et Christus posuit manum suam super aliam maxillam et strinxit eam ad se, et ista fidelis Christi audivit sibi dici ista verba: Antequam iacerem in sepulcro tenui te ita astrictam. . . . Et ipsa erat in laetitia maxima inenarrabiliter.

184. On Angela's "transgressive" stance and the way in which it challenges Jacques Lacan's views of female mysticism, see Christina Mazzoni, "On the (Un)Representability of Woman's Pleasure: Angela of Foligno and Jacques Lacan," in *Gender and Text in the Later Middle Ages,* ed. Jane Chance, pp. 239–62.

185. *Memoriale* 8 (ed., 338.21–25): . . . de homine suspenso per gulam, qui, ligatis manibus post tergum et velatis oculis, suspensus per funem remansisset in furcis et viveret, cui nullum auxilium, nullum omnino sustentamentum vel remedium remansisset.

186. On Angela's apophaticism, see Lachance, *Spiritual Journey*, pp. 370–85; and "Introduction, *Angela of Foligno*, pp. 69–78. For attempts to distinguish the meanings of *in tenebra* and *cum tenebra* (not exactly clear in the text), see the edition, pp. 358–59 nn. 5-6; and Lachance, *Angela of Foligno*, pp. 349–51 n. 172.

187. *Memoriale* 9 (ed., 360.80–81): Et in illa Trinitate quam video cum tanta tenebra videtur mihi stare et iacere in medio. Although Angela does not develop an explicit Trinitarian teaching, it is clear from this and other references that the dark aspect of the final stage involves sharing in the very life of the Trinity (cf. 372.209, 378.292, 390.418–19).

188. This phrase, which is reminiscent of Song 2:16, had a considerable history in medieval poetry, as well as in mysticism. Its use, primarily in Germany, has been investigated by Friedrich Ohly, "Du bist mein, Ich bin dein. Du in mir, Ich in dir. Ich du, Du Ich," in *Kritische Bewahrung: Beiträge zur deutschen Philologie. Festschrift für Werner Schröder*, ed. Ernst-Joachim Schmidt (Berlin: Erich Schmidt, 1974), pp. 371–415.

189. *Memoriale* 9 (ed., 380.299–301): Et video et intelligo quod illas operationes divinas et illud profundissimum abyssum nullus angelus et nulla creatura est ita larga et capax quod posset illud comprehendere.

190. *Memoriale* 9 (ed., 384.341–43): Et facit in anima multas operationes divinas cum multo maiori gratia et cum tanto profundo et inerrabili abysso, quod solum illud praesentare Dei, sine aliis donis, est illud bonum quod sancti habent in vita aeterna. Cf. 384.353–56.

191. *Memoriale* 9 (ed., 394.451–55): Et anima mea non potuit tunc comprehendere semetipsam, unde et si anima, cum sit creata et finita et circumscripta, non potest comprehendere semetipsam, quanto minus Creatorem Deum immensum et infinitum comprehendere poterit? For the notion of God and the soul as dual (and mutual) abysses, see McGinn, "The Abyss of Love," especially pp. 109–10 on Angela.

192. *Memoriale* 9 (ed., 388.399–404): ... tamen intus in anima mea est una camera in qua non ingreditur aliqua laetitia nec tristitia nec delectatio alicuius . . . , sed est ibi illud omne bonum. . . . Et in illo manifestare Dei, quamvis ego blasphemem dicendo et male dicendo illud quia non possum illud loqui. . . .

193. This was already recognized by Joseph Maréchal, *Études sur la psychologie des mystiques*, 2:292–95.

194. Instruction 23 (ed., 616.57–58): Omnes illi qui erunt amatores et sequaces istius paupertatis, doloris et despectus mei, isti sunt filii mei legitimi; et isti tales sunt filii tui, et non alii. Instruction 26 (ed., 628.48-49): Et dixit: Tu habebis filios, et istam benedictionem habent omnes, quia omnes filii mei sunt tui, et tui sunt mei. The description of Angela's death in Instruction 36 (ed., 724–36) is especially revealing for a study of the relation between the saint and her circle.

195. See Instruction 2 (ed., 422–24), as well as Instructions 3 and 25 (ed., 458 and 476–78, 620–22).

196. Instruction 4 (ed., 500.177–80): Ipsi videntur transformati in Deum sic quod quasi nihil in eis aliud video quam Deum, nunc gloriosum nunc passionatum, ita quod istos videtur totaliter in se transsubstantiasse et inabyssare. The verb *inabyssare* also occurs at 404.4 and 516.103. For other references to the abyss, see Instructions 4, 19, 32, 35, 36 (ed., 486.28 and 488.40, 590.51, 668.69, 714.21, 726.32 and 736.152). On Jacopone's use of abyss language, see above pp. 127–31. In *Arbor Vitae* 4.7 (305b) Ubertino uses the phrase . . . *inabyssati de solo Christi merito gloriantur.*

Chapter 4

1. I would like to thank Barbara Newman for reading this chapter and for making a number of helpful suggestions.

2. The role of Mary Magdalene in medieval religion has been subject to a number of studies, both serious and superficial. Important recent collections of essays can be found in *Marie Madeleine dans la mystique, les arts et les lettres,* ed. Eve Duperray (Paris: Beauchesne, 1989); and *La Madeleine (VIIIe–XIIIe Siècle): Mélanges de l'École Française de Rome. Moyen Age* 104 (1992) (for Magdalene's influence on women mystics, the most important piece in this collection is that of Michel Lauwers, "'Noli me tangere': Marie Madeleine, Marie d'Oignies et les pénitentes du XIIIe siècle" [pp. 209–68]). In English, see Susan Haskins, *Mary Magdalen: Myth and Metaphor* (New York: Harcourt, Brace, 1993). Christian tradition, at least since Origen, identified the Magdalene with Mary, the sister of Martha (see Luke 10:38-42), and saw in the two sisters the paradigm of the relation of the contemplative and active lives. For Mary and Martha in relation to late medieval mystical women, see Martina Wehrli-Johns, "Maria und Martha in der religiösen Frauenbewegung," in *Abendländische Mystik im Mittelalter: Symposium Kloster Engelberg 1984,* ed. Kurt Ruh, pp. 354-67.

3. Many of the women to be considered in this chapter had a special relation to Mary Magdalene. To cite just one example, the anchoress Juette of Huy (d. 1228), as death approached her, received a vision in which the saint took her to heaven and allowed the anchoress to take on the role that she had once enjoyed of kissing Christ's feet and hearing him say, "Your sins are forgiven you, because you have loved much" (Luke 10:47-48). See the *Vita B. Ivettae Reclusae,* chap. 43, in AA.SS. Jan. 13: 884.

4. For reflections on beguine lives and the antiheretical impetus, see Patricia Deery Kurtz, "Mary of Oignies, Christine the Marvellous, and Medieval Heresy," *Mystics Quarterly* 14 (1988): 186–96.

5. As mentioned in the introduction (see p. 15 n. 59), the literature about women mystics of the later Middle Ages has become far too extensive in recent years to be easily summarized. For a brief survey, see Valerie M. Lagorio, "The Medieval Continental Women Mystics: An Introduction," in *An Introduction to the Medieval Mystics of Europe,* ed. Paul Szarmach (Albany: SUNY Press, 1984), pp. 161–93. Longer surveys can be found in Amy Hollywood, *The Soul as Virgin Wife: Mechthild of Magdeburg, Marguerite Porete, and Meister Eckhart,* chap. 2; and Peter Dinzelbacher, *Heilige oder Hexen?* Several anthologies of women's mystical texts are also useful, such as Elizabeth Alvida Petroff, *Medieval Women's Visionary Literature;* and Emilie Zum Brunn and Georgette Epiney-Burgard, *Women Mystics in Medieval Europe* (New York: Paragon, 1989). In addition, there are numerous volumes of essays on medieval women mystics, both regional and more general, such as *Frauenmystik im Mittelalter,* ed. Peter Dinzelbacher and Dieter R. Bauer (Ostfelden: Schwabenverlag, 1985).

6. Peter Dinzelbacher provides brief accounts of a number of the women not explicitly treated here in his *Christliche Mystik im Abendland.*

7. See Augustine, *De trinitate* 12; cf. the discussion in *Foundations of Mysticism,* pp. 253–55.

8. A number of recent studies have investigated this aspect of medieval mysticism from different perspectives. See, e.g., Caroline Walker Bynum, "The Female Body and Religious Practice in the Later Middle Ages," in *Fragments for a History of the Human Body,* pp. 181–238, and the same author's ". . . And Woman His Humanity: Female Imagery in the Religious Writing of the Later Middle Ages," in *Gender and Religion: On the Complexity of Symbols,* ed. Caroline Walker Bynum, Steven Harrell, and Paula Richman (Boston: Beacon Press, 1986), pp. 257–89. See also Giles Milhaven, "A Medieval Lesson in Bodily Knowing: Women's Experience and Men's Thought," *Journal of the American Academy of Religion* 57 (1989): 341–72; and the same author's *Hadewijch and Her Sisters: Other Ways of Loving and Knowing.* Further discussions can be found in Ulrike Wiethaus, "Sexuality, Gender, and the Body in Late Medieval Women's Spirituality: Cases from Germany and the Netherlands," *Journal of Feminist Studies in Religion* 7 (1991): 35–52; and in some of the papers in *Framing Medieval Bodies,*

ed. Sarah Kay and Miri Rubin (Manchester/New York: Manchester University Press, 1994), especially Walter Simons, "Reading a saint's body: rapture and bodily movement in the *vitae* of some thirteenth-century beguines," pp. 10–23.

9. For Origen's importance as initiator of the doctrine of the spiritual senses, see *Foundations of Mysticism*, pp. 121–24. For other uses of the theme, see the indices under "Senses, spiritual," in *Foundations of Mysticism* and *Growth of Mysticism*, and the various studies cited in the relevant notes.

10. On Bernard's use of the spiritual senses, see *Growth of Mysticism*, pp. 185–90.

11. Gregory of Nyssa, *Homilies on the Song of Songs* 1.1: . . . metenegkosan eis apatheian to pathos . . . (*Gregorii Nysseni in Canticum Canticorum*, ed. Herman Langerbeck [Leiden: Brill, 1960], 27.11–12). See Bernard McGinn, "Tropics of Desire: Mystical Interpretation of *The Song of Songs*," in *That Others May Know and Love: Essays in Honor of Zachary Hayes, OFM*, ed. Michael F. Cusato and F. Edward Coughlin (St. Bonaventure: Franciscan Institute, 1997), 143–47, on Gregory's use of the spiritual senses.

12. In this connection Anne Clark Bartlett has noted some interesting parallels between descriptions of erotic union with Christ in Middle English devotional literature and medieval medical descriptions of female orgasm, though her suggestion that mystical descriptions follow a standard four-stage progress to full union is scarcely true of all mystics (*Male Authors, Female Readers: Representation and Subjectivity in Middle English Devotional Literature* [Ithaca: Cornell University Press, 1995], pp. 128–41).

13. There are prior examples in Eastern Christian mysticism, notably among the fourth-century Messalians and in the case of Simeon the New Theologian (d. 1022).

14. See James of Vitry, *VMO* 1.1.12 (639F): Nec hoc dixero ut excessum commendam, sed ut fervorem ostendam.

15. To cite just two of the early-thirteenth-century works to be treated below, see, e.g., *Vita S. Christinae Mirabilis*, prol. (AA.SS. Jul. 24:650C): Fatemur quidem, et verum est, narrationem nostram omnem hominis intellectum excedere, utpote quae secundum cursum naturae fieri nequaquam possent, cum tamen sint possibilia Creatori . . . ; and the *Vita S. Julianae* 1.3.14 (AA.SS. Apr. 5:448A): Quod si de nimietate, Christi Virgo credatur excessisse, habet certe excessus hujusmodi apud pias mentes reverentiam suam.

16. For a discussion of Richard's treatise, see *Growth of Mysticism*, pp. 415–18.

17. On the *ordo caritatis*, see *Growth of Mysticism*, pp. 149–57 and passim.

18. See Barbara Newman, *From Virile Woman to WomanChrist*, pp. 122–36. Newman studies five woman mystics; once again, however, note that this theme is not restricted to women, as the case of Meister Eckhart demonstrates.

19. Matthew Paris, *Chronica majora*, ed. Henry Richards Luard, 7 vols., Rolls Series (London: Longman, 1877), 4:178 (sub 1243): Eisdemque temporibus, quidem, in Alemannia praecipue, se asserentes religiosos, in utroque sexu, sed maxime in muliebre, habitum religionis, sed levem, susceperunt, continentiam et vitae simplicitatem privato voto profitentes, sub nullius tamen sancti regula coartatae, nec adhuc ullo claustro contenti.

20. The rule for the Paris beguinage was edited by Karl Christ, "*La Regle des fins amans:* Eine Beginenregel aus dem Ende des XIII. Jahrhunderts," in *Philologische Studien aus dem romanisch-germanischen Kulturkreise*, ed. B. Schädel and W. Mulertt (Halle: n.p., 1927), pp. 173–213. We also know that James of Troyes, the future Pope Urban IV, drew up a rule for *beguinae clausae* about 1246.

21. For an overview of the history of the Cistercian nuns, see Louis J. Lekai, *The Cistercians: Ideals and Reality* (n.p.: Kent State University Press, 1977), chap. 22. The most complete account of the institutional development of the early Cistercian nuns, with a special concentration on Belgium, is that of Janet I. Summers, "'The Violent Shall Take It by Force': The

First Century of Cistercian Nuns, 1125–1228" (Ph.D. diss., University of Chicago, 1986). On the inner life and spirituality of the female Cistercians, see the papers collected in *Hidden Springs: Cistercian Monastic Women,* ed. John A. Nichols and Lillian Thomas Shank, 2 vols. (Kalamazoo: Cistercian Publications, 1995). For the Cistercian nuns in Belgium, see Simone Roisin, *L'hagiographie cistercienne dans la diocèse de Liège au XIIIe siècle* (Louvain: Bibliothèque de l'Université, 1947), and "L'efflorescence cistercienne et le courant féminin de pieté au XIIIe siècle," *Revue d'histoire ecclésiastique* 39 (1943): 342–78; Roger De Ganck, "The Cistercian Nuns of Belgium in the Thirteenth Century," *Cistercian Studies* 5 (1970): 169–87; and the same author's *Beatrice of Nazareth in her Context,* 2 vols. (Kalamazoo: Cistercian Publications, 1991); as well as Martinus Cawley, "The Trinity in the *Mulieres religiosae* of Thirteenth-Century Belgium," *Monastic Studies* 17 (1986): 167–90.

22. For a summary of this ambivalence, see chap. 5 in Herbert Grundmann, *Religious Movements in the Middle Ages.*

23. This survey is based upon Summers, "'The Violent Shall Take It,'" chap. 5.

24. By 1228 there were already fourteen convents in the diocese of Liège alone. For these figures and a more complete discussion, see Summers, "'The Violent Shall Take It,'" chap. 7. All together, in the "Pays-bas-réunis," that is, Belgium, Holland, and the adjoining parts of northern France, there were eighty Cistercian nunneries by 1252 (ibid., pp. 236–37).

25. One exception, to be treated in the final section of this chapter, is the recluse Juette of Huy. An illustration of a holy woman who lived a variety of forms of religious life can be found in the career of Juliana of Mont-Cornillon (1193–1258), well known for her role in propagandizing for the establishment of the new eucharistic feast of Corpus Christi. The house of which she was prioress followed the Rule of St. Augustine, but when she was compelled to leave the house because of internal struggles, she and her companions lived a life close to that of beguines until they were taken in by the Cistercian nuns at Salzinnes. Juliana's *Vita,* written by a cleric of Liège appears in AA.SS. Apr. 5:437–77 and has been translated by Barbara Newman, *The Life of Juliana of Mont-Cornillon* (Toronto: Peregrina, n.d.). For Juliana's mystical raptures, often connected with the reception of the Eucharist, see *Vita* 1.2.11–12, 1.5.28, and 2.3.11.

26. The following list is divided into three categories according to the predominant form of religious life:

I. *Beguine*

1) Mary of Oignies (1171–1213)–*Vita* by James of Vitry (AA.SS. Jun. 23:630–66)

2) Mary of Oignies–*Supplementum* by Thomas of Cantimpré (AA.SS. Jun. 23:666–78)

3) Odilia (d. 1220)–*Vita* by a cleric of Liège (*Analecta Bollandiana* 13 [1894]: 197–287)

4) Christina (the Astonishing) of St. Trond (1150–1224)–*Vita* by Thomas of Cantimpré (AA.SS. Jul. 24:650–60)

5) Margaret of Ypres (1216–1237)–*Vita* by Thomas of Cantimpré (*Archivum Fratrum Praedicatorum* 18 [1948]: 106–30)

II. *Cistercian*

6) Ida of Nivelles (1199–1231)–*Vita* by Goswin of Villers in Chrysostom Henriquez, ed., *Quinque prudentes virgines* (Antwerp, 1690), 199–298.

7) Lutgard of Aywières (1182–1246)–*Vita* by Thomas of Cantimpré (AA.SS. Jun. 16:187–209)

8) Alice of Schaarbeck (1215–1250)–*Vita* by a Cistercian monk (AA.SS. Jun. 11: 471–77)

9) Beatrice of Nazareth (ca. 1200–1268)–*Vita* by her confessor in *The Life of Beatrice of Nazareth,* translated and annotated by Roger De Ganck (Kalamazoo: Cistercian Publications, 1991)

10) Ida of Lewis (d. ca. 1273)–*Vita* possibly by a monk of Villers (AA.SS. Oct. 29: 100–124)

11) Ida of Leuven (ca. 1211–ca. 1290)–*Vita* by a Cistercian (AA.SS. April 13:156–89)

12) Beatrice of Zwijveke (thirteenth century)–*Vita* by a Cistercian in *Ons Geestlijk Erf* 23 (1949): 225–46

13) Catherine of Parc-des-Dames (d. ca.1300)–*Vita* possibly by a Cistercian (AA.SS. Mai. 1:537–39)

14) Elizabeth of Spaalbeek (d. 1304)–*Vita* by Philip of Clairvaux in *Catalogus Codicum Hagiographicorum Bibliothecae Regiae Bruxellensis* (Brussels, 1886), 1:362–78

III. Other

15) Juette of Huy (d. 1228)–*Vita* by Hugh of Floreffe (AA.SS. Jan. 13:145–69)

16) Juliana of Mont-Cornillon (1193–1258)–*Vita* by a cleric of Liège (AA.SS. Apr. 5:437–77)

This wealth of *vitae* of female mystics fell off sharply in the fourteenth century, though there are a few examples, such as the *Vita* of the beguine Gertrude of Delft (d.1358) in AA.SS. Jan. 6:348–53.

27. For the role of the Eucharist for women mystics, see especially Caroline Walker Bynum, "Women Mystics and Eucharistic Devotion in the Thirteenth Century," in *Fragmentation and Redemption*, pp. 119–50.

28. For a sketch of Thomas's life and works, see Alfred Deboutte, "Thomas de Cantimpré," DS 15:784–92. On Thomas as hagiographer, consult Simone Roisin, "La méthode hagiographique de Thomas de Cantimpré," in *Miscellanea historica in honorem Alberti de Meyer* (Louvain: Bibliothèque de l'Université, 1946), 1:546–57. In English, there is considerable information on Thomas in Ernest W. McDonnell, *The Beguines and Beghards in Medieval Culture.* On the role of the Dominicans in Belgium at this time, see Gilles Meersseman, "Les débuts de l'ordre dès frères prêcheurs dans le Comté de Flandre (1224–1280)," *Archivum Fratrum Praedicatorum* 17 (1947): 5–40; and "Les frères prêcheurs et le mouvement dévot en Flandre au XIIIe siècle," *Archivum Fratrum Praedicatorum* 18 (1948): 69–130 (containing an edition of Thomas's *Vita de Margarete de Ypris*).

29. The *Bonum universale de apibus,* or *Liber apum,* written ca. 1256–61, was edited by Georgius Colvenerius and published at Douai in 1627 (I wish to thank John van Engen for making a copy of this rare work available to me). In comparing human society to a beehive, Thomas illustrates the virtues appropriate to the various states of life through a large collection of interesting *exempla.* The contemplative life, as illustrated especially by friars and *mulieres sanctae,* is treated, e.g., in 1.9 and 13, 2.13, 32-33 (examples of levitation), 40, 41 (on the *iubilus*), 45, 46 (miraculous illuminations), 49 (a beguine expires in ecstasy), 51 (a beguine filled with divine fire), 52 (Lutgard), and 54.

30. See Herbert Thurston, S.J., "Christina of Saint-Trond," in *Surprising Mystics* (Chicago: Regnery, 1955), p. 147 (the essay originally appeared in the Jesuit periodical *The Month* in 1922).

31. E.g., Robert Sweetman, "Christine of St. Trond's Preaching Apostolate," *Vox Benedictina* 9 (1992): 67–97. See also Margot H. King, "The Sacramental Witness of Christina Mirabilis: The Mystic Growth of a Fool for Christ's Sake," in *Peace Weavers: Medieval Religious Women II,* ed. John A. Nichols and Lillian Thomas Shank (Kalamazoo: Cistercian Publications, 1987), pp. 145–64; and Amy Hollywood, *Soul as Virgin Wife,* pp. 45–46. For a reading of Christina as a "demoniac saint," see Barbara Newman, "Possessed by the Spirit: Devout Women, Demoniacs, and the Apostolic Life in the Thirteenth Century," *Speculum* 73 (1998, forthcoming).

32. The *Vita Christinae Mirabilis* (hereafter VMC) is found in AA.SS. Jul. 24, and will be

cited here by book and chapter with the page and column in parentheses. At the end of his "Prologue," Thomas provides an overall tripartite structure, describing how he will present Christina's nourishment (*nutrita*), education (*educata*), and deeds (*gesta*)–see VMC Prol. 3 (650D). *Pace* Margot King ("The Sacramental Witness of Christina *Mirabilis*," pp. 149–56), I do not see any link between this tripartite structure and William of St. Thierry's three stages of the spiritual life: *animalis-rationalis-spiritualis.*

33. VMC 5.56 (659F): Et quid aliud in omni vita sua Christina clamavit, nisi poentitentiam agere, et paratos esse homines omni hora? Hoc verbis multis, hoc fletibus, hoc ejulatibus, hoc clamoribus infinitis, hoc exemplo vitae plus docuit, plus clamavit, quam de aliquo praecedentium vel subsequentium scripto vel relatione percepimus. . . . There is a translation by Margot H. King, *The Life of Christina Mirabilis* (Toronto: Peregrina, 1995), but I have preferred to make my own versions.

34. Christina's sense that her body has become a "good" resurrected body is also hinted at in the odd reversal found in VCM 5.47–49 (658E–659A), in which the saint begins with a typical medieval attack on the wretched body, but then shifts to condemning the "miserable soul" and praising the "most beloved body."

35. For Aelred's notion of *spiritualis amicitia* and its relation to mysticism, see *Growth of Mysticism,* pp. 316–21.

36. Brian Patrick McGuire, "The Cistercians and Friendship: An Opening to Women," in *Hidden Springs,* 1:171–200.

37. Caesarius of Heisterbach, *Libri VIII Miraculorum* 1.5, as found in Alfons Hilka, *Die Wundergeschichten des Caesarius von Heisterbach* (Bonn: Publikationen der Gesellschaft für Rhenische Geschichtkunde XLIII:III, 1939), 24. The *Libri VIII Miraculorum* is a continuation of Caesarius's better-known *Dialogus Miraculorum.*

38. John Coakley, "Friars as Confidants of Holy Women in Medieval Dominican Hagiography," in *Images of Sainthood in Medieval Europe,* pp. 222–46, especially 225–28 on Margaret.

39. The *Vita Margaritae* was edited by Meersseman in "Les frères prêcheurs et le mouvement dévot en Flandres au XIIIe siècle," pp. 106–30. It will be cited here using the abbreviation VM with chapter followed by page number in parentheses.

40. VM 6 (ed., 109): Qui cum forte Margaretam in habitu seculari inter multas feminas coniectis oculis inspexisset, vidit quodammodo divino instinctu eam, quam nunquam antea viderat, habilem ad Dei graciam suscipiendam et vas electionis, Christo revelante, futuram. Cumque vocasset eam et ille admoneret eam secularia cuncta respuere, dixit sine ulla retractatione quod Saulus: "Domine, quid me vis facere?". . . . mundumque statim perfecte relinquens.

41. Margaret can be described as a beguine in the most primitive sense, that is, a *mulier religiosa* who lives at home but marks out her special way of life by continence, asceticism, and special devotion.

42. After Margaret's death, Siger is described as a co-worker of her first miracle (chap. 53); he also demands control of her relics (chap. 54; see ed., 128–29).

43. VM 13 (ed., 112): . . . . excepto tamen solo spirituali patre eius, per quem salutem fuerat consecuta. Ad huius verba suspensa sedebat et eius colloquia incorporabat sibi anima illius, velut corpus cibum quo vivit.

44. Thomas's *Vita S. Lutgarde* (hereafter VL), composed between 1246 and 1248, exists in two versions. The better-known long version is to be found in AA.SS. Jun. 16:234–63. This is what will be used here, cited by book and section with the column reference in parentheses. There is an English translation, *The Life of Lutgard of Aywières by Thomas of Cantimpré,* translated with notes by Margot H. King (Saskatoon: Peregrina, 1987), but I have preferred to make my own translations. Guido Hendrix in his article "Primitive Versions of Thomas of Cantimpré's *Vita Lutgardis,*" *Citeaux* 29 (1978): 153–206, argues for a shorter form of this text found in a Brussels manuscript as representing Thomas's first attempt and not a later adaptation.

45. The threefold structure is announced in the Prologus (234B): Vitam piae Lutgardis utcumque descripsi; tribus libris opus distinguens, secundum triplicem statum in anima, inchoantium, proficientium, et perfectorum. The theme is reprised in 2.43 (253AC) according to the image of the three beds (*lectuli*) of the Song of Songs (see Song 3:1 and 1:15), a Cistercian motif probably suggested by William of St. Thierry (see *Growth of Mysticism*, pp. 240–44).

46. Considerable literature has been devoted to Lutgard's mystical spirituality. Thomas Merton wrote a book on her (*What are These Wounds? The Life of a Cistercian Mystic: Saint Lutgarde of Aywières* [Milwaukee: Bruce, 1950]), though he thought it one of his least successful. See also Léonce Reypens, "Sint Lutgards mystieke opgang," *Ons Geestelijk Erf* 20 (1946): 7–49; Alfred Deboutte, "Sainte Lutgarde et sa spiritualité," *Collectanea Cisterciensia* 44 (1982): 73–87, and "Lutgarde," DS 9:1201–4. Three essays in *Hidden Springs* (1:211–81) are devoted to Lutgard: Amandus Bussels, "Saint Lutgard's Mystical Spirituality"; Margot King, "The Dove at the Window: The Ascent of the Soul in Thomas of Cantimpré's Life of Lutgard of Aywières"; and Alfred Deboutte, "The *Vita Lutgardis* of Thomas of Cantimpré." The most recent contribution is Jean-Baptiste Lefèvre, "Sainte Lutgarde d'Aywières en son temps (1182–1246)," *Collectanea Cisterciensia* 58 (1996): 277–335.

47. Devotion to the open wound (*vulnus*) in Christ's side can be found in twelfth-century writers, like Anselm and Bernard of Clairvaux. Emphasis on the bleeding heart itself was the next stage in this trajectory. This emphasis, which after many transformations eventually produced the establishment of the feast of the Sacred Heart (1765), was developed by a line of female visionaries (especially the nuns of Helfta to be considered in chap. 6) that reaches down to Margaret Mary Alocoque (1647–1690). For an overview, see Auguste Hamon, "Coeur (Sacré)," DS 2:1023–46; for theological reflections Karl Rahner's "Part Five: Devotion to the Sacred Heart," in *Theological Investigations*, vol. 3 (New York: Seabury, 1974), pp. 321–52, is still valuable.

48. VL 1.2 (237D): Blanditias inepti amoris ulterius non requiras; hic jugiter contemplare quid diligas, et cur diligas: hic totius puritatis delicias tibi spondeo consequendas.

49. VL 1.3 (237E): . . . et quasi columba meditans, in fenestra ad introitum solaris luminis, ostium crystallinum arcae typicae corporis Christi pertinaciter observabat. This unusual symbol is partly reminiscent of biblical texts on the *columba* as an image of contemplation (especially Isa. 38:14; 59:11; and 60:8) and also seems to reflect a passage from William of St. Thierry's *De contemplando Deo* 3 (ed. SC 61:64), which refers to the wound in Christ's side as the *ostium archae*, that is, the physical manifestation (like the *arca testamenti* of Exodus 25–26) of the presence of God.

50. On this motif, see André Cabassut, "Coeurs (Changement des, Échange des)," DS 2:1046–51.

51. VL 1.12 (239D): Cui Dominus: Quid vis? Volo, inquit, cor tuum. Et Dominus, Quin ego potius et cor tuum volo. Cui illa: Ita fit Domine, sed tamen sic, ut cordis tui amorem cordi meo contemperes et in te cor meum possideam, omni tempore tuo munimine jam securum. Facta est ex tunc communicatio cordium quin potius unio spiritus increati et creati per excellentiam gratiae, et hoc est quod Apostolus dicit: Quae adhaeret Deo, unus spiritus efficitur. For a text close to the above in William, see the *Expositio in Cantica Canticorum* 94 (ed. SC 82:222), and the discussion in *Growth of Mysticism*, pp. 264–67.

52. This is particularly evident later in the *Vita Lutgardis* in the two extended analyses of the saint's role as "bride of Christ" found in 2.42–43 (252E–253D) and 3.9 (256CF), where Thomas employs many of the themes and biblical texts, especially from the Song of Songs, used by Bernard and William of St. Thierry.

53. VL 1.14 (240AB) indicates that this type of vision was frequent whenever she gazed on an image of the crucifixion. A subsequent chapter (1.19 [240AB]) has a presentation of a related theme, one also involving drinking bodily fluids. Here Lutgard sees Christ in the form

of a lamb positioning himself with both hooves on her shoulders in order to suck forth a miraculous melody from her mouth. The nutritive and erotic connotations of such descriptions have evoked considerable study in recent years. The complex interchange between human experiences of eating and sexual intercourse and modes of presenting contact with God are too varied for easy summary. I have tried to indicate some of my own perceptions in two essays: "The Language of Love in Christian and Jewish Mysticism," in *Mysticism and Language*, ed. Steven Katz (New York: Oxford University Press, 1992), pp. 202–35; and "Mysticism and Sexuality," *The Way. Supplement* 77 (1993): 46–53.

54. For the history of the community at Aywières, see Summers, "'The Violent Shall Take It,'" pp. 254–67. According to VL 1.22 (242AB) Christina the Astonishing encouraged Lutgard in making this transfer. VL 2.3 (244AB) also recounts how Lutgard's prayers delivered James of Vitry from temptation, while 2.9 (245E) speaks of Mary of Oignies prophesying Lutgard's miracles on her deathbed in 1213. All this gives us some sense of how closely the leading figures of the new mysticism in Lotharingia were connected.

55. See VL 2.2 (243F) for the first fast, which was initiated by the appearance of the Blessed Virgin asking the nun to do penance for the conversion of Albigensian heretics and "bad Christians," and 2.9 (245DE), where Jesus with his bloody wounds asks her to fast for all sinners. A third seven-year fast is recounted in the third book. On Lutgard as a type of female "co-redemptrix," see Deboutte, "The *Vita Lutgardis*," pp. 263–71; and Barbara Newman, *From Virile Woman to WomanChrist*, pp. 119–22. This aspect of Lutgard's spiritual powers is also evident, e.g., in 3.15 (258AB), where the saint, in Pauline fashion, asks to be deleted from the book of life unless God grants her wish to pardon a sinner under her protection.

56. VL 3.17 (258D): . . . et nimirum perfecte sentirent, quod cum immenso tripudio supernorum, ipse praesentialiter salutis nostrae princeps Jesus, animam illius ad delicias evocaverit paradisi.

57. Our basic source for Beatrice's life is the anonymous *Vita Beatricis*, edited by Léonce Reypens and reprinted with an English translation in *The Life of Beatrice of Nazareth 1200–1268*, translated and annotated by Roger De Ganck assisted by John Baptist Hasbrouck (Kalamazoo: Cistercian Publications, 1991). Beatrice's surviving Middle Dutch treatise, *The Seven Experiences of Loving*, was edited by Léonce Reypens and Joseph Van Mierlo, *Beatrijs Van Nazareth: Seven Manieren van Minne* (Leuven: Vlaamsche Boekenhalle, 1926). A considerably revised Latin version of this work was incorporated into the *Vita*. There are English translations (of both versions) in *The Life of Beatrice*, pp. 286–331, and of the Dutch alone in Edmund Colledge, *Mediaeval Netherlands Religious Literature* (London: Heinemann, 1965), pp. 19–29. Neither the *Vita* nor the *Seven Manieren van Minne* achieved wide popularity–there are four manuscripts of the former and three of the latter. In English, considerable information about Beatrice and other contemporary Belgian mystics can be found in R. De Ganck's two volumes *Beatrice of Nazareth in her Context* and *Towards Unification with God* (Kalamazoo: Cistercian Publications, 1991). See also Amy Hollywood, *Soul as Virgin Wife*, pp. 29–39; Emilie Zum Brunn and Georgette Epiney-Burgard, *Women Mystics in Medieval Europe*, pp. 69–94; Mary Ann Sullivan, "An Introduction to the *Vita Beatricis*," and Ritamary Bradley, "Love and Knowledge in the *Seven Manners of Loving*," in *Hidden Springs*, 1:345–76; and Ritamary Bradley, "Beatrice of Nazareth (c. 1200–1268): A Search for her True Spirituality," in *Vox Mystica: Essays on Medieval Mysticism in Honor of Professor Valerie M. Lagorio*, ed. Anne Clark Bartlett et al. (Cambridge: D. S. Brewer, 1995), pp. 57–74. There is a rich literature in Dutch, some of which will be cited in subsequent notes. In German (translated from Dutch), see Herman Vekeman, "Beatrijs van Nazareth: Die Mystik einer Zisterzienserin," in *Frauenmystik im Mittelalter*, pp. 78–98; and especially the fine treatment in Ruh, *Geschichte*, 2:137–57. For an extensive bibliography, consult Gertrud Jaron Lewis, *Bibliographie zur deutschen Frauenmys-*

tik des Mittlelalters: Mit ein Anhang zu Beatrijs van Nazareth und Hadewijch, by Frank Willaert and Marie-José Govers, pp. 325–50.

58. The *Vita* will be cited according to book and chapter with the page and (where necessary) line numbers within parentheses. For Beatrice's education, see 1.3 (24–26). The passage about gathering books on the Trinity is found in 3.7 (246.11–13). *The Seven Manners of Loving* will be cited according to the edition of Reypens by page and line. In this treatise Beatrice cites the Latin Vulgate twice (33.76–77, 34.104) and St. Augustine in Latin once (38.158–59).

59. On Rupert's mystical journal, see *Growth of Mysticism,* pp. 328–33.

60. Hollywood, *Soul as Virgin Wife,* p. 31 (see the whole analysis on pp. 29–37). The chaplain, who does not seem to have been a Cistercian, remains anonymous, but he did have a fairly extensive theological education, as is shown by his lengthy defense of Beatrice's claim to have beheld the divine essence. See 2.19, which describes this "seraph" vision as follows: Ibi diuinam essentiam in plenitudine glorie sue, perfectiissimeque maiestatis sue potentia, continentem omnia, gubernantem uniuersa, disponentem singula, clara contemplationis acie, si fas est dicere, videre promeruit . . . (202.66–204.68). The chaplain's theological explanation can be found on 204–8. For another comparison of the two texts, see Herman Vekeman, "Vita Beatricis en Seuen Manieren van Minne: Een vergelijkende studie," *Ons Geestelijk Erf* 46 (1972): 3–54.

61. *Vita* 1.10 (58–66). The *Vita* recounts other important spiritual friendships in her life, both with women (e.g., 1.4 [32]) and with men (e.g., 3.12 [278]). On Ida of Nivelles (1199–1231), see the articles of Martinus Cawley and Claire Boudreau in *Hidden Springs,* 1:305–44.

62. De Ganck hazarded the guess that the original spiritual journal might have been destroyed (ca. 1275) because of attacks on women's speculations on the Trinity (*Life of Beatrice of Nazareth,* pp. xxviii–xxxii). But the papal inquisitor Robert le Bougre was already active from ca. 1235 to ca. 1245 in the diocese of Cambrai, in which Nazareth was located, and Hadewijch tells us that he had a beguine executed for her views regarding *minne.* See Charles Homer Haskins, "Robert le Bougre and the Beginnings of the Inquisition in Northern France," in *Studies in Mediaeval Culture* (Oxford: Clarendon Press, 1929), pp. 219–29.

63. We have no real way of determining the relative dating of Beatrice's treatise in relation to Hadewijch's writings, which probably begin in the 1240s (see Ruh, *Geschichte,* 2:137, 151–52, for a discussion). *The Seven Manners of Loving* does not appear to come down to us in a pure form, as its editor Léone Reypens argued in his article, "De *Seven Manieren van Minne* Geinterpoleerd?" *Ons Geestelijk Erf* 5 (1931): 287–322.

64. For some examples of each of these characteristics: (1) penance–1.5, 2.3, 3.1 (36–40, 116–18, 214–20); (2) devotion to the passion–1.14–15, 2.16, 3.7, 3.12 (88–92, 134, 248–50, 278); (3) the role of the Eucharist, especially in relation to mystical experiences–1.13, 1.18, 2.11, 2.15, 2.16, 3.2, 3.4, 3.5, 3.11 (82, 102–4, 154–56, 180–82, 188, 224, 234, 238, 276–78); (4) trials as a "Dark Night"–2.12 (158–68); and (5) the psychosomatic effects of mystical consciousness–1.11 (unrestained laughing and the feeling of levitation), 1.16 (*iubilus* as laughing or dancing), 2.16 (dilated heart and flowing of blood), 3.4 (raving, dancing, bodily collapse), 3.8 (frenzy and bodily collapse) (72, 942–96, 186–88, 232–36, 254–58).

65. These are among the key themes of the *Vita,* and will also appear in *The Seven Manners.* For *insania/vesania,* see, e.g., 1.11, 2.16, 3.4, 3.8 (72.96–97, 188.79, 232.21, 254.4–7, and 256.43–66); *insatiabilitas desiderii* occurs, e.g., 2.3, 3.4, 3.9 (122.134, 236.65–66, 258.10–13); *vehementia* is one of the most frequent terms in the text. For one good example see 3.4 (236.69–82).

66. Sullivan notes that the severe ascetical practices mentioned in the *Vita* do not appear in *The Seven Manners* ("An Introduction to the *Vita Beatricis,*" p. 350).

67. See Bradley, "Love and Knowledge in the *Seven Manners of Loving,*" pp. 363–64.

68. Although Hadewijch's letters can be described as treatise-like, they are not technically mystical tractates. In the treatise Beatrice speaks not in an autobiographical way, recounting her own visions and experiences of God, but as a teacher conveying mystical wisdom. Neither does she at any time use the topos of the "weak woman."

69. Without getting into the difficult issue of whether or not Cistercian mystics, especially Bernard of Clairvaux, may have adapted courtly themes, it is clear that as early as Richard of St. Victor's *De quatuor gradibus violentae caritatis* (ca. 1160s) we find influence from courtly literature in mysticism (see *Growth of Mysticism,* pp. 415–18). In the thirteenth century there is the interesting example of the Cistercian Gerard of Liège (ca. 1250), who in his *Quinque incitamenta ad Deum amandum ardenter* uses contemporary Old French love songs to illustrate the qualities of loving God (see André Wilmart, "Les traités de Gérard de Liège sur l'amour illicite et sur l'amour de Dieu," *Analecta Reginensia* [Rome: Biblioteca Apostolic Vaticana, 1933], pp. 205–47).

70. On the relation between mysticism and love poetry in general, see Peter Dronke, *Medieval Latin and the Rise of the European Love Lyric,* 2 vols. (Oxford: Clarendon Press, 1968), 1:57–70. On the term *fin'amour,* see Edmund Reiss, "Fin'Amors: Its History and Meaning in Medieval Literature," *Medieval and Renaissance Studies* [Duke University] 8 (1979): [74]–[99]. There are a number of studies of the role of *minne* in the mystical women of northern Europe. See, e.g., Kurt Ruh, "Beginenmystik: Hadewijch, Mechthild von Magdeburg, Marguerite Porete," in *Kleine Schriften: Band II, Scholastik und Mystik im Spätmittelalter,* 2:237–49; Elizabeth Wainwright-deKadt, "Courtly Literature and Mysticism: Some Aspects of Their Interaction," *Acta Germanica* 12 (1980): 41–60; and Joris Reynaert, "Hadewijch: mystic poetry and courtly love," *Medieval Dutch Literature in its European Context,* ed. Erik Kooper (Cambridge: Cambridge University Press, 1994), pp. 208–25.

71. See Newman, "*La mystique courtoise:* Thirteenth-Century Beguines and the Art of Love," in *From Virile Woman to WomanChrist,* pp. 137–67, especially 137–39. Newman advances her claim through an analysis of the three beguines: Hadewijch, Mechthild of Magdeburg, and Marguerite Porete, who will be considered in the next chapter; but Beatrice could also be added to the list of exponents of *la mystique courtoise,* as Newman notes on p. 139.

72. For some further reflections on this, see my essay "The Language of Love in Christian and Jewish Mysticism."

73. Saskia Murk-Jansen, "The Use of Gender and Gender-Related Imagery in Hadewijch," in *Gender and Text in the Later Middle Ages,* p. 53.

74. The use of male terms for God was never universal, as the employment of *sapientia* and other feminine names (even by Augustine—see *Foundations of Mysticism,* p. 260) indicates.

75. Among those not treated here, to list only a few: (1) descriptions of natural settings, often as introductory framing devices (*Natureingang*); (2) personifications of psychological faculties; (3) metaphors of warfare and the "game" of courtliness; (4) the contrast between noble folk and base; (5) the fusion of ethical and aesthetic values; (6) the importance of gift-giving; and (7) the "tests" of true love.

76. See the conclusions of Herman Vekeman in his detailed study of *minne* in Beatrice ("Minne in 'Seuven Manieren van Minne' van Beatrijs van Nazareth," *Cîteaux* 29 [1969]: 285–316), who says (in the English summary): "'Minne' as a concept contains the totality of Beatrijs' experience of divine love. Next to its ability to express the existential value of divine love, this concept excels in flexibility to explain intelligibly the whole phenomenon of divine love. The concrete significance of the concept must therefore be determined out of its close context in 'Seven Manieren van Minne'" (p. 316). See also De Ganck, *Towards Unification with God,* pp. 469–71.

77. *Van seuen manieren van heiliger minne* (hereafter SV) 3.3–4 (page and line in the

Reypens edition): Seuen manieren sijn van minnen, die comen vten hoegsten, ende keren weder ten ouersten. The term *manieren,* generally translated as "manners," is rich and ambiguous. Insofar as it expresses the internal modalities of *minne* within the soul, it might be translated by "experiences," but this would subjectivize the range of meanings implied in *minne,* especially its overarching divine referent. The notion of the *circulus amoris* found in this passage has been compared to a text in William of St. Thierry's *Orationes meditativae* 6.7: Amor enim ad te, Domine, in nobis illuc ascendit, quia amor in te huc nos descendit (ed., SC 324:110). For translations of the Middle Dutch of the *Van seuen manierien* I have depended on the versions of Colledge and De Ganck compared with the Reypens text, but in some details I have accepted the suggestions of Saskia Murk-Jansen, whose assistance I am grateful to acknowledge.

78. The interconnective, rather than successive, role of the "manners" has been emphasized by Ruh, *Geschichte,* 2:146 and 156; cf. Bradley, "Love and Knowledge in the *Seven Manners of Loving,*" pp. 362–63 and 368.

79. On the significance of these three characteristics of the soul in its original state, see De Ganck, *Beatrice of Nazareth in her Context,* 1:135–46. The same motif appears in *Vita,* e.g., 3.11 (276.40–43). On Beatrice's *imago Dei* theology, see Else Marie Wiberg Pedersen, "Image of God-Image of Mary-Image of Woman: On the Theology and Spirituality of Beatrice of Nazareth," *Cistercian Studies* 29 (1994): 209–20. The emphasis on recovering the soul's *vriheit* throughout the text (see, e.g, 4.15, 14.18–19, 24.22, 27.52) is Beatrice's form of the *spiritus libertatis* theme (cf. 2 Cor. 3:17), found among Cistercian mystics, like William of St. Thierry and Aelred, and increasingly popular in the thirteenth century.

80. SM 4.21–26: Ende dan ghevuelt si dat al hor sinne sijn geheilicht in der minnen ende har wille es worden minne, ende datsi so diepe es versonken ende verswolgen int afgront der minnen, ende selue al es worden minne (De Ganck trans., 305.) The following passage (4.27–35) praises this absorption in a quasi-poetic form.

81. See McGinn, "The Abyss of Love," in *The Joy of Learning and the Love of God: Studies in Honor of Jean Leclercq,* pp. 103–6 on Beatrice.

82. On the meaning of *orewoed,* the equivalent of the Latin *insania amoris,* see De Ganck, *Towards Unification with God,* pp. 390–96; and Ruh, *Geschichte,* 2:151–52. The term was employed by Beatrice and Hadewijch, and also by John Ruusbroec, but it later fell out of use.

83. SM 5.40–49: Ende so dunct hare, dat har adren ontpluken, ende hare bloet verwalt, ende hare march verswijnt, ende hare been vercrencken, ende hare borst verbrent, ende hare kele verdroget, so dat hare anscijn ende al har ede gevuelen der hitten van binnen, ende des orwoeds van minnen. Si geveult oec die wile, dat een gescutte geet dicwile dor har herte toter kelende vort toten hersenen, also of si har sins gemissen soude. (Here I have combined both the Colledge and De Ganck translations to give what seems to me a more effective reading.) Herman Vekeman argues that we have here an example of the special form of wounding, the *transfixio cordis,* later associated with Teresa of Avila (*"Dat waren scachte die diepe staken:* Beatrijs van Nazareth [1200–1268], Mechthild von Hackeborn [1241–c.1299], Geertrui de Grote [1256–ca.1301] en Theresia van Avila [1515–1582]: *vulnus amoris* en *transfixio,*" *Ons Geestelijk Erf* 67 [1993]: 3–19).

84. SM 6.4–5: . . . si noch andre maniere van minnen, in naerren wesene ende in hogeren bekinne (my translation). On the role of love and knowledge in the seven manners, especially the fifth and sixth, see Bradley, "Love and Knowledge in the *Seven Manners of Loving,*" pp. 363–68.

85. SM 7 consists of 171 lines in Reypens's edition, more than twice as long as any other section. The Latin text is quite different, not least because it omits the final hundred lines.

86. This key term of early vernacular mysticism (*gebruken* in Beatrice; *ghebrukene* in

Hadewijch; *gebruchunge* in Mechthild of Magdeburg) is based upon the conception of *fruitio Dei* going back to Augustine, but it takes on new accents in the vernacular theologians. See Ruh, *Geschichte,* 2:180.

87. SM 7.8–14: . . . in die ewelicheit der minnen, ende in die onbegriplicheit, in die witheit, ende die ongerinlike hoecheit, ende in die diepe afgronde der godheit, die es al in alle dinc, ende die obegripelec bluiet bouen alle dinc, ende die onwandelec, al-wesende, al-mogende, al-begripende, ende al-geweldeleke werkende (I have adopted and modified both the Colledge and De Ganck translations here).

88. On epektasis in the Flemish women mystics, see De Ganck, *Towards Unification with God,* pp. 569–91 (pp. 586–90 on Beatrice).

89. SM 7.164–66: Daer wert die siele geenicht met haren brudegome, ende wert al een geest met heme in onscedeliker trouwen ende eweliker minnen. This is the only mention of the Bridegroom in the text.

90. For notes on the relationship and historical development of the beguines and these Italian groups, see Romana Guarnieri, "Beguines beyond the Alps and Italian *Bizzoche* between the 14th and 15th Centuries," *Greyfriars Review* 5 (1991): 93–104; and, more fully, the same author's article "Pinzochere," in DIP 6:1722–49. A rich collection of studies relating to these Italian women can be found in Anna Benvenuti Papi, *"In Castro Poenitentiae": Santità e società femminile nell'Italia medievale* (Rome: Herder, 1990), part of which is available in English as "Mendicant Friars and Female Pinzochere in Tuscany: From Social Marginality to Models of Sanctity," in *Women and Religion in Medieval and Renaissance Italy,* pp. 84–103.

91. This judgment was directly connected to the life and teachings of Marguerite Porete and hence will be treated in more detail in the following chapter.

92. *Lamprecht von Regensburg: Sanct Francisken Leben und Tochter Syon,* ed. Karl Weinhold (Paderborn: Schöningh, 1880), p. 341: diu kunst ist bî unsern tagen / in Brábant und in Baier-landen / undern wiben úf gestanden. / herre got, waz kunst is daz, / daz sich ein alt wip baz / verstét dan witzige man? For thirteenth-century French critiques of beguines, see Alfons Hilka, "Altfranzösische Mystik und Beginentum," *Zeitschrift für romanische Philologie* 47 (1927): 121–70.

93. For a summary of these relations and some of the particular mendicant legislation dealing with beguines, see Grundmann, *Religious Movements,* pp. 143–44. For Germany, see also John B. Freed, *The Friars and German Society in the Thirteenth Century* (Cambridge, Mass.: Mediaeval Academy of America, 1977), especially chap. 1; and his article "Urban Develop-ment and the 'Cura monialium' in Thirteenth-Century Germany," *Viator* 3 (1972): 311–27.

94. Gilbert of Tournai's *Collectio de scandalis ecclesiae* was edited by Autbertus Stroick in *Archivum Franciscanum Historicum* 24 (1931): 33–62. For his attack on the beguines, see #25 (pp. 61–62).

95. Both women are included in the group of lesser female mystics of late medieval Germany by Peter Dinzelbacher ("A Plea for the Study of the Minor Female Mystics of Late Medieval Germany," *Studies in Spirituality* 3 [1993]: 91–100).

96. Among the earliest treatments of Christina is the interesting essay by Ernest Renan, "Une Idylle monacale au XIIIe siècle: Christine de Stommeln," in *Nouvelles études d'histoire religieuse* (Paris: Lévy, 1884), pp. 355–96. In English the first serious consideration was by Herbert Thurston, "Peter and Christina," first published in *The Month* in 1928 and later incor-porated into his *Surprising Mystics,* pp. 1–26. Thurston was tempted to write off the whole story as a romance, but eventually argued that Christina suffered from "hysterical neurosis" and her "tale of horrors" was communicated to her eager recorders, especially the gullible *Magister Johannes,* when she was in trance states (see especially pp. 22, 25–26). See also McDonnell, *Beguines and Beghards in Medieval Culture,* pp. 344–55.

97. See especially the treatment by Aviad Kleinberg, *Prophets in Their Own Country,* pp. 50–98. In English, John Coakley has penetrating comments on Christina and Peter ("Friars as Confidants of Holy Women," in *Images of Sainthood in Medieval Europe,* pp. 228–33). In German there are treatments in Ruh, *Geschichte,* 2:116–20; and Dinzelbacher, *Geschichte der abendländische Mystik,* pp. 212–13, and *Heilige oder Hexen?,* pp. 32–35; as well as the article of Anna Martin, "Christina von Stommeln," *Mediaevistik* 4 (1991): 179–263, which I have not seen.

98. On Peter, see Volker Schmidt-Kohl, "Petrus de Dacia, ein skandinavischer Mystiker des 13. Jahrhunderts," *Zeitschrift für Religions- und Geistesgeschichte* 18 (1966): 255–62; and Tryggve Lundén, "Pierre de Dacie," DS 12:1550–51.

99. The *Acta B. Christinae Stumbelensis* was first partially edited by Daniel Papebroch in AA.SS. Jun. 22:270-454. The improved, but still partial, edition of Johannes Paulson, *Petri de Dacia Vita Christinae Stumbelensis,* Scriptores latini medii aevi Suecani 1 (Gothenberg, 1896) is not available to me, so I will cite from the AA.SS. Later editions have made most of the other parts of the collection available. The best study is Peter Nieveler, *Codex Iuliacensis: Christina von Stommeln und Petrus von Dacien, ihr Leben und Nachleben in Geschichte, Kunst und Literatur* (Mönchengladbach: Kühlen, 1975). The Einsiedeln abridgment can be found in *Vita B. Christinae Stumbelensis ex manuscriptis Petri de Dacia et Johannis Capellani in Stumbel,* ed. Isak Collijn (Uppsala: Almqvist & Wiksell, 1936). I disagree with Kleinberg (*Prophets,* pp. 56–58), who thinks that this complicated mass of materials was itself a *vita.* It is difficult to imagine that a writer as rhetorically skillful as Peter could have intended this.

100. The letters are divided into two groups: (a) the first thirty (here assigned Roman majuscule numbers), which are chronologically arranged in book 2 of the AA.SS. edition; and (b) letters xxxi–lxiii (to which I will assign small Roman numbers), which are found in book 5 without chronological ordering. Christina's letters are all in the first group and can be numbered (with some correcting of the misprints in the AA.SS) as follows: ## II (301AB), IV (301D–303D), VII (306B–307E), XIII (311F–312C), XVI (318B–319B), XVII (319B–320C), XVIII (320C–321A), XIX (321AC), XXI (323F–324C), XXIV (329F–335B), XXV (335E–337E), XXVII (339D–340B), XXVIII (340D–343D), XXIX (343D–344A).

101. Christina was able to read Latin, since her prayer book plays an important role in some of the devil's tricks, but she could not write it. The letters were dictated, with some of them speaking in the first person, others in the third about the beguine; some even mix both voices. It is also difficult to know how much editing Peter may have done. Still, something of Christina's own voice survives.

102. Coakley, "Friars as Confidants," p. 232.

103. The chief authority for the dating of the various events of the life of Peter and the documents relating to Christina is Jarl Gallen, *Le province de Dacie de l'Ordre des Frères Prècheurs* (Helsingfors: Soderstrom, 1946), pp. 225–44.

104. *Acta* 2.42 (314C): Cum ergo duo iremus pariter, moesti et tristes de imminenti separatione, et plura suspiria quam colloquia commisceremus, et dixi: Carissima Christina, tempus advenit, ut ab invicem separemur. Vale in Domino, carissima. Quae haec audiens nihil respondit, sed pallio faciem operuit, et super terram resedit, flens amarissime et abundantissime.

105. A selection of the letters between Peter and Christina and their circle has been translated into German with a sensitive introduction by Wilhelm Öehl, *Deutsche Mystikerbriefe des Mittelalters 1100–1550* (Munich: Georg Müller, 1931), pp. 246–75.

106. Ep. IV (301EF): Propter quod contristata sum, quia post recessum vestrum nullus est, coram quo possim vel audeam ita facere: cum omnes timeam, et non sit mihi cum eis sicut vobiscum. For some other expressions of her pain at separation from her beloved friar and

pleas that he return, see, e.g., Ep. XIII (311E–312A), Ep. XVI (318C and 319A) and Ep. XXI (324C).

107. *Acta,* lib. 5, ep. xxiv (425DF): O Amantissima mea! O cordis mei intima medulla; rogo te, oculos attollamus et cor erigimus ad Deum, in quo omnia sunt unum: et ex eo, et in eo nos inveniemus, in quantum unum sumus, qui in nobis in plurima dividimur. O Carissima! utinam te ore ad os alloqui possem, et tecum etiam corporali praesentia commorari! . . . quod et rogo quotidie Deum ut hoc faciat ante meam mortem, quacumque data occasione.

108. Ep. XXIII (329B): Sive ergo a vobis ego, sive vos a me quaeratis an vos diligam vel a vobis diligar; certitudinaliter responderi potest ab utroque: Quia diligo, et diligor: et ideo tertiam inducam personam, ut facilius elucidem veritatem intentam. Si quis ergo a me quaereret an Christinam diligerem; tota fiducia responderem, Diligo. Et si amplius prosequeretur, dicens et inquirens dilectionis causam, et rationem cur Christinam diligerem: ex optima conscientia dicerem; Quia propter Christum.

109. In Ep. XXIV (332D) Christina sees Peter in a night vision wearing a ring with the inscription, *Iesus Christus est vestrorum amborum fides aeterna.* For the spiritual marriage between Peter and Christina, see Schmidt-Kohl, "Peter von Dacia," p. 260; and Kleinberg, *Prophets,* pp. 85–87.

110. On the second visit, hearing the hymn "Jesu dulcis memoria" sends Christina into ecstasy (*mentis excessum* [282D–283A]). On the fourth and twelfth visits, Peter witnesses her reception of the stigmata (285AD, 297F–298F), while on visit 8 Christina sings a wordless ecstatic *iubilus* (291CE). Raptures are also described as occuring during visits 5, 6, 7, 10, 11, and 12, often after receiving the Eucharist.

111. As noted by Thurston, *Surprising Mystics,* pp. 5–21, who himself wrote a book entitled *Ghosts and Poltergeists.*

112. Kleinberg also emphasizes the martyr image in Peter's presentation of Christina (*Prophets,* p. 59).

113. Another example of such a mystical "formula" is found when the beguine is described in the language of monastic mysticism as combining ecstasy and the ordering of charity: . . . quia mente exceditis Deo frequenter, et in vobis caritatem ordinat decenter (327F). The emphasis on the ordering of charity seems gratuitous, especially since Christina is not described as practicing the active charitable works associated with most beguines, e.g., care of the sick and lepers, etc.

114. Kleinberg, *Prophets,* pp. 57–58, 87–89.

115. For some examples of these ecstasies as mentioned by the scribes, see, e.g., Epp. XXIV (331F, 332D, 334E); XXV (337A); XXVIII (340E, 341A, 341C).

116. This text comes from the abbreviated *Vita* edited by Collijn (71): A seculo enim non est auditum hominem sic horribiliter et manifeste a daemonibus cruciari.

117. The most important of these texts is Ep. X (309C–311E), in which Peter discusses mystical union and transformation, citing both Dionysius and John Scottus Eriugena. Here he also expresses his desire to share in the delights of mystical union *through* Christina (310F).

118. Dinzelbacher, *Heilige oder Hexen?* pp. 32–34.

119. At least part of Christina's obsession with the devil may have depended on Peter as audience. After his death in 1289 the beguine ceased to suffer diabolical attacks and faded from public notice.

120. For a survey of the role of the demonic in Christian spirituality, consult the multi-author article "Démon" in DS 3:141–238.

121. Volume 3 of *Die christliche Mystik* deals with "Demonic Mysticism," and volume 4 with diabolical possession and witches. Naturally, Görres made considerable use of Christina; see *Die christliche Mystik,* 4 vols. (Regensburg/Landshut: Manz, 1836–42), e.g., 1:343–46; 2:249–52 and 416; 3:445–56 and 492–95.

122. Blannbekin is briefly considered in Ruh, *Geschichte*, 2:132–36. The most extensive treatments of the beguine are by Peter Dinzelbacher; see his *Christliche Mystik im Abendland*, pp. 214–15; and especially "Die 'Vita et Revelationes' der Wiener Begine Agnes Blannbekin (d. 1315) im Rahmen der Viten- und Offenbarungsliteraur ihrer Zeit," in *Frauenmystik im Mittelalter*, pp. 152–77. See also Anneliese Stoklaska, "Weibliche Religiosität im mittelalterliche Wien unter besonderer Berücksichtigung der Agnes Blannbekin," *Religiöse Frauenbewegung und mystische Frömmigkeit im Mittelalter*, ed. Peter Dinzelbacher and Dieter Bauer (Cologne/Vienna: Böhlau, 1988), pp. 165–84.

123. The *Vita et Revelationes* survives in four mss. and was first published by the learned Benedictine, Bernard Pez, in 1731. A Middle High German version, probably a later translation, is lost. There is a new critical edition by Peter Dinzelbacher and Renate Vogeler, *Leben und Offenbarungen der Wiener Begine Agnes Blannbekin (d. 1315)* (Göttingen: Kümmerle, 1994). The work will be cited by chapter (235 in all) with page number in parentheses. Some of Agnes's revelations are dated, mostly to the 1290s. Given the Franciscan authorship of the work, some have thought that Agnes eventually joined one of the houses of Franciscan tertiaries known to have existed in Vienna, but this is doubtful (see Stoklaska, "Weibliche Religiosität," pp. 183–84).

124. On references to Agnes reading, see, e.g., *Vita* chaps. 127 (284) and 196 (408).

125. *Vita* chap. 39 (124): Festinabat quoque eo citius fieri begina, ut posset saepius communicare.

126. A good illustration of her loyalty can be found in the vision recounted in chap. 211 (434–36). After compline one night, she sees a beautiful maiden dancing around the altar of the Blessed Virgin. The maiden represents her faith, which is described as "proud," because as she says: Ego superbior et glorior super omnes sectas et errores, quae putridae sunt in conspectu Dei.

127. On the role of the wounds of Christ, see, e.g., *Vita* chaps. 5–6 (70–72), 19 (86–a reference to Francis as stigmatic), 55 (150–52), 113 (254), 137 (306–8), 140–41 (310–14), 170 (354–56), 190 (396–98) and 233 (476–78).

128. *Vita* 23 (94): Item dixit, quod post istam visitationem vel revelationem frequentius habeat revelationes a domino et consolationes spirituales, ita quod a minus semel infra diem naturalem. . . . Ait enim, quod, quando vult vacare contemplationi, convertit aciem mentis ad quaecunque eorum vult, quae ei revelata sunt in visione domini. . . . Et persaepius accidit, ut ibi rapiatur in exstasim, et exterioribus sensibus sopitis, cor intus vigilet . . . . Est autem ista exstasis subitanea. In the same passage the friar reports that whereas Agnes earlier had taken spiritual delight from the beauty of the church and its art, after this light vision she did not need such exterior triggers. Later, in chapter 131 (296–98), a divine voice distinguishes two kinds of raptures, a perfect form enjoyed by St. Paul and St. John, and rapture "into a flow of divine light where frequently secrets are opened, as God wills." Agnes recognizes that the vision at the beginning of the *Vita* belongs to this latter type.

129. Agnes's revelation also contradicted one given to a far more popular later seer, Birgitta of Sweden (see Dinzelbacher, "Die 'Vita et Revelationes,'" pp. 152–53). On the relics of the foreskin, see J. Sauer, "Praeputium Domini," *Lexikon für Theologie und Kirche*, ed. Konrad Hoffman and Michael Buchberger, 2nd ed. (Freiburg-im-Breisgau: Herder, 1936), 8:434–35.

130. Hadriani Pontii, *Epistola ad amicum . . .* (Frankfurt/Leipzig, 1735), pp. 6–8. Pontius also attacked other aspects of Blannbekin's revelations.

131. *Vita* 195 (406): Tantamque in anima sensit spiritus dulcedinem et nihilominus in carne sua tota non libidinosam, sed castam dulcorationem, ut illi utrique delectationi scilicet animae et corporis nullam sciret prorsus delectationem super terram posse comparari, nihilque esse sub caelo, quod sibi placere posset in comparatione illius gaudii, quo replebatur in illa utraque suavitate animae et carnis.

132. *Vita* 179 (370): Sicque se sensit deo in deo unitam, ut, quidquid vellet, quidquid desideraret, quaecunque scire cuperet, omnia ei praesto essent.

133. Although the same Latin term was used for both, in order to distinguish the northern beguines from the southern French followers of the radical Spiritual Franciscans, medievalists generally prefer to term the latter "beguins," the usage that is followed here. See Robert E. Lerner, "Beguins," in *The Dictionary of the Middle Ages*, 2:162–63.

134. *Bernard Gui: Manuel de l'Inquisiteur,* ed. and trans. Guy Mollat (Paris: Société d'édition "Les Belles Lettres," 1964), 1:108–10: Bequinorum secta, qui fratres Pauperes se appellant et dicunt se tenere et profiteri tertiam regulam sancti Francisci, modernis temporibus exsurrexit in provincia Provincie et in provincia Narbonensi et in quibusdam locis provincie Tholosane. . . . Inventum est autem per inquisitionem legitimam ac per depositiones et confessiones plurium ex ipsis, . . . quod errores suos et opiniones hujusmodi pestiferas ipsi habuerunt et collegerunt partim quidem ex libris seu opusculis fratris Petri Johannis Olivi, . . . videlicet ex postilla ejusdem super Apocalipsam quam habent tam in latino quam etiam transpositam in vulgari. . . . The nomenclature for the sect includes the forms *bequini/ae* as well as *beguini/ae.* The most detailed study remains that of Raoul Manselli, *Spirituali e beghini in Provenza.*

135. Largely for this reason I have chosen to present the beguin Na Prous Boneta in this chapter with other women who did not belong to recognized orders, rather than with the Franciscan women treated in chapter 3.

136. A seventeenth-century copy of the court record of the inquisition of Na Prous Boneta survives. The text has been edited by William Harold May, "The Confession of Prous Boneta Heretic and Heresiarch," in *Essays in Medieval Life and Thought: Presented in Honor of Austin Patterson Evans* (New York: Columbia University Press, 1955), pp. 3–30. See also Daniela Müller, "Die Prozess gegen Prous Boneta: Begine, Ketzerin, Häresiarchin (1325)," in *Ius et historia: Festgabe für Rudolf Weigand,* ed. Norbert Höhl (Würzburg: Echter, 1989), pp. 199–221. For discussions of Na Prous, see Manselli, *Spirituali e beghini,* pp. 239–49; Gordon Leff, *Heresy in the Later Middle Ages,* 1:213–17; and Newman, *From Virile Woman to WomanChrist,* pp. 195–98 and 215–18.

137. The only woman to have advanced a comparably radical message was the mysterious Guglielma of Milan (d. 1281), who was said to be an ecstatic and stigmatic by her followers, the Guglielmite sect of Milan that was crushed by the inquisition in 1300. According to this group, Guglielma was the incarnation of the Holy Spirit and her successor Manfreda of Pirovano was the pope of a new spiritual church. See Stephen Wessley, "The Thirteenth-Century Guglielmites: Salvation through Women," in *Medieval Women: Studies in Church History, Subsidia 1,* ed. Derek Baker (Oxford: Blackwell, 1978), pp. 289–303; and especially Newman, *From Virile Woman to WomanChrist,* pp. 185–95 and 212–15.

138. Confession (ed., 7): . . . dominus Jesus Christus transportavit eam in spiritu scilicet in anima usque ad primum coelum et cum fuit ibi vidit dictum Jesum Christum in forma hominis et in divinitate sua, qui apparuit sibi, quae loquitur, et ostendit cor suum perforatum quasi ad modum portulae unius parvae lanternae, et quod ex ipso corde exiverunt radii solares. . . . [E]t tunc ipsa appropinquavit se de ipso, et posuit caput suum infra corpus ipsius Christi, et non vidit aliud nisi talem claritatem qualem sibi Christus dederat in radiis supra-dictis. . . .

139. Confession (ed., 8): . . . fuit sibi data a Deo alta contemplatio et gratia contemplandi in coelum et videndi dominum nostrum Jesum Christum et oratio continua et continuus sen-timens de nostro siegneur. . . .

140. Confession (ed., 10): . . . asserens ipsa loquens quod extunc fuit secum tota Sancta Trinitas in spiritu.

141. Confession (ed., 10–11). This seems to have taken place fifteen years previous to the

visions–that is, in 1306–but the account is not always clear. Olivi's tomb, a frequent place of pilgrimage and devotion for the beguins, especially on his feast day of March 14, was destroyed in 1318. See David Burr, *The Persecution of Peter Olivi,* p. 86. As Barbara Newman points out (*From Virile Woman to WomanChrist,* pp. 196–97 and 216), Na Prous seems to believe that she and Olivi functioned as co-redeemers for the church of the new age.

142. Confession (ed., 11): Item quod ita complete dederat sibi ipse Deus totam divinitatem in spiritu quam complete ipsam dederat suae matri virgini et eius Filio; et quod tota humana natura non erat sufficiens ad petendum la veritat nisi Deus dedisset sibi Spiritum sanctum. Item quod illa divinitas quam Deus dedit sibi loquenti, formavit sibi unum corpus desperit de praecisiori et puriori intellectu, quem ipsa habebat . . . . Item quod Deus dixit sibi: *beata virgo Maria fuit donatrix Filii Dei et tu eris donatrix Spiritus Sancti.* . . . The claim is repeated several times (see, ed., 20, 22 and 25).

143. Newman, *From Virile Woman to WomanChrist,* pp. 216–17.

144. The beguin's frequent insistence on the invalidity of the sacraments (see ed., 12-13, 14–15, 16, 20, 25–26, 28) was doubtless another fatal error in the eyes of her examiners.

145. Confession (ed., 29): Item quod dixit sibi Dominus quod sicut Eva prima foemina fuit initium et causa dampnationis totius naturae humanae sue humani generis per peccatum Adae, sic: *tu eris initium et causa salvationis totius humanae naturae seu humani generis per illa verba quae facio te dicere, si credantur.*

146. See the discussion of Porete in the following chapter, pp. 255–56. Nevertheless, mystics who made comparable claims, such as the recluse Margaret the Cripple (to be treated below), were able to avoid the stake.

147. For an overview of forms of the solitary life, both eremitical and anchoritic, see Peter Anson, *The Call of the Desert: The Solitary Life in the Christian Church* (London: SPCK, 1964), which treats of "Anchorites and Anchoresses" (chap. 16). For more detailed considerations, see the articles "Reclus" in DS 13:217–28; and "Reclusione" in DIP 7:1229–45.

148. From the *Regula Reclusorum Dubliniensis* VI edited by Livarius Oliger, "Regulae tres reclusorum et eremitarum Angliae Saec. XIII-XIV," *Antonianum* 3 (1928): 178: . . . omnis vita anachoritarum comparatur vitae monachorum et eremitarum; sedet enim solus quasi heremita in deserto et debet vivere in silentio monachorum, et nullus tam duram vitam possidet quam anachorita bonus. . . . Benedicta Ward in her "Preface" to *Anchoritic Spirituality: Ancrene Wisse and Associated Works,* translated and introduced by Anne Savage and Nicholas Watson (New York: Paulist Press, 1991), p. 4, puts it this way: ". . . the solitary life seems to have been regarded officially as special and different from both lay and monastic life, though linked to both."

149. Grimlaic, *Regula solitariorum* (PL 103:573–664), much of which is dependent on the Rule of Benedict, Gregory the Great, Isidore of Seville, and other standard authorities.

150. Philippe Rouillard, "Regole per Reclusi," DIP 7:1533–36, discusses nine; see also the texts edited and studied by Oliger, "Regulae tres Reclusorum et Eremitarum Angliae Saec. XIII–XIV," *Antonianum* 3 (1928): 151–90, 299–320; 9 (1934): 37–84 and 243–68.

151. The story of Thais, the converted prostitute who became a *reclusa,* found in the *Vitae Patrum,* provided a prototype. Among the first historical witnesses to female anchorites in the West is Wiborada of St. Gall (d. 926), said to be the earliest example of a papally approved canonization.

152. For the revival of eremitism, see especially *L'eremitismo in Occidente nei secoli XI e XII: Atti della seconda Settimana internazionale di Studio Mendola, 1962,* as well as Henrietta Leyser, *Hermits and the New Monasticism: A Study of Religious Communities in Western Europe 1000-1150* (New York: St. Martin's Press, 1984).

153. A number of works have explored English anchoritic life; see especially Rotha Mary

Clay, *The Hermits and Anchorites of England* (London: Methuen, 1914); and Ann K. Warren, *Anchorites and their Patrons in Medieval England* (Berkeley/Los Angeles: University of California Press, 1985). The twelfth-century visionary and ecstatic Christina of Markyate (d. ca. 1166) lived as a recluse.

154. Cited in Oliger, "Regulae Reclusorum Angliae," *Antonianum* 9 (1934): 265: Summa omnium reclusarum sive incarceratarum urbis CCLX. This was more than all the anchorites in England, according to the figures in Warren, *Anchorites and their Patrons,* 20.

155. For a translation along with introduction and extensive notes that concentrate on the spiritual dimensions of the text, see Savage and Watson, *Anchoritic Spirituality.* Some recent investigations of the religious nature of the works include Linda Georgiana, *The Solitary Self: Individuality in the Ancrene Wisse* (Cambridge: Harvard University Press, 1981); Elizabeth Robertson, *Early English Devotional Prose and the Female Audience* (Knoxville: University of Tennessee Press, 1990); and Anne Clark Bartlett, *Male Authors, Female Readers.*

156. See the *Ancrene Wisse,* part VIII (trans., 204).

157. This is not the place to enter into the complicated issues, much discussed in recent literature, of the extent to which these texts *written by men for women* may or may not express something of what the women themselves thought. Here, they are being treated only as evidence of what was *thought* to be appropriate for a woman who had devoted herself to asceticism leading to loving union with Christ.

158. This section can be found in *The English Text of the Ancrene Riwle: Ancrene Wisse edited from Ms. Corpus Christi College Cambridge 402* by J. R. R. Tolkien, Early English Texts Society o.s. 249 (London: Oxford University Press, 1962), pp. 48–55, with the text cited on p. 55: Osculetur me osculo oris sui. That is. Cusse me mi leofmon wid the coss of his mud mudene swetest. this coss leoue sustren is a swetnesse & a delit of heorte swa unimete swete, that euch worldes sauuer is bitter ther toyeines. Ah ure lauerd wid this coss ne cussed na sawle, the luued ei thing buten him & te ilke thinges for him the helped him to habben. I will cite the translations of Savage and Watson, *Anchoritic Spirituality,* where this section is found on pp. 82–86 (quotation from p. 86).

159. See *Ancrene Wisse,* pp. 195-209, and the translation in *Anchoritic Spirituality,* pp. 189–98.

160. This appearance of the exchange-of-hearts motif, though not expressed in a biographical mode, would date to not long after that reported in the *Vita S. Lutgardis* mentioned above (p. 164–65).

161. *Ancrene Wisse,* p. 200 (trans., 192): his leofmon bihalde thron hu he bohte hire luue. lette thurlin his scheld openin his side. to schawin hire his heorte. to schawin hire openliche hu inwardliche he luuede hire. & to ofdrahen hire.

162. *Ancrene Wisse,* p. 208 (trans., 197): Rin him wid ase muche luue. as thu hauest sum mon sum chearre. he is thin to don wid al that tu wilnest.

163. For some examples, see *Anchoritic Spirituality,* pp. 217–20, 226–28, and 240–42.

164. See especially *The Wohunge of Ure Lauerd: Edited from British Museum Ms. Cotton Titus D. XVII . . . ,* by W. Meredith Thompson, Early English Texts Society o.s. 241 (London: Oxford University Press, 1958). It begins with the following list of terms of endearment (20): Iesu swete iesu. mi drud. mi derling. mi drihtin. mi haelend. mi huniter. mi haliwei . . . .

165. *The Wohunge,* 36 (trans., 256): Mi bodi henge wid thi bodi neiled o rode. sperred querfaste wid inne fowr wahes & henge i wile wid the & neauer mare of my rode cume til that i diei. For thenne schal i lepen fra rode in to reste. fra wa to wele & to eche blisse. A. iesu swa swet hit is wid the to henge. Another meditation from the same author, called *On ureisun of ure louerd,* contains similar themes and is edited by Thompson in the same volume.

166. The most noted later English example (found in one of the few anchoresses to write) is Julian of Norwich (d. ca. 1415), who will be treated in the next volume.

167. Other examples could include the Austrian recluse Wilbirg of St. Florian (ca. 1230–1289), treated in Ruh, *Geschichte*, 2:129–30. It should be pointed out that Margaret of Cortona, considered in the previous chapter (pp. 139–40), spent the last years of her life as a kind of Franciscan *reclusa*.

168. Juette's life can be found in *Beata Ivetta, sive Iutta, vidua reclusa, Hui in Belgio* in AA.SS. Jan. 13:863–87. For a study, see Isabelle Cochelin, "Sainteté laïque: L'exemple de Juette de Huy (1156–1228)," *Le moyen âge* ser. 5, 3 (1989): 397–417.

169. This *cellula in qua agonista Christi agonizabat* (chap. 51:886) was typical of that of many recluses in having both an upper room devoted solely to prayer and a lower one in which Juette and her servant (*socia*) lived and where a *fenestra* provided access to the outer world (see, e.g., chap. 31).

170. See especially *Vita* 15, 22–23, 33–34, 36, and 43 (AA.SS. Jan. 13:872, 876–77, 881, 882, 884).

171. *Vita* 23 (877): . . . ac si a dilecti sui brachiis avelli renueret, distendebatur, clamabat, angebatur tamquam vim patiens, tamquam mulier parturiens angebatur hac et illac, suspirabat ut femina amoris impatiens. . . .

172. *Vita* 36 (882): Ibi proculdubio conceperat quam habebat ad omnium salutem caritatis affectum, cuius adeo tanta vis erat, ut ad congratulationem, compassionem, consolationem, correptionem, et aedificationem videntibus et audientibus eam universis eius sermo valeret, praevaleretque dilectio.

173. *Vita* 45 (884): Sic se habente cum filiabus matre, magistra cum discipulis, appropinquabit tanto magis, quanto expectata diutius, gloriosa Christi nativitas: cuius ultimo festivitatis die, id est, die octavarum sanctae Epiphaniae Domini ex hac luce migrare debebat. Such titles were not unprecedented, since Hildegard of Bingen had been addressed as *magistra* by some of her correspondents, but in the twelfth century this was an official title of a woman monastic leader who could not be called an abbess because her house was subject to a male superior.

174. The *Vita Humilianae de Circulis*, written by the Franciscan Vito of Cortona in 1247, can be found in AA.SS. Mai 19:386–410. There are brief treatments in André Vauchez, *The Laity in the Middle Ages*, pp. 178–82, and in Elizabeth Petroff, *Body and Soul: Essays on Medieval Women and Mysticism* (Oxford: Oxford University Press, 1994), pp. 120–22, but the most detailed consideration is that of Anna Benvenuti Papi, "Una Santa Vedova," *"In Castro Poenitentiae,"* pp. 59–98. On the Italian *recluse* in general, see Papi, "'Velut in sepulchro': cellane e recluse nella tradizione agiografica italiana," in *Culto dei santi, istituzioni e classi sociali in età preindustriale,* ed. Sofia Boesch Gajano and Lucia Sebastiani (Rome: Japadre, 1984), pp. 367–455 (reprinted in *"In Castro Poenitentiae,"* pp. 263–402).

175. Umiliana's reclusion illustrates the rather free form that this withdrawal could take. She did not undergo a formal liturgical act of inclusion and was free to go out to hear Mass and take Communion (she received every Saturday). In the interior *cellula* of the family tower she devoted herself to prayer, gazing all night on the painted image of Mary and the crucified Christ. Nevertheless, there was a connecting outer room where her *domestica*, named Piecilia, lived and where people could come to visit her.

176. *Vita* 2 (389D): Nolebat enim Deus amplius accensam lucernam latere sub modio, et ideo posuit eam super candelabrum in altitudinem vitae et exempli, ut luceret omnibus qui in domo sunt, hoc est in Ecclesia militanti.

177. Umiliana is often characterized as a Franciscan, but this seems misleading. She was publicized by Franciscans as a part of their urban mission, but it is significant that St. Francis is never mentioned in the *Vita* itself.

178. *Vita* 2 (390B): . . . ut nullus a minimo usque ad magnum viam excusationis haberet, quod Deo servire non posset juxta possibilitatem suam in domo proprio et habitu seculari. . . .

179. *Vita* 3 (392F): . . . alios vero ad vitam solitariam movebat, dicens, Domum reputa solitudinem nemoris, et familiam silvestres feras, et inter eas eris velut in nemore, servando silentium et continuis orationibus insistendo.

180. *Vita* 3 (394C): . . . non impedias me verbis; quia saepe eundo per viam, et inter creaturas existendo, et audiendo praedicationes et divina, Dominum meum adeo plene reperi, ut in cella mea orationibus et devotionibus insistendo.

181. On her ecstasies and visions, see 389F–390B, 390D, 393D, 394CD, 394F, 395CD, 397B–398A, 398AB, 398F–399A and 399B (only a few of these texts will be treated here).

182. *Vita* 4 (394F): . . . vix aut nunquam erat dies, in qua raptus hujusmodi non haberet; et aliquando duobus diebus, aliquando tota die integra cum nocte, aliquando maxima parte diei, aliquando noctis parte maxima in ecstasi quiescebat hoc modo, sicut Deus propinabat. For accounts of three-day ecstasies, see 393D and 395CD.

183. *Vita* 3 (392E): Filia mea, roga pro me, quia ego sum totus siccus. . . . Cui statim tanta infusa est gratia, quod evidentissme apparet quod, recipere non posset infusae gratiae plenitudinem: et tunc ipsa Beata in talibus rapta est.

184. See *Johannes von Magdeburg, O.P.: Die Vita der Margareta contracta, einer Magdeburger Rekluse des 13. Jahrhunderts,* ed. Paul Gerhard Schmidt (Leipzig: Benno, 1992) (I will cite the text by chapter with page in parentheses). The text was not included in the AA.SS., though it was popular in the Middle Ages and still survives in ten manuscripts. There is an insightful treatment in Ruh, *Geschichte,* 2:125–29.

185. *Vita* 3 (4): Desideravit recedere a seculo et Domino in loco alique solitario deservire, sed timuit amittere despectum, quem habebat ab hominibus, parentibus et amicis, si in claustro vel reclusorio forsitan locaretur.

186. In *Vita* 63 (86) this is referred to as the *ecclesia sancti Albani,* but no such church is known in medieval Magdeburg. (The editor Schmidt [*Die Vita,* XII] thinks it may have been the church of St. Ambrose.) Some years later, because of an attack on her in a letter sent to Friar John (*Vita* 63), he arranged to move her to a new anchorhold next to the Dominican church of St. Paul. (The fact that he needed to obtain the bishop's permission for this indicates that Margaret was an official recluse.) Despite this permission, attacks on her continued–Dixerunt enim multi, quod propter malum de reclusorio exivisset, et quod deberet sicut heretica concremari (*Vita* 63; 87). Finally, apparently because of her severe headaches, she was accepted into the Cistercian convent of St. Agnes, though she appears not to have taken formal vows (*Vita* 64–65). At this time (ca. 1265) Margaret is described as approximately thirty years old; she seems not to have lived much longer. Friar John apparently composed the *Vita* soon after her death, having received a promise that he would not long outlive his spiritual friend.

187. *Vita* 1 (3): Fecit autem Deus sicut, qui preciosum thesaurum vult abscondere sacco vili, ut securius servetur. . . . Deus, qui eam elegerat, . . . illi tribuit habundanter; hoc fuit: pena, abiectio et paupertas. The formula occurs in *Vita* 7, 35, and 59 (10, 38, 73).

188. There are important analogies here to aspects of the teaching of her Magdeburg contemporary, the beguine Mechthild (see pp. 239–43), as well as the later French beguine Marguerite Porete (pp. 261–65). On the divine and human abysses, see *Vita* 21 (24–25). In chap. 27 (28–30), a brief treatise on the divine nature, God is described as both *incomprehensibilis bonitas* and by that very fact an *abissus incomprehensibilis humilitatis* who must flow down to fill those humans, especially the Virgin Mary, who also are humble (see the discussion of Mechthild, p. 225, on the "flowing down" of God to fill the lowest places). Mary is described as Margaret's constant patron and model from the beginning of her career as a recluse (see chap. 3). Margaret also had a special devotion to Mary Magdalene (e.g., chaps. 33 and 58).

189. *Vita* 24 (26): Secundum hoc, quod anima se hic a Deo elongavit ex consideratione proprie indignitatis, secundum hoc Deo illic vicinior erit.

190. At the conclusion, in defending the account against those who will not understand it, just as they cannot read Greek, or Slavic, or Hebrew, John emphasizes the internal miracles of his saint (*Vita* 70 [101]): In multis sanctis nostris temporibus per exteriora miracula est Dominus glorificatus, modo autem vult suam gloriam revelare per interiora mirabilia, que interius operatur.

191. Such was her sense of abnegation, however, that late in the *Vita* she asks Christ to stop talking to her since it consoles her too much: Domine, vox tua et allocutio tua nimis est michi gravis et magna. Non possum te pati, tu per hoc in vita ista me nimium consolaris. Consolare me, si tibi placuerit, post hanc vitam (chap. 67; 93).

192. A number of these themes find strong parallels in the mysticism of her contemporary in Magdeburg, the beguine Mechthild (see chap. 5, pp. 222–44). It is difficult to think that the two women did not know each other, especially since both were sponsored by the Dominicans of the city. Nonetheless, neither the *Vita* of Margaret nor Mechthild's *Das fliessende Licht der Gottheit* provides direct evidence for contact. A comparative study of the two mystics would be a fruitful way to pursue the question of mutual influence.

193. *Vita* 4 (7): Non propter hoc desideravit talem penam, ut haberet maius gaudium post hanc vitam . . . . Emere vel conventionem sic facere noluit cum Christo, sed ut gratia Dei, quam facturus erat in ea in celis, magis grata et accepta ei esset. . . .

194. See, e.g., *Vita* 3, 11, 44, 56, and 60 (5, 14, 47, 63, 80).

195. The *Vita* frequently employs strong adversative or paradoxical language, based on the inversion of values displayed in the cross; e.g., chap. 19 (21): Et quanto minus solatii in se quaerit, tanto plus in Deo invenit. Et quanto pauperior est in se ipsa, tanto ditior est in Deo. Et quanto plus moritur in se ipsa, tanto plus vivit et confortatur in Deo. See, e.g., chaps. 24, 36, 45, and 56. Similar passages based on mystical paradoxes occur in Mechthild's *Das fliessende Licht der Gottheit* (e.g., 1.22), as Barbara Newman has reminded me.

196. *Vita* chap. 56 (64): Si solatium tibi esset solatium, tunc istud tibi solatium non dedissem; sed quia solatium est tibi desolatium, te sum taliter consolatus. For similar expressions, see chaps. 19, 41, 59, 62 (20–21, 44, 74, 85). For occasions when she rejects divine consolations, see chaps. 54, 60, 67 (58, 77, 93).

197. *Vita* 55 (59): Tunc fuit in cruce cum Christo et desideravit salutem ecclesie et super omnia laudem Dei. For similar formulae, see chaps. 19 and 58 (23, 70). While Friar John writes the narrative of Margaret in the *Vita*, it is God himself who is the main author, writing down Margaret's sufferings in his own heart, as he tells her in chap. 45 (50): Ego sum scriptor tuus. In corde meo omnia tua gravamina sunt conscripta; et omnia in me leges et cognosces et de hoc singulariter me laudabis.

198. Margaret's concern for all, especially *peccatores, desolati, pauperes,* and *afflicti* is a constant theme of the *Vita;* e.g., chaps. 9, 38, 47, 66, and 69 (12–13, 41–42, 51–52, 91, 100).

199. *Vita* 55 (59): . . . quia in illo tempore eam mirabiliter illuminavit, et se ei in corde suo modo inconsueto ostendit, qui talis est, quod nec cor cogitare nec lingua proferre posset, nisi quis per experientiam didicisset.

200. *Vita* 55 (60): Ego in utero matris tue te singulariter preelegi, eo tempore, quando volui homo fieri–maximum, quod umquam feci homini, fuit, quod virginem matrem elegi. In ultimo tempore tu es modo, et maximum, quod umquam homini continget tempore tuo, hoc continget in te. Therefore, Margaret has become the spiritual equivalent of Mary; cf. chap. 56 (63): Ego et mater mea et tu in singulari familiaritate simul erimus in eternum . . . ; and chap. 57 (65), which applies Luke 1:35 to the recluse.

201. *Vita* 55 (62): . . . tamen preter me solum nunquam ita in corde sicut tu aliquis luit mundum. Similar expressions are found in chap. 56 (62): Tu enim es vas, in quod ipsa caritas est transfusa, et cuicumque de cetero dabitur, volo, quod ex te ei detur.

202. This experience was apparently the source for Margaret's later subtle teaching con-

cerning the *discretio spirituum,* that is, the ways to distinguish between true divine messages and diabolical simulations; see *Vita* 67 (93–95).

203. See *Vita* 60 (77) for another expression of the co-redemptix theme. The mystic as co-redeemer, already seen with Na Prous Boneta, will be important also for the three beguine mystics to be studied in the next chapter.

204. *Vita* 67 (95): ... tunc cor Dei est unitum animae, quasi sit ipsius animae proprium cor....[Q]uia vident in se ipsis, quasi in oculis Dei se viderent, quia eorum oculi sunt oculi Dei.

205. *Vita* 68 (99): ... quia ita secura efficitur, quasi iam domi haberet, quod ei promissum fuerat diu ante. This summarizes the detailed description of the characteristics of union provided in the later part of chap. 67 and through chap. 68 (ed., 96–99).

Chapter 5

1. This chapter, the longest of the volume, was read in draft form by several friends who made a number of valuable suggestions. I especially want to single out Saskia Murk-Jansen and Gordon Rudy, who gave me useful comments on the section devoted to Hadewijch, and Frank Tobin and Patricia Z. Beckman, who read and commented on the Mechthild section.

2. A number of studies have begun to explore the thematic relations among these beguines; see, e.g., Frances Gooday, "Mechthild of Magdeburg and Hadewijch of Antwerp: a Comparison," *Ons Geestelijk Erf* 48 (1974): 305–62; Kurt Ruh, "Beginenmystik: Hadewijch, Mechthild von Madgeburg, Marguerite Porete," in *Kleine Schriften: Band II, Scholastik und Mystik im Spätmittelalter,* 2:237–49, and "L'amore di Dio in Hadewijch, Mechthild di Magdeburgo e Margherita Porete," in *Temi e problemi nella mistica femminile trecentesca* (Todi: Convegni del Centro di Studi sulla Spiritualità Medievale XX, 1983), pp. 85–106; Georgette Epiney-Burgard, "Hadewijch d'Anvers, Mechthilde de Magdebourg: Thèmes communs," *Ons Geestelijk Erf* 66 (1992): 71–87; and especially Barbara Newman, "*La mystique courtoise*" in *From Virile Woman to WomanChrist,* pp. 137–67.

3. The editions of Hadewijch's works will be cited below. There is one full English translation, *Hadewijch: The Complete Works,* translation and introduction by Mother Columba Hart (New York: Paulist Press, 1980). I will generally cite from this version unless otherwise noted, although it has been criticized as being rather loose at times. Much of the literature about Hadewijch is in Dutch and relatively inaccessible to English readers. For an extensive bibliography, see Gertrud Jaron Lewis, *Bibliographie zur deutschen Frauenmystik des Mittlelalters: Mit ein Anhang zu Beatrijs van Nazareth und Hadewijch,* by Frank Willaert and Marie-José Govers, pp. 351–410 (listing 452 items to 1980). An essential survey of Hadewijch's language can be found in Joris Reynaert, *De beeldspraak van Hadewijch* (Tielt: Studiën en tekstuitgaven van Ons Geestelijk Erf, 1981). There is a good recent interpretation of Hadewijch's mysticism in Ruh, *Geschichte,* 2:158–225. For a succinct introduction, see Paul Mommaers, "Hadewijch," in *Die deutsche Literatur des Mittelalters: Verfasserlexikon,* ed. Kurt Ruh et al. (Berlin: Walter de Gruyter, 1981), 3:368–78.

4. Hadewijch cites passages from Richard (Letter 10), Bernard (Letters 15 and 20), and William (Letter 18). Her admiration for Augustine is evident in Vision 11. Further work needs to be done on the beguine's relation to her sources; see Joseph Van Mierlo, "Hadewijch en Willem van St. Thierry," *Ons Geestelijk Erf* 3 (1929): 45–59; and Paul Verdeyen, "De invloed van Willem van Saint-Thierry op Hadewijch en Ruusbroec," *Ons Geestelijk Erf* 51 (1977): 3-19.

5. For an appreciation of some aspects of Hadewijch's style, see Saskia Murk-Jansen, "The Mystic Theology of the Thirteenth-Century Mystic, Hadewijch, and its Literary Expression,"

in *The Medieval Mystical Tradition in England: Exeter Symposium V,* ed. Marion Glasscoe (Cambridge: D. S. Brewer, 1992), pp. 117–27.

6. The *Strophische Gedichten* were edited by Joseph Van Mierlo in two volumes in 1942, but I will use the more recent edition of Edward Rombauts and Norbert De Paepe, *Hadewijch, Strofische Gedichten: Middelnederlandse tekst en moderne bewerking met een inleiding* (Zwolle: Willink, 1961). For an important study, see Norbert De Paepe, *Hadewijch Strofische Gedichten: Een studie van de minne in het kader der 12e en 13e eeuwse mystiek en profane minnelyrik* (Ghent: Secretariat van de Koninklijke Vlaamse Academie voor Taal-en Letterkunde, 1967). Ruh provides a good survey in *Geschichte,* 2:163–82. See also Wilhelm Breuer, "Philologische Zugänge zur Mystik Hadewichs: Zu Form und Funktion religiöser Sprache bei Hadewijch," in *Grundfragen christlicher Mystik,* ed. Margot Schmidt and Dieter R. Bauer (Stuttgart-Bad Canstatt: frommann-holzboog, 1987), pp. 103–21. In English, consult Tanis M. Guest, *Some aspects of Hadewijch's poetic form in the "Strofische Gedichten"* (The Hague: Nijhoff, 1975); and Elizabeth Alvida Petroff, "Gender, Knowledge, and Power in Hadewijch's *Strofische Gedichten,*" in *Body and Soul: Essays on Medieval Women and Mysticism,* pp. 182–203.

7. Twenty-nine *Mengeldichten* are ascribed to Hadewijch in some manuscripts, but scholarly research indicates that only the first sixteen are certainly authentic (the remaining thirteen PC, the product of Pseudo-Hadewijch, date from the fourteenth century and will be considered later). The edition used here is that of Joseph Van Mierlo, *Hadewijch: Mengeldichten* (Antwerp: N.V. Standaard, 1952). The recent work of Saskia Murk-Jansen, *The Measure of Mystic Thought: A Study of Hadewijch's Mengeldichten* (Göppingen: Kümmerle, 1991), argues that PC17–24 are close to Hadewijch's own works and might possibly have been composed by her, so that only PC25–29 are definitely by the Pseudo-Hadewijch. For reactions to this view, see Ruh, *Geschichte,* 2:182–91; and Guido da Baere, "De Mengeldichten of Hadewijch mit een janusgezicht," *Millennium: Tijdschrift voor Middeleeuwse studies* 7 (1993): 40–51. For a recent, unconvincing argument that all the *Mengeldichten* belong to Hadewijch, see Mary A. Suydam, "The Politics of Authorship: Hadewijch of Antwerp and the *Mengeldichten,*" *Mystics Quarterly* 22 (1996): 2–20.

8. There are really only eleven visions in the book, since V2–3, V7–8 and V13–14 constitute single showings. The Visions were edited by Joseph Van Mierlo in two volumes (1924–25), but I will cite from the more recent text of H. W. J. Vekeman, *Het Visioenenboek van Hadewijch, Uitgegeven naar handschrift 941 van de Bibliotheek der Rijksuniversiteit te Gent* (Nijmegen-Bruges: Dekker & Van de Vegt-Orion, 1980). (The Vekeman edition has a different line numeration from that of Van Mierlo and the Hart translation which follows the latter.) See Herman W. J. Vekeman, "Angelus sane nuntius: Een interpretatie van het Visioenenboek van Hadewijch," *Ons Geestelijk Erf* 50 (1976): 225–59; Frank Willaert, "Hadewijch und ihr Kreis in den 'Visionen,'" in *Abendländische Mystik im Mittelalter,* pp. 368–87; and Ruh, *Geschichte,* 2:191–208.

9. The edition used is that of Joseph Van Mierlo, *Hadewijch: Brieven,* 2 vols. (Antwerp: N.V. Standaard, 1947). Thirty-one letters are ascribed to the beguine in the manuscripts, but strong arguments suggest that L 28 is not authentic (see the summary and discussion in Ruh, *Geschichte,* 2:212, 225–30). On the letters, see Joris Reynaert, "Attributieproblemen in verband met de 'Brieven' van Hadewijch," *Ons Geestelijk Erf* 49 (1975): 225–47; Paul Mommaers and Frank Willaert, "Mystisches Erlebnis und sprachliche Vermittlung in den Brieven Hadewijchs," in *Religiöse Frauenbewegung und mystische Frömmigkeit im Mittelalter,* pp. 117–51; and Ruh, *Geschichte,* 2:209–25.

10. Ruh, *Geschichte,* 2:211: . . . die Gottesliebe als zentrales und (fast) einziges Thema hat in den Briefen andere Dimensionen als in den Visionen; man möchte sagen: Der Sicht *in*

patria steht diejenige *in via* gegenüber, wobei aber der Blick auf den jeweils anderen Bereich immer offenbleibt.

11. Though Hadewijch sees herself as a bride in V 10 and V 12, and Christ is referred to as the Bridegroom there and elsewhere (e.g., L 24.31), her mysticism does not feature nuptial language as *the* central theme, as has been sometimes claimed.

12. Like many other female mystics, Hadewijch took Mary Magdalene as a model for someone who "was one in unity of *minne*" and thus became an apostle to others; see PC 3.50–62 (ed., 22).

13. Paul Mommaers, "Preface," in *Hadewijch: The Complete Works*, pp. xi–xxiv (an excellent brief presentation of the essentials of Hadewijch's mysticism).

14. This is confirmed by her critical remarks about the dangers of spiritual sweetness, e.g., L 4.77–79, 6.210–14, 10.15–50 and 15.75–80.

15. PS 27.66–67 (ed., 200): Die hare lief dore minnen, die sijn fijn, / Ende beide out ende vroet. . . .

16. Hadewijch, like all medieval mystics, had several words at her command to express love. While *minne* is her favored and most varied term, she also employs *caritate* (generally to refer to love of neighbor) and also uses the term *lief* (loved one) to refer to Christ and at times to the soul.

17. According to one calculation, *minne* appears 987 times in the PS alone! Almost everyone who has written on Hadewijch has analyzed her treatment of *minne*. Among the more insightful discussions, see Tanis M. Guest, "Hadewijch and Minne," in *European Context: Studies in the history and literature of the Netherlands presented to Theodoor Weevers*, ed. P. K. King and P. F. Vincent (Cambridge: Modern Humanities Research Association, 1971), pp. 14–29; Paul Mommaers, "Bulletin d'histoire de la spiritualité: L'Ecole néerlandaise," *Revue d'ascetique et de mystique* 49 (1973): 477–88 (discussing N. de Paepe's book), and the same author's "Preface," in *Hadewijch: Complete Works*, pp. xvi–xxiv; Esther Heszler, "Stufen der Minne bei Hadewijch," in *Frauenmystik im Mittelalter*, pp. 99–122; Joris Reynaert, "Hadewijch: mystic poetry and courtly love," in *Medieval Dutch Literature in its European Context*, pp. 208–25; Newman, "*La mystique courtoise*," pp. 145–48 and 153–57; and Murk-Jansen, "The Mystic Theology of Hadewijch," pp. 122–27.

18. As Breuer points out ("Philologische Zugänge zur Mystik Hadewijchs," pp. 117–18), this brief expression summarizes the paradoxical character of Hadewijch's mystical language: "Wenn 'Minne alles' ist bzw. wenn Minne die Minne ist, ist der Inhalt leer und gefüllt, nichts und alles zugleich. Man kann sagen: die Leere ist die Fülle" (p. 117).

19. PS 22.15–19 (ed., 160–62): Dat ghebod dat ic bekinne in minnen natuere / Dat brinct mine sinne in avontuere: / En heeft forme, sake noch figuere; / Doch eest inden smake alse creatuere; / Hets materie miere bliscape . . . (Hart translation slightly altered).

20. L 24:1–2 (ed., 208): Jc sal v segghen sonder voeghen: en laet v niet men dan Minne ghenoeghen.

21. PS 24.60 (ed., 178): Ic en hebbe el niet: ic moet op minne teren.

22. A survey of the personified language of *minne* can be found in Reynaert, *De Beeldspraak*, pp. 333–64.

23. PS 19.50–53 (ed., 142): Ay, die gheweldeghe wondre minne, / Die al met wondre verwinnen mach, / Verwinne mi, dat ic di verwinne, / In dine onverwonnenne cracht.

24. L 12.1-2 (ed., 101): God si v god ende ghi hem Minne. God gheue v te leuene der Minnen werc in allen dinghen der ter Minnen behoren.

25. PC 15.49–53.: Ay minne ware ic minne / Ende met minne / minne u minne / Ay minne om minne / gheuet dat minne / de minne al minne volkinne (here I use the edition and translation of Murk-Jansen, "The Mystic Theology of Hadewijch," p. 124, but retain the word *minne*).

26. There is an extensive treatment of these names in the first part of Reynaert, *De Beeld-spraak,* pp. 41–186.

27. See especially her comment in L 24.104-07 (ed., 212). On Hadewijch's use of scripture, see Reynaert, *De Beeldspraak,* pp. 403–23; and the same author's "Mystische Bibelinterpretation bei Hadewijch," in *Grundfragen christlicher Mystik,* pp. 123–37.

28. On Richard's treatise, see *Growth of Mysticism,* pp. 416–17. For a comparison, consult Esther Heszler, "'Dat helle es hare hoecste name': Das XVI Mengeldicht Hadewijchs als Auseinandersetzung mit dem Traktat 'De IV gradibus violentae caritatis' Richards von St. Viktor," in *Religiöse Erfahrung: Christliche Positionen im Wandel der Geschichte,* ed. Walter Haug and Dietmar Mieth (Munich: Beck, 1992), pp. 171–88.

29. PC 16.25–30 (ed., 78–79): Hare band doet al voeghen / Jn en ghebruken, in een genoeghen. / Dit es die band, die al dat bint / Dat deen den anderen dorekint / Jn pine, in rast, in orewoet, / Ende etet sijn vleesch ende drinct sijn bloet . . . .

30. *Orewoet* is found seven times in the PS, five in the PC, twice in the Visions, and never in the letters (which do, however, have an equivalent in L 22.236: *woede sonder hope*). The term, whose etymology is still obscure, is one that Hadewijch shares with Beatrice. For comments on the word, see Reynaert, *De Beeldspraak,* pp. 377–81; Hart, *Hadewijch: The Complete Works,* p. 375 n. 19; Ruh, *Geschichte,* 2:178–79.

31. Augustine, *Confessions* 7.10.16 (PL 32:742).

32. Song 2:16 was one of Hadewijch's favorite scriptural passages. It appears no fewer than nine times in PS: 3.60–63, 7.83, 12.67, 13.50, 25.9, 27.46, 34.47, 36.92, and 38.44; as well as three times in the L: 13.14, 14.38, and 19.4–5. See Reynaert, "Mystische Bibelinterpretation bei Hadewijch," pp. 129–37, for a treatment of some of the biblical passages especially favored by the beguine.

33. PC 16.77–80 (ed., 80): Al dat vallen ende dat op staen, / Dat nemen, dat gheuen, dat ontfaen / Ontsteket ende blusschet bi orewoede / die cole hare name. . . .

34. PC 16.92–102 (ed., 81): Alse dit vier wert dus ouerghinghe / So eest hem alleens wat vertreet: . . . / Troest met gode inden hemel te sine / Ochte in die helsche pine: / Dies es desen viere al een; / Het verberret al dat ye gheeren, / Om doemen noch om benedien / En es oec, dies maghie lien.

35. PC 16.122–24 (ed., 82): Jn enen cussenne sonder sceiden; / dat cussen enicht scone / Jn enen wesenne .IIJ. persone. The trinitarian dimension of love-union with God is heightened in the summary of the seven names that concludes the poem (16.169–212), especially lines 191–96 (ed., 84–85): Die wellheyt ende die orewoet / Worpse dan in die diepste vloet, / Die grundeloes es ende altoes leuet / Ende metten leuenne hen drien een gheuet / Gode ende menschen in ene minne: / Dits drieheit bouen alle sinne.

36. PC 16.129–30 (ed., 82): Dat vloyen ende dat weder vloyen die ene dore andere. There are a number of other similar expressions of the basic Neoplatonic dynamic of the *exitus/reditus* theme in Hadewijch; e.g., L 12.60–64 (ed., 104).

37. PC 16.149–64 (ed., 83): Hare seuende name dat es helle / Der minnen daer ic aue quelle. / Want si al verslindet ende verdoemt . . . / ghelijc dat die helle al verderuet / Ende men in hare niet el en verweruet / Dan onghenade ende sterk pine, . . . / Al verslonden ende al verswolghen / Jn hare grundelose natuere, / Sinken in hitten, in coulde elke vre, / Jnder minnen diepe, hoghe deemsterheit. / Dit gheet bouen der hillen arbeit (Hart translation altered). This theme of the hellish cruelty of divine *minne* is present in many places; see, e.g., her complaint that God "has been more cruel to me than any devil ever was" (L 1.56–82; ed. 18–19), or her description of how she wrestled with the terrible power of love in V 13 to be treated below.

38. L 20.1–3 (ed., 170): . . . die heuet .xij. vren die de Minne berueren vte hare seluen Ende bringense weder in haer seluen.

39. The importance of L 30 was highlighted in one of the first modern studies of Hade-wijch's mysticism, Joseph Van Mierlo, "Hadewijch: Une mystique flamande du treizième siècle," *Revue d'ascétique et de mystique* 5 (1924): 269–89, 380–404, especially 391–93.

40. The role of *minne* in the inner life of the Trinity appears in other texts. In PS 29.41–46, for example, the Father keeps the Son who is *minne* hidden within his bosom until Mary dis-closes him to us. See also L 17.67–77 and L 22.264–78, as well as the discussion in Heszler, "Stufen der Minne," pp. 102–4.

41. L 30.77–80 (ed., 254): Mer woude de edel redene vanden redeleken mensche haer werdeghe scout verstaen Ende volghen den gheleide dat hem de Minne soude gheuen in hare lant. . . .

42. L 30.151–54 (ed., 258): . . . Ende daer versament werden, daer dat grote licht die clare blixeme hier vore gescoten heuet, Ende di starke donder daer na gheslaghen heuet (Hart translation slightly altered).

43. L 30.173–76 (ed., 258): Dan selense emmermeer met ere vren manen Ende ghelden enen wesene, Jn enen wille, Jn enen hebbene, Jn enen ghebrukene (Hart translation altered).

44. E.g., in the PS, see 14.11–18 and 65–72, 16.101–3, 18.15–21, 40.33–36. See also L 18.174–88.

45. PS 43:43–49 (ed., 298): Ay, weerde natuere, minne fine,/ Wanneer maecti mijn natuere so fijn / Al uwer natueren ghenoech te sine? / Want ic ghenoech al woude sijn. / So waren al mine andere dine, / Ende daertoe die uwe algader mijn: / Ic woude in uwen brant verblaken.

46. PS 43.92–98 (ed., 302): Men sal al minne om minne begheven; / Hi es vroet die minne om minne beghevet. / Al eens sij sterven ochte leven: / Om minne sterven es ghe-noech ghelevet. / Ay, minne, ghi hebt mi langhe verdreven; / Maer in welken so ghi mi ver-drevet,/ Ic wille u, minne, al minne waken. This passage finds a parallel in L 13.34–44 (ed., 115) with its teaching on doing without the satisfaction of love in order to satisfy love.

47. For considerations of this vision, see Ruh, *Geschichte*, 2:201–8; and A. A. Bardoel, "On the Nature of Mystical Experience in the *Visions* of Hadewijch: A Comparative Study of the Unitive and the Intellectual Traditions," *Ons Geestelijk Erf* 66 (1992): 338–40.

48. The distinction between "in the spirit" and "above, or beyond, the spirit" (*bhuten den gheeste*) may have been suggested to Hadewijch by a passage in Richard of St. Victor's *De arca mystica* 5.12 (PL 196:181D–182C), contrasting John's apocalyptic visions *in spiritu* with the *sine spiritu* ecstasy of the Queen of Sheba (see 2 Chron. 9:4). V 3, 4, 7, 10, 11 and 12 all refer only to visions in the spirit; while V 5, 6, 9, 10 and 13–14 refer to both forms. For a further study of this terminology, see Bardoel, "On the Nature of Mystical Experience in the *Visions* of Hadewijch," pp. 324–28.

49. V 13.20-22 (ed., 161): . . . die nie moeder gods der volcomene dracht en waren. . . . The theme of being, in imitation of Mary, a "mother of God," already met with in Francis of Assisi, is found elsewhere in Hadewijch (e.g., L 30.200-02, and especially PC 14). On the motherhood motif in Hadewijch, see Reynaert, *De Beeldspraak*, pp. 293–300.

50. On the role of the seraph in medieval mysticism, see the discussion of Francis's vision in chapter 1, pp. 61–63. In V 4 (ed., 62-73) Hadewijch sees a seraph who is Christ.

51. On the vision of the divine form and face in Jewish mysticism, see Elliot R. Wolfson, *Through a Speculum that Shines: Vision and Imagination in Medieval Jewish Mysticism* (Princeton: Princeton University Press, 1994).

52. For William's teaching on the *facies Dei*, see *Growth of Mysticism*, pp. 261–64.

53. The language is not restricted to the visions. For the *minnen anschijn,* see, e.g., L 6.130–37, L 18.151–53, L 20.81–96, PS 12.36–46, PS 14.18, PC 3.78. The "countenance of God" or "countenance of the Beloved" appears in L 18.119, as well as in V 1, V 6, V 8 and V 12.

54. Notice of the divine countenance (*vultus/facies*) also occurs in Mechthild of Madgeburg. For some references to this theme in both Mechthild and Hadewijch, see Grete Lüers, *Die Sprache der deutschen Mystik des Mittelalters im Werke der Mechthild von Magdeburg* (Munich: Reinhardt, 1926; reprint, Darmstadt: Wissenschaftliche Buchgesellschaft, 1966), pp. 128–29.

55. V 13.79–84 (ed., 163): Ende di seraphin die mine es / ende di mi daer brachte hi hief mi op ende alte hant saghic in die oghe des anschijns enen setel / ende daer op sat de minne gheciert in die vorme van eenre coninghinnen/.

56. Claims to be superior to Mary were among the errors mentioned by Albert the Great (ca. 1270) in his list of the heresies of a group who had appeared in the Swabian Ries. See the *Compilatio de novo spiritu*, edited by Wilhelm Preger, in *Geschichte der deutschen Mystik*, 2 vols. (Leipzig: Dorffling & Franck, 1874–93), 1:461–69 (## 31, 70, 74, and 93). The "three glorified forms" of love (*drie ghecierde wesene* [13.142–44]) that Hadewijch sees and possesses appear to be a reference to the Trinity (cf. 13.291–99). Ruh (*Geschichte*, 2:201–2), comparing the role of the seraphim in V 13 with other angelic appearances in V 1, 4, and 8, notes a process of ascension through all the angelic hierarchies in Hadewijch's mystical trajectory. This indicates knowledge of the Dionysian CH, but the beguine does not appear to have had contact with the writings of Thomas Gallus.

57. V 13.198–203 (ed., 171): Dese waren de ghene die oetmoedecheit begheuen hadden tusschen hen ende hare lief bi vriheiden van minnen Ende di kinnesse hadden ghenomen tusschen hen ende haren god. . . . The reference to the "freedom of love" highlights another of the key themes that Hadewijch shared with other thirteenth-century mystics. For some important treatments of freedom, see, e.g., L 4.84–85, 18.150–60, 19.20–26, 31.26–27; PS 2.99, 4.37–38, 15.53–54, 23.48, 24.54–57, 36.90–91, 40.21–24, 42.38–40; PC 1.108 and 176–78, 2.94. In the visions there is an extended treatment in V 11.99–161 (ed., 133–37). On this important theme, see Reynaert, *De Beeldspraak*, pp. 382–92.

58. V 13.220–23 (ed., 171): Ende dat achtende es gherijnnesse van ghebrukene / die al af doet datter redenen behoert ende lief in lief een valt. . . . The notion of the "touch (*gherinen*) of love," sometimes bringing pain and sometimes fruition, is found in many texts in Hadewijch, especially in the Poems in Stanzas; see, e.g., L 6.361–66, 20.109–10; PS 5.18–21, 7.24, 11.97–102, 12.24–26, 21.27–31, 24.14–17, 25.35–36, 33.25–28, 38.45–46, 39.10; PC 9.39. According to Léonce Reypens, "Ruusbroec-Studien, I. Het mystieke 'gherinen,'" *Ons Geestelijk Erf* 12 (1938): 158, the term may originate in Hugh of St. Victor.

59. V 13.226–34 (ed., 171–73): . . . so maendense alle vren dat ghebrukenesse ende ongheloefden haren lieuen minnen niet / ende dochte hen datse allene minden ende hen minne niet en hulpet. Die ontrouwe maectse so diep dasse die minne al verwielen ende si gaen hare met sueten ende met sueren ane/. For further texts on *ontrouwe*, see especially L 8.27–71 and PC 10.87–102. There are helpful comments in Ruh, *Geschichte*, 2:206–7 and 221; and John Giles Milhaven, *Hadewijch and Her Sisters: Other Ways of Loving and Knowing*, pp. 57–72.

60. The *Lijst der Volmaakten* can be found in *Het Visioenenboek*, pp. 192–207, with a helpful commentary on pp. 241–46. This enigmatic enumeration of those who have received the eighth gift of love contains important references for the dating of the list (and presumably at least part of Hadewijch's literary career) to ca. 1250. See Murk-Jansen, "The Mystic Theology of Hadewijch," pp. 118–19.

61. V 8.132–34 (ed., 109): Gheleide alle de ongheleidde / na hare werdecheit / daerse van mi toe ghemeint sijn/.

62. The metaphor of mystical death, however, plays an important part in the beguine's mysticism. See Reynaert, *De Beeldspraak*, pp. 321–32.

63. V 13.319–23 (ed., 177): Doe ghine mi ghebruken als te voren ende ic viel in die grondelose dipte ende quam buten den gheeste op die vre daer men nemmermeer af segghen en mach/.

64. V 14.16–21 (ed., 181): . . . dat was ene cracht van sijn selues wesene: / hem god te sine met minen doeghene na heme / ende in heme ghelijc dat hi mi was doe hi mensche leuede te mi. . . .

65. In V 14.58–59 (ed., 183) she says the "being," or "manner of existence" (*wesen*), of the throne is the *wesen gods*.

66. On this aspect of the *Visioenenboek,* see Willaert, "Hadewijch und ihr Kreis," and Ruh, *Geschichte,* 2:202–3. The passage in V 14.74–91 matches other expressions of spiritual friendship found in such texts as L 25–26 and 29. On spiritual friendship in Netherlandish mysticism, see Herman W. J. Vekeman, "Vriendschap in de Middelnederlandse mystiek: De plaats van Ruusbroec," in *Jan Van Ruusbroec: The sources, content and sequels of his mysticism,* ed. Paul Mommaers and Norbert De Paepe (Leuven: Leuven University Press, 1984), pp. 124–41.

67. Hadewijch's gender reversal language, especially her frequent descriptions of herself as a bold knight pursuing the unattainable "Lady Love," has been studied by Saskia Murk-Jansen, "The Use of Gender and Gender-Related Imagery in Hadewijch," in *Gender and Text in the Later Middle Ages,* 55–66.

68. Other important texts for Hadewijch's teaching on God as one and three include L 17, PS 29 and PC 4.

69. The poem belongs to Hildebert, but Hadewijch may well have thought it was by Abelard, whom she seems to have read and to some degree admired. For the text, see PL 171:1411: Super cuncta, subter cuncta; / extra cuncta, intra cuncta. / (a) Intra cuncta, nec inclusus; / (b) extra cuncta, nec exclusus; / (c) super cuncta, nec elatus; / (d) subter cuncta, nec substratus. Hadewijch treats the four paradoxes in the following order: (c) in 22.25–83; (d) in 22.84–101; (a) in 22.102–250; and (b) in 22.251–371. A brief treatment of related paradoxes is to be found in V 6.90–100 (ed., 67).

70. L 22.110–13 (ed., 192): Alle die waren ende sijn ende wesen selen, ia in welken hen behoert te sine, hi ghebruket siere weldegher wondere daer met in alre volre glorien.

71. This trinitarian image imprinted on the soul is, of course, standard Augustinian theological anthropology rooted in Augustine's *De trinitate* and well known to most medieval theologians.

72. L 22.179–82 (ed., 195): Dese wech leidse herde diepe in gode: Want die grote onthope leidse ouer alle stercke ende dore alle passagen Ende in allen ghewarighen staden. The *onthope* of this passage is closely allied to the *ontrouwe* considered above.

73. In L 22.218–20 Hadewijch briefly notes a fifth way, that of people of simple faith who go to God through outward service.

74. L 22.252–55 (ed., 198): . . . want hine rustet in ghene dinc dan in die druusteghe nature siere vloyender vloedegher vloede, die al omme ende al overvloeyen.

75. For studies of the language of "flowing" in reference to the Trinity and to describe mystical union, see Lüers, *Die Sprache der deutschen Mystik,* pp. 278–85; and Ruh, "Die trinitarische Spekulation in deutscher Mystik und Scholastik," in *Kleine Schriften,* 2:30–36.

76. V 1.299–303 and 313–16 (ed., 40): Ende in midden onder die sciue drayede een wiel / soe vreeslike omme / ende die soe eyseleke was aen te siene / dat hemelrike ende ertrike daer af verwondren mochte ende uervaren / . . . . Die diepe wiel die soe vreeselike donker es / Dats die godleke gebrukelecheit in haren verhoelnen stormen/.

77. V 1.341–45 (ed., 41): Stant op / Want du best in mi op ghestaen / sonder beghin gheheel vri / ende sonder val / Want du begheert hebs een met me te wesenne/.

78. Although Hadewijch does not use the technical vocabulary of exemplarism, the importance of preexistence in the divine exemplar in her thought has rightly been stressed by Louis Bouyer, *Women Mystics* (San Francisco: Ignatius Press, 1993), pp. 25–35; and Epiney-Burgard, "Hadewijch d'Anvers, Mechthilde de Magdebourg," pp. 74–76. On the shift in ways of understanding *unio mystica,* see McGinn, "Love, Knowledge, and *Unio mystica* in the West-

ern Christian Tradition," in *Mystical Union in Judaism, Christianity, and Islam: An Ecumenical Dialogue,* ed. Moshe Idel and Bernard McGinn (New York: Continuum, 1996), pp. 59–86.

79. For Origen's teaching on the eternal preexistence of all things in the mind of the Logos, see, e.g., his *Commentary on John* 1.114 and 244.

80. On Augustine, see, e.g., *De diversis quaestionibus* 83, q. 46; *De Trinitate* 6.10.11; *De Genesi ad litteram* 4.24.41 and 5.15.33. For a brief sketch of the development of the Christian interpretation of the divine ideas in the Word, see Bernard McGinn, "Platonic and Christian: The Case of the Divine Ideas," in *Of Scholars, Savants, and their Texts: Studies in Philosophy and Religious Thought. Essays in Honor of Arthur Hyman,* ed. Ruth Link-Salinger (New York: Peter Lang, 1989), pp. 163–72. The mystical use of this theme, with particular reference to Marguerite Porete, has been studied by Joanne Maguire, "Nobility and Annihilation in Marguerite Porete's Mirror of Simple Souls" (Ph.D. diss., University of Chicago, 1996).

81. See, e.g., William's *Meditatio* 1.8.1–4 (ed. SC 324:46).

82. See, e.g., L 6.29–35 and 337–43; L 18; L 19.37–45; and L 29.85–91.

83. V 4.77–82 (ed., 67): . . . euen gheweldech / ende in gheliken dienste / ende in alre ghelikere glorien / ende in ere werdeghe gheweldecheit / ende in enen verdraghelikere ghenadecheit Jn allen eeuweleken wesene/.

84. V 4.92–105, (ed. 67–69): Nu sich mi eneghe gheeenech dinen gheminded / ende mine gheminde sidi ghemeint met mi / Dese gheheele hemele / die du sies dia hare sijn ende mine / Ende die du saghes alse twee conincriken / die verwoest waren / dat was onser tweer menscheit / eer si vol wies / Jc wies wore / ende nochtan bleuen wi effene / Ende ic quam in mijn rike ghisteren / ende ghi wiest na / nochtan bleuen wi effene / Ende si sal volwassen heden / ende met die comen marghen in hare rike / ende nochtan bliuen effene mit mi/.

85. V 11.27–31 (ed., 129): . . . gheeste die hen seluen verholen sijn in die diepheit / daer ic af segghe ende die niets en ghemissen dan datse daer in dolen / (Hart translation slightly altered). This mystical theme of the birth of the divine Word in the soul, found in a number of Cistercian authors, such as Guerric of Igny (see *Growth of Mysticism,* pp. 283–84), was to be richly developed by Meister Eckhart. For an overview, see Hugo Rahner, "Die Gottesgeburt: Die Lehre der Kirchenväter von der Geburt Christi aus dem Herzen der Kirche und der Gläubigen," in *Symbole der Kirche* (Salzburg: Otto Müller, 1964), pp. 13–87.

86. V 11.79–83 (ed., 133): Die outheit oec die ic hadde dat was inder naturen ven eweleken wesene uolcomenleke al wasic vander vtterster naturen toecomende/.

87. The remainder of V 11 is a consideration of the *minne* that sacrifices everything, even itself, in order satisfy its true nature.

88. The vision later identifies the whirlpool with the divine Unity (V 12.130–34): Si toense oec bekint dore elken persoen der driuoldichaeit in die enecheit die daer so diep wiel was onder die wonderleke vreseleke sciue/ daer hi in sat die de bruut ontfaen soude/.

89. V 12.187–92 and 206–10 (ed., 155–57): Ende met dien saghic mi seluen ontfaen een vanden ghenen die daer sat in dien wiel op die lopende sciue / ende daer wardic .i. mede in sekerheiden der enecheit / . . . . Jn die diepheit saghic mi verswolghen/ daer ontfinghic sekerheit met diere vormen ontfaen te sine in mijn lief / ende mijn lief also in mi / (Hart translation modified).

90. Hadewijch employs a range of terminology here, not only *afgront* but also the roughly equivalent terms *wiel* ("whirlpool"), *diepheit* ("depth"), *grondeloesheit* ("bottomlessness"), etc. In what follows I am drawing on my article "The Abyss of Love" in *The Joy of Learning and the Love of God: Studies in Honor of Jean Leclercq,* pp. 106–8. See also the treatments in R. Vanneste, "Over de betekenis van enkele abstracta in de taal van Hadewijch," *Studia Germanica* 1 (1959): 34–40; Breuer, "Philologische Zugänge zur Mystik Hadewijchs," pp. 109–11; and the references in Lüers, *Die Sprache der deutschen Mystik,* pp. 119–22.

91. Bernard of Clairvaux, Quad 4.3 (*Sancti Bernardi Opera* 4:370).

92. William of St. Thierry, *Expositio in Cantica Canticorum* 132 (SC 82:282).

93. L 18.69–79 (ed., 154–55): . . . daer es de ziele ene grondeloesheit daer god he seluen ghenoech met es, Ende sine ghenoechte uan hem seluen altoes te vollen in hare heuet, Ende si weder altoes in heme. Siele es een wech vanden dore vaerne gods in sine vriheit van sinen diepsten; Ende god es een wech vanden dore vaerne der zielen in hare vriheit, Dat es in sinen gront die niet gheraect en can werden, sine gherakene met hare diepheit; Ende god si hare gheheel, hine waer hare niet ghenoech (Hart translation slightly altered).

94. L 12.44–49 (ed., 103): Mer die daer na staen der Minnen ghenoech te doene, die sijn oec ewech ende sonder gront / . . . . Ende al mindemen die oec met eweleker Minnen, si en worden oec nummermeer van Minnen gronde veruolghet. . . . For other passages in Hadewijch that express the mutual infinity of the soul and God, with or without explicit use of abyss language, see, e.g., L 19.37–45, L 22.183–200, PS 4.45–48, PC 16.185–96, V 1.224–231 and 513–23.

95. PC 12.87–90 (ed., 58): Ende dat cussen met enen eneghen monde, / Ende te vergrondenne die eneghe gronde, / Ende met enen siene te doresience al / Dat es, ende was, ende wesen sal . . . . (Hart translation slightly altered). References to the abyss or depths of love (not always mutual) are frequent in Hadewijch's poems, e.g., PS 11.76–78, 19.28, 21.20–26, 24.80; PC 10.61–64, 13.1–2, 14.7, 16.163 and 190–94.

96. On the relation between Hadewijch and Eckhart, see Saskia Murk-Jansen, "Hadewijch and Eckhart: Amor intellegere est," in *Meister Eckhart and the Beguine Mystics: Hadewijch of Brabant, Mechthild of Magdeburg, and Marguerite Porete*, pp. 17–30.

97. Mommaers has shown the insufficiency of this categorization of Hadewijch's mysticism in his "L'Ecole neérlandaise," pp. 468–73.

98. For an analysis, see Paul Mommaers, "Het VIIe en VIIIe Visioen van Hadewijch: Affectie in de mystieke beleving," *Ons Geestelijk Erf* 49 (1975): 105–32. A survey of Hadewijch's erotic terminology has been given by Reynaert, *De Beeldspraak*, pp. 301–20.

99. See also L 19.52–61 (ed., 165) describing the annihilation of the soul's will that results in the soul becoming "with him all that he himself is" (*Ende soe wertse met hem al dat selue dat hi es*). PC 3.110–14 (ed., 24) has the soul being engulfed in one love and one will in the deepest silence.

100. E.g., L 6.361–68, 13.9–16, 16.28–40, 27.38–47; PS 12.22–26, 23.34–40, 25.61–70, 34.49–56; V 9.66–72. In many of Hadewijch's descriptions of ecstasy (e.g., PS 26 and V 6) it is difficult, if not impossible, to say what form of union is being described.

101. L 9.7–14 (ed., 79–80): Ende soe dore dat ander woent, Dat haerre en gheen hem seluen en onderkent. . . . Ende ene soete godlike nature doer hen beiden vloyende, Ende si beide een dore hen seluen, Ende al eens beide bliuen, Ja ende bliuende / (Hart translation altered).

102. V 10.74–82 (ed., 123–25): Siet hier dit es mijn bruut / die heeft doergaen alle uwe ambachte metter volmaecter minnen / Wies minne es soe starc daerse bi alle dus wassen / Ende hi seide / sich hier bruut ende moeder du heues mi alse allene go ende mensche connen leuen/.

103. L 6.227–48 (ed., 64). The proper form of *imitatio Christi* is the major theme of this letter; see 6.86–145, 160–70, 227–370. For other texts that talk about the necessity of "living God and man," see, e.g., L 18.1–12, PC 16.191–96, V 1.373f., V 6.129–36, V 11.260–70. The wider theme of the imitation of Christ in his human life and suffering is frequently discussed in the beguine's works; see, e.g., L 1.8–17, 15.16–35, 16.28–40, 22.285–327, 29.85–95, 30.84–99 and 123–44; PS 30.28–30; PC 9.7–15, 12.129–42; V 8.39–67, and 12.134–62.

104. L 15.29–35 (ed., 125): Hi wrachte met wakender caritaten, ende hi gaf ter Minnen al sijn herte ende al sine ziele Ende al sine crachte. Dit es die wech dien ihesus wiset ende selue

es, Ende dien hi selue ghinc, daer dat eweghe leuen in leghet Ende die ghebrukenisse der waerheit sijns vader glorie/. On the use of these biblical texts in Hadewijch, see Reynaert, "Mystische Bibelinterpretaton bei Hadewijch," pp. 130–32.

105. The importance of this paradoxical formulation has been emphasized by Murk-Jansen, *The Measure of Mystic Thought,* pp. 103–13 and 163–66; and "The Mystic Theology of Hadewijch," pp. 126–27. She points to the reception of the eighth gift of love in V 13.220–39 (ed., 171–73) as a good example, although the phrase does not appear there. Explicit formulations, however, are characteristic of PC 17–24; e.g., PC 17.19–21: *Men moet crighen / Jn dat ontbliuen / Saelt sijn goet . . .* (ed., 87).

106. See Mommaers, "Preface," in *Hadewijch: Complete Works,* pp. xix–xxiv; and "Bulletin d'histoire de la spiritualité: L'Ecole néerlandaise," pp. 485–87. Other studies of Hadewijch have also emphasized this paradoxical notion of union; e.g., Epiney-Burgard, "Hadewijch d'Anvers, Mechthilde de Magdebourg. Thèmes communs," pp. 81–84.

107. L 29.46–50 (ed., 244): . . . dat mi niet en behoerde te hebbene bliscap noch rouwe en gheen, groet noch clene, Sonder van dien dat ic mensche was, Ende dat ic gheuoelde Minne met Minleker herten . . . .

108. PS 33.25–28 (ed., 236): Sat ende hongher, beide in een, / Dat es der vrier minnen leen, / Als ye den ghenen wale scheen / Die minne met haerre natueren ghereen. The following lines (29–40) expand upon the paradox. For comparable expressions of Hadewijch's epektasis of *minne,* see L 12.13–30 and 16.9–20.

109. L 23.27–29 (ed., 206): Ende leuet in enighen vlite met ons, ende laet ons inder soeter Minnen leuen. leuet gode ende hi v ende ghi ons/.

110. See, e.g., Hart, "Introduction," *Hadewijch,* pp. 35–41; Willaert, "Hadewijch und ihr Kreis in den 'Visioenen'"; Mommaers and Willaert, "Mystisches Erlebnis und Sprachliche Vermittlung in den Briefen Hadewijchs."

111. See, e.g., L 3.26–37, 6.54f., 16.56–80, 20.70–80, 24.1–15, 29.61–84; and PC 12.37–44, etc.

112. L 2.122–49 (ed., 29–30). There is a similar passage in V 11.203–30 (ed. 139–41).

113. The problems involved in this letter have been discussed by Ruh, *Geschichte,* 2:222–24, who also cites previous treatments.

114. L 17.39–43 (ed., 141): Ende dit hoerdi altoes dat ict altoes gherarden hebbe bouen al; Ende oec leuede ict bouen al, ende diende daer inne ende wrachte ouerscone tote dien daghe dat mi verboden wart/.

115. L 17.74–77 (ed., 143): Want in dat ghebruken van Minnen en was nie noch en mach ander werc sijn dan dat enighe ghebruken, daer die eneghe moghende godheit Minne met es.

116. Another problematic aspects of her boldness is the strange incident described in V 5.40–70 (ed., 77–79), where she upbraids herself for having been a "Lucifer" in freeing from hell four souls among the living and dead. This incident has been variously interpreted; some taking it literally, others metaphorically. See the discussion in Newman, *From Virile Woman to WomanChrist,* pp. 124–27. For a detailed study of this text in relation to the whole range of the beguine's thought, see Bernard Spaapen, "Hadewijch en het vijfde Visioen," *Ons Geestelijk Erf* 44 (1970): 7–44, 113–41, 353–404; 45 (1971): 129–78; 46 (1972): 113–99.

117. See Paul Mommaers, "Hadewijch: A Feminist in Conflict," *Louvain Studies* 13 (1988): 58–81, for the context.

118. See Charles Homer Haskins, "Robert le Bougre and the Beginnings of the Inquisition in Northern France," in *Studies in Mediaeval Culture.*

119. For a summary, see Mommaers, "Bulletin d'histoire de la spiritualité: L'Ecole néerlandaise," pp. 473–77. More will be said about this heresy in the treatment of Marguerite Porete below.

120. On Hadewijch's audience, see Willaert, "Hadewijch und ihr Kreis," pp. 380–81; and Breuer, "Philologisches Zugänge," pp. 118–21.

121. L 2.86-89 (ed., 28): Dient scone ende en wilt el niet Ende en ontsiet el niet ende laet de minne vrileken met hare seluen ghewerden/. Want minne volloent al comtse dicke spade/.

122. For an introduction to Mechthild, see Alois M. Haas, "Deutsche Mystik," in *Die deutsche Literatur im späten Mittelalter 1250–1370*, ed. Ingeborg Glier (Munich: Beck, 1987), pp. 245–54. Other introductions can be found in Margot Schmidt, "Mechthilde de Madgebourg," DS 10:877–85; and Hans Neumann, "Mechthild von Magdeburg," in *Die deutsche Literatur des Mittelalters: Verfasserlexikon*, 6:260–70. Two early studies of Mechthild still retain much value: Jeanne Ancelet-Hustache, *Mechthilde de Magdebourg (1207–1282): Étude de psychologie religieuse* (Paris: Champion, 1926); and especially Grete Lüers, *Die Sprache der deutschen Mystik des Mittelalters im Werke der Mechthild von Magdeburg*, also first published in 1926. The best recent summary of Mechthild's mysticism is that of Kurt Ruh in *Geschichte*, 2:245–92. Frank Tobin's *Mechthild von Magdeburg: A Medieval Mystic in Modern Eyes* (Columbia, SC: Camden House, 1995) supplies a good critical introduction to modern scholarship on Mechthild, most of which is in German. Recent English studies of Mechthild are uneven. For a complete listing of pre-1980 bibliography, see Lewis, *Bibliographie zur deutschen Frauenmystik des Mittelalters*, pp. 164–83 (166 items).

123. The edition employed here will be that of Hans Neumann, *Mechthild von Magdeburg: Das fliessende Licht der Gottheit*, 2 vols. (Munich: Artemis, 1990, 1993). The text will be cited under the abbreviation FL followed by book and chapter with the page and line number in parentheses where necessary. Neumann's edition supersedes that of Gall Morel, *Offenbarung der Schwester Mechthild von Magdeburg oder Das fliessende Licht der Gottheit* (Regensburg, 1869; reprinted, Darmstadt: Wissenschaftliche Buchgesellschaft, 1963). There are three English translations, by far the best of which is that of Frank Tobin, *The Flowing Light of the Godhead* (Mahwah: Paulist Press, 1998). I will generally employ the Tobin translation, unless otherwise noted.

124. For a summary, see Hans Neumann, "Beiträge zur Textgeschichte des 'Fliessenden Lichts der Gottheit' und zur Lebensgeschichte Mechthilds von Magdeburg," in *Altdeutsche und altniederländische Mystik*, ed. Kurt Ruh (Darmstadt: Wissenschaftliche Buchgesellschaft, 1964), pp. 175–239. The critical approach has been advanced by Ursula Peters, *Religiöse Erfahrung als literarisches Faktum: Zur Vorgeschichte und Genese frauenmystischer Texte des 13. und 14. Jahrhunderts*, pp. 52–67 and 116–29. For an evaluation, see Tobin, *Mechthild von Magdeburg*, pp. 127–32.

125. On the role of the Dominicans and the care of religious women, see Herbert Grundmann, *Religious Movements in the Middle Ages*, pp. 92–109 and 124–30; for a corrective of some of Grundmann's views, consult John B. Freed, "Urban Development and the 'Cura Monialium' in Thirteenth-Century Germany," *Viator* 3 (1972): 311–27. Mechthild's brother Baldwin became a Dominican, as we learn from FL 4.26 and 6.42.

126. For the influence of Wichmann, see Ruh, *Geschichte*, 2:286–88 and 292–95.

127. This view has been challenged by Peters, *Religiöse Erfahrung*, pp. 116–22, but it still seems basically plausible.

128. Most authorities, including the editor Hans Neumann, detect no ordering principle in these books, but Hans-Georg Kemper has suggested that the first four books should be considered as a single composition on the basis of the remarks in FL 4.28 and that their structural principle is laid out at the beginning of FL 6.6 (211.5–6) in the four themes of *minne-gerunge-rúwe-vorhte*). See Kemper, "Allegorische Allegorese: Zur Bildlichkeit und Struktur mystischer Literatur (Mechthild von Magdeburg und Angelus Silesius)," in *Formen und Funktionen der Allegorie*, ed. Walter Haug (Stuttgart: Germanistische Symposien 3, 1978), pp. 96–98.

129. For more on Helfta and its mystics, see the following chapter (pp. 267–82).

130. The Latin text, entitled the *Lux divinitatis fluens in corda veritatis,* is available in vol. 2 of the *Revelationes Gertrudianae et Mechtildianae,* ed. the monks of Solesmes [Louis Paquelin] (Paris/Poitiers: Oudin, 1875–77), pp. 423–643. It survives in two Basel manuscripts. The ordering of the books and chapters is different in the Latin version. On Mechthild's relation to the learned Latin tradition, see John Margetts, "Latein und Volkssprache bei Mechthild von Magdeburg," *Amsterdamer Beiträge zur älteren Germanistik* 12 (1977): 119–36.

131. According to Wolfgang Mohr, "Darbietungsformen der Mystik bei Mechthild von Magdeburg," in *Märchen, Mythos, Dichtung: Festschrift zum 90. Geburtstag Friedrich von der Leyens,* ed. Hugo Kuhn and Kurt Schier (Munich: Beck, 1963), p. 375: "Es [Mechthild's mysticism] steht nicht deutlich in einer einzigen Linie historischer Kontinuität, sein geschichtlicher Ort ist urtümlicher, vieldeutiger und weniger greifbar bedingt, und es ist eine so einmalige und einsame Leistung, dass so gut wie keine Nachwirkung davon ausging."

132. It is not impossible, though unlikely, that Mechthild read Hadewijch. There are a number of interesting parallels (as well as real contrasts) between the two beguines. Considerable literature has been devoted to the relation between these two great mystics. See especially Hans Neumann, "Mechthild von Magdeburg und die mittelniederländische Frauenmystik," in *Medieval German Studies: Festschrift Presented to Frederick Norman* (London, 1965), pp. 231–46; Frances Gooday, "Mechthild of Magdeburg and Hadewijch of Antwerp: A Comparison," *Ons Geestelijk Erf* 48 (1974): 305–62; K. Ruh, "Beguinenmystik: Hadewijch, Mechthild von Magdeburg, Marguerite Porete," in *Kleine Schriften,* 2:137–49; and Elisabeth Wainwright-de Kadt, "Courtly Literature and Mysticism: Some Aspects of Their Interaction," *Acta Germanica* 12 (1980): 41–60.

133. Mechthild uses the term *gottesfrünt* a number of times, an early example of this mystical term in the German language. See, e.g., FL 1.22 (19.73), 1.44 (32.94), 3.10 (91.58), 6.1 (208.33), and 7.31 (279.5). On the community context of the work, see Ulrike Wiethaus, *Ecstatic Transformation: Transpersonal Psychology in the Work of Mechthild of Madgeburg* (Syracuse: Syracuse University Press, 1996), pp. 23–26.

134. This prologue (4.1–5.11) is to be distinguished from the Latin prologue added by the Dominican translators (1–2). The recent debate on the prologue is summarized in Tobin, *Mechthild von Magdeburg,* pp. 134–36.

135. FL 1.prol (4–5; titles italicized here): *Dis buoch sol man gerne enpfan, wan got sprichet selber dú wort.* Dis buoch das sende ich nu ze botten allen geistlichen lúten beidú boesen und guoten, wand wenne die súle vallent, so mag das werk nút gestan, und ez bezeichent alleine mich und meldet loblich mine heimlicheit. Alle, die dis buoch wellen vernemen, die soellent es ze nún malen lesen. *Dis buoch heisset ein vliessendes lieht der gotheit.* "Eya herre got, wer hat dis buoch gemachet?" "Ich han es gemachet an miner unmaht, wan ich mich an miner gabe nút enthalten mag." "Eya herre, wie sol dis buoch heissen alleine ze dinen eren?" "Es sol heissen ein vliessende lieht miner gotheit in allú dú herzen, dú da lebent ane valscheit" (Tobin translation slightly altered). The notion of reading the book nine times (the number of the choirs of angels) seems to suggest that, like the Bible, it should be constantly meditated upon through a kind of *lectio divina.*

136. The position that God is the speaker has been upheld by the editor Hans Neumann, as well as Eberhard Nellmann, *"Dis buoch ... bezeichent alleine mich:* Zum Prolog von Mechthilds 'Fliessendem Licht der Gottheit,'" in *Gotes und der werlde hulde: Literatur im Mittelalter und Neuzeit. Festschrift für Heinz Rupp zum 70. Geburtstag,* ed. Rüdiger Schnell (Bern/ Stuttgart: Francke, 1989), pp. 200–205; and Nigel Palmer, "Das Buch als Bedeutungsträger bei Mechthild von Magdeburg," in *Bildhafte Rede in Mittelalter und früher Neuzeit: Probleme ihrer Legitimation und Funktion,* ed. Wolfgang Harms and Klaus Speckenbach (Tübingen: Niemeyer, 1992), pp. 217–35.

137. FL 3.1 (74:37–39): Nu voerhte ich got, ob ich swige, und voerhte aber unbekante lúte, ob ich schribe. Vil lieben lúte, was mag ich des, das mir dis geschiht und dike geschehen ist? (Tobin translation slightly modified).

138. FL 2.26 (68.9–11): . . . die warheit mag nieman verbrennen. der es mir us miner hant sol nemen, der sol starker denne ich wesen. Das buoch ist drivaltig und bezeichnet alleine mich (my translation).

139. I am grateful to Michael Curschmann of Princeton University for this suggestion.

140. Ibid. (69.27–29): . . . die irdenschen hohsten berge moegent nit enpfan die offenbarunge miner gnaden, wan die vluot mines heligen geistes vlússet von nature ze tal. Bynum (*Jesus as Mother: Studies in the Spirituality of the High Middle Ages*) captures this aspect of Mechthild's understanding of her position as a woman when she writes: "Thus she embraces her femaleness as a sign of her freedom from power. And exactly this freedom makes her a channel through which God acts" (pp. 241–42).

141. Ibid. (69.32–33). This important text provides the title for Marianne Heimbach's study of Mechthild's authority and teaching, *"Der ungelehrte Mund" als Autorität: Mystische Erfahrung als Quelle kirchlich-prophetischer Rede im Werk Mechthilds von Magdeburg* (Stuttgart/Bad Canstatt: frommann-holzboog, 1989).

142. Other texts scattered through the FL also defend the book against its detractors and emphasize its divine status; see, e.g., FL 3.1 (79.174–78); 3.20 (99–100), where five great prophets of the Old Testament are said to illuminate the book; 4.2 (114.128–34); 5.12 (166); 6.1 (206.163–64); and 6.43 (251), an editor's addition.

143. FL 5.34 (195.41–45): Dis buoch sende ich nu ze botten allen geistlichen lúten, bedú den boesen und den guoten, wan swenne die súle valent, so mag das werk nit gestan. Ich sage dir werlich,...in diesem buoch stat min herzebluot geschreiben, das ich in den jungsten ziten anderwarbe wil giessen. Mechthild's interest in apocalypticism is reflected not only in the specific chapters devoted to the topic (e.g., FL 4.27 and 6.15) but also in her sense of presentiality to the last events as the summation of *Heilsgeschichte*. For insightful comments, see Hans Urs von Balthasar, "Mechthilds kirchlicher Auftrag," in *Mechthild von Magdeburg: Das Fliessende Licht der Gottheit*, translated with an introduction by Margot Schmidt (Einsiedeln: Benziger, 1955), pp. 28–38; and Palmer, "Das Buch als Bedeutungsträger," pp. 230–33. See also my forthcoming article "'To the Scandal of Men, Women are Prophesying': Female Seers in the High Middle Ages," in *Waiting in Fearful Hope*, ed. Christopher Kleinhenz and Fanny LeMoine (forthcoming).

144. *Lux divinitatis*, prologus (ed. Solesmes, 436): Legenda est autem haec scriptura pie, et religiose intelligenda, et secundum morem aliarum sanctarum scripturarum, sane et fideliter. . . . Auctor quippe ejus Pater et Filius et Spiritus Sanctus est, materia ejus Christus et Ecclesia est, et Satanas cum corpore suo. Modus agendi, historicus et mysticus; finis vero, praesentis vitae ordinatio, et praeteritorum utilis recordatio, et prophetica insinuatio futurorum. On the significance of this passage, see Palmer, "Das Buch als Bedeutungsträger," pp. 217–21. Similarly, in the letter that Henry of Nördlingen sent to Margarete Ebner recommending the work, he says of it: "Eia! ich man euch als des gutz, das got in im selber ist und in diszem buch bewiszt hat" (Philipp Strauch, *Margaretha Ebner und Heinrich von Nördlingen, ein Beitrag zur Geschichte der deutschen Mystik* [Freiburg: Mohr, 1882], p. 246).

145. On the forms of literary presentation employed in the FL, a good introduction is that of Wolfgang Mohr, "Darbietungsformen der Mystik bei Mechthild von Magdeburg," in *Märchen, Mythos, Dichtung*, pp. 375–99.

146. See Introduction, pp. 25–30. The import of the 1980s debate between Peter Dinzelbacher and Siegfried Ringler over the "reality" of medieval visions has been summarized by Tobin, *Mechthild von Magdeburg*, pp. 110–22. Mechthild also demonstrates the typical late-

medieval concern for distinguishing between delusive visions sent by the devil and authentic heavenly ones; see, e.g., FL 2.19 (51.48–56), 2.24 (60.47–62), 4.15 (129–30), and 7.7 (262–63). Margot Schmidt shows that for the beguine the heavenly *gustus* experienced in the spiritual sense of taste is the central criterion for true visions ("Elemente der Schau bei Mechthild von Magdeburg und Mechthild von Hackeborn: Zur Bedeutung der geistlichen Sinne," in *Frauenmystik im Mittelalter*, pp. 137–39).

147. Frank Tobin has studied the relation of Mechthild to the Augustinian teaching on visions in "Medieval Thought on Visions and its Resonance in Mechthild von Magdeburg's *Flowing Light of the Godhead*," in *Vox Mystica: Essays on Medieval Mysticism in Honor of Professor Valerie M. Lagorio*, pp. 41–53. Though Tobin does not claim for Mechthild any direct knowledge of Augustine, he argues that her teaching on the three heavens (see FL 2.19) reflects a broad acquaintance with Augustinian categories.

148. For an example of what seems like an intellectual vision in Mechthild, see FL 6.1 (203.78–205.113). For Mechthild's combining pictorial spiritual visions with the immediate and intuitive apprehension of divine truths characteristic of intellectual visions, see, e.g., FL 2.3 (39–41) and 3.1 (72–79, especially 73.23–74.41).

149. Lüers was the first to emphasize the importance of metaphor and symbol in understanding Mechthild (*Die Sprache der deutschen Mystik*, pp. 1–54). This strategy has been commented upon by many later students of Mechthild; see, e.g., von Balthasar, "Mechthilds kirchlicher Auftrag," pp. 27–28; Mohr, "Darbietungsformen," pp. 383–85; Margot Schmidt, "Versinnlichte Transzendenz bei Mechthild von Magdeburg," in *"Minnichlichiu gotes erkennusse": Studien zur frühen abendländischen Mystiktradition*, ed. Dietrich Schmidtke (Stuttgart-Bad Canstatt: frommann-holzboog, 1990), pp. 62–88.

150. Mechthild's visions make for interesting comparisons with those of Hadewijch, though direct parallels are rare (compare, however, the eucharistic vision in FL 2.4 with Hadewijch's V 7).

151. Tobin, *Mechthild of Magdeburg*, "Introduction," p. 11.

152. Mohr, "Darbietungsformen," 378.

153. This aspect of Mechthild's book was first emphasized by Haas, *Sermo Mysticus: Studien zu Theologie und Sprache der deutschen Mystik* (Freiburg: Universitätsverlag, 1979), pp. 77–79 and 105–6, and has been developed by Ruh, *Geschichte*, 2:256, and Amy Hollywood, *The Soul as Virgin Wife*, pp. 57–61.

154. There has been considerable study of the dialogical form of the FL in German. The first major work was that of Heinz Tillmann, *Studien zum Dialog bei Mechthild von Magdeburg* (Marburg: Kalbfleisch, 1933) (see the summary in Tobin, *Mechthild of Magdeburg*, pp. 48–50), who estimated that a third of the text is dialogical. More recently, see especially Walter Haug, "Das Gespräch mit der unvergleichlichen Partner: Der mystische Dialog bei Mechthild von Magdeburg als Paradigma für eine personale Gesprächsstruktur," in *Das Gespräch*, ed. Karlheinz Stierle and Rainer Warning (Munich: Fink, 1984), pp. 251–79. See also Ruh, *Geschichte*, 2:256–58; and in English, Hollywood, *The Soul as Virgin Wife*, pp. 61–65.

155. Haug, "Das Gespräch mit dem unvergleichlichen Partner," p. 268: "Niederschrift und Lektüre, d.h. die literarische Existenz des *Fliessende Lichts* ist somit ausgespannt zwischen der einstigen Erfahrung und dem Wiedereintreten in den mystischen Prozess." The four levels that Haug identifies are: (1) the past of a recounted mystical experience; (2) the timeless mystical experience as such; (3) the nontemporal theological consideration of the experience; and (4) the present in which the mystic writes (see pp. 258–59). These form a complex series of interactions summarized on pp. 266–68. Haug's approach has proven stimulating to other investigators; see, e.g., Alois M. Haas, who suggests an expansion to five levels ("Mechthilds von Magdeburg dichterische *heimlichkeit*," in *Gottes und der werlde hulde: Literatur im Mittelalter*

und Neuzeit. Festschrift für Heinz Rupp zum 70. Geburtstag, ed. Rüdiger Schnell (Bern/Stuttgart: Francke, 1989), pp. 210–11.

156. FL 1.1 (5–7). See the comments on this by Tobin, *Mechthild of Magdeburg,* p. 13.

157. FL 1.2 (8.17–18): So swebent si fúrbas an ein wunnenreiche stat, da ich nút von sprechen wil noch mag.

158. Ibid. (9.40–43): Disen gruos mag noch muos nieman enpfan, er si denne úberkomen und ze nihte worden. In disem gruosse wil ich lebendig sterben, das moegen mir die blinden heligen niemer verderben, das sint die da minnent und nit bekennent (my translation). A clue concerning the blindness of those holy people who love without knowing can be found in 1.21 (16.1–2): Minne ane bekantnisse dunket die wisen sele ein vinsternisse, bekantnisse ane gebruchunge dunket si ein hellepin, gebruchunge ane mort kan si nit verklagen. The Latin softens this attack on "holy people" by rendering *nec ab hoc voto ignorantium me deterrebit simplicitas (Lux divinitatis* 4.11; ed., 559).

159. FL 1.5 (11.15): Dise qwale muesse dich bestan,/ niemer muesset du ir entgan (my translation with an attempt to suggest the poetic form).

160. FL 1.28 (22.8): Du darft mich nit me leren. . . .

161. I exclude Dante for the moment—a supreme poet with mystical elements in his writings, but not a mystic. Most authors who have treated Mechthild comment briefly on the role of poetry in her work. For helpful studies, see Alois M. Haas, "Mechthild von Magdeburg. Dichtung und Mystik," in *Sermo mysticus,* pp. 67–103; and "Mechthilds von Magdeburg dichterische *heimlichkeit,*" in *Gottes und der werlde hulde,* pp. 206–23; Hans-Georg Kemper, "Allegorische Allegorese," in *Formen und Funktionen der Allegorie,* pp. 90–125; and Ruh, *Geschichte,* 2:258–61.

162. Haas surveys some of the literature (*Sermo mysticus,* pp. 99–103 and 128–35).

163. Hans Urs von Balthasar puts it thus in commenting on the poetry of John of the Cross: "The center of the mystic act is beyond the center of the poetic act. The center of the latter is on the periphery of the former, even though the poem is conceived in the more secret womb of mystical experience; the poem is the echo of the experience, testifying and referring and pressing back into it" (*The Glory of the Lord: A Theological Aesthetics* [San Francisco: Ignatius, 1984], 3:126).

164. See Wiethaus, *Ecstatic Transformation,* pp. 26–28, making use of the research of Tillmann, *Studien zum Dialog.*

165. Kemper, "Allegorische Allegorese," pp. 92–96. The first illustration that Kemper uses, the erotic dialogue in FL 3.3 (80.2-81.27) based on Song 8:14 and 2:4, can be compared to the way in which Bernard of Clairvaux discussed the connection between the biblical book and the book of experience (see *Growth of Mysticism,* pp. 185–86). Nevertheless, Bernard's *literary* exposition usually adheres to the standard procedures of biblical allegorical exegesis, following these with an appeal to experience, whereas in Mechthild personal experience occupies the foreground throughout.

166. FL 4.12 (127.107): Mere ie ich tieffer sinke, / ie ich suesser trinke. For other examples of such closure, see, e.g., 1.4, 4.5, 5.4. Sometimes, the heightened emotional summary comes in the middle of a chapter, e.g., 2.3, 2.4, 3.1, 3.5, 7.8, often as part of a dialogue.

167. FL 2.15 (48): Swelch mensche wirt ze einer stunt / von der warer minne reht wunt, / der wirt niemer me wol gesunt, / er enkússe noch den selben munt, / von dem sin sel ist worden wunt (my translation with an attempt to convey the poetic form of the original).

168. Wiethaus, *Ecstatic Transformation,* p. 43.

169. Of course, Mechthild often says that her experience of God is inexpressible, as do all mystics (see, e.g., FL 2.19, 2.25, 3.1, 5.12, 6.39, 6.40 and 7.25).

170. This point has been emphasized by Haas, *Sermo mysticus,* pp. 82–83; and *Die deutsche*

Literatur im späten Mittelalter, pp. 247, 252–53. For a collection of texts, see Lüers, *Die Sprache der deutschen Mystik,* pp. 278–85.

171. FL 7.25 (275.2–12): . . . so gruos ich di hoehin, . . . die wunderlichen einunge der heligen drivaltekeit, da alles das us gevlossen ist unbewollen, das do was, das ist, das iemer wesen sol, da muos ich ie wider in. Wie sol mir das geschehen? Ich muos wider kriechen, wan ich schuldig bin. . . . Ich muos vliegen mit tubenvreden. . . . Ich muos sweben an allen dingen über mich selber; als ich allermuedest bin, so kumme ich wider in . . . . Gloria tibi trinitas! (my italics). Mechthild often refers to the soul as a dove (e.g., 1.11, 1.14–15, 1.18, 1.34, 2.17, 2.24, 3.23, 5.11, and 5.31).

172. Mechthild has a wide range of unusual images for the Trinity that cannot be taken up here. In FL 2.3 (39.14) the Trinity is compared to a crossbow; in 2.3 (40.23–25) to musical harmony (cf. 3.9). FL 2.24 (59.17–34) pictures the Trinity as chalice-bearer, chalice, and wine (cf. 5.25). For a sketch of Mechthild's teaching on the Trinity, see Margot Schmidt, "'die spilende minnevluot': Der Eros als Sein und Wirkkraft in der Trinität bei Mechthild von Magdeburg," in *"Eine Höhe über die nichts geht": Spezielle Glaubenserfahrung in der Frauenmystik,* ed. Margot Schmidt and Dieter R. Bauer (Stuttgart/Bad Canstatt: frommann-holzboog, 1986), pp. 80–89; and Frank Tobin, "Mechthild of Magdeburg and Meister Eckhart," in *Meister Eckhart and the Beguine Mystics,* pp. 52–56.

173. Note that *gotheit* usually signifies the Father in Mechthild, but because all three persons are one divinity, *gotheit* can also be ascribed to the Son (e.g., FL 7.1; ed., 256.93).

174. FL 5.26 (186.8–21): Ich bin ein usvliessende brunne, den nieman mag verstoppfen, aber der mensche mag villihte sin herze selber mit eime unnützen gedank verstoppfen, das dú ungeruewige gotheit, dú iemer mere arbeitet ane arbeit, nit in sin sele mag vliessen. . . . Ich bin ein widerkomende richtuom, den nieman behalten mag, wan alleine dú ie gevlos und iemer gevliessen sol von gotte, du kumt alles wider mit sime sune. . . . Ich bin ein unúberwunden kraft der warheit. . . . Ich bin also stark an miner ungescheidenheit, das mich gescheiden nieman mag noch zerbrechen an miner ganzen ewekeit (Tobin translation slightly modified). Although Mechthild does not apply the language of flowing directly to the Holy Spirit here, it is found in many other passages (see, e.g., FL 2.3, 3.1, 5.11, 7.1, 7.24, and especially 6.32; ed. 240.8–9). There are a number of other places where Mechthild speaks directly of the trinitarian flowing into itself; e.g., FL 3.1 (75.68–72), where the three persons are seen in terms of circumincessive light, and 3.9 (86.1–10).

175. For this aspect of Mechthild's teaching on the soul, see Sonja A. Buholzer, *Studien zur Gottes- und Seelenkonzeption im Werk der Mechthild von Magdeburg* (Bern/Frankfurt: Peter Lang, 1988), chap. 1 and the summary on pp. 177–81.

176. Images of light and radiance are perhaps as prevalent as those of flowing in the FL and often interact with them. For some major appearances of light imagery, see, e.g., 1.22, 2.2–3, 2.7, 2.19, 3.9, 3.12, 3.20–21, 3.24, 4.3, 5.1, 5.27, 5.31, 6.39, 7.7, 7.27, 7.32 and 7.63.

177. FL 6.41 (250.6–11): . . . ein spiegel wart gesehen in dem himmelriche vor der brust einer ieglichen sele und lip. Dar in schinet der spiegel der heligen drivaltekeit und git warheit und bekantnisse aller der tugenden, die der lip ie begieng, und aller der gabe, die dú sele in ertrich ie enpfieng. Da von schinet der here gegenblik von einer ieglichen persone wider in der hohen majestat, da si usgevlossen hat. The motif of the mirror is richly developed by Mechthild. FL 6.16 and 7.1 (226.20, 257.107) are like 6.41 in identifying the Trinity as an "eternal mirror," and the same appears to be the case in 3.11 (91.1). In 3.1 (75.69), however, the *spiegel* is the *gotheit* of the Father. In 7.7 (263.16–17) *goetlichen bekantnisse* is a "clear mirror," and in 7.17 and 18 (269.56 and 271.32–33) Jesus Christ is the mirror, both for Lady Conscience and for the Eternal Father. Finally, in 7.14 (267.7–10) Mechthild, like Clare of Assisi (see p. 69), sees the nuns of her community as mirrors both here and hereafter.

178. FL 1.22 (16.4–5): Der suosse tove der unbeginlicher drivaltikeit hat sich gesprenget us dem brunnen der ewigen gotheit in den bluomen der userwelten maget. . . . Cf. 6.39 (248–49).

179. On Mechthild's teaching that her soul, and all souls, participate in the Trinity through its overflowing goodness, see, e.g., FL 4.12, 5.6, 6.8, 6.32, and 6.37.

180. The most important texts are FL 1.22, 3.9, and 4.14 (16–19, 86–89, and 127–29).

181. FL 1.22 (18.35–40): Eya, wa wart únser loser brútgovm? In dem jubilus der heligen drivaltikeit, do got nit me mohte sich enthalten in sich selben, do mahte er die sele und gab sich ir ze eigen von grosser liebe. . . . Du hast gesprochen von minem aneginne, nu sage ich dir werlich: Ich bin in der selben stat gemachet von der minne. . . . (Tobin translation altered). It is interesting that Mechthild uses the term *iubilus*, the ecstatic song ascribed to women mystics, for the inner delight of the Trinity.

182. For more on the importance of Mary, see, e.g., FL 2.3, 5.23, and 6.39 (39–41, 174–81, and 248–49). On the role of Mary in Mechthild's thought, see Buholzer, *Studien zur Gottes- und Seelenkonzeption,* pp. 165–71.

183. FL 3.9 (87.50–88.52): Ich bin got aller goetten, du bist aller creaturen goettinne und ich gibe dir mine hanttrúwe, das ich niemer verkiese. . . .

184. FL 4.14 (128.18–20): Die selber ander persone was ein nature worden mit Adames menscheit, e er sich verboesete mit den súnden. This teaching, which scholastic theology speaks of as the eternal predestination of Christ, is also suggested in Hadewijch and later found explicitly in Julian of Norwich.

185. Ibid. (128.27–28): Der mensche hat volle nature in der heiligen drivaltikeit, und die geruochte got ze machende mit sinen goetlichen henden.

186. Mechthild, however, thought that the bodies given to Adam and Eve were different from the deformed bodies we now possess; see FL 3.9 (87.40–49).

187. Ibid. (129.42–44): Da spilet ovge in ovge und da flússet geist in geiste und da rueret hant ze hande und da sprichet munt ze munde und da gruesset hertz in hertzen. Alsus eret der wirt bi siner siten die husfrovwen (Tobin translation modified). There is a comparable passage in FL 2.25 (67.131–68.139).

188. For more on Mechthild's understanding of the body, see Hollywood, *The Soul as Virgin Wife,* pp. 23–25, 73–86.

189. FL 6.31 (238–40). In 6.36 (244–45) Mechthild also defends herself against someone who had attacked her vision of John the Baptist saying Mass (see 2.4). On these texts, see my forthcoming article "Visions and Critiques of Visions in Late Medieval Mysticism."

190. Ibid. (239.28–240.32): Rehte ze glicher wis als eni clot und allú ding waren in gotte besclossen ane sclos und ane túr. Das niderste teil des klotes das its ein grundelosú vestenunge beniden allú abgrúnde, das oberste teil des clotes das ist ein hoehi, da nút úber ist, das umbezil des clotes das ist ein cirkel unbegriffenlich. The notion of God as an infinite sphere has an ancient pedigree, on which see Dietrich Mahncke, *Unendliche Sphäre und Allmittelpunkt: Beiträge zur Genealogie der mathematischen Mystik* (Halle, 1937). Mechthild's description is related to the noted second proposition of the *Liber XXIV Philosophorum* cited by theologians as early as Alan of Lille (see *Theol. reg.* 7 in PL 210:627A): Deus est sphaera intelligibilis cuius centrum est ubique et circumferentia nusquam. On Mechthild's use of the image, see Margetts, "Latein und Volkssprache bei Mechthild," pp. 129–36.

191. On the contemporary church and its apocalyptic future, see especially FL 4.3, 4.27, 6.15, 6.21 and 6.26.

192. For some treatments, see Margot Schmidt, "'minne dú gewaltige kellerin.' On the Nature of *minne* in Mechthild of Magdeburg's *fliessende licht der gottheit,*" *Vox Benedictina* 4 (1987): 100–125; Newman, *From Virile Woman to WomanChrist,* pp. 143–58; and Ruh,

Geschichte, 2:261–75 (who cautions against overemphasizing the courtly dimension to Mechthild's eroticism on p. 288).

193. Gooday, "Mechthild of Magdeburg and Hadewijch of Antwerp," p. 321, estimates that Hadewijch uses *minne* over two thousand times, while Mechthild mentions it around five hundred times. Important treatments of *minne* can be found in many chapters of the FL, especially 1.1–5, 1.17, 1.28, 1.44, 1.46, 2.2, 2.6, 2.15, 2.22–25, 3.3, 3.5, 3.9–10, 4.5, 4.12, 4.15–16, 4.19, 5.4, 5.25, 5.30–31, 5.35, 6.1, 6.20, 6.25–26, 6.30, 7.7, 7.15–16, 7.24, 7.27, 7.31, 7.37, 7.45, 7.48, 7.55 and 7.61.

194. FL 2.19 (49.5–8): Du bist drivaltig an dir, du maht wol gottes bilde sin: Du bist ein menlich man an dinem strite, du bist ein wolgezieret juncfrovwe in dem palast vor dinem herren, du bist ein lustlichú brut in dinem minnebette gottes! (Tobin translation modified). The virile image, as we have seen, is also strong in Hadewijch.

195. Mohr claims: "Dies geistliches Buch der Mechthild ist vielleicht die kühnste erotische Dichtung, die wir aus dem Mittelalter besitzen" ("Darbietungsformen," p. 393).

196. Haas puts it this way: "Sie [Mechthild] interpretiert nicht mehr das Hohelied, sie erfährt es wie Hadewijch" (*Die deutsche Literatur im späten Mittelalter,* p. 250).

197. FL 2.22 (55.16–56.22): . . . den werdesten engel Jhesum Christum, der da swebet oben Seraphim, der mit sinem vatter ein ungeteilet got muos sin. Den nim ich minstú sele in den arm min und isse und trinke in und tuon mit im, swas ich wil. Das mag den engeln niemer geschehen. Wie hohe er wonet ob mir, sin gotheit mir niemer so túre, ich muosse ir ane underlas allú gelide volbewinden; so mag ich niemer mere erkuolen. Of course, the soul does have to "cool down," as we shall see below; but in the ecstatic moment this cannot be envisaged. The language of heating and cooling is frequent in Mechthild (e.g., FL 1.44, 3.23, 4.12 and 5.4).

198. FL 5.25 (185.23–29): . . . ich mag ir nút vollen heimlich wesen, si well sich rehte muessig und blos an minen goetlichen arm legen, und das ich muos mit ir spilen. Wan darumbe han ich mich in ir gewalt geben, . . . und si sol iemer me in miner heligen drivaltikeit mit sele und mit libe sweben und spilen sat und ertrinken als der visch in dem mere. The image of the fish in the sea to describe the soul's delight in God was also seen in Beatrice's *Seven Manners of Loving* (see p. 173).

199. FL 7.16 (268.5–7): Ich habe din begert e der beginne. Ich gere din und du begerest min. Wa zwoei heisse begerunge zesamen koment, da ist die minne vollekomen.

200. See, e.g., FL 1.3, 2.24, 2.25, 3.5, 3.9, 7.18, and 7.58.

201. In FL 1.4 (10.4–8) Christ places the bride into his glowing heart so that they embrace and attain a union in which "she turns to nothing and is transported out of herself" (*so wirt si ze nihte und kumet von ir selben*). In the union described in 2.6 (45.1–11) God says to the soul: *Swen du súfzest, so zúhest du min goetlich herze in dich.*

202. The *brutbette* is a frequent image in FL, e.g., 1.3, 1.19, 1.44, 2.2, 2.19, 2.23, 2.25, 3.9, 3.10, 5.11, 5.34, 6.1, 7.30, etc.

203. FL 1.44 (27–33). In the presentation of this text, I will use Tobin's translation, with a few modifications. The term "spiritual sexuality" is suggested by Ulrich Müller, "Mechthild von Magdeburg und Dantes Vita Nova oder erotische Religiosität und religiöse Erotik," in *Liebe als Literatur: Aufsätze zur erotischen Dichtung in Deutschland,* ed. Rüdiger Krohn (Munich, 1983), pp. 163–76.

204. Many students of Mechthild have commented on this chapter. For a recent treatment, see Ruh, *Geschichte,* 2:264–68.

205. In FL 7.37 (286) Christ is described as a fair youth of about eighteen years of age.

206. Ibid. (27.14–28.22). Images of clothing and unclothing play an important role in the FL. The soul must prepare itself for God by clothing itself with the virtues, but must also be

ready to strip itself naked for ultimate union. Proper stripping, however, involves a paradoxical reclothing in the nakedness of the crucified Christ. Besides FL 1.44, see, e.g., 2.23, 3.1, 5.25, and 6.1. For a study, see the unpublished paper of Patricia Zimmerman Beckman, "Ritual Clothing and Nakedness in Mechthild of Magdeburg's Journey to Mystical Union."

207. Ibid. (29.36–37): Unde muos der jungeling singen alsus: "Dur mich in dich und dur dich von mir." "Gerne mit dir, noete von dir."

208. Ibid. (30.68–31.74): Der visch mag in dem wasser nit ertrinken, / der vogel mag in dem luft nit versinken, / das golt mag in dem fúre nit verberben, / . . . wie moehte ich denne miner nature widerstan? / Ich mueste von allen dingen in got gan, / der min vater ist von nature, / min bruoder von siner moenscheit, / min brútegovm von minnen / und ich sin brut ane anegenge.

209. Ibid. (32.90–92): So geschihet da ein selig stilli / nach ir beider willen. / Er gibet sich ir / und si git sich ime. / Was it nu geschehe, das weis si, / und des getroeste ich mich. Note again, the splitting of the voices of the soul and Mechthild as narrator, as in FL 1.2. The play closes with an allusion to the brevity of the mystical experience.

210. See Lüers, *Die Sprache der deutschen Mystik,* pp. 308–9, for some examples.

211. On the divine *gruos,* see, e.g., FL 1.2 (7.1–8), 1.5 (11.11), 1.14 (14.1), 2.3 (39.1–12), 4.2 (110.12), 5.18 (169.1), 6.1 (204.106), and 6.39 (249.5). William Seaton in "Transforming of Convention in Mechthild of Magdeburg," *Mystics Quarterly* 10 (1984): 64–72, notes that having the Divine Lover bestow the *gruos* subverts the conventions of courtly literature.

212. A number of traditional theological issues concerning *unio mystica* could be taken up with regard to Mechthild, but the genius of her mystical teaching is scarcely to be captured through the exploration of such issues. Among these is the relation of love and knowledge in union, where the beguine teaches the continuing importance of *bekantnisse,* or the *intelligentia amoris,* in consciousness of God. See, e.g., FL 1.21, 1.44 (28.32–29.35), 2.19, 4.2 (110.26–111.39), 5.4 (156.24–157.41), and 7.8. Mechthild, like other contemporary mystics, was also concerned with false views of mystical union. In the late text FL 7.47 (292–93) she attacks those who claim that "they shall enter into the eternal Godhead" (*das si sich in die ewigen gotheit wellen ziehen*), but who neglect "the eternal humanity [i.e., of Christ] that hovers in the eternal Godhead" (*du entbekentest ovch die ewigen menscheit, die da swebet in der ewigen gotheit*).

213. These are two of the three metaphors that occur in a passage in Bernard of Clairvaux's *De diligendo Deo* 10.27 (*Sancti Bernardi Opera* 3:143), but they were widely used and there is no need to think that Mechthild may have actually read the Cistercian.

214. Besides the passage in FL 1.44 cited above (*ir sint so sere genatúrt in mich*), see, e.g., FL 2.6 (45.7), where Mechthild speaks of becoming "one being" with God (*so werden wir zwoei ein sin*); cf. 2.25 (64.52–54).

215. FL 6.1 (203.80–83): Swenne der mensche bettet in cristanem gelovben mit einem also demuetigem herzen, das er enkein creature beniden im enmag erliden, und mit also ellendiger sele, das im allú ding muessent entwichen in sime gebette ane got alleine, so ist er ein goetlich got mit dem himmelschen vatter. Mechthild's language of detachment (*ellendiger sele*) is different from that later employed by Meister Eckhart. This should not be taken to imply all lack of connection between Mechthild and Eckhart. See Frank Tobin, "Mechthild of Magdeburg and Meister Eckhart," in *Meister Eckhart and the Beguine Mystics,* pp. 44–61; and Bardo Weiss, "Mechthild von Magdeburg und der frühe Meister Eckhart," *Theologie und Philosophie* 70 (1995): 1–40.

216. Ibid. (204.87–103): Swenne aber der mensche erbeit in rehter nutz durch ware not mit der selben liebin, da er mitte gebettet hat, so ist er ein menschliche got mit Christo. . . . Swenne alleine der mensche dur gottes liebi und nit mit irdensche miete den tumben leret und den súnden bekeret und den betruebten troestet und den verzwivelten wider zuo gotte

bringen, so ist er ein geistlich got mit dem heligen geist . . . so ist er ein gantz persone mit der heligen drivaltikeit . . . so wirt si denne mit got ein got, also das er wil, das wil si und si moegent anders nit vereinet sin mit ganzer einunge (Tobin translation modified). For some other texts on the trinitarian character of mystical union, see, e.g., FL 2.22, 3.9, 3.15, 4.8, 4.12, 6.32, and 6.39.

217. FL 7.3 (260.17–19): Din kintheit was ein gesellinne mines heligen geistes; din jugent was ein brut miner menscheit; din alter ist nu ein housvrovwe miner gotheit. Note again the trinitarian structure.

218. FL 6.20 (229.3–230.13): Dise gabe, die in disem buoche stat geschriben, di hat mir got in drier hande wise geben. Allerest mit grosser zartekeit, da nach mit hoher heimelicheit, nu mit sweren pinen; da wil ich gerner inne bliben denne in den andern zwein. . . . Aber der minne nature ist, das si allerest vlússet von suessekeit, dar nach wirt si riche in der bekantnisse, zem dritten male wirt si girig in der verworfenheit (Tobin translation modified).

219. FL 7.45 (291.14–15): . . . das ist die spilende minnevluot, die von got heimlich in die sele vlússet und si wider mit siner kraft nach ir maht. The hapax legomenon *spilende minnevluot* has been studied by Schmidt, "'die spilende minnvluot': Der Eros als Sein und Wirkkraft," pp. 74–80. As Frank Tobin has reminded me, the verb *spilen* in Middle High German also has the sense of light shimmering, or "playing," on a surface, so the phrase might also be rendered "the shimmering flood of love."

220. The notion of a sinking love that flows down in humility appears in Richard of St. Victor's *De quatuor gradibus violentae caritatis* 39 and 42 (see *Ives: Épitre à Severin sur la charité. Richard de Saint-Victoire: Les quatre dégres de la violent charité*, ed. Gervais Dumeige [Paris: Vrin, 1955], pp. 167, 171), but Mechthild's mode of developing the theme appears original.

221. FL 4.12 (123–27). This aspect of Mechthild's mysticism has been well treated by Haas, *Sermo mysticus*, pp. 91–99 and 113–19; Ruh, *Geschichte*, 2:270–75; and Buholzer, *Studien zur Gottes- und Seelenkonzeption*, pp. 158–60.

222. This tension will be overcome at the time of the resurrection of the body, as Mechthild beautifully expresses it in FL 6.35 (243–44).

223. In FL 4.13 (127) Mechthild insists that the entire work of the writing of her book springs from an experience involving both the spiritual and the bodily senses: Ich enkan noch mag nit schriben, ich sehe es mit den ovgen minere sele und hoer es mit den oren mines ewigen geistes und bevinde in allen liden mines lichamen die kraft des heiligen geistes. On the role of the spiritual senses in Mechthild, especially the central sense of taste, see Schmidt, "Elemente der Schau bei Mechthild von Magdeburg und Mechthild von Hackeborn: Zur Bedeutung der geistlichen Sinne," in *Frauenmystik im Mittelalter*, pp. 123–51.

224. Ibid. (123.22–23): Mir smekket nit wan alleine got, / ich bin wunderliche tot. Appeal to the *mors mystica* is frequent in Mechthild; see FL 1.2, 1.3, 1.28, 3.23, 4.19, 5.25, 6.26, and 7.21. For Mechthild's place in the tradition, see Alois M. Haas, "Mors mystica–Ein mystologisches Motiv," in *Sermo mysticus*, pp. 446–49.

225. FL 4.12 (124.45–47): Do sprach únser herre: "Wie lange wilt du hie wesen?" / Die brut sprach: "Eya, entwich mir, lieber herre, und la mich fúrbas sinken durch din ere."

226. Ibid. (125.65–69): Hie nach kam die stete vroemedunge gottes und bevieng die sele so sere alumbe, das dú selig sele sprach: "Siest willekomen, vil selig vroemedunge, wol mir das ich ie geboren wart, das du, vrovwe, nu min kamererin solt sin; wan du bringest mir ungewone vroede und unbegrifflich wunder und dar zuo ungetreglich suessekeit. Aber, herre, die suessekeit solt du von mir legen und la mich dine vroemedunge han."

227. Ibid. (125.76–77): . . . nu mir sine vroemedunge bekemer ist denne er selber si.

228. Mechthild loves mountain symbolism, often speaking of Christ as a mountain; see, e.g., FL 2.21, 3.15, 4.3, 4.18, 5.24, and 6.21.

229. Ibid. (157.32–41): Die minnenreiche sele sinket harnider in dem zuge der ungruntlichen diemuetekeit und wichet ie vor dem, was ir got ze liebe tuot .... der licham sinket ovch vil sere, wenne er sinem viande dienet. ... Die sele sinket noch fúrbas, wan si merer maht hat denne der licham. Si sinket mit grossem vlisse in die nidersten stat, di got in siner gewalt hat. O, wie getar ich dise stat den nemmen, die der sinkenden diemuetekeit nit erkennent.

230. Ruh (*Geschichte*, 2:286–88) suggests that Mechthild depends on Wichmann of Arnstein for this metaphor.

231. Unlike other thirteenth-century mystics, Mechthild uses the abyss (*abgrunde*) as a negative image of the depths of hell (e.g., FL 1.8, 3.1, 3.7, 3.21, 5.34, 6.16, 7.18).

232. FL 3.10 (89–91). For this passage, see 89.5–6: Si wirt gevangen in der ersten kúnde, / so got si kússet mit suesser einunge. A comparable text, emphasizing how the sisters of Helta participate in the mysteries of Christ's death and resurrection, can be found in FL 7.53 (299–300).

233. Ibid. (90.26–40): Si treit ir crúze in einem suessen wege, wenne si sich gotte werlich in allen pinen gibet. Ir hovbt wirt gesclagen mit einem rore, wenne man ir grosse helikeit glichet einem tore. Si wirt an dem crútze so vaste genegelt mit dem hammer der starken minnlovffe, das si alle creaturen nit moegent wider gerueffen. ... Si hanget ovch hoch in dem suessen luft des heligen geistes gegen der ewigen sunnen der lebendigen gotheit an dem crútze der hohen minne, das si vollen dúrre wirt von allen irdischen dinge (Tobin translation slightly modified).

234. For more on the role of the passion in the FL, see 1.28–29, 2.3, 2.24, 3.2, 3.9, 4.2, 5.24, 5.34, 6.24, 6.31, 6.37, 7.1, 7.11, 7.26, and 7.35.

235. FL 1.35 (24–25): Du solt minnen das niht, / du solt vliehen das iht, / du solt alleine stan / und solt zuo nieman gan. / Du solt nit sere unmuessig sin / und von allen dingen wesen vri. / Du solt die gevangenen enbinden, / und die vrien twingen. / Du solt die siechen laben / und du solt doch selbe nit haben. / Du solt das wasser der pine trinken / und das fúr der minne mit dem holtz der tugende entzúnden: / So wonestu in der waren wuestenunge. Mechthild's other uses of the desert motif (e.g., FL 2.23, 6.2, and 7.53) do not go beyond standard twelfth-century understanding of the desert as the soul ready to receive Christ. Here, by using the desert in conjunction with the language of *iht* and *niht*, she at least suggests the divine desert motif that was employed by Thomas Gallus and later Meister Eckhart. (For a comparison of Mechthild and Eckhart on the desert, see Tobin, "Mechthild of Magdeburg and Meister Eckhart," pp. 48–51.) On Mechthild's sense of the necessity of service of others and loving God in creatures, see, e.g., FL 5.8, 5.35, and 6.5. The atmosphere of peaceful detachment found in this early text should be compared with those texts, such as FL 6.26 and 7.64, in which the aged Mechthild accepts her failing powers and dependence on others and looks forward to death.

236. The most recent general account of Marguerite Porete is Ruh, *Geschichte*, 2:338–66, summarizing a number of his previous studies. Among important recent accounts in English, see Michael A. Sells, *Mystical Languages of Unsaying*, chaps. 5 and 7; Amy Hollywood, *The Soul as Virgin Wife*, chaps. 4 and 7; and the papers by Sells, Hollywood, and Maria Lichtmann in part 2 of *Meister Eckhart and the Beguine Mystics*. My own study of Porete has been enriched by the privilege I have had of directing five Ph.D. dissertations relating to the beguine's thought, those of Ellen Babinsky, Amy Hollywood, Stephanie Paulsell, Joanne Maguire, and Robin O'Sullivan.

237. In 1946 Romana Guarnieri identified Latin manuscripts of the *Mirror* in the Vatican as the supposedly lost book of Marguerite. Guarnieri went on to edit the surviving Middle French text from one manuscript in "Il movimento del Libero Spirito: II, Il 'Miroir des sim-

ples ames' di Margherita Porete," *Archivio italiano per la storia della pietà* 4 (1965): 501–708. This text was reprinted, along with an edition of the Latin text by Paul Verdeyen, in *Marguerete Porete: Le Mirouer des Simples Ames,* CCCM 69 (Turnholt: Brepols, 1986). There is a modern English translation: *Marguerite Porete: The Mirror of Simple Souls,* translated and introduced by Ellen L. Babinsky (New York: Paulist Press, 1993). I will cite from the Guarnieri-Verdeyen edition with chapter followed by page and line numbers in parentheses. I will use the Babinsky translation, unless otherwise noted.

238. Contrast, for example, Edmund Colledge, who emphasizes Porete's heretical status ("Liberty of Spirit: 'The Mirror of Simple Souls,'" in *Theology of Renewal,* ed. L. K. Shook, 2 vols. [Montreal: n.p., 1968], pp. 100–117), with Jean Orcibal, who presents a more moderate evaluation ("'Le Miroir des simples ames' et la 'secte' du Libre Esprit," *Revue de l'Histoire des Religions* 175 [1969]: 35–60). More helpful is the approach of Eleanor McLaughlin, who argues that the "heretics"–at least those attacked by the Inquisition, like Marguerite–shared a common spirituality with orthodox mystics, and thus *The Mirror* is both orthodox and "Free Spirit" ("The Heresy of the Free Spirit and Late Medieval Mysticism," *Medievalia et Humanistica* n.s. 4 [1973]: 37–54).

239. See "Marguerite Porete, 'The Mirror of Simple Souls': A Middle English Translation," ed. Marion Dorion, *Archivio italiano per la storia della pietà* 5 (1968): 247.

240. This is not the place to enter into a full discussion of Marguerite's sources, though some comments will be made where appropriate. Like all vernacular theologians, she does not cite *auctoritates* in the manner of scholastic theology; but anyone who reads, for example, chap. 115 (308–9) on the Trinity, cannot fail to appreciate how deeply grounded Marguerite was in traditional Latin theology, especially Augustine, the Cistercians (Bernard and William), and Richard of St. Victor.

241. The documents concerning Porete's trial and execution were first edited in Paul Fredericq, *Corpus Documentorum Inquisitionis Haereticae Pravitatis Neerlandicae,* 1:63–65 and 155–60, but a more complete edition can be found in Paul Verdeyen, "Le procès d'Inquisition contre Marguerite Porete et Guiard de Cressonessart (1309–1310)," *Revue d'histoire ecclésiastique* 81 (1986): 48–94. The best study of the trial and its effect is that of Robert E. Lerner, *The Heresy of the Free Spirit in the Later Middle Ages* (Berkeley: University of California Press, 1972), pp. 68–84 (cf. pp. 200–208). See also Lerner, "An Angel of Philadelphia in the Reign of Philip the Fair: The Case of Guiard of Cressonessart," in *Order and Innovation in the Middle Ages: Essays in Honor of Joseph R. Strayer,* ed. William C. Jordan, Bruce McNab, and Teofilo F. Ruiz (Princeton: Princeton University Press, 1976), pp. 343–64.

242. Their *approbatio* survives in the Latin and Middle English versions of the text and can be found as chap. 140 (404–9). Two of the three evaluators cautioned that the book should be restricted in readership. Brother John (apparently an honest man) allowed that the book was so deep that he had not been able to understand it (407.18–19)!

243. According to the document of condemnation issued by the Paris theologians on April 11, 1310, the first article read: Quod anima adnichilata dat licentiam virtutibus nec est amplius in earum servitute, quia non habet eas quoad usum, sed virtutes obediunt ad nutum (see *Mirror,* chap. 8 [29.1–14]). The final article read: Quod talis anima non curat de consolationibus Dei nec de donis eius, nec debet curare nec potest, quia tota intenta est circa Deum, et sic impediretur eius intentio circa Deum (see chap. 16 [66.21–22]; cf. chap. 85 [242.20f.]). A third article, contained in the *Continuatio Chronici Guillielmi de Nangiaco,* reads: Quod anima annihilata in amore conditoris sine reprehensione conscientiae vel remorsu potest et debet naturae quidquid appetit et desiderat (concedere) (see chaps. 9 and 17 [32.21–22 and 68.1f.]). [For these articles, see Verdeyen, "Le procès," pp. 51 and 88.] Attempts to identify the other articles seem questionable, including those advanced by Edmund Colledge and Romana

Guarnieri, "The Glosses by 'M.N.' and Richard Methley to 'The Mirror of Simple Souls,'" *Archivio italiano per la storia della pietà* 5 (1968): 357–82.

244. Any careful reading of Marguerite's *Mirror* will suffice to show that she can scarcely be accused of antinomianism. To use the seventeenth-century term "quietism" of a thirteenth-century beguine, of course, is anachronistic, but the indifference to all external religious works that was condemned in the case of Miguel de Molinos in 1687 had a prefigurement in some of Porete's language about the annihilated soul's attitude toward prayer and the sacraments and even the desire for salvation. See, e.g., chaps. 9, 41, 69, 81, 85, and 90.

245. Cited in Verdeyen, "Le procès," p. 89: Multa tamen in suo exitu poenitentiae signa ostendit nobilia pariter et devota, per quae multorum viscera ad compatiendum ei pie ac etiam lacrymabiliter fuisse commota testati sunt oculi qui viderunt.

246. See Grundmann, *Religious Movements in the Middle Ages,* chaps. 6–7.

247. See Lerner, *The Heresy of the Free Spirit,* pp. 68–84; Verdeyen, "Le procès," pp. 76–77 and 84–86.

248. The text of the *Compilatio de novo spiritu* was edited by Wilhelm Preger in his *Geschichte der deutschen Mystik,* 1:461–69. For an account of the heresy, see Grundmann, *Religious Movements,* pp. 170–86; and Lerner, *The Heresy of the Free Spirit,* pp. 13–19.

249. The sixth of the eight articles constituting *Ad nostrum* refers to being freed from the virtues and almost certainly reflects article 1 from the list against Marguerite. Article 8 of *Ad nostrum* condemns the view that one should not disturb one's contemplative state to show reverence to the Eucharist, a position not unlike that found in art. 15 in Marguerite's list, though there the eucharistic reference is lacking. Article 2 of *Ad nostrum* attacks the view that the perfect person "can freely give the body whatever it wants," a position close to the article cited in William of Nangis's *Chronicon* that was apparently drawn from *Mirror,* chap. 17. Finally, *Ad nostrum* art. 3 condemns those adepts of freedom who claim they are not subject to human obedience or the church's precepts, something that might reflect Porete's attitude toward "Holy Church the Little." As Robert Lerner notes (*Heresy of the Free Spirit,* p. 83), the first article of *Ad nostrum* condemning the possibility of impeccability may echo the view attacked in Albert's *Compilatio* #94.

250. Jacqueline Tarrant shows that the council mentioned the beguines only in passing and that the partial condemnation of the movement was a work of postconciliar revision of the documents, one that was qualified by John XXII in his bull *Recta ratio* ("The Clementine Decrees on the Beguines: Conciliar and Papal Versions," *Archivum Historiae Pontificiae* 12 [1974]: 300–307).

251. None of these versions represents the beguine's original Old French text. Modern scholarship has tended to favor the Middle French version probably done after 1370 and today found only in a fifteenth-century manuscript from Cambrai (there are two lost French manuscripts), but the Latin version present in six manuscripts often gives better readings, and so I have not hesitated to employ both the French and the Latin in my citations. Two Italian translations were based on the Latin, while the Middle English translation seems based on the Middle French. The Middle English was later translated into a second Latin version. For a brief account, see Povl Skarup, "La langue du *Miroir des simples âmes* attribué à Marguerite Porete," *Studia Neophilologica* 60 (1988): 231–36. For studies of the Middle English version, see Michael Sargent, "'Le Mirouer des simples âmes' and the English Mystical Tradition," in *Abendländischer Mystik im Mittelalter,* pp. 443–65; and Nicholas M. Watson, "Melting into God the English Way: Deification in the Middle English Version of Marguerite Porete's *Mirouer des simples âmes anienties,*" in *Prophets Abroad: The Reception of Continental Holy Women in Late-Medieval England* (Cambridge: Brewer, 1996), pp. 19–49.

252. The Middle English version comes equipped with explanatory glosses by an

unknown "M.N." to show the proper interpretation of difficult passages. The use of the book in fifteenth-century Italy provoked attacks by the Observantine Franciscans and at the Council of Basle, on which see Ruh, *Geschichte,* 2:346. We can also note that Jean Gerson attacked a *Maria de Valenciennes,* almost certainly Marguerite, in his treatise *De distinctione verarum revelationum a falsis;* see *Jean Gerson: Oeuvres completes,* ed. J. Glorieux (Desclée: Paris, 1962), 3:51–52.

253. See Edmund Colledge and J. C. Marler, "'Poverty of Will': Ruusbroec, Eckhart and *The Mirror of Simple Souls,*" in *Jan van Ruusbroec: The sources, content and sequels of his mysticism,* pp. 14–47.

254. See the papers in *Meister Eckhart and the Beguine Mystics,* part 2.

255. On the "courtly" character of *The Mirror,* see Newman, *From Virile Woman to WomanChrist,* chap. 5; and Ellen Louise Babinsky, "The Use of Courtly Language in *Le Mirouer des simples ames anienties* by Marguerite Porete," *Essays in Medieval Studies* 4 (1987): 93-106, and more fully in her "A Beguine in the Court of the King: The Relation of Love and Knowledge in 'The Mirror of Simple Souls' by Marguerite Porete" (Ph.D. diss., University of Chicago, 1991).

256. Like Mechthild's *Flowing Light,* Marguerite's *Mirror* also contains poetry, though in smaller doses (see chaps. 1, 86, 88, 120–22, 132, and 139). On her poetry, see Peter Dronke, *Women Writers of the Middle Ages: A Critical Study of Texts from Perpetua (d. 203) to Marguerite Porete (d. 1310),* pp. 217–28.

257. In chap. 49 (146–48) Marguerite boldly asserts that willing nothing is higher than miracles, martyrdom, and even being raptured into heaven every day to see the Trinity as Paul was (cf. 2 Cor. 12:1–6)!

258. See Ritamary Bradley, "Backgrounds to the Title 'Speculum' in Medieval Literature," *Speculum* 29 (1954): 100–115; and Herbert Grabes, *The Mutable Glass: Mirror Imagery in Titles and Texts of the Middle Ages and English Renaissance* (Cambridge: Cambridge University Press, 1982).

259. Chap. 1 (12.37–14.43): . . . mais si loing estoit de moy et moy de luy, que je ne savoie prandre confort de moy mesmes, et pour moy souvenir de lui il me donna ce livre qui represente en aucuns usages l'amour de lui mesmes. Mais non obstant que j'aye son image, n'est il pas que je no soie en estrange païs et loing du palais ouquel les tres nobles amis de ce seigneur demourent . . . (my translation). The Latin *ab illa pace* (15.42) seems the better reading, as noted by Edmund Colledge, "The New Latin *Mirror of Simple Souls,*" *Ons Geestlijk Erf* 63 (1989): 281. For important reflections on this text, see Hollywood, *The Soul as Virgin Wife,* pp. 87–91.

260. Hollywood, *The Soul as Virgin Wife,* p. 95.

261. Paul Mommaers, "La transformation d'amour selon Marguerite Porete," *Ons Geestelijk Erf* 65 (1991): 101.

262. On the effacement of the narrating voice in the dialogue, see Hollywood, *The Soul as Virgin Wife,* pp. 92–93.

263. Charles Muscatine has shown how the personification of faculties of the soul introduced a new dimension for exploring psychological conflict and growth ("The Emergence of Psychological Allegory in Old French Romance," *Publications of the Modern Language Society* 68 [1953]: 1160–72).

264. These chapters may have been composed after the first condemnation of *The Mirror* as part of the beguine's attempt to defend her teaching. Paradoxically, they contain both sections that seem to intend to relate her thought to orthodox categories and models (chaps. 123–30), as well as some of the most daring expressions of her mysticism of annihilation (chaps. 131–39).

265. See Sells, *Mystical Languages of Unsaying*, pp. 129–30, for reflections on this.

266. These insights are further developed in the unpublished paper of Nicole Lassahn, "Apophasis in Marguerite Porete: The Role of the Dialogue Form in Constructing Meaning and Un-Meaning in the *Mirouer des simples ames*." My thanks to the author for allowing me to cite this paper.

267. In chap. 94 (263.12–14) the Latin version gives Christ a speaking role, but this seems to be a confusion of the text's intention to quote a saying of Christ from John 14:12.

268. Annihilation is found everywhere in the book. For major considerations include chaps. 7, 11, 12, 13, 19, 21, 23, 25, 41, 44, 47, 51, 52, 58, 59, 68, 71, 78, 80, 82, 83, 84, 89, 91, 93, 95, 100, 101, 109, 111, 114, 115, 117, 118, 119, 122, 131, 132, 133, 135, 136, 137, 138.

269. See Hollywood, *The Soul as Virgin Wife*, pp. 113–19.

270. E.g., chaps. 13, 21, 53–59, 82, 97–98, 101, and 119.

271. Chap. 41 (131.29–30): . . . quia uerbum hoc aperit Scripturas et non possumus per rationem apprehendere quod dicit. I follow the Latin here (rather than the French "surpasses our scriptures" [seurmonte noz escriptures (130.32–33)]), because this seems to conform better with chap. 43 in which both the French (132.17–19) and the Latin (133.12–14) agree that the "glosses" (i.e., deeper understandings) of the Bible teach about the life of the superior souls. Nevertheless, in chap. 7 the French (26.9–10) and the Latin (27.9–10) say that scripture does *not* teach about the annihilated soul. (If we can understand this passage as referring to the *outward* meaning of the Bible, the contradiction would be removed; but Marguerite does not say this explicitly.) Marguerite's attitude toward the Bible deserves further study. She rarely cites the scripture explicitly (the "Index biblicus" of the edition list thirty-seven appearances), but there are many implied citations. In several chapters, Marguerite gives her own interpretation of biblical passages, sometimes quite forcefully; e.g., chaps. 94, 103–5, and 132.

272. Chap. 96 (268.20–24): Et ainsi escripsit ceste mendiant creature ce que vous oez; et voult que ses proesmes trouvassent Dieu en elle, par escrips et par paroles. C'est a dire et a entendre, qu'elle vouloit que ses proesmes fussent parfaitement ainsi comme elle les diviseroit, ay moins tous ceulx a qui elle avoit voulente de ce dire. . . .

273. Chap. 97 (270.32–34): . . . que je mectoie en pris chose que l'en ne povoit faire ne penser ne dire, aussi comme feroit celuy qui vouldroit le mer en son oeil enclorre. . . .

274. Chap. 119 (332.8–334.22): Je me excuse, dit ceste Ame, a vous toutes celles qui demourez en nient et qui estes cheues d'amour en tel estre; car j'ay fait ce livre moult grant par paroles, qui vous semble moult petit, ad ce que je vous puis cognoistre. . . . [C]ar tout ce que l'en peut de Dieu dire ne escrire, ne que l'en en peut penser, qui plus est que n'est dire, est assez mieulx mentir que ce n'est vray dire. A comparable passage about the mendacious nature of the book is found in chap. 132 (390.37–38).

275. Chap. 66 (188.15–17): . . . mais ceste leçon n'est mie mise en escript de main d'omme, mais c'est du Saint Esperit, qui escript ceste leçon merveilleusement, et l'Ame est parchemin precieusement. . . . As a gloss on this, see the discussion in chap. 117 (310–16), where the Soul that recognizes its own wretchedness by that very act compels God to fill it and thereby becomes the exemplar of the salvation of every creature (to be treated below). The image of God writing a book in the soul or heart which must then be externalized is also used by Marguerite d'Oingt (see chap. 6, pp. 289–92). For a comparison of the two, see Stephanie Paulsell, "'*Scriptio divina*': Writing and the Experience of God in the Works of Marguerite d'Oingt" (Ph.D. diss., University of Chicago, 1993), chap. 5.

276. Chap. 101 (278.19–29 and 279.18–25): Et apertio huius libri, ait haec Anima, ita clare me uidere fecit, ut quod coegit me sibi reddere quod suum est, et accipere quod est meum. Hoc est: quod ipse est; . . . Et ego non sum; ideo iustum est quod ego me non habeam. Et lumen aperturae huius libri fecit me inuenire meum et in hoc morari. Vnde non

habeo tantum de esse, quod de ipso possit mihi aliquid esse. Ita ius iure mihi meum reddidit et ostendit nude quod non sum (my translation using both the Latin and French, but closer to the former).

277. The *apertura* occurs in chaps. 58 (168.5–21), 59 (170.10–172.21) and 61 (176.2–178.18). Marguerite's teaching may reflect Gregory the Great's notion of the *rima contemplationis* (e.g., *Homily on Ezekiel* 2.5.16–19), on which see *Growth of Mysticism*, p. 67.

278. Chap. 101 (279.27–29): Ita est de me et de libro isto, dicit haec Anima, sicut fuit de Deo et de creaturis, quando eas condidit.

279. On the audience and elitism of *The Mirror* and its root in Porete's conception of the noble lineage of the annihilated souls, see Joanne Maguire, "Nobility and Annihilation in Marguerite Porete's 'Mirror of Simple Souls'" (Ph.D. diss., University of Chicago, 1996), chaps. 4 and 7.

280. See especially chaps. 13, 19, 54, and 58 (52–54, 74, 156–58, and 172).

281. E.g., chaps. 1, 9, 17, 52, 62–63, 68, 75–76, 84–86, 96, 98, 111, 121–22, 132–33, and 139. On Marguerite's esotericism, see Bernard McGinn, "Donne mistiche ed autorità esoterica nel XIV secolo," in *Poteri carismatici e informali: chiesa e società medioevali*, ed. Agostino Paravicini Bagliani and André Vauchez (Palermo: Sellerio, 1992), pp. 153–74.

282. Chap. 132 (390.37–38): Se vous ne l'entendez, je ne le puis amender. C'est une oeuvre miraculeuse, dont l'en no vous peut, se l'en ment, nient dire.

283. Chap. 121 (338.35–40): O pierre celestielle, / dit la Sainte Trinité, / Je vous prie, chere fille, / lessez ester. / Il n'y a si grant clerc ou monde, / qui vous en sceust parler.

284. Chap. 85 (240.7–242.11): Elle ne respont a nully, se elle ne veult, se il n'est de son lineage; car ung gentilhomme ne diagneroit respondre a ung vilain, se il l'appelloit ou requeroit de champ de bataille; . . . ses ennemis n'ont plus d'elle response. The notion of nobility of lineage, frequent in *The Mirror* (e.g., chaps. 52, 58, 63, 74, 82, 89, 98, 114, 118, 121), is the courtly correlative of the theological theme of the Soul's preexistence in God to be considered below.

285. See *Foundations of Mysticism*, pp. 98–99, for reflections on how the battle over Gnostic esotericism was significant for the history of Christian mysticism. This is not to exclude the role that esoteric traditions had in the earliest strains of Christian mysticism, and even beyond. See Guy G. Stroumsa, *Hidden Wisdom: Esoteric Traditions and the Roots of Christian Mysticism* (Leiden: Brill, 1996).

286. Chap. 59 (172.29–31): . . . non mie, dit elle, pour ceulx qui le sont, mais pour ceulx qui ne la sont, qui encore le seront. . . .

287. I owe this suggestion to Joanne Maguire; see her unpublished paper, "Eriugenean Echoes in the 'Mirror of Simple Souls.'"

288. For the dual notion of salvation, see chaps. 62–63, 77 and 121. In the last passage Soul expresses her astonishment when the Holy Trinity tells her that even those who condemn her will be saved (340.66–70).

289. The theme of the Soul's attainment of freedom through annihilation is central to *The Mirror* and is crucial to those who have identified the text as belonging to the heresy of the "Free Spirit." Discussion of the Soul's freedom is found in some thirty or more chapters of the text (see especially chaps. 48, 78, 85, 103, and 133). Freedom of spirit (*libertas spiritus*), of course, is an ancient theme in the history of Christian mysticism, rooted especially in 2 Cor. 3:17. See M.-A. Dimier, "Pour la fiche *spiritus libertatis*," *Revue du moyen age latin* 3 (1947): 56–60. Whether Marguerite's conception of the soul's freedom goes beyond that of other Christian mystics depends on one's view of her whole teaching.

290. For the relations between the two churches, see chaps. 19, 41–43, 49, 51, 66, 134.

291. Modern scholarship has amply demonstrated that Marguerite's "saying farewell to

the virtues" is not antinomian in intention, as she clearly emphasizes by numerous explanations. See especially chaps. 6–9, 21, 56, 66, 82, 88, 94, 105, and 122. In contrasting the encumbered and freed souls in chap. 121 she summarizes: Tales sunt serui legis, sed ista est supra legem, non tamen contra legem, iuxta testimonium ueritatis (339.12–13).

292. Sells, *Mystical Languages,* pp. 128, 204. See also Mommaers, "La transformation d'amour," pp. 92–104, and the unpublished paper of Maguire, "Eriugenean Echoes."

293. Chap. 40 (127.7–17): Ille, dicit Amor, qui in nulla re iniustitiam habet, et tamen scit quod in nulla re iustitiam habet. Ille qui est in ista notitia de sua iniustitia, ita clare uidet, quod uidet se subtus omnem creaturam in luto peccati.... [E]t propter istum respectum est ipsa anima nichil effecta et minus quam nichil in omnibus suis respectibus. Diu est quod audiuit a Spirito sancto dictum, quod Deus ponet sua sola bonitate minimum et inferiorem in loco altiori (my translation). The coincidence of the highest and the lowest place, or the deepest valley with the highest mountain, occurs in a number of places in the *Mirror,* e.g., chaps. 9, 98, 118 (34.42–43, 272.5–8, 328.143–46). The same image is found in Mechthild, e.g., FL 2.23 (ed. 58.44–46). Ruh (*Geschichte,* 2:349) aptly compares Porete's fall of the soul into nothingness with Mechthild's alienation from God.

294. Porete's attitude toward the body is highly complex, and perhaps even fundamentally ambiguous, as noted by Hollywood, *The Soul as Virgin Wife,* pp. 109–19.

295. Chap. 108 (293.6–10): Quamdiu enim uoluntatem habui, non cessaui, donec omnino uoluntatem perdidi et nude illi eam reddidi, qui mihi eam dederat libere sua bonitate. Quia qui bene facit et cognoscit aliud quod melius fieri posset, si uocatur ad illud faciendum et non facit, peccat (my translation).

296. Chap. 117 (310.7–312.20): ... et parmy je suis exemple de salut. Mais encore, qui plus est, le salut mesmes de toute creature, et la gloire de Dieu; et vous diray comment, pourquoy, et en quoy. Pource que je suis la somme de tous maulx. Car je contiens de ma propre nature ce que mauvaistié, donc suis je toute mauvaistié. Et celluy qui est la somme de tous biens.... [E]t Dieu ne peut tort faire, car il se defferoit.... Or suis je donc toute mauvaistié, et il toute est bonté, pour quoy il m'esconvient avoir toute sa bonté, ains que ma mauvaistié puisse estre estanchee....

297. Here I follow the Latin, though the French is not different; chap. 118 (317.69-71): Et ex quo ego totam suam habeo bonitatem, necessario per mutationem amoris (Fr.: per muance d'amour) sum id quod ipse est.

298. Here again, the Latin seems preferable; chap. 117 (317.85–86): Ipsi portauerunt crucem Christi per opera bonitatis; nunc suam crucem portant (my translation). Elsewhere, Porete bases the co-redemptive status of the Free Soul on John 14:12 ("Whoever will believe in me, he will do such works as I, and still even greater works"); see chaps. 94 and 113 (262.13–16 and 306.5–8).

299. Hadewijch had emphasized that *minne* was both far and near (e.g., PS 31.49–56 and 36.122–33), but she had not developed this insight into a new trinitarian name.

300. *Loingprés* (sometimes also *esclar*), or *longe propinquum* in Latin, appears in thirteen chapters. In chap. 1 (12.25–26) as *amour loingtaigne qui luy estoit si prouchaine ou dedans d'elle,* and explicitly in chaps. 58 (168.20, 25; 171.28), 59 (173.14), 60 (174.23), 61 (176.12; 178.27–28, which identifies *Loingprés* with the Trinity), 73 (206.42), 80 (228.25), 84 (238.13 and 31f.), 88 (250.39–44), 98 (272.10), 134 (394.3), 135 (397.8–19), and 136 (399.3). For a treatment, see Ruh, *Geschichte,* 2:351–56.

301. Chap. 84 (238.12–17): ... adonc chet elle, dit Amor, de ce en ung esbahyssement [Lat: *stupefactionem*], que en nomme "nient penser du Loingprés de pres", qui est son plus proesme. Adonc vit telle Ame, dit Amor, non mie de vie de grace ne de vie d'esperit tant seulement, mais de vie divine, franchement–non mie glorieusement, car elle n'est mie glorifee ... (my translation).

302. Chap. 135 (397.8–14): Longinquum huius est magis propinquum, quia cognoscit magis de prope illus longinquum in seipso, quod continue facit eam [some MSS read *eum*] esse in unione velle eius, absque taedio alterius rei quae eveniat ei. Totum est sibi unum sine propter quid, et est nulla in tali uno. Tunc nihil habet plus facere de Deo quam Deus de ea. Quare? Quia Ipse est et ipsa non est (my translation).

303. Chap. 95 (264.6–8): Adonc n'est il cogneu, ne amé, ne loé de telles creatures, fors seulment de ce, que on ne le peut cognoistre, ne amer, ne louer.

304. See Sells, *Languages of Unsaying,* especially the "Epilogue" (pp. 206–17).

305. Since the essential thing about apophasis is its performance within the text, questions of sources and influence are always secondary. While Porete obviously knew Augustine and major twelfth-century mystics, it is not easy (and relatively unimportant) to determine what contact she may have had with the Dionysian corpus and its interpreters.

306. Porete's emphasis on divine incomprehensibility is succinctly put in chap. 11 (45.109–10): Ille solus est Deus meus, de quo nullus scit uerbum dicere (cf. chaps. 18, 30, 31, 32, 45, 81, 88, 95, 119, etc.).

307. Marguerite has other discussions of the powers of the soul and the various characteristics of annihilated souls (e.g., nine points about such souls in chaps. 5 and 11; twelve names of the soul in chap. 10). These will not be taken up here. For more on her faculty psychology, see Babinsky, *A Beguine in the Court of the King,* chap. 4.

308. Porete has another correlative pattern, that of the three kinds of life (*vie de grace-vie d'esperit-vie divine;* see chap. 59 et al.).

309. Chap. 57 (164.21–33): Amour. Pour ce, dit Amour, qu'ilz tiennent qu'il est ung estre meilleur que n'est leur estre.... Damoiselle Cognoissance ... leur enseigne le droit chemin royale, par le pays de nient vouloir. For more on the Sad Souls, see chaps. 95 and 133.

310. Ibid. (324.120–24): ... ostendit uoluntati animae aequitatem illius quod est et notitiam illius quid non est, ad mouendum uelle animae de loco in quo est ubi esse non debet, et ad illud reponendum ubi non est, tamen unde venit et ubi esse debet (my translation; the Fr. has a lacuna in part of this passage).

311. Ibid. (328.157–58): Or est toute, et si est nulle, car son Amy la fait une. In chap. 51 (150.9–10), Soul says that "the knowledge of my nothing has given me everything," and in chap. 52 Soul is once again described as "toute et nulle" (154.44).

312. Chap. 131 (376–89). Such "tests of love" are illustrated by the dialogues in Andreas Capellanus, *De amore* 1.5.

313. Hadewijch also was tortured by the thought that anyone might love God more than she; see L 11.1–9.

314. This is explicitly stated in chap. 58 (168.12–23).

315. This statement occurs in Eckhart's German Sermon 12 and elsewhere (see DW 1:201.5–6): Daz ouge, dâ inne ich got sihe, daz ist daz selbe ouge, dâ inne mich got sihet....

316. Chap. 118 (330.186–332.198): ... mais Dieu se voit de luy en elle, pour elle, sans elle; lequel (c'est assavoir Dieu) luy monstre, que il n'est fors que lui. Et pource ne cognoist ceste Ame sinon luy, et si n'ayme sinon luy, car il n'est fors que luy.... Et si n'est, fors cil qui est, qui se voit en tel estre de sa divine majesté par muance d'amour.... This is echoed in chap. 91 (258.14–16), and especially in chap. 26 (93.5–7), where the Latin reads: Talis anima habet ita claram notitiam, quod videt se nichil in Deo et Deum nichil in se. For a reflection on God as the *id quod est* who is the being of all things, see chap. 70 (197.3–9).

317. The role of Mary as the highest annihilated soul is stressed in chaps. 23, 93, and 126 (88, 262, and 362–67); the latter chapter includes an uncharacteristic meditation on Mary at the cross, similar to that found in much late medieval piety. Other saints (the apostles, Mary Magdalene [cf. chaps. 74, 86, and 93], and John the Baptist) are treated as examples of annihilated souls in chaps. 76 and 123–25.

318. Marguerite uses the Song of Songs, but sparingly, with perhaps six indirect uses; see chaps. 10 (34.9, using Song 2:7), 44 (136.11–12, using Song 2:5), 51 (152.29–30, suggesting Song 3:4), 86 (246.61, using Song 3:4), 120 (336.11, using Song 4:12 and 15), and 120 (340.56, using Song 5:2). I am grateful to Rebecca Stephens for help in identifying these citations.

319. Chap. 82 (236.50–51): . . . c'est assavoir en l'amour de l'espoux de sa jouvence, qui a l'espouse muee toute en luy. For other uses of nuptial language in *The Mirror,* see chaps. 19, 73, 74, 81, 86, 87, 118, 120, 121, and 122. In chap. 122 (346.122–41) Marguerite uses nuptial language in relation to the notion of impregnation with the divine seed.

320. Newman, *From Virile Woman to WomanChrist,* pp. 144–45, 151–57.

321. Augustine, *De trinitate* 8.3.5 (PL 42:950): Jam enim erat animus, qui converti ad id vellet a quo erat: qui autem vellet esse antequam esset nondum erat. Et hoc est autem bonum nostrum, ubi videmus utrum esse debuerit aut debeat. . . .

322. For other important passages on the Soul's prexistence in God, see chaps. 34, 35, 51, 87, 91, 101, 107, 108, 109, 111, 117, and 118.

323. Chap. 135 (397.16–17): Tunc est omnibus rebus nuda, quia ipsa est sine esse, ubi ipsa erat, antequam esset. The Soul's nudity is often associated with its preexistence. For some treatments of *nuditas,* see, e.g., chaps. 52, 89, 94, 95, 97, 11, 113, 133, and 134.

324. Chap. 137 (401.2–3): Hoc est quod uidelicet resoluatur per adnichilationem in illud primum esse, ubi amor acceperat eam.

325. Chap. 138 (401.1–403.6): Modo est in esse sui primordialis esse, quod est suum esse. Et dimisit tria et fecit de duobus unum. Quando est illud unum? Illud unum est quando anima est resoluta in illam simplicem diuinitatem, quae est unum simplex esse expansae et dilatatae fruitionis in plano scire absque sentimento supra mentem. Illud simplex esse facit in anima ex caritate quicquid anima facit, quia uelle est simplex effectum (my translation). The context of the chapter makes it clear that the "two" are the two natures of God and human; the "three" are probably the three deaths.

326. See above pp. 216–17 and 150–51. See also McGinn, "The Abyss of Love," which treats Marguerite on pp. 110-12.

327. On "abyssal" language, see chaps. 23 (88.53), 38 (122.15), 40 (126.9), 43 (136.59), 51 (150.8–9), 53 (154.3–4), 60 (177.28–31), 79 (226.49), and no fewer than five times in chap. 118 (326.134–35, 328.139, 328.154–57, 328.161, 330.176).

328. Chap. 118 (326.130–35): Or est telle Ame nulle. . . . Et si est toute, car elle voit par la profondesse de la cognoissance de la mauvaistié d'elle, qui est si parfonde et si grant, que elle n'y trouve ne commencement ne mesure ne fin, fors une abysme abyssmee sans fons; la se trouve elle, sans trouver et sans fons.

329. See, e.g., chaps. 5, 43, 64, 74, 97, 101, 134.

330. Chap. 70 (196.5–6): Je suis, dit ceste Ame, de la grace de Dieu ce que je suis. Cf. chap. 128 (370.27).

331. Admittedly, one text seems to contradict this explanation, namely, chap. 42, where the Holy Spirit tells Holy Church the Little that the Soul attains the hidden mystery of the Trinity through knowing-nothing and willing-nothing–"*not through divine nature,* for that cannot be, but through the power of Love, as it is necessary to be" (130.10–12): Non mye, dit le Saint Esperit, *par nature divine,* car ce ne peut estre, mais par la force d'amour, car ce convient il estre. Latin MSS A and C, however, read only *per naturam* here, referring to the Soul's created nature. This chapter, especially the following passage on how the Love that unifies is identical with the Holy Spirit, is close to William of St. Thierry's "Spirit-centered" notion of mystical union, on which see *Growth of Mysticism,* chap. 6.

332. For other occurrences, see chaps. 81, 84, 89, 91, 93, 100, 101, 111, and 135.

333. Chap. 81 (230.3–232.27): Or a ceste Ame, dit Amour, son droit non du nient en quoy elle demoure. Et puisque elle est nient, il ne luy chault de nient, ne d'elle ne de ses proesmes ne de Dieu mesmes. . . . [C]ar elle est tousjours en plaine souffisance, en laquelle elle noe et onde et flote et suronde de divine paix, sans soy mouvoir de son dedans et sans son oeuvre de par dehors. . . . Se elle fait aucune chose par dehors, c'est tousjours sans luy. Se Dieu fait son ouevre en elle, c'est de luy en elle, sans elle, pour elle. . . . Elle a tout donné franchement, sans nul pourquoy, car elle est dame de l'espouse de sa jouvence.

334. Chap. 82 (234.38–40): Et pource pert elle son nom en celluy, en quoy elle est de luy en luy fondue et remise de luy en luy pour elle mesmes.

335. Ibid. (234.40–236.50). For other examples of the sea, see, chaps. 28 (96.2–7); 61 (176.4–6); 79 (226.49); 80 (226.7), 81 (230.13–16); 83 (236.3–6); 91 (256.7–8); 97 (271.34); and 110 (302.32). Evagrius Ponticus had used the same image of rivers flowing into the sea to describe his notion of union in the *Letter to Melania* 6 (see *Foundations of Mysticism*, p. 154).

336. Chap. 25 (90.11–92.13): Or est telle Ame, dit Amour, si arse en la fournaise du feu d'amour, qu'elle est devenue proprement feu, par quoy elle ne sent point de, car en elle mesmes elle est feu. . . . For other uses of the fire metaphor, see, e.g., chaps. 52 (152.154.21)– the famous iron in fire example; 64 (186.10–13); 83 (236.7–10).

337. Chap. 85 (242.15–17): Ceste Ame, dit Amour, est escorchee par mortifficacion, et arse par l'ardour du feu de charité, et la pouldre d'elle gittee en haulte mer par nient de voulenté.

338. See, e.g., chaps. 58, 59, 61, 118 (168–70, 172, 176–78, 330–32). On this point, see Mommaers, "La transformation d'amour," p. 101.

339. See the discussion in Ruh, *Geschichte,* 2:349–57.

340. Simone Weil, *First and Last Notebooks,* trans. Richard Rees (London: Oxford University Press, 1970), p. 96.

Chapter 6

1. For recent work on medieval nuns, see especially Jo Ann Kay McNamara, *Sisters in Arms: Catholic Nuns through Two Millennia* (Cambridge, Mass.: Harvard University Press, 1996), as well as Patricia Ranft, *Women and the Religious Life in Premodern Europe* (New York: St. Martin's Press, 1996).

2. The emphasis given to the Cistercians nuns of Helta in this chapter, especially because of their extensive mystical writings, precludes attention to the Cistercian visionaries and ecstatics known only through their *vitae.* The most important of these are two German stigmatics, Elisabeth of Herkenrode (ca. 1248–1316) and Lukardis of Oberweimar (ca. 1262–1309). For further information on Elisabeth, see Peter Dinzelbacher, *Christliche Mystik im Abendland,* pp. 201–3; and Ruh, *Geschichte,* 2:108–9. For Lukardis, see Dinzelbacher, pp. 232–33; Ruh, 2:131–32; and Aviad Kleinberg, *Prophets in Their Own Country: Living Saints and the Making of Sainthood in the Later Middle Ages,* pp. 101–21.

3. A good recent account of the Helfta mystics can be found in Ruh, *Geschichte,* 2:296–337. The best study in English is the insightful essay of Caroline Walker Bynum, "Women Mystics in the Thirteenth Century: The Case of the Nuns of Helfta," in *Jesus as Mother: Studies in the Spirituality of the High Middle Ages,* pp. 170–262. See also Mary Jeremy Finnegan, *The Women of Helfta: Scholars and Mystics* (Athens/London: University of Georgia Press, 1991). For earlier bibliography on the Helfta mystics, see Gertrud Jaron Lewis, *Bibliographie zur deutschen Frauenmystik des Mittelalters,* pp. 159–223.

4. This account is taken from the *Liber specialis gratiae* 6.1 (ed., 375–76) (see next note):

Divinam scripturam valde studiose et mira delectatione quandocumque poterat legebat, exigens a subditis suis ut lectiones sacras amarent, et jugi memoria recitarent. Unde omnes bonos libros quos poterat, ecclesiae suae comparabat, aut transcribi a Sororibus faciebat. Studiose et hoc promovebat, ut puellae in liberalibus artibus proficerent, ita dicens, si studium scientiae deperierit, cum amplius divinam Scripturam non intellexerint, Religionis simul cultus interibit.

5. The five books of the *Legatus divinae pietatis* have been critically edited by Pierre Doyère, Jean-Marie Clément, and Bernard de Vregille in *Gertrude d'Helfta: Oeuvres spirituelles, Tomes II–V,* SC 139, 143, 255, 331 (Paris: Éditions du Cerf, 1968–86) (they will be cited here by book and chapter with volume and page reference to this edition in parentheses). There is a full English version (from older editions) in *The Life and Revelations of St. Gertrude* (Westminster: Christian Classics, 1983; reprint of the 1862 edition). A more accurate, but partial, version can be found in *Gertrude of Helfta: The Herald of Divine Love,* trans. and ed. Margaret Winkworth (New York: Paulist Press, 1993). For the seven parts of the *Liber specialis gratiae* we still depend on the edition of Louis Paquelin in vol. 2 of his *Revelationes Gertrudianae et Mechtildianae* (Poitiers/Paris: Oudin, 1877), cited here by part and chapter with the page reference in parentheses. There is no modern English version.

6. Some authors assert that the Helfta texts were originally written in German, but there is no evidence for this. Indeed, contrary evidence can be found in *Liber* 3.42 (245), a parable based on the two syllables of the Latin word *ovum*.

7. Bynum, "Women Mystics," p. 252.

8. Ibid., p. 174.

9. *Legatus* 2, prologus (II:226): . . . compulsa violentissimo impetu Spiritus Sancti, lateralem tabulam arripiens, quod corde sentiebat cum dilecto in secreto confabulans, haec ex superabundantia gratitudinis ad laudem ipsius et manu describebat. . . .

10. The *Legatus* appears to have had a relatively modest circulation in the late Middle Ages; eight fifteenth-century manuscripts are known (the SC edition uses five). It began to become popular in the sixteenth century, however, and there have been six Latin editions since then and numerous translations.

11. No manuscripts of the *Exercitia* survive, so the many modern editions and translations of this work depend on the 1536 Latin text of the Carthusian John Lansperg (1490–1539). The critical edition is by Jacques Hourlier and Albert Schmitt, *Gertrude d'Helfta: Oeuvres Spirituelles, Tome I, Les Exercises,* SC 127 (Paris: Éditions du Cerf, 1967). For an English translation, see *Gertrude the Great of Helfta: Spiritual Exercises,* by Gertrud Jaron Lewis and Jack Lewis (Kalamazoo: Cistercian Publications, 1989).

12. Ruh has justly described this *compilatrix* (whom he calls "Schwester N.") as a "key figure" in the mysticism of Helfta (*Geschichte,* 2:316). See his discussions on pp. 301–4, 314–16.

13. At least fifteen manuscripts of the Latin survive. For remarks on the manuscript tradition and the abbreviated version, see the edition of the Middle English text by Theresa A. Halligan, *The Booke of Gostlye Grace of Mechtild of Hackeborn* (Toronto: PIMS, 1979).

14. See especially Bynum, "Women Mystics," pp. 225, 246–47, 252–53, and 257–59. Ruh argues for stronger differences between Gertrude and Mechthild than the texts seem to warrant (*Geschichte,* 2:336–37). Work still remains to be done in sorting out the contributions and particular style of each of these mystical authors.

15. The liturgical character of Helfta mysticism has been noted before; see especially Cyprian Vagaggini's treatment of Gertrude in *Theological Dimensions of the Liturgy* (Collegeville, Minn.: Liturgical Press, 1976), pp. 741–803. For an important text on the universal character of the eucharistic mystery given to the church in the daily liturgy, see *Legatus* 4.14 (IV:152–62).

16. This point is brought out by Ann Marie Caron, "Taste and See the Goodness of the Lord: Mechthild of Hackeborn," in *Hidden Springs: Cistercian Monastic Women,* ed. John A. Nichols and Lillian Thomas Shank, 2:512–13. See also Felix Vernet, *Medieval Spirituality* (London: Sands, 1930), pp. 220–23.

17. One could contrast this liturgical form of contemplative appropriation of the meaning of the events of salvation history with the narrative and pictorial practice of meditation on the life of Christ found especially in Franciscan texts and discussed in chapter 3 (pp. 118–20).

18. Bynum, "Women Mystics," p. 257.

19. Significantly, Gertrude describes Christ's love for humanity as insane (*amor amens*), not her own; cf. *Legatus* 2.8.3 and 2.20.11 (II:264 and 316).

20. The terms *cor Iesu* and *cor deificatum* are usual in Gertrude, while Mechthild most often speaks of the *cor Dei.* For historical background on the devotion to the Sacred Heart of Jesus, see Hugo Rahner, "Grundzüge einer Geschichte der Herz-Iesu-Verehrung," *Zeitschrift für Askese und Mystik* 18 (1943): 61–83; Auguste Hamon, "Coeur (sacré)," DS 2:1023–46; and Jesus Solano, *Historical Development of Reparation in Devotion to the Heart of Jesus* (Rome: Centro Cuore di Cristo, 1980).

21. *Legatus* 2.23.8 (II:336–38): Addidisti etiam inter haec mihi inaestimabilem amicitiae familiaritatem impendere, diversis modis illa, nobilissimam arcam divinitatis, scilicet deificatum Cor tuum praebendo in copiam omnium delectationum mearum; nunc gratis dando, nunc ad majus inicium mutuae familiaritatis illud mihi pro meo commutando ... (translation of Winkworth, 130–31). For other texts on the exchange of hearts in Gertrude, see 4.25.6–7 (IV:242–44), and *Exercitia* 3 (I:116). For a picture of mystical union in and with the heart, see *Legatus* 4.38.7 (IV:318–20). The exchange of hearts motif had already appeared in Lutgard (see chap. 4, pp. 164–65), but no previous texts are so dominated by the *cor Iesu* motif.

22. *Liber* 1.19 (70): Et cum communicasset cor suum cum Dei Corde, velut massam auri in unum liquatum vidit, audivitque Dominum dicentem sibi: "Sic cor tuum in perpetuo adhaerebit secundum omne desiderium et delectamentum tuum."

23. *Exercitia* 6 (I:252; cf. 232, 248): ... in cruce cor tuum dulcissimum prae amore est ruptum. See especially the hymns to *amor* and the *praedilectum cor* in *Ex.* 7 (I:284–88), as well as that to Jesus (I:298–304).

24. Hugues Minguet, "Théologie spirituelle de sainte Gertrude: le Livre II du 'Heraut,'" *Collectanea Cisterciensia* 51 (1989): 330.

25. This is perhaps more evident in the affectionate character of Mechthild; see, e.g., her vision of the converted sinner in heaven (*Liber* 1.33 [112]). For theological expressions of Christ's universal saving love, see, e.g., 1.16, 1.19 and 3.5 (48–49, 67–68, 201–2).

26. Bynum, "Women Mystics," pp. 199–200.

27. On the influence of Bernard, especially on Gertrude, see Johanna Lanczkowski, "Einfluss der Hohe-Lied-Predigten Bernhards auf die drei Helftauer Mystikerinnen," *Erbe und Auftrag* 66 (1990): 17–28.

28. This is not to say that the Trinity does not often appear in the Helfta writings, but there is no speculative development on the inner life of the three persons in the manner we have seen among some of the beguines. For Gertrude's knowledge of the Fathers and Cistercians, see the "Index des citations patristiques" in *Ouevres spirituelles,* V:333–37.

29. This was well brought out for Mechthild, first by Hans Urs von Balthasar, "Einführung," in *Mechthild von Hackeborn: Das Buch des strömmenden Lob* (Einsiedeln: Johannes Verlag, 1955), pp. 7–18; and later by Alois Maria Haas, "Mechthild von Hackeborn: Eine Form zisterzienischer Frauenfrömmigkeit," in *Geistliches Mittelalter,* pp. 383–88. As a generalization, the same holds true for Gertrude.

30. Bynum, "Women Mystics," pp. 261–62. See especially her analyses of "Gertrude's

Role and Sense of Self" (pp. 196–209) and "Mechthild of Hackeborn: Role and Sense of Self" (pp. 217–27).

31. *Legatus* 5.33 (V:264): Eodem effectu quo in hac missa panem et vinum transubstantiavi omnibus in salutem, etiam omnia in libro isto conscripta caelesti benedictione mea modo sanctificavi omnibus. . . . This book of the *Legatus* also contains a defense of Mechthild of Magdeburg's FL (5.7; V:124) based on the former beguine's picture of God's holding the book in his hand (see FL 2.26).

32. 5.34 (268): . . . huic ego revera in sinu meo quasi digito proprio sigillatim quaeque sibi utilia demonstrabo. . . .

33. 5.36 (274): Et interim legentes in libello isto simpliciores,...saltem hoc vehiculo iter arripiant, et quasi manuductione beneficiorum proximi sui delectati, vacando lectionibus, meditationibus et contemplationibus, ipsi tandem gustare incipiant quam dulcis est Dominus. . . . There are other reflections on the divine authorization of the text, both by the *compilatrix* (e.g., *Legatus* 1.15) and by Gertrude herself in 2.5, 2.10, and 2.23–24. For comments on the authorization motif in the *Legatus*, see Ruh, *Geschichte*, 2:317–18.

34. For treatments of this, see Haas, "Mechthild von Hackeborn," pp. 374–76; and Ruh, *Geschichte*, 2:302.

35. *Liber* 2.43 (192–93): Cui Dominus statim apparuit, hunc librum supra Cor suum in dextera sua tenens, eam osculatus est, dixitque: "Omnia quae in hoc libro continentur scripta, a Corde meo divino profluxerunt, et refluent in ipsum." . . . Dominus respondit: "Da me in liberalitate largiflui Cordis mei, et da me in bonitate mea, et non in tua."

36. Mechthild of Hackeborn's doubts about the book, however, were not finished. In other places God still has to assure her that the book is written with his approval and full cooperation; e.g., *Liber* 5.22 and 5.31 (354–55 and 369–70). The text in 5.31, which notes that the book was approved by the abbess and a *praelatus* (the bishop of Halberstadt?), claims that eventually Mechthild herself read the book before she died and fully corrected it. In 7.17 (412–13) Gertrude has a vision of the dead Mechthild in heaven who reassures her that the book "is her greatest joy."

37. There are many studies of Gertrude's mysticism. Especially helpful are Pierre Doyère, "Doctrine spirituelle," in *Gertrude d'Helfta: Oeuvres Spirituelles, Tome II, Le Héraut*, SC 139 (Paris: Éditions du Cerf, 1968), pp. 32–57. In English, see also Thomas Lilian Shank, "The God of My Life: St. Gertrude, A Monastic Woman," in *Peace Weavers: Medieval Religious Women II*, ed. John A. Nichols and Lillian Thomas Shank, 2:239–73.

38. E.g., *Ex.* 1 (64, 72, 74, and 76). This stress on *visio facialis*, which may depend on William of St. Thierry, is found throughout the *Exercitia*, and also in *Legatus* 2 (e.g., 2.21, 24, and 38), but it is not strong in the other books of the *Legatus*. It is not a major theme in Mechthild of Hackeborn, though there is an important treatment of such a vision in *Liber* 5.30 (366 and 368).

39. Marian piety also plays a large role in the Helfta writings, but cannot be taken up here.

40. *Ex.* 3 (I:116): . . . fac me tam indissolubiliter coniungi tuo ardentissimo amori, ut prae vi dilectionis tecum essendi, sitiam mori: et foedus quod tu iniisti mecum, a me transferat cor meum, ut iam non ultra sit mecum, sed amore individuo cohabitet mecum.

41. *Ex.* 4 (I:148): Demergar in abyssum maris tuae indulgentissimae pietatis. Peream in tui vivi amoris diluvio, sicut perit stilla maris in suae plenitudinis profundo. Moriar, moriar in tuae immensae miserationis profluvio, sicut moritur scintilla ignis in fluminis impetu validissimo. Gertrude uses the language of the *abyssus* at least nine other times in the *Exercitia* and four times in the second book of the *Legatus*. Many of these uses are close to the traditional Cistercian notion of God as the *abyssus caritatis*, but when she speaks of the *abyssale profluvium*, *abyssus deitatis*, and *abyssus vitalis originis* (II: 178, 248, 302) she comes closer to the abyss language of the beguine mystics.

42. *Ex.* 4 (I:154): Ibi in dulci spiramento suaviflui spiritus tui tibimetipsi attrahe, intrahe et imbibe me. For another passage on the spiritual senses, see *Ex.* 5 (I:192–94), and for a comparison of carnal and spiritual sweetness, cf. *Legatus* 3.44 and 54 (III:198–200, 232–34). Gertrude's use of the spiritual senses has been studied by Pierre Doyère, "Sainte Gertrude et les senses spirituels," *Revue d'Ascetique et Mystique* 36 (1960): 429–46.

43. It is not possible to list all these here, but they include (1) drinking and tasting God, which produces greater hunger and thirst (158.21–22); (2) seeing God as an *excessus mentis* (158.30); (3) the face-to-face vision to come (160.54–61); (4) the kiss, the embrace, and *copulatio* of the lovers (e.g., 162.80–166.134), and even the *thalamus cubiculi interioris tuae perfectae unionis* (186.397–98); (5) the invocation of the *otium-sabbatum-quies* of contemplation (162–64 et passim); (6) union imaged as the absorption of a drop of water in the sea (170.181–82; cf. *Ex.* 6, ed. 246.640–41); (7) the *vulnus amoris* (190.429–33 and 451–52); and (8) unifying love as the kiss that is the Holy Spirit (172.203–12). Gertrude quotes 1 Cor. 6:17 as well (e.g., 170.173–74, 172.209). *Ex.* 6 (I:236.8) adds to this the famous phrase used by Bernard to describe the duration of mystical union (first found in John of Fécamp), *rara hora et parva mora* (see Bernard *Super Cantica* 23.15 in *Sancti Bernardi Opera* 1:148.20).

44. Bynum, "Women Mystics," p. 254.

45. This exercise contains one of the few explicit references to the major Cistercian theme of the *ordo caritatis* (I:256.784–85).

46. This cosmic aspect of Gertrude's mysticism is underlined by the universal call to *iubilus* in *Exercitia* 6. There are also texts in the *Legatus* (e.g., 4.6; IV:88–98), as well as in Mechthild's *Liber* (e.g., 2.20, 2.35, and 4.40 [157, 182–83, 260]) that emphasize a sense of the entire created universe as engaging in ecstatic praise of God. From this perspective an interesting comparison might be made with Francis of Assisi's *Canticum fratris solis* (see chap. 1, pp. 54–56).

47. On the second book of the *Legatus,* see especially Hugues Minguet, "Théologie spirituelle de sainte Gertrude: le Livre II du 'Heraut,'" *Collectanea Cisterciensia* 51 (1989): 147–77, 252–80, 317–38; there is also a treatment in Ruh, *Geschichte,* 2:319–33.

48. Ruh, *Geschichte,* 2:321–23.

49. *Legatus* 2.4 (II:244): ... scilicet intus in corde meo quasi corporalibus locis per spiritum cognovi impressa colenda illa et adoranda sanctissimorum vulnerum tuorum stigmata. ...

50. Johanna Lanczkowski has shown how Gertrude's devotion to Christ crucified is an expression of her desire to share in his absolute obedience to the Father ("Gertrud die Grosse von Helfta: Mystik des Gerhorsams," in *Religiöse Frauenbewegung und mystische Frömmigkeit im Mittelalter,* ed. Peter Dinzelbacher and Dieter Bauer, pp. 153-64).

51. *Legatus* 2.5.2 (II:248–50): Igitur cum post suscepta vivifica sacramenta, ad locum orationis reversa fuissem, videbatur mihi quasi de dextro latere crucifixi depicti in folio, scilicet de vulnere lateris, prodiret tamquam radius solis, in modum sagittae acutus, qui per ostentum extensus contrahebatur, deinde extendebatur, et sic per morum durans, affectum meum blande allexit.

52. *Legatus* 2.20.14 (II:318): "Ne haec causeris accede et suscipe pacti mei firmamentum." Et statim parvitas mea conspexit te quasi utrisque manibus expandere arcam illam divinae fidelitatis atque infallibilis veritatis, scilicet deificatum Cor tuum, et jubentem me perversam, more judiaco signa quaerentem, dextram meam imponere. ...

53. *Legatus* 2.21.1 (II:322). Gertrude here cites a passage from Bernard's *Super Cantica* 31.6 (see *Sancti Bernardi Opera* 1:223).

54. *Legatus* 2.21.3 (II:324). On the use of *similitudines* in Gertrude's writings, see Sister Mary Jeremy, "'Similitudes' in the Writing of Saint Gertrude of Helfta," *Mediaeval Studies* 19 (1957): 47–54.

55. *Legatus* 2.21.4 (II:326): ... tam visionem quam etiam amplexum et osculum cum caeteris amatoriis exhibitionibus pro loco, pro tempore et pro persona, te solitum congruentis-

sime temeperare, cum saepius experta sum. The passage concludes with Gertrude's assurance that this face-to-face vision was much higher than the experience of the *osculum* which she has sometimes received as often as ten times while reciting a single psalm!

56. E.g., *Legatus* 3.48.2 (III:216); 4.1.2, 4.12.3, 4.26.2 (IV:18, 164, 382 [the last passage cites Bernard's *Super Cantica* 41.3–4]); and 5.36.1 (V:274–76). In one noted text (4.2.3; IV:26), the *compilatrix* distinguishes between two modes of divine fruition: one that happens *per excessum mentis ferebatur in Deum* and is only for the usefulness of the seer; and a second that is a vision *praesentialiter facie ad faciem* and is useful for others. This seems, however, to reverse the picture given by Gertrude herself in 2.21, where the face-to-face vision is incommunicable and can only be expressed by distant similitudes. The notion of God's accommodation to the human mystic is also found in Mechthild's *Liber* 7.21 (419).

57. The most detailed analysis of *suppletio*, which may be described as both a substitution for what is lacking and a fulfillment of a perfection given, can be found in Minguet, "Théologie spirituelle," pp. 275–79. The term is found frequently in the *Legatus,* and also appears in Mechthild's *Liber* (e.g., 1.9, 2.15, 3.14, 4.23, 4.29, and 4.34).

58. *Legatus* 2.23.23 (II:348): Pro quo sit tibi laus illa aeterna quae de increato amore procedens jugiter refluit in teipsum.

59. For studies of Mechthild, besides the articles of von Balthasar and Haas mentioned above, see Ruh, *Geschichte,* 2:300–314; and two treatments by Margot Schmidt: "Mechthilde de Hackeborn," DS 10:873–77; and "Mechthild von Hackeborn," in *Die deutsche Literatur des Mittelalters: Verfasserlexikon,* ed. Kurt Ruh et al., 6:251–60. In English, see especially Ann Marie Caron, "Taste and See the Goodness of the Lord: Mechthild of Hackeborn," in *Hidden Springs,* 2:509-24. On Mechthild's religious experience, consult Otto Langer, "Zum Begriff der Erfahrung in der mittelalterlichen Frauenmystik," in *Religiöse Erfahrung: Historische modelle in christlicher Tradition,* ed. Walter Haug and Dietmar Mieth (Munich: Wilhelm Fink, 1992), pp. 229–46.

60. For a treatment of the *cor Dei* in Mechthild, see Haas, "Mechthild von Hackeborn," pp. 379–81. Devotion to the *cor Dei* or *cor Iesu* seems even more prevalent with Mechthild than with Gertrude. Roughly 112 of the 265 chapters of the *Liber specialis gratiae* discuss the theme.

61. Haas, "Mechthild von Hackeborn," p. 380: ". . . das Herz Gottes als Sinnmitte ihrer mysticischen Erfahrung einsichtig wird."

62. Gertrude also saw Christ's Heart as a *cithara* (*Legatus* 4.41.2; IV:328) and in one place describes the Heart as *quasi in organum quoddam dulcissimum singula verba et notas intonare; Legatus* 4.14.1 (IV:154).

63. There is a rich patristic background to these images, based on John 7:37–39 and 19:34, see Hugo Rahner, "De Dominici pectoris fonte potavit," *Zeitschrift für katholische Theologie* 55 (1931): 103–8.

64. *Liber* 2.16 (150): . . . illa vero reclinavit se ad vulnus melliflui Cordis Salvatoris sui unici, hauriens inde pocula omnis dulcoris et suavitatis plenissima, ibique omnis amaritudo ejus versa est in dulcedinem, et timor ejus mutatus est in securitatem. Ibi etiam de Corde Christi suavissimo esuxit fructum dulcissimum, quem assumens de Corde Dei in os suum posuit: per quod significabatur illa aeterna laus, quae de corde Dei procedit. . . . For some comparable images, see, e.g., 1.27, 1.46, and 4.1. Gertrude also drinks from Christ's heart, see, e.g., *Legatus* 4.13.4 (IV:148).

65. *Legatus* 5.27.7 (V:218–20). In *Legatus* 4.35.4 (IV:294) Gertrude also sees the *arbor caritatis* growing out of the divine heart and from it a pure stream of water coming to refresh the soul. Once she saw herself as burned-out cinder that grew into a tree through the action of Christ's blood and then rooted itself in the wound in his side (*Legatus* 3.18.5–6; III:84–86).

66. *Liber* 4.1 (258): Deinde visum est ei quod omnibus accedentibus Dominus praeberet bibere de tribus fistulis Cordis sui, simul dicens: *Bibete et inebriamini carissimi.* . . . Quo facto, Dominus ait: 'Omnes qui biberunt de Corde meo, eorum corda ego bibam.'" For other passages on the *fistulae,* see 1.1 and 7.9. Gertrude also sees herself as drawing nourishment from Christ's heart through a *fistula (Legatus* 3.26.2).

67. See Jeffrey F. Hamburger, *Nuns as Artists: The Visual Culture of a Medieval Convent* (Berkeley: University of California Press, 1997), pp. 137–75.

68. *Liber* 1.19 (61–62): Post haec ostendit ei Dominus pulcherrimum domum excelsam et ampliam nimis; intra quam vidit domunculum factam ex lignis cedrinis, interius laminis argenteis valde splendidis coopertam, in cujus medio Domino residebat. Hanc domum Cor Dei esse bene recognovit, quia multoties ipsum tali viderat forma; domuncula vero interior animam illam figurabat quae, sicut ligna cedrina imputribilia sunt, immortalis est et aeterna. . . . "Sic anima tua semper est in Corde meo inclusa et ego in corde animae tuae. Et licet in intimis tuis me contineas, ita ut intimior sim omni intimo tuo [see Augustine, *Conf.* 3.6.11], tamen divinum cor meum ita excellens et supereminens est animae tuae ut omnino inattingibile videatur, quod per hujus domus celsitudinem et amplitudinem denotatus."

69. For other appearances of the motif, see 1.8, 2.2, 2.22, 2.25, 3.1, and 3.4. The *domus Cordis Iesu* also occurs once in Gertrude; *Legatus* 4.58.2 (IV:466–68).

70. *Liber* 1.5 (19): "Pulsus Cordis mei non erunt ut caeterorum hominum, sed semper tales habui pulsus ab infantia mea usque ad mortem, indeque factum est quod tam cito moriebar in cruce. . . . Quartus pulsus, qui lenis est, humanitatis meae benignitatem figurabat, quae me omnibus amabilem et sociabilem ac imitabilem faciebat."

71. *Liber* 2.1 (135): "Veni ut poeniteas; veni ut reconciliaris; veni ut consoleris; veni ut bendicaris."

72. *Legatus* 3.51-52 (III:224–28) speaks of two heartbeats, one for the salvation of sinners and one for the salvation of the just. *Legatus* 4.4 (IV:64–66) contains a conversation between Gertrude and John the Beloved about their experience of hearing Christ's beating heart.

73. *Liber* 7.4 (395): Peracta unctione, Dominus eam inter amplexus suos amantissime suscipiens, sic per biduum sustentabat, ut vulnus dilectissimi Cordis sui ad os infirmae pateret; a quo omnem flatum quem spirabat trahere et iterum in Cor mittere videbatur. Two earlier texts (3.7 and 3.34) also say that a soul united to Christ's heart in true love draws its very breath (*spiramentum*) from him. Gertrude exchanges breaths with Christ, without mention of his heart, in *Legatus* 4.38.3 (IV:314).

74. *Liber* 7.4 (396): . . . una [i.e., Gertrude] ardentiori ducta affectu vidit animam ejus, in specie cujusdam puellae valde delicatae, coram Deo stantem, et omnem flatum quem spirabat, per vulnus sanctissimi lateris Cordi suo mellifluo immittentem, ex quo deificum Cor incontinentia propriae benignitatis et dulcedinis commutum, quoties flatum ejus sibi suscepit immissum, toties ex amoris abundantia supereffluens, per totam Ecclesiae latitudinem stillicidia gratiarum respersit, et specialiter in personas ibi presentes. This picture is to be understood in light of the discussion in 5.21 (352) in which God becomes all five senses of the dying just person, including her heart and her soul. There is nothing quite the same in Gertrude, though she does pray that at death Jesus will open the *cordis tui ostium* to her to give her access to the bridal chamber of his love (*Ex.* 7; I:298). The mediational character, however, is present in *Legatus* 3.66 and 3.73.3 (III:270 and 298), where Christ makes Gertrude's heart the channel (*canalis*) by which the love emanating from his heart is spread over the earth.

75. I would like to thank Patricia Z. Beckman, who read both this and the following section, for suggestions and corrections of some of my renderings from Middle High German.

76. For a sketch of the history of the order, both men and women, see "Premostratensi,"

DIP 7:720–46. On Premonstratensians and women, see Herbert Grundmann, *Religious Movements in the Middle Ages,* pp. 77–78, 82, 232–34.

77. For a study of Norbertine spirituality, see François Petit, *La spiritualité des Prémontrés au XIIe et XIIIe siècles* (Paris: Vrin, 1947).

78. See *Growth of Mysticism,* pp. 360–61.

79. Herman Joseph's *Vita* can be found in AA.SS. Apr. 7:686–714. His hymns and prayers have been edited by Josef Brosch, *Hymnen und Gebete des seligen Hermann Joseph im lateinischen Originaltext nebst einer deutschen Übersetzung,* Veröffentlichungen des Bischöflichen Diözesanarchivs Aachen 9 (Aachen: Bischöflichen Diözesanarchivs, 1950). The most recent study is Hermann Josef Kugler, *Hermann Josef von Steinfeld (um 1160–1241) in Kontext christlicher Mystik* (St. Ottilien: Eos Verlag, 1992). See also Petit, *La spiritualité des Prémontrés,* pp. 102–15; Jean-Baptiste Valvekens, "Hermann-Joseph (saint)," DS 7:308–11; and Dinzelbacher, *Christliche Mystik,* pp. 139–40.

80. Christina has not attracted a large literature. The best account is in Ruh, *Geschichte,* 2:121–25; see also Dinzelbacher, *Christlicher Mystik,* pp. 233–36. The brief notice in Petit, *La spiritualité des Prémontrés,* pp. 119–24, is now out-of-date.

81. The dispute about whether or not Christina's monastery was at Hane or Retters seems definitely settled in favor of the former. On Hane, see Norbert Backmund, "Das Kloster Hane (Hagen) im Bolanden (Pfalz)," *Analecta Praemonstratensia* 56 (1980): 103–4.

82. The work was been edited by Franz Paul Mittermaier, "Lebensbeschreibung der sel: Christina, Gen. von Retters, aus Ms. 324, fol. 211 sequ. der Bibliothèque nationale et universitaire de Strasbourg," *Archiv für Mittelrheinisches Kirchengeschichte* 17 (1965): 209–51; 18 (1966): 203–38. In what follows this text will be cited by volume number and page (e.g., 17.209).

83. Kurt Ruh sensibly suggests that this final section comes from the hand of a later redactor. See his analysis of the different stages in the evolution of the document edited by Mittermaier in *Geschichte,* 2:124–25.

84. E.g., O du aller lyebste sele myn (18.208); O du usserwillette bruytde myns hertzes (18.213)–these formulae are constantly repeated. Christ uses a wide variety of names for his chosen soul–house of the heart, temple, book (18.208, 220, 231); dove or turtledove (18.217, 223, 226, 227, 232); ark (18.213); throne (18.220, 226); etc.

85. *Description* 18.210: Da zofloissyn sie yn got myt eym vnsprechlichyn gebruchyn der soisser gotheit vnd lyeblicher menscheit (cf. 18.229). On *gebruchyn* in Christina, see, e.g., 17.243; 18.204, 216, 222, 228, 229, 230, 232.

86. The term *heymlicheit,* frequent with Mechthild, also occurs; see, e.g., 18.213, 214, 221, 232.

87. *Description* 18.225: Der gotliche schynne vnd daz lyecht gusset sich yn mych vnd vermenget sich zo myr vns machet van zweyn, daz ist van myner selen vnd got, eyn geist; vnd myner sele wyrt got myt gode vnd gantze vereyniget myt gode. For similar expressions, see 18.213, 227, 230, 231, 232.

88. *Description* 18.223: Du haist von genaden, daz ich hayn van naturen. See also 18.229.

89. See, e.g., *Description* 18. 207, 208, 210, 211, 212, 216, 218, 220, 222, 223, 225, 226, 227, 229, 231, 232.

90. *Description* 18.219: Myn vader ist yn myr vnd ich yn yme, vnd du byst yn vns; alles, was ich hayn, das ist dyne, vnd was du haist daz ist myn (see John 17:23). For similar formulae, see 18.218, 220, 221.

91. E.g., *Description* 18.220, 223, 227.

92. On the history of the order, see Sofia Boesch Gajano, "Storia e tradizione vallombrosane," *Bullettino dell'Istituto Storico Italiano per il Medio Evo* 76 (1964): 99–215.

93. These texts have been edited by Adele Simonetti, *I Sermoni di Umiltà da Faenza: Studio*

e edizione (Spoleto: Centro Italiano di Studi sull'alto Medioevo, 1995). The sermons will be cited here by number and line with the page of the edition in parentheses. Simonetti's introduction (XI–XCIV) is the best available study of Umiltà. For a brief notice in English, see Anna Benvenuti Papi, "Mendicant Friars and Female Pinzochere in Tuscany," in *Women and Religion in Medieval and Renaissance Italy,* ed. Daniel Bornstein and Roberto Rusconi, pp. 88–89. There is also a partial translation of some of her sermons by Richard J. Pioli in Elizabeth Alvida Petroff, *Medieval Women's Visionary Literature* (New York: Oxford University Press, 1986), pp. 247–53.

94. Two lives of Umiltà survive, a Latin text finished in 1332, which has been published in AA.SS. Mai 5:205–24; and a vernacular life of 1345, which was edited by F. Zambrini, *Vita della beata Umiltà faentina: Testo inedito del buon secolo della lingua toscana* (Imola, 1849). For a study of her life, see Simonetti, *I sermoni,* XI–XXX.

95. See, e.g., *Sermo* X.69–77 (ed., 136).

96. One of Umiltà's companions on this journey was Margaret of Faenza (ca. 1230–1330), who succeeded her as abbess of the house in Florence and who left a reputation as an ecstatic and visionary which was recorded by her Franciscan friend Peter of Florence (see the *Vita S. Margaritae Faventinae* in AA.SS. Aug. 26:847–51). Margaret's mystical experiences, such as her visions of Christ on the cross (see 849BE) and espousal with the Divine Bridegroom (850AB), are more typical of late-thirteenth-century female mysticism than Umiltà's unusual teaching.

97. Umiltà, like the monastic theologians of the early Middle Ages, was steeped in the Bible and the liturgy. The only other source for the *sermones* that can be clearly identified is Bernard of Clairvaux's Marian sermons *Missus est* (see Simonetti, *I sermoni,* XL, XLIV–XLV).

98. E.g., Sermones III.224–28; IV.199–201 and 631–33; V.170–77; IX.81–86; XI.211–13; XII.93–95; XIII.151–57.

99. See Simonetti, *I Sermoni,* XLI, LX–LXI, LXVII–LXVIII.

100. *Sermo* VI.45–52 (ed., 70): Vobis autem assero tantum per exemplum, quasi balbutiendo per similitudinem. Nam nasci non debet, nec natus est qui valeat comprehendere bene vicem, nisi Dominus, qui fuit vulneratus, qui posuit flumina in lancea et flagello, et illum dolorem gessit sic amarum, de quo sancti sibi faciunt gloriam novellam quae semper renovatur in suavitate, et in dulci amore domicellae, in illa humanitate benedicta quae gessit in suo corpore flagellum; et semper exultant gaudio videre carnem decoram.

101. Caroline Walker Bynum notes Umiltà's use of food images in several places (e.g., *Holy Feast and Holy Fast: The Religious Significance of Food to Medieval Women,* pp. 140, 145, 234, 248).

102. This image, perhaps disconcerting to modern readers, is close to a passage found in Humiltà's contemporary, James of Milan (see chap. 3, p. 118 n. 30). Christ's scourging is an important theme for Umiltà; see, e.g., *Sermo* X.105–7 (ed., 137).

103. *Sermo* X.48–49 (ed., 135): Si totum istum mundum habuissem in manibus, amore Christi ego dedissem. Cf. *Sermo* XI.325–27 (ed., 152).

104. *Sermo* XII.154–64 (ed., 161): Et scitis, fratres, quia non tantum visione, sed etiam domestica et amica locutione, et blando sermone, et gratissima responsione, missa ad universas nostras interrogationes et petitiones, largita divina potentia.... Et hoc vobis notum sit quoniam isti sunt proprii, et primi, et optimi ad nostrum auxilium et magnum subsidium apud Deum, et multa nobis patefaciunt de secretis coelestibus.

105. See *Growth of Mysticism,* pp. 353–62.

106. For accounts of Carthusian nuns, see Yves Gourdal, "Chartreux," DS 2:705–76 (especially 721–22), and "Certosine, monache," DIP 2:772–82.

107. The edition, with French translation, is by Antonin Duraffon, Pierre Gardette, and Paulette Durdilly, *Les Oeuvres de Marguerite d'Oingt* (Paris: Societé d'édition "Les Belles

Lettres," 1965). For an English translation (with some inaccuracies), see Renate Blumenfeld-Kosinski, *The Writings of Marguerite of Oingt: Medieval Prioress and Mystic* (Newburyport, Mass.: Focus Information Group, Inc., 1990).

108. Among the few studies on Marguerite is Roland Maisonneuve, "L'experience mystique et visionnaire de Marguerite d'Oingt, moniale chartreuse," *Kartäusermystik und -Mystiker*, Analecta Cartusiana 55 (Salzburg: Institut für Anglistik und Amerikanistik, 1981), pp. 81–102. The best account is by Stephanie Paulsell, "'*Scriptio Divina*': Writing and the Experience of God in the Works of Marguerite d'Oingt" (Ph.D. diss., University of Chicago, 1993).

109. The spiritual role of writing, especially within a monastic context, had been an important part of Western monasticism at least since the time of Cassiodorus (see his *Institutiones* 1.30.1). Twelfth-century authors expanded on this, arguing that all Christians, even the illiterate, must write God in their hearts (see Pseudo-Hildebert of Lavardin, *Sermo* 47, in PL 171:814–15). For this background, see Paulsell, "'*Scriptio Divina*,'" chap. 2.

110. For the connection of the two, see Paulsell, "'*Scriptio Divina*,'" especially pp. 146–49.

111. *Pagina* n. 1 (ed., 71): . . . et cepi cogitare miseriam in qua sumus dediti propter peccatum primi parentis. Et in illa cogitatione cepi tantum pavorem et tantum dolorem quod cor mihi deficere videbatur ex toto, propter hoc quod nesciebam utrum essem digna salute an non.

112. *Pagina* n. 4 (ed., 72): . . . et ideo ponebam in scriptis cogitationes quas Deus ordinaverat in corde meo ne perderem eas cum removissem illas a corde meo, et ut possem eas cogitare paulatim quando mihi Deus suam gratiam daret. . . .

113. See Paulsell, "'*Scriptio Divina*,'" pp. 9–11, 139–43, and 247–50. This is especially evident in the conclusion of the text, which asks Christ, "Domine dulcis, scribe in corde meo illud quod vis ut faciam. Scribe ibi tuam legem, scribe ibi tua mandata ut nunquam deleantur" (n. 109, ed., 88).

114. At one place (n. 7; ed., 92) Marguerite compares this exterior book of Christ's life with the book of her conscience (*el livro de sa concienci*), not unlike how Bernard of Clairvaux invited his readers to compare the book of scripture with the book of their experience (see *Growth of Mysticism*, pp. 185–90).

115. *Speculum* n. 19 (ed., 96): Li saint serant dedanz lor creatour tot assy com li peysson qui sont dedenz la mar qui beyvont toz jors a plein seins enoer et seins l'ayguy amermer. Tot assi seront li saint, quar il bevrant et mengirant la grant doucour de Deu. Et tant cont il plus en recevrent et il plus grant fayn en arent.

116. *Speculum* n. 24 (ed., 98): Ices glorious cors eret si tres nobles et si trapercans que l'on veoyt tot clarament l'arma per dedenz. Cil cors eret si tres nobles que l'on si poit remirer plus clarament que en un mirour. Ciz cors eret si tres beuz quo l'on y veit los angelos et los sains assi come se il fussant peint en lui. Maisonneuve notes the progressive character of Marguerite's perception of divine light in the three visions ("L'experience mystique et visionnaire," pp. 90-91).

117. In Letter 1 (nn. 129–31, ed., 138–40), Marguerite describes visions of Christ at the nativity and passion in a manner similar to that found in many ecstatic women of the late Middle Ages. Similarly, her *Via Seiti Biatrix Virgina de Ornaciu* shows that a woman writing a *vita* of another woman could adapt the standard topoi of sanctity, especially regarding severe asceticism and eucharistic visions, that are not featured in her own mystical accounts.

118. *Item ex Alia Epistola* n. 137 (ed., 142): . . . je ne say pas se co que est escrit ou livro est en sainti escriptura, mais je say que cilli que les mit en escrit fut si esleve en Nostro Segnour, una noyt, que li fut semblanz qui illi veut totes cetes choses.

119. For interpretations of Letter 4, see Paulsell, "'*Scriptio Divina*,'" pp. 28–33 and 209–11; and Maisonneuve, "L'experience mystique et visionnaire," pp. 93–94. The image of the *arbor eversa* also occurs in the tree allegory in Hadewijch's Vision 1 and is found in a wide variety

of religious traditions from around the world (see Mircea Eliade, *Patterns in Comparative Religion* [Cleveland/New York: Meridian Books, 1963], pp. 274–76).

120. On the early history of Dominican nuns, see L. A. Redigonda, "Domenicane (di Clausura)," DIP 3:780–93. Also important is the discussion in Grundmann, *Religious Movements*, pp. 92–109 and 124–30; and the texts in *Early Dominicans: Selected Writings*, edited with an introduction by Simon Tugwell, pp. 385–431. For a general history, see William A. Hinnebusch, *The History of the Dominican Order*, 2 vols. (New York: Alba House, 1973).

121. Dominic's only surviving piece of writing is a short letter written to this community. A translation can be found in Tugwell, *Early Dominicans*, p. 394.

122. For a sketch of Diana's life (ca. 1202–1236), see A. Alessandrini, "Andalò, Diana d'," *Dizionario Biografico degli Italiani* (Rome: Istituto della Enciclopedia Italiana, 1961), 3:48–50. In the late sixteenth century the Dominican Thomas Malvenda wrote a *Vita*, which can be found in AA.SS. Jun. 9:364–68.

123. The most detailed treatment is still that of Grundmann, *Religious Movements*, pp. 92–109 and 124–30.

124. The figures clearly demonstrate this. By 1250 there were over thirty female houses in Germany claiming affiliation with the Dominicans, almost all of which had been incorporated in the preceding five years. In 1277, German female houses numbered forty out of fifty-seven in the whole order, and by 1287 the number of German nunneries had reached seventy. Some leveling off of the growth rate occurred after this, but in 1303 the female German houses totaled 74 of 141 in the order (figures based on Grundmann, *Religious Movements*, pp. 108–9, 135, and Redigonda, "Domenicane (di Clausura)," 783).

125. On the spread of the friars in Germany, see John B. Freed, *The Friars and German Society in the Thirteenth Century*, especially the tables on pp. 22–24.

126. Grundmann, *Religious Movements*, pp. 104–5.

127. On Engelthal, see Grundmann, *Religious Movements*, pp. 98–100; and Gertrud Jaron Lewis, *By Women, for Women, about Women: The Sister-Books of Fourteenth-Century Germany* (Toronto: Pontifical Institute of Mediaeval Studies, 1996), pp. 18–19.

128. For a sketch of early Dominican spirituality, see Tugwell, "Introduction," in *Early Dominicans*, pp. 1–47.

129. See *Beati Jordani de Saxonia Epistulae*, ed. P. A. Walz, Monumenta Ordinis Fratrum Praedicatorum 23 (Rome: S. Sabina, 1951). These letters have been translated with an extensive study (and a different numeration) by Gerald Vann, *To Heaven with Diana!* (London: Collins, 1960). Vann's translations are often felicitous, but I have preferred to make my own. On Jordan's friendship with Diana, see John Coakley, "Gender and the Authority of the Friars: The Significance of Holy Women for Thirteenth-Century Franciscans and Dominicans," *Church History* 60 (1991): 450–52.

130. Ep. 52 (ed., 61): Quid igitur dicam de quam maxima magna, qua plurimum te diligo, caritate in Iesu nostro mediatore, qui mediator est non solum hominum se in Christo diligentium, sed et Dei et hominum, qui fecit utraque unum: unum enim fecit, ut Deus esset homo et homo Deus, ut homo Deum in homine et hominem in Deo diligeret. For other expressions of this *spiritualis amicitia*, see, e.g., Epp. 2, 9, 12, 13, 14, 32, 33, 36, 37, 39, 41, 42, 43, 46, 48.

131. See Ep. 29 (ed. 34–35); cf. the address to Diana as a temple for God's indwelling in Ep. 24 (ed., 28).

132. Ep. 28 (ed., 33): Ad hoc se ad horam sponsus vester subtrahit, ut ipsum ardentius quaeratis, quaesitum cum maiore gaudio inveniatis, inventum fortius, teneatis, tentum non dimittatis, sicut sponsa, quae in Canticis post multas inquisitiones et interrogationes, an aliquis dilectum eius vidisset, tandem cum invenisset, exclamavit: Tenui eum nec dimittam (Song 3:4). For another text using the bridal language of the Song of Songs, see Ep. 11 (ed., 13–14).

133. See Ep. 15 (ed., 17). For other texts that express strong personal devotion to Christ crucified, see, e.g., Epp. 17 and 41 (ed., 20–21, 46–47).

134. Ep. 56 (ed., 68): . . . nec ipsi profecto apparitione Iesu aliquatenus fraudabuntur, cum adeps pietatis coeperit ebullire, tamen non sine admiratione continuo fateantur: Nonne cor nostrum ardens erat in nobis, cum loqueretur nobis in via?

135. The mystical theory developed by Eckhart is partly rooted in the intellectual movement begun by Albert the Great at the new Dominican *studium generale* in Cologne from 1248, especially his commentaries on the Dionysian corpus; but it is not until the last decade of the thirteenth century that we can speak of the real formation of this other strand of Dominican mysticism.

136. The differences between Eckhart's mysticism and that of the Dominican women has been studied by Otto Langer, *Mystische Erfahrung und spirituelle Theologie: Zu Meister Eckharts Auseinandersetzung mit der Frauenfrömmigkeit seiner Zeit* (Munich/Zurich: Artemis, 1987); see the review by Frank Tobin in *Speculum* 64 (1989): 995–97. This distance has also been noted by Dinzelbacher, *Christliche Mystik*, pp. 315–16.

137. See Herbert Grundmann, "Die geschichtlichen Grundlagen der deutschen Mystik," in *Altdeutsche und altniederländische Mystik*, ed. Kurt Ruh (Darmstadt: Wissenschaftliche Buchgesellschaft, 1964), pp. 72–99. This issue will be taken up in detail in the next volume of *The Presence of God.*

138. Eckhart almost certainly was familiar with Porete's *Mirouer*, and he may have known Mechthild's *Das fliessende Licht*, at least through its use in Dietrich of Apolda's *Vita Sancti Dominici.*

139. For a survey with extensive documentation, see G. G. Meersseman, *Dossier de l'ordre de la pénitence au XIIIe siècle*, 2nd ed. (Fribourg: Éditions Universitaires, 1982).

140. The *Vita de B. Benevenuta de Bojanis* can be found in AA.SS. Oct. 29:145–85. The revelations and raptures are described in chaps. 6–10 (163A–173F).

141. *Vita* 10 (173BC).

142. On Margaret, see Enrico Menestò, "Margherita da Città di Castello e la memoria santa della famiglia perduta," in *Umbria sacra e civile*, pp. 167–78; M.-H. Laurent, "La plus anciene légende de la B. Marguerite de Città di Castello," *Archivum Fratrum Praedicatorum* 10 (1940): 109–31. Margaret is described as levitating, able to "see" the Eucharist despite her blindness, and as having pictures of Christ and the saints engraved on her heart (discovered by posthumous investigation). On Vanna, see Paoli Emore and Luigi G. G. Ricci, *La Legenda di Vanna da Orvieto* (Spoleto: Centro Italiano di Studi sull'alto Medioevo, 1996), especially chap. 5 (pp. 143–48) on her mystical prayer and *imitatio passionis.*

143. For a brief introduction to this material, see Alois M. Haas, "Nonnenleben und Offenbarungsliteratur," in *Geschichte der deutschen Literatur: Die deutsche Literatur im späten Mittelalter 1250-1370*, ed. Ingeborg Glier (Munich: Beck, 1987), pp. 291–99. Given the tendency to overemphasize the "experiential" side of these texts, the following remark of Haas is worth citing: "Die Texte der Frauenmystik unter die Deutsche Mystik zu reihen ist berechtigt, nicht weil sie direkter Ausdruck mystischer Erfahrung, sondern weil sie auf bestimmte Weise Ausdruck mystischer Lehre sind" (p. 295). See also the survey of Dinzelbacher, *Christliche Mystik*, pp. 315–30.

144. Gertrud Jaron Lewis, *By Women, for Women, about Women: The Sister-Books of Fourteenth-Century Germany*, p. 56. This work supersedes all previous English accounts of the *Sister Books*. There is a rich literature in German. See especially Siegfried Ringler, *Viten- und Offenbarungsliteratur in Frauenklöstern des Mittelalters: Quellen und Studien;* and his summary discussion in "Gnadenviten aus süddeutschen Frauenklöstern des 14. Jahrhunderts–Vitenschreibung als mystisiche Lehre," in *"Minnichlichui gotes erkennusse": Studien zur frühen abendländischen Mystiktradition Heidelberger Mystiksymposium vom 16.Januar 1989*, ed. Dietrich Schmidtke

(Stuttgart/Bad Canstatt: frommann-holzboog, 1990), pp. 89–104. Also important is Otto Langer, *Mystische Erfahrung und spirituelle Theologie*, as well as the brief summary of his argument in "Zur Dominikanischen Frauenmystik im spätmittelalterlichen Deutschland," in *Frauenmystik im Mittelalter*, ed. Peter Dinzelbacher and Dieter R. Bauer, pp. 341–46. There is a wealth of information in the edition and commentary on one of these books to be found in Ruth Meyer, *Das 'St. Katharinentaler Schwesternbuch': Untersuchung. Edition. Kommentar* (Tübingen: Niemeyer, 1995). I have not seen Hester Gehring, "The Language of Mysticism in South German Dominican Convent Chronicles of the Fourteenth Century" (Ph.D. diss., University of Michigan, 1957).

145. U 360.30–35 (for reference system see n. 147): Uidit enim repente uisibilter ignem diuinum de celo magno cum sonitu aduenientem super sanctum conuentum sororum deo psallencium. Et repleuit totum chorum ubi erant sorores in Deo laudibus congregate, illuminans eas adeo diuinis splendoribus, quod omnes pariter ignee apparebant.

146. For these three components, see Lewis, *By Women*, pp. 47–54.

147. In their modern editions this literature amounts to about 550 printed pages (admittedly of quite different sizes)–approximately half the size of the material we have from Helfta. A list of the nine *Sister Books* with their publication references and dates follows. Since the printed versions of these texts are often difficult to find, Lewis's *By Women* includes microfiche versions of eight of the texts, as well as a listing of known manuscripts (pp. 286–89). The following information is based on Lewis, pp. 10–31, 292, and makes use of her abbreviations to identify the books.

(A) Adelhausen near Freiburg begun about 1234 became Dominican in 1245. This book was composed ca. 1310–1320 by Anna of Munzingen and one version of it was edited by J. König, "Die Chronik der Anna von Munzingen: Nach der ältesten Abschrift mit Einleitung und Beilagen," *Freiburger Diözesan Archiv* 13 (1880): 129–236. It contains a chronicle of the history of the monastery and the lives of some thirty-four sisters.

(D) Diessenhofen (also known as Katharinenthal) in Switzerland, begun ca. 1240 also became Dominican in 1245. The book containing a chronicle, three lengthy *vitae* and over fifty shorter ones was composed ca. 1318–1343, but was added to in the later fourteenth century. For an edition with an excellent apparatus, see Ruth Meyer, *Das 'St. Katharinentaler Schwesternbuch.'*

(E) Engelthal (whose history was given above) produced a book containing a chronicle and accounts of some fifty sisters written by Christine Ebner about 1340. It was edited by Karl Schröder, *Der Nonne von Engeltal Büchlein von der Genaden Uberlast* (Tübingen: Literarische Verein, 1871).

(G) Gotteszell outside Schwäbisch-Gmünd began ca. 1240 and was accepted into the Dominican order in 1246. This *Sister Book* has a long *vita* of Adelheit of Hiltegarthausen and a dozen shorter entries. It was composed ca. 1320–1330 and was mistakenly edited as the second part of the Kirchberg book by F. W. E. Roth, "Aufzeichnungen über das mystische Leben der Nonnen von Kirchberg bei Sulz Predigerordens während des XIV. und XV. Jahrhunderts," *Alemannia* 21 (1893): 123–48.

(K) Kirchberg in Sulz, Württemberg, was founded in 1237 and was incorporated into the Dominicans in 1245. Its book was written by Elisabeth of Kirchberg, a convert from Judaism, about 1330–1340 and contains about fifteen lives. A poor edition can be found in Roth, "Aufzeichnungen . . . ," pp. 103–23.

(O) Oetenbach began as a group of beguines in Zurich in 1231, but had moved outside the city to "Otto's brook" before they became Dominicans in 1245. In 1285 the community moved back into Zurich for safety. Composed about 1340, the book contains a long account of the monastery's history and six lives. See H. Zeller-Werdmüller and Jakob Bächtold, "Die Stiftung des Klosters Oetenbach und das Leben der seligen Schwestern daselbst, aus der Nürnberger Handschrift," *Zürcher Taschenbuch* n.s. 12 (1889): 213–76.

(T) Töss began as a beguinage in Winterthur about 1233 and became Dominican in 1245. This large and wealthy community housing about 160 women produced the only illuminated manuscript of a *Sister Book* (Nürnberg municipal library, cod. Cent. V 10a). The well-known Elsbeth Stagel, Henry Suso's friend and collaborator, composed part of the text containing a chronicle and accounts of forty sisters. An unsatisfactory edition can be found in Ferdinand Vetter, *Das Leben der Schwestern zu Töss beschrieben von Elsbet Stagel* (Berlin: Weidmann, 1906).

(U) Unterlinden (*sub tilia*) in Colmar began as a house of pious widows ca. 1230 under the sponsorship of Friar Walther, the Dominican lector at Strassburg. For a time it existed outside the city at a spot called "ufmulin." It became Dominican in 1245 and moved back into the city in 1252. This Latin *Sister Book,* composed about 1320 by Katharina of Unterlinden, contains a foundation chronicle and the lives of forty nuns, frequently of some length. For an edition, see Jeanne Ancelet-Hustache, "Les *Vitae sororum d'Unterlinden:* Edition critique du manuscrit 508 de la Bibliothèque de Colmar," *Archives d'histoire doctrinale et littéraire du moyen age* 5 (1930): 317–517.

(W) Weiler was founded in 1230 as the first Dominican house in the diocese of Constance, apparently absorbing some earlier beguines. The monastery's incorporation into the Dominicans was confirmed by popes in 1236 and 1245. This book was composed about 1350 and has no chronicle, but gives the lives of twenty-seven nuns. See Karl Bihlmeyer, "Mystisches Leben in dem Dominikanerinnenkloster Weiler bei Esslingen im 13. und 14. Jahrhunderts," *Württembergische Vierteljahreshefte für Landesgeschichte* n.s. 25 (1916): 61–93.

148. Ringler, *Viten- und Offenbarungsliteratur,* pp. 352–56; "Gnadenviten aus süddeutschen Frauernklöstern," pp. 98–104.

149. For the way in which these nine houses became Dominican, see Lewis, *By Women,* pp. 179–86, who also has a good discussion of how the preaching friars executed their *cura monialium* (pp. 186–93).

150. U Prol. (ed., 335): . . . ne in obliuionem aliquando ueniant tam excellentes sorores, earumque gesta gloriosa et mirabilia opera eximie sanctitatis, et ut cum quanta gloria et religione istud sanctum monasterium sit fundatum, tam modernis quam posteris innotescat. . . .

151. See Langer, *Mystische Erfahrung und spirituelle Theologie,* pp. 60–64.

152. Not all uses of the term *iubilus* and *iubilum* need be taken as technical terms for a mystical grace of song; sometimes the word has a more generic sense of inner joy. See Ringler, *Viten- und Offenbarungsliteratur,* pp. 160–61.

153. For a survey, see Langer, *Mystische Erfahrung und spirituelle Theologie,* pp. 127–55.

154. In 1324 Eckhart visited Diessenhofen, where he spoke with the visionary Anne of Ramschwag (D 131–32). Elsbet of Beggenhofen, a nun at Oetenbach, consulted Eckhart about her spiritual experiences, and he advised her to "entrust herself to God in free detachment" (O 263). On these visits, see Lewis, *By Women,* pp. 188–91.

155. Obviously, there are some hints of themes related to Eckhart in some of the *Sister Books,* as Ringler points out with regard to the book from Oetenbach ("Gnadenviten," pp. 101–3).

156. There are a few exceptions, such as Oetenbach nun Ita of Hohenfels (O 289–40), who is described as cutting herself with knives to the bone but being miraculously cured in three days. Lewis notes the critical tone in which this story is recounted (*By Women,* pp. 244–45).

157. For stories regarding these types of asceticism, see Lewis, *By Women,* pp. 253–58. Especially noteworthy is the community aspect of the corporal flagellation described in U 340.25-31: In aduentu Domini et per omne tempus quadragessime uniuerse sorores post matutinas in capitulum diuertentes, siue ad loca alia opportuna diuersis flagellorum generibus corpus suum usque ad sanguinis effusio lacerantes crudelissime et hostiliter ceciderunt, ita quod sonus uerberancium se ubique per omne monasterium resonaret. . . .

158. U 418.13–15: ... corpus suum tamdiu hostiliter uirgis acerrimis uerberauit, donec miserante Domino tantam diuine gracie afflueniciam precordiis suis illabi persenit. ...

159. See "Maladie," DS 10:137–52.

160. For two summaries of the role of suffering and illness, see Margot Schmidt, "Leiden und Weisheit in der christlichen Mystik des Mittelalters," in *Leiden und Weisheit in der Mystik*, ed. Bernd Jaspert (Paderborn: Bonifatius, 1992), pp. 149–65, who deals with Bernard and Mechthild; and the more wide-ranging study of Alois M. Haas, "'Trage Leiden geduldiglich': Die Einstellung der deutschen Mystik zum Leiden," in *Gott Leiden. Gott Lieben: Zur volkssprachlichen Mystik im Mittelalter* (Frankfurt: Insel, 1989), pp. 127–52.

161. E 9.22–23: We ist ein gut wort, we ist ein suzez wort, we ist ein genadenrichez wort.

162. D 129.11–14: Vnser herr der gab ir vil lidens in ir leben, won si was gar krank und siech mengú jar . . . . Vnd mit ir liden wart si bereit gross gnad ze empfahen.

163. For more accounts and reflections on the role of suffering, see Lewis, *By Women*, pp. 159–61, 242–45; and Ringler, *Viten- und Offenbarungsliteratur*, pp. 169–70. Haas also notes the role that illness plays in this mystical literature ("Nonnenleben und Offenbarungsliteratur," pp. 295–96).

164. A 160; see Lewis, *By Women*, p. 144.

165. For an overview, see Hans Belting, *Likeness and Presence: A History of the Image before the Era of Art* (Chicago: University of Chicago Press, 1994). For a more general study of the role of images, both sacred and profane, see David Freedberg, *The Power of Images: Studies in the History and Theory of Response* (Chicago: University of Chicago Press, 1989).

166. For introductions to the relation between visions and mysticism in the late Middle Ages, especially among women, see, e.g., Jeffrey Hamburger, "The Visual and the Visionary: The Image in Late Medieval Monastic Devotions," *Viator* 20 (1989): 161–82; and Chiara Frugoni, "Female Mystics, Visions, and Iconography," in *Women and Religion in Medieval and Renaissance Italy*, pp. 130–64; Elisabeth Vavra, "Bildmotiv und Frauenmystik–Funktion und Rezeption," *Frauenmystik im Mittelalter*, pp. 201–30.

167. The richest treatment is that of Chiara Frugoni, *Francesco e l'invenzione delle stimmate: Una storia per parole e immagini fino a Bonaventura e Giotto* (Turin: Einaudi, 1993) as noted in chap. 1.

168. See, e.g., Henk van Os, et al., *The Art of Devotion in the Late Middle Ages in Europe 1300–1500* (Princeton: Princeton University Press, 1994); and Joanna E. Ziegler, *Sculpture of Compassion: The Pietà and the Beguines in the Southern Low countries c. 1300–c.1600* (Brussels/Rome: Institut Historique Belge de Rome, 1992). This shift of interest is also evident in more recent general works on Gothic art, especially Michael Camille, *Gothic Art: Glorious Visions*, especially chap. 3, "New Visions of God."

169. For a programmatic overview, see Jeffrey Hamburger, "Art, Enclosure and the *Cura Monialium:* Prolegomena in the Guise of a Postscript," *Gesta* 31 (1992): 108–34. Hamburger has produced two volumes on particular examples of illustrated manuscripts for nuns that are clearly of a mystical character. See *The Rothschild Canticles: Art and Mysticism in Flanders and the Rhineland circa 1300* (New Haven: Yale University Press, 1990), which contains a rich series of illuminations relating not only to the Song of Songs, the saints, and paradise, but also to mystical union and the mystery of the Trinity. Hamburger argues that the manuscript was produced in France, but for a Dutch or German nun, quite possibly a Dominican (see pp. 161–62). More recently, his *Nuns as Artists: The Visual Culture of a Medieval Convent* investigates a manuscript produced ca. 1500 by a nun at the Benedictine convent at Eichstätt.

170. See the general comments in Lewis, *By Women*, pp. 91–92 and 100–22 passim. For a detailed study of one image, see Jeffrey Hamburger, "The *Liber miraculorum* of Unterlinden: An Icon in its Convent Setting," in *The Sacred Image East and West*, ed. Robert Ousterhout and L. Brubaker (Champaign-Urbana: University of Illinois Press, 1995), pp. 147–90.

171. D 111.1-7: Die bettet eins tages vor einem bild, da únser herr an der sule stuond, vnd
begert von allem iren hertzen, das ir únser herr geb ze empfinden des seres vnd der bitterkeit
in der er was in dem zit, do er an der sul stuond. Des gewert si únser herr, vnd wurden all ir
inaeder vnd allú irú gelider als gar durch gossen mit grosser pin vnd bitterkeit, das si
empfintlich empfant der marter, di únser herr laid, do er an der sul stuond, als vil als ir
mvglich was ze enpfindenn. For some other examples, see, e.g., A 170-71 and E 11.

172. D 44.4-6: Vnd lidiget do únser herr den rehten arm ab dem crútz vnd vmb vieng si
vnd trukt si an sich (trans. Lewis, *By Women,* p. 110).

173. D 130.42-45: Si [Anne of Ramschwag] ze einem mal vor dem grossen bilde, da sant
Johannes ruowet vff únsers herren hertzen, vnd stuond sant Mie von Rettershouen hinder ir
ovch an ir gebett vnd sah, das si als luter ward als eine cristalle vnd das reht ein schin eins
liehtes von in gie. Seeing holy nuns as crystals giving off light is common in the *Sister Books*
(for references, see Meyer, *Das 'St. Katharinentaler Schwesternbuch',* pp. 197-98). On the role of
St. John, see Lewis, *By Women,* p. 116.

174. On Hedwig, see U 439-50. Among the other interesting visionaries in this longest of
the books, see Benedicta of Egenshen (350-54), Agnes of Ohenstein (354-59), Gertrude of
Colombaria (359-62), H. of Langelnheim (378-80), Herburg of Herenkeim (387-94), Adelheid of Rheinfelden (394-406), Tuda of Colombaria (428-30), Mechthild of Colombaria
(469-71), and, from a later addition to the book, Margaret of Brisach (499-504).

175. For other examples of infused theological wisdom in the *Sister Books,* see Lewis, *By
Women,* pp. 272 and 277-80. In W 70 a friar is described as praising a sister for the height of
her heavenly knowledge.

176. For comments on this life, see the apparatus in Meyer, *Das 'St. Katharinertaler
Schwesternbuch,'* pp. 258-67.

177. D 130.50-51: Gib mir das din, so gib ich dir das min. On this expression, see
Friedrich Ohly, "Du bist mein, Ich bin dein. Du in mir, Ich in dir. Ich du, du ich," in *Kritische
Bewahrung: Beiträge zur deutschen Philologie. Festschrift für Werner Schröder,* pp. 371-415.

178. D 130.55-59: Vnd disen rosen den truog si mit luter erkantnúss, mit brinnender
minn vnd mit inhitziger begird in ir hertzen bis an ir tot. Darnach do si únsern herren
empfieng, do ward ir der ander ros geben. Vnd is disem rosen erkant si got luterlich vnd
schovwet in got alles, das si wolt.

179. On the German terms for such raptures in the *Sister Books* (e.g., *gezogen, verzuecket,
entzuecht, usgezucket, verzuecket*), see the remarks in Meyer, *Das 'St. Katharinertaler Schwesternbuch,'* pp. 229-30. These are the equivalents of the familiar Latin terms *raptus-ecstasis-excessus
mentis,* as can be seen from the Unterlinden book.

180. D 131.84-85: Vnd in dirr gesiht ward ir zerkennen gegeben, das das ein kindli únser
herr was vnd das ander ir sele, vnd wie si vnd got vereinet was. In general, descriptions and
terminolgy for union with God in the *Sister Books* follow the inherited patterns of the *unitas
spiritus* tradition, though a few formulations seem stronger (see Lewis, *By Women,* pp. 139-40).

181. E.g., the first story (E 10.26-11.34) about revelations concerning Alheit's invalid baptism in which, as a child, she refuses to yield to various heavenly messengers God sends to
inform her about the fact until John the Baptist manages to convince her and gives her "a
baptism of grace" (*ein tauf der genaden*).

182. E 11.34-38: . . . an der mitwochen in der marterwochen da wird sie entzuket biz an
der osterabent, und sach ellew dev dink die an unserm herren ergangen waren, und brust daz
man in an der seul geslagen het, daz er da an dem dritten slag geblut het.

183. E 14.9-12: Da sprach di priolin zu ir: "Du tust sam ein gans: sing in dinem choer
und laz einen chor stehen." Da fledert sie mit den armen und wont, sie wer ein gans, biz die
priolin sprach: "Du bist kein gans." Da liez sie aller von der ungeperde.

184. This account constitutes the major part of the section devoted to her (55.23-59.15).

185. T 56.14–27. This *vulnus amoris* is reminiscent of Gregory the Great's notion of the first form of *compunctio,* that is, the *compunctio timoris;* see *Growth of Mysticism,* pp. 48–50.

186. T 57.13–18: . . . do sach ich das ain liecht kam von himelrich, das was unmass schoen und wunneklich, und umgab mich das und durchlucht und durchglast mich allensament, und ward min hertz rech geches verwanlet und erfület mit ainer unsaglicher und ungewonlicher froed, also das ich gar und gantzlich vergass alles des widermuottes und seres das ich da vor ie gewan.

187. T 57.36–58.5: . . . und in disem liecht, das min sel was, sach ich Got wunneklich lúchten, als ein schoenes liecht lúcht usser ainer schoener lúchtenden lucernen, und sach das er sich als mineklich und als guotlich zuo miner sel fuogt das er recht geainbart ward mit ir und sy mit im. Und in dieser minenklichen ainbarung ward min sel gesichret von Got das mir alle min súnd vergeben werind lutterlich. . . .

188. T 58.35–59.3: Und do sy wider zuo dem lib kam, do ward sy dieser froelichen beschoewd nit berobet, won das sy noch do in dem lib wonend sich seber und got in ir als lutterlich und aigenlich schowet als do sy von dem lib verzuckt was.

189. The text of Margaret's *Offenbarungen* (about seven manuscripts survive), along with Henry's letters to her (surviving in a single late manuscript) was edited by Philipp Strauch, *Margaretha Ebner und Heinrich von Nördlingen: Ein Beitrag zur Geschichte der deutschen Mystik* (Freiburg/Tübingen: Mohr, 1882 [the edition will be cited by page and line in what follows]). Unless otherwise noted, I will use the translation by Leonard P. Hindsley, *Margaret Ebner: Major Works* (New York: Paulist Press, 1993), with a useful introduction by Hindsley and Margot Schmidt. Hindsley's volume contains a bibliography to older literature on Margaret and Henry. Among recent contributions, see Ursula Peters, *Religiöse Erfahrung als literarisches Faktum,* pp. 142–55, and "Vita religiosa und spirituelles Erleben: Frauenmystik und frauenmystische Literatur im 13. und 14. Jahrhundert," pp. 105–7; Manfred Weitlauff, "'dein got redender munt machet mich redenlosz . . .': Margareta Ebner und Heinrich von Nördlingen," in *Religiöse Frauenbewegung und mystische Frömmigkeit im Mittelalter,* pp. 303–52; and Dinzelbacher, *Christlicher Mystik,* pp. 324–29. In English, see also Leonard P. Hindsley, "Monastic Conversion: The Case of Margaret Ebner," in *Varieties of Religious Conversion in the Middle Ages,* ed. James Muldoon (Gainesville: University Press of Florida, 1997), pp. 31–46.

190. For the account of her illness, which introduces the *Offenbarungen,* see ed., 1.18–6.18. Its importance has been recognized by Peters, "Vita religiosa und spirituelles Erleben," p. 105; and *Religiöse Erfahrung,* pp. 144–45. Margaret also exemplifies another aspect of late medieval women's mysticism noted above, especially as found with the Dominican nuns, that is, the use of sacred images in attaining ecstatic states, as we shall see below.

191. For notices of Henry (d. 1379), see DS 7:229–30, and Manfred Weitlauff, "Heinrich von Nördlingen," in *Die deutsche Literatur des Mittelalters: Verfasserlexikon,* 3:845–52. See also Haas, "Nonnenleben und Offenbarungsliteratur," pp. 298–99. In English, consult Debra L. Stoudt, "The Vernacular Letters of Heinrich von Nördlingen," *Mystics Quarterly* 12 (1986): 19–25. Henry's epistles are said to be the earliest collection of German vernacular letters.

192. The relations between Henry and Margaret have been evaluated in rather different ways. Contrast, for example, Schmidt and Hindsley, "Introduction," in *Margaret Ebner,* pp. 31–41, which takes the descriptions in the text at more or less face value; and Peters, *Religiöse Erfahrung,* pp. 142–55, which sees considerable use of *topoi* in the picture of the relations of the two.

193. Ep. 4 (ed., 175.61–64; trans., 37): also lieblichen kom mir für das jarzeit, als dich got mir gab. dem getrau ich und unsern fründen, allen hailigen, das er mir und aller cristenhait sunder gut bei dir und usz dir schencken welle.

194. Henry, Ep. 46 (ed., 251.33–36; my translation): . . . da dein kusche brüst vol und ubervol werden sullen, das du nit allein mein, . . . mer aller der cristenheit wol seugendiü

amin werden solt. See Bernard of Clairvaux, *Sermones super Cantica* 9.7 (*Sancti Bernardi Opera* 1:46). Margaret had read St. Bernard and mentions him several times in the *Offenbarungen*, e.g., 21.25–22.2, 104.11–18.

195. See Henry, Ep. 42 (ed., 242.39): Ich mocht noch nie vor meinen siechtagen, der mich wider an sties, dein hailig geschrift uberleszen, in der ich sundertrost meins hertzen funden und enpfunden han.

196. See *Offenbarung* (ed., 83–84; trans., 130).

197. *Offenbarungen* (ed., 114.1–4; trans., 147): Item allez daz ich gescriben han, daz wart mir as gegenwertig, so man ez von mir und uz mir scriben wolt, mit sölcher inner genade als ze der zit, do ez mir geben wart. . . . On this see Peters, *Religiöse Erfahrung*, p. 146.

198. A number of Henry's letters deal with the writing of the *Offenbarungen;* see, e.g., Epp. 32, 40, 41, 42, 50, 52. These letters also make clear that Margaret was assisted by Elsbeth Scheppach, the prioress of Maria Medingen (Margaret briefly mentions a helper, but does not provide her name).

199. For Henry's account of his translation of Mechthild's FL, see Ep. 43 (ed., 246–47). The influence of Mechthild on Margaret still needs work. Margaret certainly knew the work, but some accounts (e.g., Hindsley and Schmidt, "Introduction," pp. 37–39, 46–47, and 61–62) make claims for influence on the basis of vague resemblances that seem difficult to accept.

200. For general surveys, see "Amis de Dieu," DS 1:493–500; and "Gottesfreunde/Gottesfreundschaft," in *Lexikon des Mittelalters*, 8 vols. to date (Munich/Zurich: Artemis, 1980–), 4:1586–87; and especially Alois M. Haas, "Gottesfreunde," in *Geschichte der deutschen Literatur. Die deutsche Literatur im späten Mittelalter 1250–1370*, pp. 299–303.

201. Older accounts in English (based on nineteenth-century German scholarship), which tended to present the whole history of medieval German mysticism under the rubric of the "Friends of God" movement, claim too much for it. See, e.g., Anna Groh Seesholtz, *Friends of God: Practical Mystics of the Fourteenth Century* (New York: Columbia University Press, 1934); and Rufus M. Jones, *The Flowering of Mysticism: The Friends of God in the Fourteenth Century* (New York: Macmillan, 1939).

202. The group referred to in the letters of Henry and Margaret, active in the 1330s and 1340s, should be distinguished from the later Strassbourg circle of "Friends of God" centered on Rulman Merswin (1307–1382) and the mysterious "Gottesfreund aus dem Oberland," which will be considered in the next volume.

203. Hindsley and Schmidt, "Introduction," p. 41.

204. Margaret is not portrayed as someone who practiced special bodily castigation, though her fasting and lack of bathing (no bath for thirty years!) would be asceticism enough for most. Likewise, she is not presented as a miracle-worker. Even the mention of her levitation (ed., 48.20–24; trans., 111) seems better understood in light of an ecstatic feeling of being raised to God rather than actual physical elevation.

205. *Offenbarungen* (ed., 15.11–17; trans., 93): nun was ez an ainer fritagen naht, und was ich ob den grebern gewesen und gieng in den cor mit grosser süezkait und der schmag gieng und trang mir inne durch das hertz in alliu miniu lider, und der nam Jhesus Christus wart mir da so kreftlich geben, daz ich nitz maht geahten, und was mir, wie ich da gegenwertig bi im wär. nun was ich in ainer als grossen gnaud, daz ich mich niht kund enziehen.

206. Ed., 87.16–21; trans., 132: aber min begirde und min lust ist in dem säugen, daz ich uz siner lutern menschet gerainiget werde und mit siner inbrünstiger minne uz im enzündet werde und ich mit siner gegenwertket und mit siner süezzer genade durchgossen werde, daz ich da mit gezogen werde in daz war niezzen sines götlichen wesens mit allen minnenden selen, die in der warhet gelebt hant. The language of the divine essence (*götlichen wesen*) in this account is rare in Margaret's *Offenbarungen*, which are largely untouched by the more specula-

tive language found in some of the beguines. Another example is found in a communication of God's will to Henry that speaks of how God intends to draw him into "the desert-oneness of my Holy Godhead" (*in ziehen in daz wild ain miner hailigen gothait*) and also mentions how the soul has "flowed out" from God (see ed. 76.11–77.2).

207. Ed., 88.29-89.4; trans., 133: so ist der inder lust und begirde as stark und as creftig in mir, daz ez as creftlichen an mich gezwungen ist, ob ich ez gern von mir tet, ich meht ez von mir nit bringen alle die wile mir diu götlich gegenwertket mit as creftiger süezzer genade an lit. Margaret goes on to compare this sense of presence to that which she enjoys when she receives Christ in the Eucharist.

208. Ed., 28.5–6; trans., 100: "ich bin niht ain berober der sinne, ich bin ain erliuhter der sinne." This incident took place on February 28, 1335.

209. See, e.g., ed., 76.4–5; trans., 126.

210. This may help explain an obscure reference early in the *Offenbarungen* (ed., 9.18–20; trans., 90) in which Margaret referred to something "physically annoying" that happened to her when Christ "played" with her at night–ich markt auch, wenne unser herre mit mir in dem schlauf schimphet, daz mir dann etwaz liplichs unmuotz wolt wider warn.

211. *Offenbarungen* (ed., 21.18–20; trans., 96). This drinking from the side of Christ occurs elewhere, in desire or reality; see, e.g., ed., 33, 74, etc.

212. *Offenbarungen* (ed., 27.18–24; trans., 100): und der aller süezzest name Jhesus Cristus wart mir da geben mit ainer so grozzen minne siner lieb, daz ich nihtz gebetten moht wan emsigiu red, diu mir inwendig geben wart von der götlichen craft gottes und der ich niht widerstaun moht. . . . See the whole account in ed., 27–29.

213. The *Pater Noster* can be found in ed., 161–66; trans., 175–78.

214. The accounts are numerous; e.g., *Offenbarungen* ed., 42, 45, 50–51, 63, 65–66, 72, 91–92, 93, 105, 107, 108–9, 117–21, and 121–27.

215. See, e.g., *Offenbarungen*, 93, 108–9, 117–21.

216. Ed., 118.9–15; trans., 149: . . . do kom mir alle tag ze mittem tag diu gebunden swige mit grossem smerzen und wert biz morgen ze metin, also daz ich nit mag geliden, daz ich ain hant uf die andern leg und daz ich miniu ougen nit mag uf tuon und daz ich min zen zesamen bizze und daz ich min hende nit mag zuo tuon ze ainer fust. For the account of the causes of the silence, see ed., 117.13–114.8.

217. Ed., 119.26–120.3; trans., 150: do komen die luten rüeffe und werten di lange. und die rüef mit luter stime 'owe' und 'owe' die sint as groz, daz man si über al in dem closter und uf dem hof hörn mag. . . .

218. The key texts can be found in ed., 54, 75, 92, 111, 120, 131, and 134 (trans., 114, 125–26, 135, 145, 150, 156, and 158).

219. Ed., 125.6–10; trans., 153: in der selben naht vor metin saczte mich min herre Jhesus Cristus so gar in ain ungesprochenlich ellende gelazzenhet, as ob ich alle min tag der genade unsers herren nie enphunden het. ich het daz gancz getruwen in sin barmherzeket verlorn. . . .

220. Ed., 125.26–126.11; trans. 153: und kum nach der metin as ain fruint . . . und tet mir sin triwe helfe schin. . . . und gab mir den aller süezzesten lust in sinem hailigen liden und da mit mit den grösten smerzen und daz gröst lait, dem allez lait nit gelichen mag in diser zit. und wart mir sin liden as enphindenliche gegenwertig, as ob ez des tagez vor minen augen geschehen wer. und do muost ich uz brechen von der gewalt gotez, der in mir wörht, . . .' owe! min herre Jhesus Cristus, owe!, min herre Jhesus Cristus.'

221. See Peter Ochsenbein, "Die Offenbarungen Elsbeths von Oye als Dokument leidens-fixierte Mystik," in *Abendländische Mystik im Mittelalter: Symposium Kloster Engelberg 1984*, ed. Kurt Ruh, pp. 423–42 (with a brief selection of texts); and "Leidensmystik in Dominikanischen Frauenklöstern des 14. Jahrhunderts am Beispiel der Elsbeth von Oye," in *Religiöse*

Frauenbewegung und mystische Frömmigkeit im Mittelalter, pp. 353–72. Ochsenbein's research has shown that Elsbeth's text, excerpted and presented in anonymous fashion, was perhaps the most popular of all medieval mystical works written by a woman, surviving in thirty to fifty manuscripts (see "Leidensmystik," pp. 357–60).

222. See Peters, "Vita religiosa und spirituelles Erleben," whose final section (pp. 107–9) gives a summary under the heading "Kloster Engelthal: ein Zentrum frauenmystischer Literatur."

223. For an introduction to Christine Ebner, see Siegfried Ringler, "Ebner, Christine," in *Die deutsche Literatur des Mittelalters: Verfasserlexikon,* 2:297–302. Two important accounts are Ursula Peters, "Das 'Leben' der Christine Ebner: Textanalyse und kulturhistorische Kommentar," in *Abendländischer Mystik im Mittelalter,* pp. 402–22; and the same author's *Religiöse Erfahrung,* pp. 155–76. See also Ringler, "Die Rezeption mittelalterlicher Frauenmystik als wissenschaftlicher Problem, dargestellt am Werk der Christine Ebner," in *Frauenmystik im Mittelalter,* pp. 178–200.

224. Ringler, *Viten- und Offenbarungsliteratur,* pp. 391–444 for the text and pp. 144–331 for the commentary. For a brief presentation of Sunder, see Dinzelbacher, *Christliche Mystik,* pp. 321–22.

225. The *Revelations* were published as *Die Offenbarungen der Adelheid Langmann Klosterfrau zu Engelthal,* ed. Philipp Strauch (Strassburg: Trübner, 1878; for the history of the text, see also Ringler, *Viten- und Offenbarungsliteratur,* pp. 65–82). There are three known manuscripts, of which Strauch used only two. (In citing the text I will refer to the Strauch edition by page and line.) For a forthcoming translation and introduction, see Leonard P. Hindsley, *The Revelations of Adelheid Langmann* (Gainesville: University Press of Florida, 1998). My thanks to Prof. Hindsley for allowing me access to this helpful work. An important treatment of Adelheid can be found in Peters, *Religiöse Erfahrung,* pp. 176–88; for brief accounts, see "Langmann (Adélheide)," in DS 9:221–23; and Dinzelbacher, *Christliche Mystik,* pp. 329–30.

226. Ecstatic women, from Mary of Oignies on, were portrayed as able to release souls from purgatory through their intimate contact with God. By the time of Adelheid's *Offenbarungen* this motif takes the form of massive statistics—some dozen accounts in the text give her a tally of over 600,000 souls released!

227. See ed., 75–76; following one of the manuscripts, Hindsley rightly suggests that this incident belongs earlier in the story.

228. Ed., 92.1–3: "ich wil mein hertze gizzen in ir hertze und ir hertze in mein hertze, und wil si mit einander vereinen und wil ir peider selber hüeten."

229. Ed. 26.11–14: . . . 'sitz nider, mein libe, ich wil mit dir spuntziren' und sprach: 'mein gemeinte, mein zarte, mein schöne, mein minnensuzzez liep, unter deinen zingen ist honig.' And ed., 47.8-11: 'mein zukersüezzez und mein honigsüezzez lip, mein zarte, mein reine, du pist mein und ich pin dein. wir sein vereint und süllen vereinet ewichlichen sein. For other texts on Adelheid as the bride, see, e.g., ed., 11–12, 19–20, 22, 46–47, and 61–66.

230. Ed., 92.17–19: ich hon euch einmüetig gemachet in der einmüetikeit der heiligen driveltikeit. eu wirt gegeben in dem geben der heiligen driveltikeit (using the translation of Hindsley).

231. Ed., 41.31–42.3: "ich wil dir sagen, daz ich dein sel gezogen hon uz allen dein glidern und uz allen deinen kreften und hon si gezukt und gezogen in di wilden gotheit und in di wüest meinder gothait."

232. Ed., 65.27–66.3: mit dem selben wort, daz als süezziclich ging uz seim mund, zoh er mein arme, sündige sel in sein gotheit, daz ich nimmer gesagen kan von disem gesiht, denn daz ich das wol weizz, daz ez sich erhueb do man complet gesungen het und wert biz an den andern tag daz man messe het gesungen.

Bibliography

Accrocca, Felice. "Nodi problematici delle fonti francescane a proposito di due recenti edizioni." *Collectanea Francescana* 6 (1996): 563–96.

Alessandrini, A. "Andalò, Diana d'." *Dizionario Biografico degli Italiani,* 3:48–50. Rome: Istituto della Enciclopedia Italiana, 1961.

Allard, Guy-H. "La technique de la 'reductio' chez Bonaventure." In *San Bonaventura 1274–1974,* 2:395–416. 5 vols. Grottaferrata/Rome: Collegio S. Bonaventura, 1974.

Alszeghy, Zoltan. *Grundformen der Liebe: Die Theorie der Gottesliebe bei dem Hl. Bonaventura.* Rome: Gregorian University, 1946.

"Amis de Dieu." DS 1:493–500.

Ancelet-Hustache, Jeanne. *Mechthilde de Magdebourg (1207–1282): Étude de psychologie religieuse.* Paris: Champion, 1926.

Andres, Friedrich. "Die Stufen der Contemplatio in Bonaventuras *Itinerarium mentis in Deum* und im *Benjamin maior* des Richard von St. Viktor." *Franziskanische Studien* 8 (1921): 189–200.

Anson, Peter. *The Call of the Desert: The Solitary Life in the Christian Church.* London: SPCK, 1964.

Armstrong, Edward A. *Saint Francis: Nature Mystic. The Derivation and Significance of the Nature Stories in the Franciscan Legend.* Berkeley/Los Angeles: University of California Press, 1973.

Auerbach, Erich. *Literary Language & Its Public in Late Latin Antiquity and in the Middle Ages.* New York: Pantheon, 1965.

———. *Mimesis: The Representation of Reality in Western Literature.* Garden City, N.Y.: Doubleday, 1957.

Babinsky, Ellen Louise. "A Beguine in the Court of the King: The Relation of Love and Knowledge in 'The Mirror of Simple Souls' by Marguerite Porete." Ph.D. diss., University of Chicago, 1991.

———. "The Use of Courtly Language in *Le Mirouer des simples ames anienties* by Marguerite Porete." *Essays in Medieval Studies* 4 (1987): 93–106.

Backmund, Norbert. "Das Kloster Hane (Hagen) im Bolanden (Pfalz)." *Analecta Praemonstratensia* 56 (1980): 103–4.

Baldelli, Ignazio, and Angiola Maria Romanini, eds. *Francesco, Francescanesimo e la cultura della nuova Europa.* Rome: Istituto della Enciclopedia Italiana, 1986.

Baldwin, John W. *Masters, Princes and Merchants: The Social Views of Peter the Chanter and his Circle.* 2 vols. Princeton: Princeton University Press, 1970.

Barbet, Jeanne. "Thomas Gallus." DS 15:800–816.

———. "Introduction." In *Thomas Gallus: Commentaires du Cantique des Cantiques,* 43–61. Paris: Vrin, 1967.

———. *Un Commentaire du Cantique attribué à Thomas Gallus.* Paris/Louvain: Béatrice-Nauwelaerts, 1972.

Bardoel, A. A. "On the Nature of Mystical Experience in the *Visions* of Hadewijch: A Comparative Study of the Unitive and the Intellectual Traditions." *Ons Geestelijk Erf* 66 (1992): 318–40.

Bargiel, Taddeo. "Davide d'Augusta: Introduzione." In *Dizionario Francescano: I Mistici. Scritti dei Mistici Francescani Secolo XIII,* 177–80. Assisi: Editrici Francescane, 1995.

Bartlett, Anne Clark. *Male Authors, Female Readers: Representation and Subjectivity in Middle English Devotional Literature.* Ithaca: Cornell University Press, 1995.

———, et al., eds. *Vox Mystica: Essays on Medieval Mysticism in Honor of Professor Valerie M. Lagorio.* Cambridge: D.S. Brewer, 1995.

Bartlett, Robert. *The Making of Europe: Conquest, Colonization and Cultural Change 950–1350.* Princeton: Princeton University Press, 1993.

Bartoli, Marco. "Analisi storica e interpretazione psicanalitica di una visione di S. Chiara d'Assisi." *Archivum Franciscanum Historicum* 73 (1980): 449–72.

———. *Clare of Assisi.* Quincy, Ill.: Franciscan Press, 1993.

Bartoli Langeli, Attilio. "Gli Scritti da Francesco: L'autografia di un *illitteratus.*" In *Frate Francesco d'Assisi: Atti del XXI Convegno internazionale,* 101–59. Spoleto: Centro Italiano di Studi sull'alto Medioevo, 1994.

Bäuml, Franz H. "Varieties and Consequences of Medieval Literacy and Illiteracy." *Speculum* 55 (1980): 237–65.

Beckman, Patricia Zimmerman. "Ritual Clothing and Nakedness in Mechthild of Magdeburg's Journey to Mystical Union." Unpublished paper.

Beierwaltes, Werner. "Aufstieg und Einung in Bonaventuras mysticher Schrift 'Itinerarium mentis in Deum.'" In *Denken des Einen,* 385–423. Frankfurt: Klostermann, 1984.

Bell, David. *What Nuns Read: Books and Libraries in Medieval English Nunneries.* Kalamazoo: Cistercian Publications, 1995.

Bell, Rudolph M. *Holy Anorexia.* Chicago: University of Chicago Press, 1985.

Bell, Susan Groag. "Medieval Women Book Owners: Arbiters of Lay Piety and Ambassadors of Popular Culture." In *Sisters and Workers in the Middle Ages,* edited by Judith M. Bennett et al., 135–61. Chicago: University of Chicago Press, 1989.

Belting, Hans. *Likeness and Presence: A History of the Image before the Era of Art.* Chicago: University of Chicago Press, 1994.

Benevolo, Leonardo. *The European City*. Oxford: Blackwell, 1995.

Bennett, Judith M., et al., eds. *Sisters and Workers in the Middle Ages*. Chicago: University of Chicago Press, 1989.

Bériou, Nicole. "Autour de Latran IV (1215): La naissance de la confession moderne et sa diffusion." In *Pratique de la confession: Des pères du désert à Vatican II. Quinze études d'histoire*, 73–93. Paris: Cerf, 1983.

———. "Le prédication au béguinage de Paris pendant l'année liturgique 1272–73." *Recherches augustiniennes* 13 (1978): 105–229.

Bernards, Matthäus. "Nudus nudum Christum sequi." *Wissenschaft und Weisheit* 14 (1951): 148–51.

Beumer, Johannes. "Zwei schwierige Begriffe in der mystischen Theologie Bonaventuras ('raptus' und 'ecstasis')." *Franziskanische Studien* 56 (1974): 249–62.

Bihl, Michael. "Fr. Bertramus von Ahlen, O.F.M.: Ein Mystiker und Scholastiker, c. 1315." *Archivum Franciscanum Historicum* 40 (1947): 3–48.

Bihlmeyer, Karl. "Mystisches Leben in dem Dominikanerinnenkloster Weiler bei Esslingen im 13. und 14. Jahrhunderts." *Württembergische Vierteljahreshefte für Landesgeschichte* n.s. 25 (1916): 61–93.

———. "Die Selbstbiographie in der deutschen Mystik des Mittelalters." *Theologische Quartalschrift* 114 (1933): 504–44.

Bissen, J.-M. *L'exemplarisme divin selon Saint Bonaventure*. Paris: Vrin, 1929.

Bizziccari, Alvaro. "L'amore mistico di Jacopone da Todi." *Italica* 45 (1968): 1–27.

Blasucci, Antonio. "Frères Mineurs. III, Spiritualité Franciscaine: 1226–1517." DS 5:1315–47.

Blumenfeld-Kosinski, Renate, and Timea Szell, eds. *Images of Sainthood in Medieval Europe*. Ithaca: Cornell University Press, 1991.

Boesch Gajano, Sofia. "Storia e tradizione vallombrosane." *Bullettino dell'Istituto Storico Italiano per il Medio Evo* 76 (1964): 99–215.

Boff, Leonardo. *St. Francis: A Model for Human Liberation*. New York: Crossroad, 1982.

Bolton, Brenda. "Fulk of Toulouse: The Escape that Failed." In *Church, Society and Politics*, edited by Derek Baker, 83–93. Oxford: Blackwell, 1975.

———. "Mulieres Sanctae." In *Sanctity and Secularity: The Church and the World*, edited by Derek Baker, 77–95. New York: Barnes & Noble, 1973.

———. "Some Thirteenth Century Women in the Low Countries. A Special Case?" *Nederlands Archief voor Kerkgeschiedenis* 61 (1981): 7–29.

———. "*Vitae Matrum*: A Further Aspect of the *Frauenfrage*." In *Medieval Women*, edited by Derek Baker, 253–73. Oxford: Blackwell, 1978.

Bonnefoy, Jean-François. *Le Saint-Esprit et ses dons selon Saint Bonaventure*. Paris: Vrin, 1929.

———. "Une somme bonaventurienne de théologie mystique." *La France Franciscaine* 15 (1932): 77–86, 227–64, 311–59; 16 (1933): 259–326.

Bonner, Anthony, ed. *Selected Works of Ramon Llull (1232–1316)*. 2 vols. Princeton: Princeton University Press, 1985.

———, and Charles Lohr. "Raymond Lulle." DS 13:171–87.

Bornstein, Daniel. "The Uses of the Body: The Church and the Cult of Santa Margherita da Cortona." *Church History* 62 (1993): 163–77.

———. "Women and Religion in Late Medieval Italy: History and Historiography." In *Women and Religion in Medieval and Renaissance Italy,* edited by Daniel Bornstein and Roberto Rusconi, 1–27. Chicago: University of Chicago Press, 1996.

———, and Roberto Rusconi, eds. *Women and Religion in Medieval and Renaissance Italy.* Chicago: University of Chicago Press, 1996.

Bosl, Karl. *Armut Christi: Ideal der Monche und Ketzer, Ideologie der aufsteigenden Gesellschaftsschichten vom 11. bis 13. Jahrhundert.* Bayerische Akademie der Wissenschaften, Philosophisch-historische Klasse, Jahrgang 1981, Heft 1. Munich: Bayerische Akademie der Wissenschaften, 1981.

Bougerol, Jacques Guy. "L'aspect original de *l'Itinerarium mentis in deum* et son influence sur la spiritualité de son temps." *Antonianum* 52 (1977): 309–25.

———. *Introduction to the Works of Bonaventure.* Paterson: St. Anthony Guild Press, 1963.

———. "Jean 'de Caulibus.'" DS 8:324–26.

———. "La perfection chrétienne et la structuration des trois vies de la vie spirituelle dans la pensée de saint Bonaventure." *Études Franciscaines* 19 (1969): 397–409.

———. *Saint Bonaventure: Études sur les sources de sa pensée.* Northampton: Variorum Reprints, 1989.

Bouyer, Louis. *Women Mystics.* San Francisco: Ignatius Press, 1993.

Boyle, Leonard E. "The Inter-Conciliar Period 1179–1215 and the Beginnings of the Pastoral Manuals." In *Miscellanea Rolando Bandinelli, Papa Alessandro III,* edited by Filippo Liotta, 43–56. Siena: Accademia Senese degli Intronati, 1986.

Bradley, Ritamary. "Backgrounds of the Title *speculum* in Mediaeval Literature." *Speculum* 29 (1954): 100–115.

———. "Beatrice of Nazareth (c. 1200–1268): A Search for her True Spirituality." In *Vox Mystica: Essays on Medieval Mysticism in Honor of Professor Valerie M. Lagorio,* edited by Anne Clark Bartlett et al., 57–74. Cambridge: D.S. Brewer, 1995.

———. "Love and Knowledge in the *Seven Manners of Loving.*" In *Hidden Springs: Cistercian Monastic Women,* edited by John A. Nichols and Lillian Thomas Shank, 1:361–76. 2 vols. Kalamazoo: Cistercian Publications, 1995.

Bredero, Adriaan. "Religious Life in the Low Countries (ca. 1050–1384)." In *Christendom and Christianity in the Middle Ages,* 319–75. Grand Rapids: Eerdmans, 1994.

Breuer, Wilhelm. "Philologische Zugänge zur Mystik Hadewijchs: Zu Form und Funktion religiöser Sprache bei Hadewijch." In *Grundfragen christlicher Mystik,* edited by Margot Schmidt and Dieter R. Bauer, 103–21. Stuttgart/Bad Canstatt: frommann-holzboog, 1987.

Brooke, Rosalind B. *Early Franciscan Government.* Cambridge: Cambridge University Press, 1959.

Brufani, Stefano. "Angela da Foligno e gli Spirituali." In *Angela da Foligno Terziaria*

Francescana, edited by Enrico Menestò, 83–104. Spoleto: Centro Italiano di Studi sull'Alto Medioevo, 1992.

Brunel-Lobrichon, Geneviève. "Existe-t-il un christianisme méridional? L'exemple de Douceline: Le béguinage provençal." *Heresis* 11 (1988): 41–51.

Brunette, Pierre. "Une amitié spirituelle: François et Claire d'Assise vue par les symboles de leur itinéraire." *La vie des communautés religieuses* 47 (1989): 26–48.

———. *Essai d'analyse symbolique des Admonitions de François d'Assise.* Montréal: Pontificia Universitas Gregoriana, 1989.

———. "François et Claire." In *Sainte Claire d'Assise et sa posterité: VIIIe Centenaire de Sainte Claire,* 87–100. Paris/Montréal: Actes du Colloque de l'UNESCO, 1994.

Buholzer, Sonja A. *Studien zur Gottes- und Seelenkonzeption im Werk der Mechthild von Magdeburg.* Bern/Frankfurt: Peter Lang, 1988.

Bultmann, Rudolf. *Theology of the New Testament.* New York: Scribner, 1951.

Burr, David. "Olivi, Apocalyptic Expectation, and Visionary Experience." *Traditio* 41 (1985): 273–88.

———. *Olivi and Franciscan Poverty.* Philadelphia: University of Pennsylvania Press, 1989.

———. "Olivi on Prophecy." In *Lo statuto della profezia nel Medioevo,* edited by G. L. Potestà and Roberto Rusconi. *Cristianesimo nella storia* 17.2 (1996): 369–91.

———. *Olivi's Peaceable Kingdom: A Reading of the Apocalypse Commentary.* Philadelphia: University of Pennsylvania Press, 1993.

———. *The Persecution of Peter Olivi.* Philadelphia: American Philosophical Society, 1976.

Bussels, Amandus. "Saint Lutgard's Mystical Spirituality." In *Hidden Springs. Cistercian Monastic Women,* edited by John A. Nichols and Lillian Thomas Shank, 2:211–23. 2 vols. Kalamazoo: Cistercian Publications, 1995.

Butler, Cuthbert. *Western Mysticism.* New York: Dutton, 1923.

Bynum, Caroline Walker. "The Female Body and Religious Practice in the Later Middle Ages." In *Fragments for a History of the Human Body. Part One,* edited by Michel Feher, 160–219. New York: Zone, 1989.

———. *Fragmentation and Redemption: Essays on Gender and the Human Body in Medieval Religion.* New York: Zone Books, 1992.

———. *Holy Feast and Holy Fast: The Religious Significance of Food to Medieval Women.* Berkeley/Los Angeles: University of California, 1987.

———. *Jesus as Mother.* Berkeley/Los Angeles: University of California Press, 1982.

———. "Religious Women in the Later Middle Ages." In *Christian Spirituality II: High Middle Ages and Reformation,* edited by Jill Raitt, 121–39. New York: Crossroad, 1987.

———. *The Resurrection of the Body in Western Christianity, 200–1336.* New York: Columbia University Press, 1995.

———. ". . . And Woman His Humanity: Female Imagery in the Religious Writing of the Later Middle Ages." In *Gender and Religion: On the Complexity of Symbols,* edited by Caroline Walker Bynum, Steven Harrell, and Paula Richman, 257–89. Boston: Beacon Press, 1986.

Cabassut, André. "Coeurs (Changement des, Échange des)." DS 2:1046–51.

Cacciotti, Alvaro. *Amor sacro e amor profano in Jacopone da Todi.* Rome: Bibliotheca Pontificii Athenaei Antoniani, 1989.

———. "The Cross: Where, according to Jacopone da Todi, God and Humanity are Defined." *Studies in Spirituality* 2 (1992): 59–98.

Callaey, Frédégand. "L'influence et diffusion de l'*Arbor Vitae* de Ubertin de Casale." *Revue d'histoire ecclésiastique* 17 (1921): 533–46.

Camille, Michael. *Gothic Art: Glorious Visions.* New York: Harry M. Abrams, 1996.

———. "Seeing and Reading: Some Implications of Medieval Literacy and Illiteracy." *Art History* 8 (1985): 26–49.

Campbell, Jacques. "Gilles d'Assise." DS 6:379–82.

Capitani, Ovidio. *La concezione della povertà nel Medioevo.* Bologna: Pàtron Editore, 1974.

Carney, Margaret. "Francis and Clare: A Critical Examination of the Sources." *Greyfriars Review* 3 (1989): 15–43.

———. *The First Franciscan Woman: Clare of Assisi and Her Form of Life.* Quincy, Ill.: Franciscan Press, 1993.

Caron, Ann Marie. "Taste and See the Goodness of the Lord: Mechthild of Hackeborn." In *Hidden Springs: Cistercian Monastic Women,* edited by John A. Nichols and Lillian Thomas Shank, 2:509–24. 2 vols. Kalamazoo: Cistercian Publications, 1995.

Carozzi, Claude. "Une béguine joachimite: Douceline, soeur d'Hugues de Digne." In *Franciscains d'Oc: Les Spirituels ca. 1280–1324,* 169–201. Cahiers de Fanjeaux 10. Toulouse: Privat, 1976.

———. "Douceline et les autres." *La religion en Languedoc du XIIIe siècle à la moitié du XIVe siècle,* 251–67. Cahiers de Fanjeaux 11. Toulouse: Privat, 1957.

———. "Extases et visions chez frère Roger de Provence." In *Fin du monde et signes des temps: Visionnaires et prophètes en France méridionale (fin XIIIe–début XVe siècle),* 81–105. Cahiers de Fanjeaux 27. Toulouse: Privat, 1992.

Carpenter, David. *Revelation, History, and the Dialogue of Religions: A Study of Bhartrhari and Bonaventure.* Maryknoll, N.Y.: Orbis, 1995.

Cawley, Martinus. "The Trinity in the *Mulieres religiosae* of Thirteenth-Century Belgium." *Monastic Studies* 17 (1986): 167–90.

"Certosine, monache." DIP 2:772–82.

Chance, Jane, ed. *Gender and Text in the Later Middle Ages.* Gainesville: University Press of Florida, 1996.

Chartier, Roger. *Cultural History: Between Practices and Representations.* Ithaca: Cornell University Press, 1988.

Chase, Steven. *Angelic Wisdom: The Cherubim and the Grace of Contemplation in Richard of St. Victor.* Notre Dame: University of Notre Dame Press, 1995.

Châtillon, Jean. "Nudum Christum Nudus Sequere: Note sur les origines et la signification du thème de la nudité spirituelle dans les écrits de Saint Bonaventre." In *San Bonaventura 1274–1974,* 4:719–72. 5 vols. Grottaferrata/Rome: Collegio S. Bonaventura, 1974.

———. "Saint Anthony of Padua and the Victorines." *Greyfriars Review* 8 (1994): 347–80.

Chavero Blanco, Francisco de Asis, ed. *Bonaventuriana: Miscellanea in onore di Jacques Guy Bougerol, ofm.* 2 vols. Rome: Edizioni Antonianum, 1988.

Chenu, M.-D. *Nature, Man, and Society in the Twelfth Century.* Chicago: University of Chicago Press, 1968.

Chi erano Gli Spirituali? Assisi: Società Internazionale di Studi Francescani, 1976.

Cirino, André, and Josef Raischl, eds. *Franciscan Solitude.* St. Bonaventure: The Franciscan Institute, 1995.

Cistercians and Cluniacs: The Case for Cîteaux. Kalamazoo: Cistercian Publications, 1977.

Clark, Elizabeth A., trans. *Women in the Early Church.* Collegeville, Minn.: Liturgical Press, 1990.

Clay, Rotha Mary. *The Hermits and Anchorites of England.* London: Methuen, 1914.

Coakley, John. "Friars as Confidants of Holy Women in Medieval Dominican Hagiography." In *Images of Sainthood in Medieval Europe,* edited by Renate Blumenfeld-Kosinski and Timea Szell, 222–46.

———. "Gender and the Authority of the Friars: The Significance of Holy Women for Thirteenth-Century Franciscans and Dominicans." *Church History* 60 (1991): 445–60.

Cochelin, Isabelle. "Sainteté laïque: L'example de Juette de Huy (1156–1228)." *Le moyen âge* ser. 5, 3 (1989): 397–417.

Colledge, Edmund. "Liberty of Spirit: 'The Mirror of Simple Souls.'" In *Theology of Renewal,* edited by L. K. Shook, 100–117. 2 vols. Montreal: n.p., 1968.

———. "The New Latin *Mirror of Simple Souls.*" *Ons Geestlijk Erf* 63 (1989): 279–87.

———, and J. C. Marler. "'Poverty of Will': Ruusbroec, Eckhart and *The Mirror of Simple Souls.*" In *Jan van Ruusbroec: The sources, content and sequels of his mysticism,* edited by Paul Mommaers and Norbert De Paepe, 14–47. Leuven: Leuven University Press, 1984.

———, and Romana Guarnieri. "The Glosses by 'M.N.' and Richard Methley to 'The Mirror of Simple Souls.'" *Archivio italiano per la storia della pietà* 5 (1968): 357–82.

Constable, Giles. *Three Studies in Medieval Religious and Social Thought.* Cambridge: Cambridge University Press, 1995.

———. *The Reformation of the Twelfth Century.* Cambridge: Cambridge University Press, 1996.

"Contemplation." DS 2:1643–2193.

Cousins, Ewert. *Bonaventure and the Coincidence of Opposites.* Chicago: Franciscan Herald Press, 1978.

———. "Bonaventure's Mysticism of Language." In *Mysticism and Language,* edited by Steven Katz, 236–57. New York: Oxford University Press, 1992.

———. "Francis of Assisi: Christian Mysticism at the Crossroads." In *Mysticism and Religious Traditions,* edited by Steven Katz, 163–90. Oxford/London: Oxford University Press, 1983.

————. "Francis of Assisi and Bonaventure: Mysticism and Theological Interpretation." In *The Other Side of God: A Polarity in World Religion,* edited by Peter Berger, 74–103. Garden City, N.Y.: Anchor Press, 1981.

————. "Francis of Assisi: Nature, Poverty, and the Humanity of Christ." In *Mystics of the Book: Themes, Topics, and Typologies,* edited by R. A. Herrera, 203–17. New York: Peter Lang, 1993.

————. "The Humanity and Passion of Christ." In *Christian Spirituality II: High Middle Ages and Reformation,* edited by Jill Raitt, 375–91. New York: Crossroad, 1987.

————. "The Image of St. Francis in Bonaventure's *Legenda Major.*" In *Bonaventuriana: Miscellanea in onore di Jacques Guy Bougerol, ofm.,* edited by Francisco de Asis Chavero Blanco, 1:311–21. 2 vols. Rome: Edizioni Antonianum, 1988.

————. "Introduction." In *Bonaventure: The Soul's Journey into God. The Tree of Life. The Life of St. Francis,* 1–48. New York: Paulist, 1978.

————. "Mandala Symbolism in the Theology of Bonaventure." *University of Toronto Quarterly* 40 (1971): 185–201.

————. "Response." In *Celebrating the Medieval Heritage: A Colloquy on the Thought of Aquinas and Bonaventure,* edited by David Tracy. *The Journal of Religion. Supplement* 58 (1978): S97–S104.

Cusato, Michael F., and Edward Coughlin, eds. *That Others May Know and Love: Essays in Honor of Zachary Hayes, OFM.* St. Bonaventure: The Franciscan Institute, 1997.

da Baere, Guido. "De Mengeldichten van Hadewijch mit een janusgezicht." *Millennium: Tijdschrift voor Middeleeuwse Studies* 7 (1993): 40–51.

da Campagnola, Stanislao. *L'Angelo del sesto sigillo e l'alter Christus.* Rome: Laurentianum, 1971.

Dalarun, Jacques. "Angèle de Foligno a-t-elle existé." In *Alla Signoria: Mélanges offerts à Noëlle de la Blanchardière,* 59–97. Rome: École Française de Rome, 1995.

————. *Francesco: un passagio. Donna e donne negli scritti e nelle legende di Francesco d'Assisi.* Rome: Viella, 1994.

Dalla sequela Christi di Francesco d'Assisi all'apologia della povertà. Atti del XVIII Convegno Internazionale Assisi della Società Internazionale di Studi Francescani. Spoleto: Centro Italiano di Studi sull'Alto Medioevo, 1992.

Damiata, Mariano. *Pietà e Storia nell'Arbor Vitae di Ubertino da Casale.* Florence: Edizioni 'Studi Francescani,' 1988.

Daniel, E. Randolph. *The Franciscan Concept of Mission in the High Middle Ages.* Lexington: University of Kentucky Press, 1975.

————. "Spirituality and Poverty: Angelo da Clareno and Ubertino da Casale." *Medievalia et Humanistica* n.s. 4 (1973): 89–98.

————. "St. Bonaventure A Faithful Disciple of St. Francis? A Reexamination of the Question." In *San Bonaventura 1274–1974,* 2:171–87. 5 vols. Grottaferrata/Rome: Collegio S. Bonaventura, 1974.

————. "St. Bonaventure: Defender of Franciscan Eschatology." In *San Bonaventura*

1274–1974, 4:793–806. 5 vols. Grottaferrata/Rome: Collegio S. Bonaventura, 1974.

———. "St. Bonaventure's Debt to Joachim." *Mediaevalia et Humanistica* n.s. 11 (1982): 61–75.

———. "Symbol or Model? St. Bonaventure's Use of St. Francis." In *Bonaventuriana: Miscellanea in onore di Jacques Guy Bougerol, ofm.,* edited by Francisco de Asis Chavero Blanco, 1:55–62. 2 vols. Rome: Edizioni Antonianum, 1988.

d'Avry, David L. *The Preaching of the Friars: Sermons diffused from Paris before 1300.* Oxford: Oxford University Press, 1985.

Deboutte, Alfred. "Lutgarde." DS 9:1201–4.

———. "Sainte Lutgarde et sa spiritualité." *Collectanea Cisterciensia* 44 (1982): 73–87.

———. "Thomas de Cantimpré." DS 15:784–92.

———. "The *Vita Lutgardis* of Thomas of Cantimpré." In *Hidden Springs: Cistercian Monastic Women,* edited by John A. Nichols and Lillian Thomas Shank, 1:255–81. 2 vols. Kalamazoo: Cistercian Publications, 1995.

De Ganck, Roger. *Beatrice of Nazareth in her Context.* 2 vols. Kalamazoo: Cistercian Publications, 1991.

———. "The Cistercian Nuns of Belgium in the Thirteenth Century." *Cistercian Studies* 5 (1970): 169–87.

———. *Towards Unification with God.* Kalamazoo: Cistercian Publications, 1991.

Delaruelle, Etienne. "L'influence de Saint François d'Assise sur la piété populaire." In *Relazioni X Congresso internazionale de scienze storiche,* 3:449–66. 7 vols. Florence: G.C. Sansoni, 1955.

"Démon." DS 3:141–238.

"Denys l'Aréopagite: En Occident." DS 3:340–58.

De Paepe, Norbert. *Hadewijch Strofische Gedichten: Een studie van de minne in het kader der 12e en 13e eeuwse mystiek en profane minnelyrik.* Ghent: Secretariat van de Koninklijke Vlaamse Academie voor Taal-en Letterkunde, 1967.

Dettloff, Werner. "'Christus tenens medium in omnibus': Sinn und Funktion der Theologie bei Bonaventura." *Wissenschaft und Weisheit* 20 (1957): 28–42, 120–40.

Dewailly, L. M. "Notes sur l'histoire de l'adjectif 'apostolique.'" *Mélanges de science religieuse* 5 (1948): 141–52.

di Bernardo, Flavio. "Passion (Mystique de la)." DS 12:313–38.

Dimier, M.-A. "Pour la fiche *spiritus libertatis.*" *Revue du moyen age latin* 3 (1947): 56–60.

Dinzelbacher, Peter. *Christliche Mystik im Abendland: Ihrer Geschichte von den Anfängen bis zum Ende des Mittelalters.* Paderborn: Schöningh, 1994.

———. *Heilige oder Hexen? Schicksale auffälliger Frauen in Mittelalter und Frühneuzeit.* Zurich: Artemis & Winkler, 1995.

———. "A Plea for the Study of the Minor Female Mystics of Late Medieval Germany." *Studies in Spirituality* 3 (1993): 91–100.

———. "*Revelationes.*" Typologie des sources du moyen âge occidental, fasc. 57. Turnhout: Brepols, 1991.

———. Review of *Viten- und Offenbarungsliteratur in Frauenklöstern des Mittelalters: Quellen und Studien,* by Siegfried Ringler. *Anzeiger für deutsches Altertum und deutsche Literatur* 39 (1982): 63–71.

———. *Vision- und Visionsliteratur im Mittelalter.* Stuttgart: Hiersemann, 1981.

———. "Die 'Vita et Revelationes' der Wiener Begine Agnes Blannbekin (d. 1315) im Rahmen der Viten- und Offenbarungsliteraur ihrer Zeit." In *Frauenmystik im Mittelalter,* edited by Peter Dinzelbacher and Dieter R. Bauer, 152–77. Ostfildern bei Stuttgart: Schwabenverlag, 1985.

———. "Zur Interpretation erlebnismystischer Texte des Mittelalters." *Zeitschrift für deutsches Altertum und deutsche Literatur* 117 (1988): 1–23.

———, and Dieter R. Bauer, eds. *Frauenmystik im Mittelalter.* Ostfeldern bei Stuttgart: Schwabenverlag, 1985.

———, and Dieter Bauer, eds. *Religiöse Frauenbewegung und mystische Frömmigkeit im Mittelalter.* Cologne/Vienna: Böhlau, 1988.

Distelbrink, Balduinus. *Bonaventurae Scripta: Authentica dubia vel spuria critice recensita.* Rome: Istituto Storico Cappuccini, 1975.

Dizionario Francescano: I Mistici. Scritti dei Mistici Francescani Secolo XIII. Assisi: Editrici Francescane, 1995.

Dolicini, Carlo. "Francesco d'Assisi e la storiografia degli ultimi vent'anni: problemi di metodo." In *Frate Francesco d'Assisi: Atti del XXI Convegno internazionale,* 3–35. Spoleto: Centro Italiano di Studi sull'alto Medioevo, 1994.

Dondaine, H. F. *Le corpus dionysien de l'Université de Paris au xiiie siècle.* Rome: Edizioni di Storia e Letteratura, 1953.

Douie, Decima L. *The Nature and Effect of the Heresy of the Fraticelli.* Manchester: Manchester University Press, 1932.

Doyère, Pierre. "Doctrine spirituelle," 32–57. In *Gertrude d'Helfta: Oeuvres spirituelles, Tome II.* Paris: Cerf, 1968.

———. "Sainte Gertrude et les senses spirituels." *Revue d'Ascetique et Mystique* 36 (1960): 429–46.

Dreyer, Elizabeth Ann. "'Affectus' in St. Bonaventure's Description of the Journey of the Soul to God." Ph.D. diss., Marquette University, 1982.

Dronke, Peter. *Medieval Latin and the Rise of the European Love Lyric.* 2 vols. Oxford: Clarendon Press, 1968.

———. *Women Writers of the Middle Ages: A Critical Study of Texts from Perpetua (d. 203) to Marguerite Porete (d. 1310).* Cambridge: Cambridge University Press, 1984.

Duval-Arnould, L. "La Constitution 'Cum inter nonnullos' de Jean XXII sur le pauvreté du Christ et les Apotres: Redaction préparatoire et rédaction définitive." *Archivum Franciscanum Historicum* 77 (1984): 406–20.

Eliade, Mircea. *Patterns in Comparative Religion.* Cleveland/New York: Meridian Books, 1963.

Emmerson, Richard K., and Ronald B. Herzman. *The Apocalyptic Imagination in Medieval Literature.* Philadelphia: University of Pennsylvania Press, 1992.

Epiney-Burgard, Georgette. "Hadewijch d'Anvers, Mechthilde de Magdebourg: Thèmes communs." *Ons Geestelijk Erf* 66 (1992): 71–87.

Érémitisme." DS 4:936–82.

L'eremitismo in Occidente nei secoli XI e XII: Atti della seconda Settimana internazionale di Studio Mendola, 1962. Milan: Società editrice vita e pensiero, 1965.

Esser, Kajetan. *Origins of the Franciscan Order.* Chicago: Franciscan Herald Press, 1970.

Fin du monde et signes des temps: Visionnaires et prophètes en France méridionale (fin XIIIe– début XVe siècle). Cahiers de Fanjeaux 27. Toulouse: Privat, 1992.

Fischer, Columba. "Die 'Meditationes Vitae Christi': Ihre handschriftliche Ueberlieferung und die Verfasserfrage." *Archivum Franciscanum Historicum* 25 (1932): 3–35, 175–209, 305–48, 449–83.

Fischer, Konrad. *De Deo trino et uno: Das Verhältnis von productio und reductio in seiner Bedeutung für die Gotteslehre Bonaventuras.* Göttingen: Vandenhoeck & Ruprecht, 1978.

Fleming, John V. *An Introduction to the Franciscan Literature of the Middle Ages.* Chicago: Franciscan Herald Press, 1977.

Flood, David. *Francis of Assisi and the Franciscan Movement.* Quezon City, Philippines: FIA Publications, 1989.

Fontes Franciscani, edited by Stefano Brufani et al. Assisi: Edizioni Portiuncola, 1995.

Fortini, Arnaldo. *Francis of Assisi.* New York: Crossroad, 1981.

Francescanesimo e vita religiosa dei laici nel '200. Assisi: Università degli Studi di Perugia, 1981.

Francesco d'Assisi e il primo secolo di storia francescana. Turin: Einaudi, 1997.

Franciscains d'Oc: Les Spirituels ca. 1280–1324. Cahiers de Fanjeaux 10. Toulouse: Privat, 1976.

Frate Francesco d'Assisi: Atti del XXI Convegno internazionale. Spoleto: Centro Italiano di Studi sull'alto Medioevo, 1994.

Freed, John B. *The Friars and German Society in the Thirteenth Century.* Cambridge, Mass.: The Mediaeval Academy of America, 1977.

———. "Urban Development and the 'Cura monialium' in Thirteenth-Century Germany." *Viator* 3 (1972): 311–27.

Freedberg, David. *The Power of Images: Studies in the History and Theory of Response.* Chicago: University of Chicago Press, 1989.

Frugoni, Arsenio. "Iacopone Francescano." In *Iacopone e il suo tempo,* 73–102. Convegni del Centro di Studi sulla Spiritualità Medievale. Todi: L'Accademia Tudertina, 1959.

Frugoni, Chiara. "Female Mystics, Visions, and Iconography." In *Women and Religion in Medieval and Renaissance Italy,* edited by Daniel Bornstein and Roberto Rusconi, 130–64. Chicago: University of Chicago Press, 1996.

———. *Francesco e l'invenzione delle stimmate: Una storia per parole e immagini fino a Bonaventura e Giotto.* Turin: Einaudi, 1993.

Funk, Philipp. *Jakob von Vitry: Leben und Werke.* Leipzig/Berlin: Teubner, 1909.

Gadamer, Hans-Georg. "The Concept of Experience and the Essence of the Hermeneutical Experience." In *Truth and Method,* 310–25. New York: Seabury, 1975.

Gallen, Jarl. *Le province de Dacie de l'Ordre des Frères Prècheurs.* Helsingfors: Soderstrom, 1946.

Garcia, Bernardino. "Bonaventura da Bagnoregio: Introduzione." In *Dizionario Francescano: I Mistici. Scritti dei Mistici Francescani Secolo XIII,* 289–337. Assisi: Editrici Francescane, 1995.

Gehring, Hester. "The Language of Mysticism in South German Dominican Convent Chronicles of the Fourteenth Century." Ph.D. diss., University of Michigan, 1957.

Gennaro, Clara. "Clare, Agnes, and Their Earliest Followers: From the Poor Ladies of San Damiano to the Poor Clares." In *Women and Religion in Medieval and Renaissance Italy,* edited by Daniel Bornstein and Roberto Rusconi, 39–55. Chicago: University of Chicago Press, 1996.

Georgiana, Linda. *The Solitary Self: Individuality in the Ancrene Wisse.* Cambridge, Mass.: Harvard University Press, 1981.

Gerken, Alexander. "Identity and Freedom: Bonaventure's Position and Method." *Greyfriars Review* 4 (1990): 91–105.

————. *Theologie des Wortes: Das Verhältnis von Schöpfung und Inkarnation bei Bonaventura.* Düsseldorf: Patmos, 1963.

Geyer, Iris. *Maria von Oignies: Eine hochmittelalterliche Mystikerin zwischen Ketzerei und Rechtgläubigkeit.* Frankfurt: Peter Lang, 1992.

Giacometti, Luigi, ed. *Dialoghi con Chiara de Assisi: Atti delle Giornate di studio e riflessione per l'VIII Centenario di Santa Chiara.* Assisi: Edizioni Porziuncola, 1995.

Gill, Katherine. "Women and the Production of Religious Literature in the Vernacular, 1300–1500." In *Creative Women in Medieval and Early Modern Italy: A Religious and Artistic Renaissance,* edited by E. Ann Matter and John Coakley, 64–104. Philadelphia: University of Pennsylvania Press, 1994.

Gilson, Etienne. *The Philosophy of St. Bonaventure.* Paterson: St. Anthony Guild Press, 1965.

Glier, Ingeborg, ed. *Geschichte der deutschen Literatur: Die deutsche Literatur im späten Mittelalter 1250–1370.* Munich: Beck, 1987.

Godet, Jean-François. "A New Look at Clare's Gospel Plan of Life." *Greyfriars Review* 5 (1991 Supplement).

————. "Claire et la vie au féminin: Symboles de la femme dans ses écrits." *Laurentianum* 31 (1990): 148–75.

————. *Clare of Assisi: A Woman's Life.* Chicago: Haversack, 1991.

Gonzalez, Justo L. "The Work of Christ in Bonaventure's Systematic Works." In *San Bonaventura 1274–1974,* 4:371–85. 5 vols. Grottaferrata/Rome: Collegio S. Bonaventura, 1974.

Gooday, Frances. "Mechthild of Magdeburg and Hadewijch of Antwerp: a Comparison." *Ons Geestelijk Erf* 48 (1974): 305–62.

Goodich, Michael E. "The Contours of Female Piety in Later Medieval Hagiography." *Church History* 50 (1981): 20–32.

———. *Violence and Miracle in the Fourteenth Century: Private Grief and Public Salvation.* Chicago: University of Chicago Press, 1995.

Görres, Johann Joseph von. *Die christliche Mystik.* 4 vols. Regensburg/Landshut: Manz, 1836–42.

"Gottesfreunde/Gottesfreundschaft." In *Lexikon des Mittelalters,* 4:1586–87. Munich/Zurich: Artemis, 1980–.

Gougaud, Louis. *Devotional and Ascetic Practices in the Middle Ages.* London: Burns, Oates & Washbourne, 1927.

Gourdal, Yves. "Chartreux." DS 2:705–76

Grabes, Herbert. *The Mutable Glass: Mirror Imagery in Titles and Texts of the Middle Ages and English Renaissance.* Cambridge: Cambridge University Press, 1982.

Graff, Harvey J. *The Legacies of Literacy: Continuities and Contradictions in Western Culture and Society.* Bloomington: Indiana University Press, 1987.

Grau, Engelbert. "Das 'Sacrum commercium sancti Francisci cum domina paupertate': Seine Bedeutung für die franziskanische Mystik." In *Abendländische Mystik im Mittelalter: Symposium Kloster Engelberg 1984,* edited by Kurt Ruh, 269–85. Stuttgart: Metzler, 1986.

Greenspan, Kate. "Autohagiography and Medieval Women's Spiritual Autobiography." In *Gender and Text in the Later Middle Ages,* edited by Jane Chance, 217–36. Gainesville: University Press of Florida, 1996.

Grégoire, Réginald. "L'adage ascétique 'Nudus nudum Christum sequi.'" In *Studi storici in onore de Ottorino Bertolini,* 1:395–409. 2 vols. Pisa: Pacini, 1972.

Greven, Joseph. "Der Ursprung des Beginenwesens: Eine Auseinandersetzung mit Godefried Kurth." *Historisches Jahrbuch* 35 (1914): 44–45.

Grundmann, Herbert. "Die Frauen und die Literatur im Mittelalter." *Archiv für Kulturgeschichte* 26 (1936): 129–61.

———. "Die geschichtlichen Grundlagen der deutschen Mystik." In *Altdeutsche und altniederländische Mystik,* edited by Kurt Ruh, 72–99. Darmstadt: Wissenschaftliche Buchgesellschaft, 1964.

———. "Jubel." In *Ausgewählte Aufsätze,* 3:130–62. 3 vols. 2nd ed. Stuttgart: Hiersemann, 1978.

———. *Religious Movements in the Middle Ages.* Notre Dame, Ind.: University of Notre Dame Press, 1995.

Guarnieri, Romana. "Angela, mistica europea." In *Angela da Foligno Terziaria Francescana,* edited by Enrico Menestò, 39–82. Spoleto: Centro Italiano di Studi sull'Alto Medioevo, 1992.

———. "Beguines beyond the Alps and Italian Bizzoche between the 14th and 15th Centuries." *Greyfriars Review* 5 (1991): 93–104.

———. "Il movimento del Libero Spiritu: dalle origini al secolo XVI." *Archivio Italiano per la Storia della Pietà* 4 (1965): 351–708.

———. "Pinzochere." DIP 6:1722–49.

Guest, Tanis M. "Hadewijch and Minne." In *European Context: Studies in the history and literature of the Netherlands presented to Theodoor Weevers,* edited by P. K. King and P. F. Vincent, 14–29. Cambridge: The Modern Humanities Research Association, 1971.

———. *Some aspects of Hadewijch's poetic form in the "Strofische Gedichten."* The Hague: Nijhoff, 1975.

Haas, Alois M. "Deutsche Mystik." In *Geschichte der deutschen Literatur: Die deutsche Literatur im späten Mittelalter 1250–1370,* edited by Ingeborg Glier, 234–305. Munich: Beck, 1987.

———. "Mechthilds von Magdeburg dichterische *heimlichkeit.*" In *Gottes und der werlde hulde: Literatur im Mittelalter und Neuzeit. Festschrift für Heinz Rupp zum 70. Geburtstag,* edited by Rüdiger Schnell, 206–23. Bern/Stuttgart: Francke, 1989.

———. "Mystik als Theologie." *Zeitschrift für Katholische Theologie* 116 (1994): 30–53.

———. *Sermo Mysticus: Studien zu Theologie und Sprache der deutschen Mystik.* Freiburg: Universitätsverlag, 1979.

———. "'Trage Leiden geduldiglich': Die Einstellung der deutschen Mystik zum Leiden." In *Gott Leiden. Gott Lieben: Zur volkssprachlichen Mystik im Mittelalter,* 127–52. Frankfurt: Insel, 1989.

Hamburger, Jeffrey F. "Art, Enclosure and the *Cura Monialium:* Prolegomena in the Guise of a Postscript." *Gesta* 31 (1992): 108–34.

———. "The *Liber miraculorum* of Unterlinden: An Icon in its Convent Setting." In *The Sacred Image East and West,* edited by Robert Ousterhout and L. Brubaker, 147–90. Champaign-Urbana: University of Illinois Press, 1995.

———. *Nuns as Artists: The Visual Culture of a Medieval Convent.* Berkeley: University of California Press, 1997.

———. *The Rothschild Canticles: Art and Mysticism in Flanders and the Rhineland circa 1300.* New Haven: Yale University Press, 1990.

———. "The Visual and the Visionary: The Image in Late Medieval Monastic Devotions." *Viator* 20 (1989): 161–82.

Hamon, Auguste. "Coeur (Sacré)." DS 2:1023–46.

Hart, Mother Columba. "Introduction." In *Hadewijch: The Complete Works,* translated by Columba Hart, 1–42. New York: Paulist Press, 1980.

Haskins, Charles Homer. "Robert le Bougre and the Beginnings of the Inquisition in Northern France." In *Studies in Mediaeval Culture,* 219–29. Oxford: Clarendon Press, 1929.

Haskins, Susan. *Mary Magdalen: Myth and Metaphor.* New York: Harcourt, Brace & Company, 1993.

Haug, Walter. "Das Gespräch mit der unvergleichlichen Partner: Der mystische Dialog bei Mechthild von Magdeburg als Paradigma für eine personale Gesprächsstruktur." In *Das Gespräch,* edited by Karlheinz Stierle and Rainer Warning, 251–79. Munich: Fink, 1984.

Hayes, Zachary. "Bonaventure: Mystery of the Triune God." In *The History of Fran-*

ciscan Theology, edited by Kenan B. Osborne, 39–125. St. Bonaventure: Franciscan Institute, 1994.

———. "Christology and Metaphysics in the Thought of Bonaventure." In *Celebrating the Medieval Heritage: A Colloquy on the Thought of Aquinas and Bonaventure*, edited by David Tracy. *The Journal of Religion. Supplement* 58 (1978): S82–S96.

———. *The Hidden Center: Spirituality and Speculative Christology in St. Bonaventure*. New York: Paulist Press, 1981.

———. "Introduction." In *Works of St. Bonaventure. III, Disputed Questions on the Mystery of the Trinity*, 13–103. St. Bonaventure: Franciscan Institute, 1979.

———. "The Theological Image of St. Francis in the Sermons of St. Bonaventure." In *Bonaventuriana: Miscellanea in onore di Jacques Guy Bougerol, ofm.*, edited by Francisco de Asis Chavero Blanco, 1:323–45. 2 vols. Rome: Edizioni Antonianum, 1988.

Heaney, Seamus. *The Redress of Poetry*. New York: Farrar, Straus & Giroux, 1995.

Heerinckx, Jacques. "Les sources de la théologie mystique de S. Antoine de Padoue." *Revue d'ascetique et de mystique* 13 (1932): 225–56.

———. "S. Antoninus Patavinus auctor mysticus." *Antonianum* 7 (1932): 39–76, 167–200.

———. "Theologia mystica in scriptis fratris David ab Augusta." *Antonianum* 8 (1933): 49–83, 161–92.

Heimbach, Marianne. *Der "ungelehrte Mund" als Autorität: Mystische Erfahrung als Quelle kirchlich-prophetischer Rede im Werk Mechthilds von Magdeburg*. Stuttgart/Bad Canstatt: frommann-holzboog, 1989.

Hellmann, J. A. Wayne. "The Seraph in the Legends of Thomas of Celano and St. Bonaventure: The Victorine Transition." In *Bonaventuriana: Miscellanea in onore di Jacques Guy Bougerol, ofm.*, edited by Francisco de Asis Chavero Blanco, 1:347–56. 2 vols. Rome: Edizioni Antonianum, 1988.

———. "The Seraph in Thomas of Celano's *Vita Prima*." In *That Others May Know and Love: Essays in Honor of Zachary Hayes, OFM*, edited by Michael F. Cusato and Edward Coughlin, 23–41.

Hendrix, Guido. "Primitive Versions of Thomas of Cantimpré's *Vita Lutgardis*." *Citeaux* 29 (1978): 153–206.

Heszler, Esther. "'Dat helle es hare hoecste name': Das XVI Mengeldicht Hadewijchs als Auseinandersetzung mit dem Traktat 'De IV gradibus violentae caritatis' Richards von St. Viktor." In *Religiöse Erfahrung: Christliche Positionen im Wandel der Geschichte*, edited by Walter Haug and Dietmar Mieth, 171–88. Munich: Beck, 1992.

———. "Stufen der Minne bei Hadewijch." In *Frauenmystik im Mittelalter*, edited by Peter Dinzelbacher and Dieter R. Bauer, 99–122. Ostfeldern bei Stuttgart: Schwabenverlag, 1985.

Hilka, Alfons. "Altfranzösische Mystik und Beginentum." *Zeitschrift für romanische Philologie* 47 (1927): 121–70.

Hillgarth, Jocelyn N. *Ramon Lull and Lullism in Fourteenth Century France*. Oxford: Oxford University Press, 1971.

Hindsley, Leonard P. "Monastic Conversion: The Case of Margaret Ebner." In *Varieties of Religious Conversion in the Middle Ages,* edited by James Muldoon, 31–46. Gainesville: University Press of Florida, 1997.

———, and Margot Schmidt. "Introduction." In *Margaret Ebner: Major Works,* translated by Leonard P. Hindsley, 9–81. New York: Paulist Press, 1993.

Hinnebusch, William A. *The History of the Dominican Order.* 2 vols. New York: Alba House, 1973.

Holdsworth, C. J. "Visions and Visionaries in the Middle Ages." *History* 48 (1963): 141–53.

Hollywood, Amy. *The Soul as Virgin Wife: Mechthild of Magdeburg, Marguerite Porete and Meister Eckhart.* Notre Dame, Ind.: University of Notre Dame Press, 1995.

Hülsbusch, Werner. *Elemente einer Kreuzestheologie in den Spätschriften Bonaventuras.* Düsseldorf: Patmos, 1968.

———. "Die Theologie des Transitus bei Bonaventura." In *San Bonaventura 1274–1974,* 4:533–65. 5 vols. Grottaferrata/Rome: Collegio S. Bonaventura, 1974.

Huygens, R. B. C. "Le moine Idung et ses deux ouvrages: 'Argumentum super quatuor quaestionibus' et 'Dialogus duorum monachorum.'" *Studi Medievali,* 3a serie, 13 (1972): 291–470.

———. "Les passages des lettres de Jacques de Vitry rélatifs à S. François d'Assise et à ses premiers disciples." In *Hommages à Léon Herrman,* edited by R. B. C. Huygens, 446–53. Brussels: Collection Latomus, 1960.

Iacopone e il suo tempo, 73–102. Convegni del Centro di Studi sulla Spiritualità Medievale. Todi: L'Accademia Tudertina, 1959.

I compagni di Francesco e la prima generazione minoritica. Atti del XIX Convegno internazionale, Società Internazionale di Studi Francescani. Spoleto: Centro Italiano di Studi sull'Alto Medioevo, 1992.

Iozzelli, Fortunato. "I miracoli nella 'Legenda' di Santa Margherita da Cortona." *Archivum Franciscanum Historicum* 86 (1993): 217–61.

Iriarte, Lázaro. "Clare of Assisi: Her Place in Female Hagiography." *Greyfriars Review* 3 (1989): 173–206.

Jansen, André. "The Story of True Joy: An Autobiographical Reading." *Greyfriars Review* 5 (1991): 367–87.

Javelet, Robert. "Reflections sur l'exemplarisme bonaventurien." In *San Bonaventura 1274–1974,* 4:349–70. 5 vols. Grottaferrata/Rome: Collegio S. Bonaventura, 1974.

———. "Thomas Gallus et Richard de Saint-Victor mystiques." *Recherches de théologie ancienne et médiévale* 29 (1962): 205–33; 30 (1963): 88–121.

———. "Thomas Gallus ou les écritures dans une dialectique mystique." In *L'homme devant Dieu: Mélanges offerts au Père Henri de Lubac,* 2:99–110. 3 vols. Paris: Aubier, 1964.

Jeremy, Sister Mary. "'Similitudes' in the Writing of Saint Gertrude of Helfta." *Mediaeval Studies* 19 (1957): 47–54.

Johnson, Elizabeth A. "Marian Devotion in the Western Church." In *Christian Spir-*

ituality II: High Middle Ages and Reformation, edited by Jill Raitt, 392–414. New York: Crossroad, 1987.

Johnson, Timothy J. *Iste Pauper Clamavit: Saint Bonaventure's Mendicant Theology of Prayer.* Frankfurt/Bern/New York/Paris: Peter Lang, 1990.

———. "Poverty and Prayer in the Theology of Saint Bonaventure." *Miscellanea Francescana* 90 (1990): 19–60.

———. "Visual Imagery and Contemplation in Clare of Assisi's 'Letters to Agnes of Prague.'" *Mystics Quarterly* 19 (1993): 161–72.

Johnston, Mark D. *The Evangelical Rhetoric of Ramon Llull: Lay Learning and Piety in the Christian West around 1300.* New York/Oxford: Oxford University Press, 1996.

———. "Ramon Lull's Conversion to Penitence." *Mystics Quarterly* 16 (1990): 179–92.

———. *The Spiritual Logic of Ramon Llull.* Oxford: Clarendon Press, 1987.

Jones, Rufus M. *The Flowering of Mysticism: The Friends of God in the Fourteenth Century.* New York: Macmillan, 1939.

Kadel, Andrew. *Matrology: A Bibliography of Writings by Christian Women from the First to the Fifteenth Centuries.* New York: Continuum, 1995.

Kamber, Urs. *Arbor Amoris: Der Minnebaum. Ein Pseudo-Bonaventura-Traktat herausgegeben nach lateinischen und deutschen Handschriften des XIV. und XV. Jahrhunderts.* Berlin: Schmidt, 1964.

Katainen, V. Louise. "Jacopone da Todi, Poet and Mystic: A Review of the History of Criticism." *Mystics Quarterly* 22 (1996): 46–57.

Katz, Steven, ed. *Mysticism and Language.* New York: Oxford University Press, 1992.

Kay, Sarah, and Miri Rubin, eds. *Framing Medieval Bodies.* Manchester/New York: Manchester University Press, 1994.

Kemper, Hans-Georg. "Allegorische Allegorese: Zur Bildlichkeit und Struktur mystischer Literatur (Mechthild von Magdeburg und Angelus Silesius)." In *Formen und Funktionen der Allegorie,* edited by Walter Haug, 90–125. Germanistische Symposien 3. Stuttgart: Germanistische Symposien, 1978.

Kieckhefer, Richard. "Major Currents in Late Medieval Devotion." In *Christian Spirituality II: High Middle Ages and Reformation,* edited by Jill Raitt, 75–108. New York: Crossroad, 1987.

———. *Unquiet Souls: Fourteenth-Century Saints and Their Religious Milieu.* Chicago: University of Chicago Press, 1984.

King, Margot H. "The Dove at the Window: The Ascent of the Soul in Thomas of Cantimpré's Life of Lutgard of Aywières." In *Hidden Springs: Cistercian Monastic Women,* edited John A. Nichols and Lillian Thomas Shank, 1:225–53. 2 vols. Kalamazoo: Cistercian Publications, 1995.

———. "The Sacramental Witness of Christina *Mirabilis:* The Mystic Growth of a Fool for Christ's Sake." In *Peace Weavers: Medieval Religious Women,* edited by John A. Nichols and Lillian Thomas Shank, 2:145–64. Kalamazoo: Cistercian Publications, 1987.

Kirchberger, Clare. "Introduction." In *Walter Hilton: The Goad of Love. An Unpublished Translation of the Stimulus Amoris*, 13–44. London: Faber & Faber, 1952.

Kitzinger, Ernst. *Early Medieval Art*. Bloomington/London: Indiana University Press, 1966.

Kleinberg, Aviad M. *Prophets in Their Own Country: Living Saints and the Making of Sainthood in the Later Middle Ages*. Chicago: University of Chicago Press, 1992.

Knowles, David. "The Influence of Pseudo-Dionysius on Western Mysticism." In *Christian Spirituality: Essays in Honour of Gordon Rupp*, 79-94. London: SCM, 1975.

Kugler, Hermann Josef. *Hermann Josef von Steinfeld (um 1160–1241) in Kontext christlicher Mystik*. St. Ottilien: Eos Verlag, 1992.

Kurtz, Patricia Deery. "Mary of Oignies, Christine the Marvellous, and Medieval Heresy." *Mystics Quarterly* 14 (1988): 186–96.

Lachance, Paul. "Introduction." In *Angela of Foligno: Complete Works*, translated by Paul Lachance, 15–119. New York: Paulist Press, 1993.

———. *The Spiritual Journey of the Blessed Angela of Foligno according to the Memorial of Brother A*. Rome: Pontificium Athenaeum Antonianum, 1984.

Lagorio, Valerie M. "The Medieval Continental Women Mystics: An Introduction." In *An Introduction to the Medieval Mystics of Europe*, edited by Paul Szarmach, 161–93. Albany: SUNY Press, 1984.

Lambert, Malcolm. *Franciscan Poverty*. London: SPCK, 1961.

———. *Medieval Heresy: Popular Movements from the Gregorian Reform to the Reformation*. 2nd ed. Oxford: Blackwell, 1992.

Lambertini, Roberto, and Andrea Tabarroni. *Dopo Francesco: l'Eredità difficile*. Turin: Edizioni Gruppo Abele, 1989.

Lanczkowski, Johanna. "Einfluss der Hohe-Lied-Predigten Bernhards auf die drei Helftauer Mystikerinnen." *Erbe und Auftrag* 66 (1990): 17–28.

———. "Gertrud die Grosse von Helfta: Mystik des Gerhorsams." In *Religiöse Frauenbewegung und mystische Frömmigkeit im Mittelalter*, edited by Peter Dinzelbacher and Dieter Bauer, 153–64. Cologne/Vienna: Böhlau, 1988.

Langer, Otto. *Mystische Erfahrung und spirituelle Theologie: Zu Meister Eckharts Auseinandersetzung mit der Frauenfrömmigkeit seiner Zeit*. Munich/Zurich: Artemis, 1987.

———. "Zum Begriff der Erfahrung in der mittelalterlichen Frauenmystik." In *Religiöse Erfahrung: Historische modelle in christlicher Tradition*, edited by Walter Haug and Dietmar Mieth, 229–46. Munich: Wilhelm Fink, 1992.

———. "Zur Dominikanischen Frauenmystik im spätmittelalterlichen Deutschland." In *Frauenmystik im Mittelalter*, edited by Peter Dinzelbacher and Dieter R. Bauer, 341–46. Ostfeldern bei Stuttgart: Schwabenverlag, 1985.

"Langmann (Adélheide)." DS 9:221–23.

Lassahn, Nicole. "Apophasis in Marguerite Porete: The Role of the Dialogue Form in Constructing Meaning and Un-Meaning in the *Mirouer des simples ames*." Unpublished paper.

Laurent, M.-H. "La plus anciene légende de la B. Marguerite de Città di Castello." *Archivum Fratrum Praedicatorum* 10 (1940): 109–31.

Lauwers, Michel. "Entre Beguinisme et Mysticisme: La Vie de Marie d'Oignies (d. 1213) de Jacques de Vitry ou la définition d'une sainteté féminine." *Ons Geestelijk Erf* 66 (1992): 46–69.

———. "'Noli me tangere': Marie Madeleine, Marie d'Oignies et les pénitentes du XIIIe siècle." In *La Madeleine (VIIIe–XIIIe Siècle): Mélanges de l'École Française de Rome. Moyen Age* 104 (1992): 209–68.

———. "Expérience Béguinale et récit hagiographique: A propos de la 'Vita Mariae Oigniacensis' de Jacques de Vitry (vers 1215)." *Journal des Savants* (année 1989): 61–103.

Lazzeri, Zefferino. "L'Orazione delle cinque piaghe recitata da S. Chiara." *Archivum Franciscanum Historicum* 16 (1923): 246–49.

Leclercq, Eloi. *The Canticle of Creatures: Symbols of Union.* Chicago: Franciscan Herald Press, 1978.

Leclercq, Jean. "Women's Monasticism in the 12th and 13th Centuries." *Greyfriars Review* 7 (1993): 167–92.

Lefèvre, Jean-Baptiste. "Sainte Lutgarde d'Aywières en son temps (1182–1246)." *Collectanea Cisterciensia* 58 (1996): 277–335.

Leff, Gordon. *Heresy in the Later Middle Ages.* 2 vols. New York: Barnes & Noble, 1967.

———. *Paris and Oxford Universities in the Thirteenth and Fourteenth Centuries.* London: John Wiley, 1968.

Le Goff, Jacques. "Franciscanisme et modèles culturels du XIIIe siècle." In *Francescanismo e vita religiosa dei laici nel '200: Atti dell' VIII Convegno Internazionale,* 83–128. Assisi: Università degli Studi di Perugia, 1981.

Lekai, Louis J. *The Cistercians: Ideals and Reality.* N.p.: Kent State University Press, 1977.

Leonardi, Claudio, and Enrico Menestò, eds. *S. Chiara da Montefalco e il suo tempo.* Florence: La Nuova Italia, 1985.

Lerner, Robert E. "An Angel of Philadelphia in the Reign of Philip the Fair: The Case of Guiard of Cressonessart." In *Order and Innovation in the Middle Ages: Essays in Honor of Joseph R. Strayer,* edited by William C. Jordan, Bruce McNab, and Teofilo F. Ruiz, 343–64. Princeton: Princeton University Press, 1976.

———. "Beguines and Beghards." In *Dictionary of the Middle Ages,* 12:157–62. New York: Charles Scribner's Sons, 1982–89.

———. "Ecstatic Dissent." *Speculum* 67 (1992): 33–55.

———. "Literacy and Learning." In *One Thousand Years,* edited by Richard L. DeMolen, 165–233. Boston: Houghton Mifflin, 1974.

———. "Writing and resistance among Beguins of Languedoc and Catalonia." In *Heresy and Literacy, 1000–1530,* edited by Peter Biller and Anne Hudson, 186–204. Cambridge: Cambridge University Press, 1994.

Lewis, Gertrud Jaron. *Bibliographie zur deutschen Frauenmystik des Mittlelalters: Mit ein Anhang zu Beatrijs van Nazareth und Hadewijch,* by Frank Willaert and Marie-José Govers. Berlin: Erich Schmidt, 1989.

———. *By Women, for Women, about Women: The Sister-Books of Fourteenth-Century Germany.* Toronto: Pontifical Institute of Mediaeval Studies, 1996.

Leyser, Henrietta. *Hermits and the New Monasticism: A Study of Religious Communities in Western Europe 1000–1150*. New York: St. Martin's Press, 1984.

Little, Lester K. *Religious Poverty and the Profit Economy in Medieval Europe*. Ithaca: Cornell University Press, 1978.

Lochrie, Karma. "The Language of Transgression: Body, Flesh, and Word in Mystical Discourse." In *Speaking Two Languages: Traditional Disciplines and Contemporary Theory in Medieval Studies*, edited by Allen J. Frantzen, 129–39. Albany: SUNY Press, 1991.

Longère, Jean. *La prédication médiévale*. Paris: Études Augustiniennes, 1983.

Longpré, Éphrem. "Bonaventure (Saint)." DS 1:1768–1843.

———. "Frères mineurs. I, Saint François d'Assise." DS 5:1271–1303.

———. "Lulle, Raymond (Le Bienheureux)." In *Dictionnaire de théologie catholique*, edited by A. Vacant and E. Mangenot, 9:1072–1141. 16 vols. Paris: Letouzey et Ané, 1903–50.

———. "La théologie mystique de Saint Bonaventure." *Archivum Franciscanum Historicum* 14 (1921): 36–108.

Lopez, R. S. *The Commercial Revolution of the Middle Ages, 950–1350*. Cambridge: Cambridge University Press, 1976.

Lüers, Grete. *Die Sprache der deutschen Mystik des Mittelalters im Werke der Mechthild von Magdeburg*. Munich: Reinhardt, 1926. Reprint, Darmstadt: Wissenschaftliche Buchgesellschaft, 1966.

Lundén, Tryggve. "Pierre de Dacie." DS 12:1550–51.

Maccarrone, Michele. "Riforma e sviluppo della vita religiosa con Innocenzo III." *Rivista della storia della chiesa in Italia* 16 (1962): 29–72.

Macy, Gary. *The Banquet's Wisdom: A Short History of the Theologies of the Lord's Supper*. Mahwah, N.J.: Paulist Press, 1992.

La Madeleine (VIIIe–XIIIe Siècle): Mélanges de l'École Française de Rome. Moyen Age 104 (1992).

Maguire, Joanne. "Eriugenean Echoes in the 'Mirror of Simple Souls'." Unpublished paper.

———. "Nobility and Annihilation in Marguerite Porete's Mirror of Simple Souls." Ph.D. diss., University of Chicago, 1996.

Mahncke, Dietrich. *Unendliche Sphäre und Allmittelpunkt: Beiträge zur Genealogie der mathematischen Mystik*. Halle, M. Niemeyer, 1937.

Maisonneuve, Roland. "L'experience mystique et visionnaire de Marguerite d'Oingt, moniale chartreuse." In *Kartäusermystik und -Mystiker*, 81–102. Analecta Cartusiana 55. Salzburg: Institut für Anglistik und Amerikanistik, 1981.

Maleczek, Werner. *Das 'Privilegium Paupertatis' Innocenz III. und das Testament der Klara von Assisi: Überlegungen zur Frage ihrer Echtheit*. Rome: Istituto storico dei Cappuccini, 1995.

Manselli, Raoul. "La donna nella vita della chiesa tra duecento e trecento." In *Il movimento religiose femminile in Umbria nei secoli XIII–XIV*, edited by Roberto Rusconi, 243–55. Florence: La Nuova Italia, 1984.

————. *La "Lectura super Apocalipsim" di Pietro di Giovanni Olivi.* Rome: Istituto Storico Italiano per il Medio Evo, 1955.

————. *NOS QUI CUM EO FUIMUS: Contributo alla questione francescana.* Rome: Istituto Storico dei Cappuccini, 1980.

————. *Spirituali e Beghini in Provenza.* Rome: Istituto Storico Italiano per il Medio Evo. 1959.

————. *St. Francis of Assisi.* Chicago: Franciscan Herald Press, 1988.

Marchitielli, Elena. "L'alleanza sponsale con Cristo nelle lettere di S. Chiara a S. Agnese di Praga." *Dialoghi con Chiara d'Assisi: Atti delle Giornate di studio e riflessione per l'VIII Centenario di Santa Chiara,* edited by Luigi Giacometti, 309–22. Assisi: Edizioni Porziuncola, 1995.

Maréchal, Joseph. *Études sur la psychologie des mystiques.* 2 vols. Bruges: Beyaert-Desclée, 1924–37.

Margetts, John. "Latein und Volkssprache bei Mechthild von Magdeburg." *Amsterdamer Beiträge zur älteren Germanistik* 12 (1977): 119–36.

Martin, Anna. "Christina von Stommeln." *Mediaevistik* 4 (1991): 179–263.

Matter, E. Ann, and John Coakley, eds. *Creative Women in Medieval and Early Modern Italy: A Religious and Artistic Renaissance.* Philadelphia: University of Pennsylvania Press, 1994.

Matura, Thaddée. "Introduction." In *Claire d'Assise: Écrits,* 9–65. Paris: Cerf, 1985.

————. "Introduction." In *François d'Assise: Écrits,* 49–81. Paris: Cerf, 1981.

————. *Francis of Assisi: The Message in His Writings.* St. Bonaventure: Franciscan Institute, 1997.

————. "'Mi Pater Sancte': Dieu come père dans les écrits de François." In *L'esperienza di Dio in Francesco d'Assisi,* edited by Ettore Covi, 102–32. Rome: Editrice Laurentianum, 1982.

Mazzoni, Christina. "On the (Un)Representability of Woman's Pleasure: Angela of Foligno and Jacques Lacan." In *Gender and Text in the Later Middle Ages,* ed. Jane Chance, 239–62. Gainesville: University Press of Florida, 1996.

McCue, James F. "Liturgy and Eucharist. II, The West." In *Christian Spirituality II: High Middle Ages and Reformation,* edited by Jill Raitt, 427–38. New York: Crossroad, 1987.

McDonnell, Ernest W. *The Beguines and Beghards in Medieval Culture: With special reference on the Belgian scene.* New Brunswick: Rutgers University Press, 1954.

McElrath, Damian, ed. *Franciscan Christology: Selected Texts, Translations and Introductory Essays.* St. Bonaventure: Franciscan Institute, 1980.

McGinn, Bernard. "The Abyss of Love." In *The Joy of Learning and the Love of God: Studies in Honor of Jean Leclercq,* edited by E. Rozanne Elder, 95–120. Kalamazoo: Cistercian Publications, 1995.

————. *Antichrist: Two Thousand Years of the Human Fascination with Evil.* San Francisco: HarperSanFrancisco, 1994.

————. "Apocalyptic Traditions and Spiritual Identity in Thirteenth-Century Religious Life." In *The Roots of the Modern Christian Tradition,* edited by E. Rozanne Elder, 1–26 and 293–300. Kalamazoo: Cistercian Publications, 1984.

————. "Ascension and Introversion in the *Itinerarium mentis in Deum*." In *San Bonaventura 1274-1974*, 3:535–52. 5 vols. Grottaferrata/Rome: Collegio S. Bonaventura, 1974.

————. *The Calabrian Abbot: Joachim of Fiore in the History of Western Thought*. New York: Macmillan, 1985.

————. "The Changing Shape of Late Medieval Mysticism." *Church History* 65 (1996): 197–219.

————. "Donne mistiche ed autorità esoterica nel XIV secolo." In *Poteri carismatici ed informali: chiesa e società medioevali*, edited by Agostino Paravicini Bagliana and André Vauchez, 153–74. Palermo: Sellerio, 1992.

————. *The Foundations of Mysticism: Origins to the Fifth Century*. New York Crossroad, 1991.

————. "God as Eros: Metaphysical Foundations of Christian Mysticism." In *New Perspectives on Historical Theology: Essays in Memory of John Meyendorff*, edited by Bradley Nassif, 189–209. Grand Rapids: Eerdmans, 1995.

————. *The Growth of Mysticism: Gregory the Great through the Twelfth Century*. New York: Crossroad, 1994.

————. "The Influence of St. Francis on the Theology of the Middle Ages: The Testimony of St. Bonaventure." In *Bonaventuriana: Miscellanea in onore di Jacques Guy Bougerol, ofm.*, edited by Francisco de Asis Chavero Blanco, 1:97–117. 2 vols. Rome: Edizioni Antonianum, 1988.

————. "The Language of Love in Jewish and Christian Mysticism." In *Mysticism and Language*, edited by Steven Katz, 202–35. New York: Oxford University Press, 1992.

————. "Love, Knowledge and *Unio Mystica* in the Western Christian Tradition." In *Mystical Union in Judaism, Christianity, and Islam: An Ecumenical Dialogue*, edited by Moshe Idel and Bernard McGinn, 59–86. New York: Continuum, 1996.

————. "Marie d'Oignies and the New Mysticism." *Svensk Teologisk Kvartalskrift* 72 (1996): 97–109.

————. "Mysticism." *The Oxford Encyclopedia of the Reformation*, Hans J. Hillerbrand, Editor in Chief, 3:119–24. 4 vols. New York/Oxford: Oxford University Press, 1996.

————. "Mysticism and Sexuality." *The Way. Supplement* 77 (1993): 46–53.

————. "Ocean and Desert as Symbols of Mystical Absorption in the Christian Tradition." *The Journal of Religion* 74 (1994): 155–81.

————. "Platonic and Christian: The Case of the Divine Ideas." In *Of Scholars, Savants, and their Texts: Studies in Philosophy and Religious Thought. Essays in Honor of Arthur Hyman*, edited by Ruth Link-Salinger, 163–72. New York: Peter Lang, 1989.

————. "Pseudo-Dionysius and the Early Cistercians." In *One Yet Two: Monastic Tradition East and West*, edited by M. Basil Pennington, 200–241. Kalamazoo: Cistercian Publications, 1976.

————. Review of *Christliche Mystik im Abendland: Ihrer Geschichte von den Anfängen bis zum Ende des Mittelalters,* by Peter Dinzelbacher. *Cahiers de civilisation médiévale* 39 (1996): 121–23.

———. Review of *Geschichte der abendländische Mystik,* by Kurt Ruh. *Journal of Religion* 74 (1994): 94–96.

———. Review of *Holy Feast and Holy Fast,* by Caroline Walker Bynum. *History of Religions* 28 (1988): 90–92.

———. "The Role of Thomas Gallus in the History of Dionysian Mysticism." *Studies in Spirituality* 8 (1998): forthcoming.

———. "'To the Scandal of Men, Women are Prophesying': Female Seers in the High Middle Ages." In *Waiting in Fearful Hope,* edited by Christopher Kleinhenz and Fanny LeMoine, forthcoming.

———. "The Significance of Bonaventure's Theology of History." In *Celebrating the Medieval Heritage: A Colloquy on the Thought of Aquinas and Bonaventure. The Journal of Religion* 58 (1978 Supplement): S64–S81.

———. "Tropics of Desire: Mystical Interpretation of *The Song of Songs.*" In *That Others May Know and Love: Essays in Honor of Zachary Hayes, OFM,* edited by Michael F. Cusato and Edward Coughlin, 133–58. St. Bonaventure: Franciscan Institute, 1997.

———. "Visions and Critiques of Visions in Late Medieval Mysticism." In *Rending the Veil,* edited by Elliot R. Wolfson, forthcoming.

———. "Was St. Francis a Mystic?" In *Doors of Understanding: Conversations on Global Spirituality in Honor of Ewert Cousins,* edited by Steven Chase, 145–74. Quincy, Ill.: Franciscan Press, 1997.

———, ed. *Meister Eckhart and the Beguine Mystics: Hadewijch of Brabant, Mechthild of Magdeburg, and Marguerite Porete.* New York: Continuum, 1994.

McGuire, Brian Patrick. "The Cistercians and Friendship: An Opening to Women." In *Hidden Springs: Cistercian Monastic Women,* edited John A. Nichols and Lillian Thomas Shank, 1:171–200. 2 vols. Kalamazoo: Cistercian Publications, 1995.

McLaughlin, Eleanor. "The Heresy of the Free Spirit and Late Medieval Mysticism." *Medievalia et Humanistica* n.s. 4 (1973): 37–54.

McNamara, Jo Ann Kay. In *Sisters in Arms: Catholic Nuns through Two Millennia.* Cambridge, Mass.: Harvard University Press, 1996.

Meersseman, G. G. "Les débuts de l'ordre dès frères prêcheurs dans le Comté de Flandre (1224–1280)." *Archivum Fratrum Praedicatorum* 17 (1947): 5-40.

———. *Dossier de l'ordre de la pénitence au XIIIe siècle.* 2nd ed. Fribourg: Éditions Universitaires, 1982.

———. "Les frères prêcheurs et le mouvement dévot en Flandre au XIIIe siècle." *Archivum Fratrum Praedicatorum* 18 (1948): 69–130.

Ménard, André. "Spiritualité du Transitus." In *San Bonaventura 1274–1974,* 4:607–35. 5 vols. Grottaferrata/Rome: Collegio S. Bonaventura, 1974.

Menestò, Enrico. "Le Laude drammatiche di Iacopone da Todi: Fonti e struttura." In *Le laudi drammatiche umbre delle origini,* 105–40. Atti del V Convegno di Studio. Viterbo: Centro di Studi sul Teatro Medioevale e Rinascimentale Viterbo, 1981.

————. "Margherita da Città di Castello e la memoria santa della famiglia perduta." In *Umbria Sacra et Civile,* edited by Enrico Menestò and Roberto Rusconi, 167–78. Turin: Nuova Eri Edizione Rai, 1989.

————. "La mistica di Margherita da Cortona." In *Temi e problemi nella mistica femminile trecentesca,* 183–206. Todi: Convegni del Centro di Studi sulla Spiritualità Medievale XX, 1983.

————. *Le prose latine attribuite a Jacopone da Todi.* Bologna: Pàtron, 1979.

————, ed. *Angela da Foligno Terziaria Francescana.* Spoleto: Centro Italiano di Studi sull'Alto Medioevo, 1992.

————, ed. *Atti del convengo storico iacoponico in occasione del 750 anniversario della nascità di Iacopone da Todi, 29-30 novembre 1980.* Florence: La Nuova Italia, 1981.

————, and Roberto Rusconi, eds. *Umbria sacra e civile.* Turin: Nuova Eri Edizioni Rai, 1989.

Mens, Alcantera. "Beghine, Begardi, Beghinaggi." DIP 1:1165–80.

————. "Les béguines et les bégards dans le cadre de la culture médiévale." In *Le moyen âge* 64 (1958): 303–15.

————. *L'Ombrie italienne et l'Ombrie brabançonne: Deux courants religieux parallèles d'inspiration commune.* Études Franciscaines Supplement 17. Paris: Études Franciscaines, 1967.

————. *Oorsprong en betekenis van de Nederlandse begijnen–en begardenbeweging. Vergelijkende studie: XIIde–XIIIde eeuw.* Verhandelingen van de Koninklijke Vlaamse Academie voor Wetenschappen, Letteren en Schone Kunsten van Belgie. Klasse der Letteren, IX/7. Antwerp: Koninklijke Vlaamse Academie voor Wetenschappen, 1947.

Mercker, Hans. *Schriftauslegung als Weltauslegung: Untersuchungen zur Stellung der Schrift in der Theologie Bonaventuras.* Munich: Schöningh, 1971.

Merton, Thomas. *What are These Wounds? The Life of a Cistercian Mystic. Saint Lutgarde of Aywières.* Milwaukee: Bruce, 1950.

Meyer, Ruth. *Das 'St. Katharinentaler Schwesternbuch': Untersuchung. Edition. Kommentar.* Tübingen: Niemeyer, 1995.

Miccoli, Giovanni. "Bonaventura e Francesco." In *S. Bonaventura Francescano,* 49–73. Convegni del Centro di Studi sulla Spiritualità Medievale XIV. Todi: L'Accademia Tudertina, 1974.

————. *Francesco d'Assisi: Realtà e memoria di un'esperienza cristiana.* Turin: Einaudi, 1991.

————. "Francis of Assisi's Christian Proposal." *Greyfriars Review* 2 (1989): 132–42.

Milhaven, John Giles. *Hadewijch and Her Sisters: Other Ways of Loving and Knowing.* Albany: SUNY Press, 1993.

————. "A Medieval Lesson in Bodily Knowing: Women's Experience and Men's Thought." *Journal of the American Academy of Religion* 57 (1989): 341–72.

Minguet, Hugues. "Théologie spirituelle de sainte Gertrude: le Livre II du 'Heraut.'" *Collectanea Cisterciensia* 51 (1989): 147–77, 252–80, 317–38.

Mohr, Wolfgang. "Darbietungsformen der Mystik bei Mechthild von Magdeburg."

In *Märchen, Mythos, Dichtung: Festschrift zum 90. Geburtstag Friedrich von der Leyens,* edited by Hugo Kuhn and Kurt Schier, 375–99. Munich: Beck, 1963.

Mohrmann, Christine. *Liturgical Latin: Its Origins and Character.* Washington, D.C.: Catholic University Press, 1957.

Mollat, Michel, ed. *Études sur l'histoire de la pauvreté.* 2 vols. Paris: Publications de la Sorbonne, 1974.

Mommaers, Paul. "Bulletin d'histoire de la spiritualité: L'Ecole néerlandaise." *Revue d'ascetique et de mystique* 49 (1973): 477–88.

———. "Hadewijch." In *Die deutsche Literatur des Mittelalters: Verfasserlexikon,* edited by Kurt Ruh et al., 3:368–78. Berlin: Walter de Gruyter, 1981.

———. "Hadewijch: A Feminist in Conflict." *Louvain Studies* 13 (1988): 58–81.

———. "Preface." In *Hadewijch: The Complete Works,* translated by Mother Columba Hart, xi–xxiv. New York: Paulist Press, 1980.

———. "La transformation d'amour selon Marguerite Porete." *Ons Geestelijk Erf* 65 (1991): 88–107.

———. "Het VIIe en VIIIe Visioen van Hadewijch: Affectie in de mystieke beleving." *Ons Geestelijk Erf* 49 (1975): 105–32.

———, and Norbert De Paepe, eds. *Jan Van Ruusbroec: The sources, content and sequels of his mysticism.* Leuven: Leuven University Press, 1984.

———, and Frank Willaert. "Mystisches Erlebnis und sprachliche Vermittlung in den Brieven Hadewijchs." In *Religiöse Frauenbewegung und mystische Frömmigkeit im Mittelalter,* edited by Peter Dinzelbacher and Dieter Bauer, 117–51. Cologne/Vienna: Böhlau, 1988.

Mooney, Catherine M. "The Authorial Role of Brother A. in the Composition of Angela of Foligno's Revelations." In *Creative Women in Medieval and Early Modern Italy: A Religious and Artistic Renaissance,* edited by E. Ann Matter and John Coakley, 34–63. Philadelphia: University of Pennsylvania Press, 1994.

Moore, R. I. *The Origins of European Dissent.* New York: St. Martin's Press, 1977.

Moorman, John. *A History of the Franciscan Order: From its Origins to the Year 1517.* Oxford: Clarendon Press, 1968.

Movimento religioso femminile e Francescanesimo nel secolo XIII. Assisi: Società Internazionale di Studi Francescani, 1980.

Müller, Ulrich. "Mechthild von Magdeburg und Dantes Vita Nova oder erotische Religiosität und religiöse Erotik." In *Liebe als Literatur: Aufsätze zur erotischen Dichtung in Deutschland,* edited by Rüdiger Krohn, 163–76. Munich: Beck, 1983.

Mundy, John H. *Europe in the High Middle Ages, 1150–1309.* London: Longman, 1973.

———. *Liberty and Political Power in Toulouse, 1050–1230.* New York: Columbia University Press, 1954.

Murk-Jansen, Saskia. "Hadewijch and Eckhart: Amor intellegere est." In *Meister Eckhart and the Beguine Mystics: Hadewijch of Brabant, Mechthild of Magdeburg, and Marguerite Porete,* edited by Bernard McGinn, 17–30. New York: Continuum, 1994.

————. *The Measure of Mystic Thought: A Study of Hadewijch's Mengeldichten.* Göppingen: Kümmerle, 1991.

————. "The Mystic Theology of the Thirteenth-Century Mystic, Hadewijch, and its Literary Expression." In *The Medieval Mystical Tradition in England: Exeter Symposium V,* edited by Marion Glasscoe, 117–27. Cambridge: D.S. Brewer, 1992.

————. "The Use of Gender and Gender-Related Imagery in Hadewijch." In *Gender and Text in the Later Middle Ages,* edited by Jane Chance, 52–68. Gainesville: University Press of Florida, 1996.

Murray, Alexander. "Confession as an historical source in the thirteenth century." In *The Writing of History in the Middle Ages: Essays presented to Richard William Southern,* edited by R. H. C. Davis and J. M. Wallace-Hadrill, 275–322. Oxford: Clarendon Press, 1981.

Muscatine, Charles. "The Emergence of Psychological Allegory in Old French Romance." *Publications of the Modern Language Society* 68 (1953): 1160–72.

Neel, Carol. "The Origins of the Beguines." In *Sisters and Workers in the Middle Ages,* edited by Judith M. Bennett et al., 240–60. Chicago: University of Chicago Press, 1989.

Nellmann, Eberhard. "*Dis buoch . . . bezeichent alleine mich:* Zum Prolog von Mechthilds 'Fliessendem Licht der Gottheit.'" In *Gotes und der werlde hulde,* edited by Rüdiger Schnell, 200–205. Bern/Stuttgart: Francke, 1989.

Neumann, Eva Gertrud. *Rheinisches Beginen- und Begardenwesen: Ein mainzer Beitrag zur religiösen Bewegung am Rhein.* Mainzer Abhandlungen zur mittleren und neueren Geschichte 4. Meisenheim-am-Glan: 1960.

Neumann, Hans. "Beiträge zur Textgeschichte des 'Fliessenden Lichts der Gottheit' und zur Lebensgeschichte Mechthilds von Magdeburg." In *Altdeutsche und altniederländische Mystik,* edited by Kurt Ruh, 175–239. Darmstadt: Wissenschaftliche Buchgesellschaft, 1964.

————. "Mechthild von Magdeburg." In *Die deutsche Literatur des Mittelalters: Verfasserlexikon,* edited by Kurt Ruh et al., 6:260–70. Berlin: Walter de Gruyter, 1981.

————. "Mechthild von Magdeburg und die mittelniederländische Frauenmystik." In *Medieval German Studies: Festschrift Presented to Frederick Norman,* 231–46. London: University of London, 1965.

Newman, Barbara. "Hildegard of Bingen: Visions and Validation." *Church History* 54 (1985): 163–75.

————. "The Mozartian Moment: Reflections on Medieval Mysticism." In *Christian Spirituality Bulletin* 3.1 (Spring 1995): 1–5.

————. *From Virile Woman to WomanChrist: Studies in Medieval Religion and Literature.* Philadelphia: University of Pennsylvania Press, 1995.

Nguyên-Van-Khanh, Norbert. *The Teacher of His Heart: Jesus Christ in the Thought and Writings of St. Francis.* St. Bonaventure: Franciscan Institute, 1994.

Nichols, John A., and Lilian Thomas Shank, eds., *Hidden Springs: Cistercian Monastic Women.* 2 vols. Kalamazoo: Cistercian Publications, 1995.

————, eds. *Peace Weavers: Medieval Religious Women.* Kalamazoo: Cistercian Publications, 1987.

Nieveler, Peter. *Codex Iuliacensis: Christina von Stommeln und Petrus von Dacien, ihr Leben und Nachleben in Geschichte, Kunst und Literatur.* Mönchengladbach: Kühlen, 1975.

Nimmo, Duncan. *Reform and Division in the Franciscan Order: From St. Francis to the Foundation of the Capuchins.* Rome: Capuchin Historical Institute, 1987.

Nolan, Barbara. *The Gothic Visionary Perspective.* Princeton: Princeton University Press, 1977.

Oakley, Francis. *The Western Church in the Later Middle Ages.* Ithaca: Cornell University Press, 1979.

Ochsenbein, Peter. "Leidensmystik in Dominikanischen Frauenklöstern des 14. Jahrhunderts am Beispiel der Elsbeth von Oye." In *Religiöse Frauenbewegung und mystische Frömmigkeit im Mittelalter,* edited by Peter Dinzelbacher and Dieter Bauer, 353–72. Cologne/Vienna: Böhlau, 1988.

————. "Die Offenbarungen Elsbeths von Oye als Dokument leidensfixierte Mystik." In *Abendländische Mystik im Mittelalter: Symposium Kloster Engelberg 1984,* edited by Kurt Ruh, 423–42. Stuttgart Metzler, 1986.

Öehl, Wilhelm. *Deutsche Mystikerbriefe des Mittelalters 1100–1550.* Munich: Georg Müller, 1931.

Ohly, Friedrich. "Du bist mein, Ich bin dein. Du in mir, Ich in dir. Ich du, Du Ich." In *Kritische Bewahrung: Beiträge zur deutschen Philologie. Festschrift für Werner Schröder,* edited by Ernst-Joachim Schmidt, 371–415. Berlin: Erich Schmidt, 1974.

Oliger, Livarius. "De origine regularum ordinis S. Clarae." *Archivum Franciscanum Historicum* 5 (1912): 181–209, 413–47.

————. "Descriptio Codicis S. Antonii de Urbe." *Archivum Franciscanum Historicum* 12 (1919): 321–401.

————. "Regulae tres Reclusorum et Eremitarum Angliae Saec. XIII–XIV." *Antonianum* 3 (1928): 151–90, 299–320; 9 (1934): 37–84, 243–68.

————. "Spirituels." In *Dictionnaire de théologie catholique,* edited by A. Vacant and E. Mangenot, 14:2522–49. 16 vols. Paris: Letouzey et Ané, 1903–50.

Orcibal, Jean. "'Le Miroir des simples ames' et la 'secte' du Libre Esprit." *Revue de l'Histoire des Religions* 175 (1969): 35–60.

Osborne, Kenan B., ed. *The History of Franciscan Theology.* St. Bonaventure: Franciscan Institute, 1994.

Ozment, Steven. *The Age of Reform, 1250–1550: An Intellectual and Religious History of Late Medieval and Reformation Europe.* New Haven: Yale University Press, 1980.

Padovese, Luigi. "Clare's Tonsure: Act of Consecration or Sign of Penance?" *Greyfriars Review* 6 (1992): 67–80.

Palmer, Nigel. "Das Buch als Bedeutungsträger bei Mechthild von Magdeburg." In *Bildhafte Rede in Mittelalter und früher Neuzeit: Probleme ihrer Legitimation und Funktion,* edited by Wolfgang Harms and Klaus Speckenbach, 217–35. Tübingen: Niemeyer, 1992.

Papi, Anna Benvenuti. *"In Castro Poenitentiae":* Santità e società femminile nell'Italia medievale. Rome: Herder, 1990.

———. "Mendicant Friars and Female Pinzochere in Tuscany: From Social Marginality to Models of Sanctity." In *Women and Religion in Medieval and Renaissance Italy,* edited by Daniel Bornstein and Roberto Rusconi, 84–103. Chicago: University of Chicago Press, 1996.

———. "'Velut in sepulchro': cellane e recluse nella tradizione agiografica italiana." In *Culto dei santi, istituzioni e classi sociali in età preindustriale,* edited by Sofia Boesch Gajano and Lucia Sebastiani, 367–455. Rome: Japadre, 1984.

Parkes, M. B. "The Literacy of the Laity." In *Literature and Western Civilization: The Medieval World,* edited by David Daiches and Anthony Thorlby, 555–77. London: Aldus, 1973.

Pásztor, Edith. "Gli Spirituali di fronte a San Bonaventura." In *S. Bonaventura Francescano,* 161–79. Convegni del Centro di Studi sulla Spiritualità Medievale XIV. Todi: L'Accademia Tudertina, 1974.

Paul, Jacques. "L'érémitisme et la survivance de la spiritualité du désert chez les Franciscaines." In *La mystiques de désert dans l'Islam, le Judaisme et le Christianisme,* 133–45. N.p.: Association des Amis de Sénanque, 1974.

———. "La signification sociale du franciscanisme." In *Mouvements Franciscains et Societé Française XIIe–XIIIe siècles,* edited by André Vauchez, 9–25. Paris: Beauchesne, 1983.

Paulsell, Stephanie. "'*Scriptio divina*': Writing and the Experience of God in the Works of Marguerite d'Oingt." Ph.D. diss., University of Chicago, 1993.

Payen, J. C. "La Pénitence dans la contexte culturel des xiie et xiiie siècles." *Revue des sciences philosophiques et théologiques* 61 (1977): 399–428.

Péano, Pierre. "Jacques de Milan." DS 8:48–49.

———. "Olieu (Olivi; Pierre Jean)." DS 11:751–62.

———. "Pierre de Fossombrone (Angelo Clareno)." DS 12:1582–88.

Peck, George T. *The Fool of God: Jacopone da Todi.* University, Ala.: University of Alabama Press, 1980.

Peers, E. Allison. *Ramon Lull, a Biography.* London: Jarrold's, 1929.

Pelligrini, Luigi. "A Century Reading the Sources for the Life of Francis of Assisi." *Greyfriars Review* 7 (1993): 323–46.

———. "La prima *Fraternitas* francescana: una rilettura delle fonti." In *Frate Francesco d'Assisi: Atti del XXI Convegno internazionale,* 37–70. Spoleto: Centro Italiano di Studi sull'alto Medioevo, 1994.

Peters, Ursula. "Das 'Leben' der Christine Ebner: Textanalyse und kulturhistorische Kommentar." In *Abendländischer Mystik im Mittelalter: Symposium Kloster Engelberg 1984,* edited by Kurt Ruh, 402–22. Stuttgart: Metzler, 1986.

———. *Religiöse Erfahrung als literarisches Faktum: Zur Vorgeschichte und Genese frauenmystischer Texte des 13. und 14. Jahrhunderts.* Tübingen: Niemeyer, 1988.

———. "Vita religiosa und spirituelles Erleben: Frauenmystik und frauenmystische Literatur im 13. und 14. Jahrhundert." In *Deutsche Literatur von Frauen: Erster*

Band, Vom Mittelalter bis zum Ende des 18. Jahrhundert, edited by Gisela Brinker-Gabler, 88–109. Munich: Beck, 1987.

Peterson, Ingrid J. *Clare of Assisi: A Biographical Study.* Quincy, Ill.: Franciscan Press, 1993.

———. "Clare of Assisi's Mysticism of the Poor Crucified." *Studies in Spirituality* 4 (1994): 51–78.

———. "Images of the Crucified Christ in Clare of Assisi and Angela of Foligno." In *That Others May Know and Love: Essays in Honor of Zachary Hayes, OFM,* edited by Michael F. Cusato and Edward Coughlin, 167-92. St. Bonaventure: Franciscan Institute, 1997.

Petit, François. *La spiritualité des Prémontrés au XIIe et XIIIe siècles.* Paris: Vrin, 1947.

Petroff, Elizabeth Alvida. *Body and Soul: Essays on Medieval Women and Mysticism.* Oxford: Oxford University Press, 1994.

———. *Medieval Women's Visionary Literature.* New York: Oxford University Press, 1986.

Pfeiffer, Franz. "Bruder David von Augsburg." *Zeitschrift für Deutsches Alterthum* 9 (1853): 8–55.

Philippen, L. J. M. *De Begijnhoven, Oorsprong, geschiednis, inrichting.* Antwerp: n.p., 1918.

Piana, Celestino. "Il 'Fr. Iacobus de Mediolano Lector' autore dello Pseudo-Bonaventuriano *Stimulus Amoris* ed un convento del suo insegnamento." *Antonianum* 61 (1986): 329–39.

Potestà, Gian-Luca. "Aspetti e implicazioni della mistica cristocentrica di Ubertino da Casale." In *Abendländischer Mystik im Mittelalter: Symposium Kloster Engelberg 1984,* edited by Kurt Ruh, 286–99. Stuttgart: Metzler, 1986.

———. "Un secolo di studi sull'*Arbor Vitae:* Chiesa ed escatologia in Ubertino da Casale." *Collectanea Francescana* 47 (1977): 217–67.

———. *Storia ed Escatologia in Ubertino da Casale.* Milan: Università Cattolica del Sacro Cuore, 1980.

———. "Ubertin de Casale." DS 16:3–25.

Poulenc, Jerome. "Saint François dans le 'vitrail des anges' de l'église supérieure de la basilique d'Assise." *Archivum Franciscanum Historicum* 76 (1983): 701–13.

Pozzi, Giovanni. "The Canticle of Brother Sun: From Grammar to Prayer." *Greyfriars Review* 4 (1992): 1–21.

———, and Claudio Leonardi, eds. *Scrittrici mistiche italiane.* Genoa: Marietti, 1988.

"Premostratensi." DIP 7:720–46.

Principe, Walter H. "St. Bonaventure's Theology of the Holy Spirit with Reference to the Expression 'Pater et Filius Diligunt Se Spiritu Sancto.'" In *San Bonaventura 1274-1974,* 4:243–69. 5 vols. Grottaferrata/Rome: Collegio S. Bonaventura, 1974.

Pring-Mill, R. D. F. "The Trinitarian World Picture of Ramon Lull." *Romanistische Jahrbuch* 7 (1955–56): 229–56.

Quinn, John. *The Historical Constitution of Saint Bonaventure's Philosophy.* Toronto: PIMS, 1973.

Rahner, Hugo. "De Dominici pectoris fonte potavit." *Zeitschrift für katholische Theolo-gie* 55 (1931): 103–8.

———. "Die Gottesgeburt: Die Lehre der Kirchenväter von der Geburt Christi aus dem Herzen der Kirche und der Gläubigen." In *Symbole der Kirche,* 13–87. Salzburg: Otto Müller, 1964.

———. "Grundzüge einer Geschichte der Herz-Iesu-Verehrung." *Zeitschrift für Askese und Mystik* 18 (1943): 61–83.

Rahner, Karl. "Der Begriff der ecstasis bei Bonaventura." *Zeitschrift für Aszese und Mystik* 9 (1934): 1–19.

———. "The Doctrine of the Spiritual Senses in the Middle Ages." In *Theological Investigations XVI,* 109–28. New York: Crossroad, 1979.

———. "Part Five: Devotion to the Sacred Heart." In *Theological Investigations III,* 321–52. New York: Seabury, 1974.

———. *Visions and Prophecies.* London: Burns-Oates, 1963.

Raitt, Jill, ed., in collaboration with Bernard McGinn and John Meyendorff. *Christian Spirituality II: High Middle Ages and Reformation.* New York: Crossroad, 1987.

Ranft, Patricia. *Women and the Religious Life in Premodern Europe.* New York: St. Martin's Press, 1996.

Ratzinger, Joseph. *The Theology of History in St. Bonaventure.* Chicago: Franciscan Herald Press, 1971.

Rauch, Winthir. *Das Buch Gottes: Eine systematische Untersuchung des Buchbegriffes bei Bonaventura.* Munich: Hueber, 1961.

Raurell, Frederic. "El 'Càntic dels Càntics' en els segles XII–XIII: Lectura de Clara d'Assis." *Estudios Franciscanos* 91 (1990): 421–559.

———. "La Bibbia nella visione sponsale della *Legenda sanctae Clarae Virginis.*" In *Dialoghi con Chiara d'Assisi: Atti delle Giornate di studio e riflessione per l'Viii Centenario di Santa Chiara,* ed. Luigi Giacometti, 67–150. Assisi: Edizioni Porziuncola, 1995.

Rayez, André. "David d'Augsbourg." DS 3:42–44.

"Reclus." DS 13:217–28.

"Reclusione." DIP 7:1229–45.

Redigonda, L. A. "Domenicane (di Clausura)." DIP 3:780–93.

Régnier-Bohler, Danielle. "Literary and Mystical Voices." In *A History of Women. Vol. II, Silences of the Middle Ages,* edited by Christiane Klapisch-Zuber, 427–82. Cambridge: Belknap Press, 1992.

Reiss, Edmund. "Fin'Amors: Its History and Meaning in Medieval Literature." *Medieval and Renaissance Studies* 8, 74–99. Durham: Duke University Press, 1979.

Renan, Ernest. "Une Idylle monacale au XIIIe siècle: Christine de Stommeln." In *Nouvelles études d'histoire religieuse,* 355–96. Paris: Lévy, 1884.

Reynaert, Joris. "Attributieproblemen in verband met de 'Brieven' van Hadewijch." *Ons Geestelijk Erf* 49 (1975): 225–47.

———. *De beeldspraak van Hadewijch.* Tielt: Studiën en tekstuitgaven van Ons Geestelijk Erf, 1981.

———. "Hadewijch: mystic poetry and courtly love." In *Medieval Dutch Literature in its European Context,* edited by Erik Kooper, 208–25. Cambridge: Cambridge University Press, 1994.

———. "Mystische Bibelinterpretation bei Hadewijch." In *Grundfragen christlicher Mystik,* edited by Margot Schmidt and Dieter R. Bauer, 123–37. Stuttgart/Bad Canstatt: frommann-holzboog, 1987.

Reypens, Léonce. "Ruusbroec-Studien. I, Het mystieke 'gherinen.'" *Ons Geestelijk Erf* 12 (1938): 158–86.

———. "De *Seven Manieren van Minne* Geinterpoleerd?" *Ons Geestelijk Erf* 5 (1931): 287–322.

———. "Sint Lutgards mystieke opgang." *Ons Geestelijk Erf* 20 (1946): 7–49.

Rigon, Antonio. "San Antonio e la cultura universitaria nell'ordine francescano delle origini." In *Francescanesimo e cultura universitaria,* 67–92. Atti del XVI Convegno Internazionale. Perugia: Centro di Studi Francescani, 1990.

Ringler, Siegfried. "Ebner, Christine." In *Die deutsche Literatur des Mittelalters: Verfasserlexikon,* edited by Kurt Ruh et al., 2:297–302. Berlin: Walter de Gruyter, 1981.

———. "Gnadenviten aus süddeutschen Frauenklöstern des 14. Jahrhunderts– Vitenschreibung als mystisische Lehre." In *"Minnichlichui gotes erkennusse": Studien zur frühen abendländischen Mystiktradition Heidelberger Mystiksymposium vom 16.Januar 1989,* edited by Dietrich Schmidtke, 89–104. Stuttgart-Bad Canstatt: frommann-holzboog, 1990.

———. "Die Rezeption mittelalterlicher Frauenmystik als wissenschaftlicher Problem, dargestellt am Werk der Christine Ebner." In *Frauenmystik im Mittelalter,* edited by Peter Dinzelbacher and Dieter R. Bauer, 178–200. Ostfeldern bei Stuttgart: Schwabenverlag, 1985.

———. *Viten- und Offenbarungsliteratur in Frauenklöstern des Mittelalters: Quellen und Studien.* Munich: Artemis, 1980.

Robertson, Elizabeth. *Early English Devotional Prose and the Female Audience.* Knoxville: University of Tennessee Press, 1990.

Robillaird, J.-A. "Les six genres de contemplation chez Richard de Saint-Victor et leur origine platonicienne." *Revue des sciences philosophiques et théologiques* 28 (1939): 229–33.

Robson, C. A. *Maurice de Sully and the Medieval Vernacular Homily, with the Text of Maurice's French Homilies from a Sens Cathedral Chapter MS.* Oxford: Blackwell, 1952.

Rodriguez, Isaias. "Lévitation." DS 9:738–41.

Roisin, Simone. "L'efforescence cistercienne et le courant féminin de pieté au XIIIe siècle." *Revue d'histoire ecclésiastique* 39 (1943): 342–78.

———. *L'hagiographie cistercienne dans la diocèse de Liège au XIIIe siècle.* Louvain: Bibliothèque de l'Université, 1947.

———. "La méthode hagiographique de Thomas de Cantimpré." In *Miscellanea historica in honorem Alberti de Meyer,* 1:546–57. Louvain: Bibliothèque de l'Université, 1946.

Rorem, Paul. *Pseudo Dionysius: A Commentary on the Texts and an Introduction to Their Influence.* New York/Oxford: Oxford University Press, 1993.

Rouillard, Philippe. "Regole per Reclusi." DIP 7:1533–36.

Rubin, Miri. *Corpus Christi: The Eucharist in Late Medieval Culture.* Cambridge: Cambridge University Press, 1991.

Rudy, Gordon. "The Contemplation of God in Ramon Llull's *Liber de ascensu et descensu intellectus.*" Unpublished paper.

Ruello, Francis. "La mystique de l'Exode (Exode 3:14 selon Thomas Gallus, commentateur dionysien, d. 1246)." In *Dieu et l'Être: Exégèses d'Exode 3,14 et de Coran 20, 11-24,* 213–43. Paris: Études Augustiniennes, 1978.

Ruh, Kurt. "L'amore di Dio in Hadewijch, Mechthild di Magdeburgo e Margherita Porete." In *Temi e problemi nella mistica femminile trecentesca,* 85–106. Todi: Convegni del Centro di Studi sulla Spiritualità Medievale XX, 1983.

———. "Beginenmystik: Hadewijch, Mechthild von Magdeburg, Marguerite Porete." In *Kleine Schriften. Band II, Scholastik und Mystik im Spätmittelalter,* 237–49. Berlin: Walter de Gruyter, 1984.

———. *Bonaventura deutsch: Ein Beitrag zur deutschen Franziskaner-Mystik und -scholastik.* Bern: Francke, 1956.

———. "David von Augsburg und die Entstehung eines franziskanisches Schrifttums in deutscher Sprache." In *Kleine Schriften. Band II, Scholastik und Mystik im Spätmittelalter,* 46–67. Berlin: Walter de Gruyter, 1984.

———. *Geschichte der abendländische Mystik. Band II, Frauenmystik und Franziskaniche Mystik der Fruhzeit.* Munich: Beck, 1993.

———. *Geschichte der abendländische Mystik. Band III, Die Mystik des deutschen Predigerordens und ihre Grundlegung durch die Hochscholastik.* Munich: Beck, 1996.

———. *Kleine Schriften. Band II. Scholastik und Mystik im Spätmittelalter.* Berlin: Walter de Gruyter, 1984.

———. "Die trinitarische Spekulation in deutscher Mystik und Scholastik." In *Kleine Schriften. Band II, Scholastik und Mystik im Spätmittelalter,* 14–45. Berlin: Walter de Gruyter, 1984.

———, ed. *Abendländische Mystik im Mittelalter: Symposium Kloster Engelberg 1984.* Stuttgart: Metzler, 1986.

———, ed. *Altdeutsche und altniederländische Mystik.* Darmstadt: Wissenschaftliche Buchgesellschaft, 1964.

———, et al., eds. *Die deutsche Literatur des Mittelalters: Verfasserlexikon.* Berlin: Walter de Gruyter, 1981.

Rusconi, Roberto. *"Clerici secundum alios clericos":* Francesco d'Assisi e l'istituzione ecclesiastica." In *Frate Francesco d'Assisi: Atti del XXI Convegno internazionale,* 71–100. Spoleto: Centro Italiano di Studi sull'alto Medioevo, 1994.

———. "'Forma apostolorum': l'immagine del predicatore nei movimenti religiosi francesi ed italiani dei secc. XII e XIII." *Cristianesimo nella Storia* 6 (1985): 513–42.

———. "I francescani e la confessione nel secolo XIII." In *Francescanesimo e vita religiosa dei laici nel '200,* 251–309. Assisi: Università degli Studi di Perugia, 1981.

———. "Margherita da Cortona: Peccatrice redenta e patrona cittadina." In *Umbria sacra e civile,* edited by Enrico Menestò and Roberto Rusconi, 89–104. Turin: Nuova Eri Edizioni Rai, 1989.

————. "La predicazione minoritica in Europa nei secoli XIII-XV." In *Francesco, Francescanesimo e la cultura della nuova Europa,* edited by Ignazio Baldelli and Angiola Maria Romanini, 141–65. Rome: Istituto della Enciclopedia Italiana, 1986.

————, ed. *Il movimento religioso femminile in Umbria nei secoli XIII-XIV.* Florence: La Nuova Italia, 1984.

S. Bonaventura Francescano. Convegni del Centro di Studi sulla Spiritualità Medievale XIV. Todi: L'Accademia Tudertina, 1974.

Sabatelli, Giacomo. "Jacopone da Todi." DS 8:20–26.

————. "Jean della Verna (de l'Alverne)." DS 8:782–84.

Salter, Elizabeth. *Nicholas Love's "Myrrour of the Blessed Lyf of Jesu Christ."* Analecta Carthusiana 10. Salzburg: Institut für Englische Sprache und Literatur, 1974.

San Bonaventura 1274–1974. 5 vols. Grottaferrata/Rome: Collegio S. Bonaventura, 1974.

Sargent, Michael. "'Le Mirouer des simples âmes' and the English Mystical Tradition." In *Abendländischer Mystik im Mittelalter: Symposium Kloster Engelberg 1984,* edited by Kurt Ruh, 443–65. Stuttgart: Metzler, 1986.

Sauer, J. "Praeputium Domini." In *Lexikon für Theologie und Kirche,* edited by Konrad Hoffman and Michael Buchberger, 8:434–35. 2nd ed. Freiburg-im-Breisgau: Herder, 1936.

Savage, Anne, and Nicholas Watson, trans. *Anchoritic Spirituality: Ancrene Wisse and Associated Works.* New York: Paulist Press, 1991.

Sayers, Jane. *Innocent III: Leader of Europe 1198-1216.* London/New York: Longman, 1994.

Schlageter, J. "Die Bedeutung des Hoheliedkommentar des Franziskanertheologen Petrus Johannis Olivi (d. 1298): Argumente für eine neue Edition." *Wissenschaft und Weisheit* 58 (1995): 137–51.

Schlosser, Marianne. *Cognitio et amor: Zum kognitivien und voluntativen Grund der Gotteserfahrung nach Bonaventura.* Paderborn: Schöningh, 1990.

————. "Lux Inaccessibilis: Zur negativen Theologie bei Bonaventura." *Franziskanische Studien* 68 (1986): 1–140.

————. "Mother, Sister, Bride: The Spirituality of St. Clare." *Greyfriars Review* 5 (1991): 233–49.

Schmidt, Margot. "Elemente der Schau bei Mechthild von Magdeburg und Mechthild von Hackeborn: Zur Bedeutung der geistlichen Sinne." In *Frauenmystik im Mittelalter,* ed. Peter Dinzelbacher and Dieter R. Bauer, 137–39. Ostfeldern bei Stuttgart: Schwabenverlag, 1985.

————. "Leiden und Weisheit in der christlichen Mystik des Mittelalters." In *Leiden und Weisheit in der Mystik,* edited by Bernd Jaspert, 149–65. Paderborn: Bonifatius, 1992.

————. "Mechthilde de Hackeborn." DS 10:873–77.

———. "Mechthilde de Madgebourg." DS 10:877–85.

———. "Mechthild von Hackeborn." In *Deutsche Literatur des Mittelalters: Verfasser-lexikon,* edited by Kurt Ruh et al., 6:251–60. Berlin: Walter de Gruyter, 1981.

———. "'minne dú gewaltige kellerin': On the Nature of *minne* in Mechthild of Magdeburg's *fliessende licht der gottheit.*" *Vox Benedictina* 4 (1987): 100–125.

———. "Miroir." DS 10:1290–1303.

———. "Rodolphe de Biberach." DS 13:846–50.

———. "'die spilende minnevluot': Der Eros als Sein und Wirkkraft in der Trinität bei Mechthild von Magdeburg." In *"Eine Höhe über die nichts geht": Spezielle Glaubenserfahrung in der Frauenmystik,* edited by Margot Schmidt and Dieter R. Bauer, 80–89. Stuttgart/Bad Canstatt: frommann-holzboog, 1986.

———. "Versinnlichte Transzendenz bei Mechthild von Magdeburg." In *"Minnich-lichiu gotes erkennnusse": Studien zur frühen abendländischen Mystiktradition,* edited by Dieter Schmidtke, 62–88. Stuttgart/Bad Canstatt: frommann-holzboog, 1990.

———, and Dieter R. Bauer, eds. *Grundfragen christlicher Mystik.* Stuttgart/Bad Canstatt: frommann-holzboog, 1987.

Schmidt-Kohl, Volker. "Petrus de Dacia, ein skandinavischer Mystiker des 13. Jahrhunderts." *Zeitschrift für Religions-und Geistesgeschichte* 18 (1966): 255–62.

Schmitt, Clément, ed. *Vita e Spiritualità della Beata Angela da Foligno.* Perugia: Serafica Provincia di San Francisco, 1987.

Schmucki, Octavian. "Fundamental Characteristics of the Franciscan 'Form of Life.'" *Greyfriars Review* 3 (1991): 325–66.

———. "The Illnesses of St. Francis before his Stigmatization." *Greyfriars Review* 4 (1990): 31–61.

———. "The Mysticism of St. Francis in the Light of His Writings." *Greyfriars Review* 3 (1989): 241–66.

———. "The Passion of Christ in the Life of St. Francis of Assisi: A Comparative Study of the Sources in the Light of the Devotion to the Passion Practiced in his Time." *Greyfriars Review* 4 (1990 Supplement): 1–101.

———. "A Place of Solitude: An Essay on the External Circumstances of the Prayer Life of St. Francis of Assisi." *Greyfriars Review* 1 (1988): 77–132.

———. "The Rediscovery of the Canticle of Exhortation *Audite* of St. Francis for the Poor Ladies of San Damiano." *Greyfriars Review* 3 (1989): 115–26.

———. "Gli Scritti Legislativi di San Francesco." In *Approccio Storico-Critico alle Fonti Francescane,* 73–98. Rome: Editiones Antonianum, 1979.

———. *The Stigmata of St. Francis of Assisi: A Critical Investigation in the Light of the Thirteenth-Century Sources.* St. Bonaventure: Franciscan Institute, 1991.

———. "The Third Order in the Biographies of St. Francis." *Greyfriars Review* 6 (1992): 81–107.

Schnell, Rüdiger, ed. *Gottes und der werlde hulde: Literatur im Mittelalter und Neuzeit. Festschrift für Heinz Rupp zum 70. Geburtstag.* Bern/Stuttgart: Francke, 1989.

Schneyer, J. B. *Repertorium der lateinischen Sermones des Mittelalters für die Zeit von 1155-1350.* 9 vols. Münster: Aschendorff, 1969–80.

Schürmann, Reiner. *Meister Eckhart: Mystic and Philosopher.* Bloomington: Indiana University Press, 1978.

Schwietering, Julius. *Mystik und höfische Dichtung im Mittelalter.* Tübingen: Max Niemeyer, 1960.

Scott, Karen. "St. Catherine of Siena, 'Apostola.'" *Church History* 61 (1992): 34–46.

———. "Urban Spaces, Women's Networks, and the Lay Apostolate in the Siena of Catherine Benincasa." In *Creative Women in Medieval and Early Modern Italy: A Religious and Artistic Renaissance,* edited by E. Ann Matter and John Coakley, 105–19. Philadelphia: University of Pennsylvania Press, 1994.

Seaton, William. "Transforming of Convention in Mechthild of Magdeburg." *Mystics Quarterly* 10 (1984): 64–72.

Seesholtz, Anna Groh. *Friends of God: Practical Mystics of the Fourteenth Century.* New York: Columbia University Press, 1934.

Sells, Michael A. *Mystical Languages of Unsaying.* Chicago: University of Chicago, 1994.

Shank, Thomas Lilian. "The God of My Life: St. Gertrude, A Monastic Woman." In *Peace Weavers: Medieval Religious Women,* edited by John A. Nichols and Lilian Thomas Shank, 2:239–73. Kalamazoo: Cistercian Publications, 1987.

Simonetti, Adele. "Introduzione." In *I Sermoni di Umiltà da Faenza: Studio e edizione, XI–XCIV.* Spoleto: Centro Italiano di Studi sull'alto Medioevo, 1995.

Simons, Walter. "The Beguine Movement in the Southern Low Countries: A Reassessment." *Bulletin de l'Institut historique Belge de Rome* 59 (1989): 63–105.

———. "Reading a saint's body: Rapture and bodily movement in the *vitae* of some thirteenth-century beguines." In *Framing Medieval Bodies,* edited by Sarah Kay and Miri Rubin, 10–23. Manchester/New York: Manchester University Press, 1994.

Sisto, Alessandra. *Figure del primo francescanesimo in Provenza: Ugo e Douceline di Digne.* Florence: Olschki, 1971.

Skarup, Povl. "La langue du *Miroir des simples âmes* attribué à Marguerite Porete." *Studia Neophilologica* 60 (1988): 231–36.

Smalley, Beryl. "Ecclesiastical Attitudes to Novelty (c. 1100–c. 1250)." In *Church Society and Politics: Papers Read at the Thirteenth Summer Meeting and Fourteenth Winter Meeting of the Ecclesiastical History Society,* edited by Derek Baker. Oxford: Blackwell, 1975.

———. *The Study of the Bible in the Middle Ages.* 2nd ed. Notre Dame, Ind.: University of Notre Dame, 1964.

Smits, Luchesius. "Die Utopie des mystischen Zeitalters bei Bonaventura (1217–1274)." *Franziskanische Studien* 67 (1985): 114–33.

Solano, Jesus. *Historical Development of Reparation in Devotion to the Heart of Jesus.* Rome: Centro Cuore di Cristo, 1980.

Solignac, Aimé. "'NOYS' et 'MENS.'" DS 11:459–69.

———. "'SYNDERESIS.'" DS 14:1407–12.

Sorrell, Roger D. *St. Francis of Assisi and Nature: Tradition and Innovation in Western*

Christian Attitudes toward the Environment. New York/Oxford: Oxford University Press, 1988.

Southern, R. W. *The Making of the Middle Ages.* New Haven/London: Yale University Press, 1953.

———. *Western Society and the Church in the Middle Ages.* Baltimore: Penguin, 1970.

Spaapen, Bernard. "Hadewijch en het vijfde Visioen." *Ons Geestelijk Erf* 44 (1970): 7–44, 113–41, 353–404; 45 (1971): 129–78; 46 (1972): 113–99.

Stöckerl, Dagobert. *Bruder David von Augsburg: Ein deutscher Mystiker aus dem Franziskanerorden.* Munich: Lentner, 1914.

Stoklaska, Anneliese. "Weibliche Religiosität im mittelalterliche Wien unter besonderer Berücksichtigung der Agnes Blannbekin." In *Religiöse Frauenbewegung und mystische Frömmigkeit im Mittelalter,* edited by Peter Dinzelbacher and Dieter Bauer, 165–84. Cologne/Vienna: Böhlau, 1988.

Stoudt, Debra L. "The Vernacular Letters of Heinrich von Nördlingen." *Mystics Quarterly* 12 (1986): 19–25.

Strayer, Joseph R. *On the Medieval Origins of the Modern State.* Princeton: Princeton University Press, 1970.

Stroumsa, Guy G. *Hidden Wisdom: Esoteric Traditions and the Roots of Christian Mysticism.* Leiden: Brill, 1996.

Summers, Janet I. "'The Violent Shall Take It by Force': The First Century of Cistercian Nuns, 1125–1228." Ph.D. diss., University of Chicago, 1986.

Suydam, Mary A. "The Politics of Authorship: Hadewijch of Antwerp and the *Mengeldichten.*" *Mystics Quarterly* 22 (1996): 2–20.

Swanson, R. N. *Religion and Devotion in Europe, c. 1215–c. 1515.* Cambridge: Cambridge University Press, 1995.

Sweetman, Robert. "Christine of St. Trond's Preaching Apostolate." *Vox Benedictina* 9 (1992): 67–97.

Szabó, Titus. "Extase IV: Chez les théologiens du XIIIe siècle." DS 4:2120–26.

Szittya, Penn R. *The Antifraternal Tradition in Medieval Literature.* Princeton: Princeton University Press, 1986.

Tarrant, Jacqueline. "The Clementine Decrees on the Beguines: Conciliar and Papal Versions." *Archivum Historiae Pontificiae* 12 (1974): 300–307.

Tavard, G. H. *Transiency and Permanence: The Nature of Theology According to St. Bonaventure.* St. Bonaventure: Franciscan Institute, 1954.

Temi e problemi nella mistica femminile trecentesca. Todi: Convegni del Centro di Studi sulla Spiritualità Medievale XX, 1983.

Tentler, Thomas N. *Sin and Confession on the Eve of the Reformation.* Princeton: Princeton University Press, 1977.

Théry, Gabriel. "Saint Antoine de Padoue et Thomas Gallus." *La vie spirituelle. Supplement* 37 (1933): 94–115.

———. "Thomas Gallus: Aperçu biographique." *Archives d'histoire doctrinale et littéraire du moyen age* 12 (1939): 141–208.

———. "Thomas Gallus et Egide d'Assise: Le traité 'De septem gradibus contemplationis.'" *Revue Néoscholastique de Philosophie* 36 (1934): 180–90.

Thomas, Michael. "Zum religionsgeschichtlichen Standort der 'Meditationes vitae Christi.'" *Zeitschrift für Religions-und Geistesgeschichte* 24 (1972): 209–26.

Thouzellier, Christine. *Catharisme et Valdéisme en Languedoc à la fin du XIIe et au début du XIIIe siècle.* 2nd ed. Louvain: Nauwelaerts, 1969.

———. "La pauvreté, arme contre l'Albigéisme, en 1206." *Revue de l'histoire des religions* 151 (1957): 79–92.

Thurston, Herbert. *The Physical Phenomena of Mysticism.* Chicago: Henry Regnery, 1952.

———. *Surprising Mystics.* Chicago: Henry Regnery, 1955.

Tierney, Brian. *Origins of Papal Infallibility: A Study of the Concepts of Infallibility, Sovereignty and Tradition in the Middle Ages.* Leiden: Brill, 1972.

Tillmann, Heinz. *Studien zum Dialog bei Mechthild von Magdeburg.* Marburg: Kalbfleisch, 1933.

Tobin, Frank. "Introduction." In *Henry Suso: The Exemplar, with Two German Sermons,* translated by Frank Tobin, 38–50. Mahwah, N.J.: Paulist Press, 1989.

———. "Introduction." In *Mechthild of Magdeburg: The Flowing Light of the Godhead,* translated by Frank Tobin. Mahwah, N.J.: Paulist Press, 1998.

———. *Mechthild of Magdeburg: A Medieval Mystic in Modern Eyes.* Columbia, S.C.: Camden House, 1995.

———. "Mechthild of Magdeburg and Meister Eckhart." In *Meister Eckhart and the Beguine Mystics: Hadewijch of Brabant, Mechthild of Magdeburg, and Marguerite Porete,* edited by Bernard McGinn, 44–61. New York: Continuum, 1994.

———. "Medieval Thought on Visions and its Resonance in Mechthild von Magdeburg's *Flowing Light of the Godhead.*" In *Vox Mystica: Essays on Medieval Mysticism in Honor of Professor Valerie M. Lagorio,* edited by Anne Clark Bartlett et al., 41–53. Cambridge: D. S. Brewer, 1995.

———. Review of *Mystische Erfahrung und spirituelle Theologie: Zu Meister Eckharts Auseinandersetzung mit der Frauenfrömmigkeit seiner Zeit,* by Otto Langer. *Speculum* 64 (1989): 995–97.

Tugwell, Simon. "Introduction." In *Early Dominicans: Selected Writings,* translated by Simon Tugwell, 1–47. New York: Paulist Press, 1982.

Turner, Denys. *The Darkness of God: Negativity in Christian Mysticism.* Cambridge: Cambridge University Press, 1995.

———. *Eros and Allegory: Medieval Exegesis of the Song of Songs.* Kalamazoo: Cistercian Publications, 1995.

Turner, Sister Lilian. "The Symbolism of the Temple in St. Bonaventure's 'Itinerarium mentis in Deum.'" Ph.D. diss., Fordham University, 1968.

Underhill, Evelyn. *Jacopone da Todi, Poet and Mystic 1228–1306: A Spiritual Biography.* London: Dent, 1919.

Uribe, Fernando. "L'iter storico della Regola di S. Chiara: Una prova di fedeltà al Vangelo." In *Dialoghi con Chiara d'Assisi: Atti delle Giornate di studio e riflessione per l'VIII Centenario di Santa Chiara,* ed. Luigi Giacometti, 211–40. Assisi: Edizioni Porziuncola, 1995.

Urvoy, Dominique. *Penser d'Islam: le présupposés islamiques de l'"Art" de Lull.* Paris: Vrin, 1980.

Vagaggini, Cyprian. *Theological Dimensions of the Liturgy.* Collegeville: The Liturgical Press, 1976.

Valvekens, Jean-Baptiste. "Hermann-Joseph (saint)." DS 7:308–11.

van Asseldonck, Optatus. "'Sorores Minores': Una nuova impostazione del Problema." *Collectanea Franciscana* 62 (1992): 595–633.

———. "Sorores Minores e Chaira d'Assisi a San Damiano: Una scelta tra clausura e lebbrosi?" *Collectanea Franciscana* 63 (1993): 399–421.

———. "The Spirit of the Lord and Its Holy Activity in the Writings of St. Francis." *Greyfriars Review* 5 (1991): 105–58.

Vandenbroucke, François. "Fous pour le Christ." DS 5:752.

———. "New Milieux, New Problems from the Twelfth to the Sixteenth Centuries." In *The Spirituality of the Middle Ages,* edited by Jean Leclercq, François Vandenbroucke, and Louis Bouyer, 221–543. New York: Seabury, 1982.

Van Mierlo, Joseph. "Béguinages." In *Dictionnaire d'histoire et de géographie ecclesiastique,* 7:457–73. Paris: Letouzey et Ané, 1912–.

———. "Béguine, béguines, béguinages." DS 1:1341–43.

———. "Hadewijch en Willem van St. Thierry." *Ons Geestelijk Erf* 3 (1929): 45–59.

———. "Hadewijch: Une mystique flamande du treizième siècle." *Revue d'ascétique et de mystique* 5 (1924): 269–89, 380–404.

Vanneste, R. "Over de betekenis van enkele abstracta in de taal van Hadewijch." *Studia Germanica* 1 (1959): 34–40.

van Os, Henk, et al. *The Art of Devotion in the Late Middle Ages in Europe 1300–1500.* Princeton: Princeton University Press, 1994.

Van Si, Nguyen. "Les symboles de l'itineraire dans l'*Itinerarium mentis in deum* de Bonaventure." *Antonianum* 68 (1993): 327–47.

Vauchez, André. "François d'Assise entre littéralisme évangelique et renouveau spirituel." In *Frate Francesco d'Assisi: Atti del XXI Convegno internazionale,* 183–98. Spoleto: Centro Italiano di Studi sull'alto Medioevo, 1994.

———. "Les stigmates de Saint François et leurs détracteurs dans les derniers siècles du moyen âge." *Mélanges d'archéologie et d'histoire* 80 (1968): 595–625.

———. *The Laity in the Middle Ages: Religious Beliefs and Devotional Practices.* Notre Dame, Ind.: University of Notre Dame Press, 1993.

———. *Sainthood in the Later Middle Ages.* Cambridge: Cambridge University Press, 1997.

Vavra, Elisabeth. "Bildmotiv und Frauenmystik–Funktion und Rezeption." In *Frauenmystik im Mittelalter,* edited by Peter Dinzelbacher and Dieter R. Bauer, 201–30. Ostfeldern bei Stuttgart: Schwabenverlag, 1985.

Vekeman, Herman. "Angelus sane nuntius: Een interpretatie van het Visioenenboek van Hadewijch." *Ons Geestelijk Erf* 50 (1976): 225–59.

———. "Beatrijs van Nazareth: Die Mystik einer Zisterzienserin." In *Frauenmystik im Mittelalter,* edited by Peter Dinzelbacher and Dieter R. Bauer, 78–98. Ostfeldern bei Stuttgart: Schwabenverlag, 1985.

———. "*Dat waren scachte die diepe staken.* Beatrijs van Nazareth (1200–1268), Mechthild von Hackeborn (1241–c.1299), Geertrui de Grote (1256–c.1301) en

Theresia van Avila (1515–1582): *vulnus amoris* en *transfixio.*" *Ons Geestelijk Erf* 67 (1993): 3–19.

———. "Minne in 'Seuven Manieren van Minne' van Beatrijs van Nazareth." *Citeaux* 29 (1969): 285–316.

———. "Vita Beatricis en Seuen Manieren van Minne: Een vergelijkende studie." *Ons Geestelijk Erf* 46 (1972): 3–54.

———. "Vriendschap in de Middelnederlandse mystiek: De plaats van Ruusbroec." In *Jan Van Ruusbroec: The sources, content and sequels of his mysticism,* edited by Paul Mommaers and Norbert de Paepe, 124–41. Leuven: Leuven University Press, 1984.

Verdeyen, Paul. "De invloed van Willem van Saint-Thierry op Hadewijch en Ruusbroec." *Ons Geestelijk Erf* 51 (1977): 3–19.

———. "Le procès d'Inquisition contre Marguerite Porete et Guiard de Cressonessart (1309–1310)." *Revue d'histoire ecclésiastique* 81 (1986): 48–94.

Vergote, Antoine. *Guilt and Desire: Religious Attitudes and Their Pathological Derivative.* New Haven/London: Yale University Press, 1988.

Vernet, Felix. *Medieval Spirituality.* London/St. Louis: Sands & Herder, 1930.

Vicaire, M.-H., O.P. *Saint Dominic and His Times.* New York: McGraw-Hill, 1964.

Villamonte, Alejandro. "El Padre Plenitud fontal de la Deidad." In *San Bonaventura 1274–1974,* 4:221–42. 5 vols. Grottaferrata/Rome: Collegio S. Bonaventura, 1974.

von Auw, Lydia. *Angelo Clareno et les spirituels italiens.* Rome: Edizioni di Storia e Letteratura, 1979.

von Balthasar, Hans Urs. "Einführung." In *Mechthild von Hackeborn: Das Buch des strömmenden Lob,* 7–18. Einsiedeln: Johannes Verlag, 1955.

———. *The Glory of the Lord. A Theological Aesthetics. Vol. II, Studies in Theological Style: Clerical Styles.* San Francisco: Ignatius, 1984.

———. "Mechthilds kirchlicher Auftrag." In *Mechthild von Magdeburg: Das Fliessende Licht der Gottheit,* translated by Margot Schmidt, 28–38. Einsiedeln: Benzinger, 1955.

von Ivánka, Endre. *Plato Christianus: Übernahme und Umgestaltung der Platonismus durch die Väter.* Einsiedeln: Johannes Verlag, 1964.

Wainwright-deKadt, Elizabeth. "Courtly Literature and Mysticism: Some Aspects of Their Interaction." *Acta Germanica* 12 (1980): 41–60.

Wakefield, Walter L. *Heresy, Crusade and Inquisition in Southern France, 1100–1250.* Berkeley/Los Angeles: University of California Press, 1974.

———, and Austin P. Evans. *Heresies of the High Middle Ages.* New York: Columbia University Press, 1969.

Walsh, James. "Thomas Gallus et l'effort contemplatif." *Revue d'Histoire de Spiritualité* 51 (1975): 17–42.

Ward, Benedicta. "Preface." In *Anchoritic Spirituality: Ancrene Wisse and Associated Works,* translated by Anne Savage and Nicholas Watson, 1–5. New York: Paulist Press, 1991.

Warren, Ann K. *Anchorites and their Patrons in Medieval England.* Berkeley/Los Angeles: University of California Press, 1985.

Watson, Nicholas M. "Melting into God the English Way: Deification in the Middle English Version of Marguerite Porete's *Mirouer des simples âmes anienties.*" In *Prophets Abroad: The Reception of Continental Holy Women in Late-Medieval England,* 19–49. Cambridge: D.S. Brewer, 1996.

———. *Richard Rolle and the Invention of Authority.* Cambridge: Cambridge University Press, 1991.

Wehrli-Johns, Martina. "Maria und Martha in der religiösen Frauenbewegung." In *Abendändische Mystik im Mittelalter: Symposium Kloster Engelberg 1984,* edited by Kurt Ruh, 354–67. Stuttgart: Metzler, 1986.

Weil, Simone. *First and Last Notebooks,* translated by Richard Rees. London: Oxford University Press, 1970.

Weinstein, Donald, and Rudolph M. Bell, *Saints and Society: The Two Worlds of Western Christendom, 1000–1700.* Chicago: University of Chicago Press, 1982.

Weiss, Bardo. "Mechthild von Magdeburg und der frühe Meister Eckhart." *Theologie und Philosophie* 70 (1995): 1–40.

Weitlauff, Manfred. "'dein got redender munt machet mich redenlosz . . .': Margareta Ebner und Heinrich von Nördlingen." In *Religiöse Frauenbewegung und mystische Frömmigkeit im Mittelalter,* edited by Peter Dinzelbacher and Dieter Bauer, 303–52. Cologne/Vienna: Böhlau, 1988.

———. "Heinrich von Nördlingen." In *Die deutsche Literatur des Mittelalters: Verfasserlexikon,* edited by Kurt Ruh et al., 3:845–52. Berlin: Walter de Gruyter, 1981.

Welliver, Warman. *Dante in Hell: The 'De Vulgari Eloquentia'. Introduction, Text, Translation, Commentary.* Ravenna: Longo Editore, 1981.

Wessley, Stephen E. "James of Milan and the Guglielmites: Franciscan spirituality and popular heresy in late thirteenth-century Milan." *Collectanea Francescana* 54 (1984): 5–20.

———. "The Thirteenth-Century Guglielmites: Salvation through Women." In *Medieval Women: Studies in Church History. Subsidia 1,* edited by Derek Baker, 289–303. Oxford: Blackwell, 1978.

Whitlock, F. A., and J. V. Hynes. "Religious stigmatization: an historical and psychophysiological enquiry." *Psychological Medicine* 8 (1978): 185–202.

Wiberg-Pedersen, Else Marie. "Image of God-Image of Mary-Image of Woman: On the Theology and Spirituality of Beatrice of Nazareth." *Cistercian Studies* 29 (1994): 209–20.

Wiethaus, Ulrike. *Ecstatic Transformation: Transpersonal Psychology in the Work of Mechthild of Madgeburg.* Syracuse: Syracuse University Press, 1996.

———. "Sexuality, Gender, and the Body in Late Medieval Women's Spirituality. Cases from Germany and the Netherlands." *Journal of Feminist Studies in Religion* 7 (1991): 35–52.

Willaert, Frank. "Hadewijch und ihr Kreis in den 'Visionen.'" In *Abendländische Mystik im Mittelalter: Symposium Kloster Engelberg 1984,* edited by Kurt Ruh, 368–87. Stuttgart: Metzler, 1986.

Wilmart, André. "Les traités de Gérard de Liège sur l'amour illicite et sur l'amour de Dieu." In *Analecta Reginensia*, 205–47 Rome: Biblioteca Apostolic Vaticana, 1933.

Wolfson, Elliot R. *Through a Speculum that Shines: Vision and Imagination in Medieval Jewish Mysticism*. Princeton: Princeton University Press, 1994.

Yourcenar, Marguerite. *That Mighty Sculptor, Time*. New York: Noonday Press, 1992.

Zaehner, R. C. *Mysticism Sacred and Profane*. New York: Oxford University Press, 1961.

Zafarana, Zelina. "La predicazione francescana." In *Francescanesimo e vita religiosa dei laici nel '200*, 203–50. Assisi: Università degli Studi di Perugia, 1981.

Zeller-Werdmüller, H., and Jakob Bächtold. "Die Stiftung des Klosters Oetenbach und das Leben der seligen Schwestern daselbst, aus der Nürnberger Handschrift." *Zürcher Taschenbuch* n.s. 12 (1889): 213–76.

Zerfass, Rolph. *Die Streit um die Laienpredigt: Eine pastoralgeschichtliche Untersuchung zum Verständnis des Predigtamtes und zu seiner Entwicklung im 12. und 13. Jahrhundert*. Freiburg/Basel/Vienna: Herder, 1974.

Ziegler, Joanna E. "The *curtis* beguinage in the Southern Low Countries and art patronage: interpretation and historiography." *Bulletin de l'Institut historique Belge de Rome* 57 (1987): 31–70.

———. *Sculpture of Compassion: The Pietà and the Beguines in the Southern Low countries c. 1300-c.1600*. Brussels/Rome: Institut Historique Belge de Rome, 1992.

Zinn, Grover A. "Book and Word": The Victorine Background of Bonaventure's Use of Symbols." In *San Bonaventura 1274-1974*, 2:143–69. 5 vols. Grottaferrata/Rome: Collegio S. Bonaventura, 1974.

Zolla, Elémire. "Preface." In *Jacopone da Todi: The Lauds*, translated by Serge and Elizabeth Hughes, xi–xvii. New York: Paulist Press, 1982.

Zum Brunn, Emilie, and Georgette Epiney-Burgard, eds. *Women Mystics in Medieval Europe*. New York: Paragon, 1989.

Index of Names

Index of Scripture References (Vg)

Index of Subjects

Absence (of God), 169-70, 219-20, 240-43, 256, 301. *See also* Estrangement

Abyss, 127-32, 145, 148-51, 170, 172-73, 195, 211, 215-18, 234, 242, 250, 254, 259, 261, 263-65, 274, 285, 307

Action. *See* Contemplation

Affectus, 79-82, 103-4, 106, 109-11, 118-19, 126, 135, 151; apex affectus, 82, 85, 106, 110-11, 135

Allegory, 68, 117, 156, 180, 182, 201, 208, 213, 229-30, 246, 270, 280, 286, 291, 315-17. *See also* Bible.

Anagogy, 86, 108, 112, 121

Angels, 30, 37, 39, 63, 81, 83, 95-96, 98-99, 121, 126-27, 132, 138, 148, 173, 179, 181, 193, 195, 234-36, 274, 288, 291, 297, 304, 316. *See also* Hierarchy, Seraph.

Annihilation, 124, 126-31, 157, 198-99, 209, 247-65, 285

Anthropology, 82-85, 98, 105-8, 136, 155-56, 214-16, 232-33, 248-52. *See also* Body, *Imago Dei*, Soul.

Apocalypticism, 73-74, 94-99, 120-22, 126, 225, 235, 243

Apophatic (i.e., negative) language and theology, 14, 76-81, 83, 86-88, 104, 110-11, 121, 145, 147-51, 157, 230, 246, 256-57, 265, 297. *See also* Absence, Nothingness.

Art and mysticism, 29-30, 100, 119, 179, 225, 276, 280, 291, 302-4, 311-12

Ascent, 80-85, 93-96, 100, 104-7, 115, 127, 135, 171, 228, 231, 236, 239-40, 242, 252-55, 258, 260-61, 284, 287, 295

Asceticism, 6-9, 16, 36-37, 40, 43-45, 48, 53, 60, 113-14, 118, 120, 125-26, 138-40, 146, 150, 153, 156, 160-61, 163-65, 168, 170, 177, 186-87, 192-93, 195, 240, 267, 272, 283-84, 286, 288, 295-98, 300, 316

Authority, 4, 10, 17, 21-22, 27-28, 40, 72, 142, 149-50, 154-55, 157, 165, 199, 214-16, 222-26, 247-51, 262, 268, 272-73, 289-92, 310

Autohagiography, xii-xiii, 20, 145, 149, 222, 227, 267, 298, 301, 308-17. *See also* Hagiography.

Baptism, 184, 254, 273, 296

Beatitude, 101, 111, 190, 228, 254, 258, 281

Beauty, 63, 67, 83, 139, 146, 279, 287, 291, 308, 317

Bed. *See* Symbols, mystical

Beguin, 75, 158, 183-86

Beguine, ix, 18, 30, 32-41, 49, 127, 129, 132, 137-38, 158-64, 166-67, 169, 174-82, 190, 198, Chap. 5, 266, 268, 270, 272, 284, 294, 297, 299, 300, 310

Being, 108, 121, 210-15, 218, 234, 251, 254, 256, 258, 260, 262-65, 305, 307. *See also* Existence.

Benedictinism, 8, 158, 164, 267. *See also* Monasticism.

Bible (exegesis of), 19, 28, 30, 33, 39-40,

45, 51-52, 66, 75, 80, 84, 91-92, 96-99, 101, 103, 114, 117, 121-22, 133, 142, 148-49, 155-56, 185, 199, 203, 216, 219, 223, 225-27, 230, 249, 254, 260, 267, 270, 273, 276, 286-87, 292, 299, 310. *See also* Allegory, Song of Songs.
Birth of the Word, 52, 314
Blood, 38, 52, 126, 139, 181-82, 203, 225, 276, 287, 312
Body, 25, 37, 39, 43, 61, 77, 126, 140, 147, 155-57, 161-62, 167-68, 172-73, 181-82, 185, 188-90, 195, 199, 201, 210, 228-29, 232-34, 236, 240-42, 254-55, 275, 287, 291, 303, 305-8, 311-14. *See also* Anthropology, Soul
Book. *See* Symbols, mystical

Canons and Canonesses, 6, 34, 188, 282-83
Caritas, 19-21, 67, 102, 112, 118, 128, 130, 168, 170, 173, 177, 192, 202, 219, 220-21, 263-64, 280, 287, 296, 317; ordering of caritas, 128, 157, 281. *See also* Love.
Carthusians, 154, 158, 267, 282, 288-92
Cataphatic (i.e., positive) language and theology, 79, 81, 87, 203, 280, 284
Cathari, 7, 10, 35, 154, 185
Christ (and Christology), 12, 26, 30, 37, 39, 43, 51-52, 54, 58-64, 67-68, 71, 75, 88-92, 95-101, 106-7, 109-10, 115, 117-20, 122-24, 126-28, 132, 134, 137, 139-41, 145-49, 154, 156, 162, 164-66, 170, 176-82, 184, 187, 189-90, 192, 194, 201, 203, 210, 212, 215-16, 219-22, 229, 232, 236-42, 249, 254-55, 258, 260-61, 268, 271-72, 274, 276-78, 283-84, 287-88, 290-92, 295-96, 301, 303, 311-14
Church (and Ecclesiology), 35, 41, 44, 53, 69, 73-74, 92, 97-99, 102, 122, 154, 180, 184-86, 192, 196, 221, 226, 231, 234, 243, 245-46, 249, 252-54, 270, 272, 292-93, 309-10
Circle. *See* Symbols, mystical
Cistericans, 1-3, 10, 19, 30, 32, 35, 48, 59, 66-67, 80, 93, 105-6, 154, 158-60, 162, 164-73, 187, 189, 190-91, 194, 197, 199, 245, 258, 262, 266-83, 288, 293-94, 316
Cloud and darkness. *See* Symbols, mystical
Community (religious), 48, 66, 69, 136, 138, 150, 162, 165, 187, 191, 220, 222-23, 268, 271, 273, 275, 280, 282, 289, 291, 294, 298-300, 304, 306, 312, 315

Communion. *See* Eucharist
Compunction, 36
Consciousness (mystical), xi, 15, 20, 25, 27, 29-30, 79, 111, 115, 122, 126, 136, 147, 156-57, 167, 169, 171, 199, 209, 214, 219-20, 227, 239, 248, 256, 258-60, 262, 265, 270, 287, 289-90, 295, 301-2, 311, 319. *See also* Experience (mystical), Presence of God
Contemplation, 2, 18, 26, 29-30, 37-38, 50, 56-58, 63, 66-69, 77-78, 82, 86, 90, 94-100, 102-12, 114, 117, 119-25, 128, 134-36, 138-39, 141, 164, 181, 184, 191-92, 216, 235, 251, 254, 258, 271, 273, 288-89, 291, 295, 297, 304; contemplation and action, 14-15, 18, 34, 40, 76, 87, 94, 99, 120, 123, 191, 239, 243, 251. *See also* Vision
Conversation, x, xiii, 17-18, 22-24, 115, 123, 160, 163, 193-94, 223, 227, 268, 319. *See also* Friendship (spiritual), Gender
Conversion, 6, 32, 43-45, 57, 76, 125, 134-35, 143, 145, 161, 181, 239, 262, 268, 273, 276, 294, 300, 309
Co-redeemer, 165, 184-86, 196, 255-56, 282
Countenance of God, 114, 208-11, 214, 216. *See also* Vision
Courtly literature and mysticism, 20, 142, 168-70, 199, 200-202, 206-7, 227, 235-36, 246-48, 252, 256, 259-60, 316
Creation, 29, 51, 54-55, 88, 90-91, 97, 105, 127, 181, 205, 212, 215, 231-34, 240, 251, 255, 265, 275, 290, 307
Cura animarum, 5, 8-12, 34, 71, 174, 293

Deification. *See* Divinization
Democratization (of mysticism), 13-15, 24, 52, 69, 77, 99, 112, 118, 192, 223-25, 227, 310
Demon, 36-37, 39, 68, 147, 173, 175, 177-80, 193, 197, 241-42, 254, 287, 316
Desert, 86, 186, 192, 229, 243-44, 311 n206, 317
Devotion, 11-12, 59, 100, 115, 119, 126, 135, 139, 149, 154, 156, 158, 181, 187, 189, 193-94, 219, 221, 259, 270, 276, 278, 288, 302, 305, 309-11
Dialectic, 87, 108-10, 128, 130, 212, 234, 253-57, 259, 263